CENSUS OF INDIA 1911

Census of India 1871-1951, 9 Sets In 384 Bindings (9788121258876) Rs. 700000

Census of India 1911, 23 Vols. In 41 Bindings (9788121271271) Rs. 69000

1. India - Report (9788121275071) Rs. 2475 (Vol. I, Pt. 1)
2. India - Tables (9788121275057) Rs. 2225 (Vol. I, Pt. 2)
3. Andaman and Nicobar Islands - Report & Tables (9788121275033) Rs. 900 (Vol. II, Pt. 1 & 2)
4. Assam - Report (9788121275019) Rs. 1000 (Vol. III, Pt. 1)
5. Assam - Tables (9788121274999) Rs. 1300 (Vol. III, Pt. 2)
6. Baluchistan - Report & Tables (9788121274975) Rs. 950 (Vol. IV, Pt. 1 & 2)
7. Bengal, Bihar And Orissa And Sikkim - Report (9788121274951) Rs. 3100 (Vol. V, Pt. 1)
8. Bengal - Tables (9788121274937) Rs. 2250 (Vol. V, Pt. 2)
9. Bihar And Orissa - Tables and Bengal And Sikkim - Chapter I of Administrative Volume (9788121274913) Rs. 1800 (Vol. V, Pt. 3 & 4)
10. City of Calcutta - Report and Tables and Administrative (9788121274876) Rs. 1300 (Vol. VI, Pt. 1 & 2 & 3)
11. Bombay - Report (9788121274814) Rs. 1950 (Vol. VII, Pt. 1)
12. Bombay - Imperial Tables and Administrative Report (9788121274791) Rs. 3300 (Vol. VII, Pt. 2 & 3)
13. Bombay (Town And Island) - Report And Tables (9788121274753) Rs. 1250 (Vol. VIII, Pt. 1 & 2)
14. Burma - Report (9788121274739) Rs. 2250 (Vol. IX, Pt. 1)
15. Burma - Tables (9788121274715) Rs. 1480 (Vol. IX, Pt. 2)
16. Central Provinces And Berar - Report (9788121274692) Rs. 1475 (Vol. X, Pt. 1)
17. Central Provinces And Berar - Tables (9788121274678) Rs. 1900 (Vol. X, Pt. 2)
18. Coorg - Report And Tables Madras - Report (9788121274630) Rs. 1740 (Vol. XI & Vol. XII, Pt. 1)
19. Madras - Imperial And Provincial Tables (9788121274616) Rs. 1500 (Vol. XII, Pt. 2)
20. Madras - Administrative Report and city of Madras (9788121274593) Rs. 630 (Vol. XII, Pt. 3 & 4)
21. North - West Frontier Province - Report & Tables (9788121274579) Rs. 2150 (Vol. XIII, Pt. 1 & 2)
22. Punjab - Report (9788121274555) Rs. 3000 (Vol. XIV, Pt. 1)
23. Punjab - Tables (9788121274531) Rs. 2200 (Vol. XIV, Pt. 2)
24. Punjab - Appendices To The - Imperial Tables (9788121274517) Rs. 950 (Vol. XIV, Pt. 3)
25. United Provinces of Agra And Oudh - Report (9788121274494) Rs. 2225 (Vol. XV, Pt. 1)
26. United Provinces of Agra And Oudh - Tables (9788121274470) Rs. 4000 (Vol. XV, Pt. 2)
27. United Provinces of Agra And Oudh - Provincial Tables And Appendices (9788121274456) Rs. 570 (Vol. XV, Pt. 3)
28. Baroda - Report (9788121274432) Rs. 2000 (Vol. XVI, Pt. 1)
29. Baroda State - The Imperial Tables (9788121274418) Rs. 850 (Vol. XVI, Pt. 2)
30. Central India Agency - Report And Tables (9788121274395) Rs. 1470 (Vol. XVII)
31. Cochin - Report And Imperial Tables (9788121274371) Rs. 1150 (Vol. XVIII, Pt. 1 & 2)
32. Hyderabad State - Report (9788121274357) Rs. 890 (Vol. XIX, Pt. 1)
33. Hyderabad State - Imperial And Provincial Tables (9788121274333) Rs. 1750 (Vol. XIX, Pt. 2)
34. Kashmir - Report (9788121274319) Rs. 950 (Vol. XX, Pt. 1)
35. Kashmir - Tables (9788121274296) Rs. 1170 (Vol. XX, Pt. 2)
36. Mysore - Report (9788121274272) Rs. 1200 (Vol. XXI, Pt. 1)
37. Mysore - Tables (9788121274258) Rs. 1500 (Vol. XXI, Pt. 2)
38. Rajputana And Ajmer-Merwara - Report (9788121274234) Rs. 1470 (Vol. XXII, Pt. 1)
39. Rajputana And Ajmer-Merwara - Tables (9788121274210) Rs. 1700 (Vol. XXII, Pt. 2)
40. Travancore - Report (9788121274197) Rs. 1870 (Vol. XXIII, Pt. 1)
41. Travancore - Imperial Tables (9788121274173) Rs. 870 (Vol. XXIII, Pt. 2)

Owing to the antiquity and rarity of this book, certain pages are regrettably absent, and readability is compromised due to the blurring of the original text. If you possess any insights regarding the availability of these missing sections, kindly inform us. Your assistance is crucial in ensuring the completion of this significant work for the benefit of future generations.

CENSUS OF INDIA, 1911

VOLUME - XI

COORG

REPORT AND TABLES

VOLUME - XII

MADRAS

PART I - REPORT

J. CHARTRES MOLONY & ALFRED CHATTERTON

GYAN

Published by

Gyan Publishing House
5, Ansari Road
Daryaganj, New Delhi-110002
Phone: 011-47034999, 9811692060
E-mail: books@gyanbooks.com

Distribution Network
gyanbooks.com
India, USA, Canada, UK, Australia

ISBN: 978-81-212-7127-1 (Set) 23 Vols. In 41 Bindings

ISBN: 978-81-212-7463-0 (PB) Vol. XI & Vol. XII, Pt. I

First Published, 1912

2nd Impression 2024

Printed at: Gyan Press, Delhi.

CENSUS OF INDIA 1911

CENSUS OF INDIA, 1911.

VOLUME XI.

COORG.

REPORT AND TABLES.

BY

J. CHARTRES MOLONY, I.C.S.,
SUPERINTENDENT OF CENSUS OPERATIONS, MADRAS.

MADRAS:
PRINTED BY THE SUPERINTENDENT, GOVERNMENT PRESS.

1912.

AGENTS FOR THE SALE OF MADRAS GOVERNMENT PUBLICATIONS.

IN INDIA.

R. Cambray & Co., Calcutta.
Combridge & Co., Madras
T. Coopooswami Naicker & Co., Madras
Higginbotham & Co., Mount Road, Madras.
V. Kalyanarama Iyer & Co., Esplanade, Madras
G. C. Loganadham Brothers, Madras.
S. Murthy & Co., Kapalee Press, Madras
G. A. Natesan & Co., Madras.
P. R. Rama Iyer & Co., Madras
D. B. Taraporevala Sons & Co., Bombay.
Temple & Co., Georgetown, Madras
Thacker & Co. (Limited), Bombay
Thacker, Spink & Co., Calcutta.
Thompson & Co., Madras.

IN ENGLAND.

B. H. Blackwell, 50 and 51, Broad Street, Oxford.
Constable & Co., 10, Orange Street, Leicester Square, London, W.C.
Deighton, Bell & Co., Cambridge.
T. Fisher Unwin, 1, Adelphi Terrace, London, W.C.
Grindlay & Co., 54, Parliament Street, London, S.W.
Kegan Paul, Trench, Trübner & Co., 68–74, Carter Lane, London, E.C.
Henry S. King & Co., 65, Cornhill, London, E.C.
P. S. King & Son, 2 and 4, Great Smith Street, Westminster, London, S.W.
Luzac & Co., 46, Great Russell Street, London, W.C.
B. Quaritch, 11, Grafton Street, New Bond Street, London, W.
W. Thacker & Co., 2, Creed Lane, London, E.C.

ON THE CONTINENT.

Friedländer & Sohn, 11, Carlstrasse, Berlin.
Otto Harrassowitz, Leipzig.
Karl W. Hiersemann, Leipzig.
Ernest Leroux, 28, Rue Bonaparte, Paris.
Martinus Nijhoff, The Hague, Holland.

TABLE OF CONTENTS.

THE REPORT.

THE IMPERIAL TABLES.

THE PROVINCIAL TABLES.

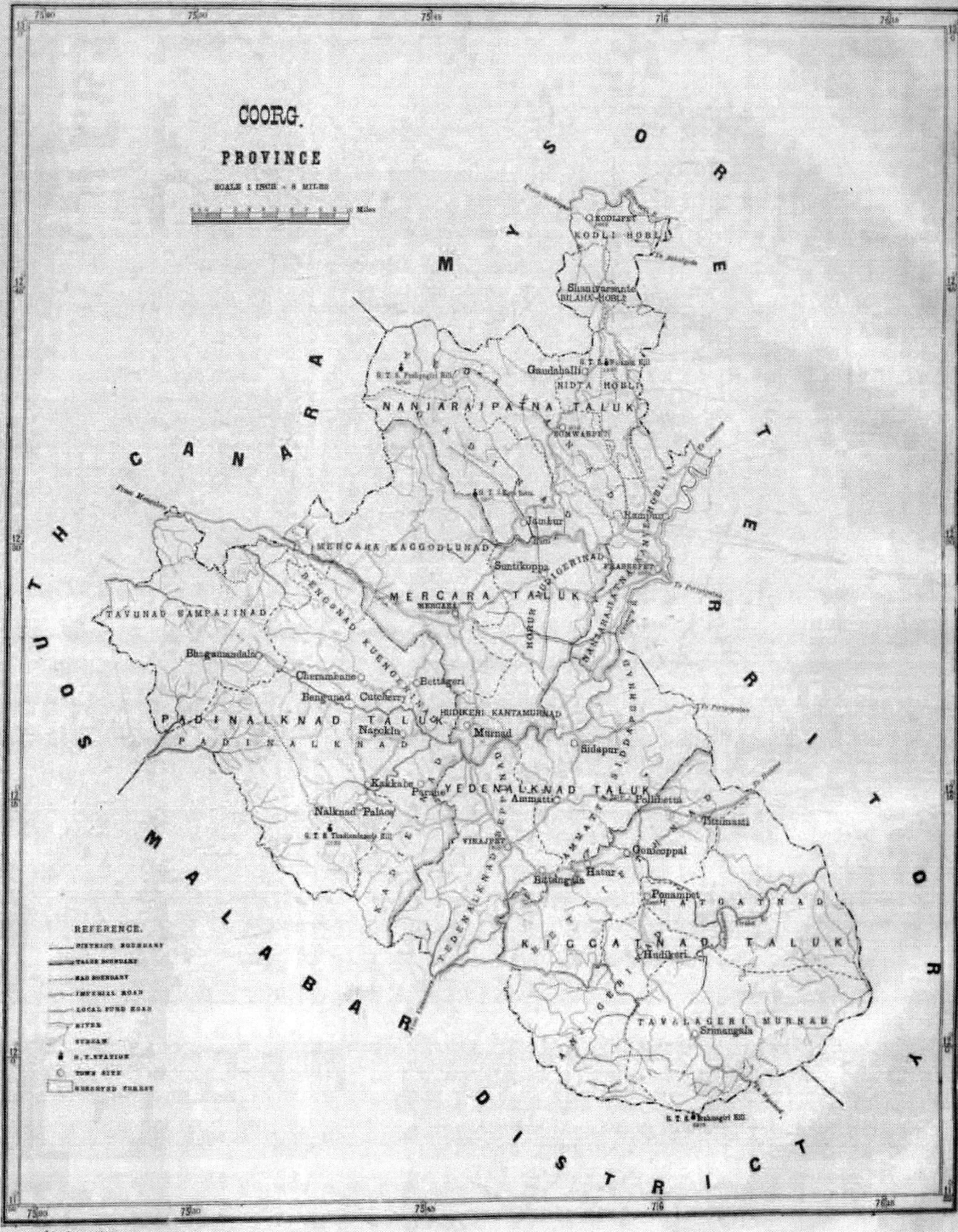

S. O. { Reg No 77
1911 { Copies 300

CENSUS OF INDIA, 1911.

COORG.

IMPERIAL SERIES—VOLUME XI.

THE REPORT AND TABLES

INTRODUCTION.

THE little province of Coorg, situated on the slopes and summits of the Western Ghats, is bounded on the north and east by the Hassan and Mysore districts of the Mysore State, and on the south and west by the Malabar and South Canara districts of Madras.

2. The area of the province, according to revenue survey, is nearly 1,600 square miles; its greatest length from north to south is 60 miles, and greatest breadth from east to west 40 miles. The old fort at Mercara stands about 3,800 feet above sea level, and this elevation is maintained for a considerable distance towards the north. Towards the east the country slopes down towards the Cauvery, the elevation of Fraserpet being some 1,100 feet lower than that of Mercara. A remarkable natural feature of South Coorg was once the bamboo jungle; a tract of land some 13 miles square being locally known as "the bamboo." This area is now for the most part under coffee.

3. Coorg is now divided for administrative purposes into five taluks, a previously existing sixth having been amalgamated with Nanjarájapatna in the year 1895–96.

4. The history of Coorg is given in detail in the Imperial Gazetteer of the province, and does not need recapitulation. It is on the whole one of sturdy independence, and loyalty of the people to their own chiefs. What appears to have been homicidal madness in the reigning family—in the walls of the Mercara fort is still shown a little den, from which, it is said, prisoners were bolted like rabbits across in palace courtyard to test the Rája's markmanship—led to the conclusion of its rule in 1834, when the Rája Víra Rájéndra Wodeyar was deposed, and the province, with the approval of the Coorgs, placed under the administration of the British Government. Its independence still persists in its recognition as self-contained administrative unit, under a Chief Commissioner, who is also British Resident in Mysore, and a Commissioner, resident in Mercara. For their loyalty during the Indian Mutiny, the Coorgs were rewarded by exemption from the Disarming Act.

5. In virtue of its existence as a separate province, the census of the little territory has always been taken separately. The first enumeration was that of 1871, which the Superintendent of 1881 considers to have been unsuccessful. This latter census was carried out by the then First Assistant Superintendent of Coorg, but those of succeeding *decennia* have been entrusted to the general supervision of the Provincial Superintendent of Census in Madras.

6. The method of taking the census of 1911 was exactly the same as that followed in the larger province; and no particular difficulties arose at any stage of the undertaking. I gladly avail myself of the opportunity to express my thanks to the Chief Commissioner, and to Messrs. Harris and Ellis, for their advice and assistance in a work to which I was able to devote but very little personal attention.

7. Here I should like to revive, with some modification, a suggestion put forward in the report of 1891 by Sir H. A. Stuart to the effect that the work of the Coorg census should in future be entrusted to a local official.

8. The actual taking of the census must necessarily be arranged by the Coorg officials. Tabulation of the information contained in the Census schedules can be most easily carried out in one of the West Coast offices of the Madras Superintendent; it would, I venture to think, be absurd to set up an extra abstraction office at Mercara, when the tables for such a small population can be prepared without trouble or delay in a large office specially entertained for census purposes. But when these tables are prepared and printed, the task of writing the report might very well be undertaken by one of the officers of the province. Statistical interest there is little or none in these small totals; intimate knowledge of the people and of prevailing economic conditions, which an outsider cannot possibly obtain in the course of a few days' hurried visit, would lend to such report an interest, wherein, I fear, my present effort is painfully lacking.

9. Local expenditure on the Census in Coorg amounted to Rs. 356. In this amount are included the cost of temporary district establishment, house-numbering charges, cost of printing circle lists, etc. Charges for abstraction and compilation, superintendence, etc., are included in the accounts for the Madras Presidency.

10. From a reader's point of view this report, necessarily brief in dealing with such a tiny population, might be written more conveniently in the form of one chapter divided into paragraphs, than broken up into a succession of very short chapters. But such arrangement would render difficult the convenient placing of the "subsidiary tables," which exhbiit in handy form percentages obtained from actual figures, or else supply information not ascertainable in the course of a general enumeration.

CHAPTER I.—DISTRIBUTION OF THE POPULATION.

THE population of Coorg returned at the census of 1911 was 174,976, which represents a decrease of nearly 6,000 souls since the previous enumeration. Such decrease is probably artificial, and will be explained in a succeeding chapter.

2. Such as it is, this population represents a density of 111 persons per square mile, with a talukwar variation of from 128 per square mile (Nanjarájapatna), to 67 per square mile (Pádinalknád). Towns are two in number, only Mercara and Vírarájéndrapet, which indeed are little more than villages, having been considered as such in this occasion; villages so called number 493. It should, however, be noted that only in the four *hoblis* of North Coorg, (the Province is divided into four *hoblis* and fifteen *náds*; the *hoblis* resembling the Mysore country, while the *náds* represent the more hilly tracts), the residential village system prevails; the inhabitants of the province elsewhere living for the most part in detached farm-houses on their lands.

3. Occupied houses have increased by nearly 3,000 in a space of ten years; the average number of houses per square mile is greater by 2 than in 1901, and by 7 than in 1881; the average number of persons per house has decreased by 3 in 30 years, and by one since the census of 1901. If real, this movement lends itself to inference of increasing prosperity, and an increasing tendency towards sub-division; on the other hand, the explanation may perhaps be found in a more precise care to distinguish each dwelling place "having a separate entrance from the common way."

4. Subsidiary tables III and IV give the distribution of the population between towns and villages; and the number per mille of the total population, and of each main religion, who live in towns. The irreverent will, I fear, look on them as solemn superfluities: 765 Parsis per 1,000 live in towns, but, all told, the Parsis of the province number 3,411.

5. Mercara town, it may be noted, has added considerably to its population, while Vírarájéndrapet has declined during the decade.

I.—Area under cultivation, etc., water-supply and crops (in acres).

Year.	Area available for cultivation.	Culturable waste other than fallow.	Current fallows.	Area cropped more than once.	Net area cropped.	Area irrigated by		Principal crops			
						Tanks	Canals.	Coffee.	Rice.	Ragi	Other food-grains
1	2	3	4	5	6	7	8	9	10	11	12
1901–02 ...	313,542	65,788	79,626	2,281	168,128	..	1,370	65,732	79,930	13,046	813
1902–03	300,078	22,313	121,480	1,544	155,735		1,370	59,417	80,694	9,998	2,396
1903–04	300,078	22,313	132,511	1,099	145,254	..	1,370	52,420	79,763	6,078	3,566
1904–05 ..	300,078	23,435	136,916	1,414	139,727		1,370	48,142	79,111	5,268	3,854
1905–06 ..	300,729	23,435	137,104	1,117	140,190		2,374	48,215	79,172	5,820	2,822
1906–07 ...	300,788	23,485	136,265	1,096	141,083		2,374	46,393	79,617	6,165	3,124
1907–08	300,783	22,119	136,488	1,647	142,176		2,537	46,108	81,121	6,866	2,368
1908–09	305,002	20,114	146,496	1,650	138,392	1,500	2,850	44,316	81,149	5,997	2 006
1909–10	310,698	20,820	150,451	1,325	139,427	1,962	2,790	43,421	81,792	5,921	2,337
1910–11	311,179	20,360	149,691	1,503	141,128	1,780	2,597	43,686	84,502	6,440	2,848

II.—Distribution of the population according to density.

Province.		Taluks with a population per square mile of					
		Under 100.		100–150		150–200.	
		Area.	Population.	Area.	Population.	Area	Population.
1		2	3	4	5	6	7
Coorg	Actual ...	820	66,634	544	67,117	218	41,225
	Ratio ..	51 8	38 1	34 4	38·3	13·8	23 6

III.—Distribution of the population between towns and villages.

Province.	Average population per		Number per mille residing in		Number per mille of urban population residing in towns with a population of		Number per mille of rural population residing in villages with a population of		
	Town.	Village.	Towns.	Villages	5,000 to 10,000	Under 5,000	2,000 to 5,000	500 to 2,000	Under 500
1	2	3	4	5	6	7	8	9	10
Coorg	4,991	335	57	943	628	372	38	551	411

IV.—Number per mille of the total population and of each main religion who live in towns.

Province.	Number per mille who live in towns.						
	Total population.	Hindu.	Musalman.	Christian.	Jain.	Parsi.	Animistic.
1	2	3	4	5	6	7	8
Coorg	57	45	206	270	670	765	...

V.—Persons per house and houses per square mile.

Province	Average number of persons per house				Average number of houses per square mile.			
	1911	1901.	1891	1881	1911	1901.	1891	1881.
1	2	3	4	5	6	7	8	9
Coorg	5	6	6	8	21	19	17	14

CHAPTER II.—MOVEMENT OF POPULATION.

THIS chapter is perhaps the only one of practical importance in dealing with the fortunes of Coorg. In it may be explained the curious fluctuations of population from decade to decade noticeable in table II, and also the apparent anomaly of increased house building to accommodate a decreasing population.

2. The explanation is really simple; it is largely a question of more or less coffee. Labourers on the coffee estates arrive about July, and return to their own affairs and crops about September. November sees a fresh influx, which does not ebb until the harvest is safely gathered in. The coffee crop of 1910–11 was comparatively light, and towards the end of February 1911, a large number of labourers had returned to their homes. The census was taken on the night of March 10th, 1911. The crop of 1911–12 was enormous, and the final paying off of labourers had not been completed everywhere, when I visited Mercara in the first week of April 1912. A census taken on March 10th of this present year would have given a widely different result.

3. These statements may be checked by a glance at a few figures. In 1901 those born in the province, and there enumerated, numbered 125,509; in 1911 the number had risen to 129,441. The decline in the total population is entirely due to a falling off of immigrants; those from Madras have declined from 29,348 to 28,581, (practically all from Malabar and South Canara); those from Mysore numbered in 1911 but 16,117, as against 24,712 of 1901.

4. It is clear that this factor of immigration renders practically valueless much of the information which the vital statistics of the province might otherwise afford. Immigration, as table XI in 1901 and 1911 shows, is preponderantly that of men, who may die, but who certainly cannot produce children. Thus in ten years (1900–1910) we find that Coorg shows an excess of 12,500 deaths over births; information as to birth and death rates for ten consecutive years will be found in subsidiary tables VI to VIII to Chapter V. The male death-rate exceeds the female in the ratio of 1,000 : 819; but among the Kodagas, or Coorgs proper, men outnumber women but slightly, and the preponderance of male births over female is not in excess of, if equal to, the normal ratio of such happenings.

5. As in the case of Madras, the classification of 'causes of death' provides us with very little additional information. Of 56 thousand deaths registered in ten years, the all-embracing "fever" accounts for 46,000.

6. Inasmuch as Coorg depends for its prosperity on coffee, some information as to the extent of land under that crop may be of interest. There were in 1901, 58 thousand acres under "mature coffee," and 31,000 acres of coffee land unplanted or abandoned. The well-known set-back which the industry experienced at the commencement of the last decade is illustrated by the figures quoted at the side. The improvement which has of late taken place is not apparent from these statistics, which show an actual decrease of cultivated acreage except in the last year. Of this I understand the explanation to be that attention is now concentrated on land really suitable for the crop, and on improvement in methods of cultivation, rather than on the attempt to secure a large acreage.

Year	Acreage under mature coffee.	Acreage unplanted or abandoned.
1901	58,393	30,977
1902	53,147	29,413
1903	51,445	35,390
1904	47,720	39,610
1905	47,657	40,095
1906	45,108	41,451
1907	45,414	40,180
1908	43,585	43,585
1909	42,773	42,452
1910	43,636	41,142

7. When the price of coffee fell, the casual cultivations of the small native owner lost alike value and interest, and Indian attention devoted itself to the cultivation of rice wherever possible. Under this crop acreage rose from 79,930 acres in 1901 to 82,502 acres in 1910. With a normal rainfall of considerably over 100

inches per annum, paddy, as might be expected, is mainly rainfed; but the small acreage under tanks and channels, such as they are, was trebled in this period. But this apparent increase, I am informed, may be accounted for by more correct calculation of areas, rather than by extended cultivation.

8. Cardamoms, grown chiefly, I was told by a Coorg, by West Coast immigrants on leased *malés*, appear to have accounted for 1,900 acres in 1910, as against 1,100 ten years earlier.

9. Pepper is a valuable "side-line" for the coffee planter, the cost of production being extremely low. Vanilla has been taken up in a small way by a few garden proprietors.

10. *Communications.*—There are no rail roads or waterways in Coorg. Four trunk roads run through the province: (1) Mysore to Tellicherry or Cannanore, (2) Mysore to Mangalore, (3) Manjurabad to Mercara, (4) Gonikoppal to the Wynaad *viâ* Ponnampet. Since the assumption of control by the British Government internal communications have been greatly improved, the policy of the old-time rulers having been to render their country as difficult of access as possible.

11. The Coorg does not appear to be much addicted to emigration. In the Madras Presidency 741 persons born in Coorg were enumerated, mostly in the districts of Malabar and South Canara; 3,071 were found in Mysore State; and three in Ceylon. The fact of a person being born in Coorg, it may be remarked, does not necessarily imply that he is a Coorg (or Kodaga) by race.

CHAPTER III.—BIRTH-PLACE.

COORG statistics supply no material for a chapter on this subject. With the exception of an insignificant minority, those enumerated in the province were born in Coorg, in Mysore State, or else in the adjoining Madras districts of Malabar and South Canara. The European population, comparatively large in proportion to the total population, is accounted for by the planting community. It has declined somewhat since 1901, but it is obviously impossible to state definitely whether this decline is real or due to temporary causes, such as the revisiting of the "old country." At the same time it may be remarked that, in point of European immigrants, 1901 too showed a falling off as compared with 1891.

CHAPTER IV.—RELIGION.

If table VI and subsidiary table I to this chapter are to be accepted without question, the ten years that have elapsed since the census of 1901 have witnessed some curious theological changes. *Hinduism* is still the faith of the majority, but has suffered severely from the inroads of *Animism*, whose followers show the incredible increase of 482 *per cent*.

2. The decrease of *Hindus* and increase of *Animists* are alike easily explicable. If, when asked his religion, a person enumerated declared himself to be a *Hindu*, such assertion was accepted without question. If, on the other hand, at his own wish, or by the whim of the enumerator, the name of his caste or tribe was entered in column 4 of the census schedule, the abstraction office without further ado wrote such person down as "*Animist*."

3. In Chapter IV of the Madras Census Report an attempt has been made to give in simple language some idea of the main ideas underlying the several philosophical systems to which Western usage has give the name of the *Hindu* religion, and to estimate the influence on, or connection with, the religious life of the general population of such abstract speculations. It is unnecessary to tread this ground again; all the more so as the returns do not raise the question in the case of the most interesting section of the population, the Kodagas, all of whom have been returned as *Hindus*.

4. At the same time, one may be pardoned for doubting the accuracy of the term *Hinduism* as a description of the religion professed by these people. True, a Kodaga described his religion to me as *Saivaism*; and a certain trace of Bráhmanical influences may be observed in the existence of a small sub-class of Amma Kodagas (not distinguished in 1901), who wear the sacred thread, abstain from meat and from intoxicating liquors, and possess and exercise, whether actully or potentially, certain priestly attributes and functions. But the main objects of the Kodaga's adoration are the river Cauvery—possibly certain *Hindu* or Bráhmanical ideas have been introduced into the manner of worship—deified heroic ancestors and miscellaneous private gods. This latter circumstance, I was told, expleins the aversion of the Coorg to migration even within the province; his god does not approve of a change to new surroundings.

5. Of the 19,227 *Animists* in the province, Yeravas and Kurubas account for 19,128. Yeravas, who have in total numbers increased by 752 during the decade, were returned *en bloc* as *Hindus* in 1901; Kurubas, with a total increase of but 204, have completely changed their religious proportion, returning 5,207 *Animists* and 2,166 *Hindus*, as against 4,794 *Hindus* and 2,375 *Animists* at the previous enumeration. The change is purely arbitrary; but the description of the culture, manners and customs of the Yeravas given in the Imperial Gazetteer of Coorg shows that they have little, if anything, in common with the social or religious ideas usually evoked in one's mind by the use of the term *Hindu*.

6. When we come to *Musalmans* and *Christians*, we tread on somewhat firmer ground. After a steady increase between 1881 and 1901 the followers of these religious systems now show a falling off in numbers

7. The actual decrease in the number of Musalmans is 511; this decrease is almost entirely on the female side. Máppillas, who number more than half the total Muhammadan population, show an increase in men with a slight falling off in women. The suggestion may be that these enterprising traders are invading the country in increasing numbers, while among the people of the country, amidst whom despite, or perhaps because of, Tipu's attempts to "honour Coorg with Islam," the religion never seems to have taken firm root, Muhammadanism is dying out.

8. The Christianity of the country is due indirectly to the ravages of Haidar and Tipu. The former, having defeated the Rája of Coorg, sent into the province a small garrison in which were found some Catholics; and for their spiritual care the Jesuit missionary at Seringapatam was wont to send yearly a visiting priest. When Tipu captured Bednur and besieged Mangalore in 1783, he deported to Seringapatam a large number of Konkani Christians, who had given assistance to the British. Escaping from Seringapatam about 1792 these people were welcomed by the ruler of Coorg, who assigned to them land at Vírarájéndrapet, assisted them to build a chapel, and obtained for their guidance a priest from Goa. The mission still exists under the charge of the Roman Catholic Bishop of Mysore, and to the present incumbent of Vírarájéndrapet, Father J. J. Cochet, I am indebted for an interesting history of the transference of spiritual jurisdiction from Goa. This history is, however, of ecclesiastical rather than general interest, and considerations of space preclude quotation.

9. Of an Indian *Christian* population of 3,208 persons, the Roman Catholic Church claims 2,830 or 882 per 1,000; its only serious competitor being the Basel Mission, whose converts number 108 per 1,000 of the Indian Christian community. While the total Christian population has declined by 130, Indian Christianity just holds its ground, its adherents having increased by 48 during the decade.

10. The absolute numbers of *Jains* and *Parsis* are too small to render comment necessary.

I.—General distribution of the population by religion.

Religion.	Actual number in 1911	Proportion per 10,000 of population in				Variation per cent. (Increase +, decrease —).			—
		1911.	1901.	1891.	1881.	1901 to 1911.	1891 to 1901.	1881 to 1891.	
1	2	3	4	5	6	7	8	9	10
TOTAL ...	***174,976***	***10,000***	***10,000***	***10,000***	***10,000***	***— 3·1***	***+ 4·4***	***— 2·9***	***— 1·9***
Hindu	188,922	7,939	8,849	9,068	9,118	— 13 1	+ 4·0	— 8·5	— 2·7
Animistic ..	19,227	1,099	183			+ 481·8			
Musalman	13,143	751	756	732	703	— 3·7	+ 7·8	+ 1·0	+ 4·8
Christian	3,553	208	204	196	177	— 3·5	+ 8·6	+ 7·6	+ 12·7
Jain	97	6	6	7	6	— 9·3	— 6·1	+ 15 2	— 2·0
Parsi .. .	34	2	2	2	1	— 17·1	+ 5 1	+ 85 7	+ 61·9

Christians (actual numbers), 1911: males 1,986, females 1,567; 1901, males 2,047, females 1,636; 1891, males 1,868, females 1,524; 1881, males 1,775, females 1,377: 1871, total 2,410.

II.—Religions of urban and rural population.

Province	Number per 10,000 of urban population who are					Number per 10,000 of rural population who are				
	Hindu	Musalman	Christian.	Animist.	Others.	Hindu.	Musalman.	Christian.	Animist	Others
1	2	3	4	5	6	7	8	9	10	11
Coorg	6,228	2,713	960	8	91	8,048	633	157	1,165	2

III.—Races and sects of Christians (actual numbers).

Sect.	European.		Anglo-Indian.		Indian.		Total.		Variation + or —.
	Male.	Female.	Male.	Female	Male	Female.	1911.	1901.	
1	2	3	4	5	6	7	8	9	10
TOTAL	*125*	*82*	*74*	*64*	*1,787*	*1,421*	*3,553*	*3,683*	*—130*
Anglican Communion	89	56	25	20	6	4	200	259	— 59
Baptist	..				2	2	4		+ 4
Congregationalist								10	— 10
Indefinite beliefs								1	— 1
Lutheran ...	4	6	2	4	177	170	363	381	— 18
Methodist	2	1	1		5	5	14	15	— 1
Presbyterian	9	5					14	24	— 10
Protestant (Unsectarian or sect not specified)	2						2		+ 2
Roman Catholic	19	14	44	40	1,590	1,240	2,947	2,959	— 12
Sect not returned ...			2		7		9	34	— 25

IV.—Distribution of Christians per mille—(a) races by sect and (b) sects by race.

Sect.	Races distributed by sect				Sect distributed by race.			
	European	Anglo-Indian	Indian.	Total.	European.	Anglo-Indian.	Indian.	Total
1	2	3	4	5	6	7	8	9
TOTAL	*58*	*39*	*903*	*1,000*	*1,000*	*1,000*	*1,000*	*1,000*
Anglican Communion ...	725	225	50	1,000	700	326	3	56
Baptist			1,000	1,000			2	1
Lutheran	28	16	956	1,000	48	43	108	102
Methodist	214	72	714	1,000	15	7	3	4
Presbyterian	1,000			1,000	68	..		4
Protestant (Unsectarian or sect not specified).	1,000			1,000	10			1
Roman Catholic	11	29	960	1,000	159	609	882	829
Sect not returned		222	778	1,000		15	2	3

CHAPTER V.—AGE.

There is nothing of peculiar interest in statistics of age in relation to Coorg. Underlying the figures are the same causes of inaccuracy as noted in the case of Madras Presidency; the disturbing influence exerted by the presence of a large number of immigrant coolies in the prime of life, can be noted in subsidiary table I, which shows that the predominant section of the people is always that of men aged 25–30.

2. Subsidiary tables VI, VII and VIII show the vital statistics of the province. The reasons which render them for census purposes unreliable have been given in Chapter II.

3. Subsidiary tables IV and V, taken for what they are worth, are not encouraging. The proportion of children to persons aged 15–40, and to married women at this age, has fallen, while the proportion of married women aged 15–40 to the general female population has risen during the last decade.

4. The decrease in the population has taken place at the age period 0–40, while the proportion of the aged (60 and over) has risen considerably.

Number per 1,000 of population at reproductive period of life.

Year.	Men.	Women.
1911	475	401
1901	473	392
1891	477	407
1881	489	482

5. Assuming, as was done in the case of Madras, that the period of reproductivity for a man is 20–45, and for a woman 15–35, the figures noted in the margin show the position of the population in this respect at the last four enumerations.

6. As a guide to the future the number of those now aged 0–10 is of some use. Twenty years hence such children, or so many of them as survive, will be the potential fathers and mothers of the rising generation in Coorg. The great rise from 1881 to 1891 is noteworthy, and it has been followed by a steady decline, until the position has again reached the level of 1881.

Number per 1,000 of population aged 0–10.

Year.	Male.	Female.
1911	198	251
1901	208	262
1891	226	284
1881	195	255

I.—Age distribution of 10,000 *of each sex in the Province.*

Age.	1911.		1901		1891.		1881.	
	Male	Female.	Male.	Female.	Male.	Female	Male	Female
1	2	3	4	5	6	7	8	9
TOTAL	*10,000*	*10,000*	*10,000*	*10,000*	*10,000*	*10,000*	*10,000*	*10,000*
0–1	216	268	275	351	221	286	205	280
1–2	141	186	81	104	151	197	130	178
2–3	220	292	205	259	251	330	136	187
3–4	218	276	182	250	263	354	182	249
4–5	210	263	212	267	228	288	186	237
0–5	1,005	1,285	955	1,231	1,114	1,455	839	1,126
5–10	977	1,225	1,121	1,398	1,146	1,388	1,118	1,421
10–15	1,051	1,161	1,185	1,293	941	988	1,133	1,166
15–20	1,041	1,052	972	964	988	1,031	1,152	1,101
20–25	1,134	1,111	1,013	1,034	1,093	1,121	1,144	1,177
25–30	1,208	1,031	1,218	1,064	1,277	1,104	1,310	1,184
30–35	962	812	1,071	839	1,032	818	1,078	855
35–40	809	567	787	543	767	540	781	546
40–45	646	531	643	527	605	529	575	460
45–50	408	381	347	285	364	269	311	256
50–55	329	362	316	350	314	327	275	291
55–60	156	152	130	130	131	115	96	99
60–65	150	199						
65–70	53	67	242	327	228	315	193	298
70 and over	76	114						
Mean age	25	24	25	23	24	23	24	23

II.—Age distribution of 10,000 of each sex and religion in the Province.

Age.	1911.		1901.		1891.		1881.	
	Male	Female	Male	Female	Male.	Female.	Male.	Female.
1	2	3	4	5	6	7	8	9
Hindu	*10,000*	*10,000*	*10,000*	*10,000*	*10,000*	*10,000*	*10,000*	*10,000*
0–5	974	1,244	984	1,239	1,152	1,465	1,089	1,420
5–10	983	1,224	1,148	1,405	1,175	1,402	914	1,148
10–15	1,069	1,233	1,198	1,304	955	996	1,153	1,181
15–20	1,068	1,072	964	959	982	1,089	1,149	1,099
20–40	4,111	3,454	4,053	3,483	4,114	3,562	4,264	3,749
40–60	1,522	1,398	1,412	1,285	1,392	1,229	1,240	1,112
60 and over	278	390	241	325	230	307	191	291
Musalman	*10,000*	*10,000*	*10,000*	*10,000*	*10,000*	*10,000*	*10,000*	*10,000*
0–5	682	1,155	647	1,114	689	1,342	685	1,258
5–10	686	1,195	833	1,279	848	1,258	723	1,060
10–15	1,050	1,022	1,095	1,157	857	876	970	993
15–20	1,165	1,011	1,073	975	1,062	984	1,212	1,111
20–40	4,546	3,611	4,479	3,646	4,730	3,807	4,759	3,871
40–60	1,574	1,526	1,609	1,431	1,593	1,363	1,419	1,294
60 and over	297	480	264	398	221	420	232	418
Christian	*10,000*	*10,000*	*10,000*	*10,000*	*10,000*	*10,000*	*10,000*	*10,000*
0–5	987	1,149	845	1,167	1,108	1,371	1,014	1,298
5–10	911	1,155	1,045	1,357	1,098	1,221	788	966
10–15	831	1,040	1,251	1,333	655	971	868	995
15–20	982	1,136	943	935	937	984	1,065	1,191
20–40	4,028	3,644	3,977	3,509	4,886	3,858	4,766	4,016
40–60	1,853	1,455	1,695	1,363	1,628	1,280	1,341	1,285
60 and over	418	421	244	336	193	315	158	254

III.—Age distribution of 1,000 of each sex in certain castes.

Caste.	Males. Number per mille aged.					Females. Number per mille aged.				
	0–5.	5–12	12–15.	15–40.	40 and over.	0–5.	5–12.	12–15.	15–40.	40 and over.
1	2	3	4	5	6	7	8	9	10	11
Ganda	114	154	75	480	177	145	183	74	430	168
Holeya	84	121	68	552	175	108	165	78	491	158
Kodaga	139	180	83	434	164	144	183	79	427	167
Lingáyat	88	163	94	473	182	98	160	86	425	231
Vakkaliga	85	135	84	499	197	103	164	86	440	207

IV.—Proportion of children and of persons over 50 to those aged 15–40; also of married females aged 15–40 per 100 females.

Province	Proportion of children of both sexes per 100.						Proportion of persons over 60 per 100 persons aged 15–40.						Number of married females aged 15–40 per 100 females of all ages.		
	Persons aged 15–40.			Married females aged 15–40.			1911.		1901.		1891.				
	1911.	1901.	1891.	1911.	1901.	1891.	Male.	Female.	Male.	Female.	Male.	Female.	1911.	1901.	1891.
1	2	3	4	5	6	7		9	10	11	12	13	14	15	16
Coorg	45·3	48·4	51·2	155·7	164·4	162·6	5·4	8·3	4·8	7·3	4·4	6·8	32·1	31·7	34·7

V.—*Variation in population at certain age periods.*

Province.	Period.	Variation per cent. in population (increase +, and decrease −).					
		All ages.	0–10.	10–15	15–40	40–60.	60 and over
1	2	3	4	5	6	7	8
Coorg	1901–1911	− 3·1	− 7·4	− 13·6	− 1·1	+ 3·6	+ 12·1
	1891–1901	+ 4·4	− 3·9	+ 33·8	+ 1·8	+ 7·2	+ 8·4
	1881–1891	− 2·9	+ 10·6	− 18·7	− 8·3	+ 8·1	+ 9·4

VI & VII.—*Reported birth and death rates by sex.*

Year.	Births						Deaths.					
	Actual			Ratio per mille of total population (census of 1901)			Actual.			Ratio per mille of population of each sex (census of 1901)		
	Total.	Males.	Females.	Total.	Males	Females.	Total.	Males	Females	Total	Males	Females.
1	2	3	4	5	6	7	8	9	10	11	12	13
1901 ...	3,401	1,686	1,715	18·83	9·38	9·50	6,590	3,690	2,900	36·49	36·81	36·09
1902 .	4,319	2,170	2,149	23·91	12·01	11·90	4,887	2,693	2,194	27·06	26·86	27·31
1903	4,787	2,444	2,343	26·51	13·53	12·97	5,676	3,086	2,590	31·43	30·78	32·23
1904	3,970	1,999	1,971	21·98	11·07	10·91	4,808	2,668	2,140	26·62	26·61	26·63
1905	4,572	2,230	2,342	25·31	12·34	12·97	4,739	2,577	2,162	26·24	25·70	26·91
1906	4,713	2,324	2,389	26·10	12·87	13·23	5,285	2,875	2,410	29·26	28·68	29·99
1907 ...	4,304	2,235	2,069	23·83	12·37	11·46	6,349	3,453	2,896	35·15	34·44	36·04
1908	4,365	2,198	2,167	24·17	12·17	12·00	6,311	3,495	2,816	34·94	34·86	35·05
1909 ...	4,981	2,497	2,484	27·58	13·83	13·75	5,084	2,819	2,265	28·13	28·12	28·19
1910	4,638	2,400	2,238	25·68	13·29	12·39	6,822	3,729	3,093	37·77	37·19	38·49

VIII.—*Deaths classified by causes.*

Year	Causes of death.						Total.
	Cholera.	Small-pox	Fevers.	Dysentery and Diarrhœa	Injuries including suicide.	All other causes.	
1	2	3	4	5	6	7	8
TOTAL	*524*	*1,194*	*45,990*	*2,029*	*359*	*6,455*	*56,551*
1901 ..	58	449	5,182	218	80	603	6,590
1902 ..	..	19	4,116	106	64	582	4,887
1903		43	4,770	137	38	688	5,676
1904 ...		16	4,054	90	52	596	4,808
1905 .	...	132	3,876	96	25	610	4,739
1906	10	234	4,266	141	24	610	5,285
1907 .	187	211	4,868	375	13	695	6,349
1908 .	114	38	5,028	408	28	700	6,311
1909 .. .	99	6	4,113	187	21	658	5,084
1910	56	46	5,717	271	19	713	6,822
Ratio per mille on total population of 1901 .. .	2·9	6·6	254·7	11·2	2·0	35·7	313·1

Note —Sexwar details are not procurable.

CHAPTER VI.—SEX.

THERE are but 799 women for every 1,000 men in Coorg. Immigration is again the explanation. Some classes obviously immigrant, such as Nāyars and Tīyans, have scarcely any women among them. But a steady fall in the proportion of women does not tally with the information given to me by a planter, who told me that the cooly, having got over his first shyness of a strange country, inclines now to bring his womankind along with him.

2. It would have been interesting, had it been possible, to take a census in the heavy crop year 1912, which followed the light year 1911. When crop is light, the planter must needs economize in his labour; and thus, so far as possible, engage men, who are more efficient than women. With a heavy crop, (and good prices), economy is not of such paramount importance; and, with demand for labour out-running the supply, the proportion of women workers must needs increase.

3. At the same time, a preponderance of men among the Kodagas, Yeravas, and Indian Christians, who may in general be assumed as natives of the province, suggests that Coorg in the matter of sex proportion ultimately agrees with Mysore rather than with Madras, although figures quoted in the preceding chapter show a general outnumbering of boys by girls at the age 0-10.

4. Inasmuch as post-puberty marriage is the rule amongst Kodagas, it is interesting to note that a defect of women here occurs for the first time at the critical age 12–15, followed by an upward movement from 15–20.

5. The extremely low proportion of women to men among Muhammadans is probably due to the fact that the Muhammadan trader or pedlar who visits the hills is even more apt than the cooly to leave his women at home.

I.—Number of females per 1,000 males at different age periods by religions at each of the last three censuses.

Age.	All religions.			Hindu.			Musalman.			Christian.		
	1911.	1901.	1891.	1911.	1901.	1891.	1911.	1901.	1891.	1911.	1901.	1891.
1	2	3	4	5	6	7	8	9	10	11	12	13
TOTAL, ALL AGES (actual population).	*799*	*801*	*804*	*808*	*818*	*823*	*565*	*609*	*603*	*789*	*799*	*816*
0–1	990	1,020	1,046	994	1,019	1,086	978	1,072	1,231	1,114	1,152	1,045
1–2	1,056	1,035	1,048	1,061	1,026	1,043	902	1,096	1,215	786	958	906
2–3	1,060	1,017	1,056	1,074	1,014	1,045	1,083	975	1,267	875	1,231	1,159
3–4	1,009	1,100	1,062	1,039	1,100	1,093	908	1,000	948	889	1,071	989
4–5	1,002	1,011	1,018	1,001	1,003	1,006	889	1,121	1,270	872	1,028	974
TOTAL 0–5 ...	*1,021*	*1,034*	*1,051*	*1,032*	*1,030*	*1,046*	*956*	*1,049*	*1,175*	*918*	*1,104*	*1,010*
5–10	1,002	996	975	1,006	1,001	982	984	935	894	1,000	1,087	907
10–15	882	874	845	925	890	858	550	644	616	988	852	1,218
15–20	807	795	840	815	814	870	491	554	580	918	793	857
20–25	783	819	825	777	839	846	452	586	605	796	858	882
25–30	684	714	695	662	741	714	507	448	496	662	689	758
TOTAL 0–30 ...	*855*	*868*	*869*	*859*	*884*	*885*	*602*	*655*	*674*	*866*	*881*	*916*
30–40	632	596	607	637	604	629	411	476	415	696	638	611
40–50	653	657	662	673	675	688	513	521	457	561	586	525
50–60	846	860	799	886	899	809	619	587	664	732	754	975
60 and over	1,089	1,084	1,111	1,136	1,108	1,100	916	920	1,143	805	1,100	1,233
TOTAL, 20 AND OVER ...	*698*	*680*	*681*	*715*	*695*	*701*	*506*	*534*	*496*	*671*	*669*	*680*

II.—Number of females per 1,000 males for certain selected castes.

Caste.	Number of females per 1,000 males.						
	All ages.	0–5.	5–12.	12–15.	15–20.	20–40.	40 and over.
1	2	3	4	5	6	7	8
Gauda	*894*	1,131	1,065	879	908	769	853
Holeya ..	*733*	942	1,004	831	721	635	661
Kodaga	*967*	1,023	1,006	934	1,108	925	1,008
Lingayat	*1,058*	1,188	1,040	968	871	975	1,340
Vakkaliga ...	*822*	996	996	845	691	735	868

CHAPTER VII.—CIVIL CONDITION.

AT the time that the census was taken the civil condition of the Coorg population was as noted in the margin; the figures are taken from subsidiary table I to this chapter. A further reference thereto shows the alterations that have occurred in this position throughout a period of thirty years.

Civil condition of 1,000 persons.

Sex.	Males.	Females
Unmarried	554	440
Married	400	387
Widowed	46	173

2. There were at this enumeration but 773 wives for 1,000 husbands. Tipu Sultan, it is true, once denounced the Coorgs as guilty of polyandry, but these figures do not really prove that that truculent potentate was justified in his suspicions. Here too we must needs discount the influence of immigration. Among Animists, the indigenous jungle tribes of the province, the proportion of wives to husbands is practically equal; the greatest deficiency is noticed among the Muhammadans, who, as already noted, are probably to a great extent but traders and pedlars not permanently resident in Coorg. Among the Kodagas themselves we see that wives exceed husbands; the explanation in all probability being that some widows or divorced women have returned themselves as married.

Wives per 1,000 husbands.

TOTAL	*773*
Hindus	764
Muhammadans	589
Christians	747
Animists	984

3. It is of interest to note that table XIV shows a few cases of infant marriage and widowhood among the Kodagas. This, a Kodaga gentleman assured me, is undoubtedly wrong; it has since occurred to me that such cases are to be explained by a tendency among settlers from the plains, who bring with them the social customs of their place of origin, to describe themselves as Kodagas; in the natural belief that, in Coorg at any rate, the social standing of the Kodaga is higher than that of the immigrant.

4. Marriage at a reasonable age is the unvarying rule among the Kodagas. Of the marriage ceremony an interesting account is given in the Imperial Gazetteer of Coorg; the chief peculiarity appears to consist in the fact that ceremonies are performed simultaneously in the houses of bride and bridegroom. Divorce on account of a woman's unfaithfulness is recognized; widow marriage apparently is not prohibited. Subsidiary table IV, compared with a similar table for 1901, shows that the proportion of widows, especially at the earlier ages, has decreased considerably.

5. The figures of Imperial tables VII and XIV, and those given in the subsidiary tables to this chapter, deal with actual totals so small that detailed analysis is not required to render them intelligible. These sections of the Coorg population which do not belong especially to the province are so small that it is impossible to take them as representative of their communities; to hang an essay concerning Māppilla marriage on the fact that there are some 7,000 Māppillas in Coorg would be obviously absurd. And as to peculiar marriage customs among the Coorgs proper, (I use the term to include Kodagas, Yeravas, Heggades, Ayiris, etc., etc.), I have no fresh or original information or knowledge.

I.—Distribution by civil condition of 1,000 of each sex, religion and main age period at each of the last four censuses

Religion, sex and age	Unmarried.				Married				Widowed.			
	1911.	1901.	1891.	1881	1911.	1901.	1891.	1881.	1911.	1901.	1891.	1881
1	2	3	4	5	6	7	8	9	10	11	12	13
All religions. Males—												
All ages	554	555	531	539	400	396	430	410	46	49	39	51
0–10	998	996	996	999	2	4	4	1	-	.	..	
10–15	990	988	982	980	10	12	18	20		..		..
15–40	478	445	405	418	489	512	565	532	33	43	30	50
40 and over	33	33	31	30	806	803	828	806	161	164	141	162

I.—Distribution by civil condition of 1,000 *of each sex, religion and main age period at each of the last four censuses*—cont.

Religion, sex and age.	Unmarried.				Married.				Widowed			
	1911.	1901.	1891.	1881.	1911.	1901.	1891.	1881.	1911.	1901.	1891.	1881.
1	2	3	4	5	6	7	8	9	10	11	12	13
All religions—cont. Females—												
All ages ...	440	446	423	398	387	378	410	410	173	176	167	192
0–10 . ..	998	997	992	995	2	3	7	5			1	
10–15	937	928	884	842	61	69	112	149	2	3	4	9
15–40 .	175	143	114	94	701	710	753	724	124	147	133	182
40 and over .	7	9	11	5	334	314	319	274	659	677	670	721
Hindu. Males—												
All ages .	560	557	584	540	393	392	426	407	47	51	40	53
0–10	999	996	996	999	1	4	4	1	..		..	.
10–15 .	991	988	981	979	9	12	19	20	..	.	...	1
15–40 ..	489	441	400	413	479	514	568	535	32	45	32	52
40 and over ..	33	32	30	27	799	797	822	803	168	171	148	170
Females—												
All ages . ..	448	451	428	402	372	373	408	408	180	176	164	190
0–10 . .	998	996	992	995	2	3	7	5	..	1	1	..
10–15 .	940	932	886	843	58	65	110	148	2	3	4	9
15–40	190	146	117	96	678	705	749	722	132	149	134	182
40 and over ..	6	9	11	5	320	312	326	279	674	679	663	716
Musalman. Males—												
All ages	547	526	499	517	421	442	479	451	32	32	22	32
0–10 . ..	996	993	996	995	2	6	4	5	2	1	..	...
10–15	987	985	988	988	13	15	12	12		..	...	
15–40 .	527	478	440	457	451	500	545	517	22	22	15	26
40 and over	34	31	37	52	866	863	890	852	100	106	73	96
Females—												
All ages	357	373	361	339	439	430	451	441	204	197	188	220
0–10	995	997	995	993	5	3	5	6	.	..		1
10–15	854	863	830	810	144	130	163	186	2	7	7	4
15–40	76	74	60	57	784	773	821	768	140	153	119	175
40 and over	6	3	7	3	303	312	262	224	691	685	781	778
Christian. Males—												
All ages ..	545	575	542	562	411	385	417	390	44	40	41	48
0–10 . .	997	1,000	993	994	3		7	6				
10–15	982	992	1,000	987	18	8		13		...	...	
15–40	506	502	459	499	468	467	518	457	26	31	28	44
40 and over .	91	78	79	38	773	796	779	808	136	126	142	154
Females—												
All ages	442	466	420	370	389	369	393	428	169	165	187	202
0–10	1,000	998	995	997		2	5	3	.	...	.	...
10–15 . ..	963	963	946	905	25	32	54	88	12	5		7
15–40	223	186	141	106	674	685	714	731	103	129	145	168
40 and over ...	27	18	21	..	344	349	248	245	629	633	731	755

II.—Distribution by main age periods and civil condition of 10,000 *of each sex and religion.*

Religion and age.	Males.			Females.		
	Unmarried	Married.	Widowed.	Unmarried.	Married.	Widowed.
1	2	3	4	5	6	7
All religions	5,541	3,997	462	4,403	3,867	1,730
0–10	1,979	3	1	2,505	5	..
10–15	1,040	11	...	1,088	71	2
15–40	2,461	2,518	169	798	3,205	570
40 and over ..	61	1,465	292	12	586	1,158
Hindu	5,603	3,928	469	4,485	3,715	1,800
0–10	1,955	2		2,463	5	...
10–15	1,058	10		1,149	72	2
15–40	2,529	2,479	167	862	3,068	595
40 and over	61	1,437	302	11	570	1,203
Musalman	5,473	4,210	317	3,574	4,339	2,087
0–10	1,864	2	3	2,887	13	.
10–15	1,037	13		872	147	2
15–40	3,009	2,575	126	852	3,622	649
40 and over .	63	1,620	188	13	607	1,386
Christian ..	5,448	4,114	438	4,422	3,893	1,685
0–10	1,893	5	..	2,304	...	.
10–15	816	15		1,002	25	84
15–40	2,533	2,342	131	1,065	3,223	191
40 and over	206	1,752	307	51	645	1,181

III.—Proportion of sexes by civil condition at certain ages by religions.

Religion.	Number of females per 1,000 males.														
	All ages			0–10			10–15.			15–40			40 and over.		
	Unmarried.	Married.	Widowed	Unmarried.	Married.	Widowed.	Unmarried.	Married	Widowed.	Unmarried.	Married.	Widowed.	Unmarried.	Married.	Widowed.
1	2	3	4	5	6	7	8	9	10	11	12	13	14	15	16
All religions ...	635	773	2,990	1,011	1,418		836	5,378	5,666	259	1,016	2,689	152	320	3,168
Hindu	647	764	3,102	1,019	1,611	.	878	5,842	4,383	278	1,001	2,888	145	321	3,219
Musalman	369	589	3,635	969	3,000	...	475	6,364		66	795	2,906	118	212	4,165
Christian	640	747	3,034	960	...	...	969	1,333		332	1·086	2,962	195	290	3,083

IV.—Distribution by civil condition of 1,000 of each sex at certain ages for selected castes.

Caste.	Distribution of 1,000 of each age by civil condition																	
	All ages			0–5			5–12.			12–20			20–40			40 and over		
	Unmarried.	Married.	Widowed.	Unmarried.	Married.	Widowed.	Unmarried.	Married	Widowed.	Unmarried.	Married.	Widowed.	Unmarried.	Married.	Widowed.	Unmarried.	Married.	Widowed.
1	2	3	4	5	6	7	8	9	10	11	12	13	14	15	16	17	18	19
Males—																		
Ganda	580	377	43	1,000	.	..	995	5	...	975	24	1	346	616	38	23	813	164
Holeya	543	406	51	1,000		.	1,000	...	..	966	34	..	359	595	46	39	787	174
Kodaga ..	640	323	37	1,000		.	998	1	1	985	15	...	407	565	28	14	818	168
Lingáyat	599	342	59	997	3	..	996	4		968	32	..	380	556	64	66	785	199
Vakkaliga ...	564	387	49	1,000	...	..	999	1	..	969	31	...	379	578	43	37	801	162
Females—																		
Ganda	486	378	136	998	2	...	995	4	1	785	211	4	42	848	110	5	400	595
Holeya	428	389	183	998	2		991	9	..	678	304	18	74	742	184	10	298	692
Kodaga	581	335	184	1,000		.	996	4	...	895	102	3	87	805	108	5	395	600
Lingáyat	386	315	299	1,000		...	986	14	..	638	350	12	47	640	3'3	1	162	837
Vakkaliga	409	347	244	1,000	.	..	994	6		694	292	14	47	706	247	8	240	752

CHAPTER VIII.—EDUCATION.

As in the Madras Presidency, ability to write a letter and to read the reply thereto, was in the Coorg census adopted as the criterion of education, or, at least, of literacy. Judged by this standard 17,443 persons, (15,277 men and 2,166 women), out of a total population of 174,976 were found to be educated. Compared with 1901, these figures show a total increase of 3,376, (2,469 men and 907 women), and subsidiary table III shows a very satisfactory proportional progress. Furthermore while the constant fluctuations, already explained, in the total population of the province are apt to render misleading proportions of which such total population forms one term, it may be noted that the floating population is almost entirely illiterate.

2. In comparison with the Madras Presidency Coorg makes a good educational showing; the proportion of literates to the total population, and among the followers of the Hindu, Musalman, and Christian religions, considerably exceeding that of the larger territory. Contrast of territories so completely disproportionate in extent and population is however hardly fair; if a comparison be drawn between Coorg and the Nilgiri hills, where general conditions are somewhat similar, it will be seen that the advantage is with the latter. At the same time, in the case of the latter district the effect on educational statistics of the large European populations of Coonoor, Wellington, and Ootacamund, must needs be discounted.

3. In regard to the literacy of particular castes, the figures given in the margin show a considerable progress among Kodagas. The comparison is vitiated to some extent by separation at this enumeration from Kodagas proper of Amma Kodagas, and of Jama Kodagas, whose low percentage of literacy must have depreciated that of the other sections with which formerly they were clubbed.

Literates per mille

Caste.	Males 1911	Males 1901	Females 1911	Females 1901
Kodaga	374	284	78	37
Jama Kodaga ...	25		1	
Amma Kodaga .	336		49	

4. Indian Christians have 313 male and 138 female literates per thousand of each sex. As Indian Christians were not in this respect differentiated from other Christian communities in 1901, it is impossible to judge whether they have advanced or receded in the matter of literacy. Their proportional figures, however, compare not unfavourably with those of the total Christian population; the falling off in English literacy noticeable in the Christian community is apparently due to a decrease in the actual numbers of Europeans and Anglo-Indians.

5. Education so far does not seem to have made much appeal to the Yeravas, who can boast but four literates in a total population of over 15,000. They can at least claim that their women are as well educated as their men, the total number of four being made up of two representatives from each sex.

6. Comparison of the number of literates at different age periods shows that among the male sex increase has been greatest at the age 20 and over, (40 per thousand), among women at the period 15–20—a fact which speaks well for educational progress amid female children in the decade.

7. From a manuscript volume of "Standing Information" compiled by Mr. L. T. Harris, I.C.S., Commissioner of Coorg, I gather that between 1901 and 1910 public schools increased in number from 77 to 91; and the pupils attending them from 4,325 to 5,910. Girls' schools increased from 4 to 7, with an increase from 179 to 606 in the number of pupils; the number of girls attending boys' schools rose from 736 to 1,205; the number of Coorg pupils from 2,769 to 3,859.

I.—*Education by age, sex and religion.*

Religion.	Number per 10,000 who are literate.											Number per 10,000 who are illiterate.		
	All ages			0–10.		10–15.		15–20.		20 and over.				
	Total.	Male.	Female.	Male.	Female.	Male.	Female.	Male.	Female.	Male.	Female.	Total.	Male.	Female.
1	2	3	4	5	6	7	8	9	10	11	12	13	14	15
All religions .	997	1,570	279	90	45	1,072	400	1,670	570	2,187	305	9,008	8,430	9,721
Hindu . ..	1,061	1,688	284	103	48	1,212	400	1,776	597	2,284	304	8,939	8,312	9,716
Musalman	1,230	1,834	160	35	9	737	330	1,585	271	2,442	173	8,770	8,166	9,840
Christian ..	2,671	3,605	1,940	845	277	2,121	2,209	4,206	2,665	4,692	2,393	7.129	6,395	8,060

II.—*English education by age, sex and religion.*

Religion.	(1911) Literate in English per 10,000											(1901) Number per 10,000.	
	Total.			0–10		10–15.		15–20		20 and over.			
	Total.	Male.	Female.	Male	Female.	Male	Female.	Male.	Female.	Male.	Female.	Male.	Female.
1	2	3	4	5	6	7	8	9	10	11	12	13	14
All religions	108	169	31	4	6	98	42	177	55	236	35	14	2
Hindu . .	99	167	15	3	7	110	41	190	35	228	10	12	...
Musalman ...	28	44		..		28		20	...	61		8	...
Christian ...	1,281	1,571	918	106	55	182	429	1,128	1,236	2,266	1,295	178	99

III.—*Progress of education since* 1891.

Province.	Number of literate per 10,000.													
	All ages.						15–20				20 and over.			
	Males.			Females.			Males.		Females.		Males.		Females.	
	1911.	1901.	1891.	1911.	1901.	1891.	1911.	1901.	1911.	1901.	1911.	1901.	1911	1901.
1	2	3	4	5	6	7	8	9	10	11	12	13	14	15
Coorg ...	1,570	1,277	1,175	279	157	90	1,670	1,620	570	367	2,187	1,725	305	164

CHAPTER IX.—LANGUAGE.

TABLE X shows the languages current in the province, and the number of persons returned as speaking each language.

2. Some changes in proportion since 1901 may be noted. *Canarese,* though it still claims most adherents, is spoken now by but 386 per 1,000 of the population, as against 424 per 1,000 ten years earlier; *Kodagu* speakers have increased from 217 to 245 per 1,000 of the population. Kodagu speakers outnumber Kodagas by 3,500; the language, which, I understand, is somewhat akin to *Canarese,* is used by other castes, such as the Āyiris, of the province.

3. The decided decrease in *Canarese* speakers, and similar though slight fallings off in those returning *Malayālam, Tamil,* and *Telugu,* as their respective vernaculars, may be attribued to the early return of coolies to their homes—a fact which will also explain the proportional increase in representation of *Kodaga.* The actual increase in the number of *Kodagu* speakers, it may be observed, is but little greater than that in the number of the Kodaga caste or race.

4. *Yerava* is returned as the mother-tongue of 14,916 persons; figures which show that the marked increase between 1891 and 1901, (from 2,587 to 13,175), was the result of more correct enumeration in the latter year. Inasmuch as the number of Yeravas (Table XIII) is 15,338, it follows that some of the caste must use the more general speech of their neighbours: the phenomenon is however not so strongly marked in 1901, when Yeravas exceeded *Yerava* speakers by 1,411.

5. *Hindōstāni* speakers have decreased by 1,100 and odd: they tally in point of numbers almost exactly with the Musalman community exclusive of Labbais and Māppillas.

6. There are but 18 Portuguese in table XIII; accordingly if a return of 67 Portuguese speakers be correct the number must include some few Goanese, or West Coast Anglo-Indians. English is returned by 345 persons—a number which exceeds by 34 the combined totals of "Europeans," "British," "Anglo-Indians," "Irish," "English," and "Scotch."

I.—Distribution of total population by language according to Linguistic Survey.

Family, sub-family, branch and sub-branch.	Group	Language.	Dialect.	Number of speakers. 1911.	Number of speakers. 1910.	Number per 10,000 of population of province (1911)
1	2	3	4	5	6	
			GRAND TOTAL ...	*174,976*	*180,607*	*10,000*
		I.—LANGUAGES OF INDIA				
Dravidian family ..	Dravida group	Tamil		4,291	5,189	452
		Malayālam		13,909	14,039	795
		...	Yerava	14,916	13,175	853
		Canarese		67,545	76,608	3,860
		..	Kurumba	4,012	4,162	229
		Kodagu or Coorgi.		42,784	39,148	2,445
		Tulu	..	14,226	12,994	813
	Andhra group	Telugu		2,688	2,974	154
			TOTAL	*164,371*	*168,289*	*9,394*
Indo-European family. Aryan sub-family. Sanskritic sub-branch.	North-west group.	Sindhi		8	7	
			Kachchi	3	29	
	Southern group	Marāthi		1,741	2,242	100
			Konkani	2,696	2,585	154
	Western group	Western Hindi	Hindōstāni	5,527	6,669	316
			Hindi	6	10	
		Rājastāni	Mārvāri	1	10	
		Gujarāti	..	129	102	8
		..	Pārsi	1	10	
		Panjābi	...	1	4	
			TOTAL	*10,113*	*11,668*	*578*

I.—Distribution of total population by language according to Linguistic Survey—cont.

Family, sub-family, branch and sub-branch.	Group.	Language.	Dialect.	Number of speakers. 1911.	Number of speakers. 1901.	Number per 10,000 of population of province (1911).
1	2	3	4	5	6	7
		I.—LANGUAGES OF INDIA—*cont.*				
Gipsy languages .	..	Lambadi ...	.. ...	60	27	4
		Kutni		4	..	
			TOTAL ..	***64***	***27***	***4***
		II.—LANGUAGES FOREIGN TO INDIA.				
Semitic family . .	......	Arabic	. .	6		. .
Indo-European family. Aryan sub-family. Iranian branch .	Romance	French	...	2	3	. .
		Portuguese ...	...	67	111	4
	Teutonic	English ...	.	345	454	20
		German .		8	22	.
			TOTAL ..	***428***	***590***	***24***
		Others	...	...	22	...

CHAPTER X.—INFIRMITIES.

On this subject there is little to be said. The number of the affected has fallen from 240 to ·92 in ten years, and each class of infirmity shows a decrease. If we can accept the returns as correct—a very doubtful question—this state of things is highly satisfactory.

I.—Number afflicted per 100,000 of the population at each of the last four censuses.

Year.	Insane.		Deaf-mute.		Blind		Leper.	
	Male.	Female.	Male.	Female	Male.	Female.	Male.	Female.
1	2	3	4	5	6	7	8	9
1911	11	10	42	59	47	45	6	...
1901 ...	16	20	59	56	45	63	6	4
1891	26	25	80	64	49	51	13	14
1881	23	18	109	85	92	90	25	23

CHAPTER XI.—CASTE, TRIBE, RACE OR NATIONALITY.

FOR the treatment of this section, the suggestion made in paragraph 7 of the introductory chapter would, I imagine, be of special import.

2 Table XIII shows the caste, tribe, race or nationality of every person enumerated in Coorg. A large number of such persons represent immigrants belonging to sections of the South Indian population in no way peculiarly representative of, or connected with, the province; and there is accordingly no justification for entering on a disquisition here as to their social or racial peculiarities. The castes peculiar to Coorg have been treated by Messrs. Holland and Richtor; in the report of 1901, Mr. Francis set forth some fresh information concerning the *Ayiris* and *Yeravas*. Devoid of personal acquaintance with the subject I can put forward nothing of that interest, which an official long resident in the Province, and conversant with the ways of its people, could doubtless supply.

3. To one small matter of detail, I may again draw attention. This is the division of the *Kodagas* of 1901 into *Kodagas*, *Amma Kodagas*, and *Jama Kodagas*. The distinction between *Kodaga* and *Amma Kodaga* has been noted in Chapter IV; as to the origin of the latter it is related that in the olden days, when strife ran high between *nād* and *nād*, or village and village, it was found necessary to exempt from the liabilities of war certain families, who should watch over the local gods and temples.

The *Jama Kodagas* are old-time immigrants from Mysore, who gained the favour of the Rāja, and received grants of land on condition of service. They are found only in Gadināḍ and Yedavanād of the Nanjarājapatna taluk; although they have adopted the Coorg dress, and, to some extent, the habits of the *Kodagas*, they remain distinct from the *Kodagas* proper.

Their fidelity to, and favour with, the Coorg Rājas are attested by the story that Vīrarāja, in exile in Benares, wrote asking that some *Jama Kodagas* of Gadināḍ might be sent to him, to be his companions and attendants.

4. In respect to increase or decrease in particular castes, sex proportion, etc., allusion has been made elsewhere in this report, where the question arose with greater appropriateness.

CHAPTER XII.—OCCUPATION.

THE information to be garnered from the various tables dealing with the subject of occupation presents no very unexpected features.

2. The principal industry of Coorg is the planting of coffee by Europeans. There does not seem to be any *ā priori* reason why one race should grow a plant better than another; still, I was informed by an expert, who occupied a position of complete disinterestedness, that Indian coffee cultivation is as a rule bad; the grower gives his garden too little manure, too much shade, and fails to keep abreast of modern improvements in agriculture. To every rule there are exceptions; and it is only fair to add that a few Indian-owned estates in the neighbourhood of Somvārpet, Mercara, and Sāntikoppa, take rank with the very best.

3. This view is confirmed by the figures of table XV-E, which show that, of 94 considerable estates enumerated, 83 are owned either by European companies, or by individual European and Anglo-Indian proprietors.

4. The number of persons shown as employed thereon, (10,812), is considerably less than that appearing in table XV-A against the item "tea, coffee, indigo, and cinchona plantations." The difference is probably represented by the small proprietors and their employēs; about almost every Coorg farm-house may be noticed some cultivation of coffee, small and careless though it may be.

5. When coffee slumped—apparently the number dependent on "planting" has fallen by nearly 7,500 in ten years—the Coorg must needs have turned his attention to other forms of agricultural employment. Figures quoted in Chapter II with respect to rice cultivation confirm this presumption, which, at the same time, receive but qualified support from the census figures: the number dependent on ordinary cultivation having increased by but 2,600 during the decade. The increase, moreover, is entirely among "dependents," actual workers of both sexes having fallen by about 2,400. Non-cultivating landowners have increased threefold, while cultivating landowners have decreased by over 4,000. The decrease, it may be remarked, is almost entirely on the female side—a fact which revives the eternal census question as to the relative accuracy of the returns at one enumeration or the other. Agricultural labourers have increased by but 787—a decrease of 810 among actual women workers setting off an increase of 1,597 among the men.

6. Although the matter is not strictly germane to the census, it is interesting to observe that many competent authorities have expressed doubt as to whether the old boom in coffee, and the subsequent slump, were unmixed boon and bane to the inhabitants of the province. The Chief Commissioner writing in 1899 remarks: "The country has been pauperized by the introduction of such a ready means of becoming rich as presented itself some years ago in the cultivation of coffee; with the higher style of living which unfortunately resulted, and especially the facility for extensive borrowing which it afforded." And another authority observes that, during their period of prosperity, intemperance gained a fearful hold on the people. This latter vice, it is agreed, is now on the wane; while in regard to the general effect of adverse fortune, the Chief Commissioner already quoted states: "There are signs that the Coorg character is slowly undergoing change in recognition of the necessity for thrifty living, and the abandonment of the foolish pride which has operated to prevent the people taking service, while it tolerated dissipation and laziness." These latter words, written some ten years ago, later observers consider to have been fully justified by subsequent events.

7. Returning to the consideration of table XV we find that "planting," and ordinary agriculture, support 143 thousand persons out of a total population of 175 thousand, and 96 thousand out of 116 thousand actual workers of both sexes. The occupational distribution of the remainder is fairly well in conformity with what the conditions of the province suggest.

THE IMPERIAL TABLES.

TABLE I.

Area, houses and population.

PROVINCE.	Area in square miles	Towns	Villages.	Occupied houses.			Population.								
				Total	In towns	In villages	Persons			Males.			Females.		
							Total.	Urban.	Rural.	Total	Urban.	Rural.	Total	Urban.	Rural.
1	2	3	4	5	6	7	8	9	10	11	12	13	14	15	16
Coorg	1,582	2	493	33,747	2,185	31,562	174,976	9,981	164,995	97,279	5,897	91,382	77,697	4,084	73,613

TABLE II.

Variation in population since 1871.

PROVINCE	Persons.					Males.					Females.					Variation (Increase +, Decrease –).				Net variation in period 1871—1911. (Increase +, Decrease –)
	1911	1901.	1891.	1881	1871	1911	1901.	1891.	1881.	1871.	1911	1901.	1891.	1881.	1871	1901 to 1911.	1891 to 1901.	1881 to 1891.	1871 to 1881	
1	2	3	4	5	6	7	8	9	10	11	12	13	14	15	16	17	18	19	20	21
Coorg	174,976	180,607	173,055	178,302	168,312	97,279	100,258	95,907	100,439	94,454	77,697	80,349	77,148	77,863	73,858	– 5,631	+ 7,552	– 5,247	+ 9,990	+ 6,664

TABLE III.

Towns and villages classified by population.

PROVINCE	Total number of inhabited towns and villages.	Population	Under 500.		500—1,000		1,000—2,000.		2,000—5,000		5,000—10,000.	
			Number.	Population.	Number	Population.	Number.	Population.	Number.	Population	Number.	Population.
1	2	3	4	5	6	7	8	9	10	11	12	13
Coorg ...	495	174,976	373	67,847	98	67,011	19	23,900	4	9,949	1	6,269

Note.—There was no town or village with a population of over 10,000 nor was there any encampment, boat or railway population.

TABLE IV.

Towns classified by population with variation since 1871.

TOWN.	Population. 1911.	1901	1891.	1881.	1871.	Variation. (Increase +, decrease −). 1901 to 1911.	1891 to 1901.	1881 to 1891	1871 to 1881.	Variation in period 1871–1911. (Increase +, decrease −)	Males 1911.	1901.	1891.	Females. 1911.	1901	1891.
1	2	3	4	5	6	7	8	9	10	11	12	13	14	15	16	17
Mercara	6,269	6,732	7,034	8,383	8,146	− 463	− 302	−1,349	+ 237	− 1,877	3,692	3,940	3,904	2,577	2,792	3,130
Vírarájéndrapet	3,712	4,283	4,447	4,576		− 571	− 164	− 129			2,205	2,527	2,613	1,507	1,756	1,834

Note.—Both the towns are municipalities, and there are no cantonments in them. Three more places treated as towns in 1901 have now been omitted as they are not municipalities, nor have they a population of 5,000

TABLE V.

Population by religion in towns.

TOWN.	Population Persons.	Males.	Females.	Hindu. Persons	Males.	Females	Musalman Persons	Males.	Females.	Christian Persons	Males	Females	Jain. Persons	Males	Females	Parsi. Persons.	Males	Females.	Animistic. Persons.	Males.	Females
1	2	3	4	5	6	7	8	9	10	11	12	13	14	15	16	17	18	19	20	21	22
Total	*9,981*	*5,897*	*4,084*	*6,216*	*3,704*	*2,512*	*2,708*	*1,683*	*1,025*	*958*	*463*	*495*	*65*	*27*	*38*	*26*	*12*	*14*	*8*	*8*	
Mercara	6,269	3,692	2,577	4,389	2,649	1,740	1,312	764	548	535	260	275	1	1		26	12	14	6	6	
Víraréjéndrapet	3,712	2,205	1,507	1,827	1,055	772	1,396	919	477	423	203	220	64	26	38				2	2	

TABLE VI.

Religion.

PROVINCE.	Population. Persons.	Males	Females	Hindu Persons.	Males.	Females.	Musalman. Persons.	Males.	Females	Christian Persons.	Males	Females	Jain Persons	Males	Females	Parsi Persons.	Males	Females	Animistic. Persons	Males	Females
1	2	3	4	5	6	7	8	9	10	11	12	13	14	15	16	17	18	19	20	21	22
Coorg	174,976	97,279	77,697	138,922	76,822	62,100	13,143	8,397	4,746	3,553	1,986	1,567	97	45	52	34	16	18	19,227	10,018	9,214

TABLE VII.

Age, sex and civil condition.

ON	AGE.	Population. Persons	Males.	Females.	Unmarried Persons	Males	Females	Married Persons	Males	Females.	Widowed. Persons	Males.	Females.
	2	3	4	5	6	7	8	9	10	11	12	13	14
	Total	*174,976*	*97,279*	*77,697*	*88,119*	*53,906*	*34,213*	*68,926*	*38,879*	*30,047*	*17,931*	*4,494*	*13,437*
	0–1	4,180	2,100	2,080	4,178	2,098	2,080	2	2				
	1–2	2,817	1,370	1,447	2,815	1,369	1,446	2	1	1			
	2–3	4,415	2,143	2,272	4,411	2,141	2,270	3	1	2	1	1	
	3–4	4,266	2,123	2,143	4,257	2,119	2,138	8	3	5	1	1	.
	4–5	4,082	2,039	2,043	4,074	2,037	2,037	7	1	6	1	1	...
	Total 0–5	19,760	9,775	9,985	19,735	9,764	9,971	22	8	14	3	3	
	5–10	19,025	9,505	9,520	18,976	9,483	9,493	48	21	27	1	1	.
	10–15	19,249	10,226	9,022	18,579	10,121	8,457	650	102	548	20	3	17
	15–20	18,295	10,125	8,170	14,212	9,575	4,637	3,900	539	3,361	183	11	172
	20–25	19,669	11,034	8,635	9,184	8,073	1,111	9,792	2,827	6,965	693	134	559
	25–30	19,705	11,698	8,007	4,579	4,316	263	13,808	6,996	6,812	1,318	386	932
	30–30	15,667	9,358	6,309	1,539	1,410	129	12,197	7,432	4,765	1,981	516	1,415
	35–40	12,280	7,873	4,407	632	570	62	9,705	6,705	3,000	1,943	598	1,345
	40–45	10,406	6,281	4,125	330	299	31	7,446	5,341	2,105	2,630	641	1,989
	45–50	6,538	3,969	2,569	138	123	15	4,487	3,349	1,138	1,913	497	1,416
	50–55	6,015	3,201	2,814	89	76	13	3,334	2,574	760	2,592	551	2,041
	55–60	2,700	1,521	1,179	41	36	5	1,432	1,152	280	1,227	333	894
	60–65	3,013	1,463	1,550	44	34	10	1,211	1,048	163	1,758	381	1,377
	65–70	1,032	512	520	13	5	8	410	346	64	609	161	448
	70 and over	1,623	738	885	29	21	8	484	439	45	1,110	278	832
	Total	*138,922*	*76,822*	*62,100*	*70,896*	*43,042*	*27,854*	*53,243*	*30,176*	*23,067*	*14,783*	*3,604*	*11,179*
	0–1	3,186	1,598	1,588	3,186	1,598	1,588						
	1–2	2,191	1,063	1,128	2,189	1,062	1,127	2	1	1			
	2–3	3,437	1,657	1,780	3,435	1,657	1,778	2		2		.	
	3–4	3,273	1,605	1,668	3,266	1,603	1,663	7	2	5			...
	4–5	3,117	1,558	1,559	3,114	1,558	1,556	3		3			...
	Total 0–5	15,204	7,481	7,723	15,190	7,478	7,712	14	3	11		.	
	5–10	15,158	7,556	7,602	15,124	7,540	7,584	33	15	18	1	1	..
	10–15	15,803	8,210	7,593	15,267	8,131	7,136	520	76	444	16	3	13
	15–20	14,823	8,168	6,655	11,767	7,736	4,031	2,911	421	2,490	145	11	134
	20–25	15,646	8,807	6,839	7,478	6,506	972	7,631	2,210	5,421	537	91	446
	25–30	15,500	9,325	6,175	3,757	3,547	210	10,681	5,483	5,198	1,062	295	767
	30–35	12,207	7,266	4,941	1,258	1,164	94	9,342	5,700	3,642	1,607	402	1,205
	35–40	9,681	6,184	3,497	523	475	48	7,532	5,228	2,304	1,626	481	1,145
	40–45	8,212	4,921	3,291	264	241	23	5,734	4,142	1,592	2,214	538	1,676
	45–50	5,196	3,094	2,102	104	94	10	3,491	2,591	900	1,601	409	1,192
	50–55	4,761	2,477	2,284	68	60	8	2,576	1,977	599	2,117	440	1,677
	55–60	2,175	1,200	975	30	25	5	1,127	906	221	1,018	269	749
	60–65	3,352	1,112	1,240	34	25	9	924	791	133	1,394	298	1,096
	65–70	850	414	436	9	4	5	330	273	57	511	137	374
	70 and over	1,354	607	747	23	16	7	397	360	37	984	281	703
	Total	*13,143*	*8,397*	*4,746*	*6,292*	*4,596*	*1,696*	*5,618*	*3,535*	*2,083*	*1,233*	*266*	*967*
	0–1	287	135	132	287	135	132			..			
	1–2	156	82	74	156	82	74						
	2–3	252	121	131	251	120	131				1	1	
	3–4	208	109	99	208	109	99						...
	4–5	238	126	112	237	125	112			..	1	1	
AN.	Total 0–5	1,121	573	548	1,119	571	548	...			2	2	..
	5–10	1,143	576	567	1,135	574	561	8	2	6		...	
	10–15	1,367	882	485	1,285	871	414	81	11	70	1		1
	15–20	1,458	978	480	1,066	939	127	372	39	333	20		20
	20–25	1,686	1,161	525	948	929	19	684	220	464	54	12	42
	25–30	1,534	1,018	516	476	466	12	962	533	429	94	19	75
	30–35	1,345	917	428	153	146	7	1,056	727	329	136	44	92
	35–40	966	721	245	49	47	2	807	643	164	110	31	79
	40–45	804	509	295	25	23	2	608	457	151	171	29	142
	45–50	541	380	161	14	13	1	400	338	62	127	29	98
	50–55	490	293	197	9	7	2	302	257	45	179	29	150
	55–60	211	140	71	5	5		129	115	14	77	20	57
	60–65	273	143	130	4	3	1	131	117	14	138	23	115
	65–70	76	40	36				33	31	2	43	9	34
	70 and over	128	66	62	2	2		45	45		81	19	62
	Total	*3,553*	*1,986*	*1,567*	*1,775*	*1,082*	*693*	*1,427*	*817*	*610*	*351*	*87*	*264*
	0–1	93	44	49	93	44	49						..
	1–2	50	28	22	50	38	22						.
	2–3	75	40	35	75	40	35			..			.
	3–4	85	45	40	85	45	40						
	4–5	73	39	34	73	39	34						
	Total 0–5	376	196	180	376	196	180					...	
	5–10	362	181	181	361	180	181	1	1			.	
	10–15	328	165	163	319	162	157	7	3	4	2		2
IAN.	15–20	373	195	178	280	187	93	92	8	84	1		1
	20–25	413	230	183	194	156	38	206	71	135	13	3	10
	25–30	394	237	157	116	108	15	253	128	125	23	6	17
	30–35	291	164	127	53	38	15	214	131	83	24	5	19
	35–40	272	168	104	25	19	6	205	137	68	42	12	30
	40–45	217	144	73	20	18	2	157	119	38	40	7	33
	45–50	159	97	62	10	7	3	106	80	26	43	10	33
	50–55	152	88	64	7	6	1	86	65	21	59	17	42
	55–60	68	39	29	5	5		41	29	12	22	5	17
	60–65	84	51	33	4	4		39	35	4	41	12	29
	65–70	28	17	11	1	...	1	13	13		14	4	10
	70 and over	36	14	22	2	1	1	7	7	..	27	6	21

TABLE VII.

Age, sex and civil condition—*concluded.*

RELIGION.	AGE.	POPULATION.			UNMARRIED.			MARRIED			WIDOWED.		
		Persons.	Males.	Females.	Persons	Males	Females.	Persons	Males	Females	Persons.	Males.	Females.
1	2	3	4	5	6	7	8	9	10	11	12	13	14
ANIMISTIC.	TOTAL	*19,227*	*10,013*	*9,214*	*9,096*	*5,153*	*3,943*	*8,592*	*4,330*	*4,262*	*1,539*	*530*	*1,009*
	0–1	632	323	309	630	321	309	2	2				...
	1–2	419	196	223	419	196	223			..	..		...
	2–3	647	323	324	646	322	324	1	1			...	
	3–4	698	363	335	696	361	335	1	1		1	1	...
	4–5	649	315	334	645	314	331	4	1	3			
	Total 0–5	3,045	1,520	1,525	3,036	1,514	1,522	8	5	3	1	1	
	5–10	2,350	1,185	1,165	2,344	1,182	1,162	6	3	3			...
	10–15	1,738	967	771	1,697	955	742	40	12	28	1	..	1
	15–20	1,631	781	850	1,092	710	382	522	71	451	17		17
	20–25	1,904	826	1,078	554	473	81	1,263	325	938	87	28	59
	25–30	2,264	1,110	1,154	224	198	26	1,902	847	1,055	138	65	73
	30–35	1,813	1,004	809	73	60	13	1,578	880	698	162	64	98
	35–40	1,355	796	559	34	28	6	1,157	695	462	164	73	91
	40–45	1,170	706	464	21	17	4	945	622	323	204	67	137
	45–50	630	392	238	9	8	1	483	335	148	138	49	89
	50–55	608	342	266	5	3	2	369	274	95	234	65	169
	55–60	242	140	102	1	1		134	101	33	107	38	69
	60–65	296	154	142	2	2		116	104	12	178	48	130
	65–70	77	40	37	3	1	2	34	29	5	40	10	30
	70 and over	104	50	54	1	1		35	27	8	68	22	46
JAIN	TOTAL	*97*	*45*	*52*	*40*	*22*	*18*	*36*	*17*	*19*	*21*	*6*	*15*
	0–1	2		2	2		2			..	..	...	...
	1–2	..						..					..
	2–3	3	2	1	3	2	1				..	...	
	3–4		..					...					...
	4–5	4	1	3	4	1	3						
	Total 0–5	9	3	6	9	3	6						
	5–10	10	5	5	10	5	5						...
	10–15	10	2	8	8	2	6	2		2			..
	15–20	4	1	3	1	1		3		3			..
	20–25	17	8	9	8	7	1	7	1	6	2	..	2
	25–30	9	5	4	1	1		7	3	4	1	1	...
	30–35	10	7	3	2	2		6	4	2	2	1	1
	35–40	2	2		...			1	1		1	1	..
	40–45	2	1	1				1	1		1		1
	45–50	10	5	5	1	1		6	4	2	3		3
	50–55	3	1	2				1	1		2	...	2
	55–60	4	2	2				1	1		3	1	2
	60–65	6	2	4				1	1		5	1	4
	65–70	1	1	..				..			1	1	
	70 and over					...		..					
PARSI	TOTAL	*34*	*16*	*18*	*20*	*11*	*9*	*10*	*4*	*6*	*4*	*1*	*3*
	0–1	..						...	..				...
	1–2	1	1	..	1	1				..	..		..
	2–3	1		1	1		1	...	..		..	...	..
	3–4	2	1	1	2	1	1	..			..		..
	4–5	1		1	1		1	..			...		...
	Total 0–5	5	2	3	5	2	3	...	..		..		...
	5–10	2	2		2	2			..	..	..		...
	10–15	2		2	2		2	...			..	...	...
	15–20	6	2	4	6	2	4				..		
	20–25	3	2	1	2	2		1	...	1		..	
	25–30	4	3	1	1	1	..	3	2	1			...
	30–35	1		1		..		1		1	...	...	...
	35–40	4	2	2	1	1	..	3	1	2		..	...
	40–45	1		1	...			1		1			...
	45–50	2	1	1	..	...		1	1		1	...	1
	50–55	1		1	..	...		..	..	..	1	..	1
	55–60		...				..						..
	60–65	2	1	1							2	1	1
	65–70			..		..		...	..			...	...
	70 and over	1	1	..	1	1	..				..	..	...

TABLE VIII.

Education by religion and age.

RELIGION.	AGE.	POPULATION. Total Persons.	Total Males.	Total Females.	Literate Persons.	Literate Males	Literate Females	Illiterate. Persons.	Illiterate. Males.	Illiterate. Females.	Literate in English. Persons.	Literate in English. Males.	Literate in English. Females.
1	2	3	4	5	6	7	8	9	10	11	12	13	14
All Religions.	Total ..	*174,976*	*97,279*	*77,697*	*17,443*	*15,277*	*2,166*	*157,533*	*82,002*	*75,531*	*1,882*	*1,642*	*240*
	0-10 .	38,785	19,280	19,505	260	173	87	38,525	19,107	19,418	20	8	12
	10-15	19,248	10,226	9,022	1,457	1,096	361	17,791	9,130	8,661	133	95	38
	15-20 .	18,295	10,125	8,170	2,157	1,691	466	16,138	8,434	7,704	224	179	45
	20 and over .	98,848	57,848	41,000	13,569	12,317	1,252	85,079	45,331	39,748	1,505	1,360	145
Hindu ...	Total .	*138,922*	*76,822*	*62,100*	*14,736*	*12,971*	*1,765*	*124,186*	*63,851*	*60,335*	*1,381*	*1,286*	*95*
	0-10 .	30,362	15,037	15,325	229	155	74	30,133	14,882	15,251	14	4	10
	10-15 ...	15,808	8,210	7,598	1,299	995	304	14,504	7,215	7,289	121	90	31
	15-20	14,823	8,168	6,655	1,848	1,451	397	12,975	6,717	6,258	178	155	23
	20 and over	77,934	45,407	32,527	11,360	10,370	990	66,574	35,037	31,537	1,068	1,037	31
Musalman.	Total	*13,143*	*8,397*	*4,746*	*1,616*	*1,540*	*76*	*11,527*	*6,857*	*4,670*	*37*	*37*	..
	0-10 .	2,264	1,149	1,115	5	4	1	2,259	1,145	1,114		...	..
	10-15	1,367	882	485	81	65	16	1,286	817	469	2	2	.
	15-20	1,458	978	480	168	155	13	1,290	823	467	2	2	...
	20 and over	8,054	5,388	2,666	1,362	1,316	46	6,692	4,072	2,620	33	33	...
Christian	Total	*3,553*	*1,986*	*1,567*	*1,020*	*716*	*304*	*2,533*	*1,270*	*1,263*	*455*	*312*	*143*
	0-10	738	377	361	23	13	10	715	364	351	6	4	2
	10-15 .	328	165	163	71	35	36	257	130	127	10	3	7
	15-20	373	195	178	133	82	51	240	113	127	44	22	22
	20 and over .	2,114	1,249	865	793	586	207	1,331	668	658	395	283	112
Animistic.	Total	*19,227*	*10,013*	*9,214*	*9*	*8*	*1*	*19,218*	*10,005*	*9,213*	*1*	*1*	...
	0-10 ...	5,395	2,705	2,690	.		..	5,395	2,705	2,690			..
	10-15 .	1,738	967	771	1		1	1,737	967	770	..		...
	15-20	1,631	781	850				1,631	781	850	...		
	20 and over	10,463	5,560	4,903		8		10,455	5,552	4,903	1	1	
Jain	Total	*97*	*45*	*52*	*36*	*30*	*6*	*61*	*15*	*46*	*1*	*1*	
	0-10 ...	19	8	11	3	1	2	16	7	9			.
	10-15	10	2	8	3	1	2	7	1	6			..
	15-20	4	1	3	2	1	1	2		2		.	.
	20 and over .	64	34	30	28	27	1	36	7	29	1	1	...
Parsi ...	Total	*34*	*16*	*18*	*26*	*12*	*14*	*8*	*4*	*4*	*7*	*5*	*2*
	0-10 ...	7	4	3	...			7	4	3			
	10-15 ...	2		2	2	..	2				..		...
	15 20	6	2	4	6	2	4						
	20 and over	19	10	9	18	10	8	1	...	1	7	5	2

TABLE IX.

Education by caste, tribe or race.

(H. = Hindu ; A. = Animistic).

CASTE, TRIBE OR RACE.	Males.			Females.		
	Population.	Literate.	Literate in English.	Population.	Literate.	Literate in English.
1	2	3	4	5	6	7
Hindu and Animistic Castes.	*86,835*	*12,979*	*1,287*	*71,314*	*1,766*	*95*
Áchári	241	74		46		
Agaru	1	1	...			
Agasa	869	26	..	778		
Agnani	68	23	4	71		
Akkasálé	562	138	1	500	5	
Ambalavási	2	1			..	
Arasu	13	2		1		
Arayan	18	1		42		
Áyiri	498	86	1	400		
Badagi	359	45		324		
Banajiga	698	167	9	585	9	
Baniya	135	14	1	14	1	
Banna	48	8		51	1	..
Bant	807	88	13	364	12	8
Basavi	3	1		13	1	
Besta	208	6		145		
Bilimagga	581	112	3	511	3	
Billava	1,512	72		756	4	
Binépatta	38	2		53		
Bóyi	221	13		222		
Bráhman	1,848	869	203	1,172	158	10
Challiya	53	2	...	4		
Chaptégára	44	15	2	37	6	
Chetti	167	36		179		
Darji	68	20		58		
Dévadiga	3	1				
Dévánga	958	297	20	883	14	
Divaramakkalu	281	21	2	267	3	..
Gániga	219	18	1	168		
Gauda	6,923	1,080	30	6,071	58	
Gauli	151	5		153		
Gauriga	127	2		126		
Golla	287	30		299		...
Hajama	418	36		386	1	...
Halépaik	18	1		21		...
Heggade	988	121	3	843	4	
Holeya	12,419	109	1	9,686	4	
Ídiga	28	3		11		
Kallukuttiga	19	4		26	1	...
Kammálan	80	16	1	87		
Kammara	30	9	3	22	1	
Kamsale	73	31	3	73		
Kanchugára	10	5		4	1	...
Kaniya	133	61	...	65	2	
Kápu	55	2	1	50		
Kávadi	23	1		10		..
Kodaga	17,106	6,401	816	16,778	1,314	74
Kodaga (Amma)	250	84	1	267	13	..
Kodaga (Jama)	2,366	60	9	2,457	8	
Kolayan	24	7		35		
Káláyiri	154	11		75	...	..
Konkani	241	58	4	216	8	..
Koracha	7	1		3		
Korama	79	8	...	67		
Kote Kshatriya	20	6	...	6		...
Koyava	105	2	..	108	...	...
Kshatriya	55	11	1	55		...
Kumbára	469	10		402	2	...
Kuruba H.	1,135	22		1,031	1	...
Kuruba A.	2,759	1	1	2,448		...
Lambádi A.	3	1	...		..	
Hindu and Animistic Castes—concld.						
Lingáyat (Siváchár)	3,697	942	23	3,361	36	..
Mádiga	1,119	7		854		
Mahrátta	1,338	75	..	807	2	
Malayáli	35	5		3	...	...
Maleya	78	18		51		
Maniyáni	314	32		7		
Marta H.	1,375	27		37	...	
Marta A.	63	4		1		
Márvári	1	1		..		..
Méda	146	4		130	1	...
Mukkuvan	18	1		2		..
Nambúdri	1	1				...
Náyar H.	1,247	292	7	157	6	...
Náyar A.	1	1				
Padárti	70	19		63		
Pánchála	133	28		107	...	...
Pandára	31	4		23		
Panika	94	14	...	78	2	
Paraiyan	60	11	1	11		...
Pennekára Konkani	4	4				..
Ráchávára	15	3	1	20	2	...
Rájput	117	59	10	92	5	...
Sámagára	8	3		6	...	...
Servegár	37	2	..	31	..	..
Sthánika	83	35	1	57		
Tacháyiri	12	7	..		...	
Tamil	23	2		10	..	
Telugu	194	26	1	87	1	
Tíyan	1,471	225	41	303	28	4
Toreya	280	8	...	346		
Uppara	151	5	...	77		...
Vaishnava	39	13	4	26	...	...
Vaisya	91	57	4	71	3	1
Vakkaliga	5,829	447	10	4,747	18	...
Vellála	653	238	54	528	20	3
Yerava H.	751	1		666	1	
Yerava A.	7,167	1	..	6,754	1	
Unclassified persons H.	14	8	...	5	1	
Unclassified persons A.	1	...	...		...	...
Others	3,663		...	1,850	...	...
Musalman	*8,397*	*1,540*	*37*	*4,746*	*76*	
Bhatkalli (Naváyat)	111	58		24	...	..
Labbai	225	104	1	107		...
Máppilla	5,032	661	7	2,184	9	..
Mémon	25	17	..	5	...	...
Moghal	53	10	1	65	1	
Pathán	397	91	4	358	14	
Saiyad	421	82	3	347	10	...
Sheik	2,053	510	20	1,869	43	..
Musalman, unspecified	50	12	1	17	...	..
Christian	*1,996*	*716*	*312*	*1,587*	*304*	*143*
Indian	1,797	560	157	1,421	196	37
Anglo-Indian	74	52	52	84	41	39
European	125	104	103	82	67	67
Jain	*45*	*30*	*1*	*52*	*6*	...
Parsi	*16*	*12*	*5*	*18*	*14*	*2*

TABLE X.

Language.

Languages.	Persons.	Males.	Females.
1	2	3	4
A. Vernaculars of India	*174,976*	*97,279*	*77,697*
(i) Vernaculars of the Province.	*57,700*	*29,428*	*28,272*
Kodagu or Coorgi ...	42,784	21,718	21,066
Yerava	14,916	7,710	7,206
(ii) Vernaculars foreign to the Province.	*116,848*	*67,603*	*49,245*
Canarese	67,545	35,471	32,074
Gujaráti	129	70	59
Hindí	6	5	1
Hindóstáni	5,527	2,975	2,552
Kachchí	3	3	.
Konkaní	2,696	1,619	1,077
Kurumba	4,012	2,147	1,865
Kutni	4	4	
Lambádi	60	34	26
Malayálam	13,909	10,906	3,003
Maráthí	1,741	1,014	727
Márvárí	1	1	
A. Vernaculars of India—*concld.*			
(ii) Vernaculars foreign to the Province—*concld*			
Pársi	1		1
Punjábí	1	1	
Sindhi	8	8	
Tamil	4,291	2,326	1,965
Telugu	2,888	1,471	1,417
Tulu	14,226	9,548	4,678
B. Vernaculars of Non-Indian Asiatic country.	*6*	*6*	
Arabic	6	6	..
C. European Languages	*422*	*242*	*180*
English	345	201	144
French ...	2	2	.
German	8	4	4
Portuguese	67	35	32

TABLE XI.

Birth-place.

Province, State or Country where born	Persons.	Males.	Females.
1	2	3	4
Total ...	*174,976*	*97,279*	*77,697*
A-I. Born within the Province.	*129,441*	*66,077*	*63,364*
Coorg	129,441	66,077	63,364
A-II. Born in Provinces and States beyond the Province.	*45,427*	*31,131*	*14,296*
(a) Adjacent Provinces and States.	*44,744*	*30,560*	*14,184*
(i) British Territory	*28,581*	*21,378*	*7,203*
Madras	28,581	21,378	7,203
(ii) Feudatory States ..	*16,163*	*9,182*	*6,981*
Madras States (including Cochin and Travancore).	46	34	12
Cochin	*35*	*27*	*8*
Travancore	*9*	*6*	*3*
Mysore	16,117	9,148	6,969
(b) Other Provinces and States.	*611*	*560*	*111*
(i) British Territory	*571*	*480*	*91*
Ajmer-Merwara	1	1	
Bengal *	8	6	2
Bombay (including Aden).	518	487	31
Burma ...	4	2	2
Central Provinces and Berar.	14	12	2
Punjab	10	9	1
United Provinces of Agra and Oudh.	16	13	3
A-II. Born in Provinces and States beyond the Provinces—*concld.*			
(b) Other Provnices and States —*concld.*			
(ii) Feudatory States	*100*	*80*	*20*
Bombay States ..	31	28	3
Hyderabad	66	49	17
Bengal States *	1	1	
Rajaputana Agency	2	2	...
(c) French and Portuguese Settlements.	*12*	*11*	*1*
B. Born in countries in Asia beyond India.	*6*	*4*	*2*
Ceylon ...	5	4	1
China	1		1
C. Born in countries in Europe.	*95*	*63*	*32*
England and Wales	64	44	20
Scotland ..	16	12	4
Ireland ..	2	2	...
France ..	6	1	5
Germany	4	3	1
Switzerland	3	1	2
D. Born in countries in Africa	*3*	*2*	*1*
Transvaal ..	1	1	...
South Africa (Unspecified)	2	1	1
E. Born in countries in America.	*2*	*2*	.
Canada ..	2	2	...
F. Born in countries in Australasia.	*2*		*2*
New Zealand	1	...	1
Tasmania	1	.	1

* Old Province

TABLE XII.

Infirmities by age.

AGE.	Population Afflicted. Persons.	Males.	Females.	Insane. Persons.	Males.	Females.	Deaf-Mutes. Persons.	Males.	Females.	Blind. Persons.	Males.	Females.	Lepers. Persons.	Males.	Females.
1	2	3	4	5	6	7	8	9	10	11	12	13	14	15	16
TOTAL	*192*	*103*	*89*	*19*	*11*	*8*	*87*	*41*	*46*	*81*	*46*	*35*	*6*	*6*	...
0–1	2	1	1			..				2	1	1		...	
1–2 ...	1	1					..		..	1	1		..	..	
2–3	2	1	1		...		1		1	1	1	...		...	...
3–4	2	1	1				2	1	1		...			...	
4–5	1	1					1	1		...	..		...	...	..
Total 0–5	8	5	3				4	2	2	4	3	1		..	
5–10	13	5	8				10	3	7	3	2	1		..	...
10–15	18	9	9				17	9	8	1		1		...	..
15–20	30	17	13	3	2	1	23	13	10	4	2	2		...	...
20–25*	22	13	9	7	5	2	10	4	6	5	4	1	1	1	...
25–30	11	5	6	1	..	1	5	2	3	5	3	2		..	
30–35	19	15	4	3	2	1	5	5	..	11	8	3	...	...	
35–40 ...	12	8	4	2	1	1	3	3		5	2	3	2	2	...
40–45 ...	11	5	6	1	1		2	..	2	7	3	4	1	1	
45–50 ..	10	5	5				4		4	5	4	1	1	1	
50–55 ...	15	5	10	1		1	2		2	11	4	7	1	1	..
55–60	4	1	3		...		2	..	2	2	1	1			...
60–65 ..	11	4	7	1		1				10	4	6			...
65–70 ..					...		..	...	..	...	...	...	...	...	...
70 and over	8	6	2					..	..	8	6	2			

* One male insane was also deaf-mute.

TABLE XII-A.

Infirmities by selected castes, tribes or races.

CASTE, TRIBE OR RACE.	Population dealt with. Persons.	Males.	Females.	Insane. Persons.	Males.	Females.	Deaf-Mutes. Persons.	Males.	Females.	Blind. Persons	Males.	Females.	Lepers. Persons.	Males	Females.
1	2	3	4		6	7	8	9	10	11	12	13	14	15	16
TOTAL ...	*174,976*	*97,279*	*77,697*	*19*	*11*	*8*	*87*	*41*	*46*	*81*	*46*	*35*	*6*	*6*	..
Gauda	12,994	6,923	6,071	1		1	2	1	1	9	5	4	...		...
Holeya	22,107	12,419	9,688	..		...	6	4	2	4	3	1	...	...	
Kodaga ...	33,886	17,108	16,778	2	2	...	33	17	16	9	5	4			...
Kuruba ...	7,373	3,894	3,479	1	..	1	4	1	3	4	3	1	..		...
Lingáyat	7,558	3,697	3,861		...		3		3						...
Mahrátta	2,145	1,338	807				1	1		3	1	2	2	2	...
Vakkaliga ...	10,576	5,829	4,747	4	2	2	8	2	6	9	3	6			...
Yerava	15,338	7,918	7,420	1	...	1	2	1	1	16	8	8	2	2	...
Others	62,999	38,153	24,846	10	7	3	28	14	14	27	18	9	2	2	...

TABLE XIII.

Caste, tribe, race or nationality.

(H = Hindu; A. = Animistic).

Caste, tribe or race.	Males.	Females.
1	2	3
Hindu and Animistic .	*86,835*	*71,314*
Áchári .	241	46
Agaru .. .	1	
Agasa . ..	869	778
Agnani .	68	71
Akkasálé .	562	500
Ambalavási .	2	
Arasu .	13	1
Arayan	18	42
Áyiri	498	400
Badagi . .	359	324
Banajiga . .	693	585
Baniya . .	135	14
Banna ..	48	51
Bant	807	364
Barike . .	..	2
Basavi	3	13
Bédaru . .	50	47
Besta . .	208	145
Bilimagga	581	511
Billava	1,512	756
Bínépatta .. .	38	52
Bóyi .. . . -	221	222
Bráhman	1,348	1,172
Budubudukala .. -	2	4
Challiya .	52	4
Chambukutti	4	...
Chaptégára	44	37
Cháródi	3	1
Chetti . . .	167	179
Darji .	68	58
Dása	6	2
Dévadiga	8	
Dévánga	958	883
Divaramakkalu .	281	267
Dombaru ..	2	4
Gániga	219	168
Gauda	6,928	6,071
Gauli	151	153
Gauriga .	127	126
Golla ...	287	299
Hajama	413	386
Halépaik . .	18	21
Heggade	988	842
Heggaaniga ..	2	
Holeya	12,419	9,688
Honniyar	14	6
Ídiga	28	11
Jógi .	24	38
Kallukuttiga	19	28
Kammálan	80	87
Kammara	30	22
Kanaka . .	7	...
Kanate	78	73
Kanchugára ..	10	4
Kaniya . . .	183	65
Kannadiyan	9	2
Kápu	55	50
Karikudumbi	6	...
Karuva	2	.
Kávadi	23	10

Caste, tribe or race.	Males	Females.
1	2	3
Hindu and Animistic —*cont.*		
Kodaga	17,108	16,778
Kodaga Amma	250	267
Kodaga Jama ...	2,368	2,457
Kolayan ..	34	35
Kóláyiri	154	75
Kolla	44	33
Konga		1
Konkani	241	216
Koracha ..	7	3
Korama	79	67
Kote Kshatriya	20	6
Koyava . ..	105	108
Kshatriya	55	55
Kudiya H. .. .	257	283
Kudiya A.	1	..
Kumbára	469	402
Kunchetiga ..	6	3
Kuruba H ..	1,135	1,031
Kuruba A . .	2,759	2,448
Kutuma ..	11	10
Lambádi H. . .	66	37
Lambádi A.	3	
Lingáyat (Siváchár)	3,697	3,861
Mádiga	1,119	854
Mahrátta	1,338	807
Malasar . . .	66	45
Malayáli . .	35	3
Maleya H	78	51
Maleya A. .	1	..
Maniyáni . ..	214	7
Marta H .	1,875	37
Marta A. ...	68	1
Márvári	1	...
Méda . ..	146	180
Mukkuvan . .	18	2
Muváyiri	10	1
Nalki		5
Nambúdri	1	.
Náyar H. ...	1,247	157
Náyar A . .	1	
Padárti	70	63
Pale H	2,887	1,214
Pale A ..	10	9
Pallava ..	25	6
Pánchála H. ..	133	107
Pánchála A.	4	...
Pandara ..	31	23
Pándavakulam ..	2	4
Panika . .	94	78
Paraiyan . .	60	641
Paravan	2	2
Parivaram H. .. .	12	7
Parivaram A ..	1	
Pennekára Konkani ..	4	
Ráchávárá	15	20
Rájput	117	92
Rangári	3	4
Sámagára	8	6
Sátáni	7	6

Caste, tribe or race.	Males.	Females.
1	2	3
Hindu and Animistic —*concld.*		
Sérvégár	37	31
Shánán	5	2
Sonegára ...	21	9
Shánika	83	57
Tacháyiri ...	12	...
Tamil	23	10
Telugu H. .	124	87
Telugu A . .	1	
Tigala .	..	1
Tíyan .	1,471	303
Toreya H. .	280	246
Toreya A .	.	1
Tuluva	10	9
Uppara .. .	151	77
Vadda H.	77	48
Vadda A	1	1
Vaishnava .	39	26
Vaisya	91	71
Vakkaliga	5,829	4,747
Valluva .	..	2
Vániyan	2	1
Vellála . -	653	588
Yerava H. .	751	666
Yerava A .	7,167	6,754
Unclassified persons H.	14	5
Unclassified persons A.	1	...
Musalman	*8,397*	*4,746*
Bhatkalli (Naváyat) ...	111	24
Labbai .. .	235	107
Máppilla	5,032	2,164
Mémon	25	5
Moghal	53	55
Pathán	397	358
Saiyad	421	347
Sheik ..	2,083	1,669
Musalman, unspecified	50	17
Christian	*1,986*	*1,567*
Indian	1,787	1,421
Anglo-Indian	74	64
British ...	1	1
English	78	52
European, unspecified .	3	2
French	1	5
German	4	1
Irish . ..	11	4
Italian		1
Portuguese ...	11	7
Scotch .	15	6
Swiss	1	3
Jain . ..	*45*	*52*
Parsi	*16*	*18*

TABLE XIV.

Civil condition by age for selected castes.

CASTE.	POPULATION.													
	TOTAL.		0–5		5–12.		12–15		15–20.		20–40.		40 and over.	
	Males.	Females.	Males.	Females.	Males.	Females.	Males.	Females	Males.	Females.	Males.	Females.	Males.	Females.
1	2	3	4	5	6	7	8	9	10	11	12	13	14	15
Gauda	6,740	6,027	771	873	1,036	1,103	505	444	740	672	2,498	1,921	1,190	1,015
Holeya	11,623	8,519	979	922	1,404	1,410	797	663	1,274	918	5,138	3,264	2,031	1,342
Kodaga	19,710	19,452	2,732	2,795	3,545	3,568	1,645	1,537	2,084	2,310	6,477	5,989	3,227	3,253
Lingáyat	3,342	3,537	292	347	545	567	315	305	379	330	1,203	1,173	608	815
Vakkaliga	5,715	4,697	484	482	774	771	478	404	645	446	2,206	1,621	1,128	973

CASTE	UNMARRIED.													
	TOTAL.		0–5.		5–12.		12–15		15–20		20–40.		40 and over.	
	Males.	Females.	Males	Females.	Males	Females.	Males	Females.	Males	Females.	Males	Females	Males	Females.
	16	17	18	19	20	21	22	23	24	25	26	27	28	29
Gauda	3,906	2,929	771	870	1,031	1,098	500	425	714	451	863	80	27	5
Holeya	6,310	3,646	979	920	1,404	1,398	796	595	1,204	477	1,847	242	80	14
Kodaga	12,620	10,331	2,731	2,795	3,539	3,555	1,636	1,514	2,036	1,930	2,633	520	45	17
Lingáyat	2,003	1,367	291	347	543	559	312	273	360	132	457	55	40	1
Vakkaliga	3,223	1,922	484	482	773	766	474	368	614	222	836	76	42	8

CASTE.	MARRIED.													
	TOTAL.		0–5.		5–12		12–15.		15–20.		20–40.		40 and over.	
	Males.	Females.	Males.	Females.	Males	Females.	Males.	Females.	Males.	Females.	Males	Females.	Males.	Females.
	30	31	32	33	34	35	36	37	38	39	40	41	42	43
Gauda	2,542	2,278	..	2	5	4	5	18	25	218	1,539	1,630	968	406
Holeya	4,725	3,316		2		12	1	66	70	414	3,056	2,422	1,596	400
Kodaga	6,362	6,510	1	..	4	13	9	23	47	369	3,662	4,819	2,639	1,286
Lingáyat	1,141	1,118	1		2	8	3	81	19	191	669	751	447	132
Vakkaliga	2,214	1,631		..	1	5	4	35	31	213	1,275	1,145	903	233

CASTE.	WIDOWED.													
	TOTAL.		0–5.		5–12.		12–15.		15–20.		20–40.		40 and over.	
	Males.	Females.	Males.	Females.	Males.	Females.	Males.	Females.	Males.	Females.	Males.	Females.	Males.	Females.
	44	45	46	47	48	49	50	51	52	53	54	55	56	57
Gauda	292	820		.		1		1	1	3	96	211	195	604
Holeya	588	1,556		..		.	...	1		27	235	600	353	928
Kodaga	728	2,611	...	.	2	..	...		1	11	182	650	543	1,950
Lingáyat	198	1,057			.	.	.	1	..	7	77	367	121	682
Vakkaliga	278	1,144	..	..	..	.	...	1		11	95	400	183	732

TABLE XV-A.

Occupation.

[*Note.*—Groups with no figures against them are omitted.]

Group number.	Description of occupation	Total actual workers and dependents.	ACTUAL WORKERS. Total. Males		Partially agriculturist. Males.	Females.	Dependents (both sexes).
			Males	Females.	Males.	Females.	
1	2	3	4	5	6	7	8
	GRAND TOTAL ..	*174,976*	*72,035*	*44,238*	*1,683*	*182*	*58,703*
	CLASS A.—PRODUCTION OF RAW MATERIALS.	144,570	56,942	39,974	485	34	47,654
	SUB-CLASS I.—EXPLOITATION OF THE SURFACE OF THE EARTH.	*144,547*	*56,922*	*39,973*	*485*	*34*	*47,652*
	Order 1.—Pasture and Agriculture	144,468	56,897	39,966	485	34	47,605
	(a) *Ordinary cultivation*	120,401	43,561	34,040		.	42,800
1 (a)	Non-cultivating landowners ...	3,709	1,072	844	..		1,793
1 (b)	Non cultivating tenants	132	44	34	.	...	54
2 (a)	Cultivating landowners	73,268	24,177	20,081			29,010
2 (b)	Cultivating tenants	8,194	3,131	2,430			2,633
3	Agents, managers of landed estates (not planters), clerks, rent-collectors, etc	7	4			...	3
4	Farm servants and field labourers	35,091	15,133	10,651			9,307
	(b) *Growers of special products and market gardening.*	22,292	12,486	5,558	420	29	4,248
5	Tea, coffee, cinchona and indigo plantations.	22,062	12,338	5,542	417	29	4,182
6	Fruit, flower, vegetable, betel, vine, areca-nut, etc., growers	230	148	16	3	...	66
	(c) *Forestry*	1,108	420	247	55	...	441
7	Forest officers, rangers, guards, etc ...	228	113	..	53	...	115
8	Wood-cutters, firewood, lac, catechu, rubber, etc., collectors, and charcoal burners.	880	307	247	2	...	326
	(d) *Raising of farm stock*	667	430	121	10	5	116
9	Cattle and buffalo breeders and keepers	245	85	96	4	5	64
10	Sheep, goat and pig breeders ..	2	...	1	...	...	1
12	Herdsmen, shepherds, goatherds, etc	420	345	24	6	..	51
	Order 2.—Fishing and hunting .	79	25	7		..	47
14	Fishing	4	4	.	.	...	...
15	Hunting	75	21	7	.	...	47
	SUB-CLASS II.—EXTRACTION OF MINERALS ..	*23*	*20*	*1*		...	*2*
18	*Order* 4.—Quarries of hard rocks—Other minerals (jade, diamonds, limestone, etc.).	23	20	1		...	2
	CLASS B.—PREPARATION AND SUPPLY OF MATERIAL SUBSTANCES.	21,792	10,972	2,833	499	96	7,987
	SUB-CLASS III.—INDUSTRY	*11,592*	*5,349*	*1,824*	*241*	*82*	*4,419*
	Order 6.—Textiles . .	279	99	64	3	3	116
22	Cotton spinning, sizing and weaving	261	98	62	3	2	101
25	Other fibres (coconut, aloes, flax, hemp, straw, etc.).	1		1	...	1	
26	Wool carders and spinners, weavers of woollen blankets, carpets, etc.	16		1			15
27	Silk spinners and weavers	1	1			...	...
	Order 7.—Hides, skins and hard materials from the animal kingdom.	1	..	1			.
32	Tanners, curriers, leather dressers, dyers, etc						
	Order 8.—Wood .	2,274	1,208	437	67	39	629
36	Sawyers, carpenters, turners and joiners, etc.	1,042	765	46	9	..	231
37	Basket makers and other industries of woody material, including leaves	1,232	443	391	58	39	398
	Order 9.—Metals	625	304	16	15	2	305
40	Makers of arms, guns, etc.	1	1		...	..	..

TABLE XV-A.

Occupation—*continued.*

Group number.	Description of occupation	Total actual workers and dependents	ACTUAL WORKERS. Total. Males.	Total. Females.	Partially agriculturist. Males.	Partially agriculturist. Females.	Dependents (both sexes)
1	2	3	4	5	6	7	8
	CLASS B.—PREPARATION AND SUPPLY OF MATERIAL SUBSTANCES—*cont.*						
	SUB-CLASS III.—INDUSTRY—*cont*						
	Order 9.—Metals—*concld*						
41	Other workers in iron and makers of implements and tools, principally or exclusively of iron.	461	196	14	15	2	251
42	Workers in brass, copper and bell metal	93	76	2			15
43	Workers in other metals (tin, zinc, lead, quicksilver, etc).	70	31				39
	Order 10.—Ceramics ...	584	188	212	17	19	184
47	Potters and earthen pipe and bowl makers	555	174	204	16	19	177
48	Brick and tile makers	29	14	8	1		7
	Order 11.—Chemical products properly so-called, and analogous.	31	19		4	...	12
51	Manufacture of aerated and mineral waters	4	3	...			1
53	Manufacture and refining of vegetable and mineral oils.	26	16		4		10
55	Others (soap, candles, lac, cutch, perfumes and miscellaneous drugs).	1	...				1
	Order 12.—Food industries ..	3,549	1,411	553	43	3	1,585
56	Rice pounders and huskers and flour grinders	595	89	303	3	1	198
57	Bakers and biscuit makers	149	40	42	2		67
58	Grain parchers, etc. ..	22	1	11		..	10
59	Butchers ...	287	95	9	3	1	183
63	Sweetmeat makers, preparers of jam and condiments, etc	118	34	29			55
65	Toddy drawers ..	2,170	1,092	138	32	1	940
66	Manufacturers of tobacco, opium and ganja	218	60	21	3		137
	Order 13.—Industries of dress and the toilet	2,242	887	431	40	15	924
68	Tailors, milliners, dress makers and darners, embroiderers on linen.	535	205	39	8		291
69	Shoe, boot and sandal makers ..	151	65	18		..	68
70	Other industries pertaining to dress, gloves, socks, gaiters, belts, buttons, umbrellas, canes, etc.	1					1
71	Washing, cleaning and dyeing	1,144	440	365	21	15	339
72	Barbers, hair-dressers and wig makers ...	410	177	8	11		225
73	Other industries connected with the toilet (tattooers, shampooers, bath-houses, etc)	1		1			
	Order 14.—Furniture industries ..						
74	Cabinet makers, carriage painters, etc. ..	1	1	...			...
	Order 15.—Building industries ...	1,039	776	60	20		208
76	Lime burners, cement workers	1	1				..
77	Excavators, plinth builders and well-sinkers ..	2	2				
78	Stone and marble workers, masons and bricklayers.	228	183	5	7		40
79	Others (thatchers, building contractors, house painters, tilers, plumbers, locksmiths, etc).	808	590	55	13		163
	Order 16.—Construction of means of transport						
80	Cart, carriage, palki, etc, makers and wheelwrights.	2	2			...	...
	Order 18.—Industries of luxury and those pertaining to literature and the arts and sciences.	875	427	24	32	1	424
84	Printers, lithographers, engravers, etc	11	6		2		5
86	Bookbinders and stitchers, envelope makers, etc.	4	2				2
88	Makers of watches and clocks and optical, photographic and surgical instruments	33	10			...	23

TABLE XV-A.

Occupation—*continued.*

Group number	Description of occupation.	Total actual workers and dependents.	ACTUAL WORKERS. TOTAL. Males.	Females.	PARTIALLY AGRICULTURIST. Males.	Females.	Dependents (both sexes)
1	2	3	4	5	6	7	8
	CLASS B.—PREPARATION AND SUPPLY OF MATERIAL SUBSTANCES—*cont.*						
	SUB-CLASS III.—INDUSTRY—*concld.*						
	Order 18.—Industries of luxury and those pertaining to literature and the arts and sciences—*concld.*						
89	Workers in precious stones and metals, enamellers, imitation jewellery makers, gilders, etc.	826	408	24	30	1	394
92	Others, including managers, persons other than performers employed in theatres and other places of public entertainment, employés of public societies, race course service, huntsmen, etc	1	1	..	...	...	
	Order 19.—Industries concerned with refuse matter.						
93	Sweepers, scavengers, dust and sweeping contractors.	90	27	26	...	...	37
	SUB-CLASS IV.—TRANSPORT	*3,089*	*2,393*	*69*	*57*	*2*	*627*
	Order 20.—Transport by water ...	10	8		4	.	2
95	Ship owners and other employés, ship brokers, ships' officers, engineers, mariners and fire men.	4	3		2	.	1
97	Boat owners, boat men and tow men	6	5	...	2	...	1
	Order 21.—Transport by road	2,837	2,265	69	30	2	503
98	Persons employed on the construction and maintenance of roads and bridges.	782	616	44	10	1	122
99	Cart owners and drivers, coachmen, stable boys, tramway, mail carriage, etc., managers and employés (excluding private servants).	1,910	1,543	22	17	1	345
101	Pack elephant, camel, mule, ass and bullock owners and drivers.	62	25	2	2		35
102	Porters and messengers	83	81	1	1		1
	Order 22.—Transport by rail	19	9		1	.	10
103	Railway employés of all kinds other than construction coolies.	17	7	..		..	10
104	Labourers employed on railway construction	2	2		1		..
105	*Order* 23.—Post office, telegraph and telephone services.	223	111		21		112
	SUB-CLASS V.—TRADE .	*7,111*	*3,230*	*940*	*191*	*12*	*2,941*
106	*Order* 24.—Banks, establishments of credit exchange and insurance—(Bank managers, money lenders, exchange and insurance agents, money changers and brokers and their employés).	91	19	28	2		44
107	*Order* 25.—Brokerage, commission and export—(Brokers, commission agents, commercial travellers, warehouse owners and employés).	3		.		...	3
108	*Order* 26.—Trade in textiles—(Trade in piece-goods, wool, cotton, silk, hair, etc)	455	263	15	25		177
109	*Order* 27.—Trade in skins, leathers and furs (feathers, horn, etc.).	81	41	1			39
110	*Order* 28.—Trade in wood (not firewood), cork, bark, etc.	68	26	19	2		23
111	*Order* 29.—Trade in metals (machinery, knife, tool, etc., sellers)	33	27				6
112	*Order* 30.—Trade in pottery	44	18	10	3		16
113	*Order* 31.—Trade in chemical products (drugs, dyes, paints, petroleum explosives, etc.)	16	5	1	1	..	10
	Order 32.—Hotels, cafes, restaurants, etc .	274	135	5	7		134
114	Vendors of wine, liquors, aerated waters, etc.	236	112	4	6		120
115	Owners and managers of hotels, cookshops, sarais, etc., and their employés.	38	23	1	1	..	14

TABLE XV-A.

Occupation—*continued*.

Group number.	Description of occupation	Total actual workers and dependents.	ACTUAL WORKERS. Total. Males.	Total. Females.	Partially Agriculturist. Males	Partially Agriculturist. Females.	Dependents (both sexes)
1	2	3	4	5	6	7	8
	CLASS B.—PREPARATION AND SUPPLY OF MATERIAL SUBSTANCES—*concld*						
	SUB-CLASS V.—TRADE—*concld.*						
	Order 33.—Trade in food-stuffs	5,885	2,888	702	146	9	2,245
116	Fish dealers	88	59	5	...	...	19
117	Grocers and sellers of vegetable oil, salt and other condiments.	2,542	1,239	336	96	7	967
118	Sellers of milk, butter, ghee, poultry, eggs, etc	31	1	9	1	..	21
119	Sellers of sweetmeats, sugar, gur and molasses	115	42	19	1		54
120	Cardamom, betel-leaf, vegetables, fruit and areca nut sellers	696	274	90	15		332
121	Grain and pulse dealers ..	1,777	730	232	80	2	815
122	Tobacco, opium, ganja, etc, sellers .	61	29		3		32
123	Dealers in sheep, goats and pigs	15	12		..		3
124	Dealers in hay, grass and fodder	15	2	11		..	2
125	*Order* 34.—Trade in clothing and toilet articles (ready-made clothing and other articles of dress and the toilet—hats, umbrellas, socks, ready-made shoes, perfumes, etc.)	9	3	1	1		5
	Order 35.—Trade in furniture . . .	47	40	1		.	6
127	Hardware, cooking utensils, porcelain, crockery, glassware, bottles, articles for gardening, the cellar, etc.	47	40	1	..	.	6
128	*Order* 36.—Trade in building materials (stones, bricks, plaster, cement, sand, tiles, thatch, etc).	64	21	24	1	...	19
129	*Order* 37.—Trade in means of transport—dealers and hirers of elephants, camels, horses, cattle, asses, mules, etc., sellers (not makers) of carriages, saddlery, etc.	3	2	...		...	1
130	*Order* 38.—Trade in fuel (firewood, charcoal, coal, cowdung, etc.).	73	1	61	..	1	11
	Order 39.—Trade in articles of luxury and those pertaining to letters and the arts and sciences.	290	93	50	1	2	147
131	Dealers in precious stones, jewellery (real and imitation), clocks, optical instruments, etc.	13	4	2	..	...	7
132	Dealers in common bangles, bead necklaces, fans, small articles, toys, hunting and fishing tackle, flowers, etc.	274	88	48	1	2	138
133	Publishers, booksellers, stationers, dealers in music, pictures, musical instruments and curiosities.	3	1	.	.		2
	Order 41.—Trade of other sorts .	225	148	22	2		55
135	Shopkeepers otherwise unspecified .	154	115	11	1		28
137	Conjurors, acrobats, fortune-tellers, reciters, exhibitors of curiosities and wild animals.	41	23	10	1		8
138	Other trades (including farmers of pounds, tolls and markets)	30	10	1	...	.	19
	CLASS C.—PUBLIC ADMINISTRATION AND LIBERAL ARTS.	*3,324*	*1,678*	*112*	*537*	*8*	*2,034*
	SUB-CLASS VI.—PUBLIC FORCE	*432*	*261*	.	*148*		*171*
	Order 2.—Army	17	6	...			11
139	Army (Imperial)						
	Order 44.—Police	415	255	.	148		160
142	Police ..	349	204	.	132		145
143	Village watchmen	66	51		16	..	15
	SUB-CLASS VII.—PUBLIC ADMINISTRATION ...	*1,171*	*476*	...	*179*	.	*695*
	Order 45.—Public administration	1,171	476	..	179		695
144	Service of the State ..	777	291	.	100	.	486
145	Service of Native and Foreign States ...	6	---	...		...	6
146	Municipal and other local (not village) service	180	92	..	18		88
147	Village officials and servants other than watchmen.	206	93	..	62	..	115

TABLE XV-A.

Occupation—*concluded.*

Group number.	Description of occupation.	Total actual workers and dependents.	ACTUAL WORKERS. Total — Males.	Total — Females.	Partially agriculturist — Males.	Partially agriculturist — Females.	Dependents (both sexes).
1	2	3	4	5	6	7	8
	CLASS C.—PUBLIC ADMINISTRATION AND LIBERAL ARTS—*concld.*						
	SUB-CLASS VIII.—PROFESSIONS AND LIBERAL ARTS.	*2,081*	*901*	*88*	*200*	*7*	*1,092*
	Order 46.—Religion	899	393	30	113	3	476
148	Priests, ministers, etc.	54	33	2	1		19
149	Religious mendicants, inmates of monastries, etc.	8	8	...			
150	Catechists, readers, church and mission service	204	98	..	85		106
151	Temple, burial and burning ground service, pilgrim conductors, ironmcisers.	638	259	28	27	3	351
	Order 47.—Law	149	38		9		111
152	Lawyers of all kinds, including kazis, muktiars and law agents.	129	33		9		96
153	Lawyers' clerks, petition writers, etc.	20	5				15
	Order 48.—Medicine	258	103	20	20	4	135
154	Medical practitioners of all kinds including dentists, oculists and veterinary surgeons.	177	75	5	13	3	97
155	Midwives, vaccinators, compounders, nurses, masseurs, etc.	81	28	15	7	1	38
156	*Order* 49.—Instruction (professors and teachers of all kinds—except law, medicine, music, dancing and drawing—and clerks and servants connected with education)	351	186	18	48		197
	Order 50.—Letters and arts and sciences ...	424	231	20	10		178
157	Public scribes, stenographers, etc.	5	...				5
158	Architects, surveyors, engineers, and their employés.	220	110	2	6		108
159	Others (authors, photographers, artists, sculptors, astronomers, meteorologists, botanists, astrologers, etc.)	117	77	8	2		82
160	Music composers, and masters, players on all kinds of musical instruments (not military), singers, actors and dancers.	83	44	10	2		28
	SUB-CLASS IX.—PERSONS LIVING ON THEIR INCOME.	*140*	*40*	*24*	*10*	*1*	*76*
161	*Order* 51.—Persons living on their income—Proprietors (other than of agricultural land), fund and scholarship holders and pensioners.	140	40	24	10	1	76
	CLASS D.—MISCELLANEOUS	*4,790*	*2,443*	*1,319*	*72*	*44*	*1,023*
	SUB-CLASS X.—DOMESTIC SERVICE	*2,318*	*1,149*	*680*	*43*	*1*	*489*
	Order 52.—Domestic service	2,318	1,149	680	43	1	489
162	Cooks, water carriers, doorkeepers, watchmen and other indoor servants.	2,055	984	679	40	1	392
163	Private grooms, coachmen, dog boys, etc.	263	165	1	3		97
	SUB-CLASS XI.—INSUFFICIENTLY DESCRIBED OCCUPATIONS	*1,882*	*1,022*	*450*	*28*	*43*	*410*
	Order 53.—Insufficiently described occupations (general terms which do not indicate a definite occupation).	1.882	1,022	450	28	43	410
164	Manufacturers, business men, and contractors otherwise unspecified	46	17	...	1	..	29
165	Cashiers, accountants, book-keepers, clerks and their employés in unspecified offices, warehouses and shops.	260	150	2	15		108
166	Mechanics otherwise unspecified	7	.	7			
167	Labourers and workmen otherwise unspecified	1,569	855	441	12	43	273
	SUB-CLASS XII.—UNPRODUCTIVE	*590*	*272*	*189*	*1*		*129*
168	*Order* 54.—Inmates of jails, asylums and hospitals.	110	77	1		...	32
169	Order 55.—Beggars, vagrants, procurers, prostitutes, receivers of stolen goods, cattle poisoners.	480	195	188	1		97

TABLE XV-B.

Subsidiary occupations of agriculturists—Actual workers only.

1 (a) Rent Receivers—Non-cultivating Landowners.

Subsidiary occupation.	Males.	Females.
1	2	3
Total actual workers ...	*1,072*	*844*
Total who have returned subsidiary occupations.	*497*	*132*
Other agricultural occupations	66	66
Tea, coffee, cinchona planters, etc.	90	40
Government servants	69	.
Traders (other than money-lenders and grain dealers).	61	8
Artisans ...	61	7
Priests	45	
Money-lenders and grain dealers ...	19	5
School masters ...	21	2
Cart owners and drivers	13	...
Others	52	4

2 (a) Rent Payers—Cultivating Landowners.

Subsidiary occupation.	Males.	Females.
1	2	3
Total actual workers	*24,177*	*20,061*
Total who have returned subsidiary occupations.	*2,811*	*615*
Other agricultural occupations ...	388	279
Cart owners and drivers, etc. ...	409	4
Government servants other than village watchmen	411	...
Tea, coffee, cinchona planters, etc ...	310	67
Washermen ...	114	97
Village watchmen	138	...
Traders (other than money lenders and grain dealers)	128	10
Money-lenders and grain dealers	101	16
Workers in precious stones, etc. ..	96	1
Blacksmiths	76	.
Potters ...	86	28
Barbers ...	69	1
Growers of fruit, flower, etc.	61	5
Carpenters ...	31	2
Workers in fibre (cocoanut, etc) ..		24
General labourers ...	19	2
Others ..	429	69

2 (b) Rent Payers—Cultivating Tenants

Subsidiary occupation.	Males.	Females.
	2	3
Total actual workers ...	*3,131*	*2,430*
Total who have returned subsidiary occupations.	*463*	*189*
Other agricultural occupations ...	186	118
Tea, coffee, cinchona planters, etc.	70	46
Artisans ...	65	16
Cart owners and drivers ...	58	
Traders (other than money-lenders and grain dealers).	14	3
Money-lenders and grain dealers ...	11	3
General labourers ...	13	1
Village watchmen ...	11	.
Priests ...	11	..
Others ...	24	2

4 Agricultural Labourers.

Subsidiary occupation.	Males.	Females.
1	2	3
Total actual workers .	*15,133*	*10,861*
Total who have returned subsidiary occupations.	*290*	*130*
Other agricultural occupations ...	78	21
Basket makers and other workers of woody materials.	47	46
Tea, coffee, cinchona planters, etc. ...	37	25
Artisans (other than basket makers, etc.) ...	31	25
Cart owners, drivers, etc. ...	26	...
Music composers, singers, actors, dancers, etc.	24	...
Village watchmen ...	18	...
Others ...	34	13

TABLE XV-E.

Statistics of industries.

Description of factory, mine, etc.	Classification of factory, etc., according to number of persons employed (including management).	Number of factories.	Total number of persons employed: Males.	Total number of persons employed: Females.	Direction, supervision and clerical work — Europeans and Anglo-Indians: Males	Direction, supervision and clerical work — Europeans and Anglo-Indians: Females	Direction, supervision and clerical work — Indians: Males.	Direction, supervision and clerical work — Indians: Females.	Skilled workmen — Europeans and Anglo-Indians: Males.	Skilled workmen — Europeans and Anglo-Indians: Females.	Skilled workmen — Indians: Males.	Skilled workmen — Indians: Females	Unskilled labourers — Age 14 and over: Males.	Unskilled labourers — Age 14 and over: Females.	Unskilled labourers — Under 14: Males.	Unskilled labourers — Under 14: Females	Remarks. N.B.—The "state of business" is indicated thus in figures— (1) Much brisker than usual. (2) Brisker than usual. (3) Somewhat brisker than usual. (4) Normal. (5) Somewhat slacker than usual. (6) Slacker than usual. (7) Much slacker than usual.
1	2	3	4	5	6	7	8	9	10	11	12	13	14	15	16	17	18
Coffee plantations—	Total ...	*94*	*7,187*	*3,625*	*47*		*138*	*3*	*2*	*2*	*252*	*107*	*6,211*	*3,045*	*537*	*468*	*Nature of power.* — *State of business.*
In which mechanical power is used.	Total ..	25	2,568	1,474	23	.	25	...	2	2	316	107	2,117	1,190	185	175	
	From 20 to 50 persons...	4	101	81	4		3	..	...	2	34	11	60	8	..	..	Water 3, Oil 1 — (4) 4
	" 50 to 100 " ...	4	175	85	1		4	..	.	...	2	.	168	85		...	Water 3 . (4) 3. Oil 1 ... . .. (6) 1.
	" 100 to 200 " ...	9	922	462	10	.	7		1	..	2		827	369	75	56	Water 3 .., Water and oil 1, Oil 5 — (1) 4. (4) 5.
	" 200 to 400 "	8	1,370	946	8	..	11	..	1		178	96	1,062	731	110	119	Steam 1, Water 1, Oil 4, Water and oil 2 — (1) 1. (4) 6. (6) 1.
In which mechanical power is not used.	Total ...	69	4,619	2,151	24		113	3	...		36		4,094	1,865	352	293	
	From 20 to 50 persons	14	362	141	2		16			.	.	.	314	115	30	26	(1) 1, (4) 8, (6) 1, (7) 1, (not stated) 3.
	" 50 to 100 " ..	32	1,588	734	13		45			.	10	..	1,389	626	131	108	(1) 1, (2) 2, (3) 1, (4) 24, (6) 1, (7) 1, (not stated) 2.
	" 100 to 200 " .	17	1,595	817	7		39	3			9	.	1,445	736	95	78	(1) 1, (2) 2, (3) 1, (4) 10, (6) 2, (not stated) 1.
	" 200 to 400 " ...	6	1,074	450	2	.	18	.			17		946	378	96	81	(1) 1, (2) 1, (3) 1, (4) 3.

Note.—Of the 94 factories, 47 are owned by companies, the directors of all of which are Europeans or Anglo-Indians. Of the private owners of the remaining 47, 36 are Europeans or Anglo-Indians, and 11 Hindus. The managers of 76 of these concerns are Europeans or Anglo-Indians.

TABLE XVI.

Occupation by selected castes, tribes or races.

CASTE, TRIBE OR RACE.	TRADITIONAL OCCUPATION.	Population dealt with. Actual workers. Males.	Actual workers. Females.	Dependents. Males.	Dependents. Females.	Number of actual workers whose traditional caste occupation was returned as their Principal means of livelihood. Males.	Principal means of livelihood. Females.	Subsidiary means of livelihood. Males.	Subsidiary means of livelihood. Females.	Number of actual workers returning their traditional occupation as their principal means of livelihood who had some subsidiary occupation. Males.	Females.	Recorded principal occupation of actual workers. I.—Exploitation of the surface of the soil. Income from rent of land. Males.	Income from rent of land. Females.	Cultivators of all kinds. Males.	Cultivators of all kinds. Females.	Agents and managers of landed estates, planters, forest officers and their clerks, rent collectors, etc. Males.	Agents and managers … Females.	Field labourers, wood cutters, etc. Males.	Field labourers … Females.	Raisers of live-stock, milkmen and herdsmen. Males.	Raisers of live-stock … Females.	Fishing and hunting. Males.	Fishing and hunting. Females.	II.—Extraction of minerals. Owners, managers, clerks, etc. Males.	Owners, managers … Females.	Labourers. Males.	Labourers. Females.
1	2	3	4	5	6	7	8	9	10	11	12	13	14	15	16	17	18	19	20	21	22	23	24	25	26	27	28
Hindu and Animistic.																											
1. Dévánga ...	Weavers ...	666	401	276	479	49	39	11		...		42	35	246	153	30	19	50	50	1	1	...				...	...
2. Ganda	Cultivators and cattle breeders.	4,642	3,330	2,098	2,697	3,858	3,017	87	25	291	63	*	*	1		549	120			22*	1*						
3. Holeya	Agricultural labourers	9,354	6,097	2,289	2,421	7,114	4,584	282	226	161	14	53	39	1,681	1,812	4		7*	16*	84	5						
4. Kodaga	Cultivators ..	12,813	10,497	7,897	8,955	11,467	10,348	162	100	769	148	*	*			218	13	71	43	10	1						
5. Kuruba	Shepherds and blanket weavers.	2,197	1,931	842	800	..						1	8	123	132	1,023	849	762	712	14*	1*						
6. Mahrátta	...	1,117	475	192	305			...				11	12	197	144	240	61	358	141	14		21	7	...	...		...
7. Lingáyat (Siváchár).	....	2,405	2,006	937	1,581							68	154	1,938	1,559	72	43	84	136	2	2				...		
8. Vakkaliga	Cultivators .	4,895	3,016	1,380	1,681	2,476	2,682	61	36	420	55	*	*	1	..	327	186	1		16	3						
9. Yerava ...	Coolies, and day labourers and labourers unspecified.	5,352	4,716	2,485	2,636	5,157	4,593	21	30	16	13	1	1	147	121	3		11*	*	33							
Musalman.																											
1. Sheik	...	1,468	392	620	1,277							21	14	193	54	157	73	50	43	7							
2. Máppilla	....	4,199	1,250	833	914							12	14	709	523	489	128	395	222	15				...			
Christian.																											
1. Indian		1,287	603	500	818	...	...					19	9	168	139	342	184	157	69	5	7	...	...	...			
2. European ...	...	105	15	20	67		...	...		...	...		...			77	3			...		...	...	...			

Note.—The figures in column 13 onwards are exclusive of those in columns 7 and 8. Asterisks have been placed against the figures in those columns which are affected by this arrangement.

TABLE XVI.

Occupation by selected castes, tribes or races—*concluded.*

RECORDED PRINCIPAL OCCUPATION OF ACTUAL WORKERS—*concld.*

CASTE, TRIBE OR RACE.	III.—Industries. Owners, managers, clerks, etc.		III.—Industries. Artisans and other workmen.		IV.—Transport. Owners, managers, ships' officers, etc.		IV.—Transport. Labourers, boatmen, carters, palki-bearers, etc.		V.—Trade.		VI.—Public Force. Commissioned and Gazetted officers		VI.—Public Force. Others.		VII.—Public Administration. Gazetted Officers.		VII.—Public Administration. Others.	
	Males.	Females.	Males	Females.	Males	Females	Males.	Females	Males	Females	Males.	Females.	Males	Females	Males.	Females.	Males	Females.
	29	30	31	32	33	34	35	36	37	38	39	40	41	42	43	44	45	46
Hindu and Animistic.																		
1. Dévánga	..	..	*5	*18			24	...	161	75							7	
2. Gauda			30	7			58	1	10	5			18				28	
3. Holeya			71	29			82		27	70			30	...			10	
4. Kodaga ...			13	1	2		12		6	1			127	..	3		143	
5. Kuruba			*258	*232			5		4	2	..				..			
6. Mahrátta	..		106	35	...	..	39		20	22	...	...	13					
7. Lingáyat (Siváchár) ..		...	17	9		...	35		137	62	..				...		9	
8. Vakkaliga	..	..	39	60			336	4	71	60			2				30	
9. Yerava	..	..	..	1	...		...									...	...	
Musalman.																		
1. Shaik			220	94			147	1	492	61			6		..		33	
2. Máppilla	..		132	95	...	...	797	1	1,340	170			1			..	3	..
Christian.																		
1. Indian	5		142	26	2		42	8	23	19			9	..		..	32	
2. European	..	..	4	...		...	...	1		...		...	4		3	...	...	..

CASTE, TRIBE OR RACE.	VIII.—Arts and Professions. Religious		VIII.—Arts and Professions. Lawyers, doctors and teachers.		VIII.—Arts and Professions. Others.		IX.—Persons living on their income.		X.—Domestic service		XI.—Contractors, clerks, cashiers, etc., otherwise unspecified.		XII.—Labourers unspecified		XIII.—Beggars, prostitutes, criminals and inmates of jails and asylums.	
	Males.	Females.	Males	Females	Males	Females.	Males	Females.	Males.	Females	Males.	Females.	Males.	Females.	Males.	Females.
	47	48	49	50	51	52	53	54	55	56	57	58	59	60	61	62
Hindu and Animistic.																
1. Dévánga			12	1	3			1	6	6	1		4		4	3
2. Gauda			11		1				38	171			15	4	3	4
3. Holeya	4		2	2	16				35	2			157	84	21	4
4. Kodaga	89		54	5	6		8	1	57	75	15		5	8	7	1
5. Kuruba				...	1				5	1			..	3	1	1
6. Mahrátta	1		2	1	3				33	26	3		41	17	20	9
7. Lingáyat (Siváchár)	37	5	2		4	2		..	5	22	3		1	4	11	8
8. Vakkaliga	2	2	4		1			...	51	9	4		26	25	8	15
9. Yerava	..			..				..					..	..		..
Musalman.																
1. Shaik	2		19		2		5	2	50	9	12		29	22	18	19
2. Máppilla	17		11	1	24			..	143	48	17		181	43	13	5
Christian.																
1. Indian	14		29	13			2		246	98	15	1	31	26	3	4
2. European	6	1	5	5	4		1	...	...	5	1	...	..			..

* Please see note at foot of table on page 45.

TABLE XVII.

Distribution of the Christian population by sect and race.

DENOMINATION.	POPULATION RETURNED.			DISTRIBUTION BY RACE.					
				European		Anglo-Indian.		Indian.	
	Persons.	Males.	Females.	Males.	Females.	Males.	Females.	Males	Females.
1	2	3	4	5	6	7	8	9	10
ALL DENOMINATIONS ...	*3,553*	*1,986*	*1,567*	*125*	*82*	*74*	*64*	*1,787*	*1,421*
Anglican Communion	200	120	80	89	56	25	20	6	4
Baptist	4	2	2					2	2
Lutheran .. .	363	183	180	4	6	2	4	177	170
Methodist	14	8	6	2	1	1		5	5
Presbyterian	14	9	5	9	5				
Protestant (unsectarian or sect not specified).	2	2		2	..	..	..	.	..
Roman Catholic	2,947	1,653	1,294	19	14	44	40	1,590	1,240
Sect not returned	9	9	.	..	.	2	..	7	...

Note.—There were no Armenians in the Provinc

TABLE XVIII.

Europeans and Anglo-Indians by age.

RACE.	ALL AGES.			0–12		12–15.		15–30.		30–50.		50 AND OVER.	
	Persons.	Males.	Females	Males.	Females	Males.	Females.	Males.	Females	Males.	Females.	Males	Females.
1	2	3	4	5	6	7	8	9	10	11	12	13	14
Europeans—													
British subjects	174	109	65	14	6		1	17	18	40	28	32	12
Others	33	16	17	4	3	.	...	2	6	7	7	3	1
Anglo-Indians ...	138	74	64	20	16		4	24	24	15	11	15	9

Note.—There were no Armenians in the Province.

THE PROVINCIAL TABLES.

TABLE I.

Area and population of taluks.

TALUK.	Area in square miles	Number of: Towns.	Number of: Villages.	Number of occupied houses.	Population 1911. Persons.	Population 1911. Males.	Population 1911. Females.	Population 1901 (both sexes).	Percentage of variation 1901 to 1911.	Percentage of variation 1891 to 1901.	Number of persons per square mile in 1911.
1	2	3	4	5	6	7	8	9	10	11	12
Total ..	*1,582*	*2*	*493*	*33,747*	*174,976*	*97,279*	*77,697*	*180,607*	– *3·1*	+ *4·4*	*111*
Kiggatnád	421	.	68	7,289	39,767	21,711	18,056	37,235	+ 6·8	+ 7·0	94
Mercara ...	227	1	56	5,995	26,604	15,727	10,877	28,767	– 7·5	+ 3·8	117
Nanjarájapatna	317	.	254	8,393	40,513	21,672	18,841	42,573	– 4·8	+ 2·1	128
Pádinálknád	399		60	4,083	26,867	14,039	12,828	28,620	– 6·1	– 6·5	67
Yedenálknád	218	1	55	8,687	41,225	24,130	17,095	43,412	– 5·0	+ 13·6	189

TABLE II.

Population of taluks by religion and education.

TALUK.	Distribution by religion: Hindu Males.	Hindu Females.	Musalman Males.	Musalman Females.	Christian Males.	Christian Females.	Animistic Males.	Animistic Females.	Parsi Males.	Parsi Females.	Jain Males.	Jain Females.	Number of literate persons: 0–15 Males.	0–15 Females.	15–20 Males.	15–20 Females.	20 and over Males.	20 and over Females.	Literate in English: Males.	Literate in English: Females.
1	2	3	4	5	6	7	8	9	10	11	12	13	14	15	16	17	18	19	20	21
Total ...	*76,822*	*62,100*	*8,397*	*4,746*	*1,986*	*1,567*	*10,013*	*9,214*	*16*	*18*	*45*	*52*	*1,269*	*448*	*1,691*	*466*	*12,317*	*1,252*	*1,642*	*240*
Kiggatnád	12,801	10,396	1,397	734	164	110	7,346	6,812	2	3	1	1	170	58	303	72	2,368	186	178	19
Mercara	13,632	9,438	1,460	915	558	470	65	39	14	15	3	...	366	145	383	100	2,547	332	693	141
Nanjarájapatna	20,374	18,124	884	474	280	117	128	120	...		6	6	283	28	311	18	1,876	52	168	6
Pádinálknád	12,606	11,763	1,380	1,048	43	11	12	6			.	.	228	78	282	68	2,282	219	161	3
Yedenálknád	17,410	12,879	3,276	1,575	947	859	2,462	2,237	...	..	35	45	222	139	412	193	3,144	463	452	71

CENSUS OF INDIA, 1911.

VOLUME XII.

MADRAS.

PART I.

REPORT.

BY

J. CHARTRES MOLONY, I.C.S.,

SUPERINTENDENT OF CENSUS OPERATIONS, MADRAS.

THE SECTION DEALING WITH INDUSTRIES AND INDUSTRIAL OCCUPATIONS IN THE PRESIDENCY

BY

ALFRED CHATTERTON, C.I.E.

MADRAS:
PRINTED BY THE SUPERINTENDENT, GOVERNMENT PRESS.

1912.

GENERAL TABLE OF CONTENTS OF THE THREE PARTS.

PART I.—VOLUME XII.

THE REPORT.

PART II.—VOLUME XII.

IMPERIAL AND PROVINCIAL TABLES.

The Imperial Tables (giving figures by Districts States, or Cities).

The Provincial Tables (giving figures by taluks or divisions).

PART III.—VOLUME XII.

THE ADMINISTRATIVE REPORT.

CENSUS OF INDIA, 1911.

MADRAS.

IMPERIAL SERIES, VOLUME XV. PROVINCIAL SERIES, PART I.

THE REPORT ON THE CENSUS.

INTRODUCTION.

The fifth decennial census of the Presidency was taken on the night of March 10th, 1911, and details of the process are set forth at length in the Administrative report, Volume XII, Part III, of the present series. But that volume is intended peculiarly for the use of future Superintendents, and is not likely to come within the ken of the general reader. Assuming that these presents do find a general reader, such person may wish for some brief account of how the thing was done; if only to rid his mind of a lingering doubt as to whether the Census Superintendent is not indebted to his imagination for many of the facts which he sets forth.

2. The vast majority of the population enumerated live in villages; and the village of Southern India bears little resemblance to the mental picture suggested by the word in its European sense. Instead of orderly rows of fairly substantial houses fronting some well-used thoroughfare, the incipient statistician finds a bewildering medley of cottages, leaf-huts, cowsheds, and straw-yards, arranged on no apparent plan, and often lying hidden in a grove, or isolated in a swamp, miles distant from any public highway. At the first glance it would seem well nigh impossible to account even for the villages of the Presidency, without seeking further to ascertain the number of houses in each such village, and that of the inhabitants in each house.

3. The problem however becomes simplified by a consideration of already existing administrative divisions. The Presidency is divided into districts, each district into divisions, each division into taluks, each taluk into firkas. If a firka contains on an average some 25 to 30 villages, the formidable total resolves already into defined units of not unmanageable size.

4. Furthermore if he essays himself to draw up the house-list of a village, the bewildered Superintendent gathers comfort from a gradually observed fact. If to him the ordinary village is merely a planless maze of blind alleys and crooked lanes, to the Karnam, who has lived there all or most of his life, this tangled skein presents no particular difficulty. Whether he actually perambulates the village, or casts up an account in the reflective ease of his verandah, it does not take him very long to set down the tale of houses, and chief occupant of each. The number of houses known, it is sufficiently easy to map them out in compact blocks of 25 to 30, to each of which an enumerator is assigned: blocks are grouped into circles under a supervisor, and circles into charges under a superintendent. When these charges are subsumed under the administrative taluks, each district has already taken census shape.

5. While this work pushes in the districts, the form of schedule leaf, on which enumeration particulars will be entered, has been settled, and the necessary translations into the vernaculars of the Presidency prepared. From the records of previous censuses it is possible to estimate with tolerable exactitude, and have printed, the number of forms that will be required; on receipt of the village houselists with proposed division into blocks, supplementary orders for printing can be given, and leaves bound into books of standard size. A twelve-leaved book will as a rule suffice for the enumeration of 25 houses.

6. But before these books can be despatched to Tahsildars for distribution to the Charge Superintendents of their taluks, and thence to the enumerators, an important step remains to be taken.

7. It is of little use to provide an enumerator with a book, and tell him to enumerate some 25 houses of a village; he must be enabled to identify the particular houses with which he has to deal. Accordingly, on each house door is painted the serial number assigned to each house by the Karnam in his initial count. This actual numbering affords at once a check on the accuracy of the original house-list, while in an index provided for the enumerator's book are posted the numbers appearing on the houses that fall to his lot, with the names of the householders.

8. Armed with this information the enumerator, some six weeks before the census night, commences the round of his block, and gradually fills up details for the persons living therein. On the actual night he visits each house, and checks the correctness of the entries already made. Next morning the enumerators meet their circle supervisors at some place previously appointed: the entries in each book are totalled by sexes, and these totals, with the books, are sent to the Tahsildar of the taluk. From such material that sore toiled man makes out the total population of his taluk, and sends the figures to the Collector. The Collector combines these returns into the total of his district, and telegraphs the figures to the Census Commissioner for India, and to the Superintendent of the Province. These figures are published as the *Provisional Totals*. The provisional totals appeared in print seven days after the census. Allowing for travellers by sea, enumerated after the actual census night, they varied but by 3,600, or ·0086 per cent., from the totals as finally ascertained.

9. Meanwhile each Tahsildar has packed up the books which he has received, and forwarded them to the Central Abstraction office. Here they are issued in regular order to a staff of copyists, who copy the particulars noted against each person on to a slip. These slips are sorted into various combinations, and the Imperial and Provincial tables represent the figures ascertained by these sortings.

10. In addition to the good citizens whom the enumerator worries in their households, there are on any given night a certain number of persons travelling in trains: others are following their occasions on foot or in the humble bullock cart; while some thousands will be found assembled together listening to the soulful tom-tom at festal gatherings.

11. To the presumably literate first or second class railway passenger a form is provided by the guard of the train: this he is requested to fill up and deliver to the station-master when he alights. For the third-class multitude a more elaborate procedure is necessary.

12. Fortunately the simple Indian is disposed to regard the arrival or departure of a train rather as an arbitrary dispensation of Providence than as an occurrence preordained by a Traffic Superintendent. It follows that the traveller is apt to arrive in good time at his station of departure. At every station in the Presidency enumerators were appointed, who enumerated as many as possible of those who announced their intention of travelling by a train timed to start at or after 7 P.M. To each such person was given a ticket, on which was printed in seven languages the word "*enumerated.*" Every person descending unpossessed of such ticket throughout the night was enumerated at the station of arrival; while at 6 A.M. (or as near as might be) on March 11th every running train was stopped, and those yet unaccounted for were gathered in.

13. For travellers by road police and toll gate-keepers account, or are supposed to do so. Festival centres are ascertained beforehand, and a special staff of enumerators detailed thereto.

14. The tale of the census is not yet finished. In certain jungle tracts, such as the hills of Vizagapatam and Ganjám, nocturnal wanderings, if not impossible, are at least unadvisable; in the Javádi hills of North Arcot, and the Attapádi valley of Malabar, native talent does not suffice, and literate enumerators "go bitterly," (*vide* district reports), from the plains. From the Laccadive and Amindivi Islands the schedules must get sailed to the main land. In all such tracts the census had perforce to be taken by day, and at times fixed with reference to the seasonal unhealthiness of such places, and the period required for getting in the returns.

15. Suppose the census safely taken, the provisional totals added up, the schedule books committed to the mercy of the railway companies, and the country at peace. Subsequent proceedings alluded to in paragraph 9 perhaps deserve a somewhat fuller treatment.

16. There are some 70 languages current in Madras, but of these six alone, (Tamil, Telugu, Malayálam, Canarese, Oriyá and English), are offered to the choice of the schedule writer. Offices for dealing with Tamil and English matter suggest themselves in Madras, Malayálam work obviously must be done in Malabar, Oriyá in Ganjám. South Canara is now the obvious centre for Canarese, although in 1901, owing to lack of railway communication with South Canara, the work was got done at Calicut by clerks toilsomely persuaded thither. Telugu remains, and it would at first seem a fairly obvious plan to send such schedules to the Telugu country. But these Telugu returns require a staff far larger than that needed in any language save Tamil, and accommodation for some 800 men is not easily found outside Madras.

17. Accordingly six offices, three for Tamil, and three for Telugu, were opened in Madras.

18. In 1901, these offices were perforce scattered through the city in various buildings, for which a considerable rent had to be paid. In 1911, fortune and the courtesy of the Army Department provided free the disused Gun Carriage Factory, a vast building with accommodation for thousands of workers. Here then were the offices opened; beginning with an experimental strength of 50, by 8th April they contained 500.

19. The Gun Carriage Factory was but space unadorned; some matter of furniture was needed ere work could move in right earnest. For the habit of modern schools has lost an art to the Madrasi; the youthful scholar no longer drives the quill with any tolerable comfort or speed, while squatting cross-legged on the floor. Such chairs and tables may be bought; but who would buy if he could borrow, and in former years most accommodating lenders were the University of Madras, and the Commissioner for Government Examinations. Now, the University Examinations were in full swing just when the census abstraction offices would open: the Commissioner's furniture was either in use at his own examinations, or boarded out with schools, who used it in return for giving it storage. Even with new chairs and tables bought for Rs. 1,300, the offices worked at nothing like their proper strength till May 1st, when 1,075 men were engaged. The few figures in the margin give some idea of what might have been but for this furniture difficulty.

	Number of abstractors employed.
May 8th	1,195
May 16th	1,394
May 23rd	1,443

20. And yet it is only fair to doubt whether, with all facilities for furniture, many more men than a thousand could have found work before the end of April. With the exception of the schedule books for Madras city, it was not till about March 20th that packages from the districts began to arrive; but then they came in van loads. Statistical use and honoured custom seem to demand a calculation of how many times these schedule books piled atop of each other would reach to heaven, carpet the path from John of Groats to Lands End if strewed lengthways, encircle the earth tacked page to page. It is perhaps sufficient to state that an average

schedule book contains fifteen pages of very thin paper 20 inches long by 8⅓ in breadth; and that there were some 30—40 tons of such books. They filled to overflowing the basement of the hospital building in the factory—two great halls measuring 90′ × 18′ each—and overflowed into the verandahs. Before the books could be given out for posting, they had to be arranged by circles, charges, taluks, and districts, and stored in orderly fashion upon racks. The task was far beyond the powers of a record-keeper with two assistants, but the accident, that kept two Deputy Superintendents and some 25 to 30 Supervisors unemployed at their proper work for about twenty days, rendered their services available for this task.

21. Slip copying, sorting, and compilation, have been described generally in the reports of 1901, and in detail in the administrative reports of that year, and that of 1911. It is unnecessary to tread again the well-trodden ground.

22. Slip copying ended on 17th June 1911. From a maximum of 462 in seven hours on 3rd April, some posters after practice attained the almost incredible figure of 1,737 per day. Sorting rates varied for each table, but the appended maximum figures give some idea of the speed attained.

Week ending	1st July	... 6,600	Ordinary sorting.
Do.	15th July	... 8,800	do.
Do.	29th July	... 7,800	(Partly ordinary and partly occupation sorting).
Do.	5th August	... 5,500	Occupation sorting.
Do.	12th August	... 7,100	Do.

23. The time occupied with census work, and the exact cost of the undertaking it is not easy to state with absolute accuracy. With the preparation of the Imperial tables and report proper are associated certain provincial details, such as the compilation of village statistics for every district in the Presidency, revision of the statistical portions of the District Gazetteers, etc. Furthermore these remarks as regards time and money must necessarily be written before the census offices are finally closed, before the report and tables are published, and before the final accounts for printing are rendered.

24. The first Imperial Table (No. VII, part 1) was sent to Press on August 25th, 1911; the last (No. XV-A, part 2) on January 8th, 1912. At the end of April 1912 all Imperial tables had been printed, revised, reprinted, and submitted for approval to the Census Commissioner for India. The striking of tables finally approved by him had been commenced.

The report, with the exception of these present paragraphs, had been written, printed, revised; and stood in clean proof ready for striking.

The tables for the Province of Coorg had been printed and revised; the report for that Province written but not printed.

The "Administrative Report," which deals with the organization and accomplishment of the census, had been sent to Press.

"Village statistics" for all districts of the Presidency, and for the Pudukkóttai State, had been completed.

The revision of the statistical volumes of District Gazetteers had been put in hand.

25. The accounts of the census are maintained in a two-fold form: (*a*) departmental, (*b*) financial. Departmental accounts show everything actually paid out in connection with the work; the financial accounts admit certain abatements, such as salaries which in the ordinary course of things would have to be paid, irrespective of whether a census was toward or not.

From the beginning of April 1910 to the end of March 1911 departmental accounts showed an expenditure of two lakhs, sixty-two thousand rupees; which exceeded the total of the financial accounts by some thirty-six thousand rupees. Adding the estimated cost of printing, salaries disbursed in the opening months of the year 1912–1913, and deducting recoveries from municipalities, Native States, from sale of paper and furniture, etc., the total cost of the census may be estimated at two lakhs, sixty-three thousand rupees, on departmental account, or two lakhs, fourteen thousand rupees, on financial. The heaviest item of expenditure was naturally the maintenance of the nine large abstraction offices, of which the departmental cost amounted approximately to one lakh, sixty thousand rupees.

26. To all who have helped me in this work I wish to express, however imperfectly, my acknowledgments. To all Collectors and other district officers, who carried through the troublesome task of the actual enumeration with admirable promptitude and care. To the superintendents of the abstraction offices Messrs. A. Narayana Aiyangar, T. Arokiaswami Pillai, A. K. Kuppusawmi Aiyar, T. Ranganadhan Mudaliyar, C. Mohideen Khan, R. Dorasawmi Aiyar, M. Venkata Rao, K. N. Choyikutti and M. Thiadi; who directed their huge establishments with unfailing energy and care. To Mr. Fisher, Superintendent of the Government Press, Mr. Gilbert, Deputy Superintendent, and their subordinates, who carried out the enormous mass of work, which the census entails on them, with wonderful speed and accuracy; and who met every demand, (and there were many of them), for extra schedules, proofs, reprintings, etc., with unfailing courtesy. To Mr. C. S. Gopal Aiyar, who had charge of the records of the abstraction offices, Messrs. S. Shanmugam Pillai and V. Muttusawmi Aiyar, who kept the accounts and paid the workers, and to Mr. S. Ramasawmi Aiyangar, who prepared the subsidiary tables for each chapter of this report.

27. To those who have assisted me in the writing of the report I have endeavoured to render my thanks in the text itself. If, as is too probable, I have omitted any name, oversight, not ingratitude, I may plead as my excuse. To one in particular I owe an especial debt—my late personal assistant Mr. S. Dandapani Aiyar. His industry and accuracy as regards clerical detail have been described by my predecessor of 1901; in wider matters of arrangement and ideas I have come to look on him as a collaborateur rather than as a subordinate.

CHAPTER I.—DISTRIBUTION OF THE POPULATION.

(a) The Presidency and its Peoples.

Madras, the southernmost province of British India, is bounded on the west, south, and east, by the open sea. Its northern boundary, running from west to east, touches on the Presidency of Bombay, the Mysore State, the Dominions of His Highness the Nizam, the Central Provinces, and the newly constituted Province of Bihar and Orissa. The area of the Presidency, the feudatory states of Travancore and Cochin, and the Province of Coorg, being excluded for the purposes of the present census, is 143,924 square miles: its greatest length from north-east to south-west being approximately 950 miles, and its maximum width 450 miles.

2. Travancore and Cochin conduct their own census operations, and publish their own reports: the small states of Pudukkóttai, Banganapalle, and Sandúr, are, for the purpose of census, included in the charge of the Madras Provincial Superintendent.

3. The area of the Presidency has recently received a trifling addition by the transference from the Central Provinces of the Nugur taluk. But in the ten years that have elapsed since the last census, modifications in its internal administrative structure have been considerable. The 22 administrative districts of 1901 have resolved into 25.* Guntúr district has emerged from a shuffling of the boundaries of Kistna, Gódávari, and Nellore; the Madura of 1901 presents itself as Madura and Ramnad; while North Arcot, after a projected cessation of existence, finds re-incarnation in the forms of North Arcot and Chittoor. Twenty-three new taluks have come into being, while the boundaries of some 50 more have been affected by transfers of area.

4. Though administrative changes come and go, the natural features of a country remain unaltered. A detailed description of each district and state would but leave confusion worse confounded in the mind of a reader unacquainted with the Presidency, but each of the six natural divisions presents some sufficient element of distinction, either in physical circumstance, or in the characteristics of its people. On this latter peg may be hung some brief description of the *Agency division* and its primitive inhabitants.

5. Typical of such people is the Khond—Kui, he calls himself—a short, thickset, good-humoured, jungle man. He lives in a cabin built of rough hewn planks, has a predilection for toddy, and an aversion to education; generally speaks the truth, worships singularly unpleasant devils in a strangely unpleasant manner, and in his worldly affairs exhibits a deplorable, but eminently cheerful, disregard for the morrow. Of admirable physical development, he likes to set off his beauty with a white flower stuck in his top-knot; but the most noticeable article of his attire is his *tangi*, an axe with brass bound handle, wherewith on reasonable occasion he batters earnestly the flinty head of his brother Khond. The gentler sex, in whose ears straws as yet unreplaced by brass rings denote, if not maiden meditation, at least an element of non-permanency in attachment, afford small material for speculation to a modern clothes-philosopher; a cloth tied round the waist, *et practerea nihil*, satisfies the simple taste that declines the immodesty of an upper cloth.

6. Here too are found the Savara, a matter of fact not very interesting person, the graceless vagrant Pano, the hill Oriya exercising a patriarchal form of Government as Patro of a muttah, and his trading brother from the plains.

* Or 26, if Anjengo be considered as a "district."

7. Descending eastwards and south through the plains, where the Oriya ploughs beneath his matinée hat, curiously devised from a shallow basket turned upside down and tied beneath his chin, we come to the country of the Telugus. Nine districts in the Presidency return Telugu as their official vernacular, but Gódávari, Kistna, and Guntúr, in the *East Coast Division* (*North*), are pre-eminently the home of this people. Here, in the great deltas of the Kistna and Gódávari rivers, irrigation and rice growing become the dominant features of the country; in 1910–1911 Gódávari grew 664,173 acres of rice and other irrigated crop, Kistna 966,497 acres. and Guntúr 327,874 acres.

8. The prosperity conferred on the *East Coast Division* (*North*) by the Kistna and Gódávari irrigation system is apparent to the eye, and finds its proof in the statistics of density of population, and revenue accruing to the State. Yet for the human beings, with whom the census deals, this water-induced prosperity may be not altogether unattended with disadvantage. A rice field is a pleasant thing to contemplate, and profitable to possess; but its cultivation implies residence in a quagmire hardly conducive to physical, or indeed moral, excellence. Few people may die of starvation in the deltas, but many live a prey to rheumatism, malaria, spleen, litigation, and kindred ills; while it is questionable, and questioned by many of the more thoughtful dwellers in these districts, whether the easy certainty of a crop has not dulled the industry, and caused a forgetfulness of the old skill in husbandry, which the former struggle against adverse nature demanded.

9. This point is accentuated for the visitor to the *Deccan division*, where at first glance the great black plains, the aching wildernesses of stone, the bare dusty roads, and summer air half dust and wholly heat, realise vividly the abomination of desolation. Yet longer stay discovers a fascination in these dour lands, and closer acquaintance wakens a sentiment of admiration for the tall grave Reddi, struggling manfully in truncated breeches against the obstinacies of nature. Without the prop of irrigation he has learned a sage economy of effort; his "*pani pudhu*" denotes, not so much a disinclination to work, as a recognition that it is foolish to squander industry, of which the reward is not sure. "It is better," he says, "to die of starvation than of overwork;" he is born with a resolve not to die of a combination of the two. Educational and other statistics show the Deccan ryot backward, but in truth the contrast of his fine physique, and shrewd mother wit, with the cultured anæmia of his statistically more advanced fellow countryman, is not altogether to his disadvantage.

10. The black plains of the Deccan are obvious to any one: it is not so easy to set down a general characteristic for the Tamil country, that constitutes the *fourth* and *fifth divisions*. "Colour and shade" may seem vague if not self contradictory: yet it may suggest a mental picture not altogether inaccurate. The treeless ugliness of the grey Deccan villages gives place to many coloured clusters of houses, some whitewashed, some bright with red tiled roofs, some thatched; all as a rule built near, or amid, overshading trees. Bleak dusty roads are exchanged for pleasantly overarched avenues, a curious tinge of red showing through the surface. Though irrigation abounds, the effect suggested is rather an added fertility to a country not unpromising, than the sodden wealth of the great deltas of the East Coast

11. If we turn from the country to its inhabitants, the thought arises that, as the Deccan ryot has found salvation in his struggles with Nature, so the peculiar excellencies of the Tamil are in a sense reflected in the characteristics of his mother tongue—"*ce langage criard, obscur, et mal articulé.*" Few would call Tamil beautiful; yet its great harsh words, that one can almost bite as they pass the teeth, the stubborn inelasticities of its construction, suggest a certain doggedness in the people, who have subdued such an untractable organ to their daily use. The Tamil ryot has not, as a rule, the natural advantages that have abated the need for intelligence in the Eastern deltas, nor have his wits been sharpened, like those of the Deccan countrymen, by necessity of not squandering effort that Nature may render fruitless. To win his bread he must work, but if he works he can have a tolerable sureness of success. Without undue deprecation of the Tamil's natural

endowments, we may find the explanation for his pre-eminence in standardised education, and affection for the careful business of the city, in a marked capacity for dogged work, or that capacity for taking pains once defined as genius.

12. Even the jaded railway traveller of modern days can scarcely fail to notice the remarkable scenic contrast, which the rounding of the corner of the Western Ghauts presents to his eyes. But more striking than any mere change in the physical configuration of the country, is the thought that here, in the *West Coast Division*, the Indian leads a life comprehensible, at least in appearance, to the stranger. To the European, elsewhere it seems inexplicable that the well-to-do farmer of the village, or prosperous, educated business man of the town, should not look for air, space, and such obvious agreements of life, as his position would seem to indicate, and his means procure. Yet the rich ryot of Tanjore or Kistna does not seem desirous of surroundings more amenable than the soggy lanes of his village afford; the shopkeeper of the towns finds a sufficient relaxation in the dusty noise of his unattractive street; in his grimy *paracheri*, the cooly, freed from the uninterest of his daily toil, bolts a pessimistic meal. Here, in the *West Coast Division*, the huddled squalor of the eastern villages gives place to the solid comfort and freedom of substantial homesteads scattered over the country side; the pleasant airy buildings of the western cities form a charming contrast to the stewing houses of the eastern towns. Here too, at the teashops which flourish on all sides, even the cooly finds time to refresh himself in a manner more suggestive of humanity than of the furtive gobbling of a cat or dog.

13. In this home of orthodoxy the strange strict caste system is far more intelligible to the heretic than its laxer presentation in the East. If the aristocratic Nambúdri, living secluded in his country house, considers that certain of his fellow-countrymen do pollute him by their contiguity, he, to some extent at least, lives up to his own ideal of spotless cleanliness, and aloofness from the common herd, and does not expect recognition for a non-apparent sanctity obtruded in the forum; the Tíyan's good humoured recognition of the claims of long descent has not for him implied acquiescense in degradation.

14. There may be another side to this pleasant picture, and to disciples of the strenuous life, this graceful aristocratic people, contentedly watching their cocoanuts grow in their lotus land, may recall the great and jolly nation of the Doasyoulikes, who sat beneath the wild flapdoodle tree. The richness of the country is in a large measure due to the abundant rainfall, which in turn, combined with the heat, induces in the native a Turkish bath like indolence, not less surely, if less perceptibly, than in the foreigner. Yet the bustle of the Máppilla bazaars compares not unfavourably with the dustiest strenuousness of Tuticorin, while in education, and especially female education, Malabar enjoys an honoured eminence in the Presidency.

(b) Density of the Population.

15. From a general description of the Presidency and its inhabitants, one passes naturally to a consideration of the degree of density where with these latter burden the earth's surface. The argument of this chapter rests on a somewhat firmer basis than that of its successor, inasmuch as it deals with the undoubted existence of people rather than with the causes which modify that existence.

16. A population of 291 souls to the square mile now represents the average density of occupation of the Presidency. Figures quoted in the margin permit comparison in this respect with some few European and other countries. But, as would be expected from the heterogeneity of countries, climates, and peoples prevailing in Madras, the extremes from which this mean is deduced differ somewhat widely; ranging as they do from a sparse 80 per square mile in the Agency division, to a five-fold greater density (429 per square mile) in the south-east.

Density per Square Mile.

England and Wales	619
Ireland	135
Germany	311
France	189
Russia	67
Spain	100
Roumania	135
Turkey	94
Egypt	940
Japan	334
China proper	266

17. Whatever be the vicissitudes that may attend colonization and development of a new country, it may be assumed that in Southern India density of population has now to a great extent adjusted itself to local possibility of subsistence and to climatic conditions.

18. Although variations in the decennial rates of increase or decrease, which may be seen in subsidiary table I to Chapter II, suggest possibilities of an ultimate change in the relative positions of districts, or of natural divisions not utterly dissimilar, it is on the whole improbable that, within any appreciably restricted period, the cumulative effect of such changes will be so marked as to render their consideration a matter of present necessity. The suggestion is confirmed indeed by the figures of the table referred to, which show that since the enumeration of 1891 the order of density among natural divisions has remained unaltered, while changes in district position have been so slight as to be for practical purposes immaterial.

19. The figures in the margin show that, with the exception of the decade 1871–1881, in which occurred the great famine of 1877, progress in regard to density has been fairly constant for a number of years: and such progress may be accepted as an indication that the question of overpressure of population on the land is not as yet one of practical emergency. In support of, or at least in relation to this argument, there are certain lines of enquiry, which may be pursued with a view to ascertain how far the density of certain representative districts or taluks has reached a point beyond which further progress is unsafe, if not impossible; and whether a surplus population at one point can be utilised to supplement an apparent deficiency at another. For our purpose we shall need to anticipate the existence of succeeding chapters, in so far as to borrow some of the facts or theories which they set forth.

	Mean density per square mile.
1911	291
1901	269
1891	251
1881	217
1871	220

20. If man does not live by bread alone neither can he live without it; and in the last resort the population of a tract, at least in Madras, is mainly determined by the amount of food that its soil can and does produce. Here as yet the development of industry and of urban life is, and perhaps will for ever be, too small to demand consideration of a population which buys its food rather than produces it. Agricultural statistics set forth in subsidiary table I supply us with certain standards by which to estimate the present possibilities of each district.

21. I use the word "present" advisedly. As a guide to the future, the utility of these figures is vitiated by the vagueness of the terms "cultivable" and "cultivated."

22. Exclude sheet rock, sand, roads, rivers, uncleared jungle, and such like, and there is not much of the land's surface uncultivable; that on which something cannot be grown. The Deccan ryot, who hastily scratches a few inches of stony surface soil, throwing thereon some scanty handful of castor or millet seed, is a cultivator, equally in name if not in degree, with the careful Tamil, who assiduously ploughs, manures and weeds his securely irrigated rice field. From this same subsidiary table I it may be seen that if the districts be ranked, first in accordance with the proportion of their several areas considered "cultivable," and then according to area of actual cultivation, their respective places in each classification will differ widely. If going further we consider the nature of crop cultivated, we shall see that in those districts, whose density of population in respect to cultivated area is highest, density is as a rule proportional to the extent of rice cultivation. Thus South Canara, which stands fifteenth in point of density proportional to total area, stands second in respect of density proportional to cultivated area, and first in regard to extent of such cultivated area under rice. Similar figures for Chingleput will be six, four, and three; for Vizagapatam five, one, and eleven.

23. Or, in other words, the power of a district to support its population is determined by the quality rather than the quantity of its cultivable area, and modified by an intensiveness rather than by an extensiveness of cultivation.

District.	Rank according to	
	Density proportional to total area.	Increase during past decade.
Tanjore	1	23
Gódávari	2	8
Kistna	14	5
Bellary	20	29
Anantapur	24	28
Vizagapatam	5	25
South Canara	15	22
Malabar	4	16

24. Tanjore, in respect to total area the most densely populated district of Southern India, in point of increase during the decade ranks but twenty-third among the Madras districts and states (excluding Madras city and Anjengo). For convenient reference the rank of a few typical districts in these two connections may be exhibited in the margin.

25. Tanjore supports its 2,362,639 souls on a cultivation of 1,331,941 acres. Of its cultivated area, the district irrigates 990,308 acres, and of this 836,282 acres from Government cana's. Its cultivation, apart from the quality of the cultivators, may therefore be assumed as potentially good; and from the fact that in respect of population proportional to cultivated area the district stands but sixth in the presidency, with an average density of 1,135 persons per cultivated square mile, we may deduce that, whatever be the cause of tardy increase, over-pressure of population on the soil is not primarily responsible.

26. Vizagapatam, with 1,549 persons per cultivated square mile, and a small percentage of increase during the decade, is more liable to the charge of over-population. Its rank in respect of density proportional to total area is somewhat surprisingly high, inasmuch as no more than 37·8 per cent. of its extent is claimed as fit for cultivation. At the same time of such cultivable area as it possesses it utilises but 62·7 per cent., and has therefore a sufficient margin on which to fall back. Although not an irrigation district in the sense in which the term may be applied to districts commanded by the great canal systems, such as Tanjore, Kistna, and Gódávari, it yet, with a normal rainfall of 40·88 inches per annum, manages to devote an appreciable percentage (31·6) of its cultivated area to the production of rice. It is however possible to push too far this theory as to the intimate connection between density of population and extent of rice cultivation, as the following figures will show. The Ganjám agency, twelfth in rank as regards population per square mile of cultivated area, has but 34·6 per cent. of such area under rice; the agency of Vizagapatam, with rice growing on 58·2 per cent. of its cultivated land, occupies but twenty-fourth place in the same classification.

27. Bellary twentieth district in point of density proportional to total area, and lower still if population be considered in relation to cultivated area, requires 2,425,557 acres for the maintenance of its 969,436 inhabitants. Gódávari uses 822,367 cultivated acres for 1,445,957 persons; Anantapur requires 1,928,633 acres for a population of 963,223. By further reference to subsidiary table I we find that Tanjore claims but 72·6 per cent. of its surface as cultivable, against the 77·5 per cent. of Bellary: of its cultivable area it utilises some 9 per cent. less than the thinly populated Deccan district. Gódávari has 72 per cent. of its area capable of cultivation, and of this extent cultivates over 70 per cent. Anantapur at the bottom of the scale can cultivate 69 per cent. of its total area, and turns to account more or less profitable over 66 per cent. of its opportunities.

28. While the examination already made of figures relating to Tanjore gives ground for belief that density of population in the district has not as yet assumed the characteristic of dangerous over-pressure on the soil, the argument of Chapter II suggests that no appreciable advance in the percentage of decennial increase need be expected. Bellary and Anantapur, for all their popular leanness, we may deem unlikely to attract a much closer settlement. In point of increase during the past decade their respective positions (29th and 28th) are lowly; twentieth and twenty-fourth in point of population related to total area, their rank (29th and 27th) in respect of population proportional to cultivated area is lower still. If

the argument of Chapter III, paragraph 3, be accepted, the sources on which they could draw for immigrants—the remaining Deccan districts—are in no better case than themselves.

29. Of the other districts selected Gódávari, and still more so Kistna, in the East Coast Northern division appear to exhibit certain potentialities of increase. Second in regard to absolute density, Gódávari ranks eighth in point of increase during the decade, and eighth in respect of pressure of population on its cultivated area. Of its 531,772 irrigated acres 378,299 are irrigated by Government canals, a source which in Kistna feeds 812,628 acres out of a total of 896,540. The latter district, which with a population of 1,997,535 stands fourteenth in the Presidency in point of density, and fifth in respect of progress during the decade, has as yet but 742 persons per cultivated square mile; a proportion less than half that of its northern and less fertile neighbour Vizagapatam. Malabar, fourth and third in regard to the two standards of density hitherto adopted, stands sixteenth in point of increase. It now supports the largest population of any district in the Presidency (3,015,119) * on the cultivation of 55·5 per cent. of its cultivable area, which latter amounts to 63·6 of the total extent of the district. For its irrigation it depends on rain; with a normal rainfall, of well-nigh 117 inches per annum it may well do so.

30. Subsidiary table II shows the talukwar distribution of density throughout the Presidency and in the natural divisions, while subsidiary table IV, Chapter II, shows the percentage of increase in each class of taluk throughout the decade. From the first of those statements it may be seen that taluks with such low densities as 0–100, 100–150, and 150–200 per square mile, occupy a very considerable proportion of the area of the Presidency, and that a greater density than 500 persons to the square mile is comparatively rare. The second statement shows that on the whole increase has been greatest at the weakest point, although for reasons to which allusion will be made in the succeeding chapter, the reality of increase in the Agency division is open to some suspicion. A further proof of the theory already advanced as to the ability of Madras to support its present population is afforded by the figures in column 10 of this table, which show that even in the most densely populated areas increase has been by no means inconsiderable.

31. Following the principle hitherto adopted of dealing with a few representative districts taken from each part of the Presidency, it may be of interest to exhibit the density of some districts and their taluks in greater detail.

District.	Number of taluks.	100 to 150.	150 to 200.	200 to 300.	300 to 400.	400 to 450.	450 to 500.	500 to 600.	600 to 700.	700 to 750.	750 to 800.	800 to 900.	900 to 1,000.	1,050 and over.
Tanjore	11	...	...	1	2	...	...	...	1	2	2	...	2	1
Gódávari	8	...	...	...	1	...	...	4	...	1	1	1	...	...
Anantapur	9	5	3	1	...	...	...	...	...	...	...	...	...	...
Bellary	9	2	6	1	...	...	..	...	...	..	...	..	...	...
Kistna	13	...	1	6	1	1	1	1	1	1	...	...	...	...
Malabar	11	1	...	...	...	2	2	...	1	2	...	.	...	3

32. Of the taluks whose density far exceeds the customary limit of the Presidency that in the Tanjore district is the Kumbakónam taluk. Malabar has three such; but such is the varying nature of the country that the density found in Ponnáni taluk, which averages more than 1,200 persons to the square mile, is not considered as representing unfairly the state prevailing with 10 miles of the sea board

* Unless Vizagapatam and its agency tracts be considered as together forming one district.

throughout the district. At the same time, as may be seen from Chapter II, here, if anywhere, the shoe of population pinches, or is in the near future likely to pinch, the foot of accommodation.

33. *Houses.*—Although in the mild climate of Southern India shelter from the elements is not of such paramount importance and necessity as in more inclement lands, yet man needs some sort of abode wherein to bestow himself and his belongings; as a gregarious animal he congregates in villages, cities, or towns.

34. A house was for census purposes defined as "the residence of one or more families, and having a separate entrance from the common way." This definition includes alike Government House and the Paraiyan's hut; but all embracing as it may appear difficulties would now and then arise. On the census night I sought perplexedly the residence of one Muniyan in a city *parachéri*: a friendly neighbour banged against a sheet of tin, which leant against the side wall of a cabin, and forth on all fours came Muniyan. His lair was certainly his residence, and it had a separate entrance from the common way—two in fact, one at either end. But it is a nice point whether it could be considered a house.

35. The description of a standard Indian house in various districts has been so often given that its repetition here is needless. Nor indeed is there any one description that will include alike, (at least as regards external appearance), the isolated farmstead of Malabar, the cottages of the eastern village street, and the city lodging house.

36. From statistics such as those given in subsidiary table VII showing the number of houses per square mile, and average number of inmates per house for each natural division, there is little inference to be drawn. Fifty houses scattered over a square mile represent ample accommodation, but exactly the same statistical result is given by fifty houses huddled together in an inappreciable fraction of the same area.

37. The stately homes of the Presidency number 7,916,490, a figure which represents an increase of approximately 10 per cent. since 1901. House room has therefore increased more rapidly than has population; but theories as to relief of overcrowding based on a foundation so indefinite as the nature of the Indian house are of somewhat problematical value.

38. In the fact that, whilst population and houses increase, the average number of persons per house shows little or no change, it may be possible to see some trace of the individualistic tendencies of to-day, which favour disappearance of the old Hindu joint family system. This system has been assumed by lawyers * as the normal condition of the Hindu family; the assumption has been vehemently combated by Mr. J. H. Nelson.† As to the correctness of either view it is not for me to decide, but there can be little doubt as to the practical truth of the following words: "It is an undoubted fact that year by year thousands of Hindu families "resident in the Madras Province are in effect permanently broken up, by one or "more members going to a distant place or to distant places, he or each of them "hoping to make a fortune for himself solely. The pressure of poverty, the love "of adventure, and the desire to escape the terrors of the law, are constantly "operating powerfully on many thousands of individuals in this part of the world "as elsewhere, and the informal division of families is rapidly becoming a common "occurrence in every part of Madras."

39. The question becomes more real if considered in relation to the larger cities; and in Madras city, house accommodation has increased by more than 7 per cent. in comparison with a rise of less than 2 per cent. in the population. The improvement here is in all probability real, as the trend of population and building alike in Madras is from the old city proper in the north to the open spaces on the southern side, where new buildings required for the increasing population must now be erected under some measure of sanitary supervision and control.

* "Joint undivided family is the ordinary status of the Hindu"—Norton's "Leading Cases."
† "A View of the Hindu Law"—J. H. Nelson.

40. At the same time there are some few other indications that a real improvement is in progress. An increase in general urban population between 1891 and 1901 of 25 per cent. outstripped by 4 per cent. increase in urban accommodation, while increases in village population and in houses available, or at least occupied, were exactly equal at 5 per cent. In the decade now under consideration the urban and village increase of occupied houses surpasses, albeit slightly, the urban and village increase of population.

41. *Village.*—A "village" is the unit of revenue administration, and the word used thus does not necessarily connote material existence or present habitation. In the Agency tracts, especially, there exist numerous "villages," in which no one now resides. Clubbing and splitting of villages for revenue purposes is an every day feature of settlement; the revenue village may frequently include two or more residential villages; or on the other hand a village, to all outward seeming one and indivisible, may enjoy a theoretically dissevered existence.

42. It is therefore idle to draw conclusions from increase or decrease apparent in the number of villages existing at successive enumerations. For the little that they are worth I give the marginal figures. From the figures of subsidiary table III to this Chapter it is abundantly clear that the Madrasi is a village dweller. Even in the East Coast southern division, which contains five of the largest cities in the Presidency, 841 per 1,000 of the population live in villages, and of these the majority in villages with a population ranging from 500 to 2,000. Town dwellers are still fewer in the central division of the East Coast, which contains the capital of the Presidency, and the predilection of the rustic for a comparatively small village is still more strongly marked.

	Number of towns and villages.
1911	54,623
1901	55,423
1891	57,596

43. Subsidiary tables V and VI give certain particulars as to the towns and cities of the Presidency. Of the latter the Province claims thirteen, of the former two hundred and sixty-seven.

44. With the term "*city*" one is apt to associate certain external appearances: broad streets of substantial shops, cheap and ready methods of communication (tramways, etc.), considerable public buildings, factories and marts. In the statistics of a city one looks to find a certain density of houses and population, in India an excess of males over females, a high percentage of immigrants, and of literacy. Judged by these standards it is permissible to question whether the Southern Presidency, despite the wealth of information afforded by the subsidiary tables and Imperial Tables VII and VIII, in truth possesses a "city." The capital itself suggests but faintly

"The citys congregated peace of homes and pomp of spires"

and in such loose aggregation of villages as Salem and Cuddalore one scarcely discovers any peculiarly urban characteristics.

45. Taking however possession of 50,000 inhabitants, the criterion adopted to this census as a valid claim to "cityship" in Madras, the first noticeable point is that Coimbatore and Bellary, though included, have fallen below the required standard, while the population of Salem has noticeably decreased. Herein is but the effect of a cause to which further allusion will be made in Chapter II; namely temporary evacuation induced by plague. Conjeeveram and Cocanada have joined the ranks; and indeed the bustle of the latter's port, and its apparent attractiveness to immigrants do something to justify a claim to inclusion.

46. The striking increase of Madura, in external appearance not altogether uncity-like, is undoubtedly due to industrial development, especially in the line of weaving; an inference strengthened by the reversal of the proportion of the sexes during the decade. In a lesser sense the same may be said of Trichinopoly, headquarters of a considerable railway system. Kumbakónam claimed by its friends as the Cambridge of the South, and of more equivocal renown in Tamil slang, strives and thrives apace through the decade despite occasional municipal misadventures;

but, though both have increased in absolute numbers, the strenuous hum of city life is hardly apparent to the visitor to Tanjore and Negapatam. If the projected transfer of the South Indian Railway workshops to Trichinopoly takes place, it is not unlikely that Negapatam will in the forthcoming decade fall from its present estate.

47. Statistics of density and literacy in cities are also included in subsidiary table VI. Certain abnormal variations in regard to density, such as may be seen in the cases of Kumbakónam and Calicut, are to be accounted for by survey revision of the areas of the cities, or by disregard of a fraction lower than ·50 in making the calculation. In point of literacy the percentage, as might be expected, is higher than that of the surrounding country, but in no case even among men does it reach 50 per cent. of the total population, while the literacy of women is still practically a negligible existence.

48. The religious distribution of the urban population is seen in subsidiary table IV. The figures therein found, which show that of the three main religions of the Presidency Muhammadanism is in proportion to its total following most strongly represented in urban life, are of little added interest to any one acquainted with local circumstance. Save on the West Coast, where his proportion of town dwellers is at its lowest, the Muhammadan is rarely an agriculturist; trade, and the minor handicrafts which the poorer brethren affect, require a somewhat larger field than that afforded by the village community for their convenient and profitable exercise.

49. Of rather more general interest appears to be the fact that urban life, in so far as it exists, is markedly the characteristic of the Tamil. Of 13 cities all but three belong to this people; of 280 towns and cities combined, with a population of 4,919,476 souls, 165 supporting 3,102,764 persons are in the Tamil country.

50. "*Towns*" as defined for census purposes included all municipalities and cantonments, and "every other continuous collection of houses inhabited by not less than 5,000 persons, which the Provincial Superintendent may decide to treat as a town." Local consideration suggested the inclusion of some additional 10 towns, which do not fulfil these conditions.

51. On this basis the Presidency now contains 267 towns exclusive of cities. Some few more villages were tentatively included in the list as likely to fulfill the requisite conditions; but subsequent consideration led to their exclusion.

52. A few instances have been given of cities which are in the main but aggregations of villages. Distinction between village and town is still more difficult, many so-called towns differing in nothing save in number of inhabitants from their rural neighbours.

53. Between 1891 and 1901 the urban population of the Presidency increased by 25 per cent., as compared with an increase of but 5 per cent. in the rural population. The decade which has just concluded has witnessed a considerable change, urban increase having fallen to 15 per cent., while that in the countryside has risen to 8 per cent. The marked increase in urban population between 1891 and 1901 was explained in the latter year as in all probability due to the attraction of higher wages, and greater freedom from caste restriction offered by town life; but if this explanation were correct the drift towards the town might have been expected to continue. A more probable explanation is perhaps to be found in the contrast between the agricultural possibilities of the two decades described in Chapter II; a succession of favourable seasons, by rendering the work most congenial to the Indian villager fairly abundant and certain, must have to a large extent arrested the townward quest of work. Caste fetters, which may gall an infinitesimal minority, whose oriental conservatism is in some sort disturbed by the influences of western culture, sit lightly, as will be suggested in a later chapter, on the vast majority of the people, to whom these strange restrictions serve as natural and convenient guides of daily life.

54. A striking feature of the change between the decades has been the practical cessation of increase in the City of Madras. On the census of the capital city the liberality of the Municipal Corporation has enabled me to publish a special report, and therein the attempt has been made to give detailed reasons for results, which, it must be admitted, came as a surprise to most people. Recapitulation is needless, but the greater potentialities there suggested of extra Indian emigration, as compared with movement from village to town, or district to district, may be taken as of some general application throughout the Presidency.

55. Subsidiary table V gives, in somewhat complicated form, information as to the rate of progress throughout a considerable number of years in towns classified in accordance with size. From the fact that increase appears greatest at the lowest end of the scale may be drawn confirmation of the opinion, suggested in paragraph 28, that the Madras town is in most cases nothing other than a somewhat overgrown village.

56. Imperial table IV shows decennial variations of every town in the Presidency. To labour through each item therein set forth would be a long and, on the whole, unprofitable task. Fluctuations apparently violent can be in many cases explained by alteration of area and exclusion of outlying hamlets, as in the case of Dharmavaram, and other towns of Anantapur, or of Gúdúr in the Nellore district; by occurrence or non-occurrence of religious festivals at the time of enumeration, as in the case of Tiruvottiyúr; by plague scare, or recovery from plague scare, as in the cases of Salem, Coimbatore, Tiruppattúr, and Vániyambádi. The contrasted figures of the latter two towns are especially interesting, inasmuch as in 1901 Vániyambádi had lost much of its population to Tiruppattúr, while in the decade that has just concluded its emigrants have returned. Mangalore, to some extent affected by plague, does not as yet seem to reap the full benefit of railway connection with the rest of the Presidency; Tellicherry and Cannanore on the West Coast extension have doubled the increase of the preceding decade. An increase of 2,616 in Masulipatam, against one of 698 between 1891 and 1901, indicates the presence of a new railway connection with Bezwáda, which has itself added nearly 9,000 to its strength. Guntúr advances steadily: Berhampur at the northernmost end of the Presidency, after standing still between 1891 and 1901 has gained 5,727 new inhabitants; Tuticorin in the extreme south has increased by more than 12,000.

I.—Density, water-supply and crops.

District and Natural Division.	Mean density per square mile in 1911.	Percentage of total area.		Pecentage to cultivable area of		Percentage of cultivated area which is irrigated.	Normal rainfall.	Percentage of gross cultivated area under—					
		Cultivable.	Net cultivated.	Net cultivated.	Double cropped.			Rice.	Cholam, cumbu and ragi.	Other food crops and pulses.	Groundnut.	Cotton.	Other crops.
1	2	3	4	5	6	7	8	9	10	11	12	13	14
Province ...	***291***	***58·0***	***37·9***	***65·3***	***8·6***	***25·9***	***43·09***	***28·2***	***30·5***	***20·4***	***2·4***	***6·1***	***12·4***
Agency	***80***	***39·5***	***13·4***	***33·8***	***1·1***	***40·7***	***51·83***	***50·5***	***16·7***	***15·8***	***0·1***	***0·3***	***16·6***
Agency, Ganjám ...	101	30·5	12·7	59·3	...	...	56·77	34·6	7·4	21·9	0·3	0·2	35·6
" Vizagapatam.	81	49·1	15·6	31·8	1·3	53·7	56·23	58·2	15·2	14·3	0·0	0·4	11·9
" Gódávari ...	56	17·7	6·9	39·1	1·8	12·3	42·49	21·1	41·6	16·4	...	...	20·9
East Coast (North)...	***332***	***62·6***	***41·4***	***65·9***	***12·7***	***37·3***	***37·97***	***37·2***	***26·5***	***17·6***	***0·1***	***3·1***	***15·5***
Ganjám	382	61·3	46·5	81·0	16·5	43·5	45·12	56·3	16·1	14·0	0·3	0·1	13·2
Vizagapatam	472	37·8	23·7	62·7	23·9	47·7	40·88	31·6	30·8	18·2	...	1·0	18·4
Gódávari	568	72·2	50·8	70·4	21·3	49·6	39·78	51·2	8·4	18·8	...	0·9	21·2
Kistna	338	81·5	50·8	62·4	8·9	45·5	35·96	50·0	22·2	9·5	0·0	3·5	14·8
Guntúr	296	73·3	57·8	78·8	11·6	13·5	31·60	14·4	31·0	21·0	0·0	7·5	23·1
Nellore	167	58·8	29·3	49·7	5·6	36·7	34·50	24·0	45·2	20·1	0·0	2·8	7·9
Deccan	***145***	***60·7***	***45·0***	***74·1***	***3·4***	***7·7***	***24·39***	***5·7***	***38·0***	***34·5***	***0·9***	***13·0***	***7·9***
Cuddapah	152	44·2	27·5	62·1	7·1	19·7	27·84	11·4	50·6	17·4	2·6	8·4	9·6
Kurnool	123	52·8	41·4	78·4	2·7	4·7	25·76	4·2	39·3	35·3	0·4	14·5	6·3
Banganapalle ...	154	86·3	77·6	89·9	0·6	1·2	24·52	0·6	48·5	20·9	0·1	26·6	3·3
Bellary	170	77·5	66·5	85·8	1·5	2·7	22·56	1·7	38·7	36·2	0·2	17·8	5·4
Sandúr	84	61·0	47·1	77·3	...	1·4	22·99	0·1	68·1	24·6	0·0	0·1	7·1
Anantapur	143	69·0	45·1	65·4	4·0	10·2	23·69	9·1	28·0	42·1	1·3	7·6	11·9
East Coast (Central).	***362***	***53·6***	***37·5***	***69·9***	***11·5***	***27·6***	***40·18***	***24·0***	***39·1***	***17·9***	***7·3***	***3·0***	***8·7***
Madras *	19,210	...			...	...	49·00	...	...	...	...	...	...
Chingleput	457	57·8	39·9	69·1	14·9	53·4	45·11	62·3	15·0	6·9	3·5	...	12·3
Chittoor	218	36·4	19·1	52·6	9·9	47·6	32·81	28·7	44·7	12·9	2·5	0·1	11·1
North Arcot	399	51·8	36·6	70·8	16·9	30·4	37·78	36·0	29·2	16·1	9·2	0·0	9·5
Salem	280	54·6	38·1	69·7	10·1	11·4	34·86	10·3	46·3	31·5	2·4	0·7	8·8
Coimbatore	294	58·6	43·2	73·6	8·7	17·4	36·85	4·3	57·9	18·3	1·6	11·0	6·9
South Arcot	561	66·4	51·1	76·9	11·4	32·0	44·86	81·6	24·6	13·0	23·8	0·2	6·8
East Coast (South)...	***429***	***72·9***	***52·1***	***71·4***	***7·4***	***32·7***	***32·41***	***29·5***	***30·0***	***18·3***	***2·9***	***9·9***	***9·4***
Tanjore	634	72·6	55·7	76·8	6·1	68·9	44·23	75·7	4·9	7·2	5·0	0·2	7·0
Trichinopoly	427	77·5	50·9	65·7	8·3	18·8	32·29	17·1	51·1	15·7	4·6	3·4	8·1
Pudukkóttai	350	Statistics not available.					31·09		Statistics not available.				
Madura	393	61·3	46·2	75·5	7·9	25·9	30·71	19·4	36·5	22·1	3·2	10·0	8·8
Rámnád	343	80·1	64·1	79·9	5·2	34·2	28·91	19·5	24·5	26·4	0·7	19·5	9·4
Tinnevelly	411	77·0	49·8	64·7	8·2	20·9	27·25	18·5	26·0	22·0	0·0	19·9	13·6
West Coast	***400***	***53·7***	***27·0***	***50·4***	***12·7***	...	***110·16***	***60·1***	***0·9***	***4·7***	***0·1***	...	***34·2***
Nilgiris	118	39·4	10·3	26·1	1·2	...	68·44	7·4	3·4	22·9	...	0·1	66·2
Malabar	520	63·6	35·3	55·5	11·7	...	116·69	53·7	0·9	2·9	0·1	...	42·4
Anjengo	5,572	92·0	88·5	96·2	...	...	...	...	...	...	...	...	100·0
South Canara ...	297	43·0	19·3	44·9	17·5	...	145·35	80·2	0·7	6·9	...	...	12·2

* The whole area of Madras city is treated as "not available for cultivation" for the purposes of agricultural returns.

II.—Distribution of the population (000-s omitted) classified according to density.

Natural Division.	Taluks or divisions with a population per square mile of—															
	Under 100.		100–150.		150–200.		200–300.		300–400.		400–500.		500–700.		700 and over.	
	Area.	Population.	Area.	Population.	Area.	Population.	Area.	Population.	Area.	Population.	Area.	Population.	Area.	Population.	Area.	Population.
	2	3	4	5	6	7	8	9	10	11	12	13	14	15	16	17
Province	*15,730*	*968*	*25,959*	*3,078*	*21,828*	*3,666*	*19,631*	*4,948*	*25,631*	*9,008*	*18,201*	*8,150*	*9,987*	*5,775*	*6,947*	*6,277*
	10·9	*2·3*	*18·0*	*7·3*	*15·2*	*8·8*	*13·6*	*11·8*	*17·9*	*21·5*	*12·6*	*19·5*	*6·9*	*13·8*	*4·9*	*15·0*
Agency	11,156	585	7,610	818	1,015	174	...	...	...	...	..	..	..	...	...	...
	58·6	*37·1*	*38·2*	*51·9*	*5·2*	*11·0*	...	...	.		..	...	..	...	...	...
East Coast (North)	...	...	3,689	454	5,475	902	5,469	1,417	9,228	3,283	2,109	984	4,485	2,585	1,351	955
	...	...	*11·6*	*4·3*	*17·3*	*8·6*	*17·2*	*13·5*	*29·3*	*31·2*	*6·7*	*9·2*	*14·0*	*24·1*	*3·9*	*9·1*
Deccan	2,609	218	13,054	1,637	8,114	1,389	2,543	576	...	..	.	...	...		...	...
	9·9	*5·6*	*49·6*	*42·9*	*30·8*	*36·4*	*9·7*	*15·1*	...	...	...	...	...	...	...	...
East Coast (Central)	..	...	1,606	169	5,426	898	7,690	1,950	5,509	1,902	6,592	3,085	3,232	1,807	1,344	1,564
	...	...	*5·1*	*1·5*	*17·3*	*7·9*	*24·5*	*17·1*	*17·5*	*16·7*	*21·0*	*27·1*	*10·3*	*15·9*	*4·3*	*13·8*
East Coast (South)	403	22	...	...	...	...	3,810	866	9,407	3,308	6,489	2,769	1,687	1,019	2,647	2,285
	1·7	*0·2*	...	...	...	...	*13·8*	*8·4*	*39·3*	*32·2*	*27·1*	*28·9*	*7·1*	*10·0*	*11·0*	*22·3*
West Coast	1,562	148	..	...	1,798	308	619	139	1,487	590	3,011	1,332	643	414	1,705	1,473
	14·4	*3·4*	...	...	*16·6*	*7·1*	*5·7*	*3·2*	*13·7*	*12·0*	*27·8*	*30·7*	*6·0*	*9·6*	*15·8*	*34·0*

III.—Distribution of the population between towns and villages.

Natural Division.	Average population per		Number per mille residing in		Number per mille of urban population residing in towns with a population of				Number per mille of rural population residing in villages with a population of			
	Town.	Village.	Towns.	Villages.	20,000 and over.	10,000 to 20,000.	5,000 to 10,000.	Under 5,000.	5,000 and over.	2,000 to 5,000.	500 to 2,000.	Under 500.
1	2	3	4	5	6	7	8	9	10	11	12	13
Province ...	*17,570*	*680*	*117*	*883*	*514*	*301*	*175*	*10*	*54*	*295*	*500*	*151*
Agency	...	119	...	1,000	...	...	...	...	9	40	148	803
East Coast (North) ...	15,240	806	96	904	420	357	209	14	42	310	506	142
Deccan	11,960	970	107	893	228	443	329	...	24	266	620	90
East Coast (Central).	21,183	769	134	866	585	265	138	12	45	255	550	150
East Coast (South)...	17,909	872	159	841	534	296	165	5	72	347	471	110
West Coast	20,716	1,298	81	919	708	156	108	28	110	331	501	58

IV.—Number per mille of the total population and of each main religion who live in towns.

Natural Division.	Number per mille who live in towns.									
	Total population.	Hindu.	Musalman.	Christian.	Animistic.	Jain.	Buddhist.	Parsi.	Jew.	Brahmo.
1	2	3	4	5	6	7	8	9	10	11
Province ...	*117*	*107*	*244*	*200*	*12*	*106*	*904*	*924*	*817*	*969*
Agency	...	...	...	...	..	...	...	...	...	...
East Coast (North) ...	96	92	227	103	52	1,000	1,000	739	...	1,000
Deccan	107	86	275	114	21	380	875	788	...	...
East Coast (Central) ...	134	118	449	319	81	89	923	970	800	984
East Coast (South) ...	159	145	380	179	...	840	830	1,000	1,000	947
West Coast	81	63	98	304	19	22	563	998	1,000	995

V.—Towns classified by population.

Class of Town.	Number of towns of each class in 1911.	Proportion to total urban population.	Number of females per 1,000 males.	Increase per cent. in the population of towns as classed at previous census.				Increase per cent. in urban population of each class from 1871 to 1911.	
				1901 to 1911.	1891 to 1901.	1881 to 1891.	1871 to 1881.	(a) In towns as classed in 1871.	(b) In the total of each class in 1911 as compared with the corresponding total in 1871.
1	2	3	4	5	6	7	8	9	10
* TOTAL ...	*280*	*100·0*	*1,027*	+ *14·5*	+ *24·6*	+ *13·7*	—*35·3*	+ *5·1*	
I. 100,000 and over	3	15·8	965	+ 7·8	+ 12·6	+ 11·5	+ 2·1	+ 20·5	+ 95·3
II. 50,000—100,000	8	9·9	1,021	— 5·1	+ 9·7	+ 12·8	+ 12·3	+ 45·9	+ 72·5
III. 20,000— 50,000	40	25·7	1,019	+ 11·7	+ 12·8	+ 12·7	+ 4·9	+ 35·2	+ 85·3
IV. 10,000— 20,000	105	30·1	1,054	+ 3·8	+ 18·0	+ 10·7	+ 6·5	+ 53·0	+ 99·7
V. 5,000— 10,000	113	17·5	1,057	+ 6·8	+ 37·2	+ 14·8	— 8·9	+ 47·3	— 66·6
VI. Under 5,000	11	1·0	1,020	+ 26·6	+ 85·0	+ 50·5	...	...	+ 100·0

* The percentages in columns 5 to 9 are worked on the total variation in urban population between decade to decade.

VI.—Cities.

Cities.	Population in 1911.	Number of persons per square mile.	Number of females to 1,000 males.	Proportion of foreign born per mille.	Number of Literates per Mille.		Percentage of variation.				
					Males.	Females.	1901 to 1911.	1891 to 1901.	1881 to 1891.	1871 to 1881.	Total 1871 to 1911.
1	2	3	4	5	6	7	8	9	10	11	12
Madras	518,660	19,210	946	334	421	129	+ 1·8	+12·6	+11·5	+ 2·1	+ 30·5
Madura	134,130	19,161	999	150	412	50	+26·6	+21·2	+18·5	+42·0	+158·0
Trichinopoly	123,512	15,439	1,006	189	433	86	+17·9	+15·6	+ 7·3	+10·8	+ 61·4
Calicut	78,417	7,129	928	41	352	112	+ 1·9	+16·5	+15·8	+19·0	+ 63·5
Kumbakônam	64,647	16,162	1,064	122	470	57	+ 8·3	+ 9·9	+ 8·4	+12·7	+ 45·5
Tanjore	60,341	7,543	1,097	81	456	79	+ 4·3	+ 6·4	− 0·6	+ 4·9	+ 15·7
Negapatam	60,168	12,034	1,006	185	415	55	+ 5·2	− 3·4	+10·0	+11·0	+ 24·0
Salem	59,153	14,788	1,024	33	285	27	−16·2	+ 4·3	+33·6	+ 1·3	+ 18·3
Cuddalore	56,574	5,143	1,020	145	339	60	+ 8·3	+10·3	+ 8·7	+ 8·1	+ 40·4
Cocanada	54,110	9,018	1,032	247	266	71	+12·5	+18·6	+40·5	+61·8	+208·3
Conjeeveram	53,864	13,466	1,036	188	445	56	+16·7	+ 8·5	+14·2	+ 0·1	+ 44·3
Coimbatore	47,007	11,752	1,009	98	420	87	−11·4	+14·4	+19·0	+10·4	+ 33·1
Bellary	34,956	3,496	892	131	286	62	−40·0	− 2·1	+11·2	+ 3·3	+ 32·5

VII.—Persons per house and houses per square mile.

Natural Division.	Average number of persons per house.			Average number of houses per square mile.		
	1911.	1901.	1891.	1911.	1901.	1891.
1	2	3	4	5	6	7
Province ...	5	5	5	55	50	47
Agency	5	4	5	17	16	15
East Coast (North)	5	5	5	65	59	54
Deccan	5	5	5	29	27	27
East Coast (Central)	6	5	6	62	57	53
East Coast (South)	5	5	5	84	77	72
West Coast	6	6	6	72	66	61

CHAPTER II.—MOVEMENT OF POPULATION.

THE title of this chapter implies that variation in the population of the Presidency, due to the working of the natural forces, birth and death, as well as to the more mechanic influences of emigration and immigration.

2. Even were trustworthy materials available for the work, it would be of little interest to draw a comparison between such happenings in bygone days and in the present century. The shadowy conflicts of Pándiyan, Chóla, and Chéra dynasties, the nose-cropping forays of Tirumala and his peers, the glory and downfall of Vijayanagar and Madura, are unrealisable in contrast with the carefully recorded monotony of to-day, when Meicondan has left his forest home for the more efficient atmosphere of the law courts.

3. Statistics as to the religions and occupations of some forty-two million people, based on the enquiry of a single night, imply a sufficient deprecation of their own existence. But if the numbering of the people shows anything in truth, it must show the number of people actually existing at a particular moment in 1911; which may safely be compared with that of those existing at some fixed time at each previous decade. For although all figures may be, and probably are, inaccurate, it is on the whole unlikely that the percentage of inaccuracy has latterly varied to any very significant extent from decade to decade.

4. If then this chapter's discussion were to proceed merely by showing the positive figures of increase or decrease for the Presidency, or even for each district and each city, the ground would be firm enough. But such method would show nothing beyond what one might naturally expect, namely that in a decade unmarked by any great or widespread natural calamity there has been a certain increase.

5. There are certain figures and returns in the light of which the crude census totals may be examined: in Europe the examination to a few, and its results to many, are interesting and valuable. Such are statistics relating to births, deaths, age or marriage.

6. Marriage registration in Southern India does not exist, and it has hitherto been customary to doubt whether that of births and deaths can be seriously regarded. The village officer, source of all Indian information, is the recorder of his village, and it well may be that, amid the toils of keeping accounts and collecting *mamuls*, he pays scant heed to what he and his friends consider the idle curiosity of an eccentric Sircar.

7. Still of more concrete value than speculation as to the workings of the village munsif's tortuous soul will be some figures, extracted from the vital statistics of the Presidency, and compared with those disclosed by the census.

8. The census of 1901 was taken on March 1st, that of 1911 on March 10th; statistics of birth and death are compiled according to the calendar year. For all practical purposes the slight difference between the two periods may be ignored and the increases according to both calculations contrasted as in the margin.

Increase shown by	Total.	Males.	Females.
Registration ...	2,797,197	1,435,021	1,362,176
Census	3,175,780	1,531,641	1,644,139

9. When we remember that registration is not enforced over the whole area of the Presidency, it seems but natural that the census increase should exceed that shown by registration. The difference is small (378,583), and the registration figures of Madras, when examined with reference to those of India, contain a certain

inherent probability of accuracy. The total excess of census over registration in India is 2,361,658, and this excess is accounted for almost entirely under the head of males (1,866,735). This condition is reversed in the case of Madras, where the excess is mainly on the female side (281,963); a state of things rendered entirely probable by the reluctance of the Madras parent to proclaim abroad the advent of a daughter.

10. But at the same time there is something to be said on the other side. Roughly speaking, all persons aged 0—10 at the census must have been born in the registration decade under reference; age is rarely accurate to a couple of months in India. To obtain the deaths among those so born, a certain amount of calculation and adjustment is necessary, in order to avoid inclusion of the deaths of children born prior to 1900. The method of this calculation is somewhat too long for detailed exposition; its result gives us 3,081,539 deaths (males 1,621,922, females 1,459,617) among this particular section of the people. The results of registration may then be summarised as in the margin; while those returned on the census night as at the age period 0—10 are as follows: total 11,137,786; males 5,495,796, females 5,641,990. The surprising difference between the two sets of statistics at their commencement, contrasted with their practical coincidence at the close, can be explained, and the explanation helps us to a just estimation of the worth of the vital statistics and of some aspects of the census returns. In the first place, as these figures suggest, registration of deaths is undoubtedly far more accurate than that of births. A birth to the simple Indian is a matter of no importance; he has not grasped, nor probably heard of, d'Ivernois' method of estimating the worth of a government, and the happiness of its subjects, by the contrast of the number of children born with the ages at which such children die. But a death is a different matter. Even in a country village disposal of an adult body cannot be overlooked; while neglect of an infant death affords too obvious an opening for the enemy's false case to admit of carelessness. In the second place the accuracy of census age-returns, as will be noted in a succeeding chapter, is open to very considerable suspicion. Especially is this the case in regard to girls unmarried between the ages of 10 and 15; there can be little doubt that many such have been returned as under 10 though in reality considerably older.

Number of	Total.	Males.	Females.
Births during decade.	11,314,152	5,777,672	5,536,480
Deaths at 0—10 ...	3,081,539	1,621,922	1,459,617
Survivors aged 0—10.	8,232,613	4,155,750	4,076,863

11. But granting a certain accuracy to the registration of the fact of death, this accuracy serves us little for the purposes of the present chapter, if unaccompanied with a certain measure of probability in the recorded causes of death. Here adaptation to European terminology of the traditional classification of all maladies as "hot" or "cold," is apt to drive the *vaidyan*, expert adviser of the village registrar, to the all-embracing classification of "fever," a fairly regular concomitant, it must be admitted, if not immediate cause of death in the East Thus of a registered total of 4,342,651 deaths in the decade, 2,920,761 have been ascribed to fever. For more conclusive arguments as to the causes of movement in the population we must fall back on cholera and plague, both fairly easy of identification.

12. The average annual mortality from cholera for the decade has been 61,689; an average which, if we exclude the epidemics of 1901 and 1906, 1907, 1908, when deaths from this cause numbered 81,370, 142,811, 81,565 and 141,970 respectively, sinks to 28,196 per annum for a period of six years.

13. Plague—fortunately a rare visitant in Southern India—claims an annual mortality of 6,887. Without the deaths of 1902 and the two succeeding years, (a total of 44,211), this average would be but 3,522. But the effect of a recurrence of plague at the time the census was taken is but too evident in a contrast of the figures of 1901 and 1911 for the cities Salem, Coimbatore and Bellary.

Years.	Salem.	Coimbatore.	Bellary.
1911	59,153	47,007	34,956
1901	70,621	53,080	58,247

District.			Increase per mille of population.	
			1901–1911.	1891–1901.
Presidency	...	...	84	72
Salem ...	...	...	40	143
Coimbatore	...	..	69	105
Bellary ...	...	...	23	75
			Deaths from Plague.	
			February.	March.
Presidency	...	...	1,070	808
Salem ...	...	...	487	403
Coimbatore	...	...	187	129
Bellary ...	...	...	256	178
Deaths.			Male.	Female.
Total ...	...	...	4,342,651	4,174,304
Under 1	...	...	1,086,361	936,373
10–15	...	...	161,733	145,614
15–20	...	...	148,194	182,636
20–30	...	...	314,385	385,308
30–40	...	...	350,668	330,145

14. Evacuation of a plague-affected city does not, it is true, necessarily imply a disappearance of its population from this world of time. But that plague affected these districts as a whole, the marginal figures suggest; the suggestion is to some extent confirmed by the recorded number of deaths from this cause about the time of the census.

15. Some further reflections are suggested by further figures extracted from these vital statistics. The first is the high proportion of infant deaths to the total mortality; the second is the sudden change in the death proportion between male and female, to the disfavour of the latter, which commences at the period 15–20 and ends at the period 30–40. Of both phenomena an explanation may be found in the universality of marriage, and of marriage too often untimely and unprovident. The subject will be treated more fully in Chapter VII; but Southern India seems hardly to recognise as yet that the national desideratum is not a huge number of random marriages, with a consequent horde of children absolutely certain to die off like flies, but a steady keeping up of numbers at an efficient age.

16. Immature maternity can but result in sickly children, and physically injured mothers. And even with all allowance for the inevitable risks of motherhood, the contrasted death figures for the sexes at the normal child-bearing age of women suggest that there is here a vast amount of wastage and preventible misery. The following words from an acknowledged authority are worth attention:—

"Midwifery in India is still in an awful condition. It is the common habit and custom in almost all districts to hand over the women in labour to the care of one of the dirtiest, most backward, illiterate, ignorant and superstitious classes, the barber midwife. The result of this custom is that untold misery, and unnumbered unnecessary deaths, are meted out to the parturient women of this country by these untrained and unclean practitioners. I do not exaggerate. Every medical practitioner in this country will substantiate this statement.

* * * * *

"If a nation is to be judged, as some hold that it should be judged, by the way women are treated, then India's place on the list of nations must indeed be very low." *

17. Abandoning vital statistics we may glance at certain natural conditions and mechanical changes of the last decade and of that preceding. Interwoven with these reflections may be a consideration of the general increase in the population disclosed by succeeding enumerations.

Decade.			Increase per cent.
1901–1911	...	...	8·3
1891–1901	...	...	7·2
1881–1891	...	...	15·7†

18. The abnormal increase of the decade 1881–91, is easily explicable as the rebound following on the terrible famine of 1877–78. Its diminution in the succeeding decade may indicate a return to more normal conditions; the improvement disclosed by the last census, while partly due to the fact that, owing to the heavy child mortality of the great famine, the number of persons at reproductive ages during

* Lt.-Col. Giffard, I.M.S., at the opening of a new Medical School in connection with the Maternity Hospital, Madras.

† Taken on unadjusted area of the Presidency.

the decade 1891–1901 was probably somewhat low, may also suggest that the Presidency is settling down to a jog-trot of prosperity.

19. This opinion however may be accepted with some reservation. In his report on the decennium 1891–1901 Sir Frederick Nicholson describes it as "one of almost uninterrupted bad seasons"; his analysis of the facts on which he bases this opinion may be quoted in full.

"Although the decade which ended in 1890 had been on the whole one of favourable seasons, it closed gloomily owing to widespread failure of crop over the greater part of the Tamil districts, and in some parts of Cuddapah, consequent on a failure of the north-east monsoon rains of that year: and though the strain was in part removed by rain in January 1891, yet in March of that year an area of 7,600 square miles was so far affected that relief works and relief kitchens were opened in several districts. As the year wore on, and the usual south-west monsoon rains were delayed, and to a large extent failed, distress was prolonged and intensified, though relieved by the later rains, which were generally good in the southern half of the Presidency. In the Deccan districts and the northern part of Nellore, however, distress deepened into famine, and at the end of March 1892, an area of 22,700 square miles with a population of 3½ millions was in distress. Relief operations were carried on from February 1891 to September 1892; the largest numbers on relief being an average of 88,681 workers, and 1,094 gratuitously relieved, in June 1892. The cultivating season of 1892 was, on the whole, favourable in the northern half of the Presidency, but in the extreme south, owing to a phenomenal failure of the north-east monsoon, much loss of crop ensued; but the pressure was mitigated to a large extent by the migration of the people to favoured localities, and later on, in March 1893, by copious showers. The next two years were, on the whole, favourable, but the season of 1895, not so much so; and it closed with unfavourable late rains. Notwithstanding this, in June 1896 prices had receded from the high level caused by previous unfavourable seasons, and were becoming normal. In that year, the south-west monsoon set in fairly; but the rainfall of September—the most critical month of the year—was scanty over the Deccan, parts of North Arcot, and in the Circars. The north-east rains were copious over the south of the Presidency, but in the northern half extensive local failure of crop occurred, which, coupled with the demand for grain in other parts of India, forced up prices at a time when the demand for labour was reduced to a minimum. Relief operations again became necessary, and in March 1897 an area of nearly 16,000 square miles with a population of more than 3½ millions was affected. These operations were continued far into the year, and in July there was an average of 557,719 relief workers employed, besides 215,495 persons relieved gratuitously, and relief was not closed until November. It was continued so far into the year owing to the delay in the proper setting in of the rains of 1897, especially in the Deccan, for elsewhere, although rather late, the early rains were favourable. The later rainfall was, however, a general failure, and the rains ceased early, causing much injury to the crops, and this necessitated the granting of some relief in Nellore up to July 1898. In 1898, the early rains were abundant, and though those of the south-west monsoon were rather late in beginning, they were generally good, and the season was, on the whole, favourable. In 1899 again the early rains were copious, but those of the south-west monsoon were extremely deficient, over the greater part of the Presidency. Later on, however, the rainfall was generally good, and the season was favourable as a whole, except in parts of the Deccan districts, but at the beginning of 1900 an area of 6,500 square miles, with a population of about a million, was so far affected as to claim the closest attention. The cultivating season of 1900 opened favourably, and the rains of the early part of the south-west monsoon were good, though there was a considerable deficiency in August; but September was favourable though the north-east monsoon was deficient and ceased very early."

20. Fortunately the decade that has just closed offers no parallel to this somewhat gloomy record. An unfavourable agricultural season in 1904–1905 resulted in a certain scarcity in Chingleput, Nellore and Kurnool; but from reports published on the subject it appears that distress was neither very serious nor very widespread. I was myself in Kurnool, (or Banganapalle State to be more accurate), at this time, and though the year was bad nothing like a famine prevailed. Test works and a poorhouse were started in Chingleput the extent and cost of relief operations being as noted.

Date on which relief		Number of persons relieved.	Direct cost.
Opened.	Closed.		
			RS.
August 7th, 1905.	November 15th, 1905.	68,236	21,272

Note.—Each person is counted separately for each day relieved.

Date on which relief		Number of persons relieved.	Direct cost.
Opened.	Closed.		
			Rs.
March 1st, 1908.	October 22nd, 1908.	78,753	12,911

Note.—Each person is counted separately for each day relieved.

21. In 1908 distress prevailed in the Ganjám district, being localised chiefly in the Khond and Savara villages of the Peddakimedi Zamindari, the Mohiri Khond villages of Berhampur taluk, and a tract lying north of the Rushikulya river. Relief afforded in the form of works, poor houses and famine kitchens is summarised in the margin.

22. Ganjám suffered further misfortune in the shape of a heavy cyclone on October 26th, 1909. About 873 villages were affected, in which some 11,000 houses were destroyed, and 20,000 injured; the value of the damages being estimated at Rs. 4,00,000. Crops and gardens suffered to an extent of about Rs. 3,00,000; about 2,000 cattle, sheep, and goats were killed, and 62 persons lost their lives.

23. It may be that the diminution of increase in 1901 was to some extent real, not merely comparative; but the distresses of that decade were probably not so marked in their effects as to produce anything in the nature of a rebound in that which succeeded. Discussion of this question involves examination of the age periods of the people, and may with advantage be postponed to Chapter V, which treats exclusively of this subject.

24. Extension of irrigation, of roads, and of railways, does not in a land long and closely settled, and one whose social customs afford a barrier well nigh impenetrable to colonization from without, indicate such actual or potential increase in the population as in a land which still relies for its development on the advent of the colonist. Yet figures relating thereto may be quoted for what they are worth, as showing a progressive adaptation of the land's surface to the needs of a larger population. Extension of irrigation is a potent safeguard against the vicissitudes of seasons; if it be objected against railways and roads, especially the former, that they tend to destroy the habit of grain storage against an evil day, it is a fair answer that they also equalise distribution, and, as between province and province, or district and district, prevent co-existent extremes of plenty and scarcity.

25. The following figures exhibit the development of irrigation at various periods—extents are given in square miles:—

Source of irrigation.	Average, 1884–1885 to 1889–1890.	Average, 1890–1891 to 1899–1900.	1900–1901.	1903–1904.	1910–1911.
Total ...	9,444	9,137	9,330	9,756	15,505
Government canals	8,972	4,067	4,378	4,388	5,421
Private canals	42	44	39	37	352
" Tanks	3,569	3.098	2,939	3,381	5,635
" Wells	1,494	1,705	1,730	1,677	2,200
Other sources	367	223	244	273	1,897

26. Prophecy in this connection is an essay of doubtful value, but the figures at the side give an approximate idea of the area now commanded by some of the great irrigation systems, and of the area which these systems may ultimately command. Obviously it does not follow that the goal will be reached by 1921; on the contrary, as these are old and already well tried sources, extension will probably be slow.

—	Area commanded (acres) 1910–1911.	Ultimate area (acres).
Gódávari delta	744,992	765,730
Kistna delta	711,275	725,000
Cauvery delta	902,769	919,540
Pennér river canal ...	151,679	165,885

District.	Name.	Acreage.
Guntúr	Bhavanási	841
Nellore	Mopád	12,500
Kurnool	Venkatápuram ...	1,700
Vizagapatam ...	Nágavalli	31,200
Kurnool	Siddápúr	4,250

27. In respect of new irrigation it is possible that the projects referred to in the margin, or at least some of them, may have entered the sphere of actual existence when the next numbering of the people comes about.

Areas in square miles.

Year.	Total area cropped.	Area of food crops.	Area of rice crops.
Average, 1884–1889.	37,250	30,161	9,225
„ 1890–1899.	41,647	33,278	10,255
1900–1901 ...	43,506	34,859	10,300
1903–1904	46,125	36,289	12,139
1907–1908	59,353	46.771	16,559
1909–1910	56,857	44,919	16,187

28. Transition from these statistics to those of area cropped and details of crop is obvious.

29. It should be borne in mind that the abnormal development of later years is apparent rather than real, being induced by the inclusion for the first time in 1907 in these statistics of the figures for zamindari areas. To the same cause may be assigned the shrinkage of crop area in 1909–10, as compared with 1907–08. Statistics for the latter year, founded largely on estimate or guesswork, have assumed more reliable if more modest proportions three years later.

30. *Railways.*—There were in 1911 some 3,800 miles of railway serving the Presidency, as against 2,100 in 1891, and 3,500 in 1904. Although the decade shows no such important work as the line from Madras to Northern Frontier of Ganjám that marked its predecessor, mention may be made of the line from Bezwáda to Masulipatam, through the rich delta of the Kistna; extension of the West Coast line to Mangalore, the capital of South Canara; and the line which banished the nightmare jutka gallop (*experto crede*) from Dhone to Kurnool.

31. *Roads.*—There were at the end of the decade some 22,000 miles of metalled, and 4,000 miles of unmetalled roads in the Presidency. No new roads of great importance appear to have been laid during the decade. * Salem and Coimbatore, with nearly 1,800 metalled miles apiece, head the list; closely followed by Malabar with 1,603. Vizagapatam accounts for some 1,400 miles of metal, North Arcot for 1,600; Cuddapah, Madura and South Canara, have each more than 1,000 miles. This class of road, it may be observed, is not of paramount necessity in the "black cotton plains" of the Deccan and Tinnevelly, inasmuch as in the dry season, when cartage is required, the fields themselves give going for bullock carts probably easier than does a permanent road of the type usually encountered in the mofussil. An increase of substantial highways, could such be built without prohibitive expense, through the irrigation districts of Kistna, Gódávari, and Tanjore, could scarcely fail to aid materially in developing still further the resources of these territories.

32. *Emigration.*—Figures relating to emigation and immigration are, for reasons described in the census report of 1901, a somewhat broken reed for the leaning of the statistician. In point of district detail, they are open to the special objection that the emigrant is almost invariably described as a native of the district wherein his port of embarkation, or the dépôt at which he arranges for his passage, is situated. Thus in the figures available of emigrants to Ceylon, Salem, Coimbatore, and North Arcot, to give a few examples, are unrepresented. But a statement compiled for me by the respresentative of the Ceylon Labour Commission shows that, in a period

* The figures that I have obtained are for districts as they stood prior to the introduction of Sir William Meyer's redistribution scheme.

of five years (1905–1909), 15,689, 8,246 and 11,694 persons respectively left these districts for the island.

33. Such information as I have been able to obtain shows a nett loss to the Presidency of 647,793 in ten years, as compared with one of 444,859 in the previous decade. For convenient reference I quote in the margin figures of emigration to those parts of the world outside India most affected by the native of Madras.

Emigrants from Madras to—	
Natal	45,740
Straits Settlements	447,036
Burma	1,160,522
Ceylon	1,501,623

34. It may be of some interest to give a few details as the castes of emigrants. For this information I am again indebted to the Ceylon Labour Commissioner, who at all times has spared no pains in complying with my manifold requests. In the five-year period above referred to there passed through his hands 42,493 *Paraiyans*, 28,596 *Pallans*, 15,759 *Kallans*, 13,738 *Vellálas*, 18,066 *Ambalakárans* and 9,753 *Agamudaiyans*. For the spiritual care of the wayfarers five *Bráhmans* had perforce to suffice.

35. It is obvious that much of this emigration is merely temporary, and by no means in the nature of permanent expatriation. The traveller to Ceylon is a harvester in the tea gardens of the island ; the Straits Settlements call loudly for a few seasons labour in their rubber plantations; the rice mills of Burma are reported to be run well nigh entirely by Madrasi workmen, who in due course return to their native land. Burma appears to have given us back nearly 1,000,000, of her Madras emigrants, Ceylon 400,000, the Straits Settlements 266,000.

36. The pros and cons of this emigration question deserve perhaps a moment's consideration. Anxiety at depletion of the country's labour supply has been significant at sundry agricultural conferences, and has at times suggested governmental interference : of the manner of the coolies' going, the following description is sufficiently lachrymose :—

> "Many thousands are shipped away to Penang every year for use in the plantations. Some are recruited by authorized agents, but the majority goes on its own account. Packed like sardines in a tin, sea sick and wretched, they make the five days' journey under conditions which would be intolerable to a white man. But the cooly takes it all with the mute philosophy of his kind, ready to endure anything and face anything for the sake of a few rupees, which may save his children from starvation, and his house from the clutches of the money-lender." *

37. Yet there is another side to this question. Probably nothing more than this outgoing has helped the Indian Paraiyan † to realise that cultivation of his high caste neighbour's land for a precarious handful of rice is not all that life has to offer: if his race suffers hardships in some of these new lands, he can at least murmur with some measure of satisfaction to his more aristocratic fellow sufferer "it is now unto thee as unto this last." A few figures may be given relative to the savings brought from abroad by returning emigrants, and to amounts remitted by them to their friends or relatives at home.

38. Between 1901 and 1910, 17,250 persons returned from Natal bringing with them Rs. 24,20,164; during the same period 2,225 persons remitted by money order Rs. 13,95,300. From Mauritius 2,659 persons returned with Rs. 13,127; from Fiji 35 persons remitted Rs. 3,515.

39. The voyage is probably quite sufficiently unpleasant. Yet returned emigrants whom I have questioned do not appear to find in it a subject for a tale of woe.

40. *Interprovincial migration.*—From the Superintendents of other provinces I have received information concerning more than one million persons born in the

* S. P. Hyatt. "Off the beaten track."

† At Negapatam a Bráhman chided a Paraiyan who barged into him on the quay. To which the Paraiyan "I have taken off my caste and left it with the Port officer. I won't put it on again till I come back." I have heard of "depressed classes," or at least of depressed individuals, evolving into substantial farmers with the aid of the money earned and saved in foreign countries.

Madras Presidency, but enumerated elsewhere. When it is remembered that the Madras labourer frequently returns as his birth place his taluk or his village, rather than his district, and that a knowledge of the taluks, or even districts of provinces other than his own, is rarely possessed by the average enumerator, or abstracting clerk, the information supplied is somewhat remarkably accurate, "Madras unspecified" accounting for less than 20 per cent. of the total number.

41. Of provinces across the sea, Burma and Ceylon, as might be expected, account for the greater number of our emigrants A remarkable variation in sex proportion is observable; of quarter of a million Madrasi emigrants to Burma, over 200 thousand are men; while in Ceylon, women contribute 182 thousand to a total of approximately 448 thousand. In the Burmese return "Madras unspecified" accounts for the major portion of those enumerated; but the districts, which claim the greater number of those whose birth-place has been ascertained, (Ganjám, Vizagapatam and Gódávari), are certainly those from which emigration to Burma most prevails. Ceylon has returned the birth-places of its Madrasi immigrants with extraordinary accuracy, the majority coming, as one might expect, from the southern districts of Tanjore, Trichinopoly, Madura and Tinnevelly. In the Straits Settlements were enumerated some 58 thousand Madrasis, among whom men outnumbered women in the proportion of four to one.

42. Of provinces or states within India, Mysore has taken from us more than quarter of a million souls (well nigh three times as many as she has given), with a fairly equal ratio between the sexes. North Arcot, with more than 57 thousand persons, is her largest contributor; closely followed by South Canara with nearly 49 thousand. Frontier contiguity is a readily apparent reason in the latter case as it is in the case of 52 thousand immigrants from Bellary and Anantapur; but an emigration of more than 41 thousand people from "Madras" indicates the difficulty experienced in obtaining a correct return of birth place. Travancore has enumerated nearly 50 thousand Madrasis, natives for the most part of the adjoining district of Tinnevelly; of some 30 thousand found in Cochin five sixths came from Malabar. Sex proportion in these emigrants to Travancore and Cochin is practically equal, which suggests that the emigration may be permanent; but an overwhelming preponderance of men among the Madrasis found in Coorg, combined with the fact that practically all there found are natives of Malabar or South Canara, indicates the temporary migration of labour to the coffee estates on the plateau. Eastern Bengal and Assam account for 36 thousand persons, nearly all of whom come from the northernmost districts of Ganjám and Vizagapatam, to which labour recruiters for the Assam gardens look mostly for their workmen. Bombay shows some 35 thousand Madrasis, the greater number coming apparently from Madras City; but, as already noted, the opportunity for error, when the province and its capital possess the same name, is obvious. The figures for Hyderabad, I have not received in time for inclusion in this report.

43. So much for the Presidency as a territorial whole. Before devoting space to an analysis of the progress of the whole into the progress of its component parts, it will be well to glance at the movement of the four great religious sections into which the Presidency is divided.

44. The subject may appear one belonging essentially to Chapter IV, wherein indeed it is treated in some of its aspects. But that chapter deals with the progress of religion; increase or decrease among people professing a religion is more germane to this present train of thought.

45. The population of the Presidency has increased by 84 per mille during the decade. In the same period Hindus have increased by 81 per thousand, Muhammadans by 116, Christians by 163; while Animists have declined by 5 per mille.

46. Inasmuch as Hinduism is not a proselytizing religion, its only apparent possibilities lie in natural increase; and at the same time it is exposed to defections caused by Muhammadan and Christian conversions. Moreover, while Hinduism undoubtedly tends to absorb Animists, *en bloc* if not individually, a tendency which accounts for Animistic decrease during the decade, the theological whim

of the enumerator, exemplified in the case of the Nellore *Yánádis*, may sweep away abruptly a considerable number of its adherents.

47. Such are the efforts devoted to the spread of Christianity in India that its greater increase need occasion no surprise. Between Hinduism and Muhammadanism arises the question whether there is anything in the social habit of the latter religion more favourable to rapid natural increase. This question is usually answered in the affirmative; the reasons alleged for such answer being the more generous diet permissible to a Muhammadan, his freedom from the pernicious custom of immature marriage, and from sterile widowhood among his womenkind. There are however certain considerations which give ground for pause and reflection before a too implicit acceptance of this answer. As compared with the high caste Hindu the Muhammadan may eat meat; the express prohibition of his religion against intoxicating drink gives him an advantage over the Hindu of the lower sort. But, inasmuch as the rank and file of southern Muhammadans are not amongst the most prosperous, it is questionable whether they can afford flesh food to any great extent; and whether such flesh as they can procure has a more nutrient, or in any way better effect, than a grain and vegetable diet. On the other hand, abstinence from alcohol may be counterbalanced, it is feared, by the Muhammadan's greater predilection for intoxicating or narcotic drugs.

48. In respect of avoidance of immature marriage, Chapter VII shows that the Muhammadan has the advantage of his Hindu fellow countryman, but it is questionable whether this is sufficient to counterbalance the harm that enforced seclusion of women must necessarily do to the community. In regard to female widowhood in general, and premature widowhood in particular, counsel is somewhat darkened by the fact that all Muhammadan widows may remarry, while the prohibition against remarriage is not of universal application throughout the several strata of Hinduism. Taking however 10,000 women of each religion, Hinduism has 1,892 of that number widowed against 1,745 of Islam: in point of premature widowhood the advantage is with the Hindus, whose widows aged 0—35 number 1,856 of 10,000 widowed, the corresponding figures of the Muhammadans being 2,029.

49. The better classes apart, occupation and residence are factors with some bearing on this question. As seen by Chapter I the Muhammadan, much more than the Hindu, is a town dweller; and the petty commerce and industry, in which he finds employment, is not in the nature of things so favourable to physical well-being as the country life and agricultural employment of the poor Hindu. An indirect confirmation of this view is obtained from the fact that among *Máppillas*, the agriculturists of the community, increase is considerably greater (139 per mille), than among the general body of Muhammadans. At the same time this increase as a natural happening needs to be discounted, in view of the greater activity in proselytism on the West Coast, of which Chapter IV makes mention.

50. The contrast of British territory with the feudatory states, whose statistics this volume includes, is of little interest. In comparison with their surroundings the extent and population of the latter are microscopic, and the marginal figures for the last two decades are too easily explicable to need lengthy comment. The unfavourable decade 1891–1901 told hardly on these little states, especially those of the Deccan, which showed a positive decrease; the slight increase of all three together being entirely due to the influence of the Pudukkóttai figures. The marked improvement of the last ten years is the obvious rebound after a season of adversity. Political comparisons and arguments, besides being objectionable, are in this case futile, inasmuch as, from a variety of causes, all three states were more or less directly under British control for a considerable portion of the last decade.

—	Percentage of increase	
	1901–1911.	1891–1901.
British Territory	8·3	7·3
Feudatories	9·7	0·9

Natural division.	1901–1911.		1891–1901.	
	Rank.	Rate of increase per cent.	Rank.	Rate of increase per cent.
East Coast, Central.	4	8·0	1	9·1
East Coast, North.	2	9·8	2	8·8
West Coast ...	5	7·1	3	6·3
East Coast, South.	3	8·2	4	5·4
Deccan	6	3·8	5	5·3
Agency	1	16·7	6	2·4

51. Turning to comparison of movement in natural divisions and districts, it is essential to bear in mind the states precedent and subsequent to movement. In point of density the rank of the natural divisions remains unchanged from 1901, but in regard to rate of increase there has been considerable variation as the marginal figures show.

52. From the sudden acceleration of progress in the Agency division it would be unsafe to draw any conclusion. In point of density, this division with its several component parts is still at the bottom of the scale, and is likely to remain so. It is no doubt sparsely populated, but, from what I have seen of it, I should doubt if the land is capable of adaptation to the needs of an appreciably greater population, while its seasons of unhealthiness, and the peculiarities of its inhabitants, peculiarities probably less acceptable to the Hindu than to the European, render colonization unlikely. The greater progress of the decade may as probably be ascribed to better enumeration as to any other cause : this is especially noticeable in the case of the Vizagapatam Agency, which has changed from a decrease of 1 per cent. to an increase of 20 per cent., and where the Collector reports that some 245 villages, with a present population of 29,845, do not figure in the census returns of 1901.

53. Turning to the plains divisions, on whose statistics more reliance can be placed, we find the Deccan division low down both in actual density and in rate of progress. Two of its components, it is true, Banganapalle and Sandúr, in this latter respect outstrip the rest of the Presidency ; but of this phenomenon an explanation has been suggested in paragraph 50, and is confirmed by the fact that Banganapalle, for the most part exceedingly fertile, is now but on a level in point of density with the adjoining district of Cuddapah, while the population of Sandúr per square mile is less than half that of Bellary.

54. Conditions of life in Cuddapah, Kurnool, and Bellary are such as to favour a sparsity of population, and a slow rate of increase. Although holdings are larger than in the south, the farmer, whether he lives on the cholam that he grows, or buys food-stuff with the price of his cotton, requires a greater acreage for his livelihood than the rice grower. Individually the inhabitants of these tracts, in point of physical fitness, are probably equal to, or surpass, those of milder natural divisions, but the rigours of the climate, while bracing to the fit, do not favour the idle or physically weakly.

55. Examination in greater detail of vital satistics for the years 1901–10 shows that, taking the figures given for what they are worth, the birth rate of Cuddapah for each of the ten years was lower than that of the Presidency, as is that of Kurnool for eight of these years. In four years the death rate of Cuddapah was higher than the Presidency rate, that of Kurnool in six years. The birth rate of Bellary was higher than that of the Presidency in five years, but in every year save 1907 the death rate exceeded that of the rest of the Presidency.

56. This Deccan division is land-locked ; and industry, as opposed to agriculture, tends to flourish in the reasonable neighbourhood of the sea. The same natural circumstance precludes to a great extent extra Indian immigration, which may temporarily deplete a district, but in the long run is apt to raise the general level of prosperity by the return of the emigrant in much better case than when he started. And the reluctance of the Deccan ryot to seek fortune elsewhere is exemplified in the story of the Kurnool Reddis, who, when invited to Heaven, made enquiries as to the extent of black cotton soil there to be found, and respectfully declined the invitation.

57. In the south-eastern division the birth rates of Tanjore and Tinnevelly exceed that of the Presidency in every one of the ten years 1901–10 ; but

consequent increase is checked by a similar excess of deaths in every year in Tanjore, and in all save one in Tinnevelly. The large emigration from Negapatam, already referred to, must exercise a potent influence in relieving overpressure in Tanjore, as does that to Ceylon in the case of Tinnevelly. On the side of increase must be reckoned the inflow of money resulting sooner or later from this emigration, the well established industry and activity of Tuticorin, and the rapidly rising industrial importance of Madura city.

58. Malabar and South Canara, the main districts of the West Coast division, occupy 16th and 21st place in regard to percentage increase throughout the decade. In birth rate Malabar surpasses the Presidency average in seven years out of ten; South Canara excels it in eight years, and equals it in one. The death rate is higher in nine years out of ten in South Canara, and in five in Malabar. In point of population compared to cultivated area, these districts, as already noted, occupy second and third place respectively; which fact, combined with their comparatively slow rate of increase, may suggest that possibility of popular progress can only lie in enlargement of the proportion of cultivated to cultivable land. Although on the sea board, Canara and Malabar can hardly look to emigration westwards as an outlet for their surplus population; emigration to the east involves the crossing of India to a port of embarkation. Language and custom form a barrier to internal migration; the Malayali in particular, as seen in table XI, is reasonably loth to leave his own country, which has attracted a regular section of Tamil immigrants; who, though many of them have been born in Malabar, yet remain differentiated from the true West Coast people.

59. In the north-east division the slow increase of Vizagapatam, (4·2 per cent.), rendered credible by the position of the district in regard to density of population, is somewhat surprising in view of the abnormally low death-rate with which sanitary reports credit the district. The inhabitants may indeed observe with solicitude the precepts of the sagacious Vidura, and avoid "the rays of the rising sun, the smoky flame of the burning ground, the secret embraces of bad old women, the use of dirty water, the eating of curds and rice at night, wherein length of days slips away"; and may follow scrupulously his practical, but alas! unquotable regimen of daily life, but the probability is greater that something is amiss with these vital statistics. Of the abnormal increase in the rate for the years 1906 and 1908 I can find no detailed explanation; and although in eight years out of ten the birth-rate of the district was below that of the Presidency, the variation was not at all so strongly marked as in the complementary return.

Year.	Death-rate per mille.	
	Presidency.	Vizagapatam.
1901	21·8	14·6
1902	20·2	15·1
1903	22·2	18·1
1904	22·5	18·4
1905	21·4	18·8
1906	27·4	29·8
1907	24·3	19·1
1908	26·2	27·7
1909	21·8	19·6
1910	24·7	22·4

60. To examine in detail the reasons for variaton of population in each of the 250 and odd taluks, into which the Madras districts are divided, would require a separate volume. It must be remembered that the territorial redistribution of the Presidency has necessitated creation, by adjustment, of population for taluks, which in 1891 and 1901 did not exist; and alteration of figures for many, which, with an altered area, still retain their old names. The consequent necessity for discounting error is therefore so obvious as to require no further mention.

61. To the reasons for abnormal increase in the Vizagapatam Agency, or rather in parts of it, allusion has already been made. A decrease of nearly 27 per cent. in the Koraput taluk of the same district is considered by the Collector as genuine, and due to a large migration of Khonds to the points at which increase has been greatest. This migration is accounted for by (1) want of land for *pódu* cultivation, the hereditary employment of the Khond, and the possibility of getting such land in Padwa and Nowrangapur taluks; (2) the nomadic instinct of the Khond; (3) want of capital (ploughs, cattle, etc.) for cultivation, which causes emigration as farm servants; (4) bad crops.

62. The Collector of Ganjám considers the greater rate of increase in his district, as compared with that in the previous decade, to be due to three general causes, to which he also assigns talukwar variations. These causes are (1) more accurate enumeration, (2) absence of epidemics and famine during the decade, (3) a favourable season in 1910–11, which induced many of the labouring classes, who usually migrate at harvest time to Rangoon and other places, to remain behind.

63. In Goomsur taluk a portion of the increase is attributed to the settlement of Khonds and other hill tribes in the plains; in Berhampur to settlement from outside for purposes of trade and agriculture; in Ramagiri (Agency) to immigration from Parlákimedi, caused by forest reservation operations in the latter area. In Chicacole taluk, where increase is lowest in the district, and lower than in the previous decade, emigration is assigned as the reason.

64. The Collector of Nellore considers as somewhat abnormal the rate of increase in Darsi, Kanigiri, and Podili taluks. These parts of the district appear to have suffered from scarcity twice in the decade ending with 1900; once in 1891–92, and again in 1898–99, with the result that labourers then left their homes in large numbers in search of work, and returned in the more favourable decade which followed. The same reason may be applicable to Udayagiri, where increase would have been greater but for a wave of bad public health, which also affected the neighbouring taluk of Atmakúr. Rápur taluk, which shows a decrease, contains several mica mines once employing a large floating population of labourers. Many of these mines, which were being worked at the time of census in 1901, had closed down, and such closure must have contributed in large measure to the decrease. In Atmakúr cholera prevailed at the time of enumeration; a slight decrease in Gúdúr, and a low percentage of increase in Polúr, Nellore, and Kandukúr are reported to be due to emigration to the Straits Settlements and elsewhere. Kovur is affected by malaria and general unhealthiness, and the tract was already somewhat congested in point of population.

65. In Bellary, a high percentage of increase in Alúr taluk is attributed to influx of labourers from neighbouring tracts at the cotton picking season. Bellary taluk has suffered badly from plague, a cause which may also account for lack of improvement in Hadagalli after the fall between 1891 and 1901; plague prevailed in Hospet, and large tracts along the river have been evacuated on account of the prevalence of malaria. Adóni was comparatively free from plague, but has lost several of its large villages to the newly constituted taluk of Siruguppa.

66. In respect of Kurnool the decade 1891–1901 was one of bad seasons; while during 1901–11 the district was comparatively prosperous. In bad years the inhabitants of the Cumbum and Markapur taluks migrate to the Kistna delta, and in a lesser degree to Kurnool, Nandikotkur, Nandyál and Sirvel, the canal fed taluks of their own district. The greater increase of these taluks, as compared with their neighbours, between 1891 and 1901 is thus explained, as is their diminished progress in the last decade. Pattikonda suffered severely in the scarcity of 1897, and its large percentage of increase now is probably the rebound after adversity. Dhone, which shows the highest rate of increase in the district (14·2), bears testimony to the value of railway extension, a line from Dhone to Kurnool having been opened during the decade that has passed.

67. In Guntúr the Collector considers the result of the census to be very much what might have been anticipated. Tenáli and Répalle taluks are commanded by the Kistna channels, and are markedly prosperous. Palnád taluk, where increase is smallest, is a stony and unfertile tract: increase in Vinukonda and Narasaraopet is possibly attributable in some degree to overflow from other taluks, where increase has been very marked for the last 20 years. As a whole the district is extremely fertile; it has been free from plague, and has not suffered severely from any other epidemic, nor from malaria.

68. Going further south the increase in five taluks of South Arcot, namely, Chidambaram, Tirukkóyilúr, Villupuram, Gingee, and Tindivanam is assigned by the

Collector in the first place to certain general causes, such as (1) greater accuracy of enumeration; (2) freedom from epidemics and from severe famine; (3) decrease of emigration; a point noticed in the special report on Madras city. Secondly, increase has been greatest where ground-nut cultivation is most extensive, and the census was taken at the time of harvest, when a large number of immigrant coolies were employed. In Villupuram taluk the large railway works may partially account for an increase of nearly 5,000 in the population of the town, and exercise some influence on that of the taluk generally.

69. The Collector of North Arcot considers the marked increase in the Arkónam, Arni, Cheyár, Wálája and Wándiwásh taluks of his district to be due to the influence of a favourable agricultural decade, the season of 1896–97 in the previous decennium having been exceedingly bad. In Gudiyáttam and Kangundi taluks this seasonal improvement was not so strongly marked, and the increase during the decade is consequently nearer the normal for the Presidency. In Tirupattúr an outbreak of plague occurred just about the time of the census, and the cessation of increase, which the figures show, is probably the result of temporary evacuation.

70. Of Rámnád, the Collector observes that the prosperity of Srívilliputtúr, Aruppukkóttai, and Sáttúr has of late increased by leaps and bounds, largely owing to the increased cultivation of cotton. In Srívilliputtúr taluk there has been a considerable extension of irrigation under wells, and the fact that a tile factory has recently been established there may be taken as indicating increasing wealth, was much as it suggests a demand for a better class of dwelling-house.

71. The marked change in the fortunes of the Ambásamudram and Nángunéri taluks of the Tinnevelly district is explained by the Collector as due to the abnormal figures obtained in 1891. In that year the paddy harvest of Ambásamudram, which attracts coolies from Nánguuéri, was in full swing at the time of census, and subsequent fluctuations are due to the more normal situation encountered at the last two enumerations. The increase in Srívaikuntam taluk reflects the growing prosperity of Tuticorin and Srívaikuntam towns; although the most notable section of the latter's population, the Vellálas of Fort, Chapter XI shows to be on the verge of extinction. Tiruchendúr owed its large increase in 1901 to the occurrence at census time of an important religious festival; it is a poor taluk and bad seasons with consequent emigration have checked its rate of increase.

72. The increase of the Salem district during the period 1891–1901, the Collector considers to have been abnormal. In that decade the population of the district increased by more than 212 thousand souls; an increase of half this amount, the Collector observes, would have been more readily explicable. The set back which has occurred during the decade now under reference may be explained as due to plague, which continually afflicts the Hosúr taluk, and which by its marked occurrence in Salem town spreads panic in the Salem taluk. Uttangarai taluk is unhealthy, and from Krishnagiri there is said to be a considerable stream of emigration to Ceylon.

73. On the West Coast the settlements of Anjengo and Tangasseri have now been excluded from the Cochin taluk of Malabár. In the Wynaad, coffee planting fared poorly during the decade 1891–1901; in the succeeding ten years the opening up of tea cultivation has brought back prosperity. In Ernád, six rubber estates were opened in the decade; in Ponnáni, increase has been stimulated by an increasing demand for the products of the cocoanut.

74. In South Canara, Udipi and Coondapoor are said to have been comparatively free from the fever which checked their growth between 1891 and 1901. On the other hand dysentery is said to have prevailed in Kásaragod; whose cooly population have also become more migratory in their habits since the recent opening of railway communication with other parts of the district. Plague has visited Mangalore town at intervals since 1902, and in the taluk dysentery is said to have claimed nearly 10,000 victims in the last ten years. In 1894 the Amindivi

Islands suffered severely from cholera, and the results of the visitation are to be seen in the figures for 1901; better health, and increasing prosperity, due to improvement in the price of cocoanut products, explain the improvement shown by 1911.

75. The Nilgiri district is somewhat abnormal, and population here varies largely in accordance with the state of the planting industry. Increase in the Ootacamund and Coonoor taluks is small as compared with that between 1891 and 1901, when planting throve, and numerous coolies from the plains were to be found on the hills. In Gúdalúr taluk there was a heavy fall in the population of 1901 compared with that of 1891, due no doubt to the failure of gold mining companies in the neighbourhood, and to the abandonment of coffee estates. The increase of the last decade may be attributed to the large extension of tea planting which has taken place.

I.—Variation in relation to density since 1891.

District and Natural Division.	Percentage of variation Increase (+) Decrease (—)		Net variation 1891 to 1911.	Mean density per square mile.		
	1901 to 1911.	1891 to 1901.		1911.	1901.	1891.
1	2	3	4	5	6	7
Province ...	+ ***8·3***	+ ***7·2***	+ ***16·1***	***291***	***269***	***251***
Agency	+ ***16·7***	+ ***2·4***	+ ***19·5***	***80***	***68***	***67***
Agency, Ganjám	+ 9·1	+ 4·5	+ 14·0	101	92	88
„ Vizagapatam ...	+ 20·0	— 1·0	+ 18·8	81	67	68
„ Gódávari	+ 14·9	+ 17·4	+ 34·9	56	49	42
East Coast (North)	+ ***9·8***	+ ***8·8***	+ ***19·5***	***332***	***302***	***278***
Ganjám	+ 10·7	+ 6·8	+ 17·6	382	345	325
Vizagapatam	+ 4·2	+ 7·2	+ 11·7	472	453	422
Gódávari	+ 12·4	+ 9·2	+ 22·7	568	505	462
Kistna	+ 14·5	+ 14·3	+ 30·9	338	295	258
Guntúr	+ 13·9	+ 13·3	+ 29·0	296	260	230
Nellore	+ 4·2	+ 2·8	+ 7·1	167	160	156
Deccan	+ ***3·8***	+ ***5·3***	+ ***9·3***	***145***	***140***	***133***
Cuddapah	+ 1·6	— 0·3	+ 1·3	152	149	150
Kurnool	+ 7·2	+ 6·6	+ 14·4	123	115	108
Banganapalle	+ 21·9	— 9·1	+ 10·8	154	127	139
Bellary	+ 2·3	+ 7·5	+ 10·0	170	166	154
Sandúr	+ 20·8	— 1·7	+ 18·8	84	70	71
Anantapur	+ 3·2	+ 8·2	+ 11·7	143	139	128
East Coast (Central)	+ ***8·0***	+ ***9·1***	+ ***17·8***	***362***	***335***	***307***
Madras	+ 1·8	+ 12·6	+ 14·6	19,210	18,865	16,760
Chingleput	+ 7·8	+ 9·1	+ 17·1	457	426	391
Chittoor	+ 5·6	+ 4·7	+ 10·6	218	207	197
North Arcot	+ 12·0	+ 6·5	+ 19·3	399	356	334
Salem	+ 4·0	+ 14·3	+ 18·8	280	270	236
Coimbatore	+ 6·9	+ 10·5	+ 18·1	294	275	249
South Arcot	+ 12·2	+ 7·6	+ 20·7	561	500	465
East Coast (South)	+ ***8·2***	+ ***5·4***	+ ***14·1***	***429***	***396***	***376***
Tanjore	+ 5·2	+ 0·8	+ 6·0	634	602	598
Trichinopoly	+ 7·2	+ 5·0	+ 12·6	427	398	379
Pudukkóttai	+ 8·3	+ 2·0	+ 10·4	350	323	317
Madura	+ 12·8	+ 11·1	+ 25·3	398	318	314
Rámnád	+ 9·2	+ 4·7	+ 14·3	343	314	300
Tinnevelly	+ 8·0	+ 8·3	+ 17·0	411	381	353
West Coast	+ ***7·1***	+ ***6·3***	+ ***13·8***	***400***	***374***	***352***
Nilgiris	+ 5·1	+ 11·6	+ 17·3	118	112	100
Malabar	+ 7·8	+ 5·6	+ 18·9	520	453	457
Anjengo	+ 15·7	+ 9·7	+ 26·8	5,572	4,817	4,393
South Canara	+ 5·8	+ 7·4	+ 13·2	297	282	263

II.—*Comparison with vital statistics.*

District and Natural Division.	In 1901–1910 total number of		Number per cent of population of 1901 of		Excess (+) or deficiency (–) of births over deaths.	Increase (+) or decrease (–) of population of 1911 compared with 1901.	
	Births.	Deaths.	Births.	Deaths.		Natural population.	Actual population.
1	2	3	4	5	6	7	8
Province ...	***11,406,386***	***8,593,737***	***29·5***	***22·3***	***+ 2,812,649***	***+ 1,205,479***	***+ 4,547,484***
East Coast (North)	***2,896,678***	***2,030,427***	***30·3***	***21·2***	***+ 866,251***	***+ 3,338,580***	***+ 2,498,568***
Ganjám	462,615	301,825	30·0	19·6	+ 160,790	+ 220,506	+ 679,594
Vizagapatam	594,521	422,114	28·7	20·4	+ 172,407	+ 262,725	+ 1,118,785
Gódávari (a)	517,225	381,199	35·8	26·4	+ 136,026		
Kistna (a)	613,647	432,180	35·2	24·8	+ 181,467	+ 722,248	+ 700,239
Guntúr (b)	369,041	228,859	24·8	15·4	+ 140,182		
Nellore (a)	339,629	264,250	26·7	20·8	+ 75,379		
Deccan Division	***1,132,988***	***983,390***	***28·7***	***24·9***	***+ 149,598***	***+ 154,404***	***+ 136,543***
Cuddapah	329,385	295,752	25·5	22·9	+ 33,633	+ 27,461	+ 14,204
Kurnool	262,654	211,872	30·1	24·3	+ 50,782	+ 64,071	+ 63,144
Banganapalle	8,215	5,974	25·5	18·5	+ 2,241	— 252	+ 7,080
Bellary (c)	296,043	272,285	30·9	28·4	+ 23,758	+ 39,827	+ 24,548
Anantapur	236,691	197,507	30·0	25·1	+ 39,184	+ 23,797	+ 27,567
East Coast (Central)	***3,397,728***	***2,566,994***	***31·5***	***23·8***	***+ 830,734***	***+ 836,512***	***+ 874,715***
Madras	196,864	224,374	38·7	44·1	— 27,510	+ 512	+ 9,314
Chingleput	454,018	331,276	34·6	25·2	+ 122,742	+ 106,875	+ 95,977
North Arcot	624,257	449,021	28·3	20·3	+ 175,236	+ 189,455	+ 234,746
Salem	682,909	521,651	31·0	23·7	+ 161,258	+ 138,151	+ 80,301
Coimbatore	644,516	468,194	29·3	21·3	+ 176,322	+ 153,189	+ 156,064
South Arcot	795,164	572,478	33·8	24·4	+ 222,686	+ 298,830	+ 298,313
East Coast (South)	***2,664,745***	***1,972,669***	***29·7***	***22·0***	***+ 692,076***	***+ 836,969***	***+ 749,827***
Tanjore	751,379	596,107	33·5	26·6	+ 155,272	+ 122,494	+ 117,660
Trichinopoly	469,208	338,306	32·5	23·4	+ 130,902	+ 110,627	+ 109,674
Pudukkóttai	73,729	62,575	19·4	16·4	+ 11,154	+ 28,103	+ 31,446
Madura	661,852	464,702	23·4	16·4	+ 197,150	+ 387,487	+ 309,783
Tinnevelly	708,577	510,979	33·1	23·9	+ 197,598	+ 188,308	+ 181,264
West Coast	***1,314,247***	***1,040,257***	***32·5***	***25·7***	***+ 273,990***	***+ 305,216***	***+ 287,831***
Nilgiris	32,339	29,460	29·0	26·4	+ 2,879	+ 15,950	+ 7,181
Malabar (d)	904,997	714,164	32·8	25·5	+ 190,833	+ 225,098	+ 220,186
South Canara	376,911	296,633	33·2	26·1	+ 80,278	+ 64,1[illegible]8	+ 60,514

(a) Up to 1904, the statistics in columns 2 to 6 are for areas of old districts.
(b) Statistics in columns 2 to 6 are for 1904 to 1910.
(c) Includes Sandúr.
(d) Includes Anjengo but excludes Laccadive Islands.

Note.—(1) The statistics in this table are adjusted for the areas of districts as they stood in 1901.
(2) The 'natural population' in column 7 represents those born and enumerated in the Presidency only.

III.—*Variation by taluks or divisions classified according to density.*

(a) *Actual variation.*

Natural division.	Decade.	Variation in Taluks or Divisions with a population per square mile at commencement of decade of							
		Under 100.	100–150.	150–200.	200–300.	300–400.	400–500.	500–700.	700 and over.
1	2	3	4	5	6	7	8	9	10
Province ...	1901-1911	+ ***217,100***	+ ***211,936***	+ ***50,348***	+ ***566,499***	+ ***851,627***	+ ***644,011***	+ ***394,291***	+ ***280,790***
	1891-1901	+ 79,263	+ 161,927	+ 275,378	+ 618,164	+ 640,521	+ 273,530	+ 416,275	+ 123,697
Agency	1901-1911	+ ***183,959***	+ ***42,010***	......	......	......	......	......	......
	1891-1901	+ 44,746	− 12,902	......	......	......	......	......	......
East Coast (North)	1901-1911	......	+ ***66,404***	+ ***894***	+ ***255,362***	+ ***261,686***	+ ***159,201***	+ ***162,373***	+ ***35,632***
	1891-1901	......	− 57	+ 90,827	+ 165,706	+ 213,611	+ 113,212	+ 190,918	......
Deccan	1901-1911	+ ***16,568***	+ ***87,212***	+ ***21,164***	+ ***13,197***	......	......	......	......
	1891-1901	+ 20,704	+ 104,151	+ 49,791	+ 10,892	......	......	......	......
East Coast (Central)	1901-1911	+ ***3,705***	+ ***16,310***	+ ***23,099***	+ ***163,086***	+ ***146,672***	+ ***338,526***	+ ***91,659***	+ ***59,464***
	1891-1901	+ 11,800	+ 49,744	+ 123,079	+ 247,282	+ 197,600	+ 94,084	+ 57,412	+ 93,894
East Coast (South)	1901-1911	+ ***2,284***	......	......	+ ***127,113***	+ ***349,775***	+ ***110,646***	+ ***59,655***	+ ***132,560***
	1891-1901	+ 1,297	......	......	+ 178,015	+ 183,746	+ 43,037	+ 84,146	− 950
West Coast	1901-1911	+ ***10,584***	......	+ ***5,191***	+ ***7,741***	+ ***93,494***	+ ***35,638***	+ ***60,604***	+ ***53,134***
	1891-1901	+ 716	+ 20,991	+ 11,676	+ 21,269	+ 46,965	+ 23,197	+ 83,799	+ 30,753

IV.—Variation by Taluks or Divisions classified according to density—cont.

(b) *Proportional variation.*

Natural division.	Decade.	Variation per cent. in Taluks or Divisions with a population per square mile at commencement of decade of							
		Under 100.	100–150.	150–200.	200–300.	300–400.	400–500.	500–700.	700 and over.
1	2	3	4	5	6	7	8	9	10
Province ...	1901-1911	+ 15·1	+ 6·6	+ 2·0	+ 9·1	+ 8·7	+ 9·7	+ 7·9	+ 7·3
	1891-1901	+ 5·3	+ 4·9	+ 7·9	+ 9·0	+ 7·2	+ 6·2	+ 8·8	+ 4·0
Agency	1901-1911	+ 20·9	+ 8·9	......	......	......	......	......	......
	1891-1901	+ 5·0	- 3·0	......	......	......	......	......	......
East Coast (North)	1901-1911	......	+ 8·6	+ 0·2	+ 13·7	+ 10·2	+ 10·7	+ 8·4	+ 8·3
	1891-1901	......	- 0·0	+ 9·7	+ 8·4	+ 9·6	+ 9·6	+ 11·2	...
Deccan	1901-1911	+ 5·9	+ 5·1	+ 2·4	+ 1·7	......	......	......	......
	1891-1901	+ 6·0	+ 6·6	+ 3·9	+ 3·7	......	......	......	......
East Coast (Central)	1901-1911	+ 3·2	+ 6·7	+ 2·7	+ 9·1	+ 7·9	+ 9·3	+ 10·7	+ 5·1
	1891-1901	+ 11·5	+ 13·2	+ 18·5	+ 10·9	+ 10·0	+ 4·4	+ 7·2	+ 8·8
East Coast (South)	1901-1911	+ 11·6	......	......	+ 7·9	+ 8·5	+ 11·1	+ 6·0	+ 7·7
	1891-1901	+ 7·1	......	......	+ 8·8	+ 4·9	+ 7·2	+ 7·9	- 0·1
West Coast	1901-1911	+ 7·7	......	+ 1·7	+ 5·9	+ 7·6	+ 6·7	+ 6·5	+ 10·3
	1891-1901	+ 0·5	+ 12·2	+ 11·9	+ 6·2	+ 5·0	+ 4·6	+ 7·8	+ 6·3

CHAPTER III.—BIRTH-PLACE.

Of the 41,870,160 persons who constitute the population of the presidency all save 253,877 were born within its limits. The strangers within our British gates number 252,060, those in the Feudatory States 1,817.

2. Statistics already quoted in Chapter II show that the Madrasi is not unwilling to make a sufficient journey, such as that to Natal, the Straits Settlements, Burma or Ceylon, if at the end thereof he descries the possibility of solid pecuniary advantage. But that he is little addicted to wandering about within his own bounds becomes clear from an examination of the figures in Table XI, which show that, with the natural exception of Madras city, over 900 persons per thousand born in each district were there enumerated; the proportion ranging from 996 per 1,000 in South Canara to 932 per 1,000 in Nellore.

3. In one respect this table has proved unexpectedly satisfactory. The territorial redistribution of the Presidency about the time that the census was taken was calculated to cause considerable confusion in respect of district of birth; at census classes it proved a hard saying for the would-be enumerator that the birth of a citizen of Madanapalle, or of Srívilliputtúr, should be credited to districts which had not then attained actual existence. At the census of 1901 Banganapalle State apparently gave birth to but 12 of its 32,264 inhabitants; a return due to the fact that, for the dwellers in those parts, Kurnool district and Banganapalle are alike Kurnool, but distinguished as "Company's territory," and "Moghal territory."

4. The reasons for this disposition are really not far to seek. The majority of the inhabitants of the Presidency are of the small farmer, or agricultural-labourer classes, and such in every country are rooted fairly firmly in their native soil. To break their ties with home a definite and sufficient reason is needed, and in Micawber-like migration from one natural division to another such reason is not found. A parallel may be drawn from the case of Ireland, a country whose most marked characteristic is emigration. From Ireland there is a steady outflow to America, because America holds out a fairly certain prospect of better things. But migration within Ireland, from north to south, from east to west is, I should say, comparatively rare, inasmuch as there is no adequate reason for making the change. Similarly in Madras, the labourer is apt to go to Burma or Ceylon; but the small farmer is not in the least likely to better his condition by a move from Anantapur to Tinnevelly; or the labourer by transferring himself from Trichinopoly to Ganjám. In fact so marked are the differences between the natural divisions of the Presidency, that such move would be equivalent to a speculative emigration of the Irish labourer to (say) Normandy; where prospect of remunerative employment is not appreciably greater than in his native land, and where differences of language, race, and climate, are obstacles sufficiently apparent to the dullest intellect. Add the enormous areas of the Madras natural divisions, the cost and imperfection of communications, and the rural Wilhelm Meister is seen justified in his conclusion that, if his America is not immediately at hand, it is at least nowhere else within the Presidency.

5. That the Madrasi may be of an even more stay-at-home nature than figures indicate, is suggested to me by remembrance of a curious fact, which I noticed on my preliminary tours of instruction in connection with the census. A native (say) of Malabar, who emigrates to Tanjore, and whose children are there born, will as a rule, unless corrected, return the birth place of such children as Malabar. The case is similar in regard to any other district; the explanation being that district of birth, especially if strongly differentiated by nature from district of residence, is regarded as conferring a certain "nationality," which the possessor is loth to abandon for himself or for his children.

6. Even in the case Madras city and Chingleput, where the ratio described in paragraph 2 falls to 856, and 913 per 1,000, respectively, migration is statistical rather than real. Of 58,000 persons born in Madras city but enumerated elsewhere, 20,000 were enumerated in Chingleput; a fact which in all probability implies no more than that they happened to live, or to be, on the night of enumeration outside the municipal boundary. A further 18,000 were found in the adjacent districts of North Arcot, Chittoor, South Arcot, and Nellore; Tanjore, Trichinopoly, and Madura, account for 7,000 more, of whom by far the greater part are found in the cities of those districts.

7. If Chingleput has borrowed from Madras, it has returned in larger measure. Of 126,204 emigrants from that district 69,576 are found in the city; while 11,835, 21,524, and 9,151, are respectively in the districts of Chittoor, North Arcot, and South Arcot, whose frontiers march with those of Chingleput.

8. Or, to sum up the matter in a few words, internal migration in the Presidency can be in almost every case explained by recognition of the arbitrary nature of district boundaries. The emigrants from Ganjám and Vizagapatam will, as a rule, be found on the other side of an imaginary line; for the balance the well-known influx of labourers from these districts into the Kistna Delta will account. Of 23,593 emigrants from Anantapur, 19,718 are found in Bellary, Cuddapah, and Kurnool; of 23,980 from Bellary, an appreciable number are found only in Anantapur, Kurnool, and the little state of Sandúr, which is actually in Bellary district.

9. From Indian provinces and states outside Madras immigration is inconsiderable, and has fallen from 245,916 in 1901 to 238,730 in 1911. As was the case ten years ago, so at present these visitors in our midst come mainly from the neighbouring states of Mysore and Hyderabad, and number 153,424, as against 151,816 in 1901. The Hyderabad immigrants are localised, as one might expect, in Kistna, Guntúr, Kurnool, Bellary, and the Gódávari Agency, all districts touching the Nizam's frontier; those from Mysore territory are found on the other side of the frontier in Anantapur, Bellary, Coimbatore, Salem, North Arcot, the Nilgiris, Malabar and South Canara. Bombay immigrants, numbering 17,301 are found mainly in the trans-frontier districts of South Canara (2,700), and Bellary (5,831), while a considerable number (2,376) were enumerated in Madras city.

10. In regard to types of migration, *i.e.*, temporary and permanent, it is difficult to draw any conclusion from the census figures. A large preponderance of males suggests among the upper classes a temporary outgoing for purposes of business, with the ultimate prospect of return. Such may be the state of things among the Bombay immigrants to Madras city, or to Anantapur. Among the labouring classes the explanation does not hold good: the 66,613 Vizagapatam emigrants in Kistna are probably for the most part agricultural labourers, who will in due course make their way back; their equality of sex proportion (33,973 males, 32,640 females) is due to the fact that in their walk of life men and women work alike.

11. Sex disproportion among emigrants from Malabar is strongly marked (19,762 males, 10,610 females), and in the majority of cases can be explained by the reluctance of the Malabar woman to leave her home; a subject treated at some length in Thurston's "Castes and Tribes of Southern India." This sex disproportion is noticeable in every district except Rámnád, where the proportions are males 2,589, females 3,027. Search in the records afforded no explanation of this curious phenomenon. The immigrants are found mainly in the Sáttúr taluk, where too the sex disproportion is most clearly marked (males 784, females 1,337). In this taluk Malayálam speakers are comparatively few, and their sex proportion tallies with that generally found in the case of Malabar emigrants (males 298, females 72). Furthermore the "Malayálam caste" people found in Rámnád number only 526. It would therefore seem tolerably clear that these people, whatever they may be, are not genuine Malayális. The suggestion has been put forward that they may be Tamil speaking Travancoreans, and that enumerators failed to distinguish between Travancore and Malabar.

12. Migration across an imaginary frontier is probably permanent, and in most cases suggests that an individual has only moved a short space; if a man, to the neighbourhood of his lands or business, if a woman, to her husband's home. It is customary among Hindu women to return to their parent's home for their first confinement; consequently, if the locality of birth has been given accurately, there may be many persons actually born on one side of a dividing line whose permanent home is on the other.

13. The preponderance of women among the emigrants from Madras city confirms a suggestion made in the special report on the figures of the Presidency town, that for one reason or another women are leaving the city in increasing numbers.

I.—Immigration (actual figures 000's omitted).

District and Natural Division where enumerated.	Born in: District or Natural Division. Total.	Males.	Females.	Contiguous Districts in Province. Total.	Males.	Females.	Other parts of Province. Total.	Males.	Females.	Contiguous parts of other Provinces, etc. Total.	Males.	Females.	Non-contiguous parts of other provinces, etc. Total.	Males.	Females.	Outside India. Total.	Males.	Females.
1	2	3	4	5	6	7	8	9	10	11	12	13	14	15	16	17	18	19
Province ...	*41,616*	*20,474*	*21,142*	...	...	...	...	...	...	*209*	*101*	*108*	*30*	*21*	*9*	*15*	*10*	*5*
East Coast (North) and Agency—	*11,987*	*5,885*	*6.102*	*31*	*15*	*16*	*20*	*11*	*9*	*42*	*20*	*22*	*6*	*4*	*2*	*1*	*1*	...
Ganjám*	2,197	1,033	1,164	15	7	8	4	2	2	4	2	2	1	1	...	...	...	...
Vizagapatam* ...	3,166	1,550	1,616	15	7	8	4	2	2	3	2	1	2	1	1	...	...	...
Gódávari*	1,530	751	779	97	48	49	17	9	8	1	...	1	8	4	4	...	...	..
Kistna	1,835	911	924	47	24	23	89	48	41	24	11	13	2	1	1	...	...	.
Guntur	1,622	818	804	64	33	31	8	5	3	3	1	2	1	...	1	...	...	...
Nellore	1,296	650	646	22	10	12	9	4	5	...	...	...	1	1	...	...	...	...
Deccan	*3,712*	*1,888*	*1,824*	*26*	*13*	*13*	*14*	*7*	*7*	*58*	*26*	*32*	*4*	*2*	*2*	*1*	*1*	...
Cuddapah	872	444	428	17	7	10	4	2	2	...	...	...	1	1	...	...	...	...
Kurnool	889	451	438	35	15	20	3	2	1	7	3	4	1	...	1	...	...	...
Banganapalle ...	31	17	14	7	3	4	1	..	1	...	...	...	..	...	...	...	...	...
Bellary	916	465	451	18	8	10	7	4	3	25	11	14	3	2	1	1	1	...
Sandúr	10	5	5	3	1	2	..	...	...	...	...	..	1	1	...	...	...	
Anantapur	907	468	439	25	12	13	6	3	3	24	10	14	1	1	...	...	...	...
East Coast (Central)	*10,135*	*5,546*	*5,589*	*121*	*58*	*63*	*36*	*23*	*13*	*16*	*7*	*9*	*57*	*29*	*28*	*5*	*3*	*2*
Madras	345	173	172	70	35	35	82	46	36	...	...	...	19	11	8	3	2	1
Chingleput ...	1,321	669	652	51	21	30	30	14	16	...	...	...	4	2	2	...	...	...
Chittoor	1,172	598	574	50	23	27	9	5	4	7	3	4	1	1	...	...	...	...
North Arcot ...	1,823	909	914	109	45	64	21	12	9	5	2	3	2	1	1	1	1	...
Salem	1,732	861	871	19	8	11	5	3	2	11	5	6	...	...	...	...	..	...
Coimbatore ...	2,070	1,021	1,049	30	15	15	5	3	2	11	5	6	...	...	...	...	...	...
South Arcot ...	2,272	1,135	1,137	67	27	40	10	5	5	12	5	7	1	...	1	...	...	...
East Coast (South)	*11,115*	*4,869*	*5,246*	*95*	*41*	*54*	*30*	*17*	*13*	*9*	*5*	*4*	*9*	*5*	*4*	*5*	*3*	*2*
Tanjore	2,275	1,082	1,193	50	21	29	30	16	14	3	1	2	3	2	1	2	1	1
Trichinopoly ...	1,987	971	1,016	105	43	62	11	7	4	...	...	...	3	2	1	1	...	1
Pudukkóttai ...	376	184	192	33	11	22	2	1	1	...	...	...	...	...		1	1	...
Madura	1,861	912	949	43	20	23	26	13	13	...	...		2	1	1	1	.	1
Rámnád	1,600	758	842	49	24	25	8	4	4	.	...	...	1	...	1	...	...	...
Tinnevelly	1,767	852	915	6	3	3	11	6	5	5	3	2	1	1	...	...		...
West Coast... ...	*4,263*	*2,084*	*2,179*	*18*	*10*	*8*	*13*	*7*	*6*	*33*	*20*	*13*	*5*	*4*	*1*	*3*	*2*	*1*
Nilgiris	80	40	40	16	10	6	9	5	4	11	7	4	1	1	...	2	1	1
Malabar	2,983	1,464	1,519	9	5	4	4	2	2	14	7	7	4	3	1	1	1	...
Anjengo	5	2	3	...	...	...	...	...	...	1	1	.	...	..	...	...	..	...
South Canara ...	1,183	569	614	5	3	2	1	1		4	3	1	2	2	...	...	...	...

* Including Agency.

II.—Emigration (*actual figures 000's omitted*).

District and Natural Division of birth.	Expenditure in: District or Natural Division.			Contiguous district in Province.			Other parts of Province.			Other Provinces.			Outside India.		
	Total.	Males.	Females.	Total.	Males.	Females.	Total.	Males.	Females.	Total.	Males.	Females.	Total.	Males.	Females.
1	2	3	4	5	6	7	8	9	10	11	12	13	14	15	16
Province ...	***41,616***	***20,475***	***21,141***	...	...	...	...	...	...	***757***	***438***	***319***	***652***	***422***	***230***
East Coast (North) and Agency	***11,987***	***5,885***	***6,102***	***36***	***17***	***19***	***23***	***14***	***9***	***140***	***94***	***46***	***4***	***3***	***1***
Ganjám *	2,197	1,033	1,164	9	4	5	11	6	5	77	47	30	...	...	..
Vizagapatam *	3,167	1,550	1,617	95	46	49	72	37	35	37	26	11	...	...	...
Gódávari *	1,530	751	779	28	14	14	6	3	3	21	18	3	1	1	...
Kistna	1,835	911	924	17	9	8	22	11	11	2	1	1	1	1	...
Guntúr	1,622	818	804	33	16	17	13	7	6	...	...	...	...	...	
Nellore	1,296	650	646	70	35	35	25	16	9	2	1	1	1	1	...
Deccan	***3,712***	***1,888***	***1,824***	***26***	***13***	***13***	***13***	***7***	***6***	***74***	***36***	***38***	***2***	***1***	***1***
Cuddapah	873	445	428	33	16	17	6	3	3	12	6	6	...	...	...
Kurnool	889	451	438	36	15	21	4	2	2	...	...	...	...	...	...
Banganapalle	31	17	14	...	...	...	..	...	...	...	...	...	...	...	...
Bellary	916	465	451	18	8	10	6	3	3	34	17	17	..	...	...
Sandúr	10	5	5	...	...	..	...	...	...	..	...	...	...	...	...
Anantapur	907	468	439	22	10	12	2	1	1	28	13	15	...	...	...
East Coast (Central) ..	***11,135***	***5,546***	***5,589***	***154***	***73***	***81***	***19***	***11***	***8***	***172***	***93***	***79***	***96***	***55***	***41***
Madras	346	173	173	20	9	11	38	19	19	64	36	28	11	7	4
Chingleput	1,321	668	653	119	54	65	7	4	3	5	3	2	7	4	3
Chittoor	1,172	598	574	28	13	15	6	3	3	...	...			...	...
North Arcot	1,822	909	913	62	27	35	36	19	17	59	31	28	17	10	7
Salem	1,731	861	870	88	40	48	17	9	8	26	13	13	39	22	17
Coimbatore	2,070	1,022	1,048	54	27	27	11	6	5	15	8	7	9	5	4
South Arcot	2,272	1,135	1,137	76	28	48	18	7	6	2	1	1	13	7	6
East Coast (South) ...	***10,115***	***4,869***	***5,246***	***61***	***26***	***35***	***44***	***25***	***19***	***60***	***34***	***26***	***333***	***196***	***137***
Tanjore	2,275	1,062	1,198	66	28	38	26	14	12	10	7	3	60	35	25
Trichinopoly	1,987	971	1,016	78	31	47	11	6	5	5	3	2	103	56	47
Pudukkóttai	376	184	192	19	6	13	1	1	...	...	...	...	18	10	8
Madura	1,861	912	949	35	16	19	33	15	18	11	7	4	82	48	34
Rámnád	1,600	758	842	28	13	15		...	...	2	1	1	...	...	...
Tinnevelly	1,767	853	914	25	13	12	30	16	14	34	17	17	70	47	23
West Coast	***4,263***	***2,084***	***2,179***	***6***	***4***	***2***	***22***	***14***	***8***	***118***	***78***	***40***	***13***	***10***	***3***
Nilgiris	80	40	40	1	1	...	4	3	1	2	1	1	...	...	..
Malabar	2,983	1,463	1,520	14	10	4	16	10	6	45	27	18	12	10	2
Anjengo	5	2	3	...	..		.	.	...	...	..	...	..	...	...
South Canara	1,183	569	614	3	2	1	2	1	1	72	51	21	...	...	..
Unspecified	..	...	...	...	...	...	...	...	...	***193***	***152***	***41***	***204***	***157***	***47***

Note.—(1) In columns 11 to 13, the immigrants into Hyderabad State are not included.

(2) ,, 14 to 16, particulars of district of birth were received only from Ceylon.

(3) The principal foreign colonies in which the persons shown under unspecified in columns 14 to 16 were enumerated are :—(i) Federated Malay States (95,435 males, 29,121 females); (ii) Straits Settlement (46,385 males, 11,951 females; (iii) Mauritius (7,615 males, 3,967 females); (iv) Johore (4,120 males, 743 females) ; (v) Fiji (3,211 males, 1,353 females) ; (vi) Seychelles (246 males, 13 females) ; (vii) Southern Rhodesia (104 males, 9 females) ; (viii) other colonies (26 males, 1 female).

(4) Figures from other provinces were not received for working out the number of persons born in the frontier districts of this Province and enumerated in the contiguous parts of those provinces.

* Including Agency.

III.—Proportional migration to and from each district.

District and Natural Division.	Number per mille of actual population of						Number of females to 1,000 males amongst			
	Immigrants.			Emigrants.			Immigrants.		Emigrants.	
	Total.	From contiguous districts.	From other places.	Total.	To contiguous districts.	To other places.	From contiguous districts.	From other places.	To contiguous districts.	To other places.
1	2	3	4	5	6	7	8	9	10	11
East Coast (North) and Agency.	*4*	*2*	*2*	*5*	*3*	*2*	*1,034*	*826*	*1,150*	*649*
Ganjám	8	6	2	9	4	5	1,082	502	1,167	771
Vizagapatam	6	5	1	58	30	28	1,121	628	1,068	942
Gódávari	69	59	10	20	17	3	1,038	406	989	838
Kistna	69	24	45	19	8	11	987	872	890	1,025
Guntúr	43	38	5	27	19	8	964	785	1,057	805
Nellore	24	17	7	71	52	19	1,166	1,055	1,002	574
Deccan	*11*	*7*	*4*	*11*	*7*	*4*	*1,068*	*918*	*1,094*	*780*
Cuddapah	28	18	5	44	37	7	1,392	1,047	1,111	850
Kurnool	41	37	4	48	38	5	1,288	862	1,416	752
Banganapalle	219	195	24	10	9	1	1,712	1,364	953	643
Bellary	26	19	7	25	19	6	1,248	780	1,393	978
Sandúr	210	195	15	26	21	5	1,428	899	1,114	14
Anantapur	33	27	6	25	23	2	1,191	822	1,264	596
East Coast (Central)	*14*	*11*	*3*	*15*	*13*	*2*	*1,101*	*568*	*1,118*	*796*
Madras	292	134	158	112	38	74	1,090	786	1,328	1,052
Chingleput	58	36	22	90	85	5	1,410	1,125	1,201	662
Chittoor	48	40	8	28	23	5	1,141	1,057	1,248	813
North Arcot	66	55	11	50	31	19	1,449	781	1,303	871
Salem	14	11	3	59	50	9	1,240	781	1,186	882
Coimbatore	17	14	3	31	26	5	1,019	819	1,028	817
South Arcot	33	29	4	37	32	5	1,494	986	1,726	936
East Coast (South)	*12*	*9*	*3*	*10*	*6*	*4*	*1,293*	*774*	*1,355*	*778*
Tanjore	34	21	13	39	28	11	1,408	882	1,402	861
Trichinopoly	55	50	5	43	37	6	1,481	695	1,497	812
Pudukkóttai	86	82	4	49	46	3	1,946	868	1,990	942
Madura	36	23	13	35	18	17	1,212	953	1,245	1,092
Rámnád	35	30	5	17	17	...	1,090	1,001	1,137	676
Tinnevelly	10	4	6	31	14	17	1,098	815	986	850
West Coast	*7*	*4*	*3*	*7*	*2*	*5*	*792*	*792*	*550*	*554*
Nilgiris	208	134	74	49	10	39	618	859	642	267
Malabar	4	3	1	10	5	5	716	682	413	667
Anjengo	11	...	11	6	...	6	...	1,259	...	1,333
South Canara	5	4	1	4	2	2	411	502	416	608

Note.—Columns 5 to 7 are worked out on absolute figures relating to persons born and enumerated in this Presidency only.

III-A.—Immigration per 10,000 of population.

Natural Division, District or State of enumeration.	Born in India. In Natural Division, District or State where enumerated.	In contiguous districts or States.	In non-contiguous territory.	Born in Europe.	Born in all other countries.
1	2	3	4	5	6
Province ...	*9,939*	*50*	*7*	*2*	*2*
Agency and East Coast (North)	*9,917*	*60*	*23*	...	...
Ganjám	9,893	85	22	...	...
Vizagapatam	9,927	55	17	1	...
Gódávari	9,255	593	151	1	...
Kistna	9,188	355	457	..	...
Guntúr	9,555	393	52	...	..
Nellore	9,759	165	76	...	...
Deccan	*9,730*	*220*	*48*	*2*	...
Cuddapah	9,758	186	56	..	...
Kurnool	9,503	452	45	...	...
Banganapalle	7,760	1,953	287	...	...
Bellary	9,452	448	97	3	...
Sandúr	7,459	1,944	593	3	1
Anantapur	9,414	510	75	1	.
East Coast (Central)	*9,793*	*120*	*82*	*3*	*2*
Madras	6,658	1,341	1,943	43	15
Chingleput	9,394	364	238	3	1
Chittoor	9,463	456	81	...	...
North Arcot	9,296	581	120	...	3
Salem	9,800	167	32	1	..
Coimbatore	9,779	192	28	1	...
South Arcot	9,619	333	46	1	1
East Coast (South)	*9,855*	*101*	*39*	*1*	*4*
Tanjore	9,628	224	141	1	6
Trichinopoly	9,481	495	69	1	4
Pudukkóttai	9,119	814	48	...	19
Madura	9,629	226	142	1	2
Rámnád	9,646	298	54	..	2
Tinnevelly	9,868	63	66	1	2
West Coast	*9,834*	*116*	*42*	*6*	*2*
Nilgiris	6,704	2,273	881	132	10
Malabar	9,893	77	25	3	2
Anjengo	8,273	1,529	171	7	21
South Canara	9,899	79	21	1	...

IV.—*Migration between natural divisions (actual figures, 000s omitted).* (*Compared with* 1901.)

Natural Division in which born.		Number enumerated in Natural Division.						Total born in each Natural Division.
		Agency.	East Coast (North).	Deccan.	East Coast (Central).	East Coast (South).	West Coast.	
1		2	3	4	5	6	7	8
TOTAL ...	1911	*1,566*	*10,473*	*3,752*	*11,292*	*10,240*	*4,294*	*41,616*
	1901	*1,317*	*9,523*	*3,867*	*10,722*	*8,938*	*4,008*	*38,375*
Agency and East Coast (North).	1911	1,565	10,428	24	32	2	...	12,045
	1901	1,317	9,469	24	27	2	1	10,840
Deccan	1911	...	23	3,712	16	1	...	3,752
	1901	...	24	3,818	13	1	...	3,856
East Coast (Central) ..	1911	...	23	13	11,135	111	26	11,306
	1901	...	26	22	10,569	110	28	10,755
East Coast (South) ...	1911	...	4	2	94	10,115	5	10,220
	1901	...	3	2	102	8,822	6	8,935
West Coast	1911	...	1	1	15	11	4,263	4,291
	1901	...	1	1	11	3	3,973	3,969

Note.—The figures for 1901 are not adjusted for changes in area during 1901–1911.

V.—*Migration between the province and other parts of India.*

(i) *Madras Presidency.*

Province.	Immigrants to Madras.			Emigrants from Madras.			Excess (+) or deficiency (−) of immigration over emigration.	
	1911.	1901.	Variation.	1911.	1901.	Variation.	1911.	1901.
1	2	3	4	5	6	7	8	9
Province ...	*155,478*	*162,694*	− *7,216*	*756,852*	*639,079*	+ *117,773*	− *601,374*	− *476,385*
British Territory ...	*36,907*	*54,723*	− *17,816*	*385,328*	*304,408*	+ *80,920*	− *348,421*	− *249,685*
Ajmer-Merwara ...	120	35	+ 85	218	157	+ 61	− 98	− 122
Andamans and Nicobars.	65	38	+ 27	1,489	1,299	+ 190	− 1,424	− 1,261
Assam	204	153	+ 51	34,509	21,571	+ 12,938	− 34,305	− 21,418
Baluchistan	126	23	+ 103	135	146	− 11	− 9	− 123
Bengal	6,547	9,720	− 2,747	13,168	20,800	+ 9,673	− 6,621	− 10,580
Bihar and Orissa ...	426			16,805			− 16,379	
Bombay	17,804	24,234	− 6,930	33,631	30,388	+ 3,248	− 16,327	− 6,149
Burma	2,021	1,502	+ 519	248,064	189,810	+ 58,254	− 246,043	− 188,308
Central Provinces and Berar.	6,291	14,071	− 7,780	5,357	8,879	− 3,522	+ 934	+ 5,192
Coorg	741	631	+ 110	28,583	29,351	− 768	− 27,842	− 28,720
North-West Frontier Province.	82	...	+ 82	72	...	+ 72	+ 10	...
Punjab	875	1,044	− 169	1,050	915	+ 135	− 175	+ 129
United Provinces of Agra and Oudh.	2,105	3,272	− 1,167	2,247	1,597	+ 650	− 142	+ 1,675
Native States and Agencies.	*118,571*	*107,971*	+ *10,600*	*371,524*	*334,671*	+ *36,853*	− *252,953*	− *226,700*
Assam States	...	...	...	10	...	+ 10	− 10	...
Baroda State	320	304	+ 16	228	207	+ 21	+ 92	+ 97
Bengal States	...	...	+ 975	1,074	7,118	+ 12,655	− 18,793	− 7,118
Bihar and Orissa States.	975			18,694				
Bombay States ..	1,518	194	+ 1,324	1,853	1,964	− 111	− 335	− 1,770
Central India Agency.	503	479	+ 24	1,033	1,128	− 95	− 530	− 649
Central Provinces States.	915	...	+ 915	4,863	13,563	− 8,700	− 3,948	− 13,563
Cochin State	9,643	7,078	+ 2,565	30,488	33,201	− 2,713	− 20,845	− 26,123
Kashmir State ...	28	32	− 4	27	9	+ 18	+ 1	+ 23
Mysore State	92,732	89,430	+ 3,302	263,417	236,775	+ 26,642	− 170,685	− 147,345
Punjab States ...	...	...	...	39	22	+ 17	− 39	− 22
Rajputana Agency ...	1,491	1,488	+ 3	283	177	+ 106	+ 1,208	+ 1,311
Travancore State ...	10,446	8,966	+ 1,480	49,511	40,508	+ 9,008	− 39,065	− 31,537
United Provinces States.	...	...	...	4	9	− 5	− 4	− 9

Note.—The figures for Hyderabad State are not included as the statistics of Madras emigrants into that state for 1911 have not been received in time to be included in this table.

V.—*Migration between the province and other parts of India*—cont.

(ii) *Madras—British Territory.*

Province.	Immigrants to Madras.			Emigrants from Madras.			Excess (+) or deficiency (−) of immigration over emigration.	
	1911.	1901.	Variation.	1911.	1901.	Variation.	1911.	1901.
1	2	3	4	5	6	7	8	9
Province ...	*175,843*	*183,909*	− *8,066*	*802,784*	*705,355*	+ *97,429*	− *626,941*	− *521,446*
British Territory ...	*36,493*	*54,428*	− *17,935*	*384,589*	*304,376*	+ *80,213*	− *348,096*	− *249,948*
Ajmer-Merwara ...	120	35	+ 85	218	157	+ 61	− 98	− 122
Andamans and Nicobars.	65	38	+ 27	1,489	1,299	+ 190	− 1,424	− 1,261
Assam	204	158	+ 51	34,497	21,571	+ 12,926	− 34,293	− 21,418
Baluchistan	126	23	+ 103	135	146	− 11	− 9	− 123
Bengal	6,537	9,668	− 2,705	13,168	20,271	+ 9,694	− 6,631	10,608
Bihar and Orissa ...	426			16,797			− 16,371	
Bombay	16,952	24,061	− 7,109	33,629	30,383	+ 3,246	− 16,677	− 6,322
Burma	1,991	1,495	+ 496	247,360	189,810	+ 57,550	− 245,369	− 188,315
Central Provinces and Berar.	6,281	14,059	− 7,778	5,357	8,879	− 3,522	+ 924	+ 5,180
Coorg	737	628	+ 109	28,581	29,348	− 767	− 27,844	+ 28,720
North-West Frontier Province.	79	...	+ 79	72	...	+ 72	+ 7	...
Punjab	874	1,038	− 164	1,044	915	+ 129	− 170	+ 123
United Provinces of Agra and Oudh.	2,101	3,230	− 1,129	2,242	1,597	+ 645	− 141	+ 1,633
Native States and Agencies	*139,350*	*129,481*	+ *9,869*	*416,195*	*400,979*	+ *17,216*	− *278,845*	− *271,498*
Assam States	...	...	...	10	...	+ 10	− 10	...
Baroda State	318	294	+ 24	228	207	+ 21	+ 90	+ 87
Bengal States ...	975	...	+ 975	1,070	6,424	+ 13,340	− 1,070	− 6,424
Bihar and Orissa States.				18,694			− 17,719	
Bombay States ...	1,518	161	+ 1,357	1,853	1,964	− 111	− 335	− 1,803
Central India Agency.	503	477	+ 26	1,038	1,128	− 95	− 530	− 651
Central Provinces States.	915	...	+ 915	4,862	13,563	− 8,701	− 3,947	− 13,563
Cochin State	9,641	7,073	+ 2,568	30,485	33,184	− 2,699	− 20,844	− 26,111
Kashmir State ...	28	32	− 4	27	9	+ 18	+ 1	+ 23
Mysore State	92,503	89,277	+ 3,226	263,362	236,733	+ 26,629	− 170,859	− 147,456
Madras States ...	21,046	21,746	− 698	46,734	67,081*	− 20,347	− 25,686	− 45,335
Punjab States	..	...	...	39	22	+ 17	− 39	− 22
Rajaputana Agency ...	1,484	1,487	− 3	283	177	+ 106	+ 1,201	+ 1,310
Travancore State ...	10,417	8,934	+ 1,483	49,511	40,478	+ 9,033	− 39,094	− 31,544
United Provinces States.	...	...	...	4	9	− 5	− 4	− 9

* Imperial Table XI of 1901 shows that, out of 32,264 persons enumerated in Banganapalle State, 31,150 were born in Kurnool District.

V—*Migration between the province and other parts of India*—cont.

(iii) *Madras—Feudatories.*

Province.	Immigrants to Madras.			Emigrants from Madras.			Excess (+) or deficiency (—) of immigration over emigration.	
	1911.	1901.	Variation.	1911.	1901.	Variation.	1911.	1901.
1	2	3	4	5	6	7	8	9
Province ...	***683***	***531***	+ ***152***	***802***	***805***	— ***3***	— ***119***	— ***274***
British Territory ...	***414***	***295***	+ ***119***	***739***	***32***	+ ***707***	— ***325***	+ ***263***
Assam	...	...	...	12	..	+ 12	— 12	...
Bengal	10			..				
Bihar and Orissa ...	...	52	— 42	8	29	— 21	+ 2	+ 28
Bombay...	852	173	+ 179	2	...	+ 2	+ 350	+ 173
Burma	30	7	+ 23	704	...	+ 704	— 674	+ 7
Central Provinces and Berar.	10	12	— 2	...	...	...	+ 10	+ 12
Coorg	4	3	+ 1	2	3	— 1	+ 2	...
North-West Frontier Province.	3	...	+ 3	...	...	...	+ 3	...
Punjab	1	6	— 5	6	...	+ 6	— 5	+ 6
United Provinces of Agra and Oudh.	4	42	— 38	5	...	+ 5	— 1	+ 42
Native States and Agencies.	***269***	***236***	+ ***33***	***63***	***773***	— ***710***	+ ***206***	— ***537***
Baroda State	2	10	— 8	...	...	...	+ 2	+ 10
Bengal States	...	...	...	4	689	— 685	— 4	— 689
Bihar and Orissa States.	...	...	...	...			...	
Bombay States ...	...	33	— 33	...	...	...	...	+ 33
Central India Agency ...	...	2	— 2	...	...	...	...	+ 2
Central Provinces and Berar States.	...	...	...	1	...	+ 1	— 1	...
Cochin State	2	5	— 3	3	17	— 14	— 1	— 12
Mysore State	229	153	+ 76	55	42	+ 13	+ 174	+ 111
Rajaputana Agency ..	7	1	+ 6	...	...	...	+ 7	+ 1
Travancore State ...	29	32	— 3	...	25	— 25	+ 29	+ 7

CHAPTER IV.—RELIGION.

(1) Hinduism.

Although intances have not been wanting at previous censuses of a misplaced zeal, which led a minor official to swell the number of his fellow believers by hasty inclusion of any dusky Gallio, or to seek a mild satisfaction in attributing to his enemy theological views tending parlously to damnation, we may safely assume that the average enumerator does not demand from his victims a reason for the faith that is in them, but courteously accepts their word for whatever profession they may choose to make.

2. The fact of the immense numerical preponderance of the Hindus over followers of other creeds is as patent at this census as at those precedent to it. Viewing the Presidency as a whole, the marginal figures show the distribution according to religious profession of 10,000 of its people. If we descend to the greater detail of natural divisions, we find that the index of Hinduism varies from 9,419 per 10,000 in the East Coast Central Division, to 6,808 in the Agencies, and 7,043 on the West Coast. Of the districts which constitute these divisions, Vizagapatam* is pre-eminently Hindu, with 9,869 per 10,000 of its population professing adherence to that faith; while only in the Ganjám Agency, and the tiny enclave of Anjengo, where Animists and Christians respectively predominate, are Hindus in a minority.

Hindus	8,892
Muhammadans	660
Christians	289
Animists	153
Others	6

3. Still acceptance of a fact need not preclude search for its explanation, nor need such search involve the dangers apparently attendant on the questioning of the fact.

4. It is well to remember that the strict connotation of the word Hinduism is racial and social rather than theological. European convention has applied the general term to the theology of those Indians who do not profess adherence to some other definitely named faith, or an absolute denial of all religious faiths. Thus alone the term "Hindu" figures so largely in column 4 of our census schedules; for the ordinary Indian, when asked for his faith, is wont to specify his sect (Vaishnavite, Saivite, Smárta, etc.), or possibly his caste—answers which the enumerator as a rule, though not invariably, subsumes under the general head Hindu.

5. To this aspect allusion has already been made in Chapter II, where were mentioned the possibilities of increase among Hindus, other than natural. On such other increase a chapter on the religion of Hinduism should be silent, for Hinduism, in its present acceptance at any rate, is non-proselytizing.

6. At the same time we may admit that Hinduism is in a sense acquisitive. If it strains at the individual gnat it can swallow with cheerfulness the tribal camel: some slight profession of faith, and moderate proficiency in the nice conduct of ceremony are sufficient to secure for an aspiring Animistic tribe (gods included) admission within the pale.

7. But this facile, though oft given, explanation does scant justice to its great subject. If Hinduism accepts the nominal adherence of unlettered masses, it shows itself no less potent to retain a devotion which many of the most able of Southern India will scarcely pay to an empty name.

* Here we see a foreshadowing of a difficulty to which frequent allusion will be made. Vizagapatam is in close touch with a large hill tract, where, statistics notwithstanding, "Animism" is as good a label for the faith of the inhabitants as "Hinduism."

8. For the believer, the truth of his belief affords an adequate explanation of its widespread acceptance. To the non-Hindu, it may well occur that Hinduism owes much of its success to the fact that it is in its essentials but a pure system of metaphysical doctrine, to which a man may give assent, without the obligation, expressed or implied in less philosophical religions, to mould his life on particular lines; and at the same time is a system peculiarly in harmony with the material environment of the minds to which it is presented.

9. Ethical considerations apart, mankind has always sought in his religion an explanation of the primal mysteries of his being: whence he came, his relation to the place wherein he finds himself, his ultimate destination. Judaism, Christianity, Muhammadanism have for their adherents cut the Gordian knot of perplexity with the sword of revelation. To their believers they offer a solution of these difficulties eminently comprehensible and satisfying: abandoning the search for unity, they present the readily intelligible duality of God and his creation.

10. More subtly philosophic than their western neighbours, Hindu thinkers have recognized the difficulties underlying the theory that something could be created out of nothing, that part of this something should return to its original nothingness, while part should possess inherently a patent of immortality. Man—this latter part—forms, as is only to be expected, the most emergent study of the human philosopher, who, viewing the matter without prejudice, must find it inexplicable that man prospectively immortal, should not be retrospectively so. Absolute mortality (annihilation) is rendered improbable by the fact of man's being here at all: for if he can come into one existence, there is nothing inherently improbable in the theory that he can pass into another. If he is in one, and can pass into another, surely he must come from yet a third.

11. To these questionings Hinduism appears to offer a ready answer by its doctrine of re-incarnation, to which all Hindus render at least an unthinking allegiance. Yet, to the sceptic, this doctrine would seem to be rather the allegorical representation of a truth, than an objective truth in itself. For in the popular doctrine of re-incarnation is not involved that of the persistence of a conscious personality; and on strict examination it seems incredible that a man should profess the belief that formerly he was somebody else, and is to be yet a third person in the future. It needs a hard struggle to disentangle our present personality from the present phenomena of our life; we find it impossible to think the phenomena of a life past, present, or to come, without thinking into it our present personality, whatever that may be.

12. For one school of thinkers among Southern Hindus a way remained. Abandoning the theory of personality in the life antecedent and that to come, Sankara and his followers reached a certain logical consistency by the practical abnegation of personality in the present.

13. Assumption of some kind must needs be made. By this abnegation, man, and the universe surrounding him, which indeed may have no existence *apart* from him, are but the manifestation in multiplicity of the divine unity, which neither begins nor ends. Man and all other temporal manifestations that surround him pass away; man does not pass into other forms, but the divine unity continues to manifest itself in multiplicity. Thus in a sense, as a particular being, man suffers annihilation; in another sense, he is immortal; inasmuch as that which constitutes him, in virtue of its self-manifestation in him, has been from all eternity, and can never cease to be.

14. It is questionable whether this doctrine would be possible in a land whose physical circumstances tend to force the sense of personality on mankind. In harsh climates man must bestir himself to live; if he dies he suffers in the process the inconveniences of cold and hunger. He finds it hard to make a living, and the experience of hard work tends to make him work all the harder. In Southern India a living is easily got, food is cheap, clothing more or less unnecessary. Vitality is not great, death is not a rending process so much as a gentle fading

away. In the chiefest glory of the southern teachers we can trace climatic influence; if the practically bloodless propaganda of Sankara, Rámánuja, and Madhva, never

Made accurst the name of man, and thrice accursed,
The name of God,

still these three apostles scarcely possessed the fiery zeal, that won the hearts of men to Paul, Muhammad, Loyola or Wesley.

15. Widely as spread the monism of Sankara, the notion of personality died hard, in fact refused to die. Sankara gave no satisfactory reason for the divine unity choosing to manifest itself in the phenomenal world. "It must be a very ill-advised God" said Schopenhauer, himself in no better case with his theory of the phenomenal universe as the objectification of the will to live, "who knows no better way of diverting himself, than by turning into such a world as ours." Emergence of the phenomenal world through *Máya* (illusion) is but a verbal solution of the difficulty: seriously considered it raises *Máya* to a rank equal to that of divinity itself, or superior, because limitative. Thus the monists were driven to explain *Máya*, not as a power independent of God, but simply as the eternal power, or will, of God to differentiate himself, manifested as that which renders human experience possible; but the question will still remain whether this power forms an integral part of the divine nature, and therefore demands expression; in which case the absolute freedom of the divine would appear to be curtailed; or whether the exercise of such power is optional, and the divine thus ill-advised in his exercise, as *apud* Schopenhauer.

16. Furthermore, applied to human conduct, considered merely in the human aspect, such philosophy is unlikely to produce any beneficent result, if indeed it is so applicable at all. The individual can in the last resort do neither good nor harm to the world, which, as a manifestation of the divine unity, is independent of him, even while including him as part of its manifestation; he cannot influence himself, for he as individual is nothing. Man's only incentive to virtue can be the perception that it is good to be good; diverting his gaze from the possibility of result to his actions, he must attain to a greater knowledge of his unity with all things, and allow his actions to proceed solely from the degree of his knowledge. But for practical purposes we must admit that, while man, as we know him, may render his assent to the unity of all things as a possible speculation in philosophy, the probability of his digestion of such knowledge, to the extent that it will inform his conduct as a transient phenomenon, is small indeed.

17. Thus revived old dualistic faiths in the qualified dualism of Rámánuja, which distinguished man in, though not from, God; and in the more positive doctrine of Madhva, who made the severence complete.

18. But to Hinduism so described objection may as well be taken, as being but Bráhmanism pure and simple, or, more properly, a religion of the learned, neither accepted among, nor comprehended by, the majority of those, to whom in Southern India the term Hindu is applied. Of the learned no table affords us the tale and measure, but the Bráhmans, table XIII shows to number but 313 per 10,000 of the total population, and 352 of a similar number returned as Hindu: proportions far exceeded by the 565 and 635 per 10,000 of the Tamil Paraiyans alone, to whose simple souls these metaphysical aridities offer scant attraction.

19. Yet for this reason to deny at once a place in the ranks of present day Hinduism to the manifold worshippers of multifarious godlings, is no more just than it would be to question the Christianity of the Irish peasant, whose theological attention is concentrated mainly on the

"Life, death, and miracles, of Saint Somebody"

or that of his Latin confrère, who renders allegiance to

"Saint Somebody else, his miracles, life, and death."

Nor indeed in the Southern Presidency does the denial of "Hinduism" even to the lowest and most illiterate find many advocates.

20. There are, it is true, sundry mechanic criteria, in virtue of which it has, at times, been sought to determine the admissibility of classing as Hindus certain

sections of the population. Of such the following questions supply an illustration. Do the persons concerned (*a*) worship the great Hindu Gods; (*b*) enjoy the right of entrance to Hindu temples and shrines; (*c*) receive the ministrations of Bráhman priests; (*d*) possess sufficient worthiness to give water to caste Hindus; (*e*) cause pollution by touch or proximity?

21. A means of judgment is thus at first glance provided; but closer consideration will show the necessarily superficial character of a judgment resting on such foundations.

22. The most debatable Hindu may very well worship, and often does worship, the great Hindu deities.* Such worship is no necessary impediment to a simultaneous adoration of many minor godlings: the two acts of faith, as will afterwards be observed, at times co-exist even in the Bráhmans. Again, right of entrance to a temple or shrine is in no wise an essential of Hinduism. Such right is not conceded to the Shánán, who claims to be a Kshatriya, and whose Hinduism no one disputes: nor in certain cases will it be allowed to the Bráhman, as such, should he lack the ordinations or consecrations requisite for the practical, or better, ritualistic observances of religion.

23. As regards acceptance of Bráhmanical ministrations, there are many undoubted Hindus, who, in theory at least, reject the sacerdotal authority of the Bráhmans. Among such may be mentioned the Lingáyats, now rather a caste than a sect comprising many castes; and the goldsmiths, who claim a Bráhmanhood of their own. Indeed the feebleness of this criterion may well be illustrated by its application to Christianity: although the ordinary British non-conformist neither asks nor receives the religious attentions of a Catholic priest, neither party is likely to dispute the Christianity of the other.

24. Similarly may these other tests be tried and found wanting. A Bráhman does not, it is true, receive water from the hands of a Paraiyan; but neither will he drink from the hands of a Súdra. Súdra again does not invariably drink with Súdra, nor Bráhman with Bráhman. Pollution caused by touch or proximity has been publicly rejected, in theory, as an essential of religion by sundry eminent Hindus; in fact, by many more, not less pious if less vocal, in the daily practice of the railway.

25. On the details of this aspect of Hinduism I have nothing new to say. The spirits, godlings, or devils, invoked throughout the Presidency, and the method of their adoration, have been described in Bishop Caldwell's "*Demonolatry in Southern India;*" in Mr. (now Sir Harold) Stuart's census report of 1891; by the present Bishop of Madras in his "*Village Deities of Southern India;*" in Mr. Thurston's "*Castes and Tribes,*" and in the Gazetteers of the several districts. The inter-relation of castes in the matter of priesthood can likewise be studied in Mr. Thurston's work, and in the "Caste glossary" appended to the census report of 1901.

26. Whatever be their present day union or interminglement, it is difficult to imagine any original connection of the Áryan Bráhmans, and their subtle philosophies, with the gross demonolatry of the Dravidian peoples who surrounded them. Philosophic Hinduism or Bráhmanism, it has already been suggested, is rather the attempt to find an answer, without the aid of a final revelation, to an enigma probably insoluble, than a religion in the sense understood in modern days. Holding certain philosophical opinions, which they neither expected nor particularly desired their Dravidian neighbours to share, it is unlikely that the early Áryan theists made any serious efforts to obtain adherents to their way of thinking. But satisfied with the acknowledgment of their undoubted intellectual superiority, they built gradually many a connecting bridge, between their own somewhat unpractical speculations, and the extremely material demonologies of the Dravidians.

---

* At Chingleput Railway Station I conversed on religion with a man, who informed me that he was a Vaishnavite Paraiyan. It is not probable that by these words he expressed a philosophic acceptance of Rámánuja's dualism, but rather that he deemed himself a worshipper of one member of the Hindu Trinity, although his actual worship could not be performed within a Hindu shrine.

27. In virtue of these accommodations a certain community of faith exists to-day between most so-called Hindus. The Hindu of the villages and fields worships as God the great philosophic triad, much as does the unlettered Christian worshipper, whose adoration is seldom consciously devoted to any particular member of his Trinity. If X, Y and Z, objective and often highly objectionable devils, still engage a large portion of the peasant's spiritual attention, he has about him a certain atmosphere of more subtle religious ideas: prayers, hymns, which he knows by rote, and of which he comprehends the purport, although he may not understand the language. To a certain extent his *gráma dévatás*, or propitiable demons, are the saints of the West, confidential intermediaries, to whom his prayers may be sent for transmission, and to whom his every day necessities may be expounded.

28. On his side the Bráhman has undoubtedly clothed many of his abstractions in most earthly guise. For his every day external affairs a certain regard to demonic susceptibilities does at least no harm; for the due ordering of his household he has attached the sanction of religion to methods of clothing, shaving, and other natural exercises.

29. What then is the conclusion of the matter, or the present day effects of the religion known as Hinduism, among those who return it as their faith? Just as every nation is said to get the government that it deserves, so perhaps divinity manifests itself to various races in the way most suited for their acceptance; and underlying every religion are some main ideas, ultimately identical for those who care to look nearer than the external trappings. "Whosoever comes to me, through whatsoever form I reach him, all men are struggling through paths which in the end lead to me."

30. Admitting that the Bráhman came as the apostle of a higher and more spiritual faith to a people, of whom many are still in the earliest stages of Animism or anthropomorphic religion, it is hardly just to assume that his present assertion of divinely inherent superiority is the result of consistently selfish design for his own temporal aggrandizement. Probably he followed quite as much as he led the course of events; it was well that he did not level down, and in all probability it was well nigh impossible for him to level up. Had society been fit for the equality and fraternity of the Buddhists, the Bráhman could scarce have withstood a movement with such inherent claims to general acceptance.

(2) MUHAMMADANISM.

31. In contrast to the subtle theologies and metaphysics of Hinduism, the Muhammadan creed certainly possesses the merit of simplicity. "*There is no God but God: Muhammad is the messenger of God*" is a formula easily comprehensible, and in its way well nigh all embracing. To those who demur to acceptance of its second article, it may be pointed out that the prophet himself did not declare this tenet as in any way necessary to salvation; while, if the matter be viewed dispassionately and without prejudice, it is but a logical, so far as human logic goes, corollary of the essential statement. Grant the existence of one true God, and one alone, and it becomes difficult to assert that the man, who preached this faith with acceptance to the idolaters of Arabia, and whose word "has been the life guidance now of a "hundred and eighty millions of men these twelve hundred years," was *not* God's messenger.

32. It may be the natural perversity of mankind that has introduced schism and difference of interpretation into every faith originally claiming to be but the simple exposition of universal truth; or it may equally well be that a religion too implicitly accepted, and without the vitalising influences of doubt and free discussion, would itself expire of sheer inanition. Muhammadanism has been no exception to the general lot, but considerations of practical convenience forbade the recording of Muhammadan sects at the present census. Taking first the great division into Sunnis and Shiahs, the request of the Shiahs for separate enumeration has not been complied with since 1881, owing to the then ascertained paucity of their

numbers in Madras. It is however an interesting fact that the only ruling Muhammadan Chief of Southern India, the Nawab of Banganapalle, is a Shiah. Equally has been disregarded the division of the Sunnis into the schools following the four Imams; Noman, better known as Imam Abu Hanifa, or Imam Auzam; Muhammad, son of Idris, known as Imam-Shafai; Malik, son of Anas; and Ahmad, called Imam-i-Hanbal. The followers of the third and fourth of these teachers are rarely found in Southern India, possibly because the tenets of their school are rigid, and not too easy of acquisition; and though, as pointed out by Mr. Quadir Hussain Khan in his "South Indian Mussalmans," the distinction of Hanafi and Shafi, if ascertained, will at times afford a valuable clue to *racial* divergence among Muhammadans, detailed enquiry in this direction is of little use, inasmuch as the majority of Southern Moslems, although not for the considered reasons of the "Ghir Mukullid" school, are indifferent to or ignorant of these distinctions.

33. An attempt was made by means of enquiry throughout the several districts to ascertain the respective proportions of (*a*) pure-blooded Muhammadans, and (*b*) recent converts to that religion. The distinction, as pointed out by several correspondents, is technically incorrect, inasmuch as "race" and "religion" are not convertible terms; but in default of a better it is at least comprehensible.

34. Although, as might be expected, no very definite information could be obtained, most of those consulted were of opinion that the majority of Southern Muhammadans were, at one time or other, though possibly at a time very far remote from the present, adherents of some form of Hinduism. It may be possible to gauge the completeness of their absorption into Islam by a comparison of the Muhammadan population with the number of those returning Hindóstáni as their customary vehicle of speech. For, while the number of those, other than Muhammadans, habitually using this tongue in this Presidency is undoubtedly very small, its fluent use is regarded among Muhammadans as an indication of social and even religious status, the Urdu-speaking Muhammadan being wont to adopt a somewhat Bráhmanical attitude towards the Dravidian fellow believer, who still clings to his old vernacular.

35. Excluding from our calculations 1,032,757 Máppillas, whose almost universal ignorance of Urdu strikes the visitor as curious,* we are left with 1,731,710 Muhammadans; 848,061 males and 883,649 females. The Hindóstáni speaking population numbers 975,064 (table X), of whom 498,077 are men, and 476,987 women. We have thus a surplus of 349,984 Muhammadan men, and 406,662 women, over the Urdu speakers of either sex. Of this total we may look for the greater portion among the 220,999 men, and 252,316 women, of the Labbai and Dúdékula communities; the former being as a rule Tamil converts, the latter, Telugu speakers of very doubtful adherence to any creed. The balance is probably to be found among the Sheiks, whose fellowship perforce receives most new believers.

36. The conclusion thus attained would seem to be that some 56 per cent. of non-Máppilla Muhammadans, either came to this country imbued with their faith, or else received it so far back that the newness of conversion has now passed from them. It is however possible that the return of Hindóstáni speakers is somewhat greater than the reality; partly because of the converts' social desire for complete assimilation with his fellow believers, partly owing to a curious idea, noted by one correspondent as prevailing among the lower classes, that admitted proficiency in, and habitual use of, a "profane language" is apt to make one stand in peril of the judgment.

37. As may be seen from subsidiary table II, it is only in the West Coast division, and in a lesser degree in the Deccan, that the followers of Islam constitute an appreciable percentage of the population. In the total population of the Presidency they number, as already noted, but 660 per 10,000, as against the 8,892 of the Hindus. In the districts they locm largest in Malabar, home of the Máppillas,

* At the same time as noted in Onapter Xi ney are of good Muhammadan descent on one side at least, while their present seal is unquestioned.

and in South Canara, where the same sect by far predominates; in the little states of Banganapalle, and Sandúr, and the Deccan territories of Cuddapah, Kurnool, and Bellary.

38. Their rate of increase (11 per cent.), greater than that of the general population and of the Hindu community, may be attributed, in part to their more virile nature and habit of life—a doubtful point treated more fully in Chapter II—in part to the fact that Islam, unlike Hinduism, recognizes, in theory at least, the duty or desirability of proselytism. This latter supposition is strengthened by observation of an increase of 14 per cent. among the Máppilla community, who number some 37 per cent. of the total Muhammadan population, and among whom is found a more living interest in the faith than elsewhere in Southern India. Theirs is the well-known theological college of Ponnáni,* where too is found an association (Mounnath-ul-Islam Sabha), which gives religious instruction gratuitously to converts, and renders material assistance to those under instruction.

39. But if, elsewhere systematic proselytism, as most of my informants report, has now become a thing of the past, such progress, apart from natural increase, as the faith may make, must be due to its inherent attractions, or to the accommodations which it is ready to make with existing circumstances. Although the recorded exploits of Tippu and Hyder, and the silent witness afforded by the conversion of Hindu shrines to mosques, as at Penukonda where Baba Fakruddin's *miswak* blossomed and still grows, suggest that the hand of Islam was once laid heavily on Southern India, it need hardly be said that the era of forcible conversion has long since passed away.†

40. Spiritual wrestlings being out of place in a census report, it were well not to criticise the theoretical superiority or inferiority of rival faiths. But, whether from design, or from the insensible influence of environment, there can be no doubt that certain compromises now exist in Madras between Muhammadanism and Hinduism. Propitiation of disease-godlings, worship of patron saints and local deities, veneration of relics, practisings of the black art, divinations of the future, Hindu ceremonies at birth and marriage (though not as a rule at death); all practices satirized by the poet Hali ‡ abound throughout the Presidency, and render the stern simplicity of Islam more attractive for its rural followers.

41. A particular example of such compromise may for purposes of illustration be noted in the case of the Dúdékulas—a community numbering 71,612 souls, of whom

* Ponnáni is moreover the residence of a character somewhat unique in the 20th century, a saint, of whom I have received the following curious account:—

"He is called Parithaviliya Thangal, and is more than 80 years old. He seldom or never washes his person or his "scanty raiment, fasts much, speaks rarely, and sees few people. He is much reverred by Rowthars and Máppillas. "Offerings are made for him in many mosques of Malabar, and cocoanut shells are deposited for him on the road side "under trees all over South Malabar, to await collection by his agent three or four times a year. These shells are "regarded as tabu by all classes of the population, and though there is nothing to prevent any one from collecting and "selling them, the Thangal rarely has to complain of loss. He has a great reputation as a healer of the sick. The "method employed is to tap the sick person lightly with a stick; unlike Christian scientists he does not operate from "a distance. Unlike most modern saints he has no itch for money, and the cocoanut shell offerings (worth about "Rs. 1,000 a year) are appropriated by the members of his family for the maintenance of the Saint and themselves."

† Mr. Muhammad Karimulla Faruki, to whom I am indebted for an admirable note on South Indian Muhammadanism, gives me the following curious instance of Time's revenges. At Conjeeveram he discovered a stone much venerated by Hindus as possessing the power of relieving pains and other ailments. On digging up and cleaning this stone, he discovered thereon an inscription commemorating destruction of some Hindu shrine by an emissary of Aurangazeb, and the devotion of its revenues to Moslem charity! On a mosque near a Hindu temple the same enquirer found a Persian inscription, commemorating the pulling down of a temple and the erection of a mosque in its place. *Per contra*, he instances the aid lent to the Bráhmans of Conjeeveram about 1714 A.D., by sundry Muhammadan notables, in recovering the image of Vishnu from Udaiyárpálaiyam, whither it had been removed in 1689 on rumour of a Muhammadan foray.

‡ If a stranger (other than a Muslim) worships an idol he is (denounced as) a heretic.
He that says that God has a son is a heretic.
He that worships fire is a heretic.
He that attributes miracles to stars is a heretic.
But the Moslems (God bless them) have a wide field.
They can worship with impunity anything they like.
If they like they can make a prophet God.
Exalt Imams to the rank of the prophet.
Make offerings over graves day and night.
Invoke the blessings of the Martyrs.
The Unity does not suffer by these acts.
Religion is not disturbed, nor do the essentials of the faith disappear.

the majority are found in Cuddapah, Kurnool, and Anantapur. Of them, an educated Muhammadan doubts "if they ever think of such a thing as salvation." They worship their tools on Bakrid day, as do Hindus on occasion of the Dusserah; they adopt both Hindu and Muhammadan names; they do not go to mosque, or pray according to the rites of Islam, but offer promiscuous vows to Hindu godlings and Muhammadan saints. Even in their chiefest orthodoxy, the performance of Fatheha on the occasion of a death, there are certain quaintnesses. If such be not performed, the soul of the deceased is apt to become an evil spirit; while, as it undoubtedly partakes of the funeral bakemeats, the lid of the cooking vessel is kept half open during the ceremony, to save the spirit the trouble of opening it. The dreadful contingency of a Mullah not being at hand on occasion of need (the Dúdékula himself has no store of Korán verses) is thus guarded against. A bamboo tube is washed, when the Mullah is requested to repeat half a dozen Fathehas into it. The tube, thus filled with sacred breath, is stoppered with clean rags, and secured to the roof with a well washed rope. When occasion arises, the man of the house takes down and unstoppers the tube, which he passes over the cooking vessels, the while repeating the name of the deceased. Careful not to exhaust more than one of the Mullah's repetitions he closes the tube, and puts it by till occasion next calls.

42. Similarly a knife for the slaughter of sheep or fowls can be sanctified by a Mullah for a Dúdékula ignorant of the article of cutting.

43. Nagore, seven pilgrimages to which are said to equal one to Mecca, strikes the visitor as more Hindu than Muhammadan. Hinduism and Muhammadanism have here so far amalgamated that "the Hindus assist the Muhammadans in carrying their God Allah in procession"—a startling statement by one of my correspondents.

44. Moreover even beyond the broad distinctions which race, occupation, and education are wont to draw 'twixt the followers of every religion, there may be found certain traces of the Hindu "caste" idea existing among Muhammadans in Madras. Here a Muhammadan, although he may not acknowledge the eminence of a Bráhman, yet very frequently reflects his Hindu environment so far as to show a quite Bráhmanical dislike for the Pariah. The train of thought thus started may persist in his attitude towards divers members of his own community.

45. Some curious reports of sections considered "low" have reached me from various districts. At Kílakkarai and Periyapatnam in Rámnád lives a strange community busied with diving for shells, and one from which other Muhammadans keep aloof. Of a similarly circumstanced body I hear in the Nannilam taluk of Tanjore. In Kistna, the Muhammadans who follow the professions of barber, butcher or skin dealer, appear to accept among themselves the Hindu estimation of these arts. The contemptuous name (referred to in Chapter XI), bestowed by ancients of the church on new made Sheiks, scarcely suggests that all are, *primâ facie* at least, equal in the eyes of the true believer.

46. In certain communities apparently homogeneous, such as Dúdékulas and Rávuttans, we find the characteristic Hindu formation of endogamous sub-sects, territorial and occupational. Family endogamy is a Muhammadan characteristic, which, if the family be or become sufficiently large, is apt to lead to formation of a small endogamous caste.

47. But a detailed study of Hindu influences on Muhammadanism is beyond the scope of this report. Both creeds go far outside what is considered the province of religion in other countries, in the minute regulation of social and personal details of conduct: a certain resemblance in such regulation is less surprising than would be absolute difference.

48. Just as too much is habitually made of the backwardness of Muhammadans as a class, so ascription to their creed of responsibility for such backwardness as may

be, is certainly unjust. Knowledge of a foreign tongue (English)*, addiction to the clerical profession, success in passing examinations; when all is said and done, these are somewhat artificial criteria of the progress of a people. If less receptive and industrious than the Hindu in acquiring a knowledge of rule and sanctioned usage, the Muhammadan is not infrequently the readier of the two to handle a situation, which has to create not follow a precedent. That his creed is not *per se* antagonistic to the light its earlier and purer history shows. †

49. Yet the need of constructive reform within the faith to-day in Southern India few of its most ardent admirers will deny. The progress of modern thought and liberalism has abated the old priestly governance; but as yet little replacement has been attempted. Whereas a moslem friend tells me that in his youth he saw two Muhammadans publicly flogged by order of the *Jamaat* for immorality and drunkenness, that in those days the Patel commanded more influence than any modern official; to-day another writes that *Jamaats* are dead, mosques are not looked after, Muhammadan endowments are abused, the people are either ignorant of their religious duties, or else slothfully indifferent to their performance. The need is for some Socratic gadfly to sting the lazy into action, some modern Ezekiel to see new life breathed into dry bones—*Exoriatur aliquis.*

(3) Christianity.

50. Some seventy-four years ago, a celebrated philosopher, writing on the subject of religion, spoke of "300 bribed souls," "notable for immorality," as representing the result of Christian missionary enterprise in India. Even granting that the philosopher's ignorance of India was on a par with that of most intelligent dwellers in Europe, it is interesting to contrast with the assertions of the past the facts of to-day, when the Christians of the Southern Presidency alone number 1,208,515, or 289 per 10,000 of its total population.

51. Excluding 40,928 European and Anglo-Indian Christians, whose faith may be described as ready made, and whose most interesting feature is that atheism or agnosticism on their part is considered equivalent to acceptance of some form of Christianity, we find that Indian Christians have increased during the decade by 168,964 or 17 per cent.—a rate more than double that of the increase in the total population, and one which compares favourably with an increase of 8 per cent. among Hindus, and 11 per cent. among Muhammadans.

52. Granting that a marked increase of adherents is but what one might naturally expect in the case of a religion actually and avowedly proselytizing, it may be well to consider what attraction such faith can offer to those whose allegiance it desires to win.

53. There has been at all times a tendency to attribute the progress of Christianity in India to the material advantages associated with conversion. Applied to the case of converts of good position, on whom conversion frequently entails material loss and social inconvenience, the statement is absurd: in respect of the outcastes of Hinduism such criticism has a certain foundation, but, if rightly considered, is not one at which the Christian church need feel alarm. It is no more sensible to attribute the conversion of an unlettered Paraiyan solely to a reasoned preference for Christianity as a speculative doctrine, than it is just to attribute the continuance in Hinduism of the keen witted Bráhman to an admixture of selfishness and ignorance. Nowadays many missionaries are emphatically, and with justice, of opinion, that adoption of Christianity brings with it material benefit,‡ under ordinary circumstances not an unnatural consequence or concomitant, of moral and intellectual improvement, to certain classes from which converts are obtained.

* It may be seen from Chapter VIII that in proportion to their numbers the Muhammadans are but little behind their Hindu fellow countrymen in this respect.

† Such as the history of the Moors in Spain.

‡ Some candid souls among them have written to me that K.D.'s occasionally adopt Christianity in the hope of escaping police surveillance.

54. The hope of a decent life on earth is not any more, or any less, a bribe than the hope of a blissful eternity hereafter. To apologize for the conferring of such material benefits as naturally and inevitably arise from education, and especially, in India, from female education, self-respect, and escape from social thraldom, is the merest nonsense. It is neither good Christianity, nor good sense, to offer the Paraiyan the arid stone of theological speculation, while he lacks the bread of humanity. That the Paraiyan should desire to escape from the social slough, to which Hinduism has consigned him, is perfectly just and laudable; it is natural that he should look for, and fortunate that he should find in the missionary, some one who has the power and the will to assist him to the accomplishment of his desire. Absolute famine very probably does give the final impetus in many cases; the conversions of 1878 in the Nellore district were doubtless thus influenced, but are in no way discredited by the probable reasoning of the converts that, once received into the Church, they would be kept alive by the Church's best endeavour.

55. It has been assumed in the preceding paragraphs, and the assumption is corroborated by the testimony of sundry missionaries, that Christianity finds its new adherents chiefly amongst the outcastes of Hinduism. *A priori* the assumption is reasonable: a religion which teaches that all men are equal before God in merit, or lack of merit, is hard of acceptance for a man who holds as his fundamental tenet that all men are not equal, and that he himself is at the top, or near the top, of the ladder of merit. It is far easier to make Subbigadu believe that he is as good as Periyasami Aiyangar, than it is to convince Periyasami Aiyangar that he is no better than Subbigadu. Between Muhammadanism and Christianity in India, the resemblance is, in many practical, and even theoretical, respects too great to render probable any considerable transfer of allegiance from one faith to the other.

56. It is probably incorrect to imagine that Hindus, still less Muhammadans, of the better and more educated classes, are actuated by any fanatical spirit of opposition in their relation to Christianity. In general it is scarcely to be denied that the cosmopolitan apostles of modern Hinduism have borrowed, or at least derived a quickened interest in, ideas of social service, and of a faith concerned as much with the welfare of one's neighbour as the salvation of one's solitary soul, from study of the Christian writings, and from the precept and example of Christian teachers. In particular I have myself seen Bráhmans attend Christian services; I know of a Bráhman who presided at a missionary meeting; and various missionaries have informed me of material assistance in the shape of money, grain, and cattle, received from orthodox Hindus and Muhammadans. The question of caste apart, such opposition as the new-made convert has to encounter, springs often from economic rather than theological reasons. Under the Hindu system the "untouchable" occupies in the villages the position of a serf, and one of the immediate effects of conversion is the commencement of deliverance from his bondage. Thus from orthodox Malabar an Indian clergyman quaintly states as the advantages of conversion, "that the convert becomes fully entitled to the eternal peace of Heaven and has not to leave the road at the approach of a Bráhman." In Nellore several of the erstwhile serfs appeared at a recent show in the rôle of successful exhibitors of prize cattle. Entirely commendable as is this uprising, its immediate effects on village economy are disconcerting, and it is simply in accordance with human nature that some active opposition should manifest itself. The Panchama convert is reminded sharply of the debts that he or his ancestors have contracted to the village magnates; he finds it difficult if not impossible to obtain land on darkhast; water difficulties crop up; occasionally that fine old Indian war-horse, the false case, snorting takes the field. But the general testimony is that in time things adjust themselves; and that in his spiritual adviser the convert does not lack a temporal defender.

57. Turning to subsidiary table II, we find that the natural divisions range in point of Christianity, from the East Coast South, with 494 per 10,000 of its inhabitants Christian, to that of the Agencies, where, although proportional increase is greatest in later years, but 84 persons in 10,000 have as yet been gained over by

missionary endeavour. Excluding, as in some respects abnormal, the Nilgiri district, and those of Anjengo and Madras, one recognizes with a certain sense of historical fitness the pre-eminence of Tinnevelly and Rámnád (1st and 4th); in which districts, if we disregard the recent severance of the latter from Madura, the progress of Christianity will be for ever associated with the immortal names of Francis Xavier, Robert di Nobili, and Jean de Britto. Next to Tinnevelly comes South Canara, home of an old Christianity almost exclusively Roman Catholic, whose early struggles and dissensions have been set forth by Father Francisco Xavier de Santa Anna.*

58. Guntúr, third on the list with 729 per 10,000 of its population Christian, and an Indian Christian community numbering 123,486 souls, represents in the main the later activities of Baptist and Lutheran Missions, whose adherents number respectively 60,766, and 43,610. At a decent interval, follow Rámnád (Roman Catholic), Kurnool (Baptist and Anglican), Trichinopoly and Tanjore (Roman Catholic) in close order, with Christianities varying from 462 to 380 per 10,000 of their total populations. The lowly position of South Arcot (11th) may cause some surprise when it is remembered as the home of Monseigneur Bonnand, one of the finest minds of later day missionary enterprise.

59. "He," said his successor, Archbishop Laouenan, "launched India into the Catholic movement." The chronicler of the French "Foreign Missionary Society" thus describes him: "He was not a man of strikingly brilliant intellect, but he was methodical and industrious to a degree, and his powers of work were extraordinary. With unflagging enthusiasm he combined a perfect balance and candour of judgment, and that uncommon gift, *common-sense*." His powers of organization, and that keen insight into human nature, which enabled him with equal effect to offer the kindliest encouragement, as to the weary Father Fricand, or administer the sternest reproof, as to Father Mehay on the occasion of his adventure into the horse trade, can be appreciated in the history of his episcopate, which lasted from 1833 to 1861. He died at Benares when engaged in an apostolic visitation of all India. For the outside world his fame has been somewhat overshadowed by that of his remarkable, though not entirely agreeable predecessor, Father Jean Antoine Dubois.

60. But his great influence was not confined to any one district; it can be seen in the general progress of his church in the Southern (Tamil) country. In view of the comparative ill success of the Roman Catholic church among the Telugu people, deplored by the writer of a recent "History of the Telugu Christians," it is interesting to speculate as to what might have been, had not the choice of Monseigneur d'Hèbert in 1833 called Father Bonnand from this people to the episcopacy at Pondicherry.

61. Thus far Christianity in general. With the uncomfortable reflection that he were well encased in triple brass, who, in a census report, would essay an estimate of the varying degrees of spiritual attraction or merit inherent in the creeds of the several Christian Churches, we may proceed to some consideration of the figures shown in subsidiary table V.

62. Calculations based on the total figures of 1901 and 1911 show the distribution of 1,000 Indian Christians.

	1911.	1901.
Roman Catholics	579	627
Protestants (of all sects)	401	366
Syrians	20	3
Indefinite beliefs	...	4

The suggestion of these figures is that Protestantism is gaining ground on its older rival, that the Syrian church is progressing rapidly, and that disappearance of "indefinite beliefs" indicates an improving accuracy of enumeration. But in their acceptance a certain caution is necessary. The increase in Syrian Christians is confined to one district (Malabar), where progress during the decade from 1,193 to 21,016 is obviously incredible. Suspicion becomes practical certainty, when we note that, in the same

* Old Portuguese manuscript records in the possession of Father Coohet of Virarájendrapet, Coorg, translated for me by Father Anacleto, Principal of St. Bede's College, Madras.

district, Roman Catholics have decreased during the decade by an almost equally large number (16,000). The irresistible conclusion is, either that in 1901 some 16,000 Romo-Syrians were wrongly classed as Roman Catholics, or that a similar but inverted mistake has occurred at the present census. Of the two alternatives the former is by far the more probable, inasmuch as in 1901 Romo-Syrians were not separately recorded. In fact a lengthy memorial on the subject, addressed to me by the community before the census, leaves practically no room for doubt on the subject.

63. But after all allowance has been made, it is sufficiently clear that, while the Roman Catholic Church is at present preponderant, Protestantism is rapidly drawing level. If further proof be needed, it can be found in the marginal figures, which show the rate of increase per 1,000 in the Indian adherents of the several sects. In seeking an explanation we may dismiss as equally unworthy the suggestions of too zealous controversialists; on the one hand, that the Catholic Church is complacently and consciously indifferent to a retention of Hindu observances by its converts, to an extent that renders their Christianity a mere empty name; on the other, that Protestantism in many cases gains its adherents by direct bribery.

Roman Catholics	79
Anglican	259
Baptist	191
Congregationalist	459
Lutheran	350

64. Two facts are obvious. One, that Catholicism has been far longer in the field; its missionaries had penetrated into India before some of its competitors had even come into existence anywhere: the other, that Protestantism is now by far the better equipped of the two, in point of material resources, for its undertakings.

65. In the missionary system of the two churches we may notice certain salient points of difference. The Catholic missionary who arrives in India has quitted his native land for good: he remains at his post till death relieves him.* This sacrifice is not required by any Protestant mission, and is in fact prohibited by at least one. Arrived in India the Catholic missionary to a large extent cuts himself off from European society, with which his Protestant confrère keeps in touch; while the Protestant missionary is as a rule assured of a tolerable subsistence, the Catholic priest brings to its highest perfection the art of living upon nothing.

66. As to the theoretical advantages of either course there is something to be said. Prolonged and unchanging residence must undoubtedly gain for the missionary the closer acquaintance of his parishioners; severance of all ties with his native country perforce quickens his interest in the country of his adoption. Again, though it may be doubtful whether a foreigner can ever perfectly comprehend the Indian, he is at least more likely to succeed in his attempt, if he lives entirely with Indians and so, of necessity, in conformity with their mode of life: while renunciation of worldly comfort and advantage implies a certain tinge of that asceticism, which has always appealed powerfully to the religious imagination of the Hindu.

67. On the other hand, experience shows that too prolonged residence in a tropical climate is apt to sap the energy, and dull the enthusiasm of the European. Abandonment of his natural society, for one in most cases on a lower intellectual plane, may approximate priest and parishioner; but may very possibly do so by the bringing down of the priest, rather than by the uplifting of the parishioner; asceticism, however admirable and sympathetic to the Hindu, is yet somewhat reminiscent of the underlying selfishness of the Hindu ideal, wherein the penitent seeks first his own salvation; and in practical life provokes the question whether one's power of doing good is at all proportioned to the discomfort attendant on the doing.

68. But, after all, the ordering of his private life is the missionary's own affair. In forming an estimate of the appeal of Christianity to the Indian, the most important practical point to consider is the attitude adopted by the several churches

* A remarkable example is the career of Father Jarrige, whose missionary life in the country extended from 1819 to 1889.

towards the idea of caste, in which idea, inseparably bound up with the religion of most Southern Hindus, is found the chief stumbling block to conversion. This assertion was vehemently denied, it is true, by Monseigneur Laouenan: "Daily "experience proves abundantly that there is no precept of the scriptures or of the "Church which cannot be observed, and which is not observed, no Christian virtue "which cannot be practised, or which is not practised by those living in conformity "with this institution (caste)." But the Archbishop, it may be surmised, had in mind established Christianities, rather than the attempt to establish Christianity; and in respect to this latter endeavour there may be quoted against him the opinion of such early missionaries as Father Caron, S.J., who states that "this institution of "caste is a great obstacle to the progress of the gospel, especially in places where we "have but few or no Christians;" and Father de la Lane: "This (caste) is one of "those obstacles for which there is no remedy. God alone can remove it by some "extraordinary means of which we are totally ignorant."

69. To the material advantages of conversion to the outcast allusion has been made in paragraphs 52 and 53; in fairness it must be admitted that permission to maintain the gateless barrier of caste between himself and his humbler brethren may be an inducement quite as potent for the high caste man, as somewhat problematical rice and schools for the Paraiyan.

70. Broadly speaking it may be said that the Catholic Church tolerates, the Protestant Church condemns, this idea of caste. There is doubtless much argument to be advanced on either side: arguments against toleration of Indian Pharisaism suggest themselves readily enough; on the other hand it is a reasonable plea that the high caste convert comes already equipped with a social and religious philosophy, which may be directed and modified, while the attempt to force upon him a totally new scheme of life, unacceptable to a mind moulded by the tradition of centuries, is foredoomed to failure both in theory and practical result.

71. Thus for example Monseigneur Charbonnaux: "The Native congregations "of Southern India have been founded on the principle that, to be baptized, a man "need not renounce his own caste and nationality; so that though they are not "Hindus, if that word be used in a religious sense, if, on the contrary, it is used in "its natural and geographical sense, they are Hindus as well as their (fellow) "countrymen. They have always been so, and are accepted by all to be so, with "the rank and rights of their respective castes."

72. His arguments as well as those of Monseigneur Laouenan seem to be founded on the theory that caste is purely a *social* regulation. It certainly is this, but at the same time is something more: "Caste means to the Hindu more than social standing"—("History of the Telugu Christians" by a Father of the Mill Hill St. Joseph's Society).

73. The great bishop of Drusipare * smote this stubborn rock with the sledge hammer of common-sense, in a letter to his missionaries: "Imagine that the idea "of caste with which you have grown up is rooted in you as the roots of your life, "that like most Indians you cannot conceive the existence of a civilized society "*without* caste, without those external marks of religion and social standing, "which serve as a guide of daily life in your country. Imagine then that a few "strangers, whose manners and social customs horrify you, urge you to abandon the "worldly beliefs, the religious practices handed down among you from father to "son; decry the gods that you adore, and ask you to accept a religion, which you "regard as made for persons more spiritual than yourselves, and for you impracticable; ask you to accept them as your spiritual leaders, when their disciples are "but objects of contempt for you and for your fellow countrymen!! Do you think "that this outraging of your susceptibilities, of your ancient prejudices, would gain "anything from you? I think not. Show tact then; handle this people with "discretion."

* Monseigneur Bonnand.

74. The practical outcome of the matter is that among high caste people the Roman Catholic Church alone has made appreciable progress. No direct proof, it is true, can be adduced of this assertion, inasmuch as no attempt was made to ascertain the position of converts prior to conversion. It has been controverted by Monseigneur Laouenan "so far as I have been able to observe conversions to " Protestantism are comparatively more frequent among the upper castes ; among " the lower castes to Catholicism." But he admits that he puts forward this statement with hesitation, and latter day testimony seems to be against him. As an example of such may be quoted the Rev. D. Kuss : " It would appear that the " Catholic population of the Telugu-speaking people is in round numbers about " 45,000. Of this 78 per cent. is caste and 22 per cent. non-caste."

75. Finally the numerous protests made against this omission by Catholic congregations, and their objections to the inclusive term " Indian Christian," indicate with sufficient clearness that these people deem themselves to possess something which they are solicitous not to lose. The absence of such protest by any Protestant congregation may be taken as an admission that these Christians did not originally possess any caste (Paraiyans), or else have acquiesced in the idea of its abandonment.

76. The Catholic Church is one and indivisible,* Protestant sects tend rather to resemble the sands of the sea. Among non-conformist missions a tendency towards unity has of late manifested itself, resulting in the formation of the " South Indian United Church." The Union includes the London Mission, the American Madura Mission, the American Arcot Mission, and the United Free Church of Scotland. An attempt was made to tabulate the number of persons returning themselves simply as members of this union, or of any body that could be recognized as affiliated to it. The result, which may be seen in the margin, is not entirely satisfactory. The United Free Church of Scotland, it will be observed, does not figure at all ; its adherents have obviously been returned as Presbyterians *tout court* ; possibly as much because of the difficulty that the writing of the church's full name would present to the average enumerator as for any other reason. " Protestants unspecified " who number 11,040, probably include, as well as members of the Anglican Communion, many adherents of well-defined dissenting sects.

London Mission	22,045
American Arcot Mission	5,476
American Madura Mission	14,787
South Indian United Church	2,070

77. In table XVII all Christians have been classified in accordance with the established terminology of sect ; not always very happily. For example those belonging to the London Mission have been ranked under " Congregationalist," although that mission is in fact undenominational, and permits considerable latitude as to view of Church Government.

78. The Syrian Church, a thing *sui generis*, is hardly a proselytizing body, although I am informed that at times Indian Roman Catholics, at loggerheads with their parish priest, are wont to inflict an ingenious annoyance on the good man by styling themselves Romo-Syrians, or Syrian Catholics. The remarkable increase in the number of its adherents in Malabar has already been explained. South Canara is the only other district to claim any other appreciable number of the faithful ; these as in 1901 belong to the Jacobite sect.

79. In the census report of 1901 a certain amount of detail was given as to the origin of the different Syrian sects. Recapitulation is unnecessary ; all the more so as an educated Syrian, consulted on the matter, gives it as his opnion that existing differences are of little intrinsic, as opposed to accidental, importance. The interesting point about the community as a whole is its existence as an Eastern Christianity, untrammelled by European or American leading strings. Judging from the frequency of its appearances in Southern Law Courts, the faith is in no danger of dying for lack of the stimulus of internal dissension.

* Theoretically at least. Goa at times seems to have played Barnabas to the Roman Paul with tolerable spirit and success.

(4) Animism.

80. Religions in Imperial table VI, and in the sections of this chapter purporting to give a brief account of each creed, have been arranged in accordance with the numerical importance of their adherents. A closer correlation of "Hinduism" and "Animism" would be more logical and appropriate, in view of the difficulty already alluded to in paragraphs 26 and 27 *supra*, of determining the relation between the highly metaphysical * faith of the speculative Bráhman, and the more theological * views of many, if not of the majority, of the inhabitants of the Presidency.

81. Column 8 of the standard census schedule provided for entry of the faith professed by each person enumerated. But whereas the followers of well-defined creeds, such as Muhammadanism, Christianity, Buddhism, Zorastrianism, etc., were unlikely to give anything but a perfectly clear answer as to their beliefs, it was obviously an impossibility to rely on the average enumerator for a scientific discrimination between "Hinduism" and "Animism."

82. Accordingly a rough and ready criterion was applied in the abstraction offices. The entry of "Hindu" in column 8 was accepted as proof of the Hinduism of the person enumerated; while entry there of the name of his tribe, or so-called "caste," was held sufficient warrant for classing him as an Animist.

83. This procedure, adopted from previous usage, has given results satisfactory on the whole, although, as will be noted, involving some curious discrepancies in detail. In view of the assimilative nature and progressive spread of Hinduism, in the last resort a system of social governance rather than of religious faith, it is not surprising to find in the decade a decrease of 3,359, or 5 per 1,000, in the ranks of the Animists. On the other hand an Animistic increase from 3,886 to 65,780 in the district of Nellore is obviously incredible, and as obviously due to the enumerator's theological predilection, which in 1901 returned 62,609 out of 66,318 Yánádis as Hindus, and ten years later classed 64,119 out of 71,797 of the same people as, in point of religion, "Yánádis" pure and simple, and therefore "Animists." Yet the method has given a curiously interesting result, in the disclosure of some 7,000 Animists among the Kápus, whose Hinduism no one calls in question. Were such persons found in Kistna, Nellore, or Cuddapah, the return could be unhesitatingly put down as an enumerator's mistake. Their existence in the Vizagapatam agency suggests, if they be indeed the same people as the Kápus of the plains, the possibility of assimilation to their aboriginal surroundings, so complete as to render them forgetful or careless of their claim to inclusion in Hinduism.

84. Detailed enquiries as to the customs and beliefs of people generally regarded as Animistic, especially with reference to Hinduism, addressed to those in a position to have particular knowledge of the subject, found a ready and courteous response. For much valuable information I have to thank the Rev. J. J. Vulliez, Messrs. A. C. Duff, I.C.S., G. H. Welchman, G. V. Ramamurti, H. R. Bardswell, I.C.S., A. Whitehead, Dinabandha Pandu, B. H. Barlowe-Poole, and many others.

85. It may be assumed that of Animism, whatever it may be, the dwellers in the agency hill tracts are far more truly representative than the wandering tribes of the plains. Of the former I shall take as representative the Khonds and Savaras, both because I have some personal knowledge of these peoples, and inasmuch as the information furnished to me in their respect is fuller and more detailed.

86. It is true that the Khond whose dwelling neighbours on the plains tends to come under the influence of Hindu thought. Resort by the Khonds of the Udayagiri taluk to Hindu temples at Chokkapád, Bellagunta, and Kullada, a pilgrimage probably made with the pious hope of offspring, serves as an example of such tendency. But among the people as a whole there is little trace of an approximation to Hinduism. On the social side, the idea of caste, the touchstone of Hinduism, is not innate in them. The Khond potter, the Khond herdsman, and the Khond

* I use these words in the sense implied in Auguste Comte's law of the three stages. Comte would, I presume, have regarded philosophical Hinduism as a development, natural in point of time, from what is here called Animism.

cultivator will eat together and intermarry: Khond and Páno will drink together.* Restrictions there are in point of marriage; the Khond will not recognise as a Khond the offspring of a union between Khond and Dombo, or Gahanju and Khond. But this refusal springs from the European idea of class, rather than from the Indian idea of caste; the Khond regarding himself as the social superior of Dombo or Gahanju.

87. Again among this people the idea of permanence of marriage, at least on the woman's side, and of female chastity anterior to marriage does not obtain A marriage is readily dissolved; it may be for reasons, such as sterility or lack of male offspring, similar to those prevailing among Hindus; but such dissolution is no bar to another alliance on the part of the wife. The total absence of any ideas as to female chastity is sufficiently indicated by the fact that "unmarried" Khonds of either sex live, not separately and in their parents' houses, but promiscuously in a building allotted for this purpose.

88. On the purely religious side, it may be said that the Hindu doctrines of Karma and re-incarnation are absent. The former is beyond the Khond's mental grasp; as is doubtless the latter in its Hindu form. Mr. Duff mentions one case in which a Páno, at a Khond birth ceremony, suggested that the soul of an ancestor had entered into the new-born infant; but he points out that Pános, although often Khond speakers, and not too readily distinguishable by strangers from Khonds, have long had more intercourse with the Hindu plains than the Khonds. An idea of the spirit's survival after death, and of its possible temporary transference during life-time, undoubtedly exists; the belief being universal that the spirit of a man killed by a tiger guides the tiger in his search for a fresh victim; while a frequent cause of divorce is the assertion of a husband that his wife has become a nocturnal tiger, preying on the children, fowls, pigs, etc., of the village. Again on the third day after a natural death is performed a ceremony known as "*pideri tapku*" (bringing of the devil). A spider (*Kruma-croho*) is brought from the burning ground, kept for a day, and propitiated with rice, meat, and a new cloth, apparently under the idea that it represents a malignant re-incarnation of the deceased. A woman dying in child-birth becomes a "*silungudi*," a fearsome devil, whose malevolence takes the curious form of making her brothers-in-law laugh themselves to death. A precautionary measure is to nail the corpse to the pyre by forehead, hands, feet, wrists, knees, fingers, and toes.

89. It is when we descend to the detail of what the Khond does believe, from the generality of what he does not, that the difficulty of distinguishing his Animism from the Hinduism of the uncultured villager becomes fully apparent. An account of his divinities † would serve, with very small modification, for a description of the ordinary Hindu village deities and their worship.

90. Chief of the Khond gods is *Bura Pēnu* with his wife *Pitēri* (possibly a Khond form of *Pidari*). He is worshipped as god above (*Séndo Pēnu*), and god beneath (*Nēdē Pēnu*). He is the creator of mankind, and has under him a host of subordinate gods.

91. *Dondo Pēnu*, the god of punishment, dwells amid some sacred trees near every Khond village. Cut one of his trees, and you die quickly and unpleasantly.

92. *Loha Pēnu*, the god of iron, directs your arrows against the foeman, and averts their countershafts.

93. *Odu Pēnu*, god of the outside, undertakes the general surveillance of the village, which he may not enter. In his task he is assisted by *Dandere Pēnu*, the door-keeper, who guards the back of the village, for a fee of fowls and eggs; by *Darni Pēnu*, who watches the inside of the village from beneath a heap of stones,

* I saw a hillman refuse food offered by my Bráhman assistant. But in the refusal there was no idea of caste: he refused "because I do not know you, and I am afraid of you." He was quite ready to accept a meal from a local Hindu official, whom his experience had shown him to be innocent of poisoning or purging design.

† For this present account I am indebted in particular to the Rev. J. J. Vullies.

where he dwells in the fragrant companionship of a rotten egg; by *Teki Pénu*, the god of vessels, who guards the property of the house; and by *Goheli Pénu*, god of the stable, who protects the animals from marauding tigers.

94. *Karang Pénu*, the unknown god, requires propitiation when a person sickens without apparent cause; *Djodi Pénu* of the rivers protects women with child; *Oda Pénu* drives birds and beasts from the crop.

95. This list does not exhaust the worshipful capacities of the Khond. *Murdo* and *Rugo* (small-pox and cholera) figure on his list on the way from Kurtuli to Mahasingi dwells a god, whose chief activity consists in the asking for tobacco; the god of precipices is found on the road to Korada; the hot spring of *Taptapáni* receives frequent *púja*. If ancestor worship, strictly speaking, does not prevail, there are stories of *Tummeri*, who founded Tummeribund, and of the giant Khonds, who brought the Nolobhonsos to Mahasingi.

96. It may be that Khond's hilly inaccessible country, with its feverish climate, has prevented the intersection of his orbit with that of so-called Hinduism. Did opportunity offer, he would probably enter the Hindu fold, bringing with him his gods, as easily as many another Dravidian demon-worshipper has done, and receive in time a tincture of deeper and more spiritual religious ideas, with a greater fixity and seemliness in his social regulations.

97. The religious beliefs of Savaras appear to have undergone considerable modification in the decade that is past. In 1901 of 183,159 Savaras but 24,306 were classed as Hindus; a total which has more than doubled in 1911, when 56,052 out of 186,128 are so described.

98. Of the Savaras of Rámagiri, and those of Parlákimedi, I have received detailed information from Messrs. Dinabandha Pandu and G. H. Welchman. The complete disagreement of their accounts, which in each case are founded on undoubted knowledge of the people described, indicates the difficulty of any general statement as to religious belief.

99. Mr. Dinabandha Pandu divides the Rámagiri Savaras into nine sections, of which he considers five to be Hindu for all practical purposes, and four purely Animistic. Mr. Welchman considers his Savaras as so slightly tinctured with Hinduism as to be without its pale, but curiously enough finds among them some faint trace of Buddhistic ideas.

100. If they do not worship the diseases themselves, the Animistic Savaras of Rámagiri are wont to propitiate certain divinities on the outbreak of cholera or small-pox. Although one of such deities has a Hindu name, *Tákuráni*, the Savaras specifically deny its connection with the Hindu pantheon. By certain sections though not by all *Thullia*, symbolized by a stone kept in each house, with a bundle of peacocks' feathers by its side, is worshipped at the time of eating new crop; as is *Ghansi*, a deity for whom there is no material symbol. *Korono*, an earthern pot hanging from the roof and containing rice, is worshipped at seed time; for abundance of crops *Gangi*, a stone placed under a tree, is addressed. *Dwaria* and *Budima*, likewise represented by stones, are worshipped respectively at times of harvest or epidemic; *Sapua* and *Kitum* find worshippers in Chandragiri alone.

101. The Savaras of Parlákimedi, in addition to a somewhat miscellaneous worship of natural objects, are wont to call upon their ancestors, who in general are regarded as rather harmful than otherwise. In their social relations, especially in point of permanence of marriage and pre-nuptial chastity of women, they show a closer approximation to Hinduism than do their fellow Savaras of Rámagiri, whose morality appears to be on a par with that of the Khonds.

102. There are certain other lines of enquiry by which I endeavoured to obtain some precise ideas as to the spiritual beliefs and tendencies of these people. Among such may be instanced questions as to whether they accept priests or gurus from among Hindus, as to the existence among them of totemistic ideas, as to the names conferred by them on their children.

103. My informants agree that, in general, these people neither ask for, nor accept, Hindu religious attentions, nor are such proffered by undoubted Hindus. One curious exception, it is true, is noted by Mr. Duff in the case of a shrine near Digi, where a Bráhman pújári is supported by Khond offerings.

104. Father Vulliez finds three totemistic septs among the Khonds of Udayagiri and Balliguda. These septs are in the main exogamous although the strictness of prohibition is gradually growing less; the *Muttokas*, descended from a peacock's egg, seeking mates among the *Goldekas*, who spring from the egg of the *Olangpota* (a small bird), or the *Sorengas*, the lordly progeny of a dung-worm. How far each sept now reveres its totem is a matter of uncertainty: the Muttokas at least have no objection to eating the peacock.

105. Chenchu names, taken in the main from Hindu mythology, point to the correctness of classing this tribe of the Nallamalai forests as Hindus. Khond names are varied and peculiar: * certain Savaras show a predilection for the days of the week; a system of nomenclature convenient in many respects, but possibly rendering distinction of sex by name somewhat difficult.

106. Unless the padding out of a census report be regarded as a work of practical utility, it would serve no useful purpose to labour through the names of godlings adored by tribes reputed to halt between Hinduism and Animism, and the fashion of their adoration. Name and worship are but the vesture of the underlying idea, and enough has perhaps been said, to indicate the impossibility of drawing a clear distinction between popular Hinduism and so called Animistic worship. Hinduism, its adherents claim, can find accommodation for all stages of intellectual development; if, from the statistical point of view, a European atheist can be a Christian, there is no apparent reason why an Indian animist should not be a Hindu.

* I once met a Khond called Doctor. Some difficulties attendant on his entrance to the world were surmounted by a Hospital Assistant who chanced to be on the spot: the name of the infant commemorated the occasion. I know of a Toda who answers to the weird appellation of "Deadlegs;" such is the translation of his name. But apparently this is a nickname, to the bestowing of which these strange people are addicted.

I.—*General distribution of the population by religions.*

Religion or Locality.		Actual Number in 1911.	Proportion per 10,000 of Population in			Variation per cent. (Increase + Decrease −).		Net Variation.
			1911.	1901.	1891.	1901–1911.	1891–1901.	1891–1911.
1		2	3	4	5	6	7	8
Hindu.	PROVINCE ...	37,230,084	8,892	8,914	8,963	+ 8·1	+ 6·2	+ 15·0
	Agency ...	1,073,932	6,808	6,246	6,605	+ 29·2	− 2·6	+ 24·5
	East Coast, North ...	9,823,378	9,347	9,386	9,511	+ 9·4	+ 7·4	+ 17·5
	Deccan ...	3,326,845	8,721	8,781	8,903	+ 8·0	+ 3·9	+ 7·0
	East Coast, Central ...	10,709,280	9,419	9,425	9,457	+ 7·9	+ 8·7	+ 17·3
	East Coast, South ...	9,243,600	9,006	9,085	9,048	+ 7·9	+ 5·2	+ 13·6
	West Coast ...	3,053,014	7,043	7,180	7,301	+ 5·0	+ 4·5	+ 9·7
Musalman.	PROVINCE ...	2,764,467	660	644	630	+ 11·1	+ 9·6	+ 21·8
	Agency ...	4,735	30	28	26	+ 28·0	+ 7·8	+ 38·1
	East Coast, North ...	321,457	306	298	287	+ 12·9	+ 12·8	+ 27·3
	Deccan ...	404,229	1,060	1,022	980	+ 7·6	+ 9·8	+ 18·2
	East Coast, Central ...	421,875	371	365	360	+ 9·7	+ 10·5	+ 21·2
	East Coast, South ...	512,492	499	489	467	+ 10·6	+ 5·7	+ 16·9
	West Coast ...	1,100,179	2,538	2,411	2,327	+ 12·7	+ 10·1	+ 24·1
Christian.	PROVINCE ...	1,208,515	289	266	244	+ 16·3	+ 18·1	+ 37·4
	Agency ...	13,265	84	36	8	+ 176·0	+ 336·2	+ 1,103·7
	East Coast, North ...	233,458	222	186	147	+ 31·1	+ 37·8	+ 80·1
	Deccan ...	73,449	193	165	112	+ 21·4	+ 54·8	+ 88·0
	East Coast, Central ...	211,560	186	185	167	+ 9·0	+ 20·3	+ 31·0
	East Coast, South ...	506,636	494	475	464	+ 12·4	+ 8·0	+ 21·3
	West Coast ...	170,147	393	372	348	+ 13·1	+ 15·3	+ 30·3
Animistic.	PROVINCE ...	638,486	153	166	131	− 0·5	+ 35·7	+ 35·0
	Agency ...	465,597	3,078	3,691	3,257	− 1·2	+ 15·5	+ 14·2
	East Coast, North ...	131,135	125	130	54	+ 5·4	+ 161·3	+ 175·5
	Deccan ...	8,465	22	27	...	− 14·3	* ...	* ...
	East Coast, Central ...	11,869	10	11	...	+ 4·0	* ...	* ...
	East Coast, South ...	...	...	...	...	− 100·0	* ...	* ...
	West Coast ...	1,400	3	12	...	− 70·4	* ...	* ...
Jain.	PROVINCE ...	27,005	6	7	8	− 1·6	+ 0·0	− 1·5
	Agency ...	...	...	...	...	− 100·0	+ 100·0	...
	East Coast, North ...	118	...	...	...	− 21·6	+ 120·5	+ 168·1
	Deccan ...	1,688	4	5	5	− 10·5	+ 2·8	− 7·9
	East Coast, Central ...	15,149	13	14	15	+ 2·8	+ 2·9	+ 5·8
	East Coast, South ...	656	1	1	1	+ 6·0	+ 4·0	+ 0·3
	West Coast ...	9,394	22	25	28	− 6·6	− 5·3	− 1·6
Others.	PROVINCE ...	1,673	...	...	† 4	+ 119·6	+ ‡ 50·6	+ ‡ 8·3
	Agency ...	...		...	104	...	...	...
	East Coast, North ...	150	...	...	1	− 5·7	− 22·0	+ 26·3
	Deccan ...	50		...	...	− 15·1	+ 76·7	+ 66·7
	East Coast, Central ...	947	1	...	1	+ 206·1	− 61·2	+ 18·2
	East Coast, South ...	124	...	...	...	+ 217·9	− 60·6	+ 25·3
	West Coast ...	403	1	...	1	+ 101·0	− 51·2	− 1·7

* Returned no Animists in 1891. † Includes "not stated." ‡ "Not stated" excluded.

II.—Distribution by districts of the main religions.

District and Natural Division.	Number per 10,000 of the population who are											
	Hindu.			Musalman.			Christian.			Others.		
	1911.	1901.	1891.	1911.	1901.	1891.	1911.	1901.	1891.	1911.	1901.	1891.
1	2	3	4	5	6	7	8	9	10	11	12	13
Agency	***6,806***	***6,245***	***6,606***	***30***	***26***	***26***	***84***	***38***	***8***	***3,078***	***3,691***	***3,361***
Agency Ganjám ...	3,638	3,236	2,824	2	1	2	54	29	17	6,306	6,734	7,157
,, Vizagapatam ...	7,489	6,757	7,432	20	18	17	96	87	2	2,395	3,138	2,548
,, Gódávari ...	8,818	9,564	9,834	125	131	134	78	46	32	979	259	...
East Cost, North ...	***9,347***	***9,386***	***9,511***	***306***	***298***	***287***	***222***	***186***	***147***	***125***	***130***	***55***
Ganjám	9,675	9,589	9,651	29	35	34	13	14	15	283	362	300
Vizagapatam	9,869	9,632	9,876	100	108	108	28	20	16	3	240	...
Gódávari	9,771	9,787	9,798	169	175	182	57	37	24	3	1	1
Kistna	9,389	9,468	9,547	354	352	347	250	167	106	7	12	...
Guntúr	8,526	8,618	8,848	691	654	620	729	679	586	54	49	1
Nellore	8,555	9,096	9,153	616	587	563	334	284	281	495	31	3
Deccan	***8,721***	***8,781***	***8,903***	***1,060***	***1,022***	***980***	***192***	***165***	***112***	***27***	***32***	***5***
Cuddapah	8,602	8,756	8,912	1,109	1,087	985	251	207	103	38	...	...
Kurnool	8,236	8,357	8,530	1,291	1,234	1,191	450	391	278	23	18	1
Banganapalle	7,752	7,947	7,985	2,047	1,932	1,999	200	92	16	1	29	...
Bellary	8,972	8,920	8,972	966	1,008	953	46	53	59	16	19	16
Sandúr	8,047	8,162	8,326	1,893	1,805	1,640	53	33	34	7	...	...
Anantapur	9,099	9,098	9,237	831	783	738	38	30	21	32	89	4
East Cost, Central ...	***9,419***	***9,425***	***9,457***	***370***	***365***	***369***	***186***	***185***	***167***	***25***	***25***	***16***
Madras	8,019	8,062	7,936	1,141	1,126	1,176	806	804	879	34	8	9
Chingleput	9,547	9,566	9,612	225	229	227	216	202	158	12	3	3
Chittoor	9,416	9,468	9,546	478	452	429	37	33	23	69	47	...
North Arcot	9,186	9,195	9,243	601	591	580	168	168	124	45	51	53
Salem	9,669	9,647	9,643	246	253	249	85	99	106	..	1	2
Coimbatore	9,694	9,677	9,725	204	202	192	92	90	81	10	31	2
South Arcot	9,410	9,419	9,453	284	278	268	285	283	253	21	25	26
East Coast, South ...	***9,006***	***9,035***	***9,048***	***489***	***489***	***467***	***494***	***475***	***464***	***1***	***1***	***1***
Tanjore	9,062	9,062	9,076	555	546	528	380	387	383	3	3	3
Trichinopoly	9,273	9,307	9,341	312	294	274	415	399	385	...	...	...
Pudukkóttai	9,276	9,298	9,327	326	322	303	398	380	370	...	...	...
Madura	9,291	9,308	9,330	396	400	396	313	292	273	...	...	1
Rámnád	8,813	8,836	8,824	725	699	725	462	463	451	..	...	...
Tinnevelly	8,429	8,514	8,506	589	577	587	982	909	907	...	...	...
West Coast	***7,043***	***7,180***	***7,301***	***2,538***	***2,411***	***2,327***	***393***	***372***	***343***	***26***	***37***	***29***
Nilgiris	7,917	7,802	8,387	496	521	457	1,462	1,318	1,152	125	359	4
Malabar	6,660	6,807	6,922	3,162	3,015	2,907	176	173	168	2	5	3
Anjengo	2,855	2,888	2,670	397	405	332	6,748	6,707	6,998	...	...	...
South Canara	7,244	8,056	8,168	1,177	1,118	1,060	808	741	675	76	85	97

III.—Christians—Number and variations.

District and Natural Division.	Actual number of Christians in			Variation per cent.		
	1911.	1901.	1891.	1901–1911.	1891–1901.	1891–1911.
1	2	3	4	5	6	7
Madras	***1,208,515***	***1,038,854***	***879,437***	+ ***16·3***	+ ***18·1***	+ ***37·4***
Agency	***13,265***	***4,907***	***1,102***	+ ***176·0***	+ ***336·2***	+ ***1,103·7***
Agency, Ganjám	1,896	923	521	+ 105·4	+ 77·2	+ 263·9
,, Vizagapatam	9,753	3,155	139	+ 209·1	+ 2,169·8	+ 6,916·5
,, Gódávari	1,616	729	442	+ 121·5	+ 64·7	+ 265·4
East Coast, North	***233,458***	***178,045***	***129,629***	+ ***31·1***	+ ***37·3***	+ ***80·1***
Ganjám	2,367	2,426	2,292	— 2·4	+ 5·8	+ 3·3
Vizagapatam	4,983	4,191	3,014	+ 18·9	+ 39·0	+ 65·3
Gódávari	8,240	4,768	2,871	+ 72·8	+ 66·1	+ 187·0
Kistna	49,863	29,186	16,107	+ 70·8	+ 81·2	+ 209·6
Guntúr	123,707	101,225	70,470	+ 22·2	+ 43·6	+ 75·5
Nellore	44,298	36.249	34,875	+ 22·2	+ 3 9	+ 27·0
Deccan	***73,449***	***60,480***	***39,069***	+ ***21·4***	+ ***54·8***	+ ***88·0***
Cuddapah	22,408	18,196	9,103	+ 23·1	+ 99·9	+ 146·2
Kurnool	42,068	34,052	22,735	+ 23·5	+ 49·7	+ 85·0
Banganapalle	785	297	57	+ 164·3	+ 421·1	+ 1,277·2
Bellary	4,481	5,066	5,282	— 11·5	— 4·1	+ 15·2
Sandúr	71	37	39	+ 91·9	— 5·1	+ 82·1
Anantapur	3,636	2,832	1,853	+ 28·4	+ 52·9	+ 96·2
East Coast, Central	***211,860***	***194,166***	***161,452***	+ ***9·0***	+ ***20·3***	+ ***31·0***
Madras	41,814	40,958	39,742	+ 2 1	+ 3·1	+ 5·2
Chingleput	30,377	26,466	18,982	+ 14·8	+ 39·4	+ 60·0
Chittoor	4,558	3,864	2,535	+ 17·9	+ 52·3	+ 79·8
North Arcot	32,822	28.569	20,403	+ 14·9	+ 40·0	+ 60 9
Salem	15,003	16,888	15,801	+ 11·2	+ 6·9	+ 5·1
Coimbatore	19,550	17,758	14,504	+ 10·1	+ 22·4	+ 34·8
South Arcot	67,436	59,663	49,485	+ 13·1	+ 20·6	+ 36·3
East Coast, South	***506,636***	***450,885***	***417,646***	+ ***12·4***	+ ***8·0***	+ ***21·3***
Tanjore	89,814	86,979	85,371	+ 3·3	+ 1·9	+ 5·3
Trichinopoly	87,358	78,407	72,069	+ 11·4	+ 8·8	+ 21·2
Pudukkóttai	16,398	14,449	13,813	+ 13·5	+ 4·6	+ 18·7
Madura	60,510	50,019	42,148	+ 21·0	+ 18·7	+ 43·6
Rámnád	76,677	70,295	65,466	+ 9·1	+ 7·4	+ 17·1
Tinnevelly	175,889	150,736	138,779	+ 16·7	+ 8·6	+ 26·7
West Coast	***170,147***	***150,471***	***130,539***	+ ***13·1***	+ ***15·3***	+ ***30·3***
Nilgiris	17,343	14,875	11,649	+ 16·6	+ 48·9	+ 27·7
Malabar	53,015	48,262	44,557	+ 9·8	+ 19·0	+ 8·3
Anjengo	3,760	3,231	3,074	+ 16·4	+ 22·3	+ 5·1
South Canara	96,029	84,103	71,259	+ 14·2	+ 34·8	+ 18·0

IV.—Races and sects of Christians. (*Actual numbers.*)

Sect.	European and allied races.		Anglo-Indian.		Indian.		Total.		Variation + or —.
	Males.	Females.	Males.	Females.	Males.	Females.	1911.	1901.	
1	2	3	4	5	6	7	8	9	10
ALL DENOMINATIONS ...	9,151	5,754	12,651	13,372	573,433	594,154	1,208,515	1,038,854	+ 169,661
Anglican Communion ...	5,644	3,203	4,232	4,433	72,693	78,668	168,873	139,897	+ 28,976
Armenian	15	4	...	...	..	...	19	20	— 1
Baptist	153	148	167	186	70,706	70,502	141,812	119,227	+ 22,585
Calvinist	...	...	...	...	..	...	...	2	— 2
Congregationalist	113	65	107	36	18,887	18,308	37,466	25,658	+ 11,808
Greek	4	1	...	...	1	...	6	9	— 3
Lutheran	382	240	90	43	52,289	52,171	105,215	78,086	+ 27,129
Methodist	380	195	252	303	3,456	3,441	8,027	5,547	+ 2,480
Minor Protestant Denominations.	86	54	12	26	1,661	1,403	3,242	8,459	— 5,217
Presbyterian	409	221	89	112	4,216	4,507	9,554	9,271	+ 283
Protestant (Sect not specified).	356	235	282	289	5,181	4,747	11,040	...	+ 11,040
Quaker	1	1	...	...	...	...	2	...	+ 2
Roman Catholic	1,496	1,327	7,400	7,980	329,709	346,382	694,294	642,863	+ 51,431
Salvationist	11	9	1	5	2,506	2,370	4,902	2,398	+ 2,504
Syrian. Chaldæan	...	...	...	...	2	...	2	...	
Syrian. Jacobite	...	...	...	...	1,725	1,376	3,101	2,098	
Syrian. Reformed	...	...	..	...	209	177	386	...	+ 20,588
Syrian. Romo—	...	...	...	...	9,834	9,714	19,548	...	
Syrian. Unspecified	...	...	...	...	194	150	344	705	
Sect not returned	30	21	13	9	230	211	514	4,578	— 4,064
Indefinite Belief	71	30	6	...	34	27	168	91	+ 77

V.—Distribution of Christians per mille (a) *races by sect and* (b) *sects by race.*

Sect.	Races distributed by sect.				Sects distributed by race.			
	European and allied races.	Anglo-Indian.	Indian.	Total.	European and allied races.	Anglo-Indian.	Indian.	Total.
1	2	3	4	5	6	7	8	9
ALL DENOMINATIONS...	1,000	1,000	1,000	1,000	12	22	966	1,000
Anglican Communion ...	593	333	130	140	53	51	896	1,000
Armenian	1	...	...	...	1,000	...	...	1,000
Baptist	20	12	121	117	2	2	996	1,000
Congregationalist ...	12	6	32	31	5	4	991	1,000
Greek	...	...	...	...	833	...	167	1,000
Lutheran	42	5	90	87	6	1	993	1,060
Methodist	39	21	6	7	72	69	859	1,000
Minor Protestant Denominations	10	1	3	3	43	12	945	1,000
Presbyterian	42	8	7	8	66	21	918	1,000
Protestant (Sect not specified)	40	22	8	9	53	52	895	1,000
Quaker	...	...	...	...	1,000	...	...	1.000
Roman Catholic ...	189	591	579	575	4	22	974	1,000
Salvationist	1	...	4	4	4	1	995	1,000
Syrian... Chaldæan ...	...	...	...	...	...	...	1,000	1,000
Syrian... Jacobite ...	...	...	3	3	...	...	1,000	1,000
Syrian... Reformed ...	...	...	...	...	...	...	1,000	1,000
Syrian... Romo- ...	...	...	17	16	...	...	1,000	1,000
Syrian... Unspecified.	...	...	...	...	...	...	1,000	1,000
Sect, not returned ...	4	1	...	...	99	43	858	1,000
Indefinite Belief ...	7	...	...	...	601	36	363	1,000

VI.—Religion of urban and rural population.

Natural Division.	Number per 10,000 of urban population who are						Number per 10,000 of rural population who are					
	Hindu.	Musalman.	Christian.	Animistic.	Jain.	Others.	Hindu.	Musalman.	Christian.	Animistic.	Jain.	Others.
1	2	3	4	5		7	8	9	10	11	12	13
TOTAL ...	8,101	1,373	492	16	6	3	8,996	565	261	171	7	...
Agency	...	...	...	...	...	...	6,808	30	84	3,078	...	...
East Coast, North ..	8,969	724	238	67	1	1	9,387	262	220	131	...	...
Deccan	7,043	2,730	206	4	16	1	8,922	860	191	24	3	...
East Coast, Central ..	8,295	1,242	442	6	9	6	9,593	236	146	11	14	...
East Coast, South ...	8,244	1.195	557	...	3	1	9,150	368	482	...	...	...
West Coast	5,463	3,051	1,468	1	6	11	7,189	2,496	288	4	23	...

CHAPTER V.—AGE.

Of all chapters, for which custom demands inclusion in a census report, the dealing with the ages of the people is by far the most unsatisfactory from the point of view of the ordinary writer. Even were the ages returned approximately correct as they are in the better educated sections of European populations, their scientific treatment requires a mathematical proficiency not ordinarily possessed save by those whose profession lies in the exercise of such knowledge, and to which I certainly cannot lay the faintest claim. Some crude methods of figure adjustment must necessarily be learned for the general purposes of a census office; but in view of the fact that the age returns of this Province among others will be examined and adjusted by an expert, amateur effort in this direction would be little short of ridiculous.

2. The hopelessness of a literal acceptance of the ages returned at the various Madras enumerations may be seen readily enough from a few concrete examples. There were in 1891 some two and a half million of female toddlers at the ages of 5210. Ten years later, when they should have ranged from 15–20, nearly a million of these little ladies had passed away. But this loss found a sort of compensation, for in 1901 there were respectively some 22,000, and 197,000 more girls at the ages of 20–25, and 25–30, than there had been girls of 10–15, and 15–20, in 1891.

3. These figures show a certain improvement in 1911. Girls aged 0–5 in 1901, who numbered 2,679,818, are represented by 2,318,878 survivors at the ages 10–15; the loss of 361 thousand being less startling and more credible than that of a million just noticed in the previous decade. The same fairly probable rate of decrease is observable at the next age period; of 2,232,108 girls aged 10–15 in 1901, 218,658 have passed away before attaining the period 20–25. But anomalies are not slow in coming; the girls of 15–20 in 1901 have received a mysterious accession to their ranks of 294,150 at the age period 25–30 in 1911; male infants of 0–5 in 1901, clinging to life with teeth and claws, have reached the period 10–15 in 1911 losing but 34,363 of their numbers by the way.* Their brothers aged 10–15 in 1901 seem to have been more loved by the gods, for well nigh eight hundred thousand of them have disappeared from those of 20–25 years in 1911†: but the young men of 15–20 have thriven exceedingly, for on their march through the years they have enlisted 62,256 recruits ‡.

* 1901	...	...	0–5	...	...	2,548,734
1911	...	...	10–15	...	.	2,514,371
† 1901	...	...	10–15	...	...	2,474,166
1911	...	...	20–25	...	...	1,682,335
‡ 1901	...	...	15–20	...	...	1,570,483
1911	...	...	25–30	...	...	1,632,739

4. Such inferences as may be drawn from the figures as they stand are not rendered more reliable by presumption, referred to in paragraph 3, of an increasing intelligence in enumeration, or an increasing accuracy on the part of those enumerated; inasmuch as these tend to a variation from decade to decade in the percentage of error. It is however worth considering whether some attempt may not be made to assign the general causes of error underlying these strange figures.

5. First among such causes is the undoubted tendency of the general Indian to measure time and space by periods in relation to the happenings of every day life, rather than by exact arithmetical standards. In the Ceded districts the expression

Locality.	Number per 10,000 of the population (1911).			
	40-60.		60 and over.	
	Males.	Females.	Males.	Females.
Province	1,725	1,668	568	611
Agency	1,546	1,334	320	362
East Coast (North).	1,679	1,631	613	688
Deccan	1,862	1,731	654	653
East Coast (Central).	1,782	1,678	577	569
East Coast (South)..	1,789	1,793	590	645
West Coast ...	1,478	1,500	400	504

"half age" used of a man implies that he is about 25; it does not imply a general age limit of 50, for proportionately, as may be seen from the marginal figures extracted from subsidiary table II, these people are longlived; but rather that, regarding 50 as the time limit of man's full activity, a man aged 25 has accomplished half of his journey to the commencement of decline. Distance on the West Coast is frequently estimated by the number of paces that limit the approach of an outcast to his holier brother;* hours of the day everywhere by the sun's height above the horizon measured in palmyra trees. A year or two making but little difference either way, the five-year periods stand out in relief against the single intervening years, as do mile stones on a road against the furlong stones which they enclose. Hence we can understand the curious agglomeration at the decennial age periods, and roughly speaking at the middle term of these periods, shown by subsidiary table I.

6. A more specific cause of error can be assigned to the vagaries of female age periods. Whether for the reasons described in a succeeding chapter, or from un-reasoning obedience to custom, the Indian is, or has been, apt to look upon it as a potentiality of social discredit if his daughter remains unprovided with a husband at the earliest moment at which nature permits a possibility of motherhood. At the same time there may be some dim recognition that this mental attitude is not altogether self complimentary, and accordingly, once she is married, the age of the Indian daughter takes a sudden leap forward.

7. This conjecture affords a fairly plausible explanation of the curious figures of 1891 and 1901. Of the girls aged 5–10 in 1891, probably some were a great deal older, but were unmarried. The loss of a million at the age period 15–20, and the impossible increase at the two succeeding periods in 1901, may be due partly to death; but more largely to the fact that on marriage these girls were either placed in their proper age class, or their ages artificially increased.

8. The figures of 1911 regarding these female age periods may then denote, with improving accuracy of enumeration, a great and welcome step forward in the raising of the marriage age in Madras; or else, unfortunately, a wider acceptance of the pernicious custom of infant marriage.

9. Assuming as suggested in paragraph 5 that the Indian, if he does not know his exact age, has yet a fairly clear idea as to his age period,† it is worth while trying to discover what may be these age periods. Giving precedence to males, Ramaswami from 0–5 is a "child" clad in native worth, playing with his fellow urchins in the street. From 5–15 he is in some sense a school boy, whether he sits beneath the ferule of the village dominie, or that of his big brother. From 15–20 he joins the student or apprentice class, and from 20–45 exercises the vigorous functions of a householder. When he admits to 45 and more, it is probable that his sun is westering, and that his thoughts turn in Irish parlance to the "making of his soul."

10. His sister from 0–5 enjoys her childhood; and from 5 to 10 her prospective marriage distracts her parents. From 10–15 she is in a transition between her father's house and that of her mother-in-law; from 15 to 35 or 40 she strongly pounds rice and produces children; and from 40 onwards consecrates herself to religion, and the stern upbringing of her son's wife.

* A remarkable measure of distance in Southern Ireland is "the roar of an ass."

† Dr. Khaja Muhammad Hussain of Banganapalle furnished me with some illustrations confirming this theory. He enquired of some hundreds of patients their ages; although some answers were wildly absurd—a few considered such enquiries impious—yet on the whole most people were found to have a fairly correct idea as to the period of their age. After 45–50 answers became very vague; 50, 60, 70–100 were returned at random.

Men.

Year.	0–5	5–15	15–20	20–45	45 and over.
1911	1,383	2,554	876	3,587	1,650
1901	1,339	2,734	825	3,551	1,551
1891	1,482	2,475	828	3,731	1,484

Women.

Year.	0–5	5–10	10–15	15–35	35 and over.
1911	1,341	1,312	1061	3,444	2,812
1901	1,368	1,406	1,140	3,335	2,751
1891	1,524	1,346	923	3,506	2,701

11. The age position of the Presidency in this respect may be seen from the marginal figures showing the age distribution of 10,000 of each sex throughout the Presidency at the last three enumerations.

12. The age periods here chosen, it will be noted, differ from those exhibited in the subsidiary tables. There the reproductive period for men and women alike is placed at 15–40; I have retained a period of 25 years for men, but have advanced by five years its commencement and its close. The period for women I have decreased by five years, on the basis of information as to the general child-bearing age of Indian women given to me by the Superintendent of the Maternity Hospital, Madras, who has tabulated, as in the margin, the age periods of nearly 6,000 births that came under his notice between 1907 and 1909. Child-birth after 35 is of course not impossible, but Colonel Giffard considers that the majority of births after 30 took place within the limit of 35, and that, as a general standard of reproductive age for the women of Southern India, the period 15–35 is preferable to 15–40.

	Total ..	5,936
15–20	...	880
20–25	...	2,264
25–30	...	1,466
30 and over	...	1,326

13. Subsidiary table VI shows the variation of the population throughout the Presidency and its divisions at certain age periods, and in the notes appended to this table are mentioned sundry abnormal factors which have exercised a disturbing influence on the figures. The effect produced by inter-provincial and inter-district transfers is obviously unreal, but it is interesting to note that even still we have in some degree to reckon with the *sequelae* of the great famine of 1877–78.

14. The direct consequences of severe famine are fairly obvious. It kills the aged and infirm; a result rather beneficial than otherwise to the general health of the community, if consideration of such health be divorced entirely from natural human feeling. At the same time the weakly infant class, which must needs suffer directly, is for a short period even more strongly affected indirectly, owing to temporary loss of reproductive power by those then at the reproductive period of life. This latter loss however finds a compensation in the fact that the survivors of a great famine represent the survival of the fittest, and potentially the most productive; while a rebound or stimulus in the direction of actual productivity appears to be Nature's invariable method of making good her losses.

15. But although we are not yet free from the influences of this famine—they can be seen for example in the gradual increase of the number of both sexes at the ultimate age periods, and in the shortage of adolescents, (boys and girls aged 5–15), in 1891,* which must necessarily affect potentialities of increase twenty years later—the subject has received adequate discussion in previous census reports.

16. Subsidiary table VI analyses the increase of the last two decades into increases at particular age periods. The salient feature of the decade 1891–1901 was an extraordinary increase at the age period 10–15, which may be explained by the supposition that the natality of 1877–78, or survival of infants born at that time, was exceedingly low, and that those aged 14, 13, and 12 in 1891 were correspondingly few. The same cause persists in the contrast of the figures at the period 15–40 for both decades.

* *Vide* paragraph 11 *supra*.

17. Although it speaks well for the years that are past, for those to come it may not be of altogether hopeful augury that the chief increase of this decade has been at the period of old age (60 and over). But to argue that this fact *per se* augurs ill for the immediate future is hardly fair; inasmuch as the absolute number of those at this advanced age is, comparatively speaking, so small that a small absolute variation, when looked at proportionately, can easily assume a disproportionate importance. The number of these aged persons, in proportion to those in the prime of life (15–40), has not risen appreciably since 1901; and it is interesting to note that such increase as has taken place since 1891 is entirely among male section of the population. But subsidiary table V discloses some figures which look unpromising. The proportion of children, (10 and under), to the population aged 15–40, and to the number of married women of this age, is now markedly lower than it was in 1901 or 1891; while the proportion of married women aged 15–40 to the total female population is appreciably higher than in 1901, and only very slightly lower than in 1891.

18. At paragraph 11 were quoted certain figures showing the age distribution of the population in 1891, 1901, and 1911. From these it may be possible to obtain some deductions, which may serve to indicate the tendencies during each decade, and the position and prospects at the end of a twenty-year period, in comparison with the beginning. I put these speculations forward with extreme diffidence, inasmuch as they represent in some sense an excursion into hypothetical regions with which I am entirely unfamiliar.

19. The method by which the figures quoted in the margin have been obtained is sufficiently obvious. It is clear that, whatever may have been the cause, "house holders" and "infants" fared badly during the decade 1891–1901: this is as marked on the female as on male side. Grouping the second and third age periods for each sex respectively we find that these classes fared well; their significant figures being + 256 for males, and + 277 for females, as against — 143 and — 156 in the infant, and — 180 and — 171 in the household classes, for the respective sexes.

Males.

Period.	Infants.	Adolescents.		House holders.	Old people.
	0–5	5–15	15–20	20–45	45 and over.
1891–1901	— 143	+ 259	— 8	— 180	+ 67
1901–1911	— 6	— 180	+ 51	+ 36	+ 99
1911 compared with 1891.	— 149	+ 79	+ 48	— 144	+ 166

Females.

Period.	0–5	5–10	10–15	15–35	35 and over.
1891–1901	— 156	+ 60	+ 217	— 171	+ 50
1901–1911	— 27	— 94	— 49	+ 109	+ 61
1911 compared with 1891.	— 183	— 34	+ 168	— 62	+ 111

20. As to the causes of this phenomenon, we may take into consideration the after effects of 1877–78 famine, which would be strongly marked in the case of women aged 15–35 in 1901; and also the unfavourable nature of the decade 1891–1901, to which allusion has been made in Chapter II. This would have a certain effect on the adult classes, which, although best fitted for survival, have yet to meet the chiefest stress of such a time; and which, in addition to positive casualties, and actual loss of children, suffer as regards the power of reproduction. The classes at 5–20 among males, and 5–15 among females, are over the first weaknesses of infancy, but are still among the ranks of the protected rather than of the protecting. These adolescents, (the term will serve in default of a better), have carried their vitality through the next decade; as we find that in 1911 the householders, (potential fathers and mothers), have changed the number, which indicates their distribution in the total population as compared with 1901, from —180 to + 36 among men, and from—171 to + 109 among women. Their joint efforts appear to be directed

towards an amending of the lamentable infant figure of 1891–1901, for although the position of 1911 is slightly worse than that of 1901, the former year makes a far better showing in regard to the latter than did 1901 when compared with 1891.

21. Decade 1891–1901 showed then a bad position among householders and infants, but great possibilities in its adolescent strength for a speedy repair of this state of things. The ensuing decade did in a large measure actualize these possibilities. It is possible that the characteristics of the first decade will reappear in the decade 1911–21, inasmuch as the decade 1901–11 shows a weakening in adolescents, which may more than counteract the improvement in the infant index that the improved adult position is likely to effect.

22. There are certain further deductions indicated by the subsidiary tables in respect of birth and death rates, causes of death, etc. But practically all such information has been utilized, directly or indirectly, in the chapters dealing with the movement of the population, sex, civil condition, etc., and repetition here is unnecessary.

23. Subsidiary table IV, which shows the age distribution of certain castes, is based on Imperial table XIV, which was compiled for a different purpose, and wherein the population has been taken from a few representative areas, and not over the whole area of the Presidency. It does not appear to present any feature of particular interest. It may be noted that in respect of men in the prime of life the position of the Bráhman sub-divisions is strong, but in point of infants (0–5), both male and female, they compare somewhat unfavourably with other selected castes. A reason for a paucity of girls aged 12–15 has already been suggested; it is curious that among Embrándri Bráhmans the girls at this age considerably outnumber the boys.

I.—Age distribution of 200,000 *of each sex by annual periods. (All religions.)*

Age.	Males.	Females.	Age.	Males.	Females.	Age.	Males.	Females.
1	2	3	1	2	3	1	2	3
TOTAL ...	200,000	200,000						
0	5,195	5,180	37	861	664	74	223	130
1	3,421	4,105	38 ...	1,654	1,307	75	582	395
2	5,847	5,686	39	774	578	76	263	82
3	6,403	6,320	40	9,205	9,217	77	62	25
4	5,562	5,440	41	804	575	78 ...	245	113
5	6,123	6,023	42	1,523	1,305	79	435	74
6	5,526	5,610	43	736	495	80	772	809
7	4,599	4,974	44	801	587	81	48	52
8	5,763	6,557	45	4,664	3,789	82	146	109
9	3,555	3,788	46	1,073	735	83	243	76
10	7,537	7,818	47	539	407	84	198	39
11	2,162	2,350	48	1,153	898	85	273	182
12	7,431	6,455	49	592	402	86	83	64
13	2,633	2,545	50	7,037	8,086	87	75	92
14	3,248	3,235	51	643	347	88	148	34
15	4,232	3,360	52	887	731	89	86	16
16	4,936	4,442	53	501	276	90	250	125
17	1,515	1,658	54	602	630	91	130	27
18	5,083	4,972	55	2,465	2,128	92	34	24
19	1,405	1,851	56	853	590	93	13	25
20	7,784	10,294	57	318	262	94	30	8
21	1,165	1,447	58	636	525	95	22	16
22	3,454	3,601	59	248	209	96	9	3
23	1,421	1,361	60	5,194	6,028	97	1	1
24	2,444	2,332	61	338	341	98	3	1
25	7,388	8,569	62	542	532	99	...	2
26	2,282	2,464	63	290	241	100	5	6
27	1,210	1,357	64	366	252	101	...	1
28	2,500	2,640	65	1,282	1,030	102	...	...
29	804	897	66	313	236	103	...	...
30	10,078	11,946	67	217	165	104	...	...
31	828	866	68	317	262	105	...	...
32	2,387	2,174	69	194	182	106	...	...
33	639	705	70	1,808	2,111	107	...	...
34	1,200	1,083	71	82	109	108	...	1
35	6,179	6,079	72	233	173	109	...	...
36	1,914	1,420	73	71	103	110	1	1

II.—Age distribution of 10,000 *of each sex in the province and each natural division.*

Age.	1911.		1901.		1891.	
	Males.	Females.	Males.	Females.	Males.	Females.
1	2	3	4	5	6	7
Province—						
0–1	285	284	294	297	330	388
1–2	173	177	158	161	171	178
2–3	283	285	280	288	315	327
3–4	309	315	310	322	352	365
4–5	283	280	297	300	314	316
0–5	1,333	1,341	1,339	1,368	1,482	1,524
5–10	1,334	1,312	1,484	1,406	1,391	1,346
10–15	1,220	1,091	1,300	1,140	1,084	923
15–20	876	845	835	757	828	783
20–25	817	947	711	863	820	973
25–30	792	836	755	824	821	865
30–35	745	816	816	891	828	885
35–40	590	533	599	520	592	505
40–45	643	656	670	675	670	661
45–50	410	355	376	320	365	305
50–55	454	468	465	480	427	460
55–60	218	189	190	162	177	157
60–65	295	220				
65–70	94	90	520	594	515	613
70 and over	179	201				
Mean age	25·1	25·3	24·5	24·8	24·6	25·0
Agency—						
0–5	1,321	1,402	1,197	1,346	1,023	1,158
5–10	1,584	1,560	1,539	1,532	1,264	1,254
10–15	1,158	1,023	1,249	1,074	1,023	896
15–20	793	850	814	892	711	768
20–40	3,278	3,469	3,293	3,514	2,618	2,759
40–60	1,546	1,334	1,584	1,289	1,251	1,028
60 and over	320	362	324	353	291	323
Not stated	...	...	...	...	1,824	1,814
East Coast (North)—						
0–5	1,300	1,295	1,318	1,356	1391	1,456
5–10	1,414	1,371	1,445	1,393	1,459	1,396
10–15	1,303	1,131	1,357	1,154	1,246	1,087
15–20	841	806	817	754	820	771
20–40	2,850	3,077	2,829	3,057	2,892	3,088
40–60	1,679	1,631	1,682	1,624	1,612	1,548
60 and over	613	688	552	662	578	706
Not stated	...	...	...	...	2	4
Deccan—						
0–5	1,140	1,209	1,148	1,254	1,380	1,503
5–10	1,243	1,202	1,412	1,483	1,342	1,364
10–15	1,241	1,186	1,371	1,261	826	720
15–20	824	784	705	604	720	662
20–40	3,036	3,135	2,932	3,080	3,455	3,517
40–60	1,862	1,731	1,883	1,698	1,768	1,614
60 and over	654	653	549	620	506	616
Not stated	...	...	...	...	3	4
East Coast (Central)—						
0–5	1,357	1,417	1,381	1,446	1,576	1,644
5–10	1,271	1,300	1,442	1,461	1,354	1,244
10–15	1,200	1,099	1,288	1,155	994	859
15–20	899	852	817	718	809	752
20–40	2,914	3,085	2,815	3,051	3,107	3,281
40–60	1,782	1,678	1,728	1,621	1,656	1,558
60 and over	577	569	529	553	503	561
Not stated	...	...	...	...	1	1
East Coast (South)—						
0–5	1,398	1,345	1,415	1,363	1,519	1,471
5–10	1,326	1,269	1,417	1,344	1,373	1,299
10–15	1,135	989	1,188	1,020	1,044	865
15–20	858	818	837	764	847	775
20–40	2,909	3,141	2,860	3,105	2,968	3,191
40–60	1,789	1,793	1,785	1,769	1,702	1,750
60 and over	590	645	548	685	545	647
Not stated	...	...	...	...	2	2
West Coast—						
0–5	1,388	1,387	1,348	1,322	1,528	1,524
5–10	1,319	1,227	1,412	1,320	1,371	1,268
10–15	1,277	1,156	1,381	1,248	1,228	1,092
15–20	1,018	1,086	964	965	952	972
20–40	3,120	3,240	3,040	3,178	3,080	3,186
40–60	1,478	1,500	1,461	1,469	1,488	1,482
60 and over	400	504	394	503	401	523
Not stated	...	...	...	...	2	2

III.—*Age distribution of* 10,000 *of each sex in each main religion.*

Age.	1911.		1901.		1891.	
	Males.	Females.	Males.	Females.	Males.	Females.
1	2	3	4	5	6	7
Hindu—						
0–5	1,319	1,330	1,330	1,362	1,470	1,515
5–10	1,328	1,302	1,436	1,399	1,379	1,335
10–15	1,216	1,085	1,293	1,132	1,072	911
15–20	874	835	832	746	824	778
20–40	2,944	3,132	2,884	3,097	3,062	3,230
40–60	1,748	1,694	1,720	1,659	1,653	1,596
60 and over	576	622	526	605	519	620
Not stated	...	...	...	...	21	20
Mean age	25·3	25·5	24·6	24·9	24·4	24·8
Musalman—						
0–5	1,461	1,428	1,463	1,428	1,592	1,576
5–10	1,419	1,379	1,510	1,444	1,453	1,380
10–15	1,292	1,157	1,380	1,207	1,151	976
15–20	915	940	857	843	854	851
20–40	2,900	3,087	2,809	3,059	2,972	3,167
40–60	1,502	1,458	1,492	1,473	1,479	1,462
60 and over	511	551	489	546	497	586
Not stated	...	...	...	...	2	2
Mean age	23·7	24·0	23·2	23·7	23·3	23·9
Christian—						
0–5	1,442	1,417	1,429	1,434	1,581	1,591
5–10	1,361	1,358	1,517	1,486	1,470	1,438
10–15	1,244	1,159	1,356	1,230	1,139	1,019
15–20	880	916	843	828	852	858
20–40	2,892	3,079	2,756	2,998	2.983	3,097
40–60	1,622	1,541	1,603	1,513	1,541	1,465
60 and over	559	530	496	511	482	530
Not stated	...	...	...	...	2	2
Mean age	24·5	24·8	23·7	23·7	23·5	23·5
Animistic—						
0–5	1,403	1,483	1,219	1,359	808	915
5–10	1,567	1,535	1,542	1,526	1,074	1,067
10–15	1,126	1,001	1.271	1,125	801	782
15–20	784	925	824	925	532	566
20–40	3,186	3,379	3,190	3,445	1.936	2,021
40–60	1,561	1,314	1,634	1,289	953	775
60 and over	373	363	320	331	224	214
Not stated	..	...	...	...	3,677	3,710
Mean age	23·6	22·9	23·6	22·7	23·1	22·0
Jain—						
0–5	880	1,032	1,007	1,115	1,032	1,119
5–10	893	1,046	1.014	1,076	969	1,063
10–15	1,064	1,050	1,041	1,008	1.046	963
15–20	956	887	887	764	899	830
20–40	3,421	3,122	3,278	3,065	3,378	3,198
40–60	2,039	1,988	2,029	2,054	1,997	1,956
60 and over	727	925	744	908	682	874
Not stated	...	...	...	...	2	2
Mean age	28·8	29·0	28·0	28·4	27·8	28·1

IV.—*Age distribution of* 1,000 *of each sex in certain castes.*

Caste.	Males—Number per mille aged.					Females—Number per mille aged.				
	0–5.	5–12.	12–15.	15–40.	40 and over.	0–5.	5–12.	12–15.	15–40.	40 and over.
1	2	3	4	5	6	7	8	9	10	11
Balija ...	119	168	73	380	260	117	173	60	391	259
Bráhman. Tamil ...	109	152	72	412	255	111	144	59	394	292
Bráhman. Telugu ...	119	189	84	384	224	109	158	55	378	300
Bráhman. Malayálam. Embrándri ...	68	109	53	455	315	116	178	72	398	241
Bráhman. Malayálam. Nambúdri ...	100	140	64	412	284	108	135	59	394	304
Bráhman. Malayálam. Pattar ...	98	92	46	455	314	178	171	57	391	203
Bráhman. Canarese ...	116	167	69	405	243	112	164	56	418	255
Bráhman. Oríyá ...	125	194	81	387	213	128	175	63	378	256
Cheruman ...	148	178	84	411	179	134	158	69	441	198
Chetti ...	182	174	74	383	237	119	157	64	394	266
Dévánga ...	120	170	84	397	229	110	180	55	397	258
Holeya ...	157	212	96	354	181	127	167	71	415	220
Kaikólan ...	189	179	78	379	225	137	184	72	380	227
Kálingi ...	128	190	74	388	220	122	194	60	387	237
Kalinji ...	154	230	92	338	186	184	204	65	384	213
Kammálan ...	135	180	72	386	227	135	176	61	400	228
Kamsala ...	112	188	79	403	218	120	190	56	394	240
Kápu ...	112	194	76	381	237	115	193	61	389	242
Kómati ...	121	171	77	376	255	121	170	70	374	265
Mála ...	147	232	72	350	209	140	198	63	394	205
Paraiyan ...	164	195	69	357	215	162	181	53	404	200
Sále ...	116	198	69	399	223	119	186	68	395	232
Shánán ...	141	187	76	382	214	140	186	66	387	221
Tíyan ...	138	182	81	419	180	135	169	72	438	186
Vellála ...	122	170	77	392	239	128	173	70	390	244

V.—*Proportion of children under* 10 *and of persons over* 60 *to those aged* 15–40; *also of married females aged* 15–40 *per* 100 *females.*

Natural division.	Proportion of children (both sexes) per 100.						Proportion of persons over 60 per 100 aged 15–40.						Number of married females aged 15–40 per 100 females of all ages.		
	Persons aged 15–40.			Married females aged 15–40.			1911.		1901.		1891.				
	1911.	1901.	1891.	1911.	1901.	1891.	Males.	Females.	Males.	Females.	Males.	Females.	1911.	1901.	1891.
1	2	3	4	5	6	7	8	9	10	11	12	13	14	15	16
Province ...	***68***	***73***	***73***	***165***	***179***	***175***	***14·9***	***15·4***	***14·0***	***15·4***	***13·3***	***15·3***	***31·6***	***30·6***	***32·1***
Agency ...	70	66	69	170	161	164	7·9	8·4	7·9	8·0	8·8	9·2	34·6	35·5	29·8
East Coast (North) ...	71	74	75	165	176	179	16·6	17·7	15·1	17·4	15·6	18·3	31·9	30·9	31·6
Deccan ...	68	72	67	161	189	176	16·9	16·6	15·1	16·8	12·1	14·7	30·9	28·5	32·3
East Coast (Central) ...	69	77	74	166	187	177	15·1	14·4	14·6	14·7	12·8	13·9	32·0	30·4	33·1
East Coast (South) ...	69	73	73	162	178	170	15·7	16·3	14·8	16·4	14·3	16·3	31·7	30·7	32·0
West Coast ...	63	66	69	166	177	177	9·7	11·8	9·8	12·1	9·9	12·6	31·2	30·1	31·8

Note.—The figures for previons censuses, on which the above proportions are based, have not been adjusted for changes in area.

VI.—Variation in population at certain age periods.

Natural Division.	Period.	Variation per cent. in population (Increase + Decrease −). All ages.	0–10.	10–15.	15–40.	40–60.	60 and over.
1	2	3	4	5	6	7	8
Province ...	***1901–1911***	+ ***8·4***	+ ***3·9***	+ ***2·7***	+ ***11·8***	+ ***10·2***	+ ***14·7***
	1891–1901	+ ***7·2***	+ ***4·3***	(*d*) + ***31·3***	+ ***3·3***	+ ***11·7***	+ ***6·3***
Agency (*a*)	1901–1911	+ 18·4	+ 23·8	+ 11·1	+ 16·8	+ 18·5	+ 19·3
	1891–1901	+ 2·9	+ 23·0	(*d*) + 24·5	+ 27·9	+ 29·6	+ 13·4
East Coast (North)	1901–1911	+ 9.9	+ 7·3	+ 6·5	+ 11·6	+ 10·0	+ 17·8
	1891–1901	+ 8·7	+ 5·0	(*d*) + 19·4	+ 7·1	+ 13·9	+ 2·8
Deccan (*b*)	1901–1911	− 3·2	− 10·6	− 10·8	+ 2·8	− 2·9	+ 8·2
	1891–1901	+ 5·3	− 0·2	(*d*) + 79·1	− 7·8	+ 11·4	+ 9·5
East Coast (Central)	(*c*) 1901–1911	+ 5·4	− 1·7	− 0·7	+ 10·5	+ 9·0	+ 11·6
	1891–1901	+ 8·9	+ 5·5	(*d*) + 43·7	+ 1·4	+ 13·5	+ 10·8
East Coast (South)	1901–1911	+ 1·5	+ 10·3	+ 10·2	+ 17·0	+ 17·0	+ 19·3
	1891–1901	+ 5·4	+ 8·1	(*d*) + 22·1	+ 2·5	+ 7·0	+ 4·6
West Coast	1901–1911	+ 7·1	+ 4·5	− 0·7	+ 10·6	+ 8·9	+ 8·0
	1891–1901	+ 6·3	+ 0·8	(*d*) + 20·2	+ 5·7	+ 8·5	+ 3·2

Note.—The percentages are based on variations in unadjusted figures for previous censuses. For 1891, persons who have not stated their ages have been omitted in working out percentages for columns 4 to 8 but have been included for column 3.

(*a*) High increase in all age periods between 1901–11 is partly due to inclusion of Nugur in 1911. The high increase between 1891–1901 in Agency Division may be due to exclusion of 'not stated' from 1891 figures.

(*b*) Figures for 1901 include Madanapalle and Váyalpád taluks now transferred to Chittoor.

(*c*) Slight fall in two age periods only is due partly to transfer of Karór and Námakkal from this Division to Trichinopoly

(*d*) Probably due to small number of births during 1877–78 famine.

VII.—Reported birth-rate by Sex and Natural Divisions.

Year.	Number of births per 1,000 of total population. (Census of 1901). Province. Males.	Province. Females.	Agency and East Coast (North). Males.	Agency and East Coast (North). Females.	Deccan. Males.	Deccan. Females.	East Coast (Central). Males.	East Coast (Central). Females.	East Coast (South). Males.	East Coast (South). Females.	West Coast. Males.	West Coast. Females.
1	2	3	4	5	6	7	8	9	10	11	12	13
1901	13·0	12·4	13·1	12·6	12·8	12·3	13·3	12·7	12·9	12·5	11·9	11·3
1902	14·1	13·6	14·9	14·3	13·7	13·4	14·5	13·9	13·4	12·8	13·7	13·2
1903	15·7	15·1	15·8	15·3	15·3	14·8	15·7	15·0	15·1	14·5	17·2	16·3
1904	15·6	15·0	16·2	15·6	14·7	14·3	15·3	14·9	15·4	14·9	15·5	14·9
1905	16·3	15·7	17·0	16·3	14·3	15·9	15·9	15·3	16·1	15·5	18·1	17·4
1906	15·7	15·0	15·5	14·9	15·4	14·8	15·6	14·9	15·1	14·4	17·7	16·9
1907	15·6	14·9	15·5	14·7	15·0	14·6	16·1	15·4	14·8	14·1	17·0	16·1
1908	16·6	15·8	15·4	14·7	16·1	15·4	17·9	17·1	16·5	15·8	16·6	15·7
1909	16·9	16·2	16·2	15·5	15·2	14·8	17·3	16·6	16·5	15·7	19·7	18·8
1910	17·2	16·4	18·0	17·1	15·2	14·6	16·5	15·8	17·0	16·2	19·1	18·2

Note.—(1) The statistics of Europeans and Anglo-Indians are included in this table.

(2) Separate vital statistics relating to "Agency" division are not procurable; as returns are not received from parts of Ganjam and Visagapatam Agencies the population therefor has been excluded in working out proportions.

VIII.—Reported death-rate by sex and natural divisions.

Year.	Number of deaths per 1,000 of the population of each sex. (Census of 1901.)											
	Province.		Agency and East Coast (North.)		Deccan.		East Coast (Central).		East Coast (South).		West Coast.	
	Males.	Females.	Males.	Females.	Males.	Females.	Males.	Females.	Males.	Females.	Males.	Females.
1	2	3	4	5	6	7	8	9	10	11	12	13
1901	22·5	20·8	20·9	18·9	22·8	21·9	25·7	24·4	19·7	18·2	23·7	20·9
1902	20·6	19·2	18·3	16·9	23·0	22·1	22·2	21·3	20·4	18·7	19·9	17·7
1903	23·1	21·8	20·8	19·5	23·7	23·4	24·6	23·8	22·2	20·3	25·6	23·8
1904	23·1	21·6	20·0	18·2	28·5	28·0	25·7	24·6	21·6	19·9	22·3	20·6
1905	22·2	20·7	20·3	18·5	25·8	25·2	22·2	21·1	21·3	19·5	25·3	23·4
1906	28·1	26·3	29·9	28·1	29·8	29·1	26·9	25·6	27·2	24·8	27·1	25·3
1907	24·9	23·3	21·3	19·5	22·2	21·0	24·6	23·4	24·5	22·6	37·2	35·7
1908	27·1	25·2	26·4	24·0	28·3	27·0	25·8	24·2	24·8	22·2	36·6	35·9
1909	22·7	21·0	21·5	19·6	21·6	21·2	23·5	22·2	22·8	20·4	24·3	22·4
1910	25·5	23·9	26·2	24·1	29·8	29·6	23·2	22·3	25·9	23·6	24·9	22·9

Note.—See note to sub-table VII.

IX.—Reported death-rate by sex and age during the decade per mille living at same age according to the Census of 1901.

Age.	Average of decade.		1901.		1902.		1903.		1904.		1905.		1906.		1907.		1908.		1909.		1910.	
	Males.	Females.	Males.	Females.	Males.	Females.	Males.	Females.	Males.	Females.	Males.	Females.	Males.	Females.	Males.	Females.	Males.	Females.	Males.	Females.	Males.	Females.
1	2	3	4	5	6	7	8	9	10	11	12	13	14	15	16	17	18	19	20	21	22	23
All ages	**23·6**	**22·0**	**22·2**	**20·5**	**20·6**	**19·5**	**22·8**	**21·5**	**23·2**	**21·7**	**22·2**	**20·6**	**28·2**	**26·5**	**25·1**	**23·5**	**27·1**	**25·2**	**22·7**	**21·0**	**25·5**	**23·9**
Under 1 year	190·4	165·3	158·0	127·3	169·0	140·9	203·5	169·6	203·2	168·7	200·7	165·9	211·1	177·1	195·1	162·1	217·1	177·8	209·8	170·7	231·4	192·6
1—5	30·7	29·1	27·7	26·1	28·1	26·5	30·1	28·6	26·7	25·4	27·4	25·8	38·8	36·7	33·4	32·0	34·0	32·3	26·8	25·3	33·5	32·0
5—10	9·4	8·9	9·8	8·9	8·8	8·1	9·1	8·8	8·4	8·1	7·4	7·1	13·0	12·3	10·4	9·7	11·5	10·8	7·7	7·2	8·6	8·4
10—15	6·7	6·7	6·9	6·8	5·8	5·8	6·4	6·5	6·4	6·3	5·3	5·4	9·3	9·0	7·2	7·2	8·7	8·4	5·5	5·7	5·9	6·0
15—20	9·7	12·8	9·8	12·2	8·1	10·8	9·0	12·0	9·3	12·0	8·0	11·3	12·3	16·4	10·2	13·3	12·3	15·5	8·5	11·5	9·5	12·7
20—30	11·7	12·1	12·2	11·9	9·9	10·1	10.6	11·5	10·9	11·5	9·8	10·6	14·5	14·8	12·4	13·0	14·3	14·6	10·8	11·2	11·5	11·9
30—40	13·5	12·4	14·4	12·7	11·6	10·5	12·6	11·8	13·2	12·1	11·9	10·9	15·5	14·1	14·2	13·1	16·5	15·3	12·2	11·4	13·0	13·0
40—50	19·5	15·2	20·2	15·6	16·9	13·2	18·4	14·4	19·3	15·1	18·0	13·3	21·6	17·0	20·2	16·1	22·4	18·2	18·0	13·8	19·6	15·5
50—60	31·4	26·3	33·6	28·8	28·5	21·2	30·0	25·8	31·3	26·4	29·1	24·1	34·4	28·8	31·8	26·3	33·6	28·0	29·0	23·6	32·5	27·1
60 and over	71·4	66·7	66·7	62·4	57·4	54·0	66·6	63·4	69·7	66·4	70·3	65·4	82·7	77·6	73·5	68·5	75·2	69·1	70·5	65·0	81·4	75·1

Note.—The statistics of Europeans and Anglo-Indians and those relating to the Native States of Pudukkóttai and Banganapalle are excluded from this table.

X.—*Reported deaths from certain diseases per mille of each sex.*

Year.	Whole province.					Actual number of deaths in									
	Actual number of deaths.			Ratio per mille of each sex.		Agency and East Coast (North).		Deccan.		East Coast (Central).		East Coast (South).		West Coast.	
	Total.	Males.	Females.	Males.	Females.	Males.	Females.	Males.	Females.	Males.	Females.	Males.	Females.	Males.	Females.
1	2	3	4	5	6	7	8	9	10	11	12	13	14	15	16
1901 ...	81,370	42,906	38,464	2 3	2·0	4,486	4,052	6,984	6,046	19,257	16,901	6,793	5,930	5,386	5,535
1902 ...	29,769	15,782	13,987	0·9	0·8	1,184	1,142	3,308	2,710	3,494	3,062	6,920	6,175	876	898
1903 ...	27,393	14,305	13,088	0·8	0·7	751	691	7	7	3,855	3,267	6,782	5,857	2,910	3,266
1904 ...	23,109	12,045	11,064	0·7	0·6	961	837	77	46	5,941	5,357	5,046	4,789	20	35
1905 ...	16,888	8,701	8,187	0·5	0·4	3,126	2,876	1,810	1,506	3,233	3 277	342	344	190	184
1906 ...	142,811	75,047	67,764	4·2	3·7	28,047	26,240	10,311	8,911	16,967	14,757	17,603	15,557	2,119	2,299
1907 ...	81,565	41,359	40,206	2·3	2·2	3,879	3,627	2,335	2,023	10,808	9,717	10,795	9,628	13,542	15,211
1908 ...	141,970	73,684	68,286	4·1	3·7	16,824	14,522	12,075	10,621	16,561	14,118	13,920	11,800	14,304	17,225
1909 ...	39,424	20,847	18,577	1·2	1·0	549	527	2,073	1,780	7,945	6,928	7,974	6,974	2,306	2,368
1910 ...	32,594	17,223	15,371	1·0	0·8	2,661	2,433	828	746	2,141	1,756	11,526	10,401	67	35
1901 ...	26,202	13,425	12,777	0·7	0·7	4,464	4 224	1,166.	1,062	4,494	4,426	1,968	1,897	1,333	1,168
1902 ...	24,967	12,613	12,354	0·7	0·7	1,993	1,826	1,480	1,490	4,174	4,198	1,428	1,503	3,538	3,337
1903 ...	15,015	7,596	7,419	0·4	0·4	1,537	1,643	1,155	1,044	2,983	2,891	1,139	1,032	782	809
1904 ...	9,891	5,137	4,754	0·3	0·3	1,210	1,143	665	550	1,811	1,654	1,198	1,186	253	221
1905 ..	18,540	9,410	9,130	0·5	0·5	1,329	1,254	1,023	989	2,724	2,509	3,516	3,624	818	754
1906 ...	29,840	15,069	14,771	0 8	0·8	1,318	1,248	2,043	1,972	7,425	7,345	3,369	3,330	914	876
1907 ...	22,455	11,251	11,204	0·6	0·6	1,257	1,219	1,166	1,111	6,991	7,039	1,267	1,290	570	545
1908 ...	22.204	11,240	10,964	0·6	0·6	3,423	3,225	1,132	997	4,183	4,123	745	691	1,757	1,928
1909 ...	18,862	9,758	9,104	0·5	0·5	4,508	4,303	779	723	2.456	2,249	1,024	910	991	919
1910 ...	19,198	9,730	9,468	0·5	0·5	2,969	2,941	1,328	1,249	1,764	1,682	1,812	1,875	1,857	1,721
1901 ...	294,854	150,?84	144,070	8·2	7·6	55,890	52,660	20,912	19,675	37,236	37,141	17,536	17,837	19,210	16,757
1902 ...	277,689	141,408	136.281	7·9	7·4	51,538	50,042	18,158	16,807	36,636	35,932	18.562	18,554	16,514	14,946
1903 ...	314,926	159,174	155,752	8·7	8·2	59,228	58,155	18,318	17,622	39,148	38,521	23,203	23,083	19,277	18,371
1904 ...	293,269	149,719	143,550	8·3	7·7	57,321	54,562	17,628	16,590	35,865	34,312	20,478	20,482	18,427	17,604
1905 ...	265,044	135,347	129,697	7·5	7·0	55,770	53,133	15,191	14,270	25.755	24,675	19,941	19,739	18,690	17,880
1906 ...	304,926	153.526	151,400	8·5	8·2	68,252	67,743	15,797	15,179	28,114	27,909	22,592	22,600	18,771	17,969
1907 ...	284,430	145,040	139,390	8 1	7·6	58,182	55,248	14,167	12,830	29 034	28,442	21,719	21,719	21,938	21,097
1908 ...	295,834	150,321	145,513	8·3	7·8	66,437	63,662	15,394	14,598	28,647	28,156	20,576	20,675	19,267	18,422
1909	268,408	136.541	131,867	7·6	7·1	58,201	55,387	15,553	14,990	28,866	28,309	19,686	19,331	14,235	13,850
1910 ...	321,381	162,791	158,590	9·0	8·5	71,505	68.974	24,545	23,235	29,043	29,267	21 652	21,780	16,046	15,334
Diarrhœa. 1901 ...	42,084	22,224	19,860	1·2	1·0	3,121	2,510	1,015	927	9,960	9,043	3,096	2,929	5.032	4,451
1902 ...	36,633	19,034	17,599	1·1	1·0	2,925	2,453	1,268	1,103	8,408	8,187	3,518	3,297	2,915	2,559
1903 ...	49,389	25,497	23,892	1·4	1·3	3,861	3.272	2,258	2,087	10,062	9,633	3,603	3,472	5,713	5,428
1904 ...	48,063	24,516	23,547	1·4	1·3	3,202	2,800	2,922	2,745	11,011	10,745	2,962	2,933	4,419	4,324
1905 ...	51,298	26,257	25,041	1·5	1·3	2,905	2 502	2,778	2,495	11,316	11,137	2,887	2,826	6.371	6,081
1906 ...	61,588	31,595	29,993	1·8	1·6	4,542	4,135	2,468	2,228	13,192	12,551	4,444	4,378	6,949	6,701
1907 ...	60,326	30,975	29,351	1·7	1·6	3,190	3.037	1,919	1,771	11,578	10,831	4,521	4,346	9,767	9,366
1908 ...	60.874	31,159	29,715	1·7	1·6	3,988	3,756	2,285	2,087	11,180	10,763	4,369	4,085	9,337	9,024
1909 ...	48,176	24,755	23,421	1·4	1·3	3,526	2,945	1,974	1,986	9,979	9,662	3,889	3,595	5,387	5,233
1910 ...	58,117	30,008	28,109	1·7	1·5	4,924	4,420	3,163	2,978	11,411	10,955	5,198	4,955	5,312	4,801
1905* ..	5,788	3,070	2,718	0·2	0·1	1	...	2,105	1,855	555	540	2	2	407	321
1906 ...	898	464	434	0·0	0·0	11	14	180	156	127	120	...	...	146	144
1907 ...	2,872	1,529	1,343	0·1	0·1	...	...	854	770	517	475	3	...	155	98
1908 ...	3,358	1,689	1,669	0·1	0·1	...	...	395	370	805	833	1	...	488	466
1909 ...	3,844	1,964	1,880	0·1	0·1	...	...	13	10	1,648	1,657	8	3	300	210
1910 ...	4,867	2,390	2,477	0·1	0·1	4	...	80	55	1,793	1,836	397	460	116	126

* Accurate details by sexes and districts are not available previous to 1905; the number of attacks in 1901 is 3,960; deaths in 1902, 10,795; 3, 13,291; 1,904, 20,125. See footnote to the previous subsidiary table.

CHAPTER VI.—SEX.

ONE of the most interesting results obtained by the census is the knowledge of the proportion of the sexes (*a*) in India, (*b*) in the Presidency, (*c*) in each district of the Presidency. With India I am not concerned, save in so far as to remark that the ratio of the last census (953 per thousand) is the opposite to that prevailing in Europe, where, with the exception of the south-eastern corner, the women, according to the latest information available, are found to outnumber the men.

Country.	Year of census.	Number of females per 1,000 males.
England and Wales	1911	1,068
Scotland	1911	1,068
Ireland	1911	1,004
Holland	1909	1,015
German Empire	1910	1,026
Denmark	1911	1,061
Sweden	1910	1,046
Bulgaria	1905	962
Servia	1900	946
Roumania	1899	968

2. In the Madras Presidency, taken as a whole, the facts ascertained at the census of 1911 correspond to European experience; the ratio of females to males being 1032 : 1000. From subsidiary table I, it may be seen that in point both of "actual" and "natural" population this general proportion has been found to exist at the last three decennial enumerations, and the disparity in the former case appears to increase steadily if slowly as the years go by.

3. A recent statistical writer in England finds in the preponderance of women a sufficient reason for the diversion of their domestic energies towards a pressing of their claim to political recognition. Such happening is hardly as yet within the range of practical politics in Southern India, nor need our rest be disturbed by an attempt to forecast the ultimate practical result of this sex tendency.

4. At the last census the Presidency was divided into 32 territorial units. Strictly speaking Madras, including its capital, comprises 25 "districts;" but for the purposes of the census it is customary to include the States of Pudukkóttai, Banganapalle and Sandúr; and to treat separately the Agency tracts of Ganjám, Vizagapatam, and Gódávari, and little enclave of Anjengo.

5. In fourteen of these units females were found to be in defect. From this number we may exclude for present purposes the three Agency tracts, because of the probability of faulty enumeration to which attention is drawn in Chapters I and II; Madras City, because of the generally observed tendency towards a larger male population in the large cities of India; the Nilgiris, mainly because of a large immigration of male labourers to coffee and tea estates. But the figures of this district deserve some further remark, in view of the fact that the defect of women is much more strongly marked in the actual than in the natural population; while among the persons born in the Nilgiris, and there enumerated (table XI), the sex proportions are practically equal. The explanation, which local knowledge confirms, may be found in the fact that the district holds, in addition to its imported plantation labourers, a large proportion of immigrants for various other purposes, (only 670 per 1,000 of the actual population were born in the Nilgiris), to whom the climate is on the whole uncongenial, and who find it as difficult to keep their womenkind on the hills as Europeans do to keep them on the plains. Among the Badagas, characteristically the people of the district, women outnumber men, as they do among Indian Christians, who may in general be assumed to be natives of the locality where they are found.

6. Despite the evidence of table VI and subsidiary table I to this chapter, I should be inclined to add Sandúr to this list. There is no apparent reason for a sudden and marked change in the actual female population, and the variation between actual and natural population, which the figures imply, is too great to be easily credible. As exemplified in the case of Banganapalle at the census of 1901,

the return of birth-place in these tiny states lying within the confines of one British district is one of very doubtful reliability; and the purely arbitrary nature of the frontier renders a variation of the actual population, in reality small when the smallness of the total figures is considered, largely a matter of chance.

District.	Women per 1,000 men in actual population in 1911.
Guntúr	982
Nellore	996
Cuddapah	969
Kurnool	934
Bellary	975
Anantapur	949
Chingleput	993
Chittoor	988

7. However this may be we are left with eight considerable units, (I exclude Banganapalle both on account of its size, and of its practical homogeneity with Kurnool), where actual (and natural) sex proportion differs from that of Madras in general. Or in other words while the excess of females in the Presidency is 658,144, the defect in these districts is 102,795.

8. European statistics, presumably reliable, appear to show an excess of males at birth, with a reversal of the ratio in later years. The vital statistics for the Presidency, set forth in subsidiary table V, show that, so far as births are concerned, the sex ratio tallies with that of Europe. At the age periods 0–5, and 5–10, girls outnumber boys; but at the periods 10–15 and 15–20 the proportion undergoes a change, the male sex, especially at the earlier period, being in excess. From 20 to 35 females again preponderate. From 35 onwards the pendulum oscillates according to quinquennial periods, a result probably due to as much to the haphazard inaccuracy of particular age returns as anything else; but in the result there is a female preponderance of 39,103.

9. It is worth while examining these figures in connection with three main religions of the Presidency. As to the number of births among the followers of each religion information is not procurable; but, as the result of the census, all save Animism show a preponderance of females over males. At the age period 0–5 among Hindus, Muhammadans, and Christians, girls are in the majority, as they are among the first and third at 5–10, when among Muhammadans the sexes are practically equal. At 10–15 males are in excess, as they are at 15–20 among Hindus, though not among Muhammadans and Christians. From 20–25 the sex proportion in each religion tallies with that of the Presidency: from 35 onwards women are in excess among Hindus, in a minority among Muhammadans and Christians. The curious quinquennial variation already noticed is exactly the same among Hindu anb Muhammadan as in the general population, but among Christians there is a steady preponderance of men from 55 onwards.

10. The accuracy of the Indian sex returns has been challenged by continental statisticians, on the grounds that the general defect of women is due to the reluctance of the people to disclose even the existence of their womenkind. The foregoing figures show that this argument fails to touch Madras as a whole, or any considerable section of the people living therein; unless, from an observed increase in the proportion of women to men at succeeding enumerations, we conclude that the *real* number of females in the Presidency is vastly greater than that of men; a hypothesis which fails to explain local *decrease* observable in many instances. Men indeed predominate among the "Animists," and some smaller religious communities, but these people are too few in number to warrant the drawing of any general conclusion from facts observed in their particular case. Moreover the exceeding vagueness of the term "Animist," coupled with local difficulties of enumeration, renders it probable that such error, as in this case occurs, may be that of the enumerator quite as much as of those enumerated.

11. There may be a probability of error in respect to the return of girls at the nubile age, especially if such girls be unmarried. But such error is far more likely to be caused by mis-statement of age than by absolute concealment of existence. Such concealment is indeed improbable, when it is remembered that seclusion of women, other than Muhammadan or Oriyá, is comparatively rare in the Presidency, and that, while in most districts the ascertained number of Muhammadans is too small to affect appreciably the general figures, in Malabar and South Canara, which

return by far the highest percentage of Muhammadans, women preponderate, as they do in the general Muhammadan community, and among the Oriyá castes.

12. In respect to the existence of girls at the age period 10–15 a few figures may be given. They show that such constitute more than one-tenth of the total female population: their number is smallest exactly at the point at which such a return might be expected, namely in the Hindu community. Misstatement of age at this period, at least among Hindus, becomes more apparent when the proportion of unmarried girls at the age of 10–15 to the total number of girls at this age is considered, with reference to the general population of the Presidency, and to the three main religions.

Number of girls aged 10–15 per 1,000 of female population.

Total	109
Hindus	108
Muhammadans	116
Christians	116

Number of girls unmarried at 10–15 per 1,000 girls at this age.

Total	740
Hindus	723
Muhammadans	855
Christians	915

13. Subsidiary tables V and VI disclose nothing calculated to render unwarrantable the assumption that an excess of females over males is the normal condition of the Presidency. They show that male births are more numerous than female—a fact of which the accordance with general experience discounts neglect or unwillingness to register female births; the comparative equality of deaths at the age period 1–5 is due in all probability to the greater solicitude shown for boys, whose deaths at this age should outnumber those of girls; the ominous preponderance of female mortality between 15 and 30 is eloquent of the risks of Indian motherhood. That at the ultimate age period female deaths should exceed male, appears a necessary consequence of the considerable preponderance of women at this age shown by subsidiary table II.

14. To explain the general defect of women in India the existence of certain conditions, tending to produce a high female mortality, has been suggested. Among such conditions may be—

(*a*) Neglect of female infants, for whom the procuring of a husband would be an occasion of expense;

(*b*) Infant marriage, involving premature sexual intercourse and child-bearing;

(*c*) A high birth-rate, combined with unskilful midwifery;

(*d*) Confinement and semi-starvation of women at puberty, during their menstrual periods, and after child-birth.

15. But as applicable only to a particular area within the Presidency these explanations scarcely hold good; inasmuch as there is no reason to suppose that such customs exist in greater force in the eight districts concerned than elsewhere. At the same time a few figures illustrating the prevalence of immature marriage in these districts and elsewhere may be given.

16. The figures in the margin contrast the number of women married at the ages 0–15 with the total female population. Those widowed at these ages have been excluded, because presumably they are not subjected to the disturbing influences mentioned in paragraph 14 (*b*).

Number of females among whom one under 15 is married.

Guntúr	19
Nellore	32
Cuddapah	28
Kurnool	21
Bellary	19
Anantapur	24
Chingleput	37
Chittoor	33

17. In contrast with certain districts where women outnumber men these figures appear illuminative: in Malabar but one woman out of 81 is a married woman of this tender age; in Madura one of 87, in Tanjore one of 62, in South Arcot one of 38. But the explanation fails, when we notice that in Ganjám, where the proportion of women to men is highest, one woman out of every 10 is a married woman aged between 0 and 15; in Vizagapatam the proportion is even higher, being one out of 9; in Gódávari it is one out of 15; in Kistna, one out of 17.

18. A further caution is necessary. If the deficiency of females is attributable to any one or all of the causes noted in paragraph 14, it is hardly reasonable to

suppose that such causes persist with equal force in all sections of the people irrespective of race, creed or education. We might expect a surplus of females in some sections counterbalanced by a marked deficiency in others.

19. Assuming that, in the case of Hindus, difference of mother-tongue is equivalent to difference of race in Southern India, it will be of interest to note the sex proportions, according to linguistic division, in these districts and some others.

District.	Tamil.		Telugu.		Oriyá.		Canarese.	
	Males.	Females.	Males.	Females.	Males.	Females.	Males.	Females.
Guntúr	15,470	15,238	702,434	692,155	...	...	3,732	3,652
Nellore	19,689	20,272	570,911	569,610	...	...	4.292	4,389
Cuddapah	4,175	4,525	378,339	367,008	...	...	2,968	2,944
Kurnool	5,065	5,254	357,609	354,662	...	...	17,296	15,934
Bellary	9,186	10,265	251,499	242,140	...	...	167,095	166,211
Anantapur	8,836	7,983	390,362	371,474	...	...	42,068	39,780
Chingleput	553,741	549,693	110,359	110,338	...	...	...	...
Chittoor	79,518	79,925	492,913	475,628	...	...	13,547	13,923
North Arcot	715,458	726,923	154,529	157,709	...	...	14,870	15,481
Salem	635,579	651.790	170,474	167,895	...	...	28,330	28,181
Coimbatore	686,484	706,126	237,321	242,985	...	...	83,957	87,114
Ganjám	21.858	32,755	397,530	465,922	394,830	448,352	2,216	2,036
Vizagapatam	11,202	12,163	960,962	1,025,333	35,128	37,530	4,907	4,915
Gódávari	26,048	30,608	647,775	672.715	2,661	2,926	2,887	2,752

20. From these figures it can be seen that in all eight districts Telugu males outnumber Telugu females, as they do in the "normal" district of Salem. But the inference that male predominance is characteristic of the Telugus is scarcely borne out by observation of such figures as those for North Arcot, Ganjám, Vizagapatam, and Gódávari; and of the fact that the Canarese men of Bellary and Anantapur likewise outnumber the women; while a reversal of the proportion is found in the considerable Canarese population of Coimbatore.

21. But *Race* in Southern India is complicated by considerations of caste and religion as well as by those of language. Accordingly, assuming that the Hindus of Chingleput are represented by Tamils, and those of the other districts by Telugus, I have tabulated the sex proportions for each section of the people that contributed approximately 10,000 of either sex to the sum total. Inasmuch as the statement is rather unwieldy I have placed it at the back of the subsidiary tables appended to this chapter (appendix I).

22. These figures do not seem to furnish us with any solution of the problem. Male predominance is, on the whole, fairly well marked throughout all *strata* of the population; while the total numbers show that the sections dealt with are tolerably representative of the district population. It is worthy of note that omission of Canarese-speaking Hindus from the population of Bellary has considerably accentuated the deficiency of females, and that Chingleput, the one Tamil district, shows a proportionately greater number of castes wherein females outnumber males.

23. Lastly, if we take as fairly typical the districts of Chingleput, Kurnool, and Guntúr, Provincial table II gives us the proportion of the sexes in the main religious communities in each taluk of these districts, and the figures are available for the drawing of such conclusions as may suggest themselves to the ingenious reader.

24. An intolerable deal of sack to a very scanty morsel of bread represents so far, I fear, the treatment of this question. Yet the foregoing remarks may serve some useful purpose if they indicate that explanation is to be found not in the social customs or racial peculiarities of the people, but rather in the conditions of the locality in which they reside.

25. For reasons mentioned elsewhere it must be admitted that emigration returns are of little value in regard to such comparatively small areas as districts. Indeed so difficult did it prove to ascertain accurately the birth districts of Madrasis enumerated outside the Presidency that the "natural population" of districts, shown in subsidiary table I, was at first calculated solely with reference to migration within the Presidency. It may, however, be taken for granted that emigration is a factor of very small importance in at least five of these eight districts, namely Kurnool, Cuddapah, Anantapur, Bellary, and Chittoor. They are landlocked, and the idea of crossing the sea is not likely to reach, or, if it reaches, to appeal to the adventurous youth of these parts. Guntúr, Nellore, and Chingleput have a certain number of their taluks on the sea board, but possess no central ports of embarkation. And when all allowance has been made for the fact that the emigrant is usually accredited to the district wherein he embarks, it is a matter of fairly common knowledge that there is no movement from these districts comparable to the outflow, (chiefly of men), from Ganjám to Burma, from Tanjore to the Straits, from Tinnevelly and Madura to Ceylon.

26. In the fact that these eight districts very largely coincide with the "famine zone" of the Presidency, the true explanation will, I believe, be found. It is, I am aware, a generally accepted theory that women are less susceptible than men to the effects of famine; the observable mortality due directly to this cause may be smaller among them than amongst men, but, as to their greater power of resistance to privation generally, I think that there are grounds for doubt. A woman doubtless needs less food than a man, when both can get enough; but, when both are on the verge of starvation, the advantage in staying power is probably on the side of the man. If both are in receipt of non-gratuitous famine relief, the woman's task is lighter than the man's; but when both are endeavouring unaided to last through a bad time, the man has rest, for there is practically nothing for him to do; the woman cannot, (and will not), escape from the care of children, the cooking of such little food as may be procurable, and other household duties.

27. Belief in this explanation is strengthened by observation of certain changes in sex ratio. At the census of 1901 the men of Kistna outnumbered the women in the ratio of 1000 : 976. With the formation of the new Guntúr district the sex ratio changed, women now standing to men in Kistna as 1008 : 1000; the district redistribution taking away from Kistna the barren taluks of Narasaraopet, Sattenapalle, Palnád and Vinukonda.

28. Again in 1901 North Arcot was a "female" district with 1,006 women to every 1,000 men; but in this district the female predominance was entirely among the Tamils; in the Telugu section, which in point of absolute numbers was almost equal to the Tamil, men predominated. This difference was due, I believe, not to any racial peculiarity, but to the fact that the then Telugu portion of North Arcot was extremely liable to famine; it has now been absorbed in the new district of Chittoor where, as already seen, men are in excess.

29. Facts never run exactly as one would wish them to do, and it must be admitted that facts, on which this argument is based, do not afford an exception to the rule. Certain taluks of the new Kistna district such as Bezwáda, Divi and Gudiváda, which cannot be regarded as famine zones, still show a male preponderance; in Guntúr men still exceed women in Bápatla taluk, and are outnumbered by them in Palnád; in Kurnool the Nandyál and Nandikótkúr taluks with a certain extent of irrigation are comparatively prosperous; in the first the numbers of men and women are equal, in the second men outnumber women; in Kurnool taluk men predominate, while in Sirvel and Cumbum women are in the majority.

30. But these eight districts have received perhaps more than their proper share of attention : to some points of more general interest allusion may be made before the chapter closes.

31. Subsidiary table IV, which shows the number of females per 1,000 males for certain selected castes, is an obviously unsatisfactory production. It is founded on the absolute figures of Imperial table XIV, which deals with the civil condition of these castes ; and, as these figures were taken only from certain selected districts, their utilization for a different purpose does not fairly represent conditions existing throughout the entire Presidency. As a supplement I have prepared subsidiary table IV (*a*) founded on Imperial table XIII, which gives a more just view of sex ratio according to caste, tribe, and creed. The table is its own explanation, and affords support to the theory that preponderance of females is the natural condition of the Presidency ; its figures may be examined in comparison with those of appendix I, in order to ascertain how far an excess or deficiency of females noticed in particular castes (*e.g.* Kómatis, Kápus, Mádigas) in particular districts represents or misrepresents general conditions.

32. Subsidiary table III exhibits sex proportion in the different natural divisions and religions in accordance with age periods. Its most interesting features are the confirmation it affords of the theory as to misstatement of female age at the period 10–15, and the curious local variations already noted, which are to be found in the more general proportions. The comparatively large proportion of women aged 15–30 in comparison with the number of the opposite sex at the same age would seem to be an effort of nature to make good the heavy female mortality at these ages noticed in subsidiary table VI.

1.—General proportions of the sexes by natural divisions and districts.

District and Natural Division.	Number of females to 1,000 males in					
	Actual population.			Natural population.		
	1911.	1901.	1891.	1911.	1901.	1891.
1	2	3	4	5	6	
Province ...	***1,032***	***1,029***	***1,023***	***1,017***	***1,029***	***1,025***
Agency ...	***993***	***969***	***950***	...	...	...
Agency, Ganjám ...	994	976	935	...	...	...
" Vizagapatam ...	996	965	958	...	...	...
" Gódávari ...	980	974	966	...	...	...
East Coast (North) ...	***1,043***	***1,031***	***1,018***	***1,027***	***1,023***	***1,011***
Ganjám ...	1,126	1,118	1,079	1,104	1,089	1,058
Vizagapatam ...	1,042	1,047	1,023	1,032	1,024	1,010
Gódávari ...	1,035	1,041	1,028	1,016	1,036	1,026
Kistna ...	1,008	1,005	1,002	1,012	980	983
Guntúr ...	982	980	982	988	...	..
Nellore ...	996	988	985	983	981	982
Deccan ...	***969***	***969***	***966***	***967***	***966***	***965***
Cuddapah ...	969	976	974	965	972	966
Kurnool ...	984	979	975	985	973	974
Banganapalle ...	989	988	969	858	982	969
Bellary ...	975	970	962	976	977	971
Sandúr ...	1,015	979	991	912	868	889
Anantapur ...	949	951	952	949	946	948
East Coast (Central) ...	***1,007***	***1,010***	***1,010***	***1,004***	***1,014***	***1,014***
Madras ...	946	984	1,004	967	1,085	1,050
Chingleput ...	998	984	988	990	980	981
Chittoor ...	968	974	966	965	...	...
North Arcot ...	1,021	1,028	1,014	1,004	999	990
Salem ...	1,015	1,024	1,034	1,012	1,029	1,037
Coimbatore ...	1,027	1,030	1.040	1,022	1,032	1,039
South Arcot ...	1,014	1,014	1,006	1,017	1,013	1,007
East Coast (South) ...	***1,077***	***1,060***	***1,076***	***1,061***	***1,061***	***1,076***
Tanjore ...	1,104	1,105	1,090	1,090	1,105	1,093
Trichinopoly ...	1,060	1,065	1,068	1,047	1,063	1,068
Pudukkóttai ...	1,095	1,104	1,097	1,060	1,076	1,063
Madura ...	1,043	1,046	1,048	1,025	1,092	1,088
Rámnád ...	1,109	1,118	1,111	1,111	...	...
Tinnevelly ...	1,069	1,068	1,057	1,036	1,056	1,050
West Coast ...	***1,038***	***1,030***	***1,024***	***1,019***	***1,038***	***1,034***
Nilgiris ...	868	840	778	925	966	965
Malabar ...	1,034	1,024	1,018	1,020	1,026	1,020
Anjengo ...	1,071	1,102	1,113	1,048	...	...
South Canara ...	1,068	1,069	1,067	1,022	1.076	1,075

Note.—(1) The proportions in columns 2 to 4 are worked out for population adjusted to the present area of each district; but in columns 5 to 7 they are for districts as they stood at the time of each census.

(2) The figures in columns 6 and 7 are based on the female population born in and enumerated in this Presidency only. Those in column 5 include women born in Madras Presidency but enumerated outside its limits also so far as their number could be ascertained.

II.—Number of females per 1,000 males at different age periods by religions at each of the last three censuses.

Age.	All Religions.			Hindu.			Musalman.			Christian.			Animistic.			Jain.		
	1911.	1901.	1891.	1911.	1901.	1891.	1911.	1901.	1891.	1911.	1901.	1891.	1911.	1901.	1891.	1911.	1901.	1891.
1	2	3	4	5	6	7	8	9	10	11	12	13	14	15	16	17	18	19
Total all ages (actual population).	1,032	1,029	1,023	1,033	1,029	1,024	1,029	1,032	1,026	1,030	1,033	1,027	989	969	932	906	940	941
0-1	1,027	1,041	1,048	1,029	1,043	1,049	1,002	1,013	1,036	1,010	1,036	1,038	1,046	1,064	1,059	1,070	1,010	945
1-2	1,055	1,051	1,065	1,060	1,054	1,069	1,026	1,009	1,030	1,011	1,059	1,050	1,037	1,062	988	1,112	969	1,096
2-3	1,039	1,058	1,063	1,043	1,063	1,068	1,003	1,005	1,012	1,012	1,018	1,039	1,057	1,088	1,060	1,040	1,104	962
3-4	1,054	1,067	1,061	1,057	1,070	1,064	1,014	1,024	1,011	1,044	1,050	1,034	1,062	1,098	1,121	971	1,032	1,148
4-5	1,022	1.040	1,029	1,026	1.043	1,032	987	986	995	980	1,027	1,009	1,028	1,084	1,042	1,146	1,077	1,014
Total 0-5 ...	1,038	1,051	1,052	1,042	1,055	1,055	1,005	1,007	1,016	1,012	1,036	1,033	1,046	1,082	1,062	1,063	1,040	1,021
Total 0-30 ...	1,032	1,027	1,021	1,031	1,027	1,021	1,029	1.028	1,020	1.050	1,043	1,035	1,035	1,023	968	904	925	944
5-10	1,015	1,008	990	1,017	1,011	991	1,000	988	974	1,029	1,012	1,004	969	959	926	1,062	997	1,032
10-15	922	902	871	922	902	870	921	902	870	960	937	918	879	857	852	875	905	866
15-20	996	944	967	986	934	960	1,057	1,014	1,024	1,072	1,017	1,035	1,167	1,089	992	794	810	869
20-25	1,197	1,248	1,214	1,196	1,245	1,214	1,183	1,272	1,232	1,218	1,262	1,199	1,293	1,284	1,153	851	905	948
25-30	1,088	1,120	1,077	1,089	1,120	1,077	1,101	1,156	1,104	1,105	1,139	1,098	996	1,005	903	795	867	920
Total 30 and over.	1,032	1,030	1,027	1,036	1,033	1,031	1,028	1,040	1,038	993	1,014	1,009	902	872	848	909	961	936
30-40	1,043	1,025	1,003	1,047	1,027	1,004	1,030	1,022	1,001	1,017	1,042	1,005	959	956	928	829	883	839
40-50	991	978	956	994	981	955	998	1,014	997	987	978	949	814	744	759	811	898	920
50-60	1,009	1,009	1,045	1,012	1,012	1,049	999	1,027	1,042	968	972	1,028	872	811	756	989	1,031	922
60 and over ...	1,109	1,176	1,218	1,115	1,183	1,223	1,110	1,152	1,209	973	1,066	1,013	961	1,002	892	1,152	1,141	1,205
Not stated ...	...	...	949	...	.	970	...	...	1,162	...	...	...	...	...	941	...	...	1,000

III.—*Number of females per 1,000 males at different age-periods by religions and natural divisions. (Census of 1911.)*

Age.	Agency.				East Coast (North).				Deccan.				East Coast (Central).				East Coast (South).				West Coast.			
	All religions.	Hindu.	Musalman.	Christian.	All religions.	Hindu.	Musalman.	Christian.	All religions.	Hindu.	Musalman.	Christian.	All religions.	Hindu.	Musalman.	Christian.	All religions.	Hindu.	Musalman.	Christian.	All religions.	Hindu.	Musalman.	Christian.
1	2	3	4	5	6	7	8	9	10	11	12	13	14	15	16	17	18	19	20	21	22	23	24	25
Total all Ages (Actual population).	***993***	***994***	***966***	***978***	***1,043***	***1,048***	***981***	***974***	***969***	***972***	***954***	***960***	***1,007***	***1,008***	***965***	***1,021***	***1,077***	***1,069***	***1,239***	***1,080***	***1,038***	***1,054***	***1,000***	***1,012***
Total 0–5 ...	***1,054***	***1,059***	***1,131***	***1,084***	***1,039***	***1,040***	***1,000***	***1,069***	***1,028***	***1,029***	***1,035***	***937***	***1,051***	***1,053***	***1,019***	***1,021***	***1,040***	***1,044***	***1,022***	***1,003***	***999***	***1,006***	***985***	***981***
0–1	1,023	1,018	1,200	867	1,025	1,024	1,015	1,079	1,020	1,022	1,026	924	1,041	1,042	1,042	981	1,024	1,027	995	998	1,010	1,020	981	1,029
1–2	1,040	1,038	2,143	1,179	1,056	1,059	1,010	1,063	1,014	1,007	1,104	769	1,061	1,065	1,008	1,017	1,088	1,094	1,062	1,032	999	997	1,006	972
2–3	1,064	1,058	1,185	1,116	1,036	1,036	1,005	1,094	1,018	1,015	1,096	880	1,057	1,061	986	1,056	1,041	1,045	1,023	982	1,001	1,004	996	996
3–4	1,085	1,100	1,397	1,190	1,066	1,067	994	1,093	1,046	1,049	1,028	1,052	1,068	1,069	1,061	1,055	1,041	1,041	1,035	1,045	1,001	1,013	983	938
4–5	1,047	1,064	675	1,126	1,020	1,021	983	1,018	1,036	1,087	1,032	981	1,030	1,032	997	992	1,021	1,025	1,003	960	984	995	963	961
Total 0–30 ...	***1,030***	***1,032***	***964***	***1,029***	***1,034***	***1,034***	***1,003***	***1,025***	***988***	***980***	***972***	***1,019***	***1,022***	***1,022***	***1,012***	***1,062***	***1,061***	***1,054***	***1,181***	***1,107***	***1,026***	***1,035***	***1,002***	***1,030***
5–10	978	983	1,027	1,059	1,012	1,012	1,015	1,016	1,015	1,018	1,024	1,094	1,029	1,029	1,035	1,035	1,031	1,030	1,036	1,042	965	968	955	975
10–15	877	878	785	815	906	906	908	909	926	933	876	928	923	923	905	1,031	939	931	1,041	675	939	949	916	1,024
15–20	1,064	1,020	1,350	1,080	1,000	997	987	1,027	922	921	908	1,059	954	950	990	1,083	1,028	1,007	1,392	1,098	1,057	1,066	1,033	1,048
20–25	1,308	1,320	1,013	1,431	1,272	1,275	1,158	1,260	1,085	1,087	1,074	1,078	1,145	1,147	1,098	1,148	1,240	1,219	1,583	1,333	1,163	1,179	1,138	1,051
25–30	1,028	1,050	698	917	1,075	1,081	995	989	926	933	874	923	1,062	1,063	1,059	1,036	1,194	1,179	1,478	1,234	1,110	1,119	1,089	1,085
Total 30 and over ...	***922***	***923***	***968***	***849***	***1,060***	***1,071***	***942***	***870***	***938***	***942***	***922***	***890***	***981***	***982***	***935***	***986***	***1,104***	***1,094***	***1,355***	***1,076***	***1,063***	***1,090***	***996***	***997***
30–40	946	988	941	769	1,068	1,077	960	925	978	982	951	982	1,020	1,020	1,010	1,030	1,104	1,094	1,339	1,088	1,003	1,020	961	966
40–50	824	823	845	974	1,006	1,016	893	848	915	913	926	964	952	954	887	991	1,066	1,056	1,309	1,065	1,025	1,046	978	966
50–60	929	934	1,025	1,112	1,025	1,087	910	831	881	886	875	766	941	944	862	938	1,099	1,090	1,360	1,067	1,102	1,144	989	1,012
60 and over	1,124	1,162	1,397	658	1,170	1,169	1,008	832	967	980	914	766	993	996	938	927	1,177	1,168	1,468	1,077	1,306	1,357	1,180	1,132

IV.—Number of females per 1,000 *males for certain selected castes.*

Caste.	Number of females per 1,000 males.						
	All ages.	0–5.	5–12.	12–15.	15–20.	20–40.	40 and over.
1	2	3	4	5	6	7	8
Balija	1,004	992	1,036	824	942	1,058	1,001
Bráhman. Tamil	982	995	931	802	908	952	1,123
Bráhman. Telugu	994	916	832	656	863	1,024	1,328
Bráhman. Malayálam. Embrándri	612	1,047	971	821	583	522	470
Bráhman. Malayálam. Nambúdri	966	1,037	981	892	1,053	895	1,031
Bráhman. Malayálam. Pattar	623	1,201	1,155	770	767	485	402
Bráhman. Canarese	1,026	983	1,011	833	1,048	1,046	1,077
Bráhman. Oriyá	1,071	1,095	966	832	970	1,073	1,284
Cheruman	1,105	1,007	980	906	1,192	1,184	1,220
Chetti	1,132	1,026	1,018	977	1,022	1,210	1,272
Dévánga	1,001	923	1,059	649	912	1,024	1,129
Holeya	1,312	1,058	1,031	980	1,328	1,610	1,598
Kaikólan	1,087	1,022	1,066	957	990	1,054	1,047
Kalingi	1,097	1,048	1,122	888	926	1,150	1,181
Kalinji	1,238	1,060	1,096	874	1,249	1,451	1,424
Kammálan	1,071	1,078	1,041	903	1,057	1,126	1,076
Kamsala	1,028	1,104	1,039	726	928	1,081	1,131
Kápu	1,034	1,056	1,028	837	887	1,109	1,056
Kómati	1,033	1,038	1,022	941	1,041	1,022	1,074
Mála	1,027	980	917	894	1,179	1,150	1,006
Paraiyan	1,057	1,044	982	815	1,090	1,220	965
Sálé	1.018	1,041	978	1,003	1,095	981	1,063
Shánán	1,042	1,032	1,038	915	911	1,098	1,079
Tíyan	1,029	1,000	957	923	1,088	1,071	1,061
Vellála	1,017	1,028	1,023	926	858	1.065	1,084

IV (a).—Number of females to 1,000 males for certain castes (Imperial table XIII).

Caste.	Number of females to 1,000 males.
1	2
Tamil.	
Agamudaiyan	1,084
Ambalakáran	1,050
Ambattan	1,025
Andi	1,068
Bráhman	1,012
Chetti	1,048
Idaiyan	1,040
Irula	1,009
Kaikólan	1,052
Kallan	1,068
Kammálan	1,036
Kanakkan	1,003
Kuravan	1,045
Kusavan	1,036
Malaimán	1,076
Malayali	1,022
Maravan	1,052
Muttiriyan	1,005
Nattaman	1,053
Pallan	1,087
Palli	1,038
Pandáram	1,027
Pannikkan	1,069
Panisavan	1,028
Paraiyan	1,049
Pariváram	1,060
Pattanavan	982
Sembadavan	1,019
Sénaikkudaiyán	1,025
Shánán	1,040
Sudarman	1,033
Uppiliyan	1,055
Uráli	1,050
Valaiyan	1,080
Vallamban	1,111
Valluvan	1,008
Vániyan	1,050
Vannán	1,007
Védan	1,031
Vellála	1,082
Véttuvan	1,098
Yerukala	972
Telugu.	
Bagata	1,050
Balija	1,023
Bestha	965
Bhatrásu	1,083
Bógam	1,350
Bóya	965
Bráhman	1,010
Chakkiliyan	1,014
Dásari	1,067
Dévánga	1,008
Gamalla	1,006
Gándla	1,021
Gavara	1,061
Golla	1,028
Ídiga	1,061
Índra	1,147
Jálári	1,109
Janappan	1,152
Telugu—cont.	
Játapu	1,058
Jógi	984
Kalinji	1,087
Kalinji	1,260
Kamma	995
Kamsala	1,018
Kápu	1,015
Kómati	993
Konda Dora	998
Kóyi	1,020
Kummara	962
Mádiga	990
Mála	1,021
Mangala	1,039
Médara	993
Mutrácha	983
Nágavásalu	1,035
Odde	983
Perike	988
Rásu	1,003
Sále	1,010
Sáttáni	1,036
Segidi	1,215
Telaga	1,029
Togata	955
Tottiyan	1,032
Tsákala	1,016
Uppara	989
Vadugan	1,052
Velama	1,020
Yánádi	958
Yáta	1,343
Malayalam.	
Ambalavási	1,072
Bráhman	835
Chakkán	1,038
Cháliyan	1,003
Cheruman	1,101
Iluvan	1,107
Kaduppattan	1,058
Kammálan	1,050
Kanisan	1,096
Kólayán	1,069
Mannán	1,018
Mukkuvan	967
Náyar	1,079
Paniyan	976
Jívan	1,025
Véttuvan	1,027
Canarese.	
Badaga	1,020
Bant	1,054
Bédaru	1,013
Billava	1,093
Bráhman	1,045
Dévadiga	1,168
Gauda	972
Canarese—cont.	
Holeya	1,225
Jangam	1,037
Kabbéra	1,074
Kannadiyan	949
Káppiliyan	1,013
Kumbára	1,071
Kuruba	947
Kurumban	995
Lingáyat	1,028
Mogér	1,154
Pánchála	1,030
Vakkaliga	1,075
Oriya.	
Bávuri	1,289
Bhondári	1,068
Bhúmia	974
Bottada	1,006
Bráhman	1,058
Dandási	1,182
Dhóbi	1,071
Dombó	1,006
Gaudo	1,107
Haddi	1,081
Karnam	980
Kevuto	1,291
Kottíya	973
Kudumo	1,015
Odiya	1,166
Paidi	1,033
Páno	1,001
Relli	1,188
Róna	981
Sondi	992
Telli	1,077
Other Madras castes.	
Bráhman	1,007
Gadaba	961
Gond	845
Khond	1,011
Kshatriya	972
Lambádi	958
Mahráti	1,028
Patnúlkáran	1,043
Poroja	940
Rájput	978
Savara	1,016
Musalman.	
Dúdékula	985
Labbai	1,172
Máppilla	1,007
Pathán	961
Saiyad	984
Shiek	1,016
Indian Christian ...	1,036

V.—Actual number of births and deaths reported for each sex during the decades 1891–1900 *and* 1901–1910

Year.	Number of births.			Number of deaths.			Difference between columns 2 and 3. Excess of latter over former +, deficit –.	Difference between columns 5 and 6. Excess of latter over former +, deficit –.	Difference between columns 4 and 7. Excess of former over latter +, deficit –.	Number of female births per 1,000 male births.	Number of female deaths per 1,000 male deaths.
	Males.	Females.	Total.	Males.	Females	Total.					
1	2	3	4	5	6	7	8	9	10	11	12
TOTAL 1891–1900.	*4,861,953*	*4,661,843*	*9,523,796*	*3,658,487*	*3,478,134*	*7,136,621*	*– 200,110*	*– 180,353*	*+ 2,387,175*	*958·8*	*950·7*
1891 ...	471,690	453,662	925,352	383,000	365,626	748,626	– 18,028	– 17,374	+ 176,726	961·8	954·6
1892 ...	431,523	414,613	846,136	385,676	366,037	751,713	– 16,910	– 19,639	+ 94,423	960·8	949·8
1893 ...	464,837	445,337	910,174	333,388	317,220	650,608	– 19,500	– 16,168	+ 259,566	958·0	951·5
1894 ...	477,513	456,668	934,181	344,612	328,865	673,477	– 20,845	– 15,747	+ 260,704	956·3	954·3
1895 ...	499,223	478,427	977,650	337,511	322,048	659,559	– 20,796	– 15,463	+ 318,091	958·3	954·2
1896 ...	502,068	478,989	981,057	347,592	328,983	676,575	– 23,079	– 18,609	+ 304,482	954·0	946·5
1897 ...	477,434	459,392	936,826	426,001	402,397	828,398	– 18,042	– 23,604	+ 108,428	962·2	944·6
1898 ...	466,067	446,724	912,791	360,798	339,219	700,017	– 19,343	– 21,579	+ 212,774	958·5	940·2
1899 ...	534,634	514,749	1,049,383	343,598	332,286	675,884	– 19,885	– 11,312	+ 373,499	962·9	967·7
1900 ..	536,964	513,282	1,050,246	396,311	375,453	771,764	– 23,682	– 20,858	+ 278,482	955·9	947·4
TOTAL 1901–1910.	*5,777,672*	*5,536,480*	*11,314,152*	*4,342,651*	*4,174,304*	*8,516,955*	*– 241,192*	*– 168,347*	*+ 2,797,197*	*958·3*	*961·2*
1901 ...	477,490	458,259	935,749	407,975	388,165	796,140	– 19,231	– 19,810	+ 139,609	959·8	951·4
1902 ...	521,745	501,401	1,023,146	373,355	359,082	732,437	– 20,344	– 14,273	+ 290,709	961·0	961·7
1903 ...	593,713	571,367	1,165,080	419,275	407,388	826,663	– 22,346	– 11,887	+ 338,417	962·4	971·6
1904 ...	573,819	551,932	1,125,751	419,825	404,453	824,278	– 21,887	– 15,372	+ 301,473	961·9	963·4
1905 ...	599,469	576,787	1,176,256	401,406	384,717	786,123	– 22,682	– 16,689	+ 390,133	962·2	958·4
1906 ...	575,074	550,904	1,125,978	507,823	490,568	998,391	– 24,170	– 17,255	+ 127,587	958·0	966·0
1907 ...	573,041	546,129	1,119,170	449,290	433,726	883,016	– 26,912	– 15,564	+ 236,154	953·0	965·4
1908 ...	610,268	581,868	1,192,136	491,062	469,857	960,919	– 28,400	– 21,205	+ 231,217	953·5	956·8
1909 ...	621,369	594,348	1,215,717	410,589	390,977	801,566	– 27,021	– 19,612	+ 414,151	956·5	952·2
1910 ...	631,684	603,485	1,235,169	462,051	445,371	907,422	– 28,199	– 16,680	+ 327,747	955·4	963·9

N.B.—From 1900 to 1910 the figures are exclusive of Europeans and Anglo-Indians.

VI.—Number of deaths of each sex at different ages (exclusive of Europeans and Anglo-Indians).

Ages.	1905.		1906.		1907.		1908.		1909.		Total.		Average number of female deaths per 1,000 male deaths.	1910.		Average number of female deaths per 1,000 male deaths.
	Males.	Females.	Males.	Females.	Males.	Females.	Males.	Females.	Males.	Females.	Males.	Females.		Males.	Females.	
1	2	3	4	5	6	7	8	9	10	11	12	13	14	15	16	17
0–1	109,364	94,012	114,999	100,325	106,302	91,828	118,271	100,747	114,307	96,732	563,243	483,644	858·8	126,068	109,097	865·2
1–5	52,872	52,392	74,731	74,524	64,453	64,959	65,618	65,561	51,629	51,365	309,303	308,801	998·4	64,616	65,011	1006·1
5–10	19,541	18,826	34,395	32,647	27,376	25,779	30,410	28,747	20,262	19,806	131,984	125,805	949·4	22,776	22,357	981·6
10–15 ...	12,668	11,734	22,227	19,573	17,276	15,550	20,784	18,307	13,286	12,301	86,241	77,465	898·2	14,165	13,078	923·2
15–20	12,200	16,169	19,451	23,393	15,579	19,045	18,724	22,192	12,867	16,424	78,821	97,243	1233·7	14,394	18,226	1266·2
20–30	26,355	33,764	38,873	47,038	33,441	41,461	38,521	46,509	28,942	35,754	166,132	204,526	1231·2	30,806	37,868	1229·1
30–40	30,912	29,063	40,250	37,690	36,881	34,861	42,698	40,778	31,622	30,346	182,363	172,733	947·2	33,937	32,084	945·4
40–50	34,513	25,079	41,526	32,117	38,688	30,307	42,914	34,327	34,594	26,143	192,235	147,973	717·7	37,529	29,313	781·1
50–60	35,274	29,446	41,700	35,368	38,509	32,218	40,711	34,284	35,125	28,897	191,419	160,108	836·4	39,372	33,147	841·9
60 and over ...	67,707	74,212	79,671	87,996	70,785	77,718	72,411	78,410	67,955	73,709	358,529	392,047	1093·5	78,368	85,195	1087·1

Appendix I.

Caste.	Guntúr. Males.	Guntúr. Females.	Nellore. Males.	Nellore. Females.	Cuddapah. Males.	Cuddapah. Females.	Karnool. Males.	Karnool. Females.	Bellary. Males.	Bellary. Females.	Anantapur. Males.	Anantapur. Females.	Chittoor. Males.	Chittoor. Females.
1	2	3	4	5	6	7	8	9	10	11	12	13	14	15
Balija	19,622	19,421	37,766	39,205	36,457	35,448	30,961	31,585	...	...	31,848	28,041	58,836	57,706
Bóya	...	...	...	...	5,099	4,972	47,135	46,989	67,811	68,820	61,622	60,227	11,744	11,164
Bráhman	40,834	40,369	19,391	18,998	...	...	...	...	...	...	...	...	..	..
Gamalla	15,960	15,033	9,164	8,067	...	...	...	...	...	...	...	...	...	...
Golla	48,626	47,849	55,094	57,230	30,559	30,860	32,581	32,197	15,368	14,995	26,568	25,570	33,420	32,191
Kamma	149,297	147,469	51,625	53,318	9,294	8,608	...	...	...	...	22,581	21,475	48,868	47,829
Kamsala	14,914	15,078	9,630	9,082	...	...	...	...	...	...	...	...	10,694	9,982
Kápu	71,100	68,815	96,902	97,645	110,464	106,700	63,478	62,480	26,002	24,114	73,865	70,045	96,061	90,801
Kómati	37,800	40,441	24,133	24,294	13,598	13,782	19,224	18,584	...	...	...	...	9,906	9,958
Kummara	10,626	9,915	8,077	7,640	...	...	...	...	...	...	...	...	...	...
Mádigá	32,173	32,603	40,649	40,221	28,617	27,575	31,682	31,029	42 888	42,498	51,048	51,394	24,299	23,000
Mála	74,378	72,669	84,949	83,467	29,540	29,659	27,210	26,524	...	...	13,309	13,402	83,100	81,428
Mangala	9,279	9,573	...	...	...	...	...	...	...	...	...	...	...	...
Mutrácha	9,282	8,820	12,298	12,080	11,639	10,629	...	...	...	...	...	...	8,692	8,957
Odde	17,475	15,610	18,365	18,007	14,504	13,775	10,885	10,056	13,507	12,401	19,767	18,387	21,702	20,644
Sále	17,943	18,065	...	...	8,604	8,066	...	...	10,121	9,432	...	...	...	...
Telaga	66,745	65,155	...	...	...	...	...	...	...	...	...	...	...	...
Togata	...	...	...	...	12,352	11,427	...	...		...	...	...	...	...
Tsákala	25,710	25,240	17,361	17,819	12,112	11,485	12,762	12,107	...	...	10,202	9,953	12,144	11,877
Uppara	6,443	6,665	...	...	...	...	...	.	...	...	...	...	...	...
Yánádi	...	...	36,616	35,181	...	...	...	...	...	...	...	...	...	...
Dúdékula	...	...	...	...	8,977	8,101	8,707	8,558	.	...	...	...	..	...
Sheik	46,688	45,891	31,433	30,570	31,627	30,985	40,709	39,402	35,942	34,962	25,510	23,165	20,053	18,587
Indian Christian	63,136	60,358	21,882	21,906	11,316	11,086	21,190	20,795	1,582	1,590	1,648	1,448	2,138	2,137
Total ...	*778,028*	*765,034*	*575,280*	*574,175*	*374,754*	*363,053*	*346,524*	*342,256*	*213,221*	*203,812*	*337,463*	*322,107*	*441,142*	*425,211*
Total population examined ...	1,543,062		1,149,455		737,807		686,780		417,033		659,570		866,353	
Total district population ...	1,697,551		1,328,152		898,998		935,199		969,436		962,223		1,288,742	
Number of females to 1,000 males—														
On total district population ...	982		996		969		984		975		940		968	
On figures dealt with	983		998		969		988		956		954		964	

APPENDIX I—*cont.*

Caste.	Chingleput.	
	Males.	Females.
Bráhman ...	12,882	13,493
Chetti ...	8,540	8,211
Idaiyan ...	34,802	34,701
Irula ...	10,101	9,445
Kaikólan ...	16,815	17,517
Kammálan ...	13,053	12,906
Kanakkan ...	8,451	8,379
Muttiriyan ...	13,605	13,670
Palli ...	145,788	146,547
Paraiyan ...	176,500	174,029
Shánán ...	11,312	11,022
Vellála ...	47,665	45,699
Sheik ...	9,246	8,534
Indian Christian ...	13,660	13,919
Total ...	*522,370*	*518,074*
Total population examined ...	1,040,444	
Total district population ...	1,406,006	
Number of females to 1,000 males—		
(1) On total district population ...	993	
(2) On figures dealt with ...	992	

CHAPTER VII.—CIVIL CONDITION.

MARRIAGE of some sort being the normal condition of the Southern Indian, and an unmated life being regarded as little less singular than would be a clothless existence in Europe, it is hardly necessary to apologize for regarding civil condition almost exclusively in its married aspect.

2. To the estate of matrimony a certain amount of indirect attention has been devoted elsewhere in this report. But in such references the marriages of the people were considered solely as ordained for the procreation of children, and as affecting the children sprung therefrom. It may be of some interest to view the matter from the standpoint of the contracting parties, rather than from that of their presumptive offspring.

3. In any consideration of the subject it is necessary to bear in mind the somewhat different connotations of the word "marriage" in the East and in the West. In Europe the word implies legal or religious sanction for a definite social relation, wherein the contracting parties are of marriageable, or better, cohabitable, age; it implies, moreover, an obligation on the part of the husband to support his wife, if she does not possess the means of supporting him. This obligation is scarcely implicit in India; nor has marriage a particular reference to age, except in so far as that among certain sections of the population it is looked upon as advisable, or necessary, to get one's female relatives married at an age that ensures for them the maximum possibility of physical disaster. For even if we grant that marriage in infancy *can* at most mean nothing more than irrevocable betrothal, it is not an unfair assumption that this infant betrothal leads to an undertaking of the real responsibilities of the married state at the earliest age that nature permits, and at one far earlier than nature, especially in the case of girls, renders advisable.

Religion.	Males.			Females.		
	Unmarried.	Married.	Widowed.	Unmarried.	Married.	Widowed.
All religions...	5,330	4,284	386	3,728	4,415	1,857
Hindu ...	5,284	4,322	394	3,662	4,446	1,892
Muhammadan.	5,821	3,876	303	4,123	4,132	1,745
Christian ...	5,606	4,071	323	4,457	4,114	1,429

4. The marginal statement, taken from subsidiary table III, shows the distribution of 10,000 of each sex by civil condition at the census of 1911.

5. Despite then the casual improvidence with which marriage is too often entered upon, the state of the Presidency is somewhat less married than one might expect. For these figures show that more than 50 per cent. of the male population are still in the enjoyment of single blessedness; while a rather larger number of women have at one time or another changed their state—a step which in their case generally denotes a final disposal of their chances in the matrimonial lottery.

6. Of material prudence or imprudence in marrying, the census enquiry affords no means of judgment. But an automatic check on amorous inclination is supplied by the age distribution of the people; although immature marriages may be frequent, their absolute number cannot, in the nature of things, compare with that of marriages wherein the parties are of suitable age. If we assume twenty years as the age limit within which a man should not marry, and 15 as a corresponding limit for girls, the appended figures show us the marriageability of the people.

Distribution of 10,000 of each sex.

—	All religions.		Hindu.		Muhammadan.		Christian.	
	Male.	Female.	Male.	Female.	Male.	Female.	Male.	Female.
Non-marriageable.	4,763	3,744	4,732	3,717	5,087	3,964	4,927	3,934
Marriageable.	5,237	6,256	5,268	6,283	4,913	6,036	5,073	6,066

7. For the sake of greater convenience in comparison the two foregoing statements may be combined as follows :—

Distribution of 10,000 persons.	All religions.		Hindu.		Muhammadan.		Christian.	
	Male.	Female.	Male.	Female.	Male.	Female.	Male.	Female.
Married or widowed ...	4,670	6,272	4,716	6,338	4,179	5,877	4,394	5,543
Of marriageable age ...	5,237	6,256	5,268	6,283	4,913	6,036	5,073	6,066

8. In addition to age there are sundry curious obstacles to a successful entrance on the married state: many a Hindu reaches the goal over a veritable steeple-chase course. But before attending to these matters, it will be well to examine in some further detail the question of age in relation to marriage, especially among the female sex. Of its urgency the records of any social conference afford ample proof.

9. The age limits for the respective sexes being as already assumed, the following figures show some considerable existence of premature marriage or widowhood :—

Year.	Males unmarried at 0–20 per 10,000.				Females unmarried at 0–15 per 10,000.			
	All religions.	Hindu.	Muham-madan.	Christian.	All religions.	Hindu.	Muham-madan.	Christian.
1911	9,592	9,566	9,814	9,822	9,034	8,960	9,523	9,707
1901	9,661	9,669	9,849	9,858	9,114	9,052	9,535	9,740
1891	9,596	9,577	9,816	9,792	8,996	8,939	9,458	9,624

Note.—For purposes of convenience, in this and in the succeeding statement, I give only the number of the unmarried, from which the complementary number of those who are, or who have been, married may easily be deduced.

10. The question arises whether immature marriage is a tendency confined to one community of the people or spread among all; whether it is a tendency independent of the general marriage question, and one whose intensity may increase or diminish irrespective of an increasing or diminishing marriage rate; or else a custom so deeply ingrained that its fluctuations follow those of marriage in general. To these questions an examination of the position of 10,000 of each sex in the total population, and in each main religious community, with respect to marriage at the last three enumerations, appears to supply sufficient answer :—

Year.	Males unmarried.				Females unmarried.			
	All religions.	Hindu.	Muham-madan.	Christian.	All religions.	Hindu.	Muham-madan.	Christian.
1911	5,330	5,284	5,821	5,606	3,728	3,662	4,123	4,457
1901	5,524	5,484	5,983	5,838	3,897	3,835	4,281	4,623
1891	5,386	5,352	5,814	5,643	3,723	3,667	4,118	4,395

11. These figures, combined with those immediately preceding, indicate that immature marriage, while especially characteristic of the Hindu community, is yet a tendency diffused through other sections of the population; and at the same time one of such firm acceptance that its ratio varies well nigh exactly with the general frequency or infrequency of marriage.

12. It is not *prima facie* unfair to attribute the diffusion of this social tendency, as well as of many others, to Hindu influence. Hinduism comprises the vast majority of the inhabitants of the Presidency: the rival faiths of Islam and Christianity have either been recruited from its ranks, and have as yet not sloughed the heredity of centuries; or else, despite a measure of original independence, can scarce but assimilate the social influence of their mighty neighbour, which lives and moves and has its being in social regulation. In Hinduism then we may seek an explanation for the origin, if not for the continued existence of a phenomenon, which many of the most eminent among Hindus profess to deplore.

13. To the statement that premature marriage is in vogue among Hindus because the shástras enjoin it no great attention need be paid: those qualified to speak on the subject express doubt as to whether the shástras, read in the spirit rather than in the letter, contain any such positive injunction. Moreover it is permissible to question whether mankind has at any time followed a practice simply at the bidding of a writing, rather than evolved a writing from experimentally proved advisability. It has been well observed that "it is a too common practice "in this country, at once to ascribe to the mysterious influence of religion or caste "whatever may be hard to understand in the way of personal conduct; whereas "in many cases, an act that appears strange and unaccountable to a European is "done in obedience to a custom grounded on mere convenience."

14. The present conveniences of a system that burdens a boy with a wife long before he has any ability to support one, or that subjects a woman to the inevitable risks of maternity, long before Nature turns the balance of probability to the side of safety, are too successfully inapparent to render search for them a profitable adventure.

15. Adopting therefore another line of enquiry, some have found a reason for this practice in a supposed deep scepticism of the Indian as to female morality. This view does not lack a measure of support from the classics, and these, one fears, find a frequent echo in the every day utterances of many a worthy Indian citizen.

16. But if we are to measure the Hindu's estimation of his womenfolk by the utterance of dead and gone curmudgeons, it is only fair to remember that the same reproach strikes home to most other religions—certainly to Christianity. Whatever be the sum total of Christianity's work at the end of 1,900 years for her uplifting, there is no Sanskrit deprecation of woman that cannot be equalled, or excelled, by quotations from the Christian Fathers. Nor, on the other hand, is there lacking evidence to show that the woman of the Indian classics once enjoyed a freedom and estimation as great as any of her Western sisters.

17. Premature marriage, especially that of women, is generally regarded as characteristic of the Bráhman. The figures shown in column 27 of subsidiary table V lend little support to this view, save on the somewhat arbitrary hypothesis that certain sections of the non-Bráhman Hindu community, including those who profess to reject Bráhman authority, and those who, even to-day, can have little contact with, and are little influenced by, Bráhman precept and practice, have determinedly set themselves to imitate and to excel the Bráhman, in his failings rather than in his undoubted excellences.

18. More probable would seem the explanation of premature marriage which pays regard to the racial differences between the peoples now lumped together under one general head of religion, or the several, but still widely inclusive, sub-heads of language.

19. Whatever may or may not be his present degeneration, there can be little doubt that the Aryan forbear of the present day Bráhman stood for a civilization and morality infinitely higher than that of the Dravidian hordes, with which, even as a leader, he had to associate himself. From the curious students of such primitive societies we may infer that the marriage relation, not too complicated or stable in modern days, existed some centuries back as a natural simplicity, which cannot have failed to strike the more intelligent Aryan as undesirable in the extreme.

20. The premature marryings of the early Aryan we may then ascribe to two influences. First to his desire to safeguard the purity of his race, and the morality of his daughter, by securing for her a husband within her own community at the earliest possible moment; secondly to an imitation, albeit one unconscious and one much modified, of the promiscuous cohabitation which he saw about him. His reciprocal influence is shown in the permanency and sanctity which the tie has assumed among the more educated portions of the non-Bráhman community; his persistence in the needless custom of premature marriage, and his excelment therein by sundry of his imitators, can be attributed to the unintelligent application of a rule of which the purpose has been forgotten. Whereas among the primitive "Animistic" and "outcast" peoples, for whose social guidance Bráhman influence, good or bad, is practically non-existent, premature marriage is probably a lingering survival of old time promiscuity.

21. But whatever be its cause there can be little doubt of the wide prevalence of premature marriage. It may be well to consider its advantages and disadvantages in some detail. In doing so it must be remembered that it is futile to import into the word marriage, as applied to Indian facts, its European associations. The validity or propriety of a marriage is determined solely by the standards of the society to which the contracting parties belong. Thus "marriage" in Southern India may imply a relation in some respects much more rigid and unalterable, (as among Bráhmans), than in Europe; on the other hand it may denote a state of things to European eyes in no way differing from mere animal promiscuity. In ethnographic writings I have seen at times the term "incestuous" applied to certain unions, (such as that between uncle and niece), existing in Southern India. The use of such a term is obviously improper; it might with equal justice or injustice be applied by a Hindu to many marriages absolutely unobjectionable in the eyes of European Christianity.

22. The advantages and disadvantages of a social relation have twofold application; they may be considered in regard to individuals, and to the society of which such individuals form a part. If marriage means simply promiscuous sexual freedom from an early age, with a certain quasi permanency when the natural results of such relationship become apparent, (such is the description of Chenchu marriage given to me by a correspondent), the ill effect of such a state of things on the physical and moral health of the individual, and of his society, are too obvious to need detailed description. Some detailed statements by competent observers will be found in those paragraphs of Chapter XI which treat of the Khonds and Tódas; the results appear to be, as regards the individual, the spread and transmission of loathsome disease; as regards society, in the latter case at all events, racial suicide. The extremely rigid Bráhman ideal of marriage, while, by its insistence on premature marriage in the case of girls, it in a sense safeguards female chastity, must necessarily involve certain individual and social evils. In respect to the individual woman the physical effects of early sexual intercourse and premature maternity, which in most cases are the natural *sequelæ* of immature marriage, are obvious; although theoretically immature marriage on the male side is not a necessary complement to that on the female, practically it must be so to a large extent; and the physical consequences though less apparent, can hardly be less regrettable.

23. In regard to society the harmful consequences of the system may fairly be summarized thus.

24. The physical and mental quality of a community made up to an increasing extent of the offspring of immature parents must necessarily deteriorate. The conclusion is not, I think, affected by the fact adduced by a Bráhman correspondent, that his community has in recent times produced, and will doubtless continue to produce, a certain number of men, (of the women it is impossible for an outsider to judge), who in natural intellectual endowment, and in subsequent attainment, take equal rank with the intellectual aristocracy of any nation. A swallow does not make a summer; that the rank and file of this particular community are

physically frail and undergrown is a fact which may be observed, and which has frequently been stated to me positively, if regretfully, by Bráhmans themselves.

25. With premature marriage the Bráhmans, and those who follow the Bráhmanical system, have in the case of women associated irrevocability; this in its turn involving, as a natural consequence, premature and sterile widowhood. From the figures of subsidiary table V we find that Tamil Bráhmans have some 482 widows not above 12 years of age; Telugu Bráhmans 1,848; Oriyá Bráhmans 657; and Kamsalas 2,286. Whatever may be said as to theoretical beauty of a marriage sacrament irrevocable even by the death of one of the parties thereto, (logically, it may be suggested, this irrevocability should apply equally to both sexes), the practical fact remains that these widows, who can never have been wives, represent potentialities of increase lost to the community.

26. Again the absolute necessity of premature girl marriage has given rise to an evil, which, if Indian writers on the subject are to be trusted, has grown to terrible dimensions in Hindu society where such ideals prevail. It being imperative on a father to get his daughter married before she reaches a particular age, he must literally do so at all costs. In other words, he must purchase a bridegroom. The social demoralization, which must necessarily result from the cold-blooded sale of bridegrooms by themselves or by their parents, has been described with Zolæsque force by a recent Hindu novelist, who puts the following reflection into the mouth of one of his characters: "As for our caste customs and restrictions, can anything "good ever come out of such as we now have? Why, if I go to a public prostitute's "house for a night, I have to pay her handsomely, and put up with such treatment "as she is pleased to accord me. But when a man offers me his virgin daughter, "the apple of his eye, the very breath of his nostrils, a veritable gem of innocence "and purity, the heiress of a thousand generations of chaste and loving mothers, to "be my unconditional bond slave for life in implicit obedience and unswerving "faith; to cook for me, wash for me, nurse me in my sickness, cheer me in my "hopes, comfort me in my sorrow, rejoice with me in my happiness, love me for "ever, for better and for worse, whether I hate her or return her love; to cherish "and guard me like a second mother; to bear me pure and innocent children in "infinite pain, and nourish and rear them up with infinite care and trouble to "perpetuate my name; I must needs first impoverish and ruin her parents by "extorting as much money as I can from them, and make them involuntarily curse "the day when a daughter was born to them."

27. And the writer's grim descriptions of deceit and trickery arising from this practice; of a father allowing his daughter to sicken to death and forbidding aid, lest she might live unmarried through his inability to purchase her a bridegroom; of ill-matched unions, and life-long unhappiness, are endorsed by a prominent Indian journalist as "graphic and amusing (!) pictures of what obtains more or less "generally in Bráhman households in Southern India."

28. Every question has two sides. As to the advantages of that premature "marriage," which is only another name for sexual promiscuity, I have indeed heard no argument. But in favour of the Bráhmanical system of premature marriage, I have heard from Bráhmans arguments far more convincing than the poetical rhapsodies, wherewith we are at times favoured by European sentimentalists.

29. Firstly this system, as suggested in paragraph 20 *supra*, safeguarded for those who adopted it the solidarity of their community, and the virtue of their women. But it may be questioned whether such safeguards are necessary at the present age of the world. Cultural and moral difference between many castes is now so slight that, sentiment apart, the possibility of intermarriage has in it nothing terrible; in an age of peace it is not complimentary to Indian womanhood to suggest that it needs protection from itself.

30. Secondly the Bráhmanical system, if it involves a possibility of premature and sterile widowhood, by its insistence on the necessity of marriage does away with the possibility of perpetual and sterile maidenhood, which exists in other countries. Every woman gets at least one chance in the matrimonial lottery; give

her two, and probably some other must go without any. And in fact, if age returns are approximately correct, (a doubtful point), the absolute number of these infant widows given in paragraph 25 *supra* is not very great.

31. Thirdly was used the argument that, if social bonds are once relaxed, liberty in India in this respect is apt to degenerate into license. By a curiously similar line of reasoning Browning's dialectical bishop defended his acquiescence in much of what he did not at heart approve.

32. It may, however, be observed that premature and regular marriage does not necessarily connote widowhood irrevocable if premature. In point of youthful marriages by far the most conspicuous are the Kálingis and Kalinjis, two sections of the community which were not distinguished in 1901. Among one large section of the Kálingis widow remarriage is permissible, in case the widow has no *male* children; among the Kalinjis widow remarriage is permitted, subject only to the curious qualification that the brother-in-law of the widow is entitled to the first offer of her hand. Among Telagas and Besthas, writes a correspondent, 95 per cent. of the girls are married before attaining puberty; Telagas permit widow marriage without restriction; Besthas allow remarriage of "virgin widows" and childless widows, but not of "divorced widows," or widows having offspring. And of course in the Muhammadan community, which shows a considerable proportion of early marriages and youthful widows, there is no objection to the remarriage of a widow.

33. The East, or that portion of it in which we live, moves slowly, and it is scarcely possible to draw from the figures of a few decades any conclusions as to whether theoretical declamation, of which there has been plenty, against the custom of premature marriage has to any appreciable extent materialized in practical result. Figures quoted in paragraph 10 *supra*, and the greater detail of subsidiary table I, suggest an improvement between 1891 and 1901, with a deterioration in the subsequent decade. But of this the true explanation is probably to be found in the economic characteristics, described in Chapter II of the two decades. The marriage of children, which is simply an occasion of expense to their parents, becomes naturally of less frequent occurrence at a time when such parents are hard put to it to maintain themselves; and when any avoidable expenditure, which under other circumstances inclination might dictate, must be eschewed. With returning agricultural prosperity an increase in the number of early marriages, if regrettable, is not a matter for surprise.

34. Moreover, though a little leaven leaveneth the whole lump, there must be some reasonable proportion between the amount of the leaven and the size of the lump for the results of the leavening process to become perceptible. The area over which reform has to spread is so wide, the numbers to be affected are so great, that it is hardly just to conclude that progress, because non-apparent, is non-existent.

35. In regard to the particular marriage customs and conditions of particular castes there is something to be said. Such peculiarities may be considered in two aspects; namely, conditions to be fulfilled, or obstacles to be surmounted, before marriage; and conditions under which marriage exists.

36. Of the first I may utilize for an example information given to me by a Bráhman friend. His information justifies the steeplechase metaphor employed in paragraph 8; * certain of the difficulties to be overcome are purely artificial, and, in one case at least, objectionable; others betoken a considerable foresight in avoidance of too close inbreeding which the universality of marriage might otherwise occasion.

37. Necessity of marriage, and difficulty of its accomplishment, being more urgent on the side of the bride than of the bridegroom, the business may first be viewed from the standpoint of a parent anxious to marry his daughter.

* The same idea has occurred to the Hindu novelist quoted at paragraph 26. He entitles one of his stories "Hymen's Obstacle Race."

38. (*a*) He must as a rule be prepared to pay the uttermost farthing that his means will admit, or that the bargaining ability of the bridegroom, or of his representative, can secure. On this evil business enlightened Hindu opinion, of which an example has already been quoted, is vocal: time will show if practice will follow theory.

(*b*) The girl must not have attained puberty.

(*c*) The horoscopes of bride and bridegroom must agree. This is a condition of fairly universal application; and in regard to it a Bellary correspondent gives me a curious piece of information. It is to the effect that in that district parents are unwilling to see a promising match broken off, because of an impediment as to the intrinsic validity of which a considerable degree of scepticism prevails. There has accordingly arisen a class of professional matchmakers, whose duty it is to pronounce on the agreement or disagreement of horoscopes, and whose statement is accepted as final. There are means of securing that it shall be as desired.

(*d*) The omens, which occur while "marriage business" is on the *tapis*, should be favourable.

(*e*) The husband should be older than his prospective bride—a requisite which has the weighty recommendation of Shakespeare in its favour.

(*f*) The husband must be of a different *gótra* and *pravara* to his wife, and must not be within the prohibited degrees of relationship. From the first prohibition it follows that the bridegroom is unsuitable if related to the bride, however remotely, through the paternal male line. In respect of the latter a man may not marry his mother's sister's daughter; but a Dravidian influence is seen in the fact that he may now marry his mother's brother's daughter, although, strictly speaking, such union is contrary to shástraical teaching.

(*g*) Bride and bridegroom must be of the same caste and sub-caste.

39. Such, my friend considers, are the matrimonial difficulties of his community stated in a succinct form. But inasmuch as for their full appreciation they presuppose a certain acquaintance with Bráhmanism and the religion of the philosophic Hindu, he amplifies his information in respect of caste and sub-caste. It will be found embodied in those paragraphs of Chapter XI, which treat more particularly of sub-caste formation.

40. There can be no doubt that many of these restrictions, utterly senseless now from a European point of view, were originally designed with the twofold object of preserving racial purity, and of preventing too close inbreeding; and in this quality were suited to the circumstances of those among whom they prevailed. But it would certainly appear that to-day attention is concentrated on the rules rather on their object, and that the whole system needs revision and adaptation to the needs of a modern community.

41. The fact that among Nambúdri Bráhmans is found a large percentage of unmarried women at the ages 12–20, illustrates two pecularities of their social system. The first is that women marry after attainment of puberty; the second that, inasmuch as only the eldest son of a Nambúdri family marries in his own caste, the procuring of a husband is often a matter of the utmost difficulty for a father whose quiver has been filled with daughters. Possibly because of the temptations to which this difficulty gives rise, the Nambúdris possess a singularly efficient safeguard of morality, in their custom of outcasting all *men* implicated by a fallen woman, whose statement as to her lovers is considered conclusive. In a comparatively recent case a lady's victims numbered over sixty.

42. Inasmuch as the percentage of unmarried women *actat* 12–20 among Embrándri Bráhmans, who are Canarese or Tulu immigrants to Malabar, is likewise high, it may be surmised that with their occasional usurpation of the term Nambúdri, and imitation of the Nambúdri custom of contracting sambandham with Náyar women, these Bráhmans have to a certain extent adopted Nambúdri ideas with respect to the women of their own caste.

43. *Exogamy.*—Outside the Bráhman pale there arises the question of exogamous sept in relation to marriage. The existence of these septs has been noted by Thurston and other ethnological writers; a few castes among whose sub-sections

such are said to exist are the Udaiyáns, Vellálas, Kápus and Kómatis. But I have doubts as to whether this idea of exogamy presents itself as of any practical importance to the would-be benedick; *à propos* of the question a man rather aptly observed to me, "I have quite sufficient trouble in finding some one that I *can* marry, without bothering myself about those that I *cannot*." In other words such obstacles to marriage, where they exist, are as well known as *gotra* and *pravara* among Bráhmans, and probably were designed with the same object.

44. *Totemism.*—On the connection of exogamy with totemism, and on actual living belief in totemism, I have learned nothing except what has been already recorded by others. In fact there is no way of learning anything new on this obscure subject open to the superficial enquirer. As noted by Mr. Henderson in his remarks on the Gadabas, (Chapter XI), the jungle folk, among whom such ideas might be expected to prevail, are extremely shy about giving information as to their peculiarities to a stranger; to get to the bottom of their inmost thought and belief requires an acquaintance with, and a sojourn among them, which are out of the question for an ordinary official, especially if he be a foreigner. An Indian gentleman, who has studied the subject, tells me that totemism probably survives as a living faith in the inland tracts of the northern districts; and nearer the coast a tradition survives of there having been such a belief. But real information as opposed to hearsay, or to that style of information which the ordinary villager will give if he thinks that a particular answer will please his interrogator, my informant considers unprocurable; save by one who is prepared to remain for a considerable while in one locality, obtain a perfect command of the language of the people, live with them as one of themselves, and obtain his knowledge by observation, and hints here and there, rather than by direct question and answer.

45. In respect to the conditions under which marriage exists there are quaintnesses ascribed to sundry castes. It is however permissible to doubt whether such customs are not in many cases at the present day an affair of tradition, rather than of actual practice. The most striking illustration of such a state of things is the case of the Náyars, of whom Mr. W. Logan writes as follows: "The statement "that the younger cadets of the Nambúdri families live with Náyar women, merely "reproduces in English the Malayáli mode of describing the married life of these "people, and of the Náyars. It is part of the theory that the women they live with "are not wives, that they may part at will, that they may form new connections. "The fact, at any rate of recent years, is that, although the theory of the law sanc- "tions freedom in these relations, conjugal fidelity is very general. Nowhere is the "marriage tie—albeit informal—more rigidly observed or respected, nowhere is it "more jealously guarded, or its neglect more savagely avenged. Ceremonial, like "other conventionalities, is an accident, and Náyar women are as chaste and faithful "as their neighbours."

46. The proof of a pudding lies in the eating. Selecting certain castes as to whose matrimonial peculiarities statements are on record, I have tabulated their marriages by age periods in certain localities, in order to see whether theory is confirmed by statistical result. In respect of the Kallans, for example, I find the following statement made: "Marriage among the Kallans is said to depend "entirely upon consanguinity. The most proper alliance is one between a man and "the daughter of his father's sister; and if an individual has such a cousin he must "marry her, whatever disparity there may be between their respective ages. A boy "for example of fifteen must marry such a cousin, even if she be thirty or forty "years old."

47. Tabulation of Kallan marriages in the Mélúr taluk of the Madura district gives the result noted in the margin.

Age.	Males.	Females.
0–5	...	...
5–12	5	25
12–15	22	45
15–20	122	610
20–40	3,939	5,543
40 and over	3,182	1,706

For 149 husbands aged 20 and under there are 680 wives of the same age, which implies that the husbands of such wives must be the elder. At the ultimate age period there is an excess of 1,476 husbands, which may be added to the number of husbands aged 20–40. At this age period alone wives will then exceed husbands of equal or greater age by 128 alone—a number too small on which to base any general inference.

48. Similar statements have been made in respect of the Kammas of the Tamil country, the Reddis (Kápus) settled in the Tinnevelly district, and sundry other castes. Tabulation similar to that carried out for the Mélúr Kallans,* has not in any case confirmed belief in the present reality of such practices, and gives rise to the impression that tradition of what may have happened long ago, combined with observation of a few abnormal cases, may be responsible for the attribution of peculiarities to people not differing particularly from the ordinary run of mankind in their marriage customs.

49. *Marriage of cousins.*—These statements, however, allude to a matrimonial practice, which, among the Dravidians of Southern India, is more widespread, and on the whole more deleterious, than the custom of premature marriage. This is the Dravidian *menarikam*, by which a man marries his mother's brother's daughter, his sister's daughter, or father's sister's daughter. The custom is not confined to any particular caste, or appreciably limited number of castes; and, as noted in paragraph 38, the system is creeping into Bráhmanism.

50. The ill-effects of consanguineous marriage in the transmission of infirmities have been emphasized by my medical informants in the several sections of Chapter X. The extraordinary difference between theory and practice in India was strikingly illustrated for me by conversation with some followers of the custom, who, from a theoretical standpoint, and from actual observation of results, appeared fully alive to the disadvantages involved in such close inbreeding. *Video meliora proboque, deteriora sequor.*

51. As the influence which induced continuance in a practice of which they disapproved, my informants gave the inevitable Indian answer—one hinted at in paragraphs 19 *et seq.* of Chapter VIII—the conservatism and prejudice of "the females." In practical result, they also admitted, the custom kept the family together, and prevented dispersion of the family property. In this latter consideration is perhaps to be found the true explanation, suggested to me by Mr. F. J. Richards, of the system's origin. Assuming that among the Dravidian races inheritance passed in the female line, and that bequeathment from father to son was an innovation introduced by the conquering Aryans, this form of marriage represents or ensures an exact compromise between, or combination of, both systems.

52. There are other forms of cousin, or consanguineous, marriage. But all, I fancy, spring from the same idea, namely, the conservatism of property; and the general deleterious result is the same.

53. From subsidiary table IV we may learn the proportion of wives to husbands throughout the Presidency, in each of its natural divisions, and among the main religious communities of the people. Taken literally the figures suggest that on the whole polygamy is fairly frequent, and that it has increased in the Presidency in general and among Hindus in particular since the last enumeration.

54. That polygamy is possible among Hindus and Muhammadans is a well-known fact; that it should actually exist is what might be expected from the preponderance of women in the Presidency, combined with the universality of marriage. But that it is on the increase is a contradiction of human experience in general,† as well as of Indian testimony of the present day. Of these figures many general explanations can be adduced; the following may serve as examples.

55. Emigration is a factor which needs to be discounted. The proportion of wives to husbands is highest in the East Coast, northern and southern divisions,

* It was done for the Kammas of Tinnevelly and Madura, the Káppilyans of Madura, the Kunnavans of Madura, the Malayális of Salem, and the Tottiyans of Madura.

† The monogamic form of the sexual relation is manifestly the ultimate form, and any change to be anticipated must be in the direction of the completion and extension of it.—*Spencer.*

from which as noted in the chapters dealing with the movement of the people and with sex, there is a considerable seasonal outflow to Burma, the Straits Settlements, and Ceylon. The harvest labourer probably does not go to the expense of taking his women folk with him, unless he counts on their assistance in his work, or anticipates a long sojourn abroad The proportion is lowest in the Agency and Deccan divisions, to which the idea of emigration is comparatively strange.

56. The vagueness of the term "married," and the difference of its Indian application to the sexes, needs consideration. It was frequently urged at classes held for census instruction that, while there was nothing strange or improper in designating a girl of *any* age as married, the term was absurd as applied to a boy of under (say) 12 years of age. *Per contra* it was argued that while a man might, if he preferred, remain unmarried, the idea of an old maid, at least among Hindus, was inconceivable. The argument was repeated to me by a Tamil Bráhman with particular reference to the statistics for his community; the existence of girls aged 20 and upwards, who had not through *some* form or semblance of marriage, he flatly denied.

57. In the case of irregular unions, which undoubtedly exist, it is probable that the woman almost invariably claims, for census purposes at least, the status of regular marriage. Among a certain widespread community, it was stated to me, by members of other communities it is true, married life without a concubine is not looked upon as exactly respectable. I have no means of verifying this curious assertion, and so merely record it; with the observation that, if it be founded on fact, the women concerned have probably returned themselves as married.

58. The figures shown against Muhammadans in the East Coast (South) division are so curious that I have tabulated, as in the margin, the returns for each of the main districts comprised in that division. Allowing for the effect produced by territorial changes, the figures of 1911 and 1901 exhibit such similarity as to suggest that the information given to the enumerators has been correctly recorded. The figures of column 21 of subsidiary table II do not lend weight to the theory that marriage is more universal among the Muhammadan women of this division than elsewhere; although from column 3 of the same table it can be seen that the proportion of married men in the community is here lower than in other divisions, with the exception of the Agency division and the West Coast; in which latter division the proportion of married Muhammadan women is also at its lowest. The most probable explanation that I can suggest is that the Muhammadans of these districts are mainly represented by Labbais and Rávuttans, whose addiction to skin trade and general hawking leads them frequently away from home for the acquirement and disposal of their wares.

Number of wives per 1,000 husbands among Muhammadans.

District.	1911.	1901.
Tanjore	1,367	1,400
Trichinopoly	1,130	1,074
Madura	1,082	1,372
Rámnád	1,528	
Tinnevelly	1,357	1,376

59. On the other hand, it may be that polygamy among Muhammadans is really prevalent in these districts, and is necessitated by a large preponderance of Muhammadan women, which enumeration of the actual population shows as existing there. Still it may be noted that the disparity between husbands and wives is greater in each case than that between the sexes.

Muhammadan women per 1,000 men in

Tanjore	1,297
Trichinopoly	1,084
Madura	1,060
Rámnád	1,403
Tinnevelly	1,251

60. Actual and avowed polyandry is probably well nigh non-existent in the Presidency. Theoretically it may survive among many castes, as for example the Badagas of the Nilgiris, with whom the formal ceremony which enables a father to claim paternity of his child testifies to its one time existence; or among the Náyars of the West Coast; among low castes and aboriginal people the marriage tie may be exceedingly lax. But the claim of, and the co-habitation with, several husbands by

a woman is perhaps found only among the Tódas, whose women, so a missionary informs me, are beginning to awake to the physical and moral evil of the system. The awakening of such sentiment represents perhaps the only hope of survival for this luckless race.

61. In subsidiary table II will be found information as to marriage by sex, age, religion and locality. As in 1901, marriage among both sexes appear to be more common in the East Coast (North) division than elsewhere. Chapter IV shows this division to be pre-eminently Hindu is point of religion, and the weight of the Hindu figures exercises an influence in the general return. In point of early marriage of both sexes the division is conspicuous; that it should be so in respect of girl marriage is not surprising, when we recall the large proportion, noted in Chapter VI, which child wives bear to the total female population of the districts included in the division. A natural corollary of extensive infant marriage is a pre-eminence in point of child widows; those aged 10—15 number 18 per 1,000 as against the 10 per 1,000 of the Deccan; similar proportional figures for 1901 being 19 and 13.

62. The explanation usually given of this state of things is the greater orthodoxy of the Telugus, which finds expression in early marriage and widowhood. The classic comparison of Kammálans and Kamsalas is generally adduced in support; and on the present occasion this well tried friend is found reliable. Kamsalas have 484 per 1,000 of their men married as against the 411 of the Kammálans; at the age periods 5—12, and 12—20, among the male sex Kamsala figures are 29 and 264, against the 7 and 54 of the Kammálans. The return for the gentler sex is still more conclusive. At all age periods together there are 473 Kamsala women per 1,000 married, and 272 widowed, for every 421 and 172 Kammálans. The comparison of early wifehood and widowhood I give in the margin.

Civil condition of 1,000 women.

Age.	Kamsala. Married.	Kamsala. Widowed.	Kammálan. Married.	Kammálan. Widowed.
0—5 ...	13	...	1	...
5—12 ...	356	14	17	1
12—20...	804	112	430	11

63. It may however be noticed that widowhood at the ultimate age period among men is by no means as common among the men of this East Coast (North) division as elsewhere. This fact may be a testimony to the eternal optimism of the north coast man, but it is worthy of remark that his womenkind show a somewhat similar statistical tendency. There are 137 widows per 1,000 women aged 15—40 in this division; a smaller proportion than in the Deccan and on the West Coast, where the numbers are 149 and 147; at the ultimate age period there are 649 and 657 women per 1,000 widowed in the Deccan and West Coast, as against 620 in the North-East Coast.

64. These figures may betoken a considerable possibility of widow marriage in the orthodox north; but, on the other hand, they may suggest that orthodoxy presses so hardly on the widow as to hurry her promptly into the next world.

65. Why in point of elderly widowers, (40 and over), the Deccan should predominate is not exactly easy to see; unless it be due to the fact, seen in subsidiary table II to chapter V, that proportionately there are more men of this age in the Deccan than elsewhere. The number of women and widows at this age is also high: it may be a possible conclusion that the elderly people of both sexes in this harsh climate represent the survival of the fittest, and that the odds proportionately lengthen against the simultaneous survival of both parties to a union. In 1901 widows aged 40 and over were proportionately most numerous in the Deccan; the preponderance is now observable on the West Coast. The number of men and women at this age in the division has increased, but, disregarding the Agency division, it is lower on the West Coast than elsewhere.

66. The marriage ceremonies of particular peoples, castes, and tribes have frequently been described. Among the Goomsur Khonds, it is interesting to note,

the ceremonial followed suggests a survival of the idea of marriage by capture. The West Coast system, according to which among many castes a girl goes through a form of marriage with a man who is not to be her husband, is well known; as is the practice of formally marrying (by tying of a tali) a girl who dies unmarried.

67. Fictitious marriages are not unknown. A girl may marry an arrow, or tree, perhaps to escape the reproach of attaining puberty unmarried; she may marry an idol, which generally implies that she becomes a prostitute. Among some classes a man's third marriage is considered unlucky; he accordingly espouses a tree on which ill-fortune may vent its rage, and proceeds undismayed to his fourth marriage. It is customary that children in a family should be married in the order of their birth; should deformity or disease stand in the way, the road is cleared for the expectant younger brother by the marriage of his suffering senior to a plantain tree.

68. Recent legislative proposals may give some interest to a statement of the number of marriages contracted under the Indian Civil Marriage Act (Act III of 1872). The total number of such unions in the Presidency since the passing of the Act is 54; of these 46 took place between 1902 and 1911.

I.—Distribution by civil condition of 1,000 of each sex, religion and main age period at each of the last three Censuses.

Religion.	Sex and age.	Unmarried.			Married.			Widowed.		
		1911.	1901.	1891.	1911.	1901.	1891.	1911.	1901.	1891.
1	2	3	4	5	6	7	8	9	10	11
All religions.	Males	*533*	*552*	*539*	*428*	*409*	*427*	*39*	*39*	*34*
	0–5	998	998	996	2	2	4	...	...	...
	5–10	991	993	991	9	7	9	...	...	...
	10–15	962	967	961	37	32	38	1	1	1
	15–20	849	867	842	148	130	155	3	3	3
	20–40	237	255	244	736	715	784	27	30	22
	40–60	30	30	27	876	872	885	94	98	88
	60 and over ...	20	18	17	732	733	786	248	249	247
	Females ...	*373*	*390*	*372*	*441*	*419*	*436*	*186*	*191*	*192*
	0–5	994	994	990	6	6	9	...	...	1
	5–10 .. .	946	955	937	52	44	61	2	1	2
	10–15	740	759	696	252	233	294	8	8	10
	15–20	271	286	225	697	681	745	32	33	30
	20–40	31	28	31	828	820	821	141	152	148
	40–60	10	12	17	479	451	434	511	537	549
	60 and over ...	7	9	12	137	113	107	856	878	881
Hindu ...	Males	*528*	*548*	*535*	*432*	*412*	*430*	*40*	*40*	*35*
	0–5	998	998	996	2	2	4	...	...	...
	5–10	990	992	991	10	8	9	...	...	...
	10–15	958	965	958	41	34	41	1	1	1
	15–20	842	859	836	155	138	161	3	3	3
	20–40	235	258	242	739	717	785	26	30	23
	40–60	31	30	28	873	870	883	96	100	89
	60 and over ...	21	18	17	728	780	732	251	252	251
	Females ...	*366*	*383*	*367*	*445*	*422*	*438*	*189*	*195*	*195*
	0–5	994	994	990	6	6	10	...	...	...
	5–10	941	950	932	57	48	66	2	2	2
	10–15	723	743	679	268	248	310	9	9	11
	15–20	262	276	219	705	690	750	33	34	31
	20–40	29	26	30	827	819	819	144	155	151
	40–60	10	11	16	476	448	481	514	541	553
	60 and over ...	7	8	12	185	112	106	858	880	882
Musalman.	Males	*582*	*598*	*582*	*388*	*373*	*394*	*30*	*29*	*24*
	0–5	999	999	997	1	1	3	...	...	...
	5–10	997	997	997	3	3	3	...	...	...
	10–15	989	989	990	11	11	10	...	...	...
	15–20	918	934	918	78	64	81	4	2	1
	20–40	271	286	272	700	686	711	29	28	17
	40–60	23	25	26	905	901	914	72	74	60
	60 and over ...	16	22	21	776	777	786	208	201	198
	Females ...	*412*	*428*	*412*	*413*	*398*	*416*	*175*	*174*	*172*
	0–5	998	998	995	2	2	5	...	...	...
	5–10	987	987	981	12	12	18	1	1	1
	10–15	855	861	818	140	135	178	5	4	4
	15–20	268	286	222	698	681	746	39	33	21
	20–40	26	36	48	830	821	831	144	143	126
	40–60	8	20	32	458	440	433	534	540	535
	60 and over ...	5	19	26	125	107	103	870	874	871
Christian ...	Males	*561*	*584*	*564*	*407*	*385*	*407*	*32*	*31*	*29*
	0–5	998	998	996	2	2	3	..	...	1
	5–10	997	997	995	3	3	4		...	1
	10–15	989	991	990	11	9	10	...	...	...
	15–20	923	938	906	76	61	90	1	1	2
	20–40	245	261	227	735	716	754	20	23	19
	40–60	28	24	21	890	894	907	82	82	72
	60 and over ..	19	17	14	746	752	753	235	231	233
	Females ...	*446*	*462*	*440*	*411*	*390*	*408*	*143*	*148*	*152*
	0–5	997	997	993	3	3	6		...	1
	5–10	991	991	983	9	8	16	...	1	1
	10–15	915	926	887	83	71	110	2	3	3
	15–20	439	468	374	549	518	612	12	14	14
	20–40	63	53	47	836	837	845	101	110	108
	40–60	22	19	17	541	514	490	437	467	493
	60 and over ...	16	16	12	170	142	188	814	842	850

I.—Distribution by civil condition of 1,000 of each sex, religion and main age period at each of the last three Censuses—cont.

Religion.	Sex and age.	Unmarried.			Married.			Widowed.		
		1911.	1901.	1891.	1911.	1901.	1891.	1911.	1901.	1891.
1	2	3	4	5	6	7	8	9	10	11
Animistic ...	**Males**	***540***	***545***	***524***	***424***	***415***	***436***	***36***	***40***	***40***
	0–5	997	996	991	3	4	9	...	.	...
	5–10	991	992	984	9	8	16	...	...	...
	10–15	970	975	952	29	24	47	1	1	1
	15–20	826	865	668	168	129	310	6	6	22
	20–40	206	221	195	758	737	761	36	42	44
	40–60	29	23	22	874	868	862	97	109	116
	60 and over ...	23	23	18	751	723	706	226	254	281
	Females ...	***453***	***455***	***450***	***444***	***432***	***457***	***103***	***113***	***93***
	0–5	995	998	988	5	7	12	...	...	...
	5–10	985	983	979	14	16	20	1	1	1
	10–15	894	912	847	103	84	148	3	4	5
	15–20	446	503	405	537	479	568	17	18	27
	20–40	60	54	50	860	862	885	80	84	65
	40–60	18	15	13	609	550	684	373	435	353
	60 and over ...	13	17	12	288	193	246	699	790	742
Jain ...	**Males**	***515***	***527***	***526***	***420***	***413***	***416***	***65***	***60***	***58***
	0–5	997	999	998	3	1	1	...	...	1
	5–10	995	994	992	5	5	4	...	1	4
	10–15	984	985	982	15	14	15	1	1	3
	15–20	920	934	916	80	66	83	...	...	1
	20–40	369	381	374	588	579	591	43	40	35
	40–60	75	63	62	783	806	802	142	131	136
	60 and over ...	32	44	44	677	691	687	291	265	269
	Females ...	***307***	***307***	***301***	***431***	***424***	***425***	***262***	***269***	***274***
	0–5	994	994	992	6	6	7	...	...	1
	5–10	976	971	957	22	27	39	2	2	4
	10–15	774	783	704	222	262	291	4	5	5
	15–20	175	165	150	796	805	812	29	30	38
	20–40	15	13	16	798	801	774	187	186	210
	40–60	5	7	11	414	393	366	581	600	623
	60 and over ...	2	1	7	77	57	72	921	942	921

Natural Division and Religion.	Males. All ages. Unmarried.	Married.	Widowed.	0—5. Unmarried.	Married.	Widowed.	5—10. Unmarried.	Married.	Widowed.	10—15. Unmarried.	Married.	Widowed.	15—40. Unmarried.	Married.	Widowed.	40 and over. Unmarried.	Married.	Widowed.
1	2	3	4	5	6	7	8	9	10	11	12	13	14	15	16	17	18	19
Province—																		
All Religions	533	428	39	998	2	.	991	9	.	962	37	1	378	601	21	28	840	132
Hindu	528	432	40	998	2	...	990	10	...	958	41	1	374	605	21	28	837	135
Musalman	582	388	30	999	1	...	997	3	...	989	11	...	426	551	23	21	872	107
Christian	561	407	32	998	2	...	997	3	...	989	11	...	404	581	15	26	853	121
Agency—																		
All Religions	524	439	37	996	4	..	989	11	...	955	44	1	294	674	32	28	846	126
Hindu	516	447	37	996	4	...	988	12	...	949	50	1	279	689	32	28	848	124
Musalman	505	457	38	1,000	...	...	989	11	...	970	30	...	333	631	36	30	861	109
Christian	508	463	29	993	7	...	995	4	1	966	33	1	217	757	26	29	855	116
East Coast (North)—																		
All Religions	503	464	33	996	4	...	978	21	1	907	91	2	303	680	17	21	863	116
Hindu	499	467	34	996	4	...	977	22	1	902	96	2	297	685	18	22	862	116
Musalman	559	412	29	999	1	...	996	4	...	979	20	1	418	568	14	22	875	103
Christian	530	439	31	998	2	...	997	3	...	987	13	...	364	621	15	16	879	105
Deccan—																		
All Religions	534	409	57	998	2	...	991	8	1	966	32	2	421	555	24	60	753	187
Hindu	532	409	59	998	2	..	990	9	1	964	34	2	421	554	25	62	746	192
Musalman	552	406	42	998	2	...	996	4	..	982	17	1	419	562	19	35	817	148
Christian	546	409	45	998	2	...	996	3	1	967	33	...	434	545	21	61	795	144
East Coast (Central)—																		
All Religions	542	421	37	998	2	...	995	5	...	983	17	...	408	575	17	30	842	128
Hindu	541	422	37	998	2	...	995	5	...	983	17	...	405	578	17	30	841	129
Musalman	572	401	27	998	2	.	996	4	...	985	14	1	448	537	15	29	874	97
Christian	586	387	27	998	2	...	996	4	...	990	9	1	452	536	12	32	862	106
East Coast (South)—																		
All Religions	536	425	39	998	2	..	996	4	...	985	15	...	392	588	20	23	844	133
Hindu	533	427	40	998	2	.	996	4	...	984	16	..	393	586	21	23	841	136
Musalman	576	398	26	998	2	...	996	4	...	987	13	...	374	611	15	18	885	97
Christian	555	411	34	998	2	...	997	3	...	992	8	..	378	606	16	19	850	131
West Coast—																		
All Religions	578	384	38	1,000	...	...	999	1	...	993	7	...	429	537	34	16	856	128
Hindu	566	392	42	1,000	...	...	999	1	...	992	8	...	421	542	37	16	846	138
Musalman	607	363	30	1,000	..	...	1,000	...	...	995	5	...	443	525	32	11	892	97
Christian	599	371	30	1,000	...	...	1,000	..	...	997	3	...	467	518	15	35	841	124

Natural Division and Religion.	Females. All ages. Unmarried.	Married.	Widowed.	0—5. Unmarried.	Married.	Widowed.	5—10. Unmarried.	Married.	Widowed.	10—15. Unmarried.	Married.	Widowed.	15—40. Unmarried.	Married.	Widowed.	40 and over. Unmarried.	Married.	Widowed.
1	20	21	22	23	24	25	26	27	28	29	30	31	32	33	34	35	36	37
Province—																		
All Religions	373	441	186	994	6	...	946	52	2	740	252	8	82	800	118	9	387	604
Hindu	366	445	189	994	6	...	941	57	2	723	268	9	78	802	120	9	385	606
Musalman	412	413	175	998	2	...	987	12	1	855	140	5	83	798	119	8	366	626
Christian	446	411	143	997	3	...	991	9	...	915	83	2	149	771	80	21	446	538
Agency—																		
All Religions	428	447	125	993	7	...	972	27	1	836	158	6	113	801	86	17	470	513
Hindu	415	452	133	992	8	...	966	33	1	806	187	7	93	814	93	16	448	536
Musalman	354	453	193	993	7	...	971	26	3	767	228	5	40	841	119	4	334	662
Christian	461	451	88	992	8	...	982	18	...	882	114	4	119	815	66	23	560	397
East Coast (North)—																		
All Religions	321	479	200	985	15	...	858	138	4	515	467	18	41	822	137	8	372	620
Hindu	315	481	204	984	15	1	849	147	4	493	488	19	39	820	141	8	367	625
Musalman	394	434	172	996	4	...	979	20	1	803	192	5	51	842	107	6	396	598
Christian	413	450	137	997	3	...	981	18	1	827	167	6	80	838	82	15	472	513
Deccan—																		
All Religions	352	433	215	994	5	1	947	51	2	676	314	10	62	789	149	16	335	649
Hindu	346	434	220	994	5	1	943	55	2	658	331	11	63	783	154	17	326	657
Musalman	390	434	176	995	5	...	965	33	2	794	200	6	53	836	111	8	398	594
Christian	400	429	171	995	5	...	985	14	1	846	148	6	87	804	109	13	422	565
East Coast (Central)—																		
All Religions	393	436	171	996	4	...	977	22	1	805	191	4	86	813	101	10	410	580
Hindu	390	438	172	996	4	...	976	23	1	801	195	4	85	818	102	9	411	580
Musalman	414	423	163	997	3	...	991	9	...	856	141	3	72	833	95	10	377	613
Christian	475	392	133	997	3	...	992	8	...	910	88	2	197	727	76	37	444	519
East Coast (South)—																		
All Religions	388	430	182	998	2	..	987	13	...	878	120	2	100	801	99	7	407	586
Hindu	384	432	184	998	2	...	986	13	1	875	123	2	99	802	99	7	408	585
Musalman	385	423	192	997	3	...	986	13	1	853	144	3	75	817	108	6	344	650
Christian	442	409	149	997	3	...	994	6	...	956	42	2	149	772	79	13	445	542
West Coast—																		
All Religions	409	396	195	999	1	..	992	8	.	858	136	6	123	730	147	10	338	657
Hindu	395	398	207	999	1	...	990	10	.	840	154	6	123	728	154	9	324	667
Musalman	439	391	170	1,000	...	.	997	3	.	893	101	6	108	752	140	7	352	641
Christian	483	380	137	999	1	.	998	2	...	951	49	...	206	715	79	40	419	541

III.—Distribution by main age periods and civil condition of 10,000 of each sex and religion.

Religion and age.	Males.			Females.		
	Unmarried.	Married.	Widowed.	Unmarried.	Married.	Widowed.
1	2	3	4	5	6	7
ALL RELIGIONS	*5,330*	*4,284*	*386*	*3,728*	*4,415*	*1,857*
0–10	2,651	15	...	2,575	76	2
10–15	1,173	46	1	807	274	9
15–40	1,442	2,297	81	325	3,183	470
40 and over	64	1,926	304	21	882	1,576
HINDU	*5,284*	*4,322*	*394*	*3,662*	*4,446*	*1,892*
0–10	2,626	16	1	2,547	83	2
10–15	1,165	49	1	784	291	10
15–40	1,427	2,311	80	310	3,180	477
40 and over	66	1,946	312	21	892	1,403
MUSALMAN	*5,821*	*3,876*	*303*	*4,123*	*4,132*	*1,745*
0–10	2,875	5	...	2,785	20	1
10–15	1,277	14	...	989	162	5
15–40	1,627	2,101	88	334	3,213	481
40 and over	42	1,756	215	15	737	1,258
CHRISTIAN	*5,606*	*4,071*	*323*	*4,457*	*4,114*	*1,429*
0–10	2,797	6	...	2,760	15	1
10–15	1,230	13	1	1,060	96	3
15–40	1,522	2,192	58	595	3,079	322
40 and over	57	1,860	264	42	924	1,103
ANIMISTIC	*5,400*	*4,243*	*357*	*4,527*	*4,440*	*1,033*
0–10	2,951	19	...	2,987	29	2
10–15	1,092	33	1	895	103	3
15–40	1,304	2,546	120	617	3,403	285
40 and over	53	1,645	236	28	905	743
JAIN	*5,149*	*4,202*	*649*	*3,065*	*4,313*	*2,622*
0–10	1,765	7	...	2,046	30	2
10–15	1,066	17	...	812	233	5
15–40	2,142	2,090	146	194	3,157	608
40 and over	176	2,088	503	18	893	2,007

IV.—Proportion of the sexes by civil condition at certain ages for religions and natural divisions.

Natural Division and Religion.	Number of females per 1,000 Males.														
	All ages.			0–10.			10–15.			15–40.			40 and over.		
	Unmarried.	Married.	Widowed.	Unmarried.	Married.	Widowed.	Unmarried.	Married.	Widowed.	Unmarried.	Married.	Widowed.	Unmarried.	Married.	Widowed.
1	2	3	4	5	6	7	8	9	10	11	12	13	14	15	16
Province—															
All Religions	722	1,064	4,965	1,002	5,208	4,927	710	6,194	8,135	232	1,430	5,997	341	473	4,678
Hindu	716	1,063	4,956	1,002	5,343	4,927	695	6,100	8,133	225	1,422	6,132	325	473	4,641
Musalman	729	1,097	5,914	997	4,028	4.800	797	11,623	9,846	211	1,575	5 638	368	432	6,017
Christian	819	1,041	4,562	1,017	2,613	3,824	887	7,579	8,550	403	1,447	5,739	776	512	4,301
Agency—															
All Religions	812	1,010	3,351	1,002	2,375	4,737	768	3,154	5,061	407	1,252	2,777	550	502	3,661
Hindu	799	1,004	3,616	1,003	2,713	4,200	746	3,300	5,971	352	1,240	3,030	527	481	3.928
Musalman	676	958	4,880	1,059	2,750	...	581	5,625	...	115	1,270	3,189	133	383	5,982
Christian	889	953	2,934	1,064	2,455	...	744	2,815	3,000	534	1,051	2,514	733	636	3,217
East Coast (North)—															
All Religions	667	1,077	6,249	955	6,287	6,793	514	4,673	7,861	150	1,326	8,587	387	455	5,660
Hindu	661	1,080	6,336	951	6,333	6,815	495	4,620	7,843	146	1.318	8,747	383	455	5,729
Musalman	692	1,033	5,879	997	5,520	5.429	744	8,832	6,000	125	1,508	7,965	266	422	5,431
Christian	759	999	4,371	1,033	4,303	8,000	762	11,673	19,500	228	1,396	5,526	769	451	4,077
Deccan—															
All Religions	639	1,027	3,669	996	5,603	2,518	648	9,016	5,836	145	1,399	6,023	252	408	3,191
Hindu	632	1,029	3 643	994	5,567	2,278	636	9,037	5,737	147	1,394	6,088	257	402	3 150
Musalman	675	1,018	3,988	1,011	6,650	7,600	708	10,429	6,750	120	1,429	5,580	212	442	3,650
Christian	703	1,006	3,669	1,004	3,615	2,500	813	4,119	23,000	203	1,492	5,301	184	450	3,337
East Coast (Central)—															
All Religions	729	1,044	4,686	1,031	3,816	4,764	755	105,030	10,909	220	1,469	6,184	308	467	4,354
Hindu	728	1,044	4,650	1,032	3,913	4,908	752	10,578	11,588	217	1,464	6,170	294	470	4,314
Musalman	714	1 039	5 817	1,024	2,006	2,700	787	8,916	4,333	167	1,605	6,577	323	384	5,633
Christian	828	1,033	5,073	1,025	2,036	2,667	876	8,904	3,333	467	1,453	6,847	1,066	495	4,715
East Coast (South)—															
All Religions	779	1,091	4,973	1,031	2,755	3,294	837	7,428	8,500	289	1.542	5,559	330	532	4,832
Hindu	772	1,081	4,848	1,031	2,803	3,192	828	7,304	8,451	280	1,528	5,396	309	531	4,716
Musalman	828	1,316	9,283	1,023	2,797	4 000	899	12,032	12,500	286	1,912	9,846	473	531	9,139
Christian	860	1,076	4,663	1,020	1,787	4,167	940	5,016	6,143	461	1,488	5,793	689	560	4,481
West Coast—															
All Religions	735	1,070	5,280	979	7,348	3,722	812	18,341	21,906	307	1,459	4,572	683	432	5,681
Hindu	735	1,070	5,187	983	7,564	4,154	804	18,278	23,372	318	1,448	4,574	629	437	5,516
Musalman	723	1,077	5,782	970	5,338	3,333	811	18,887	19,550	256	1,496	4,513	699	414	6,769
Christian	815	1,036	4,634	977	35,000	1,500	976	17,129	4,000	453	1,422	5,545	1,181	507	4,416

V.—*Distribution by civil condition of 1,000 of each sex at certain ages for selected castes.*

Distribution of 1,000 males of each age by civil condition.

Caste.	All ages.			0–5.			5–12.			12–20.			20–40.			40 and over.		
	Unmarried.	Married.	Widowed.	Unmarried.	Married.	Widowed.	Unmarried.	Married.	Widowed.	Unmarried.	Married.	Widowed.	Unmarried.	Married.	Widowed.	Unmarried.	Married.	Widowed.
1	2	3	4	5	6	7	8	9	10	11	12	13	14	15	16	17	18	19
Balija	546	406	48	998	2	1	996	4	...	947	52	1	319	657	24	55	787	158
Bráhman: Tamil	437	509	54	998	2	..	994	6	...	740	257	3	121	854	25	35	785	180
Bráhman: Telugu	512	441	47	998	2	...	981	19	...	737	259	4	183	791	26	66	761	178
Bráhman: Malayálam: Embrándri ...	388	561	51	1,000	...	...	1,000	...	...	921	74	5	203	748	49	10	886	104
Bráhman: Malayálam: Nambúdri ...	458	508	34	1,000	...	...	1,000	...	...	936	64	...	210	766	24	40	868	92
Bráhman: Malayálam: Pattar ...	379	572	49	1,000	...	...	1,000	...	...	892	108	...	184	794	22	39	830	131
Bráhman: Canarese ...	504	439	57	1,000	..	...	998	2	...	890	106	4	201	776	23	39	759	202
Bráhman: Oriyá	472	493	35	991	9	...	976	23	1	704	288	8	111	867	22	19	854	127
Cheruman	648	409	43	1,000	...	...	1,000	...	.	926	68	6	161	784	55	8	851	141
Chetti	521	435	44	998	2	...	991	9	...	852	146	2	226	740	34	85	824	141
Dévánga	448	508	49	996	4	...	960	39	1	666	327	7	138	827	35	34	803	163
Holeya	627	338	35	998	2	..	997	3	..	970	29	1	277	690	33	20	837	148
Kaikólan	514	425	61	998	2	..	990	9	1	833	163	4	166	790	44	34	756	210
Kálingi	362	595	43	993	6	1	828	164	8	375	605	20	42	928	30	7	863	130
Kalinji	432	546	22	987	12	1	892	106	2	366	624	10	31	945	24	17	911	72
Kammálan	555	411	34	999	1	...	993	7	..	945	54	1	267	707	26	36	847	117
Kamsala	472	484	44	997	3	...	971	29	...	726	264	10	139	832	29	24	824	152
Kápu	480	482	38	997	3	..	953	46	1	730	265	5	189	789	22	33	838	129
Kómati	491	466	43	999	1	...	993	7	..	802	194	4	190	783	27	43	820	137
Mála	524	445	31	999	1	.	980	19	1	808	189	3	128	848	24	17	870	118
Paraiyan	547	428	25	998	2	...	995	5	...	923	76	1	155	828	17	18	892	95
Sále	463	492	45	998	2	...	956	43	1	742	253	5	116	846	38	25	831	144
Shánán	587	378	35	999	1	..	999	1	...	980	19	1	308	674	18	13	848	139
Tíyan	572	389	39	1,000	...	..	999	1	..	956	41	3	242	703	55	8	873	119

Distribution of 1,000 females of each age by civil condition.

Caste.	All ages.			0–5.			5–12.			12–20.			20–40.			40 and over.		
	Unmarried.	Married.	Widowed.	Unmarried.	Married.	Widowed.	Unmarried.	Married.	Widowed.	Unmarried.	Married.	Widowed.	Unmarried.	Married.	Widowed.	Unmarried.	Married.	Widowed.
1	20	21	22	23	24	25	26	27	28	29	30	31	32	33	34	35	36	37
Balija	345	424	231	993	7	...	935	63	2	387	592	21	27	797	176	12	317	671
Bráhman: Tamil	258	495	247	996	4	...	868	130	2	106	863	31	16	804	180	7	348	645
Bráhman: Telugu	235	472	293	993	6	1	719	274	7	57	878	65	18	730	257	2	299	699
Bráhman: Malayálam: Embrándri ...	356	422	222	1,000	...		993	7	...	370	604	26	23	800	177	9	316	675
Bráhman: Malayálam: Nambúdri ...	362	372	266	1,000	...	..	996	4	...	658	319	23	65	783	152	6	288	711
Bráhman: Malayálam: Pattar ...	362	494	144	1,000	...	...	953	47	...	116	871	13	7	891	102	5	441	554
Bráhman: Canarese ...	270	458	272	998	2	...	905	93	2	51	898	51	4	741	255	2	274	724
Bráhman: Oriyá	273	471	256	954	45	1	766	226	8	63	872	65	18	749	233	10	301	689
Cheruman	407	400	193	1,000	...	...	995	5	...	556	413	31	47	775	178	8	341	651
Chetti	364	431	205	996	4	...	977	22	1	532	453	15	26	828	146	15	392	593
Dévánga	257	496	247	978	21	1	692	301	7	113	844	43	24	781	195	5	305	690
Holeya	414	368	218	999	1	...	987	12	1	633	346	21	53	761	186	7	290	703
Kaikólan	432	432	136	999	1	...	968	31	1	561	430	9	67	830	103	30	511	459
Kálingi	185	597	218	915	84	1	350	632	18	27	914	59	3	827	170	2	348	650
Kalinji	254	579	167	956	44	...	513	478	9	92	870	38	17	860	123	9	416	575
Kammálan	407	421	172	999	1	.	982	17	1	559	430	11	38	831	181	14	418	568
Kamsala	255	473	272	987	13	...	630	356	14	84	804	112	11	711	278	5	291	704
Kápu	283	502	215	978	22	..	704	288	8	216	741	43	15	805	180	5	371	624
Kómati	261	484	255	995	5	...	746	247	7	63	878	59	9	763	228	3	817	680
Mála	369	467	164	995	5	...	872	125	3	280	675	45	35	825	140	17	425	558
Paraiyan	414	449	187	997	3	...	961	38	1	466	524	10	30	878	92	9	456	535
Sále	291	499	210	982	18	.	707	287	6	188	752	65	28	786	186	17	366	617
Shánán	456	383	161	999	1	.	996	4	...	778	220	2	35	857	108	11	409	580
Tíyan	437	377	186	1,000	...	.	994	6	.	604	360	36	73	747	180	12	346	642

CHAPTER VIII.—EDUCATION.

STATISTICS procured by the census enquiry are generally deemed to afford occasion for a Jeremiah-like wailing over the educational lack of the Indian, tempered at intervals with consoling reflections as to progress made.

2. If education be "the systematic instruction, schooling or training, given to the young in preparation for the work of life," it is scarcely just to draw conclusions, flattering or otherwise, as to the education of 42 million souls from the hasty enquiry of a single night as to how many people can write a letter and read the reply to it. For such was the criterion of education adopted at the present census. In other words literacy and education are not always convertible terms.

3. Reading and writing are so widespread in the West, and afford such a ready *means* towards education, that we may now take it as an axiom that an educated European can read and write. Hence we infer, somewhat illogically, that his education is the result of his reading and writing, and overlook the possibility of its attainment by other means. Yet reflection suggests that there are many whose literacy merely enables them to read rubbish, and occasionally write it; and whose education—the training of the mind that enables them to give a decent account of themselves in the battle of life—has been won in other ways. A recent writer on Agricultural Education has pointed out that the working farmer—on the whole a solid, thoughtful sort of man—is best reached, even in Europe, by oral exposition; his mechanical power of reading is not sufficient to let him deal with the meaning behind the written symbols. Cardinal Antonelli said of the Roman mob that, despite their illiteracy, their artistic judgment as a rule agreed admirably with cultivated opinion. The Madras agriculturist, the backbone of his country, and no fool at his calling, a few typical figures show as generally illiterate.

Occupation.	Population dealt with.	Literates.	Literates per 1,000.
Cultivating landowner.	973,196	153,343	158
Cultivating tenant ...	266,765	38,546	144
Farm labourer ...	543,192	11,901	22

4. Turning to table VIII we find that 3,130,250 of the 41,870,160 persons in the Presidency now satisfy, or profess to satisfy, the test of literacy. Comparison with the figures of 1891 is hardly possible, for at that enumeration to the literates was added a heterogeneous class of "learners," among whom the student for his M.A. degree, and the infant biting his paws over the alphabet, ranked alike; while the Presidency total included figures for Travancore and Cochin. Compared with those of 1901 these figures show an absolute increase of 693,046 literates, or a proportional increase of 17·9 per mille, in relation to the total population.

5. Or, to sum up the matter briefly, the general population has increased by 83 per mille during the past decade. Separating the literate sheep from the illiterate goats, we find that the former have increased and multiplied at the rate of 284 per mille, the latter at but one quarter of this rate.

6. But only 75 per thousand of the people, 138 men and 13 women per thousand of each sex, can read and write in the year of grace 1911.

7. Granting, as we have done, that a profession such as agriculture, subject to disturbing influences which man cannot control, contains in its daily exercise certain educative possibilities, yet here, as in more stereotyped occupations, the general standard of intelligence is not so high as to render superfluous some additional measure of mental training. The most obvious direction in which such might be sought is that of literary education; but before we denounce the Indian donkey for lack of zeal in his pursuit of the educational carrot, it is only fair to consider the carrot's quality.

8. Much of the primary education now offered is undoubtedly bad; mere rote work taught to children by incompetent underpaid men. An interesting light was thrown on this subject by enquiries made as to the every-day avocations of men temporarily employed in the census office. Though literate, most of these people could not by any stretch of the imagination be described as educated; and between sudden demands for cheap clerical labour they find strange and casual livings. Prominent among such casualties is pedagogy; the perpetuation of a vicious system by its products.

9. Moreover, in Southern India the path to literacy is beset with certain obstacles, which exist but in a very modified form in European countries. The fundamental difficulty inherent in the complicated and varying scripts of the Dravidian languages is even now recognized directly in the search for a simplified and universal alphabet, and perhaps indirectly in the spread of English education. The difficulty experienced in obtaining a translation of the census rules intelligible to the ordinary run of mankind, suggests that the peculiar syntactical construction of these languages, aided, it is true, by the pedantic convention which esteems literary style in Tamil or Telugu by its measure of Sanskritic unintelligibility, renders it scarcely less difficult for the "plain common Indian" than for the foreigner, to express, or understand in print, those shades of meaning, which in conversation, gesture and intonation supply.

10. There are certain further standpoints from which it is well to examine these figures. Such are religion, sex, and age.

11. Although there is no necessary connection between education and a particular form of theology, it is not surprising that the proportion of literate Christians should compare very favourably with similar returns for other religions. The proportion of 226 male literates per mille among Christians is exceeded by that of 463 per mille among the Jains; but then the Jain community of the Presidency is so exceedingly small as to forbid the drawing of general inferences as to their educational position. Christians include among their ranks, it is true, a considerable number (32,048) of ready-made literates, Europeans and Anglo-Indians, but the true explanation of their pre-eminence in education is probably to be found in the spirit in which instruction is given.

12. The old time teacher of India—I have met a few survivors—taught chiefly because he liked teaching and talking. His methods may have been odd, but he followed them because he believed in them; not because they were laid down by a code, and supervised by an inspector. Direct material return he expected neither for himself nor for his pupils: hence he was favoured in his disciples, for those who stayed with him were presumably of the true student type, and sought learning even at the cost of material loss. The method of the modern lay teacher is too often but accurate and mechanical obedience to a prescribed routine, on which he bestows neither considered approval nor disapproval. His efforts are directed, not so much to improving generally the mind and *morale* of his students, as to loading them up with answers to questions, to be discharged on some stated occasions with direct or prospective pecuniary advantage—and then forgotten. To some extent this may explain the curious discrepancy between the liberal theory and conservative practice of present day India. The high caste boy of an older day learned his superiority to the rest of mankind, and acted on such learning: his modern descendant learns the equality of all men, but learns with a view to a telling phrase in the examination hall or debating theatre, rather than to the practical ordering of his life.

13. No one will assert that the gaze of the educational missionary is entirely diverted from the possibility of worldly result: "he catches children with the bait of a good education, offering to the capable a hope of lucrative place and employment;" but at bottom his secular teaching is but a means to the altering of his flock's whole life scheme. He offers education as part of a systematic cultural plan; State schools offer reading and writing raw.

Literacy per mille.

Religion.	1911. Total.	M.	F.	1901. Total.	M.	F.
All religions	75	138	13	68	119	9
Hindu ...	72	135	11	61	116	7
Muhammadan.	87	166	11	74	141	9
Christian ...	165	226	106	143	198	91

14. The marginal statement bears out this contention. It shows that, as compared with the total population, and with the followers of Hinduism and Muhammadanism, the Christians have maintained and improved on the advantage with which they started at the commencement of the decade.

15. At the same time a certain reserve is necessary in the appreciation of these figures and arguments. A small well-defined community, other circumstances being alike, favours educational progress much more than one amorphous and unwieldy: the point is illustrated by figures relating to the Jain community quoted in the margin. The Christian and Muhammadan communities bear to that of Hinduism the proportion of but 32, and 72 per mille, respectively. Moreover the acceptance of Christianity is now practically tantamount to the placing of oneself within the reach of education; so much does secular instruction form part of the Christian missionary's scheme of things.

Population.	Total.	Males.	Females.
Jains.	27,005	14,166	12,839
Literates per mille.	257	463	29

16. Despite its great past, one scarcely sees such intimate connection nowadays between education and the faith of Islam; but at the same time that faith, far more than Hinduism, is wont to urge on its followers the small tincture of letters needed to decipher its sacred writings.

17. Furthermore the Christian and Muhammadan communities, despite internal sectarian differences, are, as a whole, well defined. Hinduism, as suggested in Chapter IV, is a term applied by European theological use to the beliefs of various peoples, who neither definitely repudiate one indefinite creed, nor accept any one of certain others more precise and fixed. Philosophic Hinduism has no need to be ashamed for the education of its followers; it is unfair to saddle it with responsibility for the educational shortcomings of heterogeneous multitudes,* whose chief claim to inclusion in the faith is that the wide tolerance of Hinduism has never definitely cast them out. And even accepting Hinduism as a whole, it is fair to recognize that this whole is in Southern India mainly rural and agricultural, and thus more independent of literacy than the Muhammadan community, which is rather urban and commercial.

18. I have said that small communities are more susceptible of education than large, other circumstances being alike. The qualification is necessary, and will explain the shortcomings of the Animists, whose poor literary case is exhibited in the margin. The term "Animist" has no particular theological meaning, and is but the label affixed to certain wandering tribes of the plains, and to the aborigines of the hills. The roving life of the former precludes school attendance; an obstacle to the education of the latter, though but one among many, is found in the fact that their languages possess no script of their own, and are, as a rule, not well suited by the script of their more civilized neighbours.

Literates per mille.

Total.	Male.	Female.
2	4	0·1

19. *Sex.*—It may not be incorrect to say that for the general welfare of Southern India in the present day progress in female, rather than in male education is significant and important. The exceeding bitter cry of the modern social reformer is ever that his struggle towards the light is hampered by the dead weight of

* Thus an early Christian writer—"The Bráhmans at the instigation of the devil, whose ministers they are, keep before the eyes of the masses a veil of superstition and ignorance, and thus secure themselves an easy living." A kindly apostle of the same school explains the success of Christian missionaries of a different sect as due "to the aid of the devil to whom they and their converts already belong."

female superstition and ignorance, that he can neither break from, nor drag with him; if a foreigner is chary of such wholesale condemnation, it cannot but strike him as curious that those who vaunt the position of the Indian woman, are wont to measure her influence by her power to place obstacles in the path of progress.

20. The propriety of making literacy the sole test of education has already been questioned. It would be a monstrous error to write down Indian womanhood as uneducated because illiterate; but it is a fair query whether illiteracy among women is not more likely to connote non-education than amongst men; and whether the effects of such illiteracy, when it exists, are not more marked and more disastrous among the higher classes than among the lower; among the well-to-do rather than among the very poor.

21. If a man does not or cannot sharpen his wits on the "three R's," he can do so to some extent in the following of his daily avocation; the smith must hammer his iron with due featness, the witness in large practice must vigilantly avoid a mixing of his facts. But a woman's part in her husband's avocation is at best small; and the higher her social rank, and the easier her worldly circumstances, the smaller it becomes. The syce's wife may have a working knowledge of how to handle and care for animals, the small farmer's better-half is to a considerable degree a practical agriculturist. But it is hard to estimate the mental opacity of the rich man's wife, to whom orthodoxy forbids reading, and whom wealth, or so called dignity, absolves from household cares and economies.

22. An addition to the community of 104 thousand literate women, of whom 37 thousand, now at the age period 10–20, will be the mothers of the coming generation, represents real step forward.

23. On this ascertained increase in female literates, rather than on statistics as to the number * of girls now under instruction, hopes for the next decade must be based. For though a spirit of enlightenment is abroad, there will arise a plaguy doubt as to the reality of these school returns. One cannot help a suspicion that in many a case a daughter appears in a school return merely as an advertisement of the liberalism of her parent. Sent an infant to the school, as to a *crêche*, she is removed at the age of 9 or 10, before she can possibly have learned anything.

24. Viewed by religions, and in relation to the total population, literate women of all religions have increased by 5 per mille, Hindu women by a similar proportion, Muhammadan by 3, and Christian by 32 per mille. As regards the total religious community, it is true that so far only Christian literate women are of appreciable account; they number 106 per mille in contrast to the 11 per mille of Hinduism and Muhammadanism. But, placing literates and illiterates in separate classes, we see that progress is being made where it most was needed. Female literates in general have increased at the rate of 577, as against their illiterate sisters' rate of 81 per mille; similar proportional figures for Hinduism are 681 and 79, for Muhammadanism 393 and 107, for Christianity 355 and 142.

25. It is in some degree possible to estimate the vitality of literary education by the division of literates by age periods. The children of 0–10 at the present enumeration will be the adolescents of 10–20 in 1921; the college students of to-day will be the *grihasthas* of ten years hence. True education ends for man with the end of all things, but, as already explained, for our present purposes a more modest connotation of the word must needs suffice.

* *Number of female scholars according to the Report of the Director of Public Instruction for* 1910–1911.

Total ...	207,932	In Traning schools ...	404
In Arts colleges ...	32	„ Other special schools ...	891
„ Professional colleges ...	11	Private institutions — Advanced ...	500
„ Secondary schools ...	33,496	Private institutions — Elementary ...	16,571
„ Primary schools ...	156,027		

26. We would naturally expect the proportion of literates per mille at the period "20 and over" to be greater than such proportions at the earlier age-periods. But if the proportionate increase at the final age-period exceeds that of the earlier periods, it is a sign that an uneducated generation is growing up.

27. Happily every indication is in the other direction. The figures noted in the margin show that the younger generation are more than holding their own, especially in the Hindu and Christian communities. Even in the case of Muhammadans it is not an unfair supposition that a trading community may seek its education at a later age than those which supply recruits to the clerical and learned profession.

Religion.	Literates (of both sexes) per mille.		
	10–15.	15–20.	20 and over.
All religions ...	72	107	103
Hindu	69	103	99
Muhammadan ...	66	111	134
Christian	202	271	211

Religion.	Increase per mille in literates of both sexes.		
	10–15.	15–20.	20 and over.
All religions ...	290	316	277
Hindu	298	307	267
Muhammadan ...	297	361	319
Christian	254	377	375

28. Figures showing proportionate increase at the various age-periods are also encouraging. They may be quoted, while in view of the special importance of female education, similar statements for that sex alone deserve a place.

A.

Religion.	Female literates per mille.		
	10–15.	15–20.	20 and over.
All religions	22	29	14
Hindu	18	24	11
Muhammadan ...	16	19	13
Christian	160	211	118

B.

Religion.	Increase per mille in female literates.		
	10–15.	15–20.	20 and over.
All religions	514	609	616
Hindu	626	690	712
Muhammadan ...	408	445	393
Christian	250	427	418

29. Statement B, it is true, hardly bears out our contention literally, but then if things are seldom quite so fair as one would wish them to be, here they are quite sufficiently fair to encourage the hope that they will yet be fairer.

30. Thus far education taken as but the equivalent of literacy. Progress in secondary, or higher education, is difficult to estimate: selection of *data* on which to found an examination is a matter on which no two persons are likely to agree. I shall take the recorded results of literacy in English, statistics supplied by the Registrar of Books, and those to be found in the University calendars for the decade.

31. There is nothing particularly meritorious in a knowledge of English *per se*: the weird reasoning of his northern fellow countryman occasionally casts up such knowledge as a reproach to the Madrasi. Still there would seem to be greater educational possibilities in a knowledge of two languages than of one; in Madras in particular, a knowledge of English affords opportunity for the commerce and interchange of ideas throughout the Presidency as a whole, as well as beyond its limits. The positive spread of this knowledge is not so far very great; it is claimed but by 66 per 10,000 of the total population; by 53 Hindu and 46 Muhammadans of a similar number. Christians, whose community includes many to whom English is the ordinary means of communication, naturally outstrip all other religions with 541 per 10,000. This department of education, as one would expect,

is almost entirely confined to one sex. Of some 19 million Hindu, and one and a half million Muhammadan women, but 3,770 and 194 respectively can read and write English. Among Christians, female literates in English number 23,124 out of a total of 613,280; but it must be admitted that the major portion of this total (14,152) belongs to the European and Anglo-Indian communities.

Nature of increase.	All religions	Hindu.	Muhammadan.	Christian.
Absolute ...	84,784	67,222	4,828	12,469
Per mille ..	442	515	613	236

32. Proportional figures deduced from absolute figures, in which one term is exceedingly great or exceedingly small, are apt to prove misleading. The marginal statement shows the progress, both absolute and proportional, made during the decade in English literacy.

Age periods.	Increase per mille.			
	All religions	Hindu.	Muhammadan.	Christian.
0–10	−40	−29	404	−68
10–15	178	246	360	15
15–20	374	421	431	226
20 and over ...	525	598	697	309

33. Subsidiary table IV shows the present position of English education by age periods: the marginal statement shows the relation of these figures to those of 1901.

34. It is a permissible supposition that the proportional decrease at the first age period in all religions, and in each religion save Muhammadanism, is due to more accurate enumeration. The absolute figures in the case of Muhammadanism are so small, (an increase from 99 to 139), as to be negligible.

Class dealt with.	Increase per mille.			
	All religions	Hindu.	Muhammadan.	Christian.
Literates ...	284	278	322	339
Literates in English.	442	515	613	233

35. A comparison of the progress of literacy in English with literacy in general may be exhibited for what it is worth.

36. The results of University examinations in 1911 are set forth in subsidiary table VIII, in a form which permits comparison with similar happenings ten and twenty years previously. There too progress is apparent, save, oddly enough, in the matter of B.L.'s.

37. Yet with no desire to disparage the success that has crowned honest endeavour, one may doubt whether such statistics be of much import, good or ill, for the due appreciation of South Indian educational life. Tacitly, if not expressly, the longer experience of western countries has accepted the ideal of educational value contained in the definition of a University as a place where young men can meet under modified control; where preparation for the examination is of greater value than in its passing. Free association and interminglement are as yet impossible in a land whose strange deifications some of her most famous sons have quaintly satirized; and the direct attachment of graduated pecuniary values to the passing of each and every examination, whether in public service—goal hitherto of all good graduates, where a man's adult capacity is measured largely by the academic success of his boyhood—or in the modern matrimonial market, cannot but depreciate the intrinsic worth of university laurels; while it endows them with a worthless worth as means to an end. Here too we may look for some explanation of the strange differentiation supposed hithereto to exist in modern India between the "educated" and the "upper" classes. Admirable as is the heroic self-sacrifice, through which a poor family sends its promising son to the University, it is too often but a curious placing out at interest of the family savings; the interest consisting in the obligation, faithfully recognized in most cases, on the

scholar to support his family on the monthly sale-proceeds of his University distinctions. The wealthy zamindar, under no necessity to provide for himself an old age pension, as yet hardly appreciates the value to his son, as an end in itself, of a University education.

38. It can hardly be argued that a great increase of published matter stands invariably for an improved intellectual activity; the tons of printed matter daily current in modern Europe do not necessarily denote, or coincide with, an era of spacious thought. But in Southern India the margin between scarcity and superfluity is still so wide that we may welcome the increase in publication shown by subsidiary table X as indicative of a growing public, to whom the art of reading is sufficiently familiar to render books and newspapers an agreement of life. We are far enough yet from the realization of the visions of the journalist, who saw, as in a glass darkly, Ramaswami leaning at even in intellectual contemplation on the five-barred gate of his paddy field, or deciphering the daily newspapers in the village smithy.

39. Education has been considered so far in relation to the Presidency as a whole, and to the main religions existing therein. Subsidiary tables II to VI afford material for some comment as to the position and progress of education in territorial divisions, and among the varying *strata* of the population represented by its several castes and tribes.

40. From our comparisons it may be as well to exclude Madras, Anjengo, and the Nilgiri Hills; the conditions existing in these three localities being somewhat different from those which obtain throughout the Presidency in general. Inasmuch as Anjengo and the Nilgiris are included in the West Coast division, we may discount the advantage in total literacy which subsidiary table II shows this division to possess; and assign pride of place to the East Coast southern territories, of which Tinnevelly heads the list in point of male literacy, and takes second place to Malabar as regards the education of its womankind. Education in Tinnevelly would appear to be in a healthily progressive state, inasmuch as the district, in addition to claiming for its men the educational place formerly occupied by those of Tanjore, shows in female literacy a considerably greater rate of increase than Malabar, and in point of English education is rapidly closing up the gap, which, at the last enumeration, separated it from Tanjore and Chingleput.

41. It is but in the nature of things that the Agency division, which in tabular arrangement is placed first, should in point of achievement occupy the last place. And for reasons already stated it is not surprising that its educational progress, even among men, should be represented by a figure less than one-third of that of its immediate superior, the Deccan. In this latter division the conditions of agricultural life are somewhat too strenuous to admit of literary dalliance; the marked paucity of scholars, both male and female, at the age of primary school-going (10–15), suggests that literary education has not as yet disclosed to the worthy householders of these stern regions a profitable field for the energies of their children.

42. If we divide the people, as Chapter IX shows that we may fairly do, into Tamils and Telugus, these subsidiary tables make it clear that educational advantage is entirely on the side of the Tamils. Yet bearing in mind the connotation, as yet artificial and unsatisfactory, of the word "education" to the present intelligence of the Madras *raiyat*, one hesitates to stigmatize as backward the second great section of the southern people, because of their apparent inappreciation of the arts of reading and writing. It is curious to note that well nigh one hundred years ago, when education as now understood in India was not, a keen observer * drew a cultural comparison between the Tamils and Telugus, much to the advantage of the latter.

* Monseigneur Bonnand—*vide* Chapter IV.

43. When we consider the obvious advantage in respect of educational facilities possessed by a city as contrasted with the country, it is somewhat surprising that the Madras cities do not make a better showing in subsidiary table II. But, as already suggested in Chapter I, the term city is to a great extent a misnomer as applied in Madras, save to the capital; while figures quoted in the margin show that the general educational average of such cities as there are is utterly depreciated by lack of attention to the instruction of women. It is curious to find that Kumbakonam, generally regarded as an educational centre, and surpassing Madras city itself in regard to the education of its sons, should occupy last place but one among these six selected cities, if judged by its achievements in female literacy. The figures of Calicut and Cocanada indeed would almost suggest that male and female education enjoy a see-saw existence in relation to each other.

City.	Number per 1,000 who are literate.	
	Male.	Female.
Madras	421	129
Kumbakonam	470	57
Calicut	352	112
Madura	412	50
Cocanada	268	71
Trichinopoly	433	86

44. In a further paraphrase of statistics bearing on education by locality there is little genuine purpose. There is no general conclusion to be drawn, that the reader cannot draw for himself; no salient figure, that the trouble of turning a page will not give him.

45. Of more possible interest is the information in regard to the literacy of particular castes and tribes, which Imperial table IX and subsidiary table VI provide.

46. It is well to observe at the commencement that the proportional contrasts, which subsidiary table VI draws between our present table IX and its predecessor of ten years back, are apt to be misleading. In 1901 Imperial table IX showed the literacy of certain selected castes, and dealt only with those castes as found in particular districts. The table as now prepared classifies all the literates of the Presidency in accordance with the social or racial groups to which they belong. This result, more complete and satisfactory than that of old, I venture to think, is due to the ingenuity of Mr. S. Dandapani Aiyar, who pointed out an easy way to its accomplishment. To sort the slips of two million eight hundred thousand Pallis to find 137 thousand literates would be a stupendous task, and one not worth the doing, if it had to be repeated for every caste and tribe of the Presidency. But inasmuch as the population *had* to be divided by caste and tribe, two objects could be accomplished at once by separating literates and illiterates generally for Imperial table VIII, and then sorting these two agglomerations separately for the purposes of table XIII. The sorting of the literate section provided table IX as it now stands; simple addition of literate to illiterate caste totals gave table XIII.

47. So much for the method. The main result, as subsidiary table VI shows, namely the general literary predominance of the Bráhman, is what might have been expected. In point of female education, it is true, the Náyars are only excelled to any appreciable extent by the Bráhmans of their own country, and their advantage over Canarese, Oriyá, and "other" Bráhmans is very clearly marked. In the peculiar traditions, if not present practice, of Malabar womankind, we may find an explanation of the prejudice against female education, which still lingers in the orthodox Hindu mind; the point is accentuated by the comparatively high percentage of literacy (167, and 210 per mille) noticeable in the Bógam and Dási castes.

48. Educationally the Bráhman is the leader of Southern India. In view of what "education" at present represents, it is permissible to consider whether the Bráhman's pre-eminence is altogether to his unmixed advantage. The point was brought home to me one day, when walking with a meteorologist and a carpenter. The meteorologist was a Bráhman, and an educated man: that is to say, having proved at certain examinations that he could speak and write indifferent English, he had thereby been enabled to follow a literary, or clerical profession, on a salary

entirely inadequate for the comfortable maintenance of himself and of his family. The carpenter, a Gallio in regard to education, followed a humbler walk of life with much more solid pecuniary advantage.

49. It is not every man's lot to go to Corinth; nor, one fears, is the intellectual endowment of each and every Bráhman sufficient for the acquirement of a literary education, that will serve him as a sufficient pecuniary stay of life. Yet to a great extent the Bráhman, whose traditional priesthood is scarcely now a practical calling, has cut himself off from all professions, save those whose practice demands some tincture of literacy; with the consequent result that he has overstocked his own market. And it is curious to notice how in this clerical market Indian opinion tends to regulate advancement by the passing of literary examinations to the disregard of practical ability; and thus to forge chains for its own community.

50. Although for the ultimate progress of the country female education is of the last importance, and though, as already noted, the tender plant shows progress, yet for present purposes the number of educated women is too small to justify comparisons based on column 2 of subsidiary table VI. Confining our attention to column 3, we shall find that literacy is found chiefly among those sections of the people whose occupations render its possession of immediate use and advantage.

51. Thus the Kómatis, the great traders of the Presidency, have more than half their men literate, and, in comparison with other castes, show a respectable percentage of English literacy. Chettis—the term is somewhat vague—traders also, show 391 men per 1,000 as literate; among artisans Kaikólans and Kammálans, with their Telugu brethren, the Kamsalas, occupy a fairly high position. It is worthy of remark that although the Tamil goldsmiths are popularly credited with greater liberalism and enlightenment than the Telugu, the latter have the advantage in female education, and in literacy in English. The connection of oil-pressing with education is not at once obvious to explain the culture of the Vániyans, whose educational champions, it is obvious, were somewhat ill chosen in 1901.

52. Among agriculturists, Kápus with 90 literates per 1,000 men compare unfavourably with the Tamil Vellálas. Vellála, it must be admitted, is a caste name of very wide comprehension; and one by no means so closely associated with agriculture as Kápu. The Kammas are in better case, but still are far below the Bants of the West Coast (184 per 1,000).

53. Oriyá castes in general, with 103 male literates per 1,000, present a somewhat better appearance than I should have imagined, judging from the difficulty experienced in finding hands for the census abstraction office at Berhampur. It should, however, be remembered that for this office literacy in the Oriyá language was essential; that the qualification is not widespread I infer from some small personal experience, from the fact that in 1901, when literacy by language was tabulated, Oriyá was not included in the list, and from the Superintendent of the Press, whom the lack of education amongst Oriyá criminals, or of criminal propensity amongst educated Oriyás much intrigues: the Oriyá convict cannot be used to supplement a deficiency of Oriyá compositors. If, indeed, Oriyá Bráhmans be excluded, the literacy of these Oriyá castes falls to 61 per 1,000; and Oriyá Bráhmans, it may be observed, occupy last place in the Bráhman educational scale.

54. The depressed brother figures poorly in educational matters. The Tamil Paraiyans, with 28 per 1,000 men literate, far outstrip such folk as Málas, Mádigas, Cherumans and Chakkiliyans—a result possibly in some measure attributable to their frequent employment in European domestic service, which so horrifies at times the Indian visitor. In an occupation not usually held in India social esteem—that of the barber—we find an appreciable percentage of literacy among the Tamil Ambattans, and the Telugu Mangalas; Tíyans and Shánáns have now honourably extricated themselves from a once despised position, and a proof of their advancement may be seen in their education. Kallan progress may denote perception of the charm of honesty, or an adaptation of the people to the greater educational

needs of their hereditary profession in the twentieth century. The Maravan, whose attachment to his neighbours' cattle has been at time a subject of unfavourable comment, has made in ten years an appreciable educational advance.

55. Among Muhammadans, the Labbais, as one would expect from their addiction to trade, far outstrip their co-religionists in the literacy of their men; although they are below the general Muhammadan level in female literacy, and in literacy in English. Máppillas, the only other selected portion of the faith, follow at a respectful distance—a fact which may be explained by their greater addiction to agriculture than the majority of their fellow-believers.

56. Christian education has been treated at some length in the earlier portions of this chapter. Figures in subsidiary table VI are given for Indian Christians alone; as might be expected, deduction of the European and Anglo-Indian communities affects considerably the figures elsewhere quoted. But, considering the social class from which the Indian Christian community is largely recruited, their educational position and progress can hardly be deemed as other than creditable.

57. A footnote to subsidiary table I gives some particulars as to education amongst different Christian sects. The predominance of the Syrian Christians in general literacy, both male and female, coupled with their apparently infrequent acquisition of English, emphasizes the fact, already alluded to in Chapter IV, of their existence as an eastern church independent of European influence. It is curious to note that the Catholic church, which surpasses its western rivals in the education of its men, occupies a humble place in regard to female education. A possible explanation may be the greater success of the Roman church in conversion of the "high caste" population, among whom orthodox prejudice dies hard.

I.—Education by age, sex and religion.

Religion.	Number per 10,000 who are literate.											Number per 10,000 who are illiterate.			Number per 10,000 who are literate in English.		
	All ages.			0-10.		10-15.		15-20.		20 and over.							
	Total.	Males.	Females.	Males.	Females.	Males.	Females.	Males.	Females.	Males.	Females.	Total.	Males.	Females.	Total.	Males.	Females.
1	2	3	4	5	6	7	8	9	10	11	12	13	14	15	16	17	18
All religions	748	1,381	134	138	33	1,178	231	1,844	288	1,984	142	9,252	8,619	9,866	66	121	13
Hindu	720	1,352	108	135	26	1,157	182	1,801	236	1,933	113	9,280	8,648	9,892	53	106	2
Musalman	874	1,662	107	111	22	1,117	157	2,079	193	2,637	127	9,126	8,338	9,893	46	92	1
Christian	1,651	2,261	1,059	357	258	2,429	1,598	3,356	2,112	3,082	1,182	8,349	7,739	8,941	541	710	377
Animistic	19	36	1	4	...	29	...	40	...	55	2	9,981	9,964	9,999	...	...	..
Jain	2,370	4,634	292	333	49	3,750	482	6,469	724	5,722	288	7,430	5,366	9,708	78	130	20

	Number per 10,000.			
	Males.		Females.	
	Literates	Literates in English.	Literates	Literates in English.
European and allied races	8,614	8,461	8,450	8,328
Anglo-Indian	7,539	7,321	7,303	7,000
Indian: Roman Catholics	2,055	407	597	134
Indian: Syrians	3,413	328	1,216	53
Indian: Others	1,955	500	1,195	181

II.—*Education by age, sex and locality.*

District and Natural Division.	Number per 10,000 who are literate.										
	All ages.			0-10.		10-15.		15-20.		20 and over.	
	Total.	Males.	Females.	Males.	Females.	Males.	Females.	Males.	Females.	Males.	Females.
1	2	3	4	5	6	7	8	9	10	11	12
Madras	***748***	***1,381***	***134***	***138***	***32***	***1,178***	***221***	***1,844***	***288***	***1,984***	***142***
Agency	***122***	***227***	***15***	***23***	***5***	***181***	***32***	***319***	***34***	***339***	***15***
Agency, Ganjám	94	183	5	21	2	174	12	300	4	265	5
,, Vizagapatam	112	212	12	22	4	140	22	277	27	319	12
,, Gódávari	217	379	50	29	9	340	106	554	122	566	51
East Coast (North)	***533***	***984***	***101***	***124***	***30***	***924***	***189***	***1,439***	***235***	***1,379***	***98***
Ganjám	546	1,116	52	143	19	967	86	1,568	105	1,711	56
Vizagapatam	346	646	62	90	21	593	110	917	124	916	62
Gódávari	592	1,049	153	121	46	1,019	287	1,640	354	1,482	146
Kistna	643	1,128	162	173	42	1,109	323	1,700	371	1,547	154
Guntúr	601	1,091	102	110	26	1,067	186	1,624	245	1,473	98
Nellore	508	920	94	95	29	812	158	1,282	235	1,233	90
Deccan	***516***	***960***	***58***	***81***	***17***	***838***	***88***	***1,294***	***124***	***1,315***	***60***
Cuddapah	543	1,008	64	118	24	969	105	1,358	136	1,308	63
Kurnool	517	965	61	74	16	831	94	1,403	145	1,325	64
Banganapalle	470	877	58	56	15	670	89	957	109	1,250	64
Bellary	533	1,002	52	61	14	805	80	1,274	106	1,442	56
Sandúr	526	986	72	29	5	740	200	1,241	258	1,457	53
Anantapur	474	873	53	79	14	770	74	1,175	115	1,192	58
East Coast (Central)	***774***	***1,416***	***136***	***137***	***34***	***1,158***	***214***	***1,812***	***291***	***2,045***	***147***
Madras	2,791	4,213	1,289	598	357	3,885	2,111	5,515	2,316	5,383	1,334
Chingleput	884	1,615	148	160	85	1,280	212	1,882	300	2,392	170
Chittoor	536	993	63	98	18	875	107	1,316	156	1,363	64
North Arcot	708	1,351	78	88	16	1,004	132	1,916	173	2,015	85
Salem	428	815	46	82	14	675	79	976	91	1,194	48
Coimbatore	624	1,175	86	121	25	2,012	144	1,602	195	1,686	88
South Arcot	838	1,607	80	155	21	1,354	144	1,974	165	2,343	84
East Coast (South)	***1,001***	***1,930***	***137***	***194***	***33***	***1,729***	***250***	***2,561***	***306***	***2,764***	***142***
Tanjore	1,119	2,186	153	212	38	1,792	276	2,887	340	3,156	158
Trichinopoly	788	1,498	118	144	28	1,310	232	1,953	273	2,141	117
Pudukkóttai	829	1,668	62	89	10	1,200	106	363	165	2,540	65
Madura	874	1,692	89	172	22	1,572	160	2,317	182	2,411	96
Rámnád	1,032	2,085	83	232	23	1,984	144	2,838	159	2,979	89
Tinnevelly	1,241	2,290	260	244	67	2,198	441	3,122	577	3,244	267
West Coast	***1,031***	***1,782***	***307***	***136***	***55***	***1,351***	***430***	***2,175***	***527***	***2,703***	***360***
Nilgiris	1,393	2,049	636	328	199	1,766	824	2,308	1,099	2,755	728
Malabar	1,110	1,899	347	141	59	1,401	471	2,247	567	2,922	418
Anjengo	2,376	2,981	1,811	231	194	3,058	2,551	4,980	3,240	4,357	2,186
South Canara	789	1,447	172	105	32	1,178	284	1,962	354	2,133	180
Cities *	***2,283***	***3,904***	***675***	***501***	***191***	***3,764***	***1,200***	***5,272***	***1,294***	***5,144***	***679***

* Excluding Madras City.

III.—*Education by religion, sex and locality.*

District and Natural Division.	Number per 10,000 who are literate.					
	Hindu.		Musalman.		Christian.	
	Males.	Females.	Males.	Females.	Males.	Females.
1	2	3	4	5	6	7
Madras	***1,352***	***108***	***1,662***	***107***	***2,261***	***1,059***
Agency	***302***	***15***	***1,627***	***52***	***1,147***	***590***
Agency, Ganjám	451	11	6,087	...	685	86
Do. Vizagapatam...	256	9	1,516	67	1,079	522
Do. Gódávari	387	43	1,560	40	2,128	1,555
East Coast (North)	***987***	***89***	***1,193***	***168***	***1,070***	***616***
Ganjám	1,132	48	3,371	410	5,455	4,057
Vizagapatam	631	52	1,489	193	5,014	3,565
Gódávari...	1,011	134	2,294	317	3,728	2,949
Kistna	1,110	140	1,459	331	1,381	753
Guntúr	1,164	94	748	64	634	243
Nellore	968	81	1,060	105	794	533
Deccan	***948***	***44***	***1,192***	***58***	***1,578***	***664***
Cuddapah	1,008	47	954	75	1,378	582
Kurnool	989	50	821	44	983	318
Banganapalle	908	50	785	86	592	110
Bellary	979	37	886	50	5,802	3,463
Sandúr	1,082	71	419	16	4,711	2,424
Anantapur	829	43	939	67	3,987	2,252
East Coast (Central)	***1,340***	***99***	***2,589***	***257***	***2,750***	***1,729***
Madras	4,060	973	3,768	757	6,338	4,953
Chingleput	1,554	112	3,171	302	2,599	1,590
Chittoor	974	53	1,344	114	2,995	2,177
North Arcot	1,266	57	2,503	219	1,344	710
Salem	768	35	2,326	188	1,705	862
Coimbatore	1,114	69	3,105	139	3,385	1,787
South Arcot	1,585	69	2 344	124	1,324	422
East Coast (South)	***1,841***	***98***	***3,017***	***83***	***2,537***	***903***
Tanjore	2,149	138	2,962	56	2,002	658
Trichinopoly	1,414	94	3,190	149	2,112	618
Pudukkóttai	1,585	59	3,585	61	2,071	139
Madura	1,589	64	3 442	101	2,544	837
Rámnád	2,034	72	2,616	43	2,334	355
Tinnevelly	2,147	124	2,982	114	3,151	1,504
West Coast	***1,944***	***327***	***1,151***	***63***	***2,915***	***1,497***
Nilgiris	1,405	143	3,655	405	5,143	3,260
Malabar	2,223	435	1,102	49	4,165	2,290
Anjengo	3,714	402	2,119	97	2,710	2,467
South Canara	1 401	116	1,355	150	1,787	730
Cities *	***3,945***	***545***	***2,920***	***235***	***5,331***	***3,256***

* Excluding Madras City.

IV.—English education by age, sex and locality.

District and Natural Division.	Literate in English per 10,000.											
	1911.										1901.	
	All ages.		0–10.		10–15.		15–20.		20 and over.		All ages.	
	Males.	Females.	Males.	Females.	Males.	Females.	Males.	Females.	Males.	Females.	Males.	Females.
1	2	3	4	5	6	7	8	9	10	11	12	13
Madras	***121***	***13***	***6***	***2***	***93***	***18***	***227***	***28***	***168***	***14***	***90***	***11***
Agency	***13***	***0·6***	***0·2***	***0·2***	***4***	***0·5***	***18***	***2***	***21***	***0·7***	***7***	***0·3***
Agency, Ganjám	2	0·2	...	...	...	...	0·7	...	5	0·3	2	...
Do. Vizagapatam ...	9	0·6	0·3	0·3	2	0·2	14	2	16	0·7	6	0·3
Do. Gódávari	44	2	0·3	0·3	2	3	65	4	72	2	27	1
East Coast (North) ...	***92***	***5***	***6***	***1***	***74***	***7***	***208***	***13***	***122***	***6***	***62***	***4***
Ganjám	71	2	4	1	67	3	162	4	102	3	45	2
Vizagapatam	87	7	7	1	72	8	184	14	115	8	65	6
Gódávari	187	9	6	2	104	12	315	17	191	10	94	6
Kistna	114	6	9	1	91	11	256	15	151	6	69	4
Guntúr	71	2	2	0·1	50	2	181	4	91	3	47	2
Nellore	72	7	5	2	61	9	151	27	91	6	58	3
Deccan	***59***	***4***	***2***	***1***	***31***	***5***	***87***	***9***	***85***	***5***	***44***	***4***
Cuddapah	47	1	2	0·1	31	2	78	4	63	2	31	1
Kurnool	53	2	1	0·3	28	1	100	7	74	2	36	1
Banganapalle	69	0·5	..	...	79	...	186	...	88	0·9	16	2
Bellary	78	9	3	2	39	13	96	17	119	10	71	9
Sandúr	89	9	...	...	24	13	123	...	142	14	49	...
Anantapur	54	5	3	2	24	4	72	8	81	7	36	5
East Coast (Central) ...	***165***	***22***	***9***	***4***	***116***	***26***	***267***	***44***	***236***	***27***	***131***	***20***
Madras	1,803	343	140	75	1,525	512	2,821	576	2,293	379	1,404	303
Chingleput	165	21	13	4	128	19	255	32	287	29	118	16
Chittoor	72	4	3	0·9	51	5	127	11	99	4	50	4
North Arcot	79	7	2	1	40	10	181	13	120	8	67	7
Salem	54	4	2	0·5	30	4	80	8	82	5	46	4
Coimbatore	86	7	3	2	54	10	149	14	124	9	62	5
South Arcot	67	4	2	0·6	50	3	105	7	97	5	56	3
East Coast (South) ...	***134***	***9***	***5***	***1***	***118***	***15***	***274***	***24***	***182***	***9***	***98***	***6***
Tanjore	193	7	6	1	167	9	407	16	259	8	160	5
Trichinopoly	142	10	5	3	124	23	310	28	188	8	101	5
Pudukkóttai	87	1	0·8	...	40	0·8	155	0·6	131	2	82	1
Madura	10·6	9	4	1	100	15	199	22	144	10	70	6
Rámnád	66	4	2	0·2	48	5	104	8	98	5	42	2
Tinnevelly	150	16	6	1	146	27	315	52	199	16	97	14
West Coast	***142***	***26***	***8***	***6***	***112***	***40***	***246***	***54***	***202***	***31***	***102***	***27***
Nilgiris	719	349	169	119	582	451	668	523	937	411	635	277
Malabar	125	17	4	2	100	24	228	37	176	19	86	15
Anjengo	892	718	73	103	571	1,131	1,745	1,265	1,848	828		
South Canara	121	22	2	4	93	35	239	49	168	23	83	14

Note.—For 1901, absolute figures have been adjusted for changes in area as far as possible; for 1891, it is not possible to get adjusted figures.

V.—*Progress of education since* 1891.

District and Natural Division.	Number of literate per 10,000.													
	All ages.						15–20.				20 and over.			
	Males.			Females.			Males.		Females.		Males.		Females.	
	1911	1901.	1891.	1911	1901	1891	1911.	1901.	1911.	1901.	1911.	1901.	1911.	1901.
1	2	3	4	5	6	7	8	9	10	11	12	13	14	15
Madras	*1,381*	*1,185*	*1,184*	*134*	*92*	*68*	*1,844*	*1,656*	*288*	*217*	*1,984*	*1,753*	*142*	*97*
Agency	*227*	*181*	*199*	*15*	*10*	*6*	*319*	*237*	*34*	*17*	*339*	*267*	*15*	*11*
Agency, Ganjám ...	188	184	159	5	4	4	300	205	4	7	265	196	5	4
Do. Vizagapatam ...	212	175	198	12	8	5	277	215	27	11	319	259	12	10
Do. Gódávari ...	379	305	303	50	35	23	654	439	122	85	566	443	51	30
East Coast (North) ...	*984*	*830*	*804*	*101*	*56*	*35*	*1,439*	*1,255*	*235*	*136*	*1,379*	*1,207*	*98*	*55*
Ganjám	1,116	890	843	52	34	24	1,568	1,187	105	70	1,711	1,386	56	38
Vizagapatam	646	608	574	62	41	25	917	908	124	103	916	867	62	42
Gódávari ...	1,049	831	758	153	75	49	1,640	1,341	354	189	1,482	1,215	146	70
Kistna	1,128	920	900	162	81	49	1,700	1,485	371	189	1,547	1,345	154	79
Guntúr	1,091	943	964	102	56	38	1,624	1,508	245	148	1,478	1,317	98	54
Nellore	920	847	863	94	55	31	1,282	1,306	235	157	1,233	1,190	90	53
Deccan	*960*	*818*	*892*	*58*	*41*	*28*	*1,294*	*1,346*	*124*	*102*	*1,315*	*1,141*	*60*	*42*
Cuddapah	1,008	879	874	64	47	25	1,358	1,412	136	118	1,308	1,152	63	38
Kurnool	965	792	843	61	42	29	1,403	1,244	145	130	1,325	1,130	64	42
Banganapalle	877	827	961	58	32	23	957	1,043	109	45	1,250	1,179	64	38
Bellary	1,002	862	1,072	52	35	38	1,274	1,428	106	85	1,412	1,245	56	38
Sandúr	986	1,085	1,019	72	51	37	1,241	1,395	258	55	1,457	1,559	53	37
Anantapur	873	737	762	53	39	20	1,175	1,293	115	85	1,192	1,086	58	50
East Coast (Central) ...	*1,416*	*1,235*	*1,247*	*136*	*99*	*71*	*1,812*	*1,674*	*291*	*247*	*2,045*	*1,851*	*147*	*104*
Madras	4,213	3,599	3,355	1289	914	665	5,515	4,995	2,316	1,945	5,383	4,690	1,834	906
Chingleput	1,615	1,442	1,566	148	100	79	1,882	1,779	300	215	2,392	2,218	170	115
Chittoor	993	878	956	63	44	29	1,316	1,365	156	116	1,363	1,248	64	48
North Arcot	1,351	1,250	1,258	78	63	55	1,916	1,647	173	155	2,015	1,962	85	65
Salem	815	675	714	46	39	27	976	917	91	98	1,194	1,029	48	38
Coimbatore	1,175	965	942	86	55	34	1,502	1,337	195	148	1,686	1,431	88	52
South Arcot	1,607	1,410	1,400	80	54	33	1,974	1,799	165	113	2,343	2,115	84	56
East Coast (South) ...	*1,930*	*1,633*	*1,624*	*137*	*86*	*56*	*2,561*	*2,192*	*306*	*206*	*2,764*	*2,415*	*142*	*85*
Tanjore	2,186	2,028	1,917	153	90	50	2,887	2,650	340	201	3,156	2,998	158	86
Trichinopoly	1,498	1,199	1,243	118	67	44	1,953	1,655	273	174	2,141	1,769	117	63
Pudukkóttai	1,668	1,562	1,475	62	42	30	368	208	165	99	2,540	2,332	65	44
Madura	1,692	1,292	1,303	89	60	40	2,217	1,777	182	156	2,411	1,932	96	62
Rámnád	2,085	1,681	1,728	83	47	31	2,838	2,367	159	101	2,979	2,512	89	52
Tinnevelly	2,290	1,952	1,982	260	174	127	3,122	2,527	577	390	3,244	2,838	267	174
West Coast	*1,782*	*1,552*	*1,514*	*307*	*247*	*219*	*2,175*	*1,975*	*527*	*452*	*2,703*	*2,390*	*360*	*293*
Nilgiris	2,049	1,718	1,325	686	494	322	2,308	2,065	1,099	878	2,755	2,332	728	560
Malabar *	1,900	1,721	1,703	350	302	276	2,251	2,098	567	516	2,924	2,666	421	366
South Canara	1,447	1,106	1,048	172	94	71	1,962	1,631	354	242	2,133	1,706	180	98

Note.—Those shown as "learning" in 1891 over the age of 15 have been treated as "literates"

* Includes Anjengo.

VI.—*Education by caste.*

Caste.	Number per 1,000 who are literate. 1911. Persons.	1911. Males.	1911. Females.	1901. Persons.	1901. Males.	1901. Females.	Number per 10,000 who are literate in English. 1911. Persons.	1911. Males.	1911. Females.	1901. Persons.	1901. Males.	1901. Females.
1	2	3	4	5	6	7	8	9	10	11	12	13
Hindu and Animistic—												
1. Agamudaiyan	**102**	208	5	**73**	149	3	**16**	33	0·2	**7**	15	...
2. Ambalakáran	**25**	49	2	**27**	55	0·7	**0·8**	1	0·3	**2**	5	0·3
3. Ambattan	**71**	141	4	**55**	110	2	**6**	13	0·2	**2**	4	0·3
4. Balija	**114**	209	20	**75**	143	8	**131**	260	5	**49**	98	1
5. Billava	**22**	42	3	**14**	26	2	**13**	26	2	**11**	21	1
6. Bóya	**11**	19	2	**4**	8	0·5	**3**	6	...	**0·5**	1	...
7. Bráhman, Tamil	**418**	719	120	**391**	736	58	**1,121**	2,227	28	**887**	1,788	15
8. Do. Telugu	**389**	682	99	**355**	673	46	**744**	1,475	21	**538**	1,084	7
9. Do. Malayálam ...	**428**	634	182	**447**	643	312	**213**	386	7	**113**	193	17
10. Do. Canarese ...	**307**	573	51	**269**	516	18	**601**	1,217	11	**254**	501	5
11. Do. Oriyá	**233**	466	12	**151**	309	4	**125**	256	2	**16**	31	1
12. Do. Others ...	**317**	560	77	**272**	498	45	**580**	1,122	41	**457**	885	26
Total Bráhmans	***371***	***654***	***93***	***308***	***578***	***44***	***782***	***1,553***	***22***	***488***	***975***	***11***
13. Chakkiliyan	**5**	9	0·7	**0·6**	1	0·2	**0·7**	1	0·1	...	...	...
14. Cherumam	**2**	3	0·4	**1**	2	0·2	**0·1**	0·2	...	...	...	...
15. Chetti	**197**	391	12	**154**	320	4	**49**	98	2	**8**	15	2
16. Dévánga	**101**	197	6	**32**	63	2	**23**	45	0·5	**6**	12	...
17. Gamalla	**19**	35	2	**10**	19	0·7	**7**	15	0·1	**3**	6	0·2
18. Golla	**14**	28	1	**5**	10	0·8	**8**	17	0·1	**5**	10	0·1
19. Holeya	**2**	3	0·7	**0·1**	0·1	...	**0·1**	0·2	...	...	...	...
20. Idaiyan	**55**	108	5	**31**	63	1	**29**	58	1	**3**	7	...
21. Ídiga	**18**	36	0·9	**5**	11	0·3	**2**	5	...	**0·6**	1	...
22. Íluvan	**53**	107	5	**41**	82	3	**13**	27	0·5	**7**	13	0·4
23. Kaikólan	**119**	228	14	**70**	129	15	**19**	38	0·7	**6**	13	...
24. Kalingi*	**36**	74	5	**25**	50	0·6	**8**	16	0·5	**2**	4	...
25. Kallan	**78**	157	4	**53**	109	2	**13**	27	0·5	**6**	13	...
26. Kamma	**65**	122	7	**25**	48	2	**10**	20	0·5	**2**	3	...
27. Kammálan (Tamil) ...	**133**	262	8	**104**	207	3	**22**	43	1	**5**	11	...
28. Kamsala	**131**	251	13	**83**	165	5	**27**	54	0·9	**12**	24	...
29. Kápu	**47**	90	4	**19**	38	0·6	**11**	22	0·3	**2**	4	0·0
30. Khond	**5**	9	0·2	**2**	3	0·0	**0·2**	0·5	...	**0·1**	0·1	...
31. Kómati	**262**	521	25	**252**	495	9	**75**	149	3	**32**	43	0·6
32. Kuravan	**32**	64	2	**3**	6	0·1	**2**	5	0·2	...	...	...
33. Kurumban	**16**	32	0·6	**8**	15	0·4	**3**	6	...	**0·5**	1	...
34. Kusavan	**51**	101	3	**36**	73	0·7	**9**	18	0·1	**0·6**	1	...
35. Mádiga	**4**	8	0·7	**1**	2	0·1	**0·5**	0·9	0·1	**0·1**	0·1	0·1
36. Mála	**7**	14	0·8	**3**	6	0·4	**2**	3	0·1	**0·5**	1	...
37. Mangala	**35**	68	3	**18**	35	1	**0·7**	14	0·2	**4**	8	...
38. Maravan	**69**	138	3	**54**	106	2	**7**	13	1	**2**	4	0·2
39. Mutrácha	**20**	39	2	**10**	19	0·4	**6**	12	0·1	**3**	6	...
40. Náyar	**261**	419	114	**244**	395	103	**148**	297	10	**76**	154	3
41. Oddé	**6**	12	0·5	**2**	4	0·2	**0·7**	1	0·0	**0·4**	0·8	...
42. Pallan	**19**	40	0·8	**12**	25	0·4	**2**	4	0·0	**0·3**	0·5	...
43. Palli	**48**	97	2	**33**	66	0·9	**10**	2	0·5	**1**	2	0·0
44. Paraiyan	**14**	28	1	**5**	10	0·3	**8**	15	0·5	**0·3**	0·6	...
45. Sále	**62**	118	6	**25**	49	1	**16**	31	1	**6**	12	...
46. Savara	**1**	2	0·2	**1**	2	0·1	...	...	...	...	...	...
47. Shánán	**92**	181	7	**79**	154	6	**15**	30	0·2	**3**	5	0·2
48. Telaga	**58**	109	10	**38**	72	5	**65**	131	2	**44**	86	1
49. Tíyan	**99**	176	23	**81**	147	16	**51**	92	12	**32**	61	4
50. Tottiyan	**33**	63	4	**23**	46	1	**2**	4	0·8	**1**	2	...
51. Tsákala	**6**	11	1	**3**	6	0·3	**2**	4	0·1	**2**	4	...
52. Uppara	**10**	20	1	**3**	5	0·4	**3**	6	...	**0·8**	1	...
53. Valaiyan	**21**	43	1	**13**	26	0·2	**0·3**	0·6	...	**0·2**	0·4	...
54. Vániyan	**163**	317	16	**74**	148	2	**6**	11	3	**2**	4	...
55. Vannán	**32**	63	2	**13**	27	0·3	**5**	10	...	**0·2**	0·3	...
56. Velama	**20**	36	5	**13**	25	0·6	**21**	41	1	**3**	6	0·2
57. Vellála	**130**	246	18	**35**	69	2	**106**	212	4	**10**	19	0·3
Musalman—												
58. Labbai	**132**	**278**	8	**92**	211	3	**16**	33	0·6	**3**	7	...
59. Máppilla	**56**	**108**	6	**45**	87	4	**5**	9	...	**3**	5	2
Christian—												
60. Indian Christian	**143**	**204**	85	**109**	162	59	**293**	441	151	**173**	272	77

Note.—For 1901, the percentages are struck on figures from Imperial table IX of that year. The statistics were then collected for certain selected districts in which the castes were found in large numbers.

* Includes Kalinji.

VII.—Number of institutions and pupils according to the returns of the Education Department.

Class of institution.	1911.		1901.		1891.	
	Number of		Number of		Number of	
	Institutions.	Scholars.	Institutions.	Scholars.	Institutions.	Scholars.
1	2	3	4	5	6	7
TOTAL ...	***30,635***	***1,215,725***	***26,926***	***850,224***	***22,028***	***644,164***
Public.						
Arts Colleges	31	3,741	41	3,279	35	3,205
Professional Colleges	5	890	6	636	5	518
Secondary Schools—						
Upper Secondary	} 806	152,413	{ 172	46,304	178	27,152
Lower Secondary			560	53,822	637	43,363
Primary Schools—						
Upper Primary	} 24,326	922,911	{ 5,164	247,857	} 17,885	505,280
Lower Primary			15,141	373,770		
Training Schools	83	2,989	74	1,612	70	1,427
Other Special Schools	93	4,618	57	3,927	29	2,192
Private.						
Advanced	375	10,478	246	5,477	131	4,074
Elementary	4,916	117,685	5,465	113,540	3,058	56,953

VIII.—Main results of University examinations.

Examination.	1911.		1901.		1891.	
	Candidates.	Passed.	Candidates.	Passed.	Candidates.	Passed.
1	2	3	4	5	6	7
Matriculation	822	164	7,798	2,427	8,029	2,381
Intermediate Examination in Arts.*	1,453	593	1,924	730	2,048	740
B.A. degree examination—						
English language division ..	1,523	626	964	488	} 458	230
Second do. ..	1,044	881	656	516		
Science division	1,374	810	869	449	540	316
M.A.	......	......	41	19	13	6
L.T.	† New 82	56	Written 108	70	} 19	7
	‡ Old 34	24	Practl. 147	51		
B L.	354	81	353	141	137	39
M.L.	14	1	3	:	2	1
L.M. & S.	23	13	2	....	96	17
M.B. & C.M.	23	2 for M.B. & C.M. § 6 for L.M. & S.	} 6	...	2	1
M.D.	2	1	......	......	......	......
B.C.E. or B.E.	Civil 10	5	Civil 4	3	} 11	1
	Mechl. 10	3	Mechl. 5	3		

* The Intermediate Examination in Arts under the New Regulations was held first in 1911, superseding the First Examination in Arts under the old By-laws.

† New Regulations. ‡ Old Regulations.

§ Six candidates who appeared for M.B. & C.M. qualified only for L.M. & S.

IX.—*Number and circulation of newspapers, etc.*

Language.	Class of newspaper (daily, weekly, etc.).	1911. Number.	1911. Circulation.	1901. Number.	1901. Circulation.
	2	3	4	5	6
	Grand Total of all languages taken together.	*316*	*263,496*	*244*	*144,961*
	Total in English ...	*79*	*67,543*	*68*	*49,652*
English	Quarterly	7	3,250	3	900
	Once in two months.	2	1,575	1	825
	Monthly	36	30,462	31	24,980
	Bi-monthly .	4	3,268	1	500
	Weekly	17	8,889	20	9,114
	Bi-weekly	4	2,310	4	2,190
	Tri-weekly	1	600	3	650
	Daily	7	16.189	5	10,493
English and Devanagari.	Monthly	1	1,000	...	...
	Total in Tamil ...	*67*	*74,436*	*65*	*38,174*
Tamil	Quarterly	1	200	...	...
	Monthly	37	55,896	16	13,680
	Bi-monthly ...	3	1,800	5	1,904
	Tri-monthly ...	1	350	..	...
	Weekly	15	8,955	28	14,210
	Bi-weekly	2	1,350	3	700
	Daily	1	2,660	2	1,400
Anglo-Tamil ...	Bi-monthly ...	2	1,500	2	900
	Monthly	2	700	4	2,050
	Weekly	1	400	2	2,280
Tamil and Grandha types intermixed.	Monthly	1	500	...	...
Sanskrit and Tamil.	Bi-monthly... ...	...	...	1	400
Telugu and Tamil.	Monthly	...	...	1	200
Anglo-Telugu and Tamil.	Monthly	1	125	1	500
	Total in Telugu ...	*48*	*37,400*	*36*	*16,025*
Telugu	Monthly	34	25,975	17	9,545
	Bi-monthly ...	4	3,900	3	950
	Weekly	6	4,525	8	3,025
	Bi-weekly	1	500	3	1,305
	Tri-weekly... ...	1	500	...	...
	Daily	...	...	1	200
Anglo-Telugu ...	Monthly	1	500	2	550
	Bi-monthly ...	1	1,500	...	...
	Weekly	...	...	1	100
Tamil and Telugu.	Monthly	...	...	1	350
	Total in Malayálam.	*56*	*44,274*	*27*	*16,220*
Malayálam ...	Quarterly	1	500	...	...
	Once in two months.	3	2,325	1	250
	Monthly	32	24,146	13	7,595
	Bi-monthly ...	3	1,228	1	200
	Tri-monthly ...	...	...	3	1,870
	Weekly	12	10,950	6	3,870
	Bi-weekly	1	750	...	...

Language.	Class of newspaper (daily, weekly, etc.).	1911. Number.	1911. Circulation.	19 Number.
1	2	3	4	5
Malayálam—*cont.*				
Anglo-Malayálam.	Eight times a year.	1	800	...
	Weekly	...	...	1
	Bi-weekly	2	3,540	1
Malayálam and Sanskrit.	Monthly	1	540	...
	Tri-monthly ...	...	...	1
	Total in Canarese...	*30*	*23,146*	*13*
Canarese ...	Quarterly	1	200	...
	Monthly	16	8,583	5
	Bi-monthly ..	...	...	3
	Weekly	5	10,762	5
Anglo-Canarese.	Monthly	1	1,000	...
	Bi-monthly ...	2	1,028	...
Sanskrit and Canarese.	Monthly	5	1,575	...
	Total in Hindóstáni.	*23*	*10,707*	*28*
Hindóstáni ...	Quarterly	1	400	...
	Monthly	10	5,450	6
	Bi-monthly ...	2	800	...
	Tri-monthly ...	...	...	1
	Weekly	7	2,882	15
	Bi-weekly	1	100	1
	Daily	1	1,000	1
Urdu and Anglo-Tamil.	Bi-weekly	1	575	1
Hindóstáni and Maráthi.	Weekly	...	...	2
Hindóstáni and Canarese.	Weekly	...	...	1
	Total in Oriyá ...	*2*	*2,800*	*1*
Oriyá	Weekly	1	1,800	...
	Monthly	1	1,000	...
Oriyá and English.	Bi-monthly ...	...	...	1
	Total in French ...	*4*	*1,260*	*4*
French	Monthly	1	260	..
	Weekly	3	1,000	3
	Bi-weekly	...	...	1
Italian	Quarterly	*1*	*800*	...
Portuguese ...	Monthly	*1*	*130*	*1*
German	Monthly in Roman character.	...	...	*1*
	Total in Sanskrit...	*5*	*1,000*	...
Sanskrit ...	Monthly	3	700	...
	Weekly	2	300	...

Note.—Figures for 1891 are not available.

X.—*Number of books published in each language.*

Language.	Number of books published in												
											Total of decade.		
	1901	1902	1903	1904	1905	1906	1907	1908	1909	1910	1901 to 1910	1891 to 1900.	1881 to 1890.
1	2	3	4	5	6	7	8	9	10	11	12	13	14
TOTAL ...	*1,166*	*1,162*	*1,217*	*1,210*	*1,237*	*1,440*	*1,574*	*2,207*	*2,740*	*3,459*	*17,412*	*9,766*	*9,590*
English	395	411	459	424	461	499	518	643	807	1,001	5,613	3,124	2,026
Latin	...	...	3	...	1	2	...	...	1	1	8	5	18
German	...	...	...	...	...	...	...	...	...	...	.	2	...
French	...	...	...	1	1	..	...	...	2	8	12	...	1
Dutch	..	...	...	...	...	...	...	2	4	4	10	...	..
Italian	...	...	2	4	3	3	1	2	2	3	20	...	..
Tamil	282	292	317	335	343	425	421	626	772	1,007	4,820	2,297	8,232
Telugu	283	237	229	233	221	265	331	362	440	704	3,255	2,347	1,575
Malayálam	57	41	39	38	50	30	47	118	133	166	719	371	790
Canarese	27	24	31	24	25	44	64	42	67	72	420	337	530
Konkani	1	8	1	...	3	4	1	1	2	6	22	6	19
Tulu	1	8	3	7	1	...	1	..	6	2	24	4	15
Badaga	...	1	...	..	...	...	...	...	...	...	1	...	2
Coorgi	...	...	...	...	...	1	...	...	1	...	2	...	2
Maráthi	...	...	1	2	...	...	...	...	...	2	5	5	5
Sauráshtra or Patnúli.	...	1	1	3	1	...	2	1	...	...	9	1	..
Tóda	...	...	...	...	...	...	...	2	...	1	3	...	...
Lushai	...	...	...	...	...	2	7	3	3	4	19	...	...
Oriyá	3	12	33	15	11	21	9	19	37	36	196	13	6
Hindóstáni	4	7	1	5	5	3	3	91	80	24	223	56	275
Arabic	2	3	...	4	6	4	20	53	79	69	240	13	80
Persian	.	..	1	...	...	...	...	2	10	1	14	4	39
Sanskrit	161	123	94	114	105	129	153	235	293	345	1,752	1,071	964
Others	...	4	2	1	...	8	1	5	1	3	25	110	11

CHAPTER IX.—LANGUAGE.

THE enumeration schedules provide a column for entry of the language habitually used by each person enumerated. To write a chapter on the figures thus obtained, in comparison with those of previous enumerations, is as an attempt to remould ancient and crumbling bricks with a very scanty allowance of fresh straw.

2. Parts A, B and C of table X give us 28 Madras vernaculars, 18 vernaculars of other Indian provinces, 9 vernaculars of Asiatic countries beyond India, and 14 European languages as in daily use throughout the Presidency.

3. The figures in the margin show, however, that much of this detail is of little interest save for the curious student of linguistics, and of no importance in regard to practical administration. With a competent knowledge of *Tamil* and *Telugu* the foreigner can converse with 784 of every 1,000 persons that he is likely to meet: *Malayálam* and *Oriyá*, third and fourth in point of numerical importance, are confined each to particular areas; namely the two northern districts of Ganjám and Vizagapatam, and the West Coast districts of Malabar and South Canara.

Persons per 1,000 of the population speaking	
Tamil ...	407
Telugu ...	377
Malayálam ...	74
Oriyá ...	38
Canarese ...	37
Hindóstáni ...	23
Total ...	956

4. Of the remaining 44 per 1,000 persons, 9 and 4 are accounted for by *Khond* and *Savara*, and are only to be found in Ganjám and Vizagapatam: *Tulu* speakers (12 per 1,000) are confined to South Canara, where, as may be seen in the margin, their speech commands far more adherents than *Canarese*, the official vernacular of the district. *Tulu* is, however, not a written language, although it has been written at times in the *Canarese* script; a fact which places it at an obvious disadvantage as a vehicle for the transaction of business on any considerable scale. *English* is the mother-tongue of 39,309 of the population; a number slightly lower than that of the European and Anglo-Indian communities, which between them include 40,928 persons. But inasmuch as 2,868 persons have returned themselves as speaking European languages other than *English*, the conclusion to be drawn from these figures is that a certain number of Indians have entered *English* as the speech habitually employed by them. That such entry is correct in point of fact will be admitted by any one conversant with the life of the Presidency; while the assumption that all Anglo-Indians habitually use *English*, or any other European language, is one of very doubtful validity.

Persons per 1,000 of South Canara population speaking	
Canarese ...	187
Tulu ...	428
Konkani ...	137
Malayálam ...	198

5. In regard to languages less important numerically, it is not unreasonable to suggest that many persons have imposed a tribal name on the language of which they speak a more or less corrupted version. Thus *Badaga* is as much *Canarese* as *American* or *Houndsditch* is English; *Irula* in Tamil peculiarized; *Konkani*, maltreated *Maráthi*; *Yerukala* or *Korava* is in practice, whatever it may be in theory, but a mish-mash of *Tamil* and *Telugu*; *Lambádi*, *Telugu* turned into thieves' patter. A philological surgeon dissecting these languages might possibly in course of time work his way down to something original and instructive; such feat has been accomplished in regard to English *Romany*. But for all practical purposes we may assume that the proportion now between original and borrowed is such that the latter completely obscures the former.

6. The possibility of a dialect being so strongly marked as to gain in time the standing of a distinct language is not strange, in view of the differences which manifest themselves in the usage of the same language in different parts of the country. Even to the hearing of a foreigner the *Tamil* of the Nilgiris differs widely from that

of Tanjore; understanding of the pure *Telugu* of Kistna by no means guarantees immediate comprehension of that spoken in Kurnool. A French writer, M. Jules Bloch, has written an article purporting to show that a competent knowledge of *Tamil* will enable the hearer to determine the caste of the person speaking. His observations as to the variation noticeable in the pronunciations of certain *Tamil* letters, for which there is no exact European equivalent, appear to be well founded; but as to the grounds to which he assigns this variation it is permissible to express a doubt. In any country it is comparatively easy for the native to draw from manner of speech certain broad inferences as to whether the person speaking is a schoolmaster or a scavenger, a banker or a bus driver; a Frenchman can probably distinguish without trouble a Marseillais from a Norman; it is not difficult for an Irishman to recognize the accent of Belfast as differing from that of Dublin, or the accent of Cork as different to either. But that caste in the abstract can have any distinguishing effect on speech is a theory which one may well question; the speech of a *Bráhman* certainly differs from that of a *Paraiyan*, but the difference is due not to an abstract theological relation of superiority and inferiority, but to the obvious fact that the present educational status and social surroundings of *Bráhman* and *Paraiyan* are markedly distinct. If an example of a difference, more subtle than that produced by the circumstances of every-day life be sought, it may be found in that trace of elaboration, or archaism, which as a rule distinguishes the language of an educated follower of the Vaishnavite form of Hinduism from that of a Smárta.

7. Certain further scepticisms arise tending towards a diminishing of the detail of table X. *Sanskrit* as the home language of 312 persons in Madras — *Credat Judæus Apella*. *Patnúli* or *Khatri* might possibly be clubbed with *Gujaráti*; it is a dialect of the latter spoken by the weavers of Rámnád, Madura and Salem, whose most distinctive feature at the present day is their extreme objection to be styled *Patnúlkárans*. *Persian* is not impossible in the case of some wandering gangs; but *Pársi* is probably a name used by aristocratic Muhammadans to distinguish their idiomatic *Hindóstáni* from the common speech of the market place.

8. Of the 25 districts into which, including Madras city as a district, the Presidency is divided, *Tamil* in 10, *Telugu* in 9, are the recognized vernaculars. *Canarese* and *Malayálam* are accredited to South Canara and Malabar respectively; in Chittoor and North Arcot *Telugu* and *Tamil* alike find place in the official list, as do *Telugu* and *Oriyá* in Ganjám. In Madras city alone is *Hindóstáni* recognized in divided prevalence with *Telugu* and *Tamil*.

9. This linguistic distribution is purely one of form and convenience; and there being no let or hindrance in any district to a person transacting his business with a Government official in whatever tongue he will, the administrative merits of the division are hardly open to question.

10. A question which is wont to arise at times is that as to the propriety of non-recognition of *Hindóstáni* as a vernacular of the Presidency. Statistical facts are against admission of the language, inasmuch as but 23 persons per 1,000 of the Presidency population return it as their vernacular; while in no district, other than Madras city, do the *Hindóstáni* speakers amount to 10 per cent. of the total population. But ability to speak a language is by no means coincident with its habitual use; and were enquiry directed rather towards ascertaining how many people in Madras can speak and understand *Hindóstáni*, the resultant figures would be widely different. Save perhaps in the agency tracts of Ganjám, Vizagapatam, and Gódávari, and, strangely enough, in the great Muhammadan stronghold of Malabar, there are few places where a tolerable knowledge of Hindóstáni will not enable the European to communicate with those about him, unaided by an English-speaking interpreter. More especially is this true of the Deccan division, in regard to which area I may illustrate the point from personal experience. In the Banganapalle State, situated between Kurnool and Cuddapah districts, statistics show 825 per 1,000 of the population as Telugu speakers, compared with 156 of the same number who habitually speak *Hindóstáni*. But *Hindóstáni* is certainly a possible and easy medium of communication in any village of the State; while in the capital, where doubtless the

presence of a Muhammadan ruler exercises an insensible influence, many *Telugu* Hindus use Hindóstáni in ordinary speech with one another.

11. While on the subject of Banganapalle, I may point to the curious entry of 24 *Oriyá* speakers shown as enumerated there. The schedule book was perfectly clear, but what these people could have been doing in Banganapalle remains a mystery. Possibly they were *Oriyá* vagrants; more probably they were wandering "Wudders" (earth diggers), who misled a careless enumerator by giving a tribe name, somewhat in sound resembling "*Oriyá*," to the language, most probably *Telugu*, spoken by them.

12. *Canarese*, as has already been seen, is hardly the representative vernacular of South Canara; *per contra*, if numbers afford any evidence, it would seem to have much stronger claims to official recognition in Bellary than has *Telugu*. The comparative paucity of *Canarese* speakers in Salem and Coimbatore, surprising to those with memories of these districts, is probably accounted for by their localization along the Mysore frontier.

13. The official division of Ganjám between *Telugu* and *Oriyá* does evident justice to both languages; the sharp distinction in respect of these languages between Vizagapatam and its agency tracts deserves a moment's notice.

14. So far as language is concerned the official distribution of other districts seems in the main to be correct. *Tamil* would appear somewhat flattered by recognition in Chittoor, as *Telugu* in North Arcot; but, as already suggested in connection with *Hindóstáni*, the currency of these languages in doubtful cases cannot be measured by the number of those who elect for one or the other as their habitual organ of speech. *Telugu* speakers are statistically few in Chingleput district; in fact the language will there be found almost as facile a method of communication as *Tamil*.

15. The questions of persistence and disappearance, or indeed of more or less extended usage, are hardly applicable to the main languages of the Presidency. *Tamil* and *Telugu* have increased, as must needs be the case, in point of absolute numbers, and in their proportion per 1,000 of the population; an absolute increase of 30,871 in *Canarese* has not sufficed to avoid a proportional fall of 2 per 1,000; *Malayálam* shows an increase of 1 per 1,000; but *Oriyá* speakers show an absolute decrease of 204,991, and a proportional fall of 8 when considered in relation to 1,000 of the population. This phenomenon is due to a decrease of 316,314 *Oriyá* speakers in Ganjám—a loss not counterbalanced by increases of 44,710, 696, and 64,483 in Ganjám Agency, Vizagapatam, and Vizagapatam Agency respectively. The proportional variation in the case of Ganjám is so remarkable as to suggest either careless enumeration at one census or the other; or else a possibility of deliberate mis-representation by *Telugu* or *Oriyá* enumerators not uninfluenced by the contentions which prevailed some five or six years back between the *Telugus* and *Oriyás* of the district. The probability that the error lies in the earlier enumeration is strengthened by an examination as to the proportion of the district's Hindu population contributed by *Telugu* and *Oriyá* castes respectively; of which examination the result may be seen in the margin. It is improbable that in 1901, when the *Telugu* castes were well nigh as strongly represented in Ganjám as the *Oriyá*, the disparity as to language in use should be so great. In 1911 *Telugu* castes appear to have diminished somewhat in numerical importance, and *Oriyá* castes very markedly so. It should however be remembered that only main castes are now shown in detail against each district: in Part II of table XIII details are given for but ten *Oriyá* castes in Ganjám as against 75 in 1901.

Number per 1,000 of population who speak

Language.	1901.	1911.
Oriyá	755	512
Telugu	203	449

Proportion per 1,000 of Ganjám population who are of

	1901.	1911.
Telugu castes	466	458
Oriyá castes	473	262

16. In respect to other and less widely spread vernaculars there is not much of interest to be said. On *Gadaba* some remarks will be found in Chapter XI by

Mr. C. A. Henderson, I.C.S., who knows the people and their language. *Khond* and *Savara* are likely to persist with the persistence of the tribes from which the languages take their name. In the case of the former it is possible to notice a curious distinction, in point of vocabulary rather than of dialect, in the agency tracts of Ganjám. One speech passes current through practically the whole of the Goomsur-Udayagiri and Balliguda taluks; but the stranger, who wishes to converse with the *Khonds* of Rámagiri-Udayagiri, will need an extensive addition of synonyms to his vocabulary, almost every village having one or two words of purely local usage.

17. *Tóda* will assuredly come to an end with the disappearance of the Tódas—a contingency not altogether remote if the speculations of Chapter XI have any validity. The language of this people is interesting because incomprehensible; to one unacquainted with it it sounds not unlike the speech of buffaloes—a fact which may explain the sympathy between the *Tóda* and his herd. Practically all *Tódas* can speak *Tamil*, or the dialect of *Canarese* current on the Nilgiris; Sir Richard Burton, or one of his biographers, appears to have made the curious mistake of imagining that they speak *Telugu*. Missionaries, who work (with, I fear, scanty success) amongst the tribe, must needs have acquired the *Tóda* language to some considerable extent; yet curiously enough some *Tódas*, whom I questioned on the point, many years ago, it is true, stated positively to me that no stranger had ever learned their language sufficiently to converse in it without the supplement of *Tamil* or *Canarese* words.

18. *Mahl* is the language of Minicoy Island; the one *Mahl* speaker in South Canara was probably a chance fisherman or sailor, temporarily landed on the coast. *Kurumba* is merely the *Canarese* of a particular hill tribe, as *Koraga* is the Tulu of a "depressed class" in South Canara.

19. In regard to European languages other than *English* there is very little to be said. *Portuguese* is the language of the Portuguese-Indian half-caste, who has now become a statistical Anglo-Indian; in all probability it is claimed as mother-tongue by many whose acquaintance with it is but perfunctory. *French* speakers are largely missionaries, male and female—a class which accounts for many languages of the European continent spoken in the Presidency.

20. I cannot, I regret to say, claim for myself the credit of being the solitary male speaker of *Irish*.

21. Subsidiary table X to Chapter VIII shows us a marked increase in vernacular publications during the decade as compared with its predecessor. Allusion has already been made to certain inherent difficulties in the Madras vernaculars, which have probably, as much as anything else, hindered the diffusion of written matter among the masses. These difficulties are now being recognized in the search for a simpler style, but the general knowledge of *English* thought, and of the *English* language, among the literary class renders much modern *Tamil*—*Tamil* will serve for a present example—exceedingly difficult, if not impossible, of comprehension for the reader who knows no language save his own. The difficulty experienced by a European in acquiring a knowledge of *Tamil* does not lie solely in the acquisition of words, but rather in the fundamental difference of thought for which language is but a means of expression. Thus, as pointed out by that stern old purist Father Dubois, a simple English thought or expression, turned literally into simple *Tamil* or *Canarese*, may in its vernacular guise be utterly unintelligible, or, if at least intelligible, utterly absurd. Undoubtedly much vernacular writing of to-day is but *English* thought expressed through an unsuitable medium: the problem, which confronts the would-be popular writer in the vernaculars of Southern India, is to express himself without Sanskritic pedantry in the common speech of the people; and yet write "vernacular thought," in place of transcribing perfunctorily into the vernacular the ideas which suggest themselves to him in English guise.

I.—Distribution of total population by language according to Linguistic Survey.

Family, sub-family branch and sub-branch.	Group.	Language.	Dialect.	Total number of speakers (000 omitted). 1911.	Total number of speakers (000 omitted). 1901.	Number per 10,000 of population of Province in 1911.	Where chiefly spoken. (District or Natural division.)
1	2	3	4	5	6	7	8
			I. Languages of India.				
Austro-Asiatic Family.		Kúrkú ...	...	...	...	...	
Munda Sub-Family.	...	Savara ...	...	166	157	40	Ganjám and Vizagapatam.
		Gadaba ...	...	43	36	10	Vizagapatam.
				209	**193**	**50**	
Dravidian Family.	Dravida group.	Tamil ...	...	17,038	15,544	4,069	East Coast Central and South Divisions.
			Irula ...	2	1	1	Nilgiris.
			Kasuva or Kasuba.	...	...	...	
			Korava or Yerukala.	43	41	10	Deccan, East Coast North and Central Divisions.
		Malayálam ...	...	3,099	2,861	740	West Coast.
		Canarese ...	...	1,562	1,531	373	Deccan, West Coast, East Coast Central and South Divisions.
			Badaga ..	39	34	9	Nilgiris.
			Kurumba ...	3	5	.1	Nilgiris.
		Kodagu or Coorgi.	...	...	...	..	
		Tulu	...	513	496	122	South Canara.
			Bellara ..	...	...	...	
			Koraga ...	2	3	...	South Canara.
		Kóta ...	...	1	1	...	Nilgiris.
		Tóda	...	1	1	...	Nilgiris.
	Intermediate languages.	Góndi ...	...	8	4	2	Vizagapatam and Gódávari Agencies.
		Kóya or Kói.	...	49	47	12	Vizagapatam and Gódávari Agencies.
	Andhra group.	Telugu ...	...	15,782	14,315	3,769	Circars and all over the Presidency.
		Khond or Kandhi.	...	371	357	89	Ganjám and Vizagapatam.
			Konda ...	19	15	5	Vizagapatam.
				38,532	**35,256**	**9,202**	
Sanskritic Sub-Branch.	Sanskrit group.	Sanskrit ...	...	...	1	...	
	North west group.	Sindhí ...	...	...	...	...	
			Kachchi ...	...	...	...	
	Southern group.	Maráthi ...	...	127	121	31	All over the Presidency.
			Konkaní ...	170	157	41	South Canara and Malabar.
			Goanese or Gomántakí.	...	...	...	
		Singhalese ...	...	...	...	...	
			Mahl ...	4	3	1	Laccadive Islands.
	Eastern group.	Oriyá ...	...	1,604	1,809	383	Ganjám and Vizagapatam.
			Porojá or Párjá.	59	26	14	Agency, Vizagapatam.
		Bengáli ...	...	1	1	..	
	Mediate group.	Eastern Hindi	Lariya or Chattisgarhi.	3	2	1	Agency, Vizagapatam.
	Western group.	Western Hindi.	Hindóstáni ...	975	889	233	Whole province.
			Hindí ...	1	3	...	
		Rájastáni ...	Márwári ...	2	1	..	
		Gujaráthi ..	...	7	7	2	Madras and Malabar.
			Patnúli or Khatri.	93	89	22	East Coast South and Central Divisions.
			Pársi ...	...	1	...	
Gipsy Languages.	...	Lambádi or Lambaháni.	...	40	34	10	
				3,086	**3,144**	**738**	

I.—*Distribution of total population by language according to Linguistic Survey*—cont.

Family, sub-family branch and sub-branch.	Group.	Language.	Dialect.	Total number of speakers (000 omitted). 1911.	Total number of speakers (000 omitted). 1901.	Number per 10,000 of population of Province in 1911.	Where chiefly spoken. (District or Natural Division.)
1	2	3	4	5	6	7	8
		II. LANGUAGES FOREIGN TO INDIA.					
SEMITIC FAMILY ...	...	Arabic ...	...	...	1	...	
		Hebrew ...	...	...	...	...	
		Syriac ...	...	...	...	...	
				...	1	...	
INDOO-EUROPEAN FAMILY.	...	...	..		...	-	
ARYAN SUB-FAMILY.	...	...	...	..	...	...	
IRANIAN BRANCH	Western group.	Persian ...	...	1	...	...	
	Romance ...	Portugese ...	...	2	2	..	
	Celtic ...	Irish ...	...	...	...	...	
	Teutonic.	English ...	...	39	38	10	Madras, Nilgiris, Malabar and Chingleput.
		German ...	...	1	...	...	
	-			43	40	10	

II.—*Distribution by languages of 10,000 of the population of each district.*

District and Natural Division.	Canarese.	Hindóstáni.	Malayálam.	Maráthi.	Oriyá.	Tamil.	Telugu.	Other Madras languages.	All other languages.	Remarks. (Chief languages included in column 9).
1	2	3	4	5	6	7	8	9	10	11
Madras Presidency...	*373*	*233*	*740*	*31*	*383*	*4,069*	*3,769*	*388*	*14*	
Agency	...	*44*	...	*21*	*3,842*	*2*	*2,164*	*3,909*	*18*	
Agency, Ganjám ...	...	1	...	...	3,778	...	171	6,049	1	Khond (4,069), Savara (1,971).
Do. Vizagapatam.	...	45	...	31	4,641	1	1,678	3,582	27	Khond (1,900), Poraja (577), Savara (516), Gadaba (261), Konda (147), Kóya (92), Gondi (76).
Do. Gódávari ...	1	111	...	10	10	9	7,964	1,894	1	Kóya (1,881).
East Coast (North).	*2*	*246*	...	*5*	*949*	*36*	*8,635*	*122*	*5*	
Ganjám	1	32	...	1	5,124	5	4,487	347	3	Savara (234), Khond (107).
Vizagapatam ...	1	68	...	2	144	8	9,606	167	9	Gadaba (73), Khond (66), Konda (19), Korava (7).
Gódávari	5	95	...	4	27	15	9,844	1	9	
Kistna	1	283	...	9	11	16	9,632	44	4	
Guntúr	2	601	...	8	4	16	9,275	91	3	
Nellore	4	500	1	8	...	201	9,260	22	4	
Deccan	*1,687*	*831*	*1*	*71*	*1*	*42*	*7,243*	*115*	*9*	
Cuddapah	21	888	...	21	...	22	8,998	48	2	
Kurnool	78	963	...	59	...	23	8,781	93	3	
Banganapalle	16	1,562	...	53	6	5	8,253	104	1	Korava (64), Lambádi (40).
Bellary	5,513	820	1	119	2	71	3,308	144	22	Lambádi (110), Korava (33).
Sandúr	6,019	1,575	6	598	...	76	1,415	302	14	Lambádi (298).
Anantapur	953	619	2	75	3	51	8,122	166	9	Lambádi (125), Korava (40).

II.—Distribution by languages of 10,000 *of the population of each district*—cont.

District and Natural Division.	Canarese.	Hindóstání.	Malayálam.	Maráthi.	Oriyá.	Tamil.	Telugu.	Other Madras languages.	All other languages.	Remarks. (Chief languages included in column 9.)
1	2	3	4	5	6	7	8	9	10	11
East Coast (Central).	*399*	*264*	*4*	*29*	*1*	*7,054*	*2,202*	*23*	*24*	
Madras	56	1,033	85	183	7	6,235	2,074	53	374	
Chingleput	87	175	1	20	...	7,958	1,780	8	21	
Chittoor	137	428	...	33	2	2,165	7,186	51	3	
North Arcot ...	142	359	2	48	...	7,775	1,646	27	6	
Salem	759	218	1	32	...	7,470	1,468	49	3	
Coimbatore	1,218	100	12	13	...	6,439	2,202	7	9	
South Arcot	86	169	...	10	...	8,899	880	2	4	
East Coast (South).	*205*	*62*	*4*	*19*	...	*8,584*	*1,046*	*75*	*5*	
Tanjore	28	48	3	56	...	9,472	810	75	8	
Trichinopoly ...	230	118	3	11	...	8,305	1,300	30	3	
Pudukkóttai ...	136	50	2	20	...	9,476	292	22	2	
Madura	607	78	3	10	...	7,262	1,830	204	6	Patnúli (204).
Rámnád	139	25	5	4	...	8,614	1,161	50	2	
Tinnevelly	50	38	8	4	...	8,933	938	25	4	
West Coast	*582*	*67*	*7,126*	*89*	...	*356*	*58*	*1,691*	*31*	
Nilgiris	1,098	828	709	84	...	3,085	381	3,901	419	Badaga (3,261), Kurumba (246).
Malabar	52	22	9,414	5	...	386	65	33	23	
Anjengo	...	...	9,257	...	...	196	2	..	545	
South Canara ...	1,871	154	1,983	803	...	9	7	5,664	9	Tulu (4,281), Konkaní (1,367).

III.—Comparison of caste and language tables.

Tribe.	Strength of tribe (Table XIII).	Number speaking tribal language (Table X).	Tribe.	Strength of tribe (Table XIII).	Number speaking tribal language (Table X).
1	2	3	1	2	3
Badaga	38,180	38,691	Kuravan	109,684	} 42,855
			Yerukala	88,241	
Bellara	191	188	Kóta	1,163	1,271
Gadaba	45,115	43,009	Kóyi	79,422	49,305
Gond	25,596	8,087	Kurumbau	144,095	3,081
Irula	100,659	2,358	Lambádi	49,418	40,305
Khond	354,940	370,693	Poroja	92,737	58,951
Konda Dora	89,775	19,106	Savara	186,128	165.777
Koraga	4,391	1,634	Tóda	748	730

CHAPTER X.—INFIRMITIES.

It has been said somewhere by Carlyle that man can only see the evil which he has been taught to see. The statement is as applicable to physical evil as to moral evil.

2. As was the case with the census generally, enquiry into the matter of the unfit and the afflicted was carried through in one night by some three hundred and sixty thousand unpaid enumerators, the method employed being that of direct personal enquiry. The question of time and method apart, of these enumerators it may be said, without deprecation or ingratitude, that practically all lacked a tincture of that special knowledge requisite for satisfactory investigation of the prevalence or existence of certain obscure diseases; while few, if any, could be expected to bestow on the subject a degree of interest and reflection, which might enable a person of general speculative habit to atone in some small measure for technical shortcoming by ingenious use of mother wit.

3. It may then be granted that unqualified opinion, however honestly given, as to the existence of such maladies as leprosy or insanity, is of no scientific value. Doubt is practically dispelled by observation of the fact that of lepers selected, presumably by those deemed competent to do so, for examination by the Indian Leprosy Commission of 1890–91, well nigh 10 per cent. were found to be untainted by the disease. Again no man, however honest, will brand his most intimate relations as insane or leprous, while there remains in his mind the faintest glimmering of doubt or hope that his fears may be unfounded. In India is found an especial reason for denial in the stigma which attaches to an unmarried woman and to her parents—a fact which may partially explain a marked sex disproportion in the leprosy returns of the last three enumerations, and in the undoubted insanity of the Madras Asylum where, at a moment of enquiry, of 448 Indian patients but 89 were women.

	Lepers.	
	Males.	Females.
1911	12,674	4,184
1901	10,216	3,362
1891	9,529	3,209

4. This general explanation may perhaps be extended to cover the fact that, save in the case of blindness in 1891, men are found to contribute more to the ranks of the afflicted than women.

5. The instructions to enumerators threw on them the responsibility of deciding who was mad or leprous. Madness, as will be seen later in the opinion of an expert, is a relative term; and in India the rural lunatic must be very mad indeed before his antics attract the particular attention of his fellow countrymen. Leprosy is a disease of long incubation and slow progression, and, save in its marked forms, may escape the notice of the unlearned sufferer as well as of the casual observer.

6. With respect to blindness and deaf-mutism instructions were more precise. A person was not to be described as blind unless absolutely without sight; as deaf-mute unless entirely without speech or hearing.

7. A little reflection will show that precision in one of these cases defeats its own object. Unless the number of persons totally devoid of sight were very great, and this is not the case in Madras, it is difficult to see what useful purpose a knowledge of such number serves.

8. Total blindness may be, and often is, the result of accident; of more practical utility would it be to ascertain, if possible, the prevalent causes, other than accident or maltreatment, of impaired sight, and to suggest methods of remedy.

9. But while I deride others I myself become a castaway, if I essay my uninstructed comment on the material which the diligent, if unreflective, enumerator has provided. I have therefore asked and received expert aid towards the writing of

this chapter; and to Lieut.-Col. Elliot, I.M.S., Dr. T. M. Nair, Captain Heffernan, I.M.S., Dr. W. Stokes, Lieut.-Col. Leapingwell, I.M.S., and the Rev. D. Gioanini, I tender my best thanks for the help that they have afforded me.

10. To the knowledge of the following sections I can lay no claim : acknowledgment that I have in great part borrowed the phrasing of letters addressed to me personally is not intended as an attempt to saddle my contributors with responsibility for my own interpolations.

Insanity.

11. There are reported to have been 8,407 insane persons in the Madras Presidency on the night of March 10, 1911 ; or, in round numbers, one in every 5,000 of the general population was mad. Sex distribution seen in subsidiary table I shows 24 males and 17 females per 100,000 of each sex as contributing to this total.

12. In the year 1901 the population of England and Wales was 32½ millions, of whom 132,654 persons, equivalent to one in 245 of the general population, were insane. If then our present census figures are to be accepted as they stand, the conclusion to be drawn is that insanity is some twenty times commoner in England than in Madras.

13. But granting that, owing to the greater stress of life in England, mental disease, and consequently insanity, is commoner there than here, the difference cannot possibly be so great as these figures suggest.

14. Of the insane in England in 1901 some 79 per cent. were under treatment in various institutions, and may therefore be regarded as undeniably mad. In Madras in 1911 only about 9 per cent. of those returned as insane were under regular surveillance, and the accommodation available would not shelter more than an additional 2 or 3 per cent. of the total number. There is therefore a possibility of excess in the untrained enumerator writing down as mad those who are not really so ; but the probability is vastly greater that he deems many undeniable lunatics as afflicted by other conditions.

15. The present attitude of Southern India in relation to insanity is curiously akin to that which obtained in mediæval Europe. Persons suffering in Madras from melancholia are deemed afflicted with "the bile" rather than as insane ; the sufferer from sundry other forms of mental disease is "bewitched" in Indian, and "spelled" in Anglo-Indian phraseology. In mediæval Europe the treatment of "*melancholia*," the black bile, much exercised the mind of the physician ; bewitchment met with undeniable recognition in the frequent burning at the stake of witches.*

16. Mental affliction in the early Christian days of Europe provided a ready road to a local reputation for sainthood. Anchorites betook themselves to caves to escape the temptations of the world ; they slept on beds of stone, and scourged themselves to "mortify the flesh ;" unnatural ideals of virginity and celibacy, existent still, it is said, with similar effects in parts of Russia,† led to self mutilation. The visual hallucinations of such persons were regarded as veritable manifestations of God or Devil; their auditory hallucinations as the special revelation of God to His chosen few. All this is madness in Europe now ; but in India the religious mendicant still wastes his life in "silent contemplation," sleeps on thorns, mutilates horribly the image in which he was made, and yet escapes remark in column 16 of the census schedule.

17. Thus, as suggested already, the explanation of the low percentage of insanity in the Presidency lies entirely in the relativity of the condition. Insanity is a social rather than a medical term, and the difference between sanity and

* The year 1891 is not so very remote. In that year, to the everlasting shame of their country and of those responsible for its enlightenment, a family in Southern Ireland burned to death one of its members, suspected of being "a fairy," but really insane.

† The sect of the "skoptzy."

insanity is largely a question of degree and environment. The point is illustrated by a comparison of the proportional figures of insanity among Bráhmans and among some other castes. There is no reason to suppose that Bráhmans suffer especially in this respect, but in their more cultured environment mental defect is more apparent, and more disconcerting, than among their less sophisticated neighbours.

Number per 100,000 returned as insane.

Bráhmans (all) ...	32
Málas ...	20
Kápus ...	14
Paraiyans ...	14

18. In respect of the particular varieties of mental disease prevailing no information could be expected from the census returns. Four hundred and seven patients actually under professional treatment were classified as in the margin.

305 as suffering from	maniacal conditions.
30 ,,	melancholia.
14 ,,	mental stupor.
20 ,,	delusional insanity.
29 ,,	congenital mental defect.

19. But these figures cannot be taken to represent the true incidence of mental disease among the people. Melancholia, as already stated, is not generally regarded as a mental disease; the result of the well-known reluctance of the Indian to place his relations, especially female relations, under restraint is that only the worst and most unmanageable cases are sent to the asylum.

20. With regard to the causes of insanity, hereditary predisposition, in India as in Europe, seems to play an important part. It is intensified by the frequency of consanguineous marriage; contributory causes are also indulgence in ganja, and other preparations of Indian hemp; sexual excess during the immature and adolescent period of life; and, to a small, but appreciable extent, the abuse of alcohol.

It is a noteworthy fact that, during the decade 1901–1911, only in four cases admitted to the Madras Asylum could insanity be attributed to the abuse of opium, or its derivative morphine.

21. In the light of the foregoing remarks detailed criticism of the figures of tables XII and XII–A, and of the subsidiary tables concerned with insanity seems hardly necessary. The number of the insane has risen from 7,757 in 1891 to 8,407 in 1911; the increase as one would expect being somewhat more marked among males than among females. Subsidiary table I shows a slight proportional decrease since 1891 of insanity in both sexes in proportion to the total population; but statistics of insanity in the Agency can hardly be taken seriously, while the figures for the East Coast Central division are necessarily affected by the existence of the central asylum at Madras.

22. Muhammadans show a marked increase of insanity, as may be noted in the margin; but most remarkable or most unfortunate of all, at least according to statistics, are the Tamil Idaiyans, whose nurseling has not turned on them a propitious eye during the decade. Their progress in infirmity is sufficiently remarkable to warrant detailed exposition: a probable explanation of their misfortune is that the abstractors have burdened them with the misfortunes of their Telugu brethren, the Gollas.

Year.	Muhammadan insane.		
	Total.	Males.	Females.
1911 ...	948	585	363
1901 ...	741	451	290
1891 * ...	890	536	354

Years.	Idaiyan.											
	Insane.			Deaf-mutes.			Blind.			Lepers.		
	Total.	Males.	Females.	Total.	Males.	Females.	Total.	Males.	Females.	Total.	Males.	Females
1911 ...	225	148	77	998	570	428	934	453	481	507	381	126
1901 ...	81	46	35	509	277	232	656	308	348	308	241	67
1891 * ...	103	57	46	663	356	307	812	351	461	307	283	74

* Includes figures for Travancore and Cochin.

DEAF-MUTISM.

23. There were 32,490 deaf-mutes enumerated in the Presidency in 1911, compared with 24,896 in 1901, and 27,398 in 1891. The proportion of the afflicted to the total population is 7·76 : 10,000; which corresponds exactly with the ratio usually accepted in Europe, where the Netherlands with 3·35, and Switzerland with 24·5 per 10,000, show the lowest and highest percentages respectively.

24. From the fact that the greatest number of deaf-mutes is found at the ages 5–10, and 10–15, it may be concluded that here too, as in the case of other infirmities, the returns are inaccurate. In deaf-mutism the predominating factor is deafness; and accordingly deaf-mutes may be classified under three heads: (1) those who are born deaf; (2) those who have become deaf after birth, and before acquiring the faculty of speech; (3) those who have become deaf after imperfect acquirement of the faculty of speech. Parents are always unwilling to admit that a child is deaf and dumb; the unwillingness is in a sense justifiable, as, even for an expert, it is not an easy matter to test the hearing power of an infant.

25. A child who becomes deaf during the first four years of its existence seldom acquires the faculty of articulate speech: should deafness come on between 4 and 7 years of age, much depends on the child's natural intelligence, and the intelligence and care of its parents and guardians. After the age of 7, save in exceptional cases, the power of speaking is generally preserved. Hence, there being no apparent reason for an accession of numbers at the period 10–15, we may infer that the correct number of deaf-mutes under 10 years of age has not been ascertained, and that the numbers given in the table are considerably below those which would be warranted by actual facts. The obtaining of a correct return Dr. Nair considers practically impossible.

26. The causes of congenital deaf-mutism are generally acknowledged to be (1) hereditary transmission, (2) consanguineous marriage. With respect to the first point 800 slips of male deaf-mutes, and 500 of females were examined; with the result that, of these numbers, 264 men and 127 women were found to be married; while the widowed of either sex were respectively 127 and 66.

27. In respect of consanguineous marriage, the peculiar caste system of India, as noted subsequently in the case of blindness, is undoubtedly responsible for a large number of such unions; and Dr. Nair states that, of the large number of deaf-mutes that come under his observation, an appreciable percentage are actually the children of consanguineous marriages. Proportional figures such as those noted in the margin, throw little further light on the question; a particular conclusion from a general premiss, as observed later, is unwarranted. The marked preponderance among Telugu Brahmans is curious, but if taken as implying an especial habit of consanguineous marriage, it is in direct contradiction to the conclusion which similar figures in respect of blindness seem to indicate.

Proportion of deaf-mutes to 100,000 persons.

Presidency	78
Tamil Bráhmans	72
Telugu ,,	89
Malayálam ,,	62
Kammálans	78
Kamsalas	76
Kápus	62
Paraiyans	71
Muhammadans	69

28. In addition to the general prevalence of consanguineous marriage, there is another factor which may operate to the detriment of the people in this connection. This is the extraordinarily long period during which mothers suckle their children: it is not uncommon in the Presidency to see mothers suckling children nearly two years of age. The point was noticed in the case of Scotland by Dr. William Farr, who observed that "in those districts, viz., Highland and Insular, where mothers suckle their infants from 14 to 18 months, deaf-mutism and blindness prevail to a very much larger extent among the people than in districts where nine and ten months is the usual limit of the nursing period."

29. Epilepsy and idiocy are not uncommonly associated with deaf-mutism in Madras; and it is of some interest to note that in respect of multiple infirmity, insanity *plus* deaf-mutism largely predominates.

30. Among the most common causes of acquired deaf-mutism are typhoid and scarlet fever, small-pox, colds followed by local inflammation, scrofula, falls and blows. With the exception of scarlet fever such causes are very generally prevalent in Southern India.

BLINDNESS.

31. On the night of March 10th, 1911, there are said to have been in the Madras Presidency 33,982 persons totally devoid of sight. This absolute total represents 81 per 100,000 of the total population, and discloses a state of affliction, which does not compare unfavourably with that of other countries, for some of which figures, taken from the report of the Committee of the Formosan Special Census investigation, (Tokio, 1909), are quoted in the margin.

Persons blind per 100,000 of total population.

England	80
Ireland	110
France	80
Germany	90
Russia	190
Italy	90
Sweden	80
Bulgaria	310
United States of America	80
Canada	70
Australia	70

32. If the further figures noted at the side are to be accepted as reliable, the number of the blind in this Presidency has decreased steadily throughout the past twenty years. But in part I of table XII, which exhibits the age distribution of this infirmity, may be noticed certain points which afford a warning that the statistical basis of our deductions is not of the soundest.

Persons totally blind.

1911	33,982
1901	34,461
1891	36,853

33. In the first place a decrease of 2,392 from 1891 to 1901, and one of 479 during the succeeding decade, can largely be accounted for by decrease of 1,743 and 509 at the ultimate age periods examined (60 years and over). Hence we are led to suspect that the general decrease may be more apparent than real, and due to a more precise care by the enumerators not to enter as blindness the extreme dimness of old age.

34. Moreover we would naturally expect from cataract, and other diseases of old age, a steady increase of blindness up to about the period 55, and thereafter a steady decrease due to death. For the strange quinquennial increase and remission, which here characterises the later age periods, there is no apparent explanation. Misstatement of age may be suggested; with, at first sight, some measure of probability. But the peculiarly systematic misstatement that acceptance of this explanation implies is a somewhat arbitrary hypothesis; and one not rendered more credible by the fact that increase here is at the quinquennial periods, while the general tendency of the uninstructed Indian is to prefer the decennial periods when giving a general estimate of his age.

35. For purposes of convenience, the causes of blindness, as met with in the southern Presidency, may be classified as (1) the preventable, (2) those for which no prophylactic measures are available.

36. We may dismiss the latter class first, as they are of far less practical concern than the former. They are mainly of the congenital type, and include the various forms of infantile cataract, of microphthalmos, and of allied congenital defects. These defects seem to be much commoner in India than in Europe, and the true explanation is probably to be found in the intermarriage of relatives.

37. Such intermarriage is doubtless facilitated, despite certain countervailing restrictions, by the caste system which informs Southern India. Although it must be remembered that deduction from the general fact, that an individual belongs to a society wherein consanguineous marriage prevails, of the particular fact, that such individual is the child of a consanguineous marriage, is arbitrary rather than scientific, still the contrast of figures taken from table XII-A affords some confirmation and illustration of this theory.

38. Difference of speech and habit, aided by, or possibly arising from, the natural formation of the country, have isolated the West Coast community from the rest of the Presidency, and, combined with caste restriction, must needs have introduced a strong element of consanguinity into marriage. The blind, although *actually* most numerous on the East Coast, are shown by subsidiary table I to be far more numerous on the West Coast than elsewhere, in *proportion* to the total population. It is worthy of notice how this excess of infirmity runs throughout the various social *strata.* Among Malayalam Bráhmans 181 persons per 100,000 are blind, as compared with 96 among Tamil, and 66 among Telugu Bráhmans. Of Náyars 144 per 100,000 are blind; of the same number 55 Kápus, 72 Vellálans, 77 Kammálans, and 86 Kómatis are afflicted. The Tamil Paraiyans have 80 per 100,000 of their number blind; the Telugu Málas and Mádigas 62 and 85 respectively: on the West Coast 204 Cherumans and 101 Tiyans of every 100,000 are blind.

39. Among Indian Christians, a community whose circumstances must favour consanguineous marriages, 98 persons per 100,000 are blind. Inasmuch as similar circumstances probably exist among the Anglo-Indian community, the fact that of them but 31 per 100,000 are blind is striking; but may in a measure be explained by their presumed avoidance of much that produces blindness in the Indian. Yet although Muhammadans intermarry closely, and although among their ranks are found those whose diligence largely contributes to the blindness of the Presidency, their percentage of blindness, (80 per 100,000), is slightly lower than that of the total population, and by no means so high as that of many Hindu castes varying widely in social rank and custom.

40. Under irremediable causes too must be included the eye defects found in children of unhealthy parents, and especially amongst the syphilitic. In theory it may be urged that such causation is preventable, but for practical purposes such argument is at present futile. The question of state regulation of prostitution lies between, and it may well be centuries before this can be taken up seriously.

41. We now come to the preventable causes of blindness. In the order of importance first place is claimed by (*a*) neglected *Trachoma* (granular ophthalmia), which affects children and adults alike. A common cause of the spread of this disease is the custom of anointing the eyelids with various powders. Such powders are kept in a common cup, into which all members of the family, or at least all who use cosmetics, dip, and thus one affected member can affect a whole household. In this, as well as in the reason referred to in paragraph 3 *supra*, may be found the explanation of the fact that the infirmity of blindness is in Madras well nigh as widespread among women as amongst men; although in various ways the former can transmit this particular affection to the latter. Neglect, improper or insufficient treatment of this disease, leads to serious *sequelæ*; and in early neglect of the disease in children may be found the reason for the remarkable increase in blindness which occurs immediately after the age period 0–5.

42. (*b*) *Ophthalmia of new-born children.*—It has long been recognized in Western countries that this bulks there as one of the greatest factors in the production of preventable blindness. If such is the case where the midwives are certificated and trained European women, and where it is the rule rather than the exception to call in medical aid in all difficult and complicated cases, it is obvious how potent an influence for evil must be the native midwife, whose qualifications and methods have already been described in Chapter II. Indian opinion appears to be waking to a consciousness of this evil, and a progressive diminution of blindness at the earliest age periods, when age is not so much a matter of uncertainty or misstatement as in later life, may be due to a gradual amelioration of these conditions. A decrease at these early ages is indeed the most hopeful feature of the general decrease noted in the second paragraph of this section.

Year.	Age period. 0–5.	5–10.
1911	938	1,631
1901	941	1,812
1891	1,322	2,016

43. (*c*) *Cataract in all its forms.*—It is often asked "why is cataract so prevalent in India?" The question is based on the well-known fact that Anglo-Indian oculists have an unrivalled experience of this disease, and rank their cataract extractions by the thousand, against the hundreds or less of European surgeons. But while cataract may be more common in the East owing to glare and heat, the explanation of the whole matter is that trained ophthalmic surgeons in southern India are few in number, and this particular work being concentrated in a few hands, instead of being diffused through many, comes prominently into notice.* The population of the administrative county of London is about 4½ millions; that of the Madras Presidency about 42 millions. London has three large eye hospitals, and in several of the general hospitals there are eye departments (about 20); Madras has one ophthalmic hospital situated in Madras city. There are many throughout the Presidency for whom resort to the city is out of the question; if the District Medical Officer lacks the training in this particular business that would enable him to seek and command the confidence of the timid shy people by whom he is surrounded, the blind lie in their homes untouched; or else resort to the Muhammadan cataract coucher, whose filthy ways and hopeless ignorance render his results appalling.

44. (*d*) *Neglect of the eyes during severe illnesses such as small-pox, typhoid, and many others.*—The patient lies for days semi-conscious, with eyes half closed. Dessicating winds blow on him, flies and dust settle on his eyes; no one thinks of protecting these delicate organs at a time when the patient's reflex protective powers are abolished or dormant. The result is corneal ulceration, with all its ghastly *sequelæ*; and another individual is thrown on his relations a hopeless burden, who might, with a little care, have taken a share in the life work of the community.

45. (*e*) *Improper treatment of the eyes at the hands of native "Vaidyans," who resort largely to irritant drugs placed within the eyelids.*—In the majority of cases these remedies are intended as treatment for conditions, which, if left alone, would get well of themselves; and even in those cases where the *prognosis* is more grave, the treatment is far worse than the disease. The *Vaidyan* does not confine himself, in doing this damage, to cases of ophthalmic affection, but frequently inserts his dangerous pastes beneath the lids of patients in the comatose, or semicomatose state, of various severe diseases. The motive is restoration to consciousness; the end attained is too frequently the abolition of vision.

46. (*f*) On every occasion when an eclipse of the sun is visible in India, cases of "Eclipse blindness" are encountered shortly afterwards. The patient looks at the phenomenon, either with the naked eye, or through insufficiently protective glass. The solar light though greatly diminished in volume has lost nothing in intensity, and, focussed by the refractive media of the eye as by a burning glass on the retina, kills that delicate structure at its most important part—the very centre of vision. The victims are usually young people, whose career of usefulness is too often ended at a stroke. For one whose case comes under notice there must be hundreds never seen. Dissemination of information on this subject immediately before an eclipse would undoubtedly save many eyes.

47. This list of preventable causes may conclude with a few, against which common sense, as distinct from professional knowledge, would form a fairly efficient safeguard. Among these are the accidents caused by the explosion of crude native fire-works, made by mixing red sulphide of arsenic and chlorate of potash, and blending with the mixture rough sand or fine gravel. Such fire-works are often prepared for the amusement of children by their elders who ought to know better. Accidents from aërated water bottles might be avoided largely by covering the bottle before opening; a little care would largely diminish accidents from thorns in the jungle, from children's nails, etc., etc.

* Lieut.-Col. Elliot tells me that he has in one morning extracted 54 cataracts at the Madras Ophthalmic Hospital.

LEPROSY.

48. The table shows an increase of 3,280 lepers since the last enumeration: of this number 2,458 are men and 822 women. The increase is most strongly marked at the later periods of life, male lepers aged 40-60 numbering 5,806 against 4,644 in 1901, and 4,123 in 1891; similar figures for females being 1,584, 1,259 and 1,203. Still a curious, and, if the returns be accurate, regrettable fact is the recrudescence of leprosy in early life, which the marginal figures suggest.

Year.	Lepers at age period 0-10. Males.	Females.
1911	124	59
1901	54	47
1891	131	80

49. Reasons have already been given for doubt as to the general trustworthiness of figures relating to infirmity; and information as to the prevalence or diminution of leprosy, and other ills, in particular districts, and among particular classes of the population, can be obtained from the various parts of table XII without need for further exposition here. It is, however, worthy of remark that one of my medical informants questions the apparent prevalence of leprosy among Paraiyans. In his experience, he states, he has met but two real lepers of this caste; while he considers that on the West Coast leprosy is more prevalent among Máppillas, Tíyans and Náyars than the figures returned indicate.

50. The origin of leprosy is a question on which medical theories differ, and one on which it would be absurd for me to express an opinion. As to its continued existence certain causes suggested by the Rev. D. Gioanini, S.J., Superintendent of St. Joseph's Leper Asylum, Mangalore, and by others, appear adequate and convincing. They are as follows: (1) absence of segregation, which results in lepers, even in advanced stages of the disease, living in the midst of their families; (2) employment of lepers in such businesses as milk-selling, cigarette-rolling, petty shop-keeping, etc.; (3) marriage of persons, either suffering from the disease in its incipient state, or in whom the virus is latent; (4) unrestricted circulation of coins and currency notes handled by lepers; (5) unrestricted use of railway carriages by lepers. In respect to the possiblity of arresting or stamping out the disease, all my informants agree in thinking that nothing can be done without legislation, which will place some restriction, at least in towns and cities, on the freedom of movement and occupation at present allowed to lepers.

51. In addition to the provision made for these unfortunates in the Leper Hospital at Madras, asylums are maintained by missionary bodies at various places throughout the Presidency. One asylum in Mangalore has been noticed already; a letter from the Superintendent of a Mission to Lepers in India and the East, dated 1907, makes mention of homes at Calicut, Mangalore, Sálúr, Rámachandrapuram, and Bápatla, wherein the average numbers of inmates at that time were 45, 6, 30, 90 and 80 respectively.

52. There are some points of general interest in respect to the infirm generally, as well as to lepers in particular, which may here be examined. Such relate to birth-place, occupation, education and civil condition.

Tabulation of the birth-place returned by each and every sufferer shows clearly that there is little or no migration of the infirm. Except in the case of Madras city, for which details are given in the margin, fully 99 per cent. of those afflicted in any way were born in the district where they were enumerated. Migration to Madras, in the case of leprosy and insanity, is easily explained by the greater facilities for treatment there obtainable; in the case of blindness and deaf-mutism, it may be accounted for by the hope of charity which a large city holds out.

Infirmity.	Total number of infirm.	Number born in Madras city.
Leprosy	278	151
Blindness	175	114
Deaf-mutism	197	150
Insanity	625	267

53. In regard to the occupations of actual workers among lepers some gruesome information is available. Nearly 6,000 persons are engaged in cultivation in various forms, which is probably the safest outlet for their energies; but 155 are

raisers of farm stock, which implies that they constantly handle animals supplying milk, ghee, cheese, etc.; 281 are connected with "industries of dress and toilet;" 59, with "food industries;" and 422, with "trade in foodstuffs." Fourteen male lepers are hotel or restaurant keepers; 17 practise medicine; 33 are in domestic service; 38 are fishermen, who probably sell their catches; 38 are schoolmasters of some sort; 11 policemen are returned as lepers; 77 lepers are engaged in religious duties, and 6 find place under "Public administration."

54. Among the insane there are some occupations which provide food for reflection.

55. Two lunatics appear to be employed on transport by rail; one is in the army. "Public administration" claims four—a surprisingly small number, and the police force but one. Twelve are in domestic service; seven are devoted to "Literature, art and science," and a similar number practice the healing art.

56. Deaf-mutes and the blind are largely concerned with the land, or else procure a living "without definite occupation." But eight deaf-mutes, and five blind men are engaged in "Public administration;" there are 29 blind medical men, and two who can neither speak nor hear. Sixteen policemen are deaf-mutes, and three are blind; three deaf-mutes have returned themselves as employed in the "Post, Telegraph and Telephone services."

57. Civil condition is a more serious subject. More than 12,000 lepers are either married or widowed, and of this number 8,500 come under the former category. The vast majority of such persons are at comparatively advanced periods of life, and it is charitable to suppose that these marriages were contracted before signs of the disease became patent. But 12 boys and one girl at the period 0–10 are married; as are 13 boys and 11 girls at 10–15.

Age period.	Married lepers.	
	Male.	Female.
20–40	2,043	710
40–60	4,025	647
60 and over	941	71

58. All entries for the insane, and those otherwise afflicted, were not examined in this connection. Of 62 slips for male lunatics, picked up long after sorting had concluded, 20 showed the person thereon described as married, and all such were above 20 years of age. Of 99 women, 39 were married, and 29 widowed; one married woman being under 15 years of age, and two more between 15 and 20. To similar information in respect of deaf-mutes allusion has already been made.

59. Among lunatics 681 males and 65 females are literate, 149 men and 46 women being literate in English. Among lepers 1,700 men and 45 women are literate; the deaf-mutes have 180 literates (120 men and 60 women), the majority of these, (51 males and 54 females), being found in Tinnevelly, where missionary enterprise is concerned with these poor people. The blind have 493 literates, of whom 465 are males; but inasmuch as blindness may come at any time, there is no positive conclusion to be drawn from these figures.

1.—Number afflicted per 100,000 of the population at each of the last three censuses.

Natural Division.	Insane.						Deaf-mutes.						Blind.						Lepers.					
	Males.			Females.			Males.			Females.			Males.			Females.			Males.			Females.		
	1911.	1901.	1891.	1911.	1901.	1891.	1911.	1901.	1891.	1911.	1901.	1891.	1911.	1901.	1891.	1911.	1901.	1891.	1911.	1901.	1891.	1911.	1901.	1891.
1	2	3	4	5	6	7	8	9	10	11	12	13	14	15	16	17	18	19	20	21	22	23	24	25
Province ...	***24***	***23***	***25***	***17***	***15***	***18***	***87***	***74***	***87***	***68***	***55***	***65***	***83***	***91***	***101***	***79***	***88***	***104***	***62***	***54***	***53***	***20***	***17***	***18***
Agency	14	19	17	10	11	11	51	50	53	42	39	37	63	95	75	65	94	71	57	79	71	25	34	29
East Coast (North) ...	24	26	29	17	19	22	89	74	100	66	53	77	71	88	100	67	91	102	69	60	62	22	20	20
Deccan	22	24	23	14	15	17	86	80	94	69	60	67	88	107	117	69	96	113	19	29	29	8	8	9
East Coast (Central) ...	23	21	23	16	18	15	93	80	93	73	59	68	75	78	88	75	75	96	72	60	56	22	17	16
East Coast (South) ...	22	18	20	15	18	14	96	72	92	74	58	71	93	88	97	88	86	108	59	42	37	17	13	13
West Coast	35	28	40	25	20	29	65	61	38	52	45	25	117	121	133	118	108	123	61	63	82	23	25	31

II.—Distribution of the infirm by age per 10,000 of each sex

Age.	Insane.						Deaf-mutes.						Blind.						Lepers.					
	Males.			Females.			Males.			Females.			Males.			Females.			Males.			Females.		
	1911.	1901.	1891.	1911.	1901.	1891.	1911.	1901.	1891.	1911.	1901.	1891.	1911.	1901.	1891.	1911.	1901.	1891.	1911.	1901.	1891.	1911.	1901.	1891.
1	2	3	4	5	6	7	8	9	10	11	12	13	14	15	16	17	18	19	20	21	22	23	24	25
TOTAL ...	10,000	10,000	10,000	10,000	10,000	10,000	10,000	10,000	10,000	10,000	10,000	10,000	10,000	10,000	10,000	10,000	10,000	10,000	10,000	10,000	10,000	10,000	10,000	10,000
0-5	79	95	109	108	91	175	407	494	447	426	521	492	301	307	407	251	289	314	19	13	49	21	57	97
5-10	428	501	437	476	461	457	1,461	1,740	1,562	1,398	1,725	1,596	551	611	641	407	440	458	79	40	89	119	83	153
10-15	721	772	602	846	802	663	1,632	1,776	1,335	1,613	1,652	1,150	668	729	582	465	517	390	207	226	282	382	431	390
15-20	769	707	751	883	846	832	1,309	1,222	1,161	1,279	1,182	1,162	596	531	561	497	431	447	393	392	420	746	642	564
20-25	1,031	940	1,083	1,048	983	961	1,174	987	1,186	1,219	1,011	1,272	619	596	666	602	521	532	580	583	640	950	788	810
25-30	1,074	1,091	1,211	989	1,026	990	940	919	910	922	929	897	640	599	567	514	498	461	607	781	885	822	869	888
30-35	1,332	1,462	1,518	1,057	1,347	1,344	838	926	885	877	986	881	638	721	673	640	681	635	1,147	1,217	1,140	1,099	1,282	1,165
35-40	1,051	1,161	1,067	880	745	908	564	526	515	515	461	433	551	551	508	465	474	438	1,105	1,088	1,078	926	907	835
40-45	1,070	1,171	1,131	1,200	1,208	1,325	614	583	630	664	608	589	807	762	756	788	784	725	1,625	1,617	1,629	1,307	1,436	1,374
45-50	725	630	558	624	606	602	339	261	281	298	274	263	591	493	469	509	452	438	1,142	1,042	1,009	867	738	707
50-55	706	700	636	833	766	795	318	263	367	327	310	439	867	910	730	946	966	876	1,214	1,326	1,192	1,126	1,199	1,169
55-60	342	340	260	362	303	236	126	84	162	145	86	129	509	414	421	513	443	464	600	561	498	485	372	499
60 and over	672	530	647	709	816	872	278	219	569	322	260	697	2,662	2,776	3,019	3,403	3,554	3,822	1,082	1,114	1,139	1,150	1,196	1,349

III.—Number afflicted per 100,000 persons of each age period and number of females afflicted per 1,000 males.

Age.	Number afflicted per 100,000.								Number of females afflicted per 1,000 males.			
	Insane.		Deaf-mute.		Blind.		Lepers.					
	Males.	Females.	Males.	Females.	Males.	Females.	Males.	Females.	Insane.	Deaf-mutes.	Blind.	Lepers.
1	2	3	4	5	6	7	8	9	10	11	12	13
TOTAL ...	***24***	***17***	***87***	***68***	***83***	***79***	***62***	***20***	***717***	***803***	***962***	***330***
0–5	1	1	27	22	19	15	1	...	928	842	821	375
5–10	8	6	96	72	34	25	4	2	795	768	726	500
10–15	14	13	117	101	46	34	10	7	841	794	682	611
15–20	21	17	131	103	57	47	28	17	824	785	818	627
20–25	30	18	126	88	63	50	44	20	729	834	956	541
25–30	32	20	104	75	67	49	63	19	660	789	789	336
30–35	42	21	98	73	71	62	95	26	569	840	984	316
35–40	42	27	84	66	78	69	115	34	598	734	828	276
40–45	40	30	84	69	105	95	156	39	802	869	959	266
45–50	42	29	72	56	120	114	171	48	617	696	845	251
50–55	37	29	61	47	159	160	164	47	835	825	1,071	306
55–60	37	32	50	52	194	215	169	51	760	925	991	267
60 and over	28	19	48	36	390	441	117	377	757	932	1,255	351

IV.—*Number afflicted per 100,000 persons of each selected caste, tribe, or race; and number of females afflicted per 1,000 males.*

Caste.	Number afflicted per 100,000.								Number of females afflicted per 1,000 males.			
	Insane.		Deaf-mutes.		Blind.		Lepers.					
	Males.	Females.	Males.	Females.	Males.	Females.	Males.	Females.	Insane.	Deaf-mutes.	Blind.	Lepers.
1	2	3	4	5	6	7	8	9	10	11	12	13
Hindu.												
1. Bráhman, Tamil ...	40	15	73	66	90	102	63	22	385	850	1,149	347
2. " Telugu ...	49	14	103	74	68	63	28	11	295	726	986	406
3. " Malayálam.	209	79	47	79	199	159	38	11	818	1,400	667	250
4. " Canarese ...	63	27	44	44	95	94	154	13	448	1,050	1,047	86
5. " Oriya ...	3	4	3	37	2	34	38	5	1,500	13,500	25,000	154
6. " Others ...	84	26	89	34	119	150	139	64	819	380	1,269	462
7. Cheruman	12	9	44	46	220	190	103	55	857	1,148	951	584
8. Chetti	23	16	44	49	54	39	33	8	718	1,173	742	250
9. Gaudo	7	12	42	34	100	76	122	6	2,000	917	845	56
10. Holeya	8	4	59	37	75	83	57	29	600	778	1,347	629
11. Idaiyan	41	21	158	114	126	128	106	34	520	751	1,062	330
12. Kamma	17	11	88	60	64	53	21	6	612	720	824	265
13. Kammálan	21	13	88	59	84	70	42	13	662	696	862	309
14. Kamsala	28	17	82	70	78	56	44	30	610	866	728	692
15. Kápu	16	12	71	53	52	53	31	12	765	758	1,022	389
16. Khond	8	4	37	21	54	31	43	19	538	561	583	447
17. Kómati	37	14	92	53	104	68	52	16	380	574	646	310
18. Kuruba	18	13	53	62	77	70	12	7	714	1,111	859	571
19. Kurumban	6	14	98	75	71	102	8	6	2,500	761	1,431	667
20. Mádiga	20	21	89	77	86	85	60	23	1,038	861	974	376
21. Mála	17	23	77	62	66	59	76	21	1,346	819	907	278
22. Náyar	38	28	79	66	135	158	54	23	787	910	1,220	454
23. Pallan	15	17	77	70	92	108	61	17	1,262	991	1,215	299
24. Paraiyan	14	14	80	68	80	79	77	24	1,024	827	1,081	327
25. Tíyan	34	27	66	49	101	101	52	20	815	757	1,025	402
26. Velama	13	13	67	54	44	43	36	9	969	821	1,009	244
27. Vellála	17	11	90	68	69	74	50	15	671	775	1,120	320
28. Musalman	43	26	82	57	86	73	57	13	621	719	870	231
Christian.												
29. Anglo-Indian	411	419	55	37	16	45	87	45	1,077	714	3,000	545
30. Indian	28	25	89	74	104	92	99	85	918	860	923	860

V.—Statement showing the number of leper patients treated (in-door and out-door) in all the hospitals of the Madras Presidency during the years 1901–1910.

District.	1901.	1902.	1903.	1904.	1905.	1906.	1907.	1908.	1909.	1910.	Number of in-door patients in 1910.
1	2	3	4	5	6	7	8	9	10	11	12
Presidency Total ...	*6,292*	*6,123*	*8,069*	*7,111*	*7,325*	*6,496*	*6,407*	*6,750*	*7,179*	*7,625*	*1,005*
TOTAL ...	*2,256*	*2,236*	*2,575*	*2,673*	*2,546*	*2,136*	*1,883*	*1,906*	*2,162*	*1,902*	*9*
Ganjám ...	459	326	474	598	624	474	445	418	557	352	3
Vizagapatam ...	948	998	842	817	750	910	734	695	773	801	3
Gódávari ...	500	570	971	970	594	253	248	338	371	350	1
Kistna ...	237	196	176	102	374	295	267	240	253	177	1
Guntúr ...		...		100	116	120	184	121	184	182	1
Nellore ...	112	148	112	86	88	84	55	94	74	90	...
TOTAL ...	*177*	*160*	*163*	*110*	*99*	*150*	*100*	*109*	*158*	*159*	*2*
Cuddapah ...	47	45	28	38	40	69	85	47	57	39	1
Kurnool ...	46	45	47	35	20	41	22	21	40	48	...
Banganapalle ...		4	2		.	...	...	.	...	...	...
Bellary ...	63	25	25	23	18	28	24	20	26	52	1
Anantapur ...	21	41	61	14	21	17	19	21	35	25	...
TOTAL ...	*1,782*	*1,601*	*1,450*	*1,483*	*1,859*	*1,593*	*1,834*	*2,059*	*1,948*	*2,082*	*750*
Madras ...	929	771	710	797	1,008	829	988	1,041	977	1,123	724
Chingleput ...	287	172	157	138	226	163	143	166	179	239	...
North Arcot ...	164	133	114	137	167	111	136	206	214	174	25
Salem ...	157	165	164	111	144	204	192	217	172	139	...
Coimbatore ...	62	77	92	93	112	108	76	118	111	80	...
South Arcot ...	233	283	218	207	202	178	299	311	295	327	1
TOTAL ...	*1,648*	*1,583*	*1,473*	*1,497*	*1,557*	*1,402*	*1,384*	*1,473*	*1,427*	*1,533*	*15*
Tanjore ...	579	472	528	560	458	344	388	421	381	417	3
Trichinopoly ...	88	148	84	117	163	130	144	157	179	201	6
Pudukkóttai ...	24	41	29	...	.	.	.	.	..	...	...
Madura ...	688	588	547	553	602	626	602	567	523	408	1
Rámnád ...		...	...	..		...	.	..	...	221	1
Tinnevelly ...	269	384	290	267	334	302	300	328	344	291	4
TOTAL ...	*928*	*531*	*2,408*	*650*	*628*	*581*	*559*	*551*	*687*	*653*	*229*
Nilgiris ...	5	7	13	10	11	8	5	4	8	7	2
Malabar ...	848	482	443	543	506	457	421	409	502	502	139
South Canara ...	75	92	1,952	97	111	116	133	138	182	144	88
Police, Railway, Private, aided and non-aided Hospitals.	*1*	*10*	...	*698*	*636*	*634*	*647*	*652*	*797*	*1,296*	...

CHAPTER XI.—CASTE.

TABLE XIII, Part I, shows us 479 sets of people, each set wearing a distinctive label. This formidable total, chiefly made up of Hindu caste names, might have been swollen indefinitely, were the titles returned by each and every person duly recorded. *Kápus*, for example, shown as a homogeneous community of 2,678,925 souls, are wont to distinguish themselves as Kuncheti, Morasa, Mótáti, Pókanáti, Velanáti, * etc.; *Bráhmans* may be classified with far greater elaboration and detail than by the crude though practical system of linguistic distinction; two and a half million *Vellálas* comprise among them a bewildering variety of sub-sects, * of which each will state that it differs from all others, but as to why it so differs, or wherein the differences lies, can rarely give an intelligible answer. Table XVII will shiver the solid block of *Indian Christians* into a dozen or more fragments; *Muhammadans*, theoretically brothers in one common faith, possess or have acquired a pretty faculty of sub-division.

2. Thus the general instruction to enumerators, that each person should describe himself according to his will and pleasure for the purposes of column 4 of the census schedule, proved a counsel of perfection rather than of practice. To its literal fulfilment there existed, even apart from all considerations of space and convenience, certain very apparent obstacles, of which a few may be set forth.

3. Best known of all caste classifications is *Manu's* fivefold division of the people into *Bráhmans*, *Kshatriyas*, *Vaisyas*, *Súdras*, and *out-casts*. *Bráhmans* we have with us, and can more or less recognize; but whatever be a *Kshatriya* in Northern India, he in Madras, despite recent large accessions to his ranks, remains a singularly elusive personage. Of *Vaisyas*, with recollections of sundry perfervid deputation still fresh in my mind, I fear to express an opinion; but their existence among us has been doubted by many, of whom at least one ingenious writer extends his scepticism to the case of the *Súdras*.

4. It was moreover necessary to warn enumerators against the entry of certain caste affixes, current indeed and recognized throughout the Presidency, but which yet fail of distinctiveness. *Rao*, for example, is the favourite affix of the Mahrátta *Bráhman*, but is assumed elsewhere by many other *Bráhmans*, and by some not *Bráhmans*; *Pillai* leaves it uncertain whether the person so described is a *Vellála*, or the *Paraiyan* butler in a European house. A similar uncertainty prevails to some degree in the case of a *Mudaliár*; while the only definite information conveyed by the term *Náyudu* is a suggestion that the bearer thereof, whatever his present rank, occupation, or dwelling, can probably speak Telugu.

5. The table shows that the enumerators, thus instructed, have performed their task well; or else that the ingenuity of the abstraction office has performed it for them. Doubts linger in my mind as to the whereabouts of one unyielding *Mudaliár*, who would be that and naught else, though offered a choice of several hundred other, and equally euphonious, caste names. *Súdras*, as in 1901, remain a modest thousand; but an increase of seventy-eight thousand *Kshatriyas*, and a disappearance of thirteen thousand *Vaisyas*, during the decade will demand some later speculation.

6. But before entering upon any detailed criticism of the results obtained, it may be well to attempt some estimate of the present day position of this caste institution in Southern India. At the outset it will be necessary to clear our minds of the

* In an appendix to the tables of 1891 over 800 sub-sects of *Kápus* and *Vellálas* are given.

idea that caste, as it now exists, bears any close analogy to the social conditions, ancient or modern, of Europe, or perhaps indeed of ancient India. If the belted knight of Merrie England objected to engage in honourable thwackings with the churl, he does not appear to have been affronted by the churlish presence in his hall, or by churlish contiguity on such roads as then existed; while in modern days the western *Bráhman* or *Kshatriya* is made, not born. The ascent of the fit is possible, although facilities for the descent of the unfit may still need a better organization. In India, the Védántic Aryans, a soma-drinking, cattle-sacrificing, roystering set, brought into contact with an inferior race in an enervating climate, may have felt themselves slipping down the ladder of supremacy, and thus bethought themselves of a system, which, accentuating their exclusiveness, might aid their desperate efforts to maintain the purity of their blood.

7. In later and more anarchical times the caste system supplied a rule of life, under which a man might get himself lived in the economy of every-day society: and, in its functional aspect, it probably kept alive the arts and crafts, which vanishing otherwise would have left the plains dwellers of India in a state of ignorant savagery comparable to that of the African Negro.

8. But in the practical life of the present day there is little trace of the existence of such ideas. "The technicalities, the uncertainties of law; the corruption of "both judges and witnesses, encourage a gambling spirit in the people" (I quote a learned professor of history) "and render the modern court for many more attractive than the old caste *pancháyat*;" despite the laborious information of subsidiary table I, experience recognizes more clearly every day that the son of a priest is not always himself of priestly character; that the descendant of a hundred sweepers in not necessarily so excellent in the quality which he should profess, as one who comes to the sweeping with a mind open and unfettered by tradition. Restrictions on intermarriage persist it is true; but despite their persistence there are not wanting present signs of their recognition as the now needless survival of old time strategy, rather than as part of a scheme which looks to the future.

9. The main positive function of caste to-day would seem to be the superabundant remedy of that deficiency in practical regulation, which was noted in Chapter IV as characteristic of an abstract philosophy generally known as the Hindu religion. At what time the lines of religion and of social discipline coalesced, or by what degrees they tended towards coalescence, it would be difficult to say; their coalescence was illustrated at some previous enumeration by objections then raised against profanation of Hinduism's *arcana* by nominal inclusion in the faith of the outcast. Their tendency to diverge, under stress of modern conditions, grew clear in 1911, when the suggestion that the outcast, rejected socially by Hinduism, was not a Hindu by religion, and possibly not a Hindu in any political sense, awoke to life a love for the depressed brother that had long lain dormant.

10. As to the theoretic defensibility, or indefensibility of the caste idea there is something to be said, before we pass to a consideration of its vitality to-day. A system which has endured so long, and under which countless millions have lived, and millions still live, with more or less content, must needs have found not a few opponents and defenders: both, it is probable, have erred at times through excess of zeal. It is a disregard of all teachings of history to assert that this system was never aught than the worse than worthless institute of a selfish theocracy; it is no less an insult to common sense to defend the revolting doctrine that some human beings are born untouchable inheritors of unknown sins, and objects of just avoidance to the portly concentration and embodiment of equally unknown virtues. So far as the equality or inequality of all mankind is concerned, it may fairly be conceded, on the one hand, that varying natural ability and varying opportunity will inevitably produce very varying results, and that intimate social connection and intercourse between persons of widely different habit of life has never been, and never is likely to be, anything but a pretence equally disagreeble to both participants; on the other, that it was a mistake to

assume that, because the social groups of one time were obviously not all of equal position, the degrees of inequality could be stereotyped, and applied for ever to the descendant groups of succeeding ages.

11. It is possible that the idea of caste has struck its roots into Hindu life as a whole too deeply for its eradication to be possible, or even particularly desirable. But the manner of the idea's presentation is certainly undergoing a change. Of small account are ideas of "social service," borrowed perhaps from Christianity, which now direct missions to the depressed classes. Such sympathy once informed Vaishnavism, whose votaries are not now the least exclusive in their daily walk and conversation; and if the "untouchable" is willing to accept himself as such, and thereby claim the commiseration of his twice-born brethren, it is unlikely that he will thus attain to, or deserve, improvement in his material or moral circumstances. More significant is the irritation produced by the social precedence tables of 1901, which has found vigorous expression on the part of many, no longer willing to admit their polluting abilities in black and white. Caste remains—there is no anarchical wish to tear up the rails on which the Indian train has run for so many centuries—so does as yet the possibility of pollution; but with his admission the protestant couples a modest abnegation of his own polluting capacities. Thus the *Shánáns* of Tinnevelly, no longer content to "pollute without eating beef," claim to be *Kshatriyas*; as do the "slightly" polluting *Pallis*. *Kammálans*, as will be suggested hereafter, are suspected of an evolution into *Bráhmanhood*; *Kómatis* disclaim alike liberality to *Mádigas* and vulpine intelligence.

12. Or, in other words, if the idea of distinction survives, and possibly waxes stronger, that of innate superiority or inferiority is being exploded from underneath, *Paraiyan Bráhmans* may manifest themselves to the startled gaze of the Census Superintendent of ten or twenty years hence.*

13. Dealing first with *Bráhmans*, we find that the caste has increased during the decade by 111,449 or 9·3 per cent. There are some curious variations in the progress of the parts of this whole. Malayálam and Canarese *Bráhmans* have remained practically stationary throughout the decade, their total increase being but 79 and 43 respectively. Tamil *Bráhmans* have thriven, and show an increase of 15·4 per cent.; followed by Oriyá *Bráhmans* with 12·3 per cent., Telugu *Bráhmans* (5·7 per cent.) and "others" (6·4 per cent.). The remarkable increase in Tamil *Bráhmans* would at first sight suggest that *Kammálans* have fulfilled a much talked of purpose, and returned themselves in large numbers as *Bráhmans*; but the suggestion is not borne out by an observed increase of 12·6 per cent. in this class; while among the Telugu *Kamsalas*, a people probably more troubled about caste than their Tamil brethren, a slower rate of increase (8·8 per cent.) corresponds to that of the Telugu *Bráhmans*. The variations in sex proportion shown in the margin do not appear to throw any light on the subject. Disregarding "other" *Bráhmans*, whose correct enumeration must always be open to some doubt, it is curious to note that in the sections showing increase the proportion of women has fallen, while it has risen considerably in the two sections which have remained stationary.

		Women per 1,000 men.	
		1911.	1901.
Tamil	Bráhmans	1,012	1,045
Telugu	"	1,010	1,040
Malayálam	"	835	822
Canarese	"	1,045	1,020
Oriyá	"	1,058	1,060
Other	"	1,007	972

14. The vagaries of the *Kshatriyas* throughout the last two decades are perplexing, but at least they serve the useful purpose of showing how little intrinsic importance can nowadays be attached to these arbitrary caste labels. In 1891, when the *Kshatriya* stalked abroad a "military and dominant" person, he numbered 155,155; in 1901, when, forsaking war, he was concerned with social precedence alone, he diminished to 80,311. In 1911, when no one cares particularly for his warlike abilities or his social standing, he has recovered his losses, and presents a solid phalanx of 158,521. Allowing as well as may be for the

* The *Badagas* of the Nilgiri Hills have put forward a claim to rank as "*Mountain Bráhmans*."

territorial redistribution of the Presidency mentioned in Chapters I and II, we may make a marginal attempt to track him to his lair. Inasmuch as the warlike spirit of the Presidency has not perceptibly diminished or increased in the last twenty years, it is scarcely worth while to look further than the whim of enumerator or enumerated for an explanation of these figures; unless indeed they typify a growing desire, already alluded to in paragraph 11, to exchange a definite, and not over much honoured, social label for one implying a vague respectability. The explanation is very probable in the case of the northern zamindar or rája, whose desire is readily communicated to his retainers; and at first sight offers some explanation for the variation in the fifth division. The *Shánáns* of Madura and Tinnevelly districts, pre-eminently the home of this aspiring class, numbered 350,027 in 1891, as against 35,283 *Kshatriyas*. Ten years later, when *Shánáns* had risen to 379,185, *Kshatriyas* had fallen to 14,573. Disgust at the lowly position assigned to them at the last enumeration may in 1911 have inspired some few *Shánáns*, whose numbers in Madura, Rámnád and Tinnevelly have risen to 409,147, or by less than 8 per cent., while *Kshatriyas* in the same districts have risen to 23,848, an increase of 63 per cent. in the decade.

Natural Division.	Kshatriyas.		
	1911.	1901.	1891.
Agency	5,402	1,785	2,510
East Coast (North) ...	85,550	43,495	65 827
Deccan	9,277	4,496	8,442
East Coast (Central) ...	24,302	9,070	33,541
East Coast (South) ...	29,386	15,640	38,604
West Coast	4,604	5,825	6,231
Total ...	158,521	80,311	155,155

15. It is scarcely worth while labouring this point. Even supposing that nine thousand and odd persons, formerly styled *Shánáns* have now preferred to return themselves as *Kshatriyas*, this absolute number is far too small to affect the figures of the great *Shánán* community in these districts, where, indeed, increase is greater than in the *Shánán* caste as a whole (6·4 per cent.).

16. But while on the subject of these *Shánáns* it may be well to consider for a moment a hint given by the census tables of 1891, which suggests that the caste is exposed to defections on another side.

17. In that year, of 278,887 *Shánáns* in the Tinnevelly district, 19,196 were returned as Christians; as were 2,052 of 71,170 in Madura. Tinnevelly, as already noted in Chapter IV, has been a particularly fruitful field for missionary enterprise, and prominent among the people that have embraced the faith are undoubtedly the *Shánáns*. Exact comparison is impossible, both because of territorial changes and of abandonment of the attempt to ascertain the caste of converts to Christianity. But between 1891 and 1901, while the *Shánáns* of Madura and Tinnevelly increased by 8·3 per cent., Indian Christians increased by 10 per cent. Between 1901 and 1911 *Shánáns* show an increase of slightly under 8 per cent. against an increase in Indian Christians of 15·5. Of the slight fall in *Shánán* increase an explanation may be found, either in an increasing number of conversions among *Shánáns*, or in a gradual abandonment by those converted of the old caste name in favour of the general term "*Indian Christian.*"

18. In view of the zeal with which various sections of the community, generally known as *Kómatis*, urged an intangible and harmless claim to be considered *Vaisyas*, it is somewhat surprising to find that the number of persons so returned has dwindled from 19,159 in 1901 to 6,042 in 1911, and that these six thousand persons are all found in Madras City; while the number of *Kómatis* has risen from 428,188 to 498,295, or by 16 per cent. A theoretical explanation may be that the arguments addressed to me on the subject were concerned mainly with the place assigned to *Kómatis* in the social precedence table of 1901, and with certain remarks in the caste glossary considered by the members of the *Kómati* caste as derogatory, rather than with the intangible difference between two abstract names. Satisfied that no attempt to estimate the social unimportance of any one would be máde on the present occasion, the *Kómatis* may have ceased to trouble themselves about the matter, and returned a name certainly of more current usage in

the Presidency. One more practical may be that the returns of Madras City were compiled by picked men, who were aware that the difference between *Kómati* and *Vaisya* was a subject of discussion; the larger staff, which dealt with the districts, in all probability regarded *Vaisya* as an affected synonym for the more generally current term.

19. *Súdras*, returned simply as such, we have already seen to be few in number. In practice it is not difficult to decide what is a present-day *Súdra*: in theory so much may be said, and has been said, as to whether the *Súdra* of Madras in any sense identical with the *Súdra* of "*Manu*," that the question is better left alone.

20. Subsidiary table II shows the increase or decrease which has occurred during the decade in the strength of the main castes of the Presidency; and, so far as possible, exhibits similar figures for the ten years immediately preceding. Notes in column 7 of this table explain, or attempt to explain, the reasons for abnormal differences, and draw attention to different methods of grouping or separation observed at the last three enumerations.

21. Beyond observing that the reader interested in the fortunes of a particular caste can ascertain its numerical advancement or decline by simple reference to this table, I find little of interest to say on the figures, which it sets forth.

22. Taking a few typical castes throughout the Presidency, we find that *Vellálas* the cultivators of the south, have increased by 6·6 per cent.: the *Kápus* of the Telugu country have fared poorly with but 4 per cent. increase, while their fellow cultivators, the *Kammas*, have added 15·6 per cent. to their numbers. A similar curious discrepancy is to be found among trading classes, *Kómutis*, as already stated, having increased by 16 per cent., against the 3·2 per cent. of the *Balijas*.

23. At the uttermost end of the scale Tamil *Paraiyans* have increased by 9·8 per cent.; Telugu *Málas* cum *Mádigas* by 7·3 per cent.; while the Canarese *Holeyas* have decreased by 8 per cent. all round, and by 6·9 per cent. in South Canara.

24. The explanation of this latter decrease may lie in the fact that the *Holeyas* are rather a medley of low castes than one caste in particular; and many *Holeyas* of 1901 may now masquerade under different names. This assumption is rendered probable by the fact that in Part II of the present table XIII the minute detail of 1901 is not reproduced. In that year 45 caste names accounted for 672,225 of a total Hindu population of 914,163 in South Canara; the list has now been curtailed to 7, and includes 509,499 of the 949,427 Hindus in the district. All castes have been recorded in Part I of table XIII, but the figures quoted in the margin suggest the query, applicable in many other cases, whether castes, whose absolute numbers are so exceedingly small, and whose fluctuations in the short space of ten years are so incomprehensible, can have any real existence as separate entities.

Caste.	1911.	1901.
Kíchagára	28	88
Killekyáta	1,319	387
Maléyava	136	239
Pánára	258	384
Stánika	255	1,469

25. The enormous strength of the Tamil *Paraiyans*, (their men constitute about one-seventh of the Tamil-speaking population of the Presidency), gives food for reflection in these present days. Sympathy with the sufferings of depressed Behemoth is in the air; much mission-to-the-depressed-classes work is on foot. But what if in India, as elsewhere, Behemoth grow suddenly conscious of his sufferings, and direct rude efforts to the amending of his lot? Telugu Behemoth is equally cumbrous, but his *Mála* head and *Mádiga* tail pull different ways; till he sees the error of his ways he is not likely to emerge from his present wallow.

26. For a curious illustration of this *Mála-Mádiga* antagonism I am indebted to Mr. H. R. Bardswell, I.C.S. It relates to "*Chindhu* dancing"—a practice which prevails in the Kóilkuntla and Nandyál divisions of Kurnool, and in the Jammalamadugu taluk of Cuddapah.

27. The dance is performed by *Mádigas*, and its main object, or certainly its main result, seems to be to infuriate the *Málas* to the pitch of frenzy. The music for the dance is played on a particular species of tom-tom called "*tappeta*," a large round instrument with the skin only on one side. This instrument is also used for the playing of "*Koluva*" music, to which no one takes exception, while the mere playing of "*Chindhu*" music is sufficient to cause trouble.

28. The dance consists in the adoption of a number of attitudes, which, Mr. Bardswell says, must be seen to be appreciated, accompanied by the waving of a cloth and the brandishing of a stick, which probably represents a sword. The origin of the dance, and the reason for its offensiveness, are alike uncertain; but Mr. Bardswell thinks that it originated in the celebration by the *Mádigas* of the rape of a *Mála* girl from the *Málapet* by one of their number. The *Málas* endeavoured to rescue the girl, but the ravisher beat them off with his sword, (now represented by the stick), and carried off in triumph the girl, and a cloth which he snatched from one of the pursuers.

29. Another interesting feature of the whole performance is that, outside the *Mála* and *Mádiga* communities, there are certain "*Chindhu*" and "*antichindhu*" groups. The latter group includes *Kómatis*, *Gándlas*, *Balijas*, *Mangalas*, and in general all who follow the "Chetti religion" (చెట్టి మతము), which appears to be, broadly speaking, Saivaism. Chief among the "*Chindhuists*" are the *Kápus*; but Mr. Bardswell supposes that all connected, in a popular sense, with Vaishnavaism and Saivaism respectively support or oppose the performance. It can of course have no real connection with these forms of religion: the *Bráhmans*, who represent philosophic Hinduism, decline, as one would expect, to associate themselves in any way with the exhibition.

30. An opinion indirectly expressed by another community on the relative positions of *Mála* and *Mádiga* is interesting. A *Chenchu* strongly objects to being called either a *Mála* or a *Mádiga*; but of two evils he much prefers the former.

31. The unwieldy proportions of the first part of table XIII are considerably modified in Part II, where only those castes or tribes are entered which include one per mille of the Presidency population; and where existence of a caste in a particular district is not noticed unless the members of such caste amount to more than one per mille of the district population.

32. Adopting a useful, if unscientific, system of linguistic and religious division, we are left with 36 Tamil, 40 Telugu, 5 Malayálam, 12 Canarese, and 11 Oriyá, castes; 9 castes of "other Madras languages;" 6 Muhammadan "tribes," and one body of "Indian Christians:" these comprising all but an unappreciable minority of the people of Madras.

33. The list may be reduced still further. Taking a district from each natural division, we find that 2 Tamil castes, 26 Telugu, 1 Canarese, 10 Oriyá and 3 "other," castes account for 1,438,050 of the total Hindu and "Animistic" population (1,863,034) of Ganjám; 1 Tamil, 25 Telugu, 3 Canarese, and 3 "other," castes for 746,388 out of 772,446 in Cuddapah; in Chingleput, a district divided between Telugus and Tamils, 21 Tamil castes, 20 Telugu castes, one Canarese, and one "other" caste, include 1,302,139 of 1,343,601 Hindus and Animists; of 2,141,196 Hindus in Tanjore, 28 Tamil, 10 Telugu, and 4 "other," castes comprise 2,092,833. Sub-division is still easier in Malabar, where 1,459,305 Hindus out of 2,008,082 are included in but five castes.

34. In the light of these figures it is worth while considering whether much of what now is talked about as caste distinction, may not be but the social and racial differences observable in every country, and between groups of countries; overlaid in India with a veneer of semi-religious tradition, to which last foreign observers have for the most part confined their attention.

35. Every self-respecting caste, it is true, can trace its proper and exclusive descent to some philoprogenitive God or Rishi; just as in Ireland there are few pretenders to respectability unconnected with ancient Milesian kings. In the

wilds of North Arcot, at some place of which I have forgotten the name, I held converse with an ancient *Kuravan*. In a curious jargon, compounded of Tamil and Telugu, he related to me the descent of his caste from somebody or something, that landed from an impossible boat on the shores of a highly improbable sea. At Srívaikuntam in Tinnevelly are found one of the oddest peoples in the world;—a tribe of *Vellálas* who live within the circle of a lofty mud wall, and deny admittance to strangers. They carry female seclusion beyond the limits of insanity, their women not being allowed to leave the houses in which they are born, much less go abroad within their fort. They are provided with incontestable proofs of their difference from everybody else, and they presented me with a printed history of themselves.

36. The happy result of their peculiarities can be seen by a consideration of a few detailed figures. The community numbers 52 males and 42 women. Of these 42 women 17 are widows, and, not being allowed to remarry, are useless for the purposes of increase. Of 18 married women at least 6 are past child-bearing age; seven unmarried women are aged 15 years or under. Of 52 men 18 are married; and 20, unmarried or widowed between the ages of 20 and 50, obviously cannot find brides within the community. The hopes of the continued existence of this people rest then on 12 married women and 7 unmarried girls; but, considering the fact that 16 married women had between them only 8 children in the last decade, those hopes cannot be considered particularly bright.

37. In reality my ancient *Kuravan* did not differ particularly from other bad old men of my acquaintance. He stole, but excused himself on the grounds that he only stole trifles such as fowls and grain, which were necessary for his support: he did not care for regular work, finding it much pleasanter to wander from village to village and see the world; he disliked jail, whither he had been a few times, on the quaint grounds that there one had always to answer the calls of nature at the same place. The Srívaikuntam *Vellálas* are probably the descendants of some old poligar and his retainers, who, having rendered themselves locally unpopular, built a fort and held on to their lives inside it. The kingly ancestors of Ireland were described with a measure of probability by an Irish Judge now deceased as a people who "roamed the boglands without a garment to cover their latter ends."

38. Or, in other words, the objection of the cultured *Bráhman* to intermarry or "interdine" with the rude if estimable *Kápu*, is not at bottom much more or much less strange than the prejudices, which in England debar the duke and his tenant-farmer from the intimate enjoyment of each other's society. Again, if Tamil and Telugu castes are more or less irrevocably distinct, despite the fact that, in point of social status and occupation, they are resolvable into complementary groups, it may be observed that similar differences are common in Europe between groups identical in status and occupation, but dissevered by the accidents of distance, language, and race. The Tamil cobbler is distinguished from his Telugu fellow-craftsman, in point of language, and by the fact that distance as a rule renders intercourse difficult; intermarriage and exchange of hospitality are almost as uncommon between the English cobbler and the French *savetier*. Higher up in the social scale we may at times light on a sub-conscious element of racial distinction or indeed antagonism; its clash with active personal inclination has been treated finely by a recent French writer. This last element of difference is especially helpful at the point at which the analogy appears to break down; namely when we observe that castes ascribed to one language are often spread through territories where another prevails, and yet keep themselves apart. It is curious, for example, to observe how, in the Ceded Districts, the Tamil and the Telugu, born in the same place, and living in perfect amity, have at bottom a certain dim indefinable hostility to each other; how even the southern *Muhammadan* of the Presidency talks the same language as the northern, prays with him, eats with him, at times intermarries with his family, and yet remains slightly apart. An amusing instance of acquired "racial antagonism" can at times be noticed in the case of Europeans domiciled in different parts of India.

39. Of obscure difference or antagonism no better illustration can be found than that which once prevailed, and which still faintly survives, between *right-hand* and *left-hand* castes. Utterly senseless to European eyes, this distinction was, according to one of my informants, of sufficiently vital import to account for the slaughter of thousands in the neighbourhood of Porto Novo and Cuddalore some seventy or eighty years ago. The fact of its existence is noted by early writers such as Sonnerat, Dubois, and Buchanan, but to explain its why and wherefore from information available is little less difficult than it would be to educe a reason for the struggles of the Guelphs and the Ghibellines from a perusal of Browning's "Sordello."

40. A theory has been propounded that this distinction is the survival of exogamous grouping precedent to the institution of the caste system. But exogamous principle will hardly account for scenes of frenzied bloodshed, which it needed the strong rule of the British Government to suppress; and such accounts as I have been able to procure point rather to some underlying idea of social, racial, or religious difference.

41. In his "*Prospectus of the Scientific Study of the Hindu Law,*" Mr. J. H. Nelson has put forward an explanation which assumes an ancient and sharply marked distinction between the artificers of the country and the agricultural, mercantile, and other classes. In proof thereof he quotes the *Mutravansi*, that "King Vijeya, who landed on the day of the death of Buddha, sent an embassy to Madura, which brought back a princess with 700 female attendants, a train of men of eighteen different classes, and also five different classes of workmen." The number eighteen is significant, inasmuch as in later days a petition dealing with the existence of the quarrel, though not with its causes, was presented to the Government of Madras by the "eighteen sorts of people of the right-hand castes of Chennapatnam." An element of religious exacerbation is then introduced by the supposition that the "eighteen sorts" of the right hand accepted the spiritual supremacy of the *Bráhmans*, which the artificers, principally the goldsmiths, ironsmiths, coppersmiths, carpenters, and masons, denied; as, in theory at least, they still do.

42. Mr. Chokkalingam Pillai, who has written to me at length concerning the havoc caused by this dispute in olden days, places its origin more simply in a dispute as to the place of honour in temples or shrines, where the old inhabitants of the peninsula, then too divided into functional groups, conducted their worship. The cause of the dispute was soon forgotten; the dispute itself waxed hotter and hotter with accessions and desertions to and from either side. His explanation, if simple, is not necessarily untrue; history affords many instances, especially where religion has been in even remote question, of disputes as absurd with consequences as direful.

43. But the division is passing, we may hope, into the limbo of things forgotten. It emerges at times in amusing form among the *Pallans* and *Chakkiliyans* of Trichinopoly, where women and men belong to different *hands*, and contention waxing high leads to "strikes," such as depicted in those comedies of Aristophanes which are not as a rule recommended for school use.

Tribes—(1) Animistic.

44. In this chapter's attempt to treat of the Animistic tribes of the Presidency the place of honour is due to the following account of the *Gadabas* of Vizagapatam Agency, furnished to me by Mr. C. A. Henderson, I.C.S.

45. "The most interesting of these peoples to my mind are the 'Munda' stock, generally known in the Jeypore Agency as *Gadabas*. They are clearly divided into three tribes, the *Bonda Porja*, the *Gutób*, (or *Bodo Gadaba*), and the *Parenga Gadaba*. I arrange them in the order of seniority as they appear to me. They cannot be mistaken; the Mongoloid cast of countenance is at times very marked, this being the case, as I have noticed, rather more often among the women than

among the men; at least among the younger men. The typical old hill man's face, as once described to me, was exemplified in the Naik of our village near Koraput, who was a *Jhodia Porja*. The face is flat and an obliquity of the eye is traceable; the hair on the face is rather scanty; the stature is short and build sturdy.

46. "The *Bonda Porja*, so-called, I take to be the most primitive. But if the general theory of the advance of these peoples from the north is sound, they would have been the farthest and most southerly outpost of the stock. They live on or below the range of Ghāts, which divides the 3,000-foot plateau from Malkangiri taluk; that is to say on the edge of the Koi country, and a most remote unvisited part of the world it is. They have been so secluded for years and generations by the circumstances of their tract of country, that I do not think I am wrong in believing them to be the most primitive and authentic remains of the Munda stock that we have. Their customs and clothing in many ways suggest that they are at a stage which the better known *Gadabas* of the upland taluks passed some time ago. Their language also as compared with the *Gutób* bears this out in some small ways. The two vocabularies are obviously of the same stock of speech, and nearly related, but the *Gutób* is the more developed.

47. "Clothing is to my mind a crucial test. The *Bonda Porja* tabu, which prevents their women clothing themselves above the waist, is well known. They supply the very patent deficiency by a mass of brass and bead necklaces, and by large heavy circular collars of brass, often of great weight. I sent my specimens to the Museum. These collars are locally made, and are jointed at one side, with a male and female clasp at the other end, which is secured by a bit of string or fibre. The loin cloth is extremely exiguous. In fact in fully developed woman it does not meet round the hips. It is half suspended from a string, and shifted round the body to meet the exigencies of the moment. They shave their heads from early childhood, and tie round them a fillet of palmyra, or a string with olive shells or little scarlet seeds on it. Compare the familiar *Bodo Gadaba* (*Gutób*) found in villages on the main road near Koraput. The women's clothing is distinctly in two parts, a kilt and an upper cloth. A little observation and reflection would, I think, convince any one that the adoption of the *upper* cloth is comparatively a recent matter. In the first place the cloths are separate; the upper cloth is not a continuation of the lower or kilt, and is not twisted over the bust, but simply knotted on one shoulder. In the second place these *Gadaba* women are not inordinately shy about showing their breasts, *e.g.*, when suckling children, and will often do so unconcernedly even in a European's presence. On one occasion, riding past, I saw a *Gadaba* woman coming from a wash. She had only got the kilt on, and the upper part of her body was quite bare—a contrast to the way in which the local Oriyá woman contrives to conceal herself as far as possible when bathing. Another point in favour of this belief is that the *Parenga* women, though they retain their tribal cloth for the kilt, have not adopted, as the *Gadabas* have done almost universally, a cloth of the same make for their upper garment, but wear an ordinary white, or would-be white, cloth on the shoulders. All three, I am convinced, till comparatively recently were unclothed above the waist; and among the remote *Bonda Porjas* the custom has persisted, backed by a pretty strong tabu, which however, curious as it may appear, does not extend to their life indoors, where they are permitted to cover themselves completely. The fillet of the *Bondas* is common among the *Gutób*, but the latter have ceased (on my theory) to shave their heads. The *Gutób* 'bustle' is unknown to the *Bondas*, why I do not know; neither is it the fashion among the *Parengas*, because 'God did not give it to us in the beginning of things,' or words to that effect."

48. "Here I insert my protest against the use of the word '*Porja*' or '*Poroja*' in any scientific account of these peoples. The word is simply the Oriyá form of the Sanskrit '*praja*,' as '*róza*' is the Oriyá for '*raja*.' Their difficulty in pronouncing the double consonant 'pr' is shown in the fact that the word

'*promano*,' an oath, is invariably pronounced '*pormano*', at least in Jeypore. The word '*Porja*' is thus explained etymologically. Its meaning is 'subject'; that is, the people overcome by the conquering Oriyá and reduced to the position of tenants, though most probably they had held their own land, (as the Ganjám *Khonds* have almost always done), previous to his advent. The word now means no more than '*rayat*.' To take *Porja* as a generic term, and assign to it the species *Bonda*, *Pengu*, *Jhodia*, etc., as done at times, is to make confusion worse confounded; and scientifically as effective as to make a generic class of *rayats*, and sub-divide them into *Kápu rayats*, *Vellála rayats*, *Oriyá rayats*, and so on.

49. "I pass to the so-called *Bodo Gadaba*, familiar to any one who has stopped in the neighbourhood of Sembliguda. Their name for themselves is *Gutób*—a fact of which I may be the first discoverer. And I believe, in default of a better explanation, that it is the origin of the name *Gadaba*, by which this people is generally known. The word '*bodo*' is of course Oriyá for 'big.' Their women's distinctive dress has been partly described above in reference to the *Bonda Porjas*. The striped pattern, and the rather gay colours of the cloths, make them conspicuous. There is some account of a tribal custom compelling the women to weave their own cloths before marriage, which is, I daresay, true enough. Then there is the bustle, of which I sent a specimen, bought off the lady's body, to the Museum. Its origin is not quite certain; it is 'to make them strong,' I was told; perhaps a child-bearing charm, or more probably a simple artificial sexual attraction to increase the apparent size of the buttocks, for which purpose it has not been entirely unknown in Europe at certain periods.

50. "The third distinctive section the *Parenga*, I was always disposed to regard as rather inferior, and possibly more mixed than the *Bodo Gadaba* strain. But I discovered from Professor Ramamurti that their language is nearly akin to the *Savara*; while on the other hand it has clear affinities with the language of the *Bondas* and of the *Gutób*, though it is not so nearly related to either as they are to each other. I think these people may be regarded as an offshoot of the *Savaras* rather than as *Gadabas*, though, being like the *Gadabas* in appearance and probably in some of their customs, and by no means dissimilar in language, they have got the latter name in Jeypore. Their women may be distinguished by the wearing of a fibre-cloth kilt, different in pattern from that of the *Gutób*, in that it consists primarily of thin coloured stripes on a white or dingy white background. The *Gutób* cloth is broadly striped in various colours. The scanty *Bonda* cloth was till very recently of a uniform brown, this being, I believe, the natural colour of the fibre-thread. At the present day such simplicity is rare, and the cloth is coloured in narrow vertical or transverse stripes with coloured cottons.

51. "The *Oláro Gadaba*, so-called, are a mystery to me. In the first place their women are outwardly indistinguishable from the *Gutób*, with whom in some places they live. In fact a *Gutób* told me that they could not be distinguished, which was fairly conclusive. At the same time '*olár*' in the *Gadaba* tongue, means a leaf. It suggests possibilities of the clothing of these people having been extremely primitive at no very recent date. I hazard a theory that, coming into the sphere of *Gadaba* influence at a time when they themselves were clothed only with the unmanufactured produce of the jungle, they adopted the dress of a civilization higher than their own, but not before they had earned the name they now bear as a nick-name. This depends on the meaning of the word *olár*, and I am quite aware of the danger of anthropological theories based on linguistics. But it may serve as a working hypothesis to explain the curious fact that these people, entirely assimilated to the Munda stock in dress, are, by all tests, of Dravidian speech. If my theory be admitted, even as a hypothesis, it needs only further to suppose that the assimilation took place before the Oriyá conquest, and that the name *Gadaba* with the characteristic nick-name prefixed, survived under the Oriyá domination. The *Oláro* probably would not have been displeased at being ranked with the tribe they had so faithfully imitated; and it is a fact that *Gutób* and *Parenga* have a certain tendency to look down upon the *Oláro*, thus suggesting that the latter are not regarded as true *Gadabas*.

52. "The *Jhodias*, called and calling themselves *Porjas*, are to be found in abundance in the neighbourhood of Koraput and Jeypore. They have no distinctive language at present in use. But this is no proof that they have not had one, and a skilled Oriyá scholar might find out from their dialect of Oriyá that they are entitled to separate recognition, by traces of affinities to the Munda or the Dravidian group. It would be a difficult matter, inasmuch they have always been near the centre of such civilization as the country affords; and are an industrious agricultural population, not at present off the beaten track, or concealed in the jungle. Their women have a distinctive dress, and a particularly neat one too. They wear white cloths, with a cerise or crimson border; neatly arranged in a fashion of their own so as to cover the upper part of the body and both shoulders completely. Their cloth is continuous and reaches to the knee. The women are of curiously short stature, but with wonderfully developed calves. The lower leg is frequently tattooed from the knee to the ankle, and so closely as to give the appearance almost of a stocking. Their 'dancing' is the best that I saw in the Agency, but the villages near Koraput have considerable practice, as they are always dancing as a show for European visitors. The men have certainly traces of a Mongolian cast of countenance, and on the whole I should be inclined to place these *Jhodias* with the Munda group, but they would be a branch very superior to the *Gadabas* if this is so.

53. "I note one error, as I take it, perpetuated in Thurston's 'Tribes and Castes.' He refers to the peculiar *Gadaba* custom of placing swings with spiked seats outside their temples, on which the pújári swings in a sort of ecstasy, and feels no pain, by virtue of the power of the goddess that is in him. I can only say that by my experience such swings are commonest in the Naurangpur taluk, where, with the exception of an isolated and rather degraded settlement in Naurangpur town, (that is to say at the extreme southern boundary of the taluk), there are no *Gadabas*. At any rate it is absurd to ascribe this spiky swing to the *Gadabas* alone, when it and similar practices are known to be quite common in many other pseudo-Hindu cults.

54. "As to the religion and customs of the *Gadabas* and their kind I can say practically nothing. I have tried to find out, but the people are very reticent, and cannot, or will not, say more than that the important events of life are the occasion for a family, tribal, or village, feed . . . . and drink. At the same time both *Bonda* and *Gutób* have a belief in, and a name for, the spirits of the departed (*sayiré* or *se'arrai*), who seem, according to their ideas, to exercise some beneficent influence on the crops. There are also gods and goddesses of the jungle. I should say that they are or were purely Animists, however the *Gutób* may have been Hinduised externally. Their position in the scale of caste is peculiar; I am certain that there are degrees of pollution among them, and that they are not all lumped together as untouchables. The *Domb*, *Ghasi*, *Haddi* and *Chachudi* are the lowest of the low, as far as my knowledge goes. But of these things they will not talk readily. I know that some of them have most elaborate mythologies and cosmic beliefs, but they never confided in me to any great extent. The *Bondas* certainly practise village exogamy; the well-known 'marriage pit' is still an institution among them, though they do not talk much about it, and will, I feel sure, deny all knowledge of it, if asked point-blank. I asked questions about birth, marriage, and death, but was never able to get any convincing answers. This is after all no new thing. First-hand research in these matters is always exposed to this difficulty. Some enquirers have not always the scientific honesty to admit it, or to allow for the possible vagaries of an interpreter."

55. Abandoning detail for the moment, it may be suggested that a consideration of more useful, though of less curious interest arises in respect to these hill tribes in general. The manner in which they do not dress, the dialect in which they make themselves incomprehensible; these are largely their own affair. But could definite, or approximately definite, information on the subject be obtained, it would be of practical value to learn how far the hill tribesman, widely different from the Hindu of the plains however he be returned, suffers or benefits by the gradual opening

up of his country, and inroad of the more sophiscated trader and settler. This question, which at times suggested itself to me when I lived among the *Khonds* of the Ganjám Agency, was raised in 1910 by Mr. Cammiade, who suggested that statistics should be compiled for the villages of the Gódávari Agency, showing, not merely the number of Hindus, Muhammadans, Christians and Animists in each village, but rather the number of genuine hill-men there found.

56. The suggestion was not acted upon, and for certain reasons is one of doubtful practicability in connection with an ordinary census. It would first be necessary to get an accurate list of castes and tribes considered to be "hill-men;" then special and detailed instructions would be needed for the enumerators, who, in these wild tracts, are difficult to find, and not, as a rule, among the most competent of their class. Were these difficulties overcome, special sortings and the printing of special tables would be necessary; for all of which work funds were not on this occasion immediately at hand. In a thorough investigation of the subject it would be necessary to add enquiries regarding alienation of land, indebtedness of the hill-men to traders from the plains, values of produce in the plains' markets, and prices paid therefor to the cultivator in the hills, increase or diminution in the consumption of intoxicants, and sundry other points—work for which the ordinary census enumerator certainly has not enough time, and probably does not possess sufficient intelligence. If the matter is not taken up beforehand as a special enquiry, my successor in 1921, with the problem thus early placed before him, may find a means to its solution.

57. This however by the way. Returning to tribes in particular, *Khonds* and *Pános*, people written well nigh to death, exhibit fluctuations during the last two decades, which suggest that at some enumeration there has been considerable confusion in their respect. It is unlikely that after losing 3 per cent. of their numbers between 1891 and 1901 the *Khonds* should increase by 12·1 per cent. during the last decade; or that the increase of the *Pános* should diminish from 32·8 per cent. between 1891 and 1901 to 16·5 between 1901 and 1911. A high rate of increase among the *Khonds* Father Vulliez, who knows the people intimately, considers improbable on account of their antenuptial promiscuity, which leads in his opinion to a low natality of children, frequent abortion, female sterility, and the spread of venereal disease. Moreover the general prosperity of this people is not likely to be furthered by drunkenness, which the Collector of Ganjám considers to have increased of late years; but at the same time both he and Father Vulliez agree that some signs of improvement in this respect are becoming manifest, following restrictions introduced in the number of shops licensed for the sale of drink.

Tribe.	Decennial increase.	
	1901–11.	1891–1901.
Khond	+ 12·1	− 3·2
Páno	+ 16·5	+ 32·8

58. *Savaras*, to whose affairs some space has been devoted in the chapter dealing with religion, present no feature of interest save a consistently slow rate of increase. As in the case of *Bráhmans* it is somewhat curious to note that the rate of increase in the last mentioned three tribes is more or less in inverse proportion to the number of women.

Tribe.	Rate of increase per cent.	Women per 1,000 men.
Savara	1·6	1,026
Khond	12·1	1,011
Páno	16·5	1,001

59. The *Tódas* of the Nilgiri hills, according to table XIII, part I, number 748: their real number is, in all probability, some 50 less.

60. At the date fixed for the general enumeration (March 10th) it was unlikely that the *Tódas* would be found in the *munds*, where they, as a rule, reside; their custom at such season being to scatter with their herds of buffaloes through the pastures on the Kundahs. A special enumeration was accordingly held on December 15, 1911, when 383 males and 293 females were enumerated. The remaining 72 *Tódas* of table XIII, part I, were found here and there at the general enumeration; and, from the similarity of the schedule entries on either occasion, it is probable that nearly all, if not all, of these latter *Tódas* represent cases of double enumeration.

Observation of this fact may serve to some extent as an explanation of the strange rise and fall in the numbers of this people, which is shown by the figures, quoted in the margin, of the last four enumerations. In view of the fact that most persons with an intimate knowledge of the *Tódas* consider that they have long been a dying people, their increase from 1881 to 1901 is strange, and renders inexplicable their sudden set-back in 1911. Of the various hypotheses propounded in explanation by far the most credible is that of double enumeration escaping notice on previous occasions; although it must be admitted that this assumption involves another—namely, that a great many really existent *Tódas* were left out of account at the census of 1881.

Year.	Tóda population.		
	Total.	Males.	Females.
1911	676	383	293
1901... ...	805	451	354
1891... ...	739	427	312
1881... ...	675	...	...

61. It is worth while to examine present *Tóda* statistics in some detail; the basis of examination will be the schedules of their special enumeration.

62. *Tódas* aged 0–10, or the survivors of those born in the last decade, number 128; 74 being boys, and 54 girls. Male *Tódas* at present aged 20–50 are 188; women aged 15–40 number 140. Assuming that there were during the period 1901–1911 125 couples at the reproductive period of life, 128 surviving children represents a low rate of healthy natality.

63. Mr. Gordon Hadfield, who probably knows more about the *Tódas* than any one now living, tells me that the race as a whole is so rotten with syphilis that miscarriages are extremely frequent; while children actually born are in many cases horribly diseased, and die off like flies. It has been suggested that immorality is only prevalent among the *Tódas* who live on the outskirts of Ootacamund, with its large servant and cooly population; and that those of the outlying country are in the main decent folk. But in fact there are few *Tódas* save in the vicinity of Ootacamund. There are 12 in Gúdalúr taluk, and 105 in Coonoor taluk. Of 559 in Ootacamund taluk 83 are within the limits of Ootacamund village: 154 are at Shólúr, and 192 at Nanjinád; both within easy reach of the town.

64. To their misfortunes drink, opium, and poverty may contribute. Of the 676 *Tódas* 561 depend on buffalo grazing for a livelihood: there are 33 coolies, and 9 beggars. Buffalo grazing is a failing stay: murrain some years back wrought havoc with the herds. For the buffalo products, such as milk, ghee, and cheese, the *Tódas* obtain advances from traders: the money they squander in drink, and have to repay it in kind at ruinous rates.

65. It has been customary, I understand, for the *Badagas* at harvest time to pay a grain tribute to the *Tódas*. The *Badagas* themselves are frequently indebted to traders, and are moreover to a considerable extent abandoning cultivation for the more secure, and, in the Nilgiris, more profitable pursuit of daily labour. There is therefore less grain to go round.

66. It is questionable whether anything is likely to arrest the decay of this curious tribe. Separate registration of their births and deaths as distinguished from those of Hindus, would at least afford a basis for closer investigation of the causes of decay. Prohibition of the sale of liquor to *Tódas*, and compulsory removal of their *munds* from the neighbourhood of the town to the open country, are remedies drastic, but possibly not impracticable in dealing with a mere handful of people.

67. The sudden appearance of some 60,000 additional Animists in the Nellore district has been explained in Chapter IV. Although in certain ideas as to caste, dress, etc., the people in question, the *Yánádis*, conform somewhat to Hindu usage, their classification as Animists is probably not incorrect: "Hinduism" in the popular sense, and "Animism" are vague and widely comprehensive terms.

68. Like most primitive people the *Yánádi* has no particular inclination towards settled work. Cultivation does not appeal to him; while he has anything

to eat he will not work; driven by the pinch of hunger he will collect and sell firewood, watch crops, hunt or fish; in fact do anything not too monotonously irksome and laborious. He cares little for education, despite some theosophical attempts in Nellore town to educate his children; and finds a simple relaxation in singing and dancing to the accompaniment of a drum.

69. The *Yánádi* marriage is, as one would expect, a somewhat free and easy affair. In contrast to Hindu practice it is generally arranged by the inclination of the contracting parties, and as readily dissolved at the caprice of either.

70. A certain social difference exists between sections of the community, founded on the nice point of eating, or not eating, refuse. The opposing sections do not eat together even food other than the questionable dish, nor do they intermarry.

71. Mr. Quadir Navaz Khan, late Collector of Nellore, to whom I am indebted for my information in regard to this tribe, considers that except in Sríharikóta, where they are still extremely backward, the *Yánádis* are, on the whole, improving, though the rate of progress is very slow; and that they possess one commendable virtue—they are not a drinking class.

72. There is an old saw, *testimonia ponderantur non numerantur*. Without indefinite space, time and industry, all of which facilities I lack, it would be impossible to go *seriatim* through the "animistic tribes" of the Presidency. It is questionable whether to do so would serve any useful purpose. From a few examples the general position of these peoples in to-day's economy of the Presidency can be learned; and, as already observed in paragraphs 55 *supra*, of most present interest in this regard is the question whether their temperament, social customs, religious ideas as now formed, are such as to admit of their absorption into the higher civilization, that is undoubtedly extending towards them; or whether, as in the melancholy case of the *Tódas*, the necessary loss of primitive virtues will be counterbalanced only by the acquisition of more sophisticated vice.

TRIBES—(2) MUHAMMADAN.*

73. The distinction drawn at the census between Muhammadan tribes is anything but satisfactory, particularly in regard to the general division into *Saiyads*, *Patháns*, *Moghals* and *Sheiks*.

74. *Saiyads*, as the term "Children of Fatima" commonly applied to them denotes, are supposed to be the descendants of Fatima, daughter of the Prophet; and as such they not unnaturally enjoy a certain degree of respect and consideration among their fellow believers. But unfortunately material inducements occasionally proved too potent for the veracity of the faithful, with the result that, in Southern India, many calling themselves *Saiyads* have really no claim to such title. The old Nawabs of the Carnatic, themselves *Sheiks*, treated *Saiyads*, it is said, with peculiar consideration, and assigned wet lands as inams for the support of these poverty-stricken saints. The natural outcome was a plenteous crop of impostors: even to this day a delicate insult may be conveyed to a *Saiyad* by calling him دھن مری کا سید (paddy-field *Saiyad*). The well-known Persian couplet, "I was a *Sheik* in the first year; in the second I became a *Páthan*; if provisions sell cheap this year I shall be a *Saiyad*," testifies to the reliance that can be placed in these tribal distinctions in modern days. A *Sheik* servant in a rich *Saiyad* family occasionally assumes the title of *Saiyad* as a mark of respect to his patron, or calls his children *Saiyads*; the *Rávuttans* of Tinnevelly, it is said, style children born on Friday "*Friday Saiyads*."

75. *Patháns* are descendants of Khais, a Sirdar of Ghor, who embraced Islam during the life-time of the Prophet, and assumed the name of Abdur Rashid.

* For much of my information regarding Muhammadanism and Muhammadan tribes I am indebted to Mr. Khaja Akber Hussain, Diwan of the Banganapalle State, and to his brother Dr. Khaja Muhammad Hussain.

From him sprung Bora, Jano, Umer, and Timmer, to whom, and to whose immediate offspring, some families in Kurnool, Cuddapah, Gódávari, etc., still trace back their genealogy; and in proof thereof affix to their names the name of their remote ancestor, (thus *Janozi*, *Alizi*, or *Timmerzi*). Such people keep strictly to themselves: they will not intermarry with *Sheiks* or *Moghals*, whom they consider beneath them; and are somewhat averse to marriage with *Saiyads*, whom they consider above them. But these families are comparatively few; throughout the greater part of the Presidency the "*Pathán* in the street" will stare blankly, if asked to what '*zi*' he belongs.

76. *Moghals* are of two kinds, (*a*) descendants of the early central Asiatic invaders, and (*b*) domiciled Iranis. The first class have become completely Indianized, and intermarry freely with their fellow believers, from whom they are indistinguishable save by the characteristic prefix or affix, "*Mirza*" or "*Baig*," to their names. The second community have held themselves apart; intermarriage even with their fellow *Moghals* in India, owing to difference in social custom and method of living, is rare. Some of these domiciled Irani *Moghals* are to be found in certain streets of Madras, where they chiefly occupy themselves with trade in indigo. I do not know if they are found elsewhere, unless there be some such families on the west coast.

77. *Sheiks* trace their origin to the first Arabic converts to Islam, and the term can also be used with some connotation of religious authority. Nasikh has a verse "When a friend offers wine why should I refuse? I am no *Sheik* nor Saint;" and Hafiz tells, "My *Sheik* said drink no wine: I said I do not lend an ear to every ass." As applied now to the Muhammadans of Southern India the term has little precise meaning. A Hindu or Christian convert becomes a *Sheik*; many *Dúdékulas* assume the title. The stern unbending *Patháns* referred to in paragraph 73 look down on all such, calling them in derision جھینگرا, a sort of fresh water crab or fish, which begins to decay immediately it is taken out of water.

78. *Máppillas*, (the name is probably derived from the Tamil மாப்பிள்ளை bridegroom), are confined to the West Coast, and constitute practically the entire Muhammadan population of Malabar. Descended from Arabs, who visited Malabar for trade and formed connections with the women of the place, they are an active bustling community in worldly matters; although, judging from their percentage of literacy (56 per 1,000), polite learning appear to have for them even still fewer attractions than for their fellow believers throughout the Presidency. To their ignorance of Urdu allusion has already been made; in their social ceremonies the use of the tom-tom, and the distribution of betel are strongly reminiscent of Hinduism. More striking still, as a survival or adoption of Hindu custom, is the marumakattáyam form of succession obtaining among the *Máppillas* of North Malabar, and generally throughout the district in respect of religious *stánams*. Their zeal for the propagation of their faith is undoubted, if the means employed to that end are at times somewhat quaint. A correspondent remarks that women employed as maid servants in *Máppilla* houses, often join their master's faith, "when their master has made it difficult for them to return to their own community."

79. *Marakkáyars*, (the word is generally taken to mean "boatman"), and *Jónagans*, (said to be derived from *Sonagam*, the Tamil equivalent for Arabia), are descendants of Arab colonists on the eastern coast. They are chiefly found in Tinnevelly and Tanjore. *Marakkáyars* number only 2,461 as against 4,651 in 1901, the decrease being in all probability due to a greater or lesser accuracy of enumeration; *Jónagans* with 8,780 as against 8,646 have remained practically stationary.

80. *Labbai*, a term which some authorities consider should only be used of east coast settlers of Arabic descent, is now a name loosely applied to all Tamil-speaking Muhammadans. Part II of table XIII shows them as inhabiting in the main the Tamil country, although an appreciable number (31,000) are found in Malabar, where they constitute three-fourths of the non-Máppilla Muhammadans. A decrease

of 1·2 per cent. *Labbais* in the decade is explained, in all probability with tolerable correctness, by the supposition that many of them have preferred the more distinctively Muhammadan classification of *Sheik*, and thus aided an increase of 13·5 per cent. in this latter section between 1901 and 1911.

81. *Rávuttans* (Cavaliers) were not classified separately at this census, or at either of its immediate predecessors. Converted from Hinduism by the persuasion of Saints whose names and honours survive to this day, such as the Nathad Vali of Trichinopoly, Saiyad Ibrahim Shahid of Érvádi, Sha-ul-Hamed of Nágore, or by the more pointed arguments of a ruler, (it is for example related of the *Nallámpillai Rávuttans* of Madura that they were *Maravan* and *Kallan* thieves, who, sentenced to lose their hands for picking and stealing, "preferred to become Muhammadans"), they are an active thriving community found in the Tamil districts of Madura, Tinnevelly, Coimbatore, North Arcot and the Nilgiris. In the latter district, it must be admitted, their business enterprise, and their large-minded views on morality, have at times elicited somewhat marked judicial comment.

82. Reference has already been made to a hint as to racial descent afforded by profession of allegiance to a particular Imam. The author of "South Indian Musalmans" observes that the teachings of Abu Hanifa, who lived in Irak between the Tigris and Euphrates "spread naturally towards the north and east, the other two directions being bounded by sand and sea. Thus the *Turkomans, Afghans* and *Central Asian Musalmans*, in fact all races which came to India by the north-west passage were of the Hanafite school of law." The fact that *Máppillas, Jónagans*, and *Marakkáyars* belong to the Shafi sect confirms theory as to their descent from Arabs, who as a rule are Shafis.

Race.

83. On the subject of *race* there is little to be said. In the chapters dealing with marriage and religion it has been suggested that many of the apparent inconsistencies of Hinduism are due to attempts to combine the religious beliefs of two races at widely different stages of intellectual development, and that certain marriage customs apparently ill advised sprang from the desire of the higher race to avoid intermixture with the lower.

84. Although *Bráhman* and *non-Bráhman* still to some extent remain apart time has obliterated much of their salient and external difference. Their present interminglement has been forcibly depicted by Mr. J. H. Nelson as follows: "Are the million and odd *Bráhmans* of the Madras Province, many of whom are as dark skinned and puny as Paraiyans, *Bráhmans* pure and undefiled, true descendants of the white-faced warriors who first overran, and in a sense civilized the north of India? I for one cannot believe that they are such."

85. Trace of Mongolian descent afforded by blue markings on the hinder parts of children was a subject proposed for enquiry. The matter is one for expert knowledge and opportunity, and unfortunately the quest failed to stir the imagination of the Madras doctors. Among the *Gadabas* of Jeypore were noted some Mongolian traits; but observation, as may be seen, was made *a fronte* rather than *a posteriori*.

86. Of somewhat more practical interest is the fate of the mixed Anglo-Indian race, wherein the marginal figures show a steady decline throughout the period covered by the last three enumerations. To those interested in the poorer classes of the community decline may not come as a surprise; whatever hard things may be said of his shiftlessness and incapacity, the poverty-stricken Anglo-Indian is confronted with the grim fact that a body with the needs of European blood will not thrive on the wages that maintain an Indian; and that, granting his intellectual capacity to be but equal to that of his Indian competitor, he must be crowded out of the field wherein he might hope for employment.

Year.	Anglo-Indians. Males.	Anglo-Indians. Females.
1911	12,651	13,372
1901	12,737	13,472
1891	13,147	13,523

87. The decline is chiefly noticeable in Madras city and in Malabar. In Madras city, it may be observed, the community is liable to somewhat artificial defections and accretions. In prosperous circumstances the pure European is at times of somewhat dusky hue; while his brother at the bottom of the scale often relies solely on his manner of dress for his differentiation from the Indian. In Malabar, where, I understand, it is not unusual for the long-domiciled Anglo-Indian to merge in the native community, the decline is statistical rather than real, being due to the separation of Malabar and Anjengo on this occasion. Anglo-Indian figures in South Canara show some curious fluctuations. A turnover from "Portuguese" to "Anglo-Indian" at the last enumeration occurred to me as a possible explanation, but examination of previous figures lent no support to the idea.

Year.	Anglo-Indians.			
	Madras City.		Malabar.	
	Males	Females.	Males.	Females.
1911	4,914	5,412	1,594	1,860
1901	5,305	5,913	1,860	2,105
1891	5,679	6,264	1,986	2,207

Anglo-Indians in South Canara.

Year.	Males.	Females.
1911	140	172
1901	76	77
1891	122	82

FORMATION OF SUB-CASTES.

88. Distinction of castes is an obvious matter; the tendency that splits a caste into innumerable *sub-castes*, which some observers consider to represent the only true castes, deserves mention.

89. That the tendency exists is proved by its results seen in Sir H. A. Stuart's elaborate appendices to the census tables of 1891; and *passim* in Mr. Thurston's "*Castes and Tribes of Southern India.*" I have found no new grain of sand that I could venture to add to the mountain of information therein contained. My contribution to the subject can only take the form of some suggested reasons for a fact, of which the existence is beyond doubt.

90. Difference is not constituted by its effects, nor by belief in the ultimate effect of such difference as exists. Roman Catholic differs from a Protestant, but the intrinsic difference is not constituted by the mutual belief of the one, that the other is more or less on the broad path; liberal from conservative, but not because of the scepticism shared by either as to the other's honesty. Distinguishing the sub-divisions of a main caste *A* by the letters *a*, *b*, *c*, *d*, etc., one may say that *X* belonging to *A* (*a*) does not differ from *Y* belonging to *A* (*b*), because their families refuse to intermarry and "interdine;" rather they refrain from these social amenities, because they differ.

91. Taking first the difference of religious, or better, philosophic belief, the difference between the monism of Sankara and the dualism of Madhva is as wide as that between heaven and earth, between pole and pole.

92. Midway between the schools of Sankara and Madhva come the followers of Rámánuja. Their doctrine possessing some elements in common with each of the other two, a greater catholicity and tolerance might be expected to prevail among the *Vaishnavas*: it is therefore in accordance with the topsy-turvy nature of human affairs that exclusiveness should be the badge of all their tribe.

93. That persons holding widely divergent religious views should express their theological difference by refusal of each other's society may seem at first sight strange; a Hindu writer thus exclaims: "It is really unaccountable that difference "of views in matters philosophical should have so acted on its (*i.e.*, the Hindu "community) social customs as to crystalize it in varying set forms, so entirely "ill-adapted to one another as to defy all attempts for the cementation of the "entire community". And a *Bráhman* friend writing to me with special reference to this philosophical division in a particular district observes: "They (these "three classes) differ in social habits, in the manner of wearing their cloths; in

"the mode of adorning their foreheads; in their fashion of speech; in ceremonial "observances, such as temple festivals, household fasts and feasts; in other ways "even as to the form of household utensils. At the same time, despite these "differences, they possess certain features of resemblance;—all men wear the "sacred thread; the private prayers offered up thrice daily are substantially the "same; the Vedic ceremonies, monthly and annual, are performed on the same "principles."

94. But difference in India manifests itself in this particular form; and, in truth, such Indian unsociability is not really much greater than that which prevails in Western countries between Protestant and Roman Catholic, Episcopalian and Non-conformist, etc. Certainly in Southern and Northern Ireland the avoidance of intermarriage, and a tacit disinclination to exchange hospitality, are scarcely less noticeable among the members of the two prevailing forms of the Christian religion than among the Indian classes of which mention has been made.

95. The question of theological difference disposed of, arises that of race, to which some reference has been made elsewhere. Difference of mother-tongue, difference of social custom originally induced by climate and locality, are so obvious, that the linguistic division of *Bráhmans* (and of other castes) stands fairly justified as representative of a racial difference. Nowhere can the persistence of this racial difference find a better illustration than in the sharp distinction prevailing in Malabar between *Nambúdri Bráhmans*, the "indigenous" *Bráhmans, Pattar Bráhmans,* who are East Coast immigrants, and are still regarded as such although their period of residence may reach back to prehistoric days, and *Embrándri Bráhmans*, who are of Tulu or Canarese origin.

96. But now arise differences much more puzzling, which find expression in the refusal of intermarriage, though not of commensality, *et vice versâ*.

97. *Smártas*, or at any rate those of whom my informant treats, are divided for matrimonial purposes into certain mutually exclusive sub-classes, of which the following will serve as examples:—

(1) *Brihacharanam*—a sub-class again subdivided into various sub-groups according to locality, *e.g.*, *Kandramánikkam, Malaináḍu, Gavarapattu, etc.*
(2) *Ashtasahasram*—again subdivided.
(3) *Vadama*—with sub-groups *Vadadésam, Chóladésam*, etc.
(4) *Váttima*—sub-divided into (*a*) those of a particular eighteen villages; (*b*) others.
(5) *Kanjanúr.*
(6) *Késiyan.*

98. In the formation of these groups a predominating influence is doubtless that of locality, to which reference will be made in treating of other castes. It is also possible that this extreme endogamy is an offspring of exogamy instituted on sound eugenic principles, but of which the original purport has been entirely forgotten.

99. At the present day intermarriage between sub-groups of the same sub-class is not invariably avoided, nor is such occurrence necessarily followed by social ostracism. But marriage between different sub-classes (*e.g.*, *Vadama* and *Brihacharanam*) does not as yet seem to be permissible.

100. Among *Vaishnavas*, the apparently comprehensible distinction between *Tengalai* and *Vadagalai* is not a bar to matrimony; but to supplement this deficiency distinctions exist, which appear to confound even those affected by them. A convert to *Vaishnavism* for example cannot find a bride among the long-established followers of his new faith; another is rejected because "he is not sufficiently pure"—"whatever that may mean" observes a *Smárta* critic.

101. Of the difference which finds its expression in relation to food, a *Vaishnava* informant cites his own puzzling case, wherein his mother and mother-in-law partake of food cooked by his wife, while neither will touch a meal prepared by the other.

102. Inasmuch as those affected by these distinctions cannot account for them, I can venture no explanation of their origin.

103. Among *Désasthas* (followers of Madhva), *Telugu* does not marry with *Maráthi*, nor, in Canara, *Saraswat* with *Konkani*; wherein we can trace racial difference. Otherwise I have not obtained information as to the existence of clean cut groups; but from a *Désastha* I learn that locality exercises in his community almost as potent a sundering influence as elsewhere.

104. Abandoning *Bráhmans* for the present, we may glance at the subject in relation to some of the great *non-Bráhman* (Dravidian ?) castes of Southern India. Here the potent causes of sub-caste formation are, I should say, (*a*) difference of locality, (*b*) difference of occupation. But before considering these influences the question may be viewed from another standpoint. Of this view, indeed, the result is to a certain extent a reflection striking at the general theory which we are endeavouring to elucidate.

105. The custom of the country, and especially of foreigners resident therein, is to use caste names of such all embracing nature as to be practically meaningless. Few caste names are better known than *Vellála*; but at the beginning of this chapter allusion has been made to the well nigh innumerable sub-castes into which the *Vellálas* are divided. From enquiries made of intelligent and educated *Vellálas*, it would appear to me that the cause of this apparent sub-division lies, not in a fissiparous tendency existing in a definite *Vellála* community, but rather in the general application of a quasi-social term to a number of communities, which have little or no connection one with the other. A Western parallel might be the use of the terms "farmer" and "working man;" all farmers and all working men have, it is true, certain points in common; but for practical purposes their divisions are so great as to admit of their separation into a myriad of practically unconnected sub-divisions.

106. The terms *Pillai* and *Mudaliyár*, which, as already observed, were not recognized as caste names because of their frequent adoption by persons of very varying degree, are the favourite affixes of the *Vellálas*. In favour of their recognition it must be admitted that these terms, for all their indefiniteness to a foreigner, have a very definite signification to those who employ them, and are used with a definite connotation in many old records and documents. I enquired of two *Vellálas* of my acquaintance, of whom one styled himself *Mudaliyár*, the other *Pillai*, what was the difference between them which forbade them to eat together or to intermarry: they replied that the question should rather be what was the similarity which would allow them to do so. The fact that both were *Vellálas*, they appeared to regard as of as little significance as the fact that both were Government servants.

107. A chain of reasoning somewhat similar might be applied to the case of the *Náyars*, who in Malabar number some 388 thousand persons. Their divisions, sub-castes, clan, etc., have been enumerated and described by Messrs. Logan, Fawcett, Thurston and others; the reason for these sub-divisions would appear to be that assigned in the Census Report of 1891 by Sir H. A. Stuart, who suggests that a definite *Náyar* community did not break up into a number of mutually exclusive social groups, but rather that numerous communities, between whom no tie or similarity existed, in course of time adopted a general social designation, which has little more precise and definite meaning than the term *Súdra*.

108. A further illustration of this theory can be found in the matter of the *Chettis*; a caste numbering, according to table XIII, over 350,000 souls. But the affix is assumed by traders generally, who may have little or nothing in common beyond the fact of being engaged in trade. Mr. Thurston enumerates some 25 distinct castes or classes possessing distinct caste or occupational appellatives, whose trading members are wont to style themselves *Chettis*. In European hearing the term calls up to mind the *Náttukóttai Chettis*, the great Indian bankers of the south, whose head-quarters are in the Tiruppattúr and Devakóttai divisions of the Sivaganga and Rámnád Zamindaris. Yet strange to say "genuine" *Chettis*, whoever they may be, affect to doubt the "*Chettihood*" of these great representatives of the name.

109. In respect of occupation, however, the banking of the *Náttukóttai Chetti* is sufficiently distinguishable, and distinctive of its followers, from the retailing of the more general *Chetti*. To illustrate the difference arising from difference of locality Mr. Thurston instances several sections of Madura *Chettis*, whose characteristic names in most cases import locality of origin, and have little or no direct connection with their social peculiarities.

110. *Chettis* are widespread, but *Náyars* are definitely associated with Malabar. The local difference between North and South Malabar is definitely marked, and North Malabar sub-divisions of *Náyars* as a rule rank higher than the corresponding divisions in the South. The sub-divisions of the North Malabar *Náyars*, which appear to have a certain local origin, are amazingly complicated; they are described in the Gazetteer of the Malabar district—a work available for those who seek further information on this matter.

111. *Taragan* (broker) *Náyars* of Angádipuram, claiming descent from a high family of Travancore, differ from the *Taragan Náyars* of Pálghát, who for purposes of marriage are confined to their own caste; while some consider *Taragan Náyars* generally to be of different local origin to the Malabar *Náyar* properly so called.

112. Of *Balijas*, and *Kápus*, I have made some enquiries on this matter. Here too locality and occupation are put forward as the main causes of sub-caste difference. The difference may find expression in refusal of intermarriage, or of commensality, or of both. A *Balija* correspondent from the Deccan quotes the names of sundry sub-divisions of the caste to be found in the Northern Circars, observing that he considers himself distinct from such people, inasmuch as he has never had, and probably never will have, occasion to mix with them. Another from the Northern Circars puts the case in a more concrete form, when describing to me a visit to Madras City where he met a fellow *Balija*, and was by him invited to a meal. "Theoretically," said my informant, "the would-be host was an undoubted *Balija*: practically, he came from a different part of the country, and I felt that we differed In India this difference finds expression in refusal to eat together—so I refused the invitation."

113. A *Kápu* of the Peddakanti sub-class I found about to undertake a very considerable journey in search of a wife for his son. Asked why the *Kápus* of the neighbourhood, of whom there were a many, would not serve his purpose, he replied that he belonged to a sub-group of his sub-class, whose members traced their origin back to a particular locality, and among such his son must marry. It is interesting to note that there were about him certain families of suitable descent, but they had broken the strict letter of the endogamous law, and intermarried in their sub-class without regard to sub-group: therefore this strict purist would have none of them. It may be suggested that local difference, with the present improved facilities of communication, should no longer carry any great weight. But in the first place those affected by this difference are frequently not in a position to avail themselves, whether from inclination or necessity, of opportunities for travel; secondly a difference obliterated in practice will frequently persist in theory. This latter fact is still more marked in occupational sub-grouping; persons being still differentiated in accordance with professions which they no longer exercise.

114. Such sub-caste difference due to the actual following of different avocations is easily intelligible. As an illustration may be recalled the five occupational groups of the *Kammálans*, of which the goldsmiths, especially in towns, have, as a rule, ceased to intermarry with the blacksmiths. Among the trading *Balijas* are the *Rálla Balijas* (traders in precious stones), *Gázula Balijas* (traders in bangles), *Gonala Balijas* (manufacturers of, or traders in, gunny cloth); these three eat with one another, but will not intermarry; and will neither eat with, nor marry with, the *Pusala Balijas*, who are supposed to travel about the country selling beads.

115. It is said that caste sub-division is at times due to the adoption of a degrading occupation by a section of the main caste. The statement is doubtless true to a certain extent, although a doubt is permissible as to whether any considerable

section of mankind has ever deliberately adopted a profession considered by it degrading. The adoption has probably been dictated by force of circumstances; as an illustration thereof may be instanced the cases of the *Veluttédans*, a sub-division of the *Náyars*, and the *Kávutiyans*, a sub-division of the *Veluttédans*, who have sunk in the social scale, the first by undertaking the work of washermen, the second that of barbers. A still more curious instance is found in relation to *Bráhmans*, among whom those who follow the ecclesiastical calling, described in subsidiary table I to this chapter as the traditional occupation of the community, are held in somewhat small social esteem. This anomaly, and the apparent contradiction of the table just mentioned by subsidiary table VIII to Chapter XII, may be explained by the fact that, if the word "priesthood" be used in its European sense, the *Bráhman* is not traditionally a priest; but rather he possesses inherently certain priestly attributes and capacities, of which the regular exercise as a profession, and for a livelihood, is regarded as undignified.

116. But it is probable that the converse of the proposition is more generally true; and that social differentiation is more often due to the relinquishment of a lowly profession for another of better repute. An illustration is afforded by the *Kammálans* of Malabar, among whom those who have abandoned the smiths' profession in general for the particular branch of the coppersmith are considered to rank above their fellows. Tradition associates the *Shánáns* with toddy-tapping, but a *Shánán*, with whom I conversed on the subject, asserted vehemently to me the superiority of his section of the community, which had abandoned toddy-drawing for agriculture. A similar and entirely natural tendency can be observed in other Indian castes, as well as throughout European society.

117. One more factor in this evolution may be noticed. When all is said and done, the ambition of every Southern Indian, as one of my Indian correspondents puts it, is to be mistaken for a *Bráhman*, or to be told that he resembles a *Bráhman*. A society originally homogeneous tends therefore to become disintegrated according to the degree in which its members adopt *Bráhmanical* usages. The pity of the matter is that in lieu of emulation of *Bráhman* culture and refinement, imitation as a rule takes the form in a lifeless adoption of such social customs as infant marriage, irrevocable widowhood, the purchase of bridegrooms, against all of which educated *Bráhman* opinion is now lifting up its voice; of abstinence from meat, which is a mere matter of personal inclination; of assumed superiority and exclusiveness, which are the failings rather than the virtues of the *Bráhmans*.

Caste Government.

118. A foreigner observing Indian life, lived in its self-imposed fetters of caste regulation, is apt to exaggerate the potency of these trammels in curtailing individual freedom. Actions, that to a foreigner indicate but a blind uncomfortable bondage to unreasonable and inconvenient social laws, may seem both natural and advantageous to one reared in the environment of such laws.

119. Although remembrance of this fact will frequently suggest a general explanation for some action otherwise inexplicable, it is becoming clear that in modern times there are certain omissions and commissions, which recommend themselves in theory to the orthodox adherent of the caste system, but from which he refrains, at least ostensibly, from a fear of certain unpleasant accruing consequences.

120. Such consequences must have a cause; penalties, save for offences against Carlyle's "Eternal Verities," do not usually inflict themselves. It is a matter of considerable interest to discover the agency through which punishment for an act, not in the general acceptance of the word, moral or immoral, can be inflicted; or the tribunal before which an act of contrition and expiation can be made.

121. It is a common phrase to speak of a man being "outcasted." But who "out-casts" him, and how is it done? At whose hands does the modern Hindu, learned in the Shástras, and the civil and criminal law bearing on defamation, experience or apprehend unpleasant consequences arising from a partiality for strange apparel, or forbidden meats and drinks?

122. The enquiry is also interesting as bearing on the question, already discussed in some of its aspects, as to whether the caste system is breaking down or extending its influence. It is frequently asserted that the facilities afforded to evangelists of reaction by the extension of roads and railways have infused new life into the dry bones of orthodoxy in South India. In proof of this assertion is quoted an increasing, or at least non-diminishing, rigidity of prejudices against inter-caste hospitality, and inter-caste marriage. But, granting that restriction here remain unalterably rigid, although the truth of the statement in regard to "inter-dining" is certainly open to question, I have offered a suggestion in paragraph 38 that a certain exclusiveness in these matters is neither unreasonable in theory nor inconvenient in practice.

123. It has been pointed out to me by an Indian gentleman that the last few years, and especially the occasion of the present census, have witnessed an extraordinary revival of the caste spirit in certain aspects. For numerous castes "*sabhas*" have sprung up, each keen to assert the dignity of the social group which it represents.

124. But assertion of the dignity of a class differs from a detailed and fussy interference with the actions of an individual; and the praiseworthy efforts of these modern associations seem, on the whole, to tend rather in the former direction. This point is emphasized by a writer on the *Kápus* of Nellore, who states that in the pursuit of the economic aggrandizement and wealth these people care but little for caste rules and caste offences; or that, in other words, offences of the individual committed within caste are ignored, attention being focussed on actions in relation to other social groups, which tend to impair the solidarity of the *Kápu* community.

125. I circulated through every district a series of questions as to the existence, constitution, and procedure of caste tribunals; the decisions therein arrived at; and the degree of respect paid to such decisions. My thanks for interesting and valuable communications are due to many gentlemen, whose names would form a list too long for detailed mention.

126. Most of my informants agree in thinking that among the better educated, or rather more modernized sections of the population, the formal caste tribunal, with its pains and penalties for individual actions unlikely to affect the community, survives only as an ineffectual tradition. The writer of an elaborate note on the caste government of the *Kammálans*, a community generally accredited with orthodoxy, concludes thus: "Much of what I have written is out-of-date tradition, "and not an affair of common knowledge. In several villages, where I sent for "members of the community, and asked them for information, a stupid stare was "all I got. At *P*, where some came forward as officials of the caste tribunal, "they had to compare notes before they could answer my questions. Enquiries "of educated and respectable members of the caste, even in Madras, were "productive of no result." A writer on the *Vellálas* observes: "No such "recognized caste tribunal exists now so far as I know; if one does exist, its "authority is very little respected. Caste judgment now amounts to nothing "more than popular and informal opinion of a man's conduct."

127. Most striking of all is the consensus of testimony that in the very citadel of orthodoxy, where the trammels of individual action should most survive, there they are found most lacking. There are few things that the high-caste Indian may not do and retain his caste, so long as he remains loyal to the strange (at least in European opinion) system of exclusiveness, devised to keep the outer world from entering within the pale of his community. The "casteman" of modern days exchanges his *dhoti* and *angavastram* for coat and trousers, crops his luxuriant topknot, dilutes his soda, preserves a discreet incuriosity as to the nature of his food and its cooking, modestly refrains from dinning the ears of Heaven with a superfluity of prayers, and the withers of orthodox society remain unwrung. But he must not as yet trample down the sacred fence by a marriage outside his particular fold; or create a possibility of such trampling, by postponing the marriage of his daughter to an age when natural feeling might clash rudely

with abstract principles. One curious attempt in this direction I have encountered in the case of a *Bráhman*, who married, or at any rate cohabited with, a non-*Bráhman* woman. Being a rich man and influential man he succeeded in getting the "thread ceremony" of their son performed by a *Bráhman* priest; and, although this son has not been recognized as a *Bráhman*, it does not appear that the father suffered any particular inconveniences in consequence of his remarkable act.

128. Such pains and penalties as may be incurred represent rather the tacit verdict of the society amid which the offender lives, than the explicit sentence of a particular authority. Among the Tamil *Smártas*, I am informed, the presiding authority is the *Guru* of Sringeri; but "his function is rather to enlighten his "flock in spiritual matters, than to interfere in their every-day social organization." I have met a *Guru* of greatest nominal import among Telugu *Bráhmans*; but his responsible advisers admitted some qualms as to the practical deference that would be paid by society to the fiats of a thirteen-year-old child; and philosophically observed that loss of positive power was counterbalanced by the zest which risk added to its exercise.

129. Excommunication then for a *Bráhman* can only mean the avoidance of his society by other *Bráhmans*. Such avoidance can have two sides; it was quaintly put to me once, when I enquired whether orthodox society had excommunicated *X*, a notorious heretic, that one might with perfect truth say that *X* has excommunicated orthodox society. The effectiveness of a social verdict must depend largely on the grounds on which it is based, and the power of society to enforce such verdict. Thus *Y* ate beef, and drank forbidden liquors, to the scandal of the orthodox; but *Y* knew the law of libel, and his wealth gave assurance of the aid of trustworthy witnesses. So society bided its time till the occasion of an annual ceremony slipped *Y's* memory, when the voice of outraged religious opinion could be heard. Whatever inconveniences *Y* experienced thereby in his life-time I do not know; but his obsequies were a discomfortable matter, inasmuch as no bearers could be found to take his corpse to the burning-ground.

130. *P*, of rigid and minute orthodoxy, simply made himself a nuisance to his neighbours. On the occasion of a death in his house *Bráhmans* excommunicated him, practically if not in theory, by refusing to attend the funeral ceremonies. *P* secured absolution by apology, and an undertaking to amend his churlish ways.

131. *Q* in pursuit of wealth crossed the sea. Having attained it, he found on his return a many candidates for the hand of his daughter. As but one could be chosen, the rejected suitors were fain to excommunicate him. But *Q*, by sagacious bribery, formed a society which excommunicated the excommunicators, and reconciliation followed a drawn battle.

132. Even on the marriage question, where the exclusiveness of the community is not endangered by union with an outsider, caste feeling appears to be losing the power of effective expression. *Bráhmanism* does not unduly put itself about to damn the attendants at a "virgin-widow" marriage, especially if they be rich and influential. Occasionally one hears of a postponement of marriage to something like a reasonable age; a trustworthy informant tells me of a curious case where a *Bráhman* put away his wife, re-married her, and with her remains in caste.

133. And in a particular case where the existence of a formal governing body is admitted, the writer remarks that the very fact of this formal existence renders caste government a mockery; the caste authorities being mere puppets in the hands of wealthy tradesmen or professional men.

134. Among the higher castes, therefore, the present position of caste government seems to be as follows :—

The formal caste tribunal has disappeared. If in a few cases it survives, and attempts to exercise some function, it is little more than a puppet show working in obedience to the pulling of unseen wires.

A caste verdict is merely the informal opinion of the society amid which a particular person lives.

Such opinion will not, as a rule, be expressed on actions which concern merely the individual doing them, but only on actions likely to affect the society of which he forms a part.

The effectiveness of such opinion depends very largely on the position and influence of the individual affected.

135. Among the lower castes the caste tribunal appears to be a more living organization; and one whose decisions have in themselves a certain possibility of enforcement. Of this there may be one or two fairly obvious explanations.

136. The southern outcast lacks the toleration that education gives; for him the smallest infringement of age-old custom is no light matter; his inappreciation of foreign courts, which transact their business in a form, and frequently in a language, which he does not understand, renders the maintenance of his home-made tribunal for him a matter of every-day necessity. Furthermore, such accounts as I have received of caste government in the stratum of society suggest that here the tribunal is really representative of, or in fact a meeting of, all persons directly interested in the ordering of a small community; its decisions deriving weight from the fact that they represent a verdict of the society amid which the individual affected must get through his life, in most cases without the possibility of change, and with which he must needs be in practical communion.

137. Corroboration of the view that the caste tribunal is concerned rather with the interests of a society, than with the delinquencies of an individual, is derived from another observed fact, which indeed contradicts to some extent the view expressed in the preceding paragraph. In many cases the ultimate adjudication rests with an authority socially unconcerned with the individuals for whom he adjudicates, but for whose propriety of conduct as a social group, his temporal position as the lord of the soil, even though such be now but a memory, or quasi-ecclesiastical superiority, may be supposed to render him in a degree responsible.

138. Thus amongst the *Nambúdris* of part of South Malabar the Rája of Cochin, a *Kshatriya*, is the final authority in caste questions; the Ambadi Kóvilagam is the ultimate head of the *Tíyan* community in the same district; and the *Náyar* overlord of the *désam* is commonly a member of the committees which deal with caste offences among *Tíyans* and *Kammálans*.

139. Of the *Odiyas* of Goomsur taluk (Ganjám) I learn that, while they possess their own grand inquisitor living at Pechabundi in the Vishnachatram Mutta, the local zamindar appears to be a person of considerable influence in caste questions, in some cases an appeal lying to him from the decision of the caste tribunal. Among the *Dombós* of Vizagapatam the caste headman is appointed by the local zamindar, at whose will the appointment is terminable. In the deliberations of the Kurnool *Kápus* the opinion of the Rája of Gudival is reported to carry, or to have once carried, considerable weight.

140. From North Arcot I have received a report of a *Kápu* caste council, interesting inasmuch as it was held, or the attempt was made to hold it, under the presidency of a *Vaishnava Bráhman*. The lowly *Málas* of the Ceded Districts are said to acknowledge a *Balija* as their supreme caste authority—a position recalling the headmanship of a *Kavarai* among the Tamil *Paraiyans*.

141. Again, so far as I have been able to learn by written and personal enquiries, an adverse verdict in respect of caste passed on an individual does not necessarily operate to his prejudice in his relations with members of other castes. A parallel may be found in the verdicts of modern professional tribunals, which may declare a person guilty of infamous or improper conduct with respect to his profession and its members, without conveying any reflection on the propriety of his conduct as a member of general society.

142. From a large number of reports I have selected the following few cases for detailed mention. But, in descending from generalities to particulars, a word of caution is necessary. When a caste is fairly wide-spread, it by no means follows that caste procedure in one district is identical with, or even resembles, that existing in another district.

143. *Khond* or *Játapu*—the terms are synonymous terms according to my informant. The village "*hanta*," who holds his appointment through a forgotten series of ancestors, rules the village with five assessors. Offences, of which mention will be made subsequently, are adjudicated upon on sworn testimony given by the parties concerned. A man excommunicated by one "*hanta*" can appeal to another: the first "*hanta*" sits with the second, and their decision is final.

144. Allusion has already been made to the caste authority of the Goomsur *Odiyas*, and the *Dombós* of Vizagapatam; the *Behara* among the *Dondasis* of Ganjám lays down caste law to his village. If one *Behara* does not recognize the decision of another, all other *Beharas* boycott him.

145. The offences of which these Oriya tribunals take cognizance are curious. The *Bottadas* of Vizagapatam deal faithfully with social nuisance by outcasting a man who stinks. To be beaten with a slipper is an indignity; but caste feeling is sacrificed to civic patriotism in the excuses made for a *Bottada* urged to *sámán*-carrying by the slipper of a police man. He suffers and is strong in the cause of the State. If a *Bottada* has children by a woman of another, but non-polluting, caste, the children will be admitted to the *Bottada* caste, but not the parents.

146. The *Dombós* of Vizagapatam add insult to injury by excommunicating the luckless wight who is eaten by a tiger.* A *Dombó* assaulted by a *Komati*, *Bráhman*, *Mangala*, or *Tsákala* falls into disgrace; politeness towards these castes is thus secured.

147. The *Dandásis* of Ganjám are reported to exercise one excellent safeguard of morality. If a man seduces a virgin, and she becomes pregnant, he must marry her. If he refuses, both are summoned before a village meeting. Water is poured on the woman and she remains guiltless; the man is excommunicated for ever.

148. TELUGU CASTES.—Allusion has already been made to their negligence in respect of offences occurring within the caste. A few concrete cases of their action in respect to relations with other castes may be quoted.

149. A *Bráhman* kept a *Kápu* woman, and had by her two sons and one daughter. The daughter married a *Kápu*, and the bridal pair, together with all the wedding guests, were excommunicated. Subsequently a marriage was planned between the daughter of one of these excommunicated guests and a rich *Kápu*. All the outcastes were re-admitted, and, in course of time, the *Bráhman's* illegitimate daughter was received into the *Kápu* caste.

150. A *Kápu* of the village *P*, while engaged in a religious ceremony, petted his illegitimate child by a potter woman. He was excommunicated by common consent of his neighbours, and the ostracism continues.

151. *E* of the village *C*, descendant of a long line of *Kápu* headmen, is reported to possess a great and conciliatory influence throughout Bellary, Kurnool, and the Nizam's Dominions. *C* of *K* being suspected of drinking water and eating food given by a *Golla*, his neighbours ceased to associate with him. *E* on his complaint held an investigation, declared him guiltless, and prevailed on society to accept his verdict.

152. Some 100 years ago an ancestor of *N* and *V*, having contracted a doubtful marriage, was ostracised. Being a rich man, he prevailed on *Kápus* of undoubted purity to marry his children. In course of time a small community of such outcasts has grown up, and the efforts of *E* are now directed to securing their amalgamation with the *Kápu* caste.

153. Among *Balijas*, called derisively by the *Kápus* "*Kalalavandlu*," or persons troubled about caste, headmen called Chettis take cognizance of such matters as sexual relation within prohibited degrees, sexual relation with a person of right-hand caste, beating or being beaten with a shoe, spitting on or being spat on by

* The idea is probably the same as that noted in Chapter IV, paragraph 88, namely, that the victim either becomes a tiger, or else aids tigers in their ill-doings.

a caste man. But despite the opinion of the *Kápus*, all my informants agree in thinking that here too the authority of the caste tribunal is waning, if it has not already waned.

154. *Málas*, (classed by a high caste writer with "other *Súdras*"), are reported by a Guntúr writer to possess a high degree of caste organization. Each village has its standing *panchâyat*, which is subordinate to a representative assembly of the "*pargana*," while above all is the headman, a *Balija* by caste. The parallel case of the Tamil *Paraiyans* has already been noted.

155. Inseparably connected with *Málas* by ties of mutual aversion, are the *Mádigas*. These latter possess a formal caste tribunal, mostly occupied with *Mála* cum *Mádiga* relations and immoralities. Yet two species of offence with which the tribunal deals are curious, namely, false accusation of a caste offence, and unjustifiable claim to social superiority.

156. In contrast to the Tamil *Kammálans*, their Telugu brethren, the *Kamsalas*, possess a fairly rigorous caste organization. Each village is said to have a committee of five to ten members, nominated by common consent, and permanent. This *panchâyat* communicates with a district committee. At the summit of the community is a high priest living at Badvel and known as "*Sarasvati Pitham.*" Under him are subordinate local authorities such as the "*Gáyatri Pitham*" who resides near Bangalore. Succession to these posts is governed by appointment by a predecessor.

157. In Guntúr, there is a district committee for caste affairs. Important original questions are sent up to this body, which sometimes gives its decision at head-quarters, and sometimes sends a member to a village. Appeals lie from the village tribunal to this committee, and thence to the *Pitham*.

158. Tamil Castes—*Pallis*.—For an elaborate report on this caste, I am indebted to a Muhammadan informant.

159. The chief authority of the caste is "*Srímat Mahávisésham Ándiyan Brahma* "*Vanniyavamsam Kshatriya Muhámaddálayam Ratna Simhásanádhipati Chakravarti* "*Svamiyayógi Srí Agilakontakodi Brahmánandanayóga Srimat Kulandai Ánanda* "*Svami*," whose awful authority resides in the Bhaváni taluk of Coimbatore district. Second in the hierarchy comes the "*Sénathipati*" followed at a respectable distance by the "*Mahánáltán.*" No. 1 is named by his predecessor; No. 2 is hereditary; as also No. 3, unless failure of the stock necessitates an election. The jurisdiction of Nos. 1 and 2 is practically universal; that of No. 3 confined to one or two taluks. Further down, each village, which must contain at least five houses of the caste, has its "*Periyathanam*," elected by the villagers over whom his jurisdiction extends, and confirmed by the *magni nominis umbra*.

160. Complaint is made by a person aggrieved to the "*Periyathanam*," who, by means of a messenger, (a low caste person), assembles a meeting. It is characteristic of all fairly rigorous caste organizations that such messenger is no chance newsbearer, but a definite person, generally not of high social position. In his judicial functions the "*Periyathanam*" is aided by a local assessor of respectability; and his findings are circulated to all "*Periyathanams*" in the neighbourhood. A person who refuses to obey a decision is "suspended" from caste; and if obdurate even after a final decision of the higher authorities, is excommunicated.

161. *Concrete cases.*—*A* fined Re. 1 for spitting on a man. *B* "suspended" for taking off his sacred thread. *C* outcasted for cohabiting with a *Paraiyan* woman.

162. In 1908 a case, interesting inasmuch as it involved questions cognizable by a Court, was decided by a caste tribunal. *X* sold land to *Y* and executed a sale deed before the money was paid. Once possessed of this legal document, *Y* would not pay the money due. Ordered to do so by the "*Periyathanam*" he refused whereupon *X* sought the aid of the ineffable name, who ordered *Y* to pay, with an addition of Rs. 21, fine for his dishonesty. *Y* declined to obey, and was totally excommunicated.

163. Yet here too reports have reached me that these old tribunals are losing their effectiveness, and that people resort more and more to ordinary courts of law.

164. *Vellálas.*—Accounts of their caste organization vary from district to district. North Arcot reports it as practically dead; Salem gives a *Bráhman* priest of Tiruchengod as exercising some authority, and states the following concrete case.

165. A complaint was made by some *Vellálas* that *P* (a widow) lived with a *Koravan*. The widow, who had emigrated to Ceylon, was outside the jurisdiction of the *guru*; but her brothers were fined Rs. 80, and those who had used the same well as the widow, Rs. 200 between them.

166. From Madura a report comes that *Vellálas* are willing to refer their differences for adjudication to any person—even a Muhammadan—in whom they have confidence.

167. *Kaikólan.*—In one report a description is given of a somewhat elaborate caste machinery existing among this social group.

168. Each village possesses its *panchâyat* and headman, elected by the villagers, and permanent when approved by the headman of the "*Nád*", (a committee chosen from some twenty villages), to which such village is affiliated. Of the *Náds*, that of Conjeeveram is supreme. An interesting point noted in this report is that trade offences are not dealt with by this caste committee, but that a common way of dealing with social offences is to stop a man from exercising his trade by placing a seal, (a cow-dung spot), on his loom.

169. *Kammálans.*—Their system of caste government as described by one informant appears to be elaborate in theory, but, as already remarked, the writer is sceptical as to its real existence and authority in these days.

170. Each village has its *panchâyat* presided over by a "*Náttánmai.*" This latter post is usually hereditary, but removals and appointments, if need be, are made by the community. It is interesting to note that the caste *purôhit* is considered as the subordinate of the "*Náttánmai*," a trace of oriental Erastianism. As to whether or not this *purôhit* is, or may be, a *Bráhman*, authorities differ.

171. The "*Náttánmai*" convenes a meeting of the committee, and questions are decided by a majority; but the "*Náttánmai*" need not accept nor give effect to a decision, unless it is unanimous. Consequently, if the "*Náttánmai*" disagrees with the majority, he can generally make his views prevail by repeated adjournments and reconsiderations.

172. A curious tradition is given here of a relation between *Kammálans* and certain *Kômatis* called *Pillai Púndavars*, (those who enter as sons). A *Kômati* shroff of Hyderabad, sentenced to decapitation, was begged off by some *Kammálans*, and out of gratitude he dedicated himself and his family as slaves to his preservers. The arrangement was ratified by the then ruler, who engraved an agreement on a copper plate; and now each *Kammálan* householder pays one-half pagoda to his *Pillai Púndavars*, the idea being that a master should support his slave.

I.—*Castes classified according to their traditional occupations* (1911).

(Strength shown in thousands.)

Group and caste.	Strength.
1	2
Grand Total ...	***41,870***
Cultivators	***8,440***
Bant	126
Gaudo	122
Kamma	1,126
Kápu	2,679
Nattamán	168
Odiya	101
Telaga	499
Tottiyan	156
Vellála	2,536
Others	932
Field labourers	***8,270***
Cheruman	255
Holeya	130
Mála	1,511
Pallan	866
Palli	2,820
Paraiyan	2,364
Others	318
Forest and hill tribes ...	***1,367***
Irula	101
Játápu	92
Khond	355
Konda Dora	90
Poroja	93
Savara	186
Yánádi	123
Others	328
Graziers and dairymen.	***33***
Fishermen, boatmen and palki bearers.	***814***
Bóya	426
Others	388
Hunters and fowlers ...	***484***
Valaiyan	359
Others	125
Priests and devotees ...	***1,562***
Bráhman Canarese ...	94
Bráhman Óriyá	148
Bráhman Tamil	480
Bráhman Telugu	461
Bráhman Others	118
Jangam	110
Others	161
Temple servants	***110***
Bards and astrologers ...	***17***
Writers	***118***
Musicians, singers, dancers, mimes and jugglers.	***78***
Traders and pedlars ...	***3,498***
Balija	1,041
Chetti	350
Kómati	498
Traders and pedlars—*cont.*	
Labbai	402
Máppilla	1,033
Others	174
Carriers by pack animals.	***50***
Barbers	***459***
Ambattan	213
Mangala	184
Others	62
Washermen	***723***
Vannán	242
Tsákala	387
Others	94
Weavers, carders and dyers.	***1,460***
Dévánga	287
Kaikólan	368
Patnúlkáran	93
Sále	359
Others	353
Tailors	***15***
Carpenters and masons.*	***103***
Potters	***353***
Kummara	134
Kusavan	153
Others	66
Blacksmiths	***8***
Gold and silver smiths.	***4***
Brass and copper smiths.	***7***
Confectioners and grain parchers.	***15***
Oil pressers	***342***
Vániyan	195
Others	147
Toddy drawers and distillers.	***2,195***
Billava	157
Gamalla	154
Idiga	261
Íluvan	121
Shánán	642
Tíyan	640
Others	220
Butchers	***1***
Leather workers	***1,355***
Chakkiliyan	526
Mádiga	808
Others	21
Basket workers and mat makers.	***308***
Kuravan	110
Yerukala	88
Others	110
Earth, salt, etc., workers and quarriers.	***739***
Odde	550
Uppara	115
Others	74
Village watchmen and menials.	***286***
Muttiriyan	87
Mutrácha	154
Others	45
Sweepers	***28***
Military and dominant.	***2,729***
Agamudaiyan	350
Ambalakáran	185
Kallan	585
Kshatriya	158
Maravan	365
Náyar	412
Rázu	103
Velama	487
Others	134
Artisans*	***980***
Kammálan, Malayálam ...	108
Kammálan, Tamil ...	559
Kamsala	295
Others	18
Cotton cleaners	***72***
Shepherds	***2,019***
Golla	904
Idaiyan	735
Kurumban	144
Kuruba	232
Others	4
Domestic servants ...	***2***
Beggars	***178***
Tumblers and acrobats.	***27***
Devil dancers, sorcerers and physicians.	***3***
Non-Indian Asiatic races.	***1,226***
Pathán	107
Saiyad	170
Sheik	893
Others	56
Non-Asiatic races ...	***15***
Anglo-Indians	***26***
Indian-Christians ...	***1,168***
Titular names	***11***
Territorial, linguistic and sectarian names.	***170***
Lingáyat	134
Others	36
Others	***2***

* Tamil and Telugu carpenters who go by the name of Kammálans and Kamsalas are shown under "Artisans." The figure under "Carpenters and masons" is therefore not complete.

II. — Variation in caste, tribe, etc., since 1891.

Caste, tribe or race.	Persons (000s omitted).			Percentage of variation increase (+), decrease (—).		Remarks.
	1911.	1901.	1891.	1901–1911.	1891–1901.	
1	2	3	4	5	6	7
Agamudaiyan	350	318	296	+10·0	+ 7·8	
Ambalakáran	185	162	167	+14·0	— 8·0	In 1891, a portion of these may have been grouped as Kallans.
Ambattan	213	200	184	+ 6·5	+ 8·4	
Balija	1,041	1,008	884	+ 3·8	+14·0	
Bant	126	119	110	+ 6·6	+ 7·8	
Billava	157	143	126	+ 9·9	+13·4	
Bóya	426	397	357	+ 7·2	+11·3	
Bráhman—						
Canarese	94	94	1,133	+ 0·0	+ 4·9	In 1891, there was no linguistic classification.
Malayálam	19	19		+ 0·4		
Oriyá	144	128		+12·3		
Tamil	480	416		+15·4		
Telugu	461	436		+ 5·7		
Others	113	106		+ 6·4		
Chakkiliyan	526	487	444	+ 8·1	+ 9·7	
Cheruman	255	253	260	+ 0·8	— 2·7	For 1891, the figures include "Pulayan."
Chetti	350	289	656	+21·0	—55·9	In 1891, probably the distinction between Chetti and Kómati was not clear.
Dévánga	287	276	226	+ 4·0	+22·2	Increase in 1891, due to some of them in the three northern districts having been returned as Dombó.
Gamalla	154	151	136	+ 1·8	+11·3	
Gauda	46	46	152	— 1·9	— 1·7	Treated as one caste in 1891.
Gaudo	122	108		+18·8		
Golla	904	855	790	+ 5·7	+ 8·3	
Holeya	136	148	155	— 8·0	— 4·8	
Idaiyan	735	695	664	+ 5·7	+ 4·7	
Idiga	261	231	155	+12·9	+49·7	In 1891, some of them returned themselves as "Indra."
Iluvan	121	111	121	+ 9·2	— 8·0	
Indian Christian	1,168	999	839	+16·9	+19·0	
Irula	101	86	72	+16·9	+19·8	
Jangam	110	102	88	+ 7·8	+16·3	
Játápu	93	76	82	+22·2	— 7·3	
Kaikólan	368	347	313	+ 6·2	+11·0	
Kálingi	83	127	115	+ 6·7	+10·0	Treated as a single caste previous to 1911.
Kalinji	52					
Kallan	535	486	410	+10·2	+18·4	
Kamma	1,126	974	850	+15·6	+14·5	
Kammálan—						
Malayálam	108	104	590	+ 3·8	+ 1·8	Not separated in 1891.
Tamil	559	497		+12·6		
Kamsala	296	272	268	+ 8·8	+ 1·5	
Kápu	2,679	2,576	2,466	+ 4·0	+ 4·5	
Khond	355	317	327	+12·1	— 3·2	
Kómati	498	428	297	+12·8	+50·6	
Vaisya	6	19				
Konda Dora	90	89	85	+ 1·2	+ 4·2	
Kshatriya	159	80	152	+97·4	—47·3	In 1891, the "Pallis" returned themselves under this name; Rásus also preferred this name.
Kummara	134	120	149	+11·5	—10·7	
Kumbhara	18	13		+39·6		
Kuravan	110	100	135	+ 9·3	+22·7	
Yerukala	88	66		+34·7		
Kuruba	232	206	337	+12·4	+ 7·2	Separate figures not available for 1891.
Kurumban	144	155		— 7·0		

II.—*Variation in caste, tribe, etc., since* 1891—cont.

Caste, tribe or race.	Persons (000s omitted).			Percentage of variation increase (+), decrease (−).		Remarks.
	1911.	1901.	1891.	1901–1911.	1891–1901.	
1	2	3	4	5	6	7
Kusavan	158	139	129	+ 9·9	+ 7·9	
Labbai	402	407	353	− 1·3	+ 15·2	
Lingáyat	135	139	108	− 2·8	+ 27·9	
Mádiga	808	755	681	+ 7·0	+ 10·8	
Mála	1,511	1,405	1,371	+ 7·6	+ 2·5	
Mangala	184	164	154	+ 11·9	+ 7·1	
Máppilla	1,033	913	823	+ 13·1	+ 10·9	
Maravan	365	339	307	+ 7·7	+ 10·3	
Mutrácha	153	176	159	− 12·9	+ 10·6	The distinction between the two castes was not very clearly observed in 1891.
Muttiriyan	87	66	34	+ 32·2	+ 91·0	
Nattamán	163	151	95	+ 7·6	+ 58·9	In 1891, most of them were returned as Udaiyán.
Náyar	412	410	394	+ 0·4	+ 4·2	
Odde	550	498	461	+ 10·4	+ 8·1	
Odiya	101	96	92	+ 5·2	+ 4·4	
Pallan	866	825	802	+ 4·9	+ 2·9	
Palli	2,820	2,554	2,395	+ 10·4	+ 6·6	
Paraiyan	2,364	2,153	2,035	+ 9·8	+ 5·8	
Pathán	107	95	109	+ 12·2	− 12·8	
Patnúlkáran	93	87	73	+ 6·5	+ 19·9	
Poroja	93	92	82	+ 0·9	+ 12·0	
Rásu	103	107	68	− 3·8	+ 56·3	In 1891, the Pallis returned themselves under this name.
Saiyad	170	152	110	+ 11·9	+ 37·6	
Sále	358	326	310	+ 10·0	+ 5·1	
Savara	186	183	182	+ 1·6	+ 0·5	
Shánán	642	603	532	+ 6·4	+ 13·4	
Sheik	893	787	619	+ 13·5	+ 27·1	
Telaga	499	383	302	+ 30·3	+ 26·5	
Tíyan	640	578	548	+ 10·6	+ 5·6	
Tottiyan	156	150	146	+ 3·5	+ 3·3	
Tsákala	387	360	327	+ 7·5	+ 10·1	
Uppara	115	110	101	+ 4·7	+ 9·4	
Valaiyan	359	360	286	− 0·4	+ 25·8	The Valaiyans of Pudukkóttai State returned themselves as "Pallis" in 1891.
Vániyan	195	171	153	+ 13·8	+ 11·7	
Vannán	242	209	229	+ 16·0	− 8·7	
Velama	487	436	382	+ 11·7	+ 14·3	
Vellála	2,536	2,379	2,221	+ 6·6	+ 7·1	
Yánádi	122	104	85	+ 17·0	+ 22·2	

CHAPTER XII.—OCCUPATION.

PART I. (*J. C. Molony.*)

NEXT to, or even surpassing in importance, a knowledge of the Presidency population is a knowledge of the ways in which such population finds the means of livelihood. Imperial table XV in its various parts, table XVI, and the subsidiary tables appended to this chapter, profess to supply such information on the subject as columns 9–11 of the enumeration schedules afforded.

2. The present arrangement of the information obtained differs materially from that employed at the census of 1901. Employment and means of livelihood, though grouped in various classes, orders, and sub-orders, were in the final resort represented then by 520 separate sorts of occupations; actual workers and dependents in each occupation were distinguished, and actual workers still further classified by sex, and according as they depended solely on the exercise of a particular occupation, or combined such occupation with the pursuit of agriculture.

3. The three distinctions last mentioned still persist, but the actual number of occupations has now been reduced to 169. These 169 occupations have been arranged in four "classes," and twelve "sub-classes," in accordance with a scheme devised by M. Bertillon to facilitate the international comparison of statistics.

4. The claim of one arrangement or of the other to preference will vary in accordance with the standpoint from which judgment is passed. Diminution of detail is certainly an advantage; the possibility of comparison between the statistics of Indian occupation and those of other countries, which M. Bertillon's scheme holds out, is at first sight attractive. On the other hand, it must be admitted that statistica lcomparison is not necessarily identical with practical; and that things cannot be made the same by affixing to them the same general name. It is possible to contrast the representation of "industry" by $5\frac{1}{3}$ million persons in Madras with its numerical representation in France; but for the businessman the question must inevitably arise, whether the content of the term—the only matter of importance to him—is at all the same in the two countries. In particular, it may be queried whether a system of classification, devised for countries where exists a clear distinction between manufacture and trade, and where the processes of manufacture are highly specialized and sharply differentiated, is suitable for Southern India; where, to a very large extent, the native manufacturer (*e.g.*, goldsmith) carries through himself each separate process of manufacture, and then sells the finished product of his industry.

5. To a drawback inherent in change of classification system from census to census attention is invited by my collaborateur; such change may very largely vitiate numerical comparison. For example, different items of spinning and weaving, distinct in 1901, are now clubbed together; with the result that it is impossible to ascertain the *real* numerical expansion or contraction of these occupations between 1901 and 1911. Statistical comparison by proportional adjustment is, of course, possible, but of little practical value, inasmuch as it tacitly assumes the very premiss in doubt—an identity of tendency throughout two decades.

6. *Sed haec hactenus.* A word as to the ground plan of this chapter may not be amiss.

7. Long before the order of table XV *et seq.* began to emerge from the chaos of the abstraction office, it was observed to me by a business man that very frequently census statistics and criticisms of industry and occupation are of little interest or importance to a practical man, inasmuch as mere statement of numerical variation, without appreciation of the uncertainty of the actual figures, and without an expert knowledge of the causes which produce such variation, is of small value.

8. The justice of such criticism being self-evident, it was but natural to seek to remedy defect. To supplement a short note written by me on the census figures of Madras city Mr. Alfred Chatterton contributed a chapter on the industries of the capital. He has with great kindness undertaken a similar task in relation to a wider area; and his contribution, which represents in fact an industrial survey of the Presidency by an expert, forms the second section of this chapter.

9. So far as possible we have sought that one work should not overlap. I attempt to treat of the agriculture or agricultural population of the Presidency, and of a few special points, such as occupations of women, suggested by the statistics; Mr. Chatterton confines himself to trade and industry.

10. Treatment of my allotted section is facilitated by the fact that here at least the principle of classification has remained unchanged; landowners, cultivating and non-cultivating, tenants similarly distinguished, and farm servants or agricultural labourers, still constituting the bulk of the agricultural population. In table XV-B, it is true, a division of those dependent on the soil for a livelihood into "rent payers" and "rent receivers" is attempted; but in regard to this Presidency it is of no great interest.

11. One small detail relating to the statistics of agricultural occupation may be explained. This is the description, at first sight nonsensical, in table XV-B, of a certain number of the purely agricultural population as partially agriculturist. The explanation is that such description applies to men or women engaged in agriculture, who carry on more than one species of agricultural occupation. Thus a zamindar, in most cases, a person who draws his chief income from the letting out of his land to others (non-cultivating landowner), frequently carries on a certain amount of cultivation on his own account; and thus ranks in some degree also as a cultivating landowner. Similarly a cultivating tenant may possess other land of his own, which he either cultivates himself or leases out for rent; a farm labourer has frequently his own little plot, over which he is the master.

12. That agriculture is the mainstay of the Presidency, as of India in general, is a fact so well known as hardly to need mention. Of a total population of 41,870,160, ordinary cultivation supports, whether as workers or dependents, 28,621,449, or 6,836 persons per 10,000. From this number, for purposes of comparison with the figures of 1901, may be excluded 74,508 persons concerned with management of estates, rent collection, etc.; when the proportion of agriculturists to the total population will be 6,818 per 10,000.

13. In 1901 there were dependent on agriculture 26,381,813 persons out of 38,623,066, or 6,831 per 10,000 of the total population.*

14. It is questionable whether the very slight movement indicated by these figures is sufficient to justify the drawing of any conclusion as to a decrease in the popularity or possibilities of agriculture. If on the one hand there can be no doubt that industrialism is in the air, and that new fields for the employment of labour and capital are being opened up, there are some considerations on the other side which it is well to bear in mind.

15. The first is the possibility, to which attention has frequently been drawn elsewhere, of inaccuracy in the census returns. In respect of employment there are two factors tending to error; firstly, the popularity or supposed "respectability" of agriculture; secondly, the heredity still associated with calling in India A man will often give as his profession that followed by his ancestors, or that which custom assigns to his caste, even though he may not actually exercise such calling himself; I can recall to mind a man who always spoke of himself, and was spoken of, as a barber, although, as a matter of fact, he was a money-lender doing a considerable business, and in all probability never handled a razor for hire in his life. On the other hand an individual plying a calling not held in general esteem, should he have any connection however slight with agriculture, is apt to return agriculture as his principal occupation.

* Excluding figures for the Laccadive Islands.

16. Furthermore, in this Presidency, the advancement of industry is bound up with the advancement of agriculture. The country provides its own raw material, the direction of sound industrial development would seem to lie in the handling of what the soil produces. The industrial advance of Madura has been mentioned; with a large increase in the number of ginning factories and in certain taluks of the neighbouring Rámnád district there has been, I learn, a marked increase in the cultivation of cotton and improvement in methods of general cultivation.

Description.	Distribution of 1,000 persons supported by agriculture. 1911.	1901.
Non-cultivating landowner ...	34	30
Cultivating " ...	461	512
Non-cultivating tenant ...	6	2
Cultivating "	225	167
Farm labourer	274	289

17. The "internal" classification of agriculturists may next be considered. Figures quoted in the margin show the distribution of 1,000 agriculturists among the five sub-divisions of agriculture. There are some features of curious interest in this return.

18. The first is a marked decrease in the number of cultivating landowners, and increase in that of cultivating tenants. Without regard to the accuracy of the representation the statistical result is surprising. There were a few questions of classification, (to that of caste reference has already been made), hotly debated when the census-taking being organized; and prominent among them was that occasioned by the conferment of occupancy right on zamindari tenants. Among such tenants there appeared to exist a widespread apprehension that return of themselves as tenants in any form would be prejudicial to their newly established right; and so frequently was the point raised, and with such obvious earnestness, that I personally anticipated the practical disappearance of the tenant class from the returns.

19. These figures, it is true, refer to the population dependent on agriculture, not to the actual workers therein. But save in one instance, the marginal figures for actual workers alone tally with those representing the total dependent population. The exception is the case of agricultural labourers, whose numbers dependent generally on agriculture have decreased by 15 per 1,000, but who, in point of actual workers, occupy practically the same position in relation to the rest of the agricultural community as they did ten years ago.

Description.	Distribution of 1,000 actual workers in agriculture. 1911.	1901.
Non-cultivating landowner ...	23	19
Cultivating " ...	426	484
Non-cultivating tenant ...	4	1
Cultivating " ...	207	151
Farm labourer	340	345

20. This result is in many ways very curious. In the first place, as mentioned in Chapter II, there is an undoubted uneasiness over the exodus of labour to foreign countries—an exodus which emigration statistics show to exist, and which is probably due to the fact that the Indian employer of agricultural labour, as in the case of other labour mentioned by Mr. Chatterton, has not yet recognized that, to keep his labourer, he must pay him properly, and treat him properly. But these figures appear to show that the proportionate number of employers and employees has not undergone any marked change. If then we grant that there is a shortage of agricultural labour in Madras, at first sight the only possible explanation would appear to be that the pick of the labour goes abroad, that which is comparatively valueless remaining behind. There are some figures which illustrate the point; it is only fair to remark that two different meanings can be read into them.

21. As can be seen from those quoted in the margin, the number of actual workers among 1,000 persons dependent on the earnings of agricultural labour has fallen. This may be taken to denote an increase of prosperity among the labouring class, which relieves a certain number of women and children, of the aged and infirm of both sexes, from the necessity of working. In point of fact, the decrease among actual female workers

Actual workers per 1,000 dependent on agricultural labour.	
1911	649
1901	662

is sufficient to counterbalance practically the increase among the men. But, considering the general circumstances of the Indian agricultural labourer, these figures may also denote a falling off in the number *fit* to work; there being few whose relations can afford to allow them to sit idle if they *can* work.

22. Possibly a better comparison is that between the actual workers in the labouring class, and workers *plus* dependents in other branches of agriculture. To the latter class the *non-workers* among the former may be of no importance; but an adequate supply of *workers* is in the end as important to the dependents of the landowner as to the landowner himself. We find that in 1901 there were 270 working labourers for every 1,000 persons, (workers *plus* dependents), supported by the other four agricultural occupations; in 1911 this number has fallen to 245.

23. A proportional increase of "workers" among non-cultivating landlords may be noted. The term "worker" is in this case inexact; but as evidence of an increasing number of landed proprietors the figures possess some interest. Of more value than statistics as to the subsidiary occupations of landowners, and occupations followed by particular castes, would be information, could it be obtained, as to how far, if at all, the land is passing from the hands of the agricultural to those of the professional or trading classes.

24. An increase in the number of non-cultivating landlords would at first sight imply that it is becoming increasingly worth while for a man to acquire land for the purpose of subletting it to others; and the supposition is strengthened by the gradual increase observable throughout the Presidency in the selling value of land of all descriptions. Yet from information derived from others, and from some small personal observation, I am inclined to think that there is room for doubt as to whether land acquirement by those who have no intention of working the land themselves, is always, or often, a practical commercial transaction. The glamour of land possession is so strong in India, that the wealthy vakil, official, or tradesman, will often buy land at a price which precludes the hope of an adequate return on his outlay; surplus cash is in fact invested in a form of security which yields no monetary repayment, but of which the possession lends a certain sense of dignity and pleasure.

25. Table XV-B, which professes to give the subsidiary occupations returned by agriculturists, serves also to show the distribution by districts of the five classes into which the agricultural population has been divided. The figures in some cases correspond with general expectation; in others they appear self-contradictory.

26. Thus, for example, the preponderance of non-cultivating landlords in Tanjore district is not surprising. The district is wealthy; widespread irrigation renders land even at a very high price, a safe "lock-up" for money; and Tanjore is to a large extent the home or favoured retreat of well-to-do lawyers and other professional men. In South Arcot, the existence of a large number of "cultivating landlords," or "peasant proprietors," is probably facilitated by the wide spread of groundnut cultivation—a crop peculiarly suitable for the small man. If both sexes be taken into account, it is true that these and subsequent considerations will need revision, but in all probability the male return of occupation is a fairly reliable indication of the conditions of a district.

27. A high proportion of cultivating tenants seems natural in the Northern Circars, where zamindaris abound, and in Chittoor; the supply of agricultural labourers one would expect to follow in the main the demand created by the presence of a large number of possible employers.

28. But some anomalies may be noticed in the returns. It seems doubtful whether Rámnád and Tinnevelly could handle their cultivation with the comparatively scanty supply of labour that the figures indicate as there available; the number of non-cultivating landlords in Cuddapah and Kurnool is surprisingly large, if the natural characteristics of these districts be considered, and if the number is contrasted with that found in more favoured localities. In Rámnád one would hardly expect the number of cultivating landlords to exceed so enormously that of cultivating tenants; the explanation may be that suggested in paragraph 18 *supra*.

29. If the particulars given of subsidiary occupation be examined in some detail, it will be seen that non-cultivating landowners in the main follow some other form of agricultural calling. Zamindars and other large landed proprietors apart, the preference given to one form of agricultural employment or the other in the census schedules is probably to a great extent a matter of chance. The entries under the headings "artisans," "priests," and "general labourers," may be attributed to the "inam" system, which, theoretically at least, provides each indispensable unit of village society with a plot of ground for his maintenance. Thus the smith, the puróhit, and the Mála labourer, have each as a rule some shadowy title to a certain extent of land, and are wont to refer to such as their chief means of subsistence. In reality there is often very little real connection between the nominal owner and his land; I have met many cases where the land had been in the practical possession and enjoyment of others for countless years; the registered owner depending entirely on fees, paid in cash or kind, for services rendered by him.

30. The same preference for agriculture as a subsidiary occupation runs through all the five sub-divisions of agricultural employment. The connection of trade and sundry other occupations with agriculture, for its proper exposition, requires much more careful analysis than table XV-B and subsidiary table V permit. The substantial landholder, who bargains with wholesale merchants for the sale of his produce, and who can hold up his surplus stocks for a rising market, is in a sense a trader, and will often describe himself as such. The poorer agriculturist may run, more or less carelessly, a petty shop in his house, under the control of some junior member of his family, on the off chance of supplementing his scanty earnings; should the needs of his own cultivation permit, he is glad to hire out himself and his bullocks for transport, to plough for a wealthy neighbour, or for raising water from a well. But it is, I think, doubtful whether the real trader or money lender embarks to any great extent on the genuine pursuit of agriculture; he may lend money on the security of land or crop, and keep the farmer practically in the position of his servant; but he will as a rule take very little interest in agriculture *per se*, as distinguished from the profit which he may obtain by entrusting an advance to an agriculturist.

31. Subsidiary tables I to V do not appear to supply much further material for general comment. Their general witness is to the well-known fact that Southern India is well nigh wholly agricultural. Progress or regress in arts and industries I could only treat by trespassing on the preserves of Mr. Chatterton, whose reasoned expositions are obviously of much greater interest and importance than could be my bald and uninstructed statistical comparison of figures.

32. Subsidiary table VIII deals with the occupations of selected castes. It may be read in connection with subsidiary table I to Chapter XI; and its information may be summarized thus. Artisan castes in the main return as their profession that with which tradition associates their caste; other castes, in general, return agriculture as their profession; as do castes to whose traditional calling some stigma is supposed to attach. This last point is illustrated by the statistics of the Shánáns, Tíyans, and Billavas.

33. The scanty proportion of Bráhmans engaged in the priestly calling bears out the suggestion of paragraph 115, Chapter XI, that priesthood is not the profession of the Bráhman, if "profession" be understood in its European sense.

34. The weaving castes (Dévánga, Kaikólan and Sále) are, on the whole, faithful to their hereditary calling. The position and prospects of the weaving industry are discussed subsequently; comment is therefore needless at this stage. As compared with other castes it may be seen that trade appears in somewhat special favour with this people as an alternative employment.

35. Tamil metal workers (Kammálans) appear to have a much greater partiality for agriculture than their Telugu brethren, the Kamsalas. If the figures of this table be compared with those of subsidiary table on the same lines prepared

at the last census, the number of Tamil artisans who follow their hereditary profession appears to have increased considerably, while a considerable decrease is apparent among the Telugus.

36. The Indian Christian is, as a rule, recruited from that *stratum* of society which finds its chief support in agricultural, or general, labour. The return of occupations followed by this community is potentially interesting, as showing the extent to which a change of religion, with the possibilities of education and advancement suggested in Chapters IV and VIII, may have widened the horizon of the convert. But to turn potential into actual information, a much more detailed census taking, and more detailed tabulation of results attained, would be needed than is possible in connection with a general census. It would be necessary, for example, to ascertain the social and material status of the convert antecedent to conversion, the period for which he or his family had belonged to the Christian faith, and the exact meaning to be attached to the occupational term returned.

37. We find that the main professions returned are "cultivating land-owner and tenant," (237 per 1,000); "artisan" (236 per 1,000), and "field and general labourer" (263 per 1,000). The first-mentioned two classes may have been recruited to some extent from those originally belonging to the third: at the same time it must be remembered that one church, (the Roman Catholic), has been decidedly successful in obtaining conversions among the "tenant farmer" class, and that a large number of these converts, whose material circumstances remain unaltered by conversion, are to be found in the percentage of "landowners and tenants." "Artisan" is a term too vague and general to convey definite information—the person so designated, especially in India, may be anything from a highly skilled workman to a mere cooly taking an unintelligent part in some industrial occupation. It is clear, however, that such an institution as the Basel Mission, which combines industrialism on a considerable scale with evangelization, must be doing an excellent work in the imparting of practical technical education to a considerable section of the Indian Christian people.

38. "Lawyers, doctors and teachers" (29 per 1,000) are probably made up for the most part of the Indian catechists and instructors attached to every mission, both in the department of direct missionary work, and in that of secular instruction, which nowadays is the practically invariable concomitant of missionary endeavour.

39. The Anglo-Indians of 1901 who enjoyed "independent means" numbered 13 per 1,000. The fact that, under the designation of "persons living principally on their income," this proportion has increased to 116 per 1,000, is explained by the present grouping under this latter designation of pensioners, scholarship-holders, persons supported by their relatives, etc., all of whom were distinguished ten years previously. A comparison of the groupings will illustrate the dangers inherent in a change of classification: in 1901 the above-mentioned groups of persons, who were not actively engaged in the pursuit of some trade or calling, numbered together 244 per 1,000 of the total Anglo-Indian working population; in 1911 the proportion has fallen to 115 per 1,000—a result which is obviously impossible. It is impracticable to draw a real comparison between these two sets of statistics.

40. Taking those for 1911, as they stand, we find that, excluding "others" (215 per 1,000), the chief stand-by of the Anglo-Indian is the profession of "contractor, clerk, cashier, etc.;" a wide description, but one which probably may be taken as denoting here the subordinate ranks of the mercantile-clerical profession. It was observed to me in this connection by a friend acquainted with the subject that a striking feature of his long experience in the conduct of large business affairs in Madras was the disappearance of the Anglo-Indian from the "upper-subordinate" posts of commerce. This he attributed in part to a prescient desire for security and pension,—prospects afforded by Government employment in certain departments of medicine, police and engineering; partly to underselling by Indian competition. Another informant, who possesses an intimate and disinterested

acquaintance with the subject, has discussed for me this latter aspect of the question. The Indian, he considers, as a clerk pure and simple, excels the Anglo-Indian, and will work at a considerably cheaper rate.

41. In respect to the former point, the proportion of Anglo-Indians in "Public administration" now stands at 61 per 1,000, as against 37 per 1,000 in "Government service" in 1901. But for a proper appreciation of the extent to which the Anglo-Indian is successful in his search for Government employment, it would be necessary to examine in detail the statistics of certain professions exercised, some partly, some entirely, in dependence upon Government. Of such may be instanced, as examples, the telegraph and postal services, which undoubtedly provide employment for many of this race; the medical profession, where, in the Indian Subordinate Medical Department, many Anglo-Indians are found; the survey establishment; and the railway service, certainly a "public service," and one in close relation to the Government of the country, if not under its direct control. This information, unfortunately, the statistics as now compiled do not provide.

42. *Occupations of women.*—Table XV, part I, shows 8,379,378 women, out of a total female population of 21,264,152, as actively engaged in the pursuit of some occupation or other. Reducing everything to a common denominator, we find that 392 women per 1,000 in British territory are "actual workers," as against 538 per 1,000 in the Native States: in these latter a similar preponderance of actual workers among men is noticeable, their figure being 668 per 1,000, as against 627 per 1,000 in British territory.

43. It will be sufficient for our purposes to consider only the women of the British districts. Of the workers there, ordinary cultivation supports 746 per 1,000; and among the cultivators 447 per 1,000 are labourers, and 532 per 1,000 either cultivating landlords or cultivating tenants, the former predominating. In the returns of 1901 we find 8,308,233 women out of 19,362,849 in British territory described as actual workers, and 121,465 of 221,221 in the Feudatory States. Proportionately these figures represent respectively 429, and 549 women, per 1,000 of the total female populations.

44. In British territory 767 women of 1,000 workers depended for a livelihood on ordinary cultivation; and in the internal classification of agriculture 446 per 1,000 were returned as labourers, and 539 per 1,000 as either cultivating tenants or cultivating landowners, the latter outnumbering the former in the proportion of about three to one.

45. So much may be said to the reality or unreality of all these figures, that it is impossible to draw from them any valid conclusion as to an increase or decrease in possibility of employment for the women of the country. The large employment of women as farm labourers for transplanting, weeding, and harvest, is an undoubted fact; a woman may have land registered in her name, whether as *pattadar* under Government or as tenant under a private individual; and in so far as she does her fair share of work, or even more than that, in the departments of agriculture above mentioned, she may be described as a working cultivator. The vital process of agriculture, however, is ploughing, and in India this work is entirely in the hands of men.

46. In the textile industries (order 6); and in such work as basket-making (order 8—wood); in food industries (order 12); and especially in rice pounding; in industries connected with dress and toilet (order 13); in petty trade especially trade in foodstuffs (order 33); a large employment of women is perfectly credible.

47. But in many other departments of labour the position occupied by women must be accepted with some degree of scepticism. In heavy work, such as iron work (order 9), carpentry (a part of order 8), masonry (order 15), the return of female workesr means nothing more than that the wives or female relations of the workers have been returned as working at the occupations of those on whom they are dependent, or else give to the workers a general unskilled assistance, which has no intimate connection with any particular trade. Of this latter meaning an apt illustration may be found in the return of 3,187 women shown as actually engaged

in the profession of toddy drawing. A woman employed in this industry may carry toddy pots, or the paraphernalia of the tapper, receive full pots handed down from the tree, hand up pots to the tapper when he starts his climb. But such work is mere general labour, and bears no special relation to the art of toddy tapping. At buildings women may be seen passing up stones, carrying mortar, drawing water for the mixing of concrete, etc.; but a woman is never an actual working mason, if the word be used in its English signification.

48. A more genuine appreciation on the part of the enumerator of what really constitutes occupation is shown in the practical disappearance of women from the ranks of actual workers among village officials. Needless to say women do not in point of fact discharge such duties, but the return under this heading in 1901 was technically justifiable, inasmuch as inam lands for village service are often registered in the names of women, who appoint deputies (gumastas) to perform the actual work incumbent on the inam holder.

49. A decrease in the number of women employed as agricultural coolies is not perhaps an unfavourable sign for those who, from these statistics of employment, endeavour to draw some conclusion as to amelioration or deterioration in the position of the women of the country. Extension of employment, which by its nature implies a certain tincture of education, among women is what one would desire to find; but unfortunately the undoubted vagueness of occupational returns renders difficult any proper estimation of the facts underlying the figures available.

50. The profession, which in Europe appears to have afforded the first outlet for women's energies, is that of attendance on the sick. In this country there certainly is no profession in which they could be employed more usefully. Yet if figures alone are to be accepted as a guide, the number of those engaged in this vocation appears to have fallen during the decade. The returns of 1901 showed 4,630 "midwives," and 328 "compounders, hospital matrons, and nurses;" the two returns are clubbed in the present statistics and comprise some 4,006 women (group No. 155).

51. But the classification of 1901 was far more useful, inasmuch as the figures of the second group showed the number of women qualified, according to modern ideas, for the exercise of their profession; these are now swamped in a horde of "midwives," whose general qualifications have been trenchantly described by an authority on the subject quoted in Chapter II.

52. The number of women engaged in the imparting of education appears to have well nigh doubled itself in ten years, if figures are to be trusted. Quite a considerable number of the fair sex (12,110) devote themselves to "letters, arts and sciences," but the fact that practically all such are found under a sub-head which includes "singers and dancers," gives rise to doubt as to whether their profession represents a modern educational development.

53. *Occupations of some particular persons.*—Allusion has been made in Chapter VIII to a drawback which appears to attach to "education" in Southern India; namely that the word too often represents but a smattering of English, which may at best qualify a boy for some wretchedly paid post in Government service, and but too often turns him adrift, unfitted for agriculture or industry, on the overstocked market of literary unemployment. The census abstraction offices, which require temporarily an enormous number of men able to read and write, are a happy hunting ground for these much-to-be-pitied victims of our educational system. A few examples of the occupations followed by individuals there engaged may be quoted—

A—His educational qualifications consisted in having "passed Lower Secondary examination;" and in 1901 he secured a temporary job on Rs. 20 in the census offices. Between 1901 and 1911 he was temporary storekeeper in an Indian workshop, ticket checker on a railway, clerk in a shop, schoolmaster, and tram conductor. In 1911 he returned to the census office to his old position—he was not really qualified for anything better—and he describes his future prospects as "trying for a clerk's post."

B—"Studied up to Lower Secondary." Sorter in 1901. Then clerk in an Indian "Fund" office; tried trading in straw for a year or so; kept accounts for a plumber; and returned to census office.

C—Sorter in 1901. Clerk in a shop. Schoolmaster. Returned to census office.

D—Temporary clerk in railway. Clerk in a European firm. Worked in the Gun Carriage Factory. Went as a clerk to Rangoon. Returned, and after three months of "keeping quiet" got a temporary job in the Ordnance Department. Thrown out of work until the census office opened. Does not know what he is going to do.

E—"Discontinued his studies early, and started as a schoolmaster." After some time joined the census offices of 1901, and after this became a "tally clerk" under a big Madras firm. Lost this owing to ill-health, and started a school. Joined census abstraction office when it opened.

F—Passed middle school examination. For some years worked as a "petty contractor," and then became clerk in a leather shop on Rs. 7. Worked in the census office of 1901. Became clerk at a mine, and went from there to a distillery. Returned to the leather shop, and quitted it for the census office. Taken on again at his old place.

G—"Middle school." An old census hand. Between whiles is a schoolmaster.

H—Gave up his studies, and lived under the protection of his relatives. Worked in the census of 1891, and existed someway till the offices opened in 1901. Then became a fitter in a railway workshop, and after that bill collector for a photographer. Out of work for sometime till the census offices opened.

I—Commenced as a teacher in a Government school in Hyderabad. Left this, and started a private school in his own village. Out of work for a long while, and then a temporary clerk in railway service. Out of work again till census offices opened.

J—Pay sheet worker on a railway. Clerk (Rs. 15) in Public Works Department for a few years; then tried the Forest Department. After this overseer in a fuel depot; then cashkeeper, and subsequently clerk, on a mica mine. Out of work when census offices opened.

K—Private clerk to a postal inspector. Then a vaccinator, and after that a temporary copyist in various Government offices. Joined census office, and had no definite prospect of employment when this job ended.

L—Plague passport clerk, acting village karnam, schoolmaster, unemployed, abstractor in the census office. No particular prospect of employment.

M—Church clerk, then a schoolmaster. Employed in the census office, and has got work as an evangelist.

N—Read up to Fourth form, and discontinued his studies to become a schoolmaster. This failed and he joined the census office. At its closing dependent on his brother—a schoolmaster.

O—Studied up to Fifth form. Temporary clerk in Settlement Department; clerk to a merchant; surveyor; cooly recruiter; municipal clerk; plague passport clerk. Out of employment when the census office took him on.

P—Unemployed before census office opened. Left census office, and wrote from the penitentiary regarding disbursement of arrears of pay due to him.

And so on. These are melancholy tales: perhaps in every country the clerical market is overstocked. But in India it appears to be overstocked with those who could have had no real hope of success when they entered it.

PART II.—INDUSTRIAL OCCUPATIONS. (*Alfred Chatterton, C.I.E.*).

PART I.—GENERAL.

54. For industries to exist there must be raw material to work upon, which may be either of local origin or imported. The finished product of one industry is often the raw material of another. It will be convenient to designate as primary industries those which deal with the products of the earth in their natural state, as examples of which we may cite such manufactures as iron, portland cement, cotton yarn, flour and sugar; reserving the term secondary industries for those which are concerned with the conversion of the output of primary industries into articles which pass into the hands of the consumer or user. Thus the manufacture of machine tools or locomotives, of cotton cloth, of bread or of confectioneries, is in each case dependent upon the products of the primary industries already enumerated.

55. The industrial status of a country is largely determined by the extent to which the primary industries are carried on, and it is the object of the fiscal regulators of most countries to encourage the importation of material in its natural state, and to exclude that which has been subjected to the processes of manufacture, which convert it into partially or wholly finished goods. With this idea Indian raw material is welcomed in the markets of Europe and America, whilst any attempt to establish an export trade in finished products is discouraged by the imposition of heavy duties. Under modern conditions the scale of operation in the primary industries is usually very large, in secondary industries the same tendency to expansion may be seen; but there are important reasons why it is not so fully developed, and all over the world there are certain local needs which can only be met by local industries.

56. The Madras Presidency is almost wholly devoted to agriculture, and, with the exception of a few cotton and jute mills, two or three sugar factories, and a cement works, it possesses no primary industries organized on modern lines, unless such preliminary industrial processes as cotton-ginning, rice-hulling, and oil-milling are included. There is no import of raw material from abroad, except for what may be called secondary industries, and much of this, as well as what is retained in the country of the local produce, is worked up by methods which as yet have been but slightly influenced by the industrial revolution which has occurred in more advanced countries.

57. For the present unsatisfactory state of affairs two reasons may be assigned. (1) The complete dissociation of the intellectual classes in the country from its industries. Manual work of any kind was looked upon as degrading, and the higher castes treated with contempt the artizans and craftsmen who carried on the industrial work of the country. Till nearly the middle of the 19th century India was scarcely affected by the industrial changes going on in Europe. Ocean freights were heavy, and the absence of facilities for transport effectively protected the whole country except in the neighbourhood of the sea ports. Manufacturers in Europe were barely able to keep pace with the growing needs of their own people, and were under no necessity to look to foreign markets; but after the opening of the Suez Canal conditions materially changed. Not only did India become more accessible by sea, but the rapid growth of the railway system opened out the interior to trade; cultivation extended, and a ready market was found for surplus produce; the standard of living began to rise, and the needs of the people could not be fully met by the primitive industrial system of the country; the export trade in raw produce stimulated the import trade in manufactured goods, the Indian markets were carefully studied, and gradually all over the country the local artizan was made to feel the pressure of an altogether novel competition. In the past his wages had been regulated by custom, and in ordinary times he lived in tolerable comfort. Some of the old industries succumbed and are never likely to

be revived, but in others the artizan has managed to struggle on, selling his labour for a gradually decreasing wage. He might have met competition by improving his methods of working, but there was no one to help him. The educated classes were not interested in his fate, and went on their way rejoicing at the gradual decrease in the price of their domestic requirements. One or two leaders more far-seeing than the rest sounded a note of warning, but they were unheeded till recently, when the educated classes began to realize that there was no place for them in the industrial life of the country. Now they are seeking a way into it, but the road is beset with difficulties and progress is very slow. This is especially true of the Madras Presidency, where the second reason for the backward state of its industries operates very strongly. This is the absence of mineral wealth. For nearly a century exploratory work has been going on, but the sum total revealed is very meagre, and there is nothing to justify the hope that in the future discoveries will be made which will alter the present situation. The most important deficiency is coal, of which only a few tons have been mined in the Gódávari district; elsewhere none has been discovered. Of iron ores there is a vast quantity, but the bulk is of a low grade, and, in the absence of cheap fuel, is worthless, as it will not pay to export it from the country or to carry it by rail to the coal fields in Northern India. Considerable deposits of manganese ore exist in the Vizagapatam district, and during the ten years ending March 1909, 952,025 tons have been exported. The metallurgical demand for this ore is considerable but not unlimited, and there are other deposits in India which are also of commercial value. Russia and Brazil are the only other countries in which mines of this ore are extensively worked, and during the Russo-Japanese War the Russian exports ceased, with the result that India for a time enjoyed a partial monopoly of the supply, and obtained highly satisfactory prices. Since Russia recommenced exporting manganese ore the demand for Indian ore has materially decreased, and consequently the price obtainable for it. There are also deposits of manganese ore in the Sandúr State in the Bellary district, but very little practical use has so far been made of them. At present prices the long lead to the coast precludes them from being worked at a profit.

58. In the Nellore district there are extensive deposits of mica, which have been mined in a primitive way for a considerable time. The industry can hardly be described as an important one, as during the past ten years the output has been 4,234 tons valued at Rs. 49,64,193. Recently there has been a falling off in the quantity of mica mined, and still more in the price per cwt. obtained for it. Some of the old mines are reported to have been exhausted, or to have reached a depth beyond which it becomes unprofitable to work them at the low prices now obtainable for mica on the European market.

59. The extraction of saltpetre from village earths in various parts of the Presidency was at one time an industry of considerable importance. It is still carried on to some extent, chiefly in the Coimbatore district, and gives employment to 490 people. The returns for the past ten years show a production of 6,833 tons valued at Rs. 13,64,689. It is doubtful if these are very accurate, as the exports from the Presidency are extremely small, and all the saltpetre manufactured is apparently for local consumption, either for the manufacture of gunpowder or for manure.

60. Magnesite of great purity exists in the Chalk Hills of Salem, but efforts to put it on the market have not met with much success. Diamonds have been found and are still occasionally found in the Ceded districts, but the matrix from whence they came has never been discovered. There are extensive old workings in the Banganapalle State, and recently some attempt has been made to see if there are any left, but so far with no great amount of success. Old gold workings are numerous, and a vigorous effort is now being made to exploit the reefs of gold-bearing quartz in the Anantapur district with considerable prospect of success. Other minerals, such as corundum, have been found in several districts, and mention may be made of the monazite sands in the extreme south of the Peninsula which are at present of considerable value as a source of thorium. Of many metals traces exist, and specimens may be found in the mineral collections of the Madras Museum, but nowhere do they exist in payable quantities. As a basis of industry

the mineral wealth of the Presidency is a negligible quantity. In regard to building materials, there is a superabundant supply of hard gneissic rock over the greater part of the country, fairly good slate and laminated limestone in the Ceded districts, in places sandstone suitable for building work but nowhere any variety of super-excellence. Clays suitable for bricks of high quality or for tiles are only found on the West Coast, and elsewhere the products of the brickfields and tile factories are of inferior quality.

61. The area of reserved forest is nearly 21,000 square miles, and the Forest Department supply yearly more than 21,000,000 cubic feet of fuel, and 3,500,000 cubic feet of timber, besides bamboos to the number of nearly 40,000,000. There is also a considerable area of privately owned forest land, which probably yields proportionately a larger amount of produce. The quantity of wood brought into Madras for fuel averages 110,000 tons a year, of which fully 90 per cent. is derived from privately owned plantations. There is no doubt that the forests are potential sources of supply, which can meet much larger demands than have ever been made on them, provided they are systematically worked for the industrial needs of the Province. The distillation of wood, and the conservation and utilization of the bye-products, might give rise to an industry of considerable magnitude. The Madras Forest Department obtains a gross revenue of more than 16 lakhs of rupees a year from minor forest produce, but the bulk of this is obtained by fees for fodder and grazing, and the only article of any considerable industrial importance is Tungédu or Avaram bark (*Cassia auriculata*), of which about two lakhs worth is collected every year and used in the local tanneries.

62. Since the mines and forests yield so little, the cultivation of the soil is the principal source of raw material for such primary industries as exist in Madras. The agricultural products of the Presidency are many and varied, and whilst some are put on the market without undergoing any industrial processes, others are subject to treatment which gives rise to industries mostly of a very simple character, although of considerable importance because the scale of operations is large.

63. The following tabular statement, extracted from the "Season and Crop Report" for 1910–11, shows in detail the area devoted to each of the crops grown in the Presidency which is subjected to preparatory processes of an industrial character before it is put on the market:—

	Area, 1910–11. ACRES.
Classification of area—	
(1) Forests	13,606,994
(2) Net area under cultivation ..	33,751,813
(3) Irrigated from Government and private canals, tanks, wells and other sources	9,922,934
Acreage under crops—	
Cereals—	
Rice	10,754,010
Oil-seeds—	
Linseed	14,131
Gingelly	815,100
Groundnut	934,135
Castor	497,823
Cocoanut	543,112
Acreage under crops—*cont.*	
Sugar—	
Sugarcane	94,879
Palmyra	88,740
Fibres—	
Cotton	2,317,045
Jute	...
Rubber	4,420
Dyes—	
Indigo	81,464
Drugs and narcotics—	
Coffee	49,097
Tea	16,737
Tobacco	218,315

64. The figures from Government villages are fairly accurate, those for zamindari villages are at the best approximations. It is only since 1907–08 that the zamindari villages have been included, and it is a matter of regret that the information regarding them has not been furnished in separate statements. Not only is comparison with previous figures now impossible, but the total figures for the Presidency in each year are made up of two returns, one of which is accurate, and the other only an approximation. Whilst deductions from the figures for Government villages can be made with tolerable certainty, the addition of the zamindari figures introduces an element of uncertainty and permits only of very broad and marked changes being clearly recognized.

65. The area under cultivation has expanded; also the area under irrigation, but to what extent is not accurately known. The following is a list of the more

important vegetable products which have to be subjected to preparatory processes before they are fit to be put on the market, though in some cases they are exported in their raw condition and subjected to these preliminary operations in the countries which import them : paddy, oil-seeds including linseed, gingelly, groundnut, castor and cocoanut; sugar, whether extracted from cane or palmyra; cotton, jute, rubber, indigo, coffee, tea and tobacco.

66. The industries to which these products give rise will be discussed in some detail later on. Here, it is only necessary to point out that during the past ten years the industrial tendencies in the Madras Presidency have mainly exhibited themselves in the supersession of hand labour by machinery driven by power derived from steam or internal combustion engines. The main factor has been the development of the use of the internal combustion engine, which enables small quantities of power to be generated both cheaply, and by methods which require no great amount of technical skill to supervise. In the deltaic districts of the Gódávari, Kistna and the Cauvery, which are almost wholly given up to the cultivation of paddy, the primitive methods of husking by hand have to a large extent been superseded by modern machinery. As the result of measures deliberately taken by Government, there has been a similar application of motive power on a small scale to the raising of water for irrigation; and finally as the result, partly of direct Government assistance, and partly as the result of progressive private effort, a number of what may be termed rural factories have come into existence, which use machine processes usually on the smallest scale that it is practicable to employ them. Such factories employ machinery for ginning cotton, crushing sugarcane, extracting palmyra fibre, pressing oil-seeds, and cutting timber. In the towns power is similarly being employed in an even more varied manner; as will subsequently appear when we come to discuss the development of the distribution of energy by electrical methods.

67. For the purposes of this chapter the information collected on the night of the census which is embodied in table XV-A of the Provincial Summary is made use of. From this table, extracts have been prepared which deal only with industrial occupations—*vide* table I appended. The total number of people so engaged is 2,075,709 or 5·01 per cent. of the total population. Owing to changes in the method of classification, a comparison with the figures in the census of 1901 is only possible in a certain number of sub-classes; and even in the broader divisions of classes there has been some transfer of sub-classes. Taking these figures as a basis for discussion of the industrial progress of the last ten years, we find that the occupation tables in a broad way reveal the effect of the developments going on in certain directions, and because they exhibit the anticipated results very clearly in instances which can be verified, they inspire confidence in their indications in cases which cannot be corroborated by other sources of information. We know that there has been, during the period under review, a strong movement in favour of the use of machinery for hulling paddy and cleaning rice, and this fact is reflected in the figures for rice pounders (group 56), who have decreased from 167,956 in 1901 to 125,674 in 1911, or by 25 per cent. Equally it is certain, from the returns regarding the consumption of yarn, that hand-loom weavers have improved their position slightly during the decade; though it is not possible to demonstrate this from the census returns, owing to the fact that the hand industry is now classed with a number of other branches of the cotton trade in group 22—cotton, spinning, sizing and weaving. The returns show that there has been a material falling off, since the numbers in 1901 were 623,783 and in 1911, 580,321, or a decrease over the whole group of 6·9 per cent. But it is probable that the whole of this occurs amongst the hand spinners, of whom there were 65,870 registered in 1901. The industry is now for all practical purposes extinct, and it is only likely to be returned as an occupation by a few old women. The almost complete elimination of the hand spinners from the returns would justify the assumption that there has been no change in the numbers engaged in the hand-loom industry. The increased outturn of the same is due to improvements in methods of working. Again, the falling off in the leather workers (group 33), who numbered in 1901, 50,795 and in 1911, 37,028—or a decrease of 27 per cent.—is accounted for by the high prices

which the raw material now realizes in the export trade, the increase in the value of which during the ten years has been 38·4 per cent.; in consequence of which ryots have in recent years largely taken to using iron buckets in place of leather for the numerous mhotes employed in lifting water from wells for irrigation. The increase in the number of silk weavers, (group 27), may be taken as an undoubted indication of a growing demand for more costly wearing apparel, and a sign of increasing wealth and prosperity among some sections of the community. This conclusion is further substantiated by the not insignificant increase in the numbers of the artizans and craftsmen who flourish when the community has money to spend on something more than the bare necessities of life; whilst the whole population has increased by 3·3 per cent. the number of silk weavers and spinners has increased by 21 per cent., jewellers by 15·6 per cent., tailors by 18·7 per cent., carpenters by 11·6, cabinet-makers by 134 per cent. and printers by 46·5 per cent.

68. An attempt is made for the first time to obtain information regarding the amount of power used in the mills, factories, and workshops; and though the returns are not quite complete, since there was no compulsion to furnish the information, yet they are very valuable as positive evidence of the present position, and supplemented by information obtained from the Inspector of Steam-Boilers and the Director of Industries, it has been possible to ascertain with a fair degree of precision the extent to which mechanical engineering and modern methods of generating power have been called in to assist hand labour.

69. The following statement, compiled from the returns furnished by the owners of factories, and from information specially collected from various sources to fill in gaps which were known to exist, shows the number of brake horse-power or indicated horse-power applied to various industries.

In respect to railway workshops the information furnished in the returns is very incomplete. The principal locomotive shops and carriage building sheds are situated at Perambore, Negapatam, and Podanur. There are also numerous smaller repair shops and running sheds where power is employed.

Industries.	Number of factories.	Horse power.					
		Steam.		Oil or gas.	Water power.	Electricity.	Total of 3, 5 and 6.
		Engines.	Boilers.				
1	2	3	4	5	6	7	8
GRAND TOTAL ..	*903*	*26,101*	*44,613*	*8,989*	*1,763*	*286*	*36,853*
Group I.—Growth of special products ...	*58*	*315*	*1,317*	*446*	*113*	...	*874*
Tea factories ...	22	38	172	307	64	...	409
Coffee plantations ...	17	25	...	120	49	...	194
Coffee curing works ...	17	252	938	19	...	...	271
Quinine factory ...	1	...	187	...	...	...	...
Saffron works ...	1	...	20	...	...	...	...
Group II.—Mines ...	*15*	*200*	*1,549*	*163*	...	...	*363*
Mica mines ...	9	51	182	24	...	...	75
Manganese mines ...	2	149	487	139	...	...	288
Gold mines ...	3	...	820	...	...	...	...
Magnesite works ...	1	..	60	...	...	...	...
Group III.—Quarries ...	*2*	*12*	*65*	...	...	...	*12*
Quarries ...	2	12	65	...	...	...	12
Group IV.—Textile industries, (a) Cotton.	*118*	*12,834*	*16,399*	*1,102*	*1,150*	...	*15,086*
Cotton ginning factories ...	51	1,040	2,750	180	...	...	1,220
Cotton presses ...	38	687	3,500	12	...	...	699
Cotton pressing and ginning factory ...	10	818	1,387	385	...	...	1,203
Cotton spinning mills ...	8	4,000	2,837	525	1,150	...	5,675
Cotton weaving mills ...	7	339	588	...	...	...	339
Cotton spinning and weaving mills ...	4	5,950	5,337	...	...	...	5,950

Industries.	Number of factories.	Horse-power. Steam. Engines.	Steam. Boilers.	Oil or gas.	Water power.	Electricity.	Total of 3, 5 and 6.
1	2	3	4	5	6	7	8
Group IV.—Textile industries, (*b*) Jute, hemp, etc.	*22*	*1,544*	*2,238*	*3*	...	...	*1,547*
Jute mills	6	1,300	1,310	...	...	...	1,300
Jute baling presses	2	55	142	...	...	...	55
Gold thread factory	1	...	35	...	...	...	...
Rope works	7	179	550	...	...	...	179
Fibre extracting works	1	...	...	3	...	...	3
Dye works	3	...	69	...	...	...	...
Coir matting factory	1	10	110	...	...	...	10
Cocoanut dessicating factory	1	...	22	...	...	...	...
Group V.—Leather and other industries.	*7*	*53*	*131*	*10*	...	...	*63*
Tanneries	4	29	64	10	...	...	39
Leather press	1	12	...	...	...	...	12
Bone crushing mills	2	12	67	...	...	...	12
Group VI.—Wood, etc., industries ...	*13*	*22*	*174*	*124*	...	*58*	*146*
Saw mills	3	...	137	36	...	50	36
Joinery works	9	22	15	88	...	8	110
Pencil factory	1	...	22	...	...	...	..
Group VII.—Metal industries	*41*	*407*	*4,948*	*406*	...	...	*813*
General engineering works	39	407	4,948	269	...	...	676
Aluminium factory	1	...	...	105	...	...	105
Tin plate works	1	...	...	32	...	...	32
Group VIII.—Glass and earthenware ...	*27*	*505*	*1,299*	*68*	...	...	*573*
Brick and tile works	26	498	1,282	68	...	...	566
Glass works	1	7	17	...	...	...	7
Group IX.—Industries connected with chemical products.	*34*	*236*	*1,352*	*165*	*500*	*22*	*901*
Chemical works	2	44	160	37	...	...	81
Cordite factory	1	...	472	...	500	...	500
Oil mills	11	77	346	50	...	15	127
Ærated waters	8	29	160	8	...	7	37
Salt refineries	4	40	52	10	...	...	50
Petroleum storage and refinery	8	46	162	60	...	...	106
Group X.—Food industries	*181*	*3,179*	*12,106*	*885*	...	...	*4,064*
Rice mills	149	1,949	7,161	540	...	...	2,489
Sugar mills	6	153	3,752	300	...	...	453
Municipal water works	14	1,046	866	15	...	...	1,061
Distilleries	3	...	120	6	...	...	6
Forage press	2	...	35	6	...	...	6
Tobacco factories	3	12	35	11	...	...	23
Breweries	3	19	117	7	...	...	26
Fish-curing yards	1	...	20	...	...	...	...
Group XI.—Industries of dress	*4*	*3*	*22*	*12*	...	...	*15*
Tailoring	1	...	...	4	...	...	4
Laundry	2	3	22	...	...	...	3
Boot and shoe factory	1	...	...	8	...	...	8
Group XIII.—Industries connected with building.	*2*	*900*	*570*	*10*	...	*5*	*910*
Cement works	2	900	570	10	...	5	910
Group XIV.—Construction of means of transport.	*18*	*247*	*35*	*615*	...	*115*	*862*
Garage	3	...	...	8	...	7	8
Coach building works	3	...	35	7	...	13	7
Railway workshops	10	247	...	600	...	...	847
Telegraph works	1	...	...	...	...	15	...
Ærial ropeway	1	...	...	...	...	80	...
Group XV.—Production and transmission of physical force.	*17*	*4,825*	*2,059*	*256*	...	*86*	*5,081*
Electric generating stations	13	4,810	1,877	252	...	...	5,062
Ice manufacture	4	15	182	4	...	...	19
Group XVI.—Industries of luxury ...	*27*	*83*	*200*	*198*	...	...	*281*
Printing presses	26	83	200	198	...	76	281
Jewellery shops	1	...	...	...	...	10	...
	317	*736*	*149*	*4,526*	...	...	*5,262*
Irrigation	317	36	149	4,186	...	...	4,222
Sewage pumping stations	...	700	...	340	...	...	1,040

70. Appendix II shows the same information distributed among the districts of the Presidency, whilst appendix III, which has been specially compiled in the office of the Director of Industries, gives all the information available regarding the application of power to the lifting of water for irrigation. From these returns it will be seen that the bulk of the power is still generated by steam-engines, but that internal combustion engines, whether using oil or gas, are rapidly coming into favour ; and it may be anticipated that ultimately they will be universally employed, except possibly for very large units of power such as are required by cotton mills, or in certain industries in which the use of steam power possesses special advantages ; as, for instance, in rice mills, where the paddy husk can be conveniently used for generating steam, but is not suitable for making gas, and in sugar works ; where large quantities of steam are required apart from power generation, and where in the refuse of cane crushing there is a large amount of fuel which can be conveniently burnt in boilers.

71. The statement of paragraph 69 has been prepared from information supplied by the Inspector of Steam-Boilers. Under the Boiler Act every steam generator working under pressure has to be licensed, and the information under this head may therefore be regarded as complete. It is not known however on what basis the horse-power of the boilers inspected has been calculated. From this statement it will be seen that the total horse-power of the steam-engines is 26,101, whilst the total horse-power of the boilers is 44,613. The difference is considerable but is easily accounted for—

(1) It is known that the list of steam-engines is incomplete ; no return, for instance, has been furnished by the Anantapur Gold mines where a boiler capacity of 820 horse-power has been licensed.

(2) The boiler capacity in most power plants is usually in excess of the engine power, so as to permit the boilers to be cut out in turn for cleaning purposes or repairs.

(3) In a variety of industrial operations steam is required for other than power purposes.

Making allowance for these items it may be assumed that the returns for engine power and boiler capacity agree tolerably well.

72. It may here be convenient to give in a tabular form a statement showing the total consumption of fuel in the Madras Presidency year by year under the following heads :—

Year.	Coal in tons.	Wood from Government forests in cubic feet.	Liquid fuel in gallons.
TOTAL ...	***3,674,382***	***194,344,521***	***3,039,018***
1901-02	276,099	14,920,279	......
1902-03	208,444	17,981,992	......
1903-04	230,298	16,927,342	......
1904-05	337,779	17,861,005	......
1905-06	331,002	19,047,180	260,205
1906-07	358,941	21,448,576	276,744
1907-08	425,968	22,563,872	350,218
1908-09	517,172	21,196,408	745,288
1909-10	532,491	19,140,625	563,897
1910-11	456,188	23,257,242	842,666

Note.—Figures for imports of liquid fuel are not given in the trade returns prior to 1905–06.

73. It may be assumed that the whole of the coal consumed in the Presidency is for the purpose of generating steam, and that the greater part is used on the railway systems. The figures for wood relate only to Government forests, and an unknown but a very large amount is also obtained from private plantations, chiefly on zamindari lands. On certain sections of the railways large quantities of wood are still burnt in the locomotives. The bulk of the steam power generated in the Presidency is in factories at no great distance from the railway, and coal is more largely consumed than might be expected, chiefly owing to the difficulty entailed by the imperfect transport arrangements in connection with the fuel supply from the forests. The bulk of the wood obtained from the forests is used for domestic purposes, and the increasing consumption serves to strengthen the contention that the material condition of the people is steadily improving.

74. Information regarding the importation of liquid fuel is only available for the last five years under review. It is partly used to make gas for lighting railway trains, but the greater portion is now employed to generate power in the oil-engines to which attention has already been drawn. Under the conditions prevailing in the Madras Presidency, where fuel of any kind is expensive, the internal combustion engine on account of its very high efficiency, especially in engines of small power, is already very largely employed, and is likely to become in time almost the sole source of power. It is not improbable that the development will be chiefly in the direction of gas plants using wood as fuel. It is certainly desirable that it should be so, as the forests can probably be made to yield about ten times as much fuel as they now do, whilst any other fuel must be obtained either from other provinces of India, or from other parts of the world. Coal comes chiefly from Bengal, either by rail or sea, although the Singareni coal field is now much more favourably situated for supplying Madras; but unfortunately most of its output goes west to serve the demands of Hyderabad and Bombay. Owing to the necessity for storing it in bulk, the supply of liquid fuel is at present a monopoly of the Asiatic Petroleum Company. Away from Madras, and especially in the neighbourhood of the forest tracts, suction gas plants worked either with wood or charcoal are undoubtedly the cheapest methods of generating power, and the tendency at the present day is to use oil engines for small units of power and gas-engines for large.

75. But very little use is made of water power. There are two large installations—one at Ambásamudram in the Tinnevelly district, where the water power is employed to drive a cotton mill, and the other in the Nilgiris where a hydro-electric station has been put up to supply power to the Government Cordite Factory at Aruvankád. Without storage works there can never be any large development of water power in this part of India, as even in the big rivers the hot weather supply becomes insignificant. The most important potential source of water power is at the outlet from the Periyár lake, where it is contended that, by a slight modification in the present system of supplying water for irrigation, 20,000 horse-power could be made available for industrial purposes, and would be readily taken up at Madura. Electricity still plays a comparatively unimportant part in the industrial life of Southern India. In the city of Madrás there is a central generating station with a maximum capacity of 3,890 kilowatts. There are also a number of small private installations chiefly to supply current for electric lighting and driving fans. Mention has already been made of the hydro-electric station in the Niligris, and besides that there are a few lighting plants in different parts of the Presidency. Two have been set up at the railway junctions of Tanjore and Trichinopoly. There are a few private installations, and most of the mills have installed a dynamo to supply the electric lighting necessary. The advantages of an electric supply are fully appreciated in Madras, and in many of the mufassal towns there is an opening for development in this direction, with gas or oil engines to drive the dynamos, and an overhead system of distribution. That much has not been done is probably due to the general prevalence of the idea that it will only pay to start work on a much larger scale than that for which capital is forthcoming.

76. *Trade.*—The following tabular statement shows the way in which the external trade of the Presidency has developed during the past ten years :—

Year.	Sea-borne trade.		oasting trade.		Rail-borne trade.		Total.	
	Imports.	Exports.	Imports.	Exports.	Imports.	Exports.	Imports.	Exports.
	RS. LAKHS.	RS. LAKHS.	RS. LAKHS.	RS. LAKHS.	RS. LAKHS.	RS. LAKHS.	RS. LAKHS.	RS. LAKHS.
1900–01	662	1,175	727	505	757	792	2,146	2,472
1901–02	773	1,185	660	470	685	592	2,118	2,247
1902–03	720	1,311	527	492	572	648	1,819	2,451
1903–04	751	1,509	511	490	681	629	1,943	2,628
1904–05	845	1,478	554	503	884	694	2,283	2,675
1905–06	777	1,560	635	530	1,082	776	2,494	2,866
1906–07	907	1,748	724	538	1,139	827	2,770	3,113
1907–08	1,025	1,877	671	580	1,121	868	2,817	3,325
1908–09	1,155	1,826	781	567	1,083	907	3,019	3,300
1909–10	946	1,952	1,016	493	1,060	891	3,022	3,336
1910–11	1,064	2,108	914	517	1,025	921	3,003	3,546

77. The principal feature has been the general rise in prices of food-grains, due to the operation of causes affecting, not India alone, but probably the whole of the world. From 1892 to 1900, a period of eight years, second-sort paddy could be obtained in Madras at an average rate of 18 measures per rupee. During the last four years the average rate has been 12 measures per rupee, or an increase in price of 50 per cent. This has of course been greatly to the advantage of the land-owning and cultivating classes, who have profited to a large extent at the expense of other sections of the community, but in so far as higher prices have been realized for many of the staple articles in the foreign export trade, the Presidency as a whole has benefited at the expense of the consuming countries.

78. The following tabular statement, extracted from the sea-borne trade and navigation returns, gives the average prices obtainable in the three years, 1900 to 1903, and in the three years, 1907 to 1910; and in the last column is shown the percentage of increase which is very important in the case of hides, skins, rice and coir—four of the most important articles exported from this Presidency :—

—	Average price, 1900–03.	Average price, 1907–10.	Percentage of increase.
Coffee per cwt.	49·52	46·33	– 6·44
Paddy "	2·56	3·45	34·8
Tea per lb.	0·633	0·656	3·66
Oils per gallon	1·426	1·506	5·61
Cotton per cwt.	26·7	28·32	6·31
Raw skins per cwt.	85·97	106·53	23·90
Tanned skins per cwt.	141·52	199·34	40·80
Tanned hides "	55·78	77·07	38·40
Seeds per cwt.	6·51	7·27	6·75
Rice "	5·32	6·35	19·35
Coir "	9·43	10·73	13·80

79. The import trade has grown *pari passu* with the export trade, and, although values have also risen, the advance in the price of manufactured goods has been small, compared with that which has obtained for nearly all the important items of produce exported. The result has been to improve materially the relative status of the agriculturist compared with the manufacturer, whether the latter be working in the country or abroad. The chief feature of the past ten years has been the development of industrial enterprise on a small scale, as exhibited by the establishment of small factories supplied with power to do work which was formerly done by hand. That this will continue to develop there seems to be but little doubt, as the high price of the staple foods grown in the country involves a corresponding rise in the wages of the working population, and rates are now so high that in almost every instance, if the scale of working be only large enough, the introduction of a power plant is invariably attended with considerable economy.

PART II.—DETAILS REGARDING SOME INDUSTRIES OF THE MADRAS PRESIDENCY.

80. The following notes on the principal industries of the Madras Presidency contain a brief summary of the information available regarding their development during the past ten years.

Aluminium industry.—Working in aluminium in India was first started at the Madras School of Arts at the end of March 1898, and in the course of a few years a considerable business was worked up which was transferred to a private company in September 1903. This company, which is known as the Indian Aluminium Company, has now a paid-up capital of Rs. 6,80,000, and it has successfully developed a large business, and possesses very completely equipped workshops in which the manufacturing operations are carried on by the most modern processes available for working in ductile metals. The following table shows the imports into India during the seven years ending April 1911 :—

Year.	Bombay.		Madras.		Cocanada.		Total.	
	CWT.	RS. LAKHS.	CWT.	RS. LAKHS.	CWT.	LAKHS.	CWT.	RS. LAKHS.
1904-05	..	...	890	1·05	...	...	890	1·05
1905-06	188	0·25	1,615	1·81	...	...	1,803	2·06
1906-07	429	0·71	1,535	2·18	...	...	1,964	2·89
1907-08	1,126	1·73	1,570	1·89	...	...	2,696	3·62
1908-09	1,158	1·03	2,275	1·91	301	0·27	3,734	3·21
1909-10	5,373	4·04	4,477	3·46	1,898	1·52	11,740	9·02
1910-11	7,875	6·38	2,336	1·78	1,573	1·08	11,784	9·24

81. The large imports into Bombay are due to the establishment of factories working on somewhat similar lines to that of the Indian Aluminium Company, but the imports into Cocanada are wholly worked up for sale by a large number of small hand working factories which have grown up in Rajahmundry, Ellore, Bezwáda, and other towns in the Northern Circars. The very rapid growth during the last two or three years is due to the low price at which the raw material in the shape of ingots and sheets can now be obtained from Europe and America. Aluminium vessels are consequently cheaper than those made of brass and copper, and the demand is steadily increasing.

82. *Brick and tile-making.*—The number of persons engaged in this industry in 1901 was 9,337, and in 1911, 11,229—an increase of 20 per cent. In Madras, and in the districts of South Canara and Malabar, there are a number of factories engaged in this industry, but elsewhere it is carried on in the very primitive fashion to meet the immediate local needs. Only on the West Coast are suitable clays to be found, and the modern development of the industry is due to the enterprise of the Basel Mission. Foreign exports, chiefly to Ceylon, average slightly over one lakh of rupees per annum, whilst the coasting trade, largely to Bombay, ranges between six and seven lakhs of rupees per annum. From appendix II it appears that there are 23 factories employing power, and in addition there are a considerable number in which all the operations are carried on by hand.

83. *Cotton.*—The cotton trade in its various branches employs more capital and gives employment to a larger number of people than any other industry carried on in the Presidency. The following statement shows the area on which cotton was grown during the last ten years, also the weight and value of the cotton exported :—

Year.	Area under cultivation in acres.	Export of raw cotton.	
		Quantity in tons.	Value.
			RS.
1901-02	1,351,200	20,558	1,12,01,272
1902-03	1,580,900	35,826	1,63,21,810
1903-04	1,665,000	44,956	2,56,52,392
1904-05	1,755,000	37,710	2,53,62,760
1905-06	1,802,899	40,023	2,28,90,047
1906-07	1,742,416	34,019	2,21,43,742
1907-08	2,159,567	52,620	3,39,10,066
1908-09	1,989,015	41,056	2,33,43,571
1909-10	2,028,538	47,169	3,18,17,443
1910-11	2,317,045	48,599	4,14,18,813

84. In 1901 there were 24,089 people engaged in cotton-ginning, cleaning, and pressing, and in 1911, 32,553—an increase of 35·1 per cent. During the period there has been a large increase in the amount of ginning done by machinery, and a corresponding decrease in hand-ginning. The marginal table shows the distribution of ginning factories and cotton presses throughout the Presidency, but it is admittedly incomplete, as there are now a considerable number of small factories employing two or three gins driven usually by oil-engines, from which no returns have been received.

District.	Number of factories.
Gódávari ...	4
Kistna ...	4
Guntúr ...	23
Bellary ...	17
Anantapur ...	4
Coimbatore ...	5
Trichinopoly ...	1
Madura ...	1
Rámnád ...	10
Tinnevelly ...	13
Kurnool ...	11
Cuddapah ...	6
	99

85. Through the operations of the Agricultural Department, chiefly by the establishment of seed farms, considerable improvements have been effected in the quality of the cotton grown in certain areas, but the most noteworthy development is in connection with the cultivation of a species of an American upland cotton known as Cambodia cotton. This crop grows best on garden land, as it requires occasional irrigation. The yield is very large and of high quality, and so far it has proved an extremely profitable crop, with the natural result that its cultivation is increasing with extreme rapidity. It is estimated that the outturn in 1911 was not less than 25,000 bales of 500 lb. each. Of the cotton grown in the Presidency, part is manufactured into yarn in the local mills, and the balance exported. The trade has been steadily growing in importance, and has now reached very large dimensions, as shown by the following figures which relate to the exports for 1910–11 :—

Countries to which exported.	RS.
British Empire—	
To United Kingdom ...	1,01,84,101
„ Ceylon ...	2,04,974
„ Hongkong ...	1,16,100
Foreign Countries—	
To Russia—Northern Ports ...	21,672
„ Sweden ...	2,46,956
„ Germany—Free Ports ...	32,16,238
„ Holland ...	7,81,869
„ Belgium ...	74,94,041
„ France ...	10,62,923
„ Spain ...	3,66,235
„ Italy ...	22,98,474
„ Austria-Hungary—Free Ports ...	18,13,214
„ Indo-China (including Cochin-China, Cambodia, etc.).	3,28,640
„ Japan ...	1,32,81,406
Coasting Trade—	
Bengal { Calcutta ...	12,74,418
Bengal { Other Ports ...	...
Bombay { Bombay ...	8,14,487
Bombay { Other Ports ...	163
British Ports within the Presidency ...	94,932
Pondicherry ...	1,66,822
Total ...	4,37,69,665

86. *Cotton spinning.*—Hand-spinning is still carried on as a cottage industry in some remote parts of the Presidency, but it has long ceased to be of any commercial importance, and is now merely a relic of an industrial system whcih has passed away. The mill industry in Madras as compared with Bombay is not highly developed. The following statistics show the progress which has been made since 1881.

Statement showing progress of the mill industry since 1881.

Number of	1881.	1891.	1901.	1907.	1908-09.	1909-10.
Mills	3	8	11	11	11	12
Looms	...	555	1,735	1,748	1,962	2,023
Spindles	48,000	173,000	288,000	308,000	319,000	339,500
Hands employed daily	1,400	5,900	12,600	16,740	18,030	18,860

87. From this it will be seen that the number of power looms at work in the Presidency is small, and the weaving trade is still mainly carried on with hand-looms. Appendix V to this chapter has been compiled with a view to ascertain the quantity of yarn consumed in the hand looms in this Presidency. The yarn used in the Presidency is either of local manufacture or imported. As the amount of yarn spun by hand may be neglected, the output of the spinning mills furnishes exact information as to the quantity of yarn manufactured. The imports are either direct from foreign sources of supply, or by coasting steamers, which carry both Indian yarn and foreign yarn originally imported into other parts of India. The rail-borne traffic includes both Indian yarn and foreign yarn imported mainly from Bombay. The sum total of these figures furnishes the quantity of yarn brought into the Presidency each year. The table also shows how this yarn is disposed of, partly by foreign export trade, partly by coastal trade to other parts of India, and partly by rail-borne trade across the land frontiers. The returns from the weaving sheds give the quantity of yarn consumed by the power looms, and the balance is the yarn worked up by the hand-looms.

88. An examination of this table in detail shows a large but irregular development of the export trade in coarse yarns, together with a big increase in the importation of foreign yarn, which is mostly of counts higher than those spun in Indian mills. In the three years from 1900 to 1903, the hand-looms used 171,935,000 lb. of yarn; whilst in the three years from 1907 to 1910 the quantity taken was 179,572,000 lb.—an increase of 4·5 per cent. This by itself would indicate some slight retrogression of the hand-loom industry, since the population during the same period has increased by 8·3 per cent.; but if account be taken of the fact that between the periods 1900—1903 and 1907—1910 the increase in the foreign yarns consumed in the Presidency amounted to 52 per cent., it will be seen that there has been a considerable amount of progress. The substitution of fine yarn for coarse means much extra work for the hand weavers, and a proportionate increase in the value of their outturn.

89. From information furnished in the Statistical Atlas of the Madras Presidency it appears that in 1900 there were 167,806 hand-looms in the Presidency distributed through the districts as shown in the following table :—

District.	Number of looms.	District.	Number of looms.
Ganjám	10,320	Salem	16,341
Vizagapatam	1,461	Coimbatore	15,040
Gódávari	5,407	Trichinopoly	4,515
Kistna	12,203	Tanjore	9,598
Kurnool	8,146	Madura	7,551
Bellary	9,284	Tinnevelly	10,196
Anantapur	2,299	Malabar	6,328
Cuddapah	11,505	South Canara	1,317
Nellore	8,325		
Chingleput	11,255	Total ...	167,806
South Arcot	6,964		
North Arcot	9,751		

90. No recent attempt has been made to estimate the number of hand-looms in the Presidency, but it is not probable that there has been any great change in the numbers. Through efforts fostered by Government there has, however,

been a marked development in the use of the fly-shuttle slay, which increases the output of each loom on an average by not less than 50 per cent. All over the country in small numbers weavers may now be found using this type of hand-loom, but on the East Coast in the Northern Circars the transformation has been on a big scale. Recently Government deputed a special officer to investigate the matter, and in 89 villages 6,528 fly-shuttle looms were actually counted. It is estimated that the total number is not less than 10,000, and indeed it is put at a very much higher figure than this by merchants engaged in the trade. A review of all the evidence available leads to the conclusion that the hand-loom industry is holding its own, and that the general increase in prosperity is leading to an increased demand for its finer products. This is borne out by the marked increase in the number of hand-loom weavers in such centres of fine weaving as Kumbakónam and Madura. In the former town the increase has been from 465 to 1,824, and in the latter from 9,353 to 15,117, the average increase in the two being 60·8 per cent.

91. The condition of the hand-loom weavers is generally assumed to have steadily deteriorated owing to the effect of competition, and of indirect evidence there is plenty in support of this idea. The weavers themselves complain that their condition has steadily become worse, that they have to work harder and that now the coarse weavers, even by the most unremitting toil, are only able to make a bare livelihood. The present census is the fifth that has been taken, and if the classification of the returns had been uniform throughout it would have been possible to state definitely whether the number of weavers was increasing or decreasing; but unfortunately there have been many changes in the methods of grouping trades or branches of a trade at each census, and it is difficult to arrive at any certain conclusion. The following tabular statement has been compiled to show what comparable returns are available since 1871 regarding those employed in the more important branches of the cotton trade :—

—	—	1871.		1881.		1891.		1901.		1911.	
Cotton-ginning, cleaning and pressing.	Mill	...	24,714	...	...	...	15,041	1,961	12,643	1,824	20,067
	Hand	24,714				15,041		10.682		18,243	
Cotton manufactures.	...	...	. .	...	188,157	...	...	...	...	...	...
Cotton-spinning and weaving.	Mill	...	...	...	...	...	7,306	6,851	6,851	...	16,615
Spinners	Hand	...	...	...	...	7,306		6,414	6,414	...	368,509
Weavers	Hand.	...	376,561	..	196,610	...	365,112	...	383,132	..	

92. From an examination of this table it is clear that in 1871 there were 376,561 weavers (males), but in 1881, 188,157 males are returned as cotton manufacturers, and the weavers only number 196,610. The total comes to 384,767, and probably includes cotton-ginners and cotton-spinners. We may assume approximately that these numbered about 20,000, and that therefore the number of weavers in 1881 was slightly over 360,000, showing a probable decrease of 15,000 weavers in the ten years. This result would not be unexpected remembering the havoc caused by the great famine of 1877. In 1891 the weavers are returned as 365,112, and in 1901 as 383,132. So far as can be ascertained these numbers are comparable, and would show a slight increase in the actual number of weavers. The figures for 1911 are reported as 385,124, but this includes all mill hands and persons engaged in power factories connected with spinning and weaving. The number of these latter is 16,615, and deducting these, we obtain that the number of hand weavers in 1911, 368,509. I think, therefore, we may safely accept the following conclusion: That in the last forty years the number of hand-loom weavers has remained practically stationary, but that owing to stress of competition they now turn out a larger amount of finished goods than was formerly the case; that is to say, the majority of them have to work harder to make a bare living. One might also

add that their lot would probably be greatly improved if they could be induced to accept outside assistance, which can only be effectively rendered by the establishment of small hand-loom weaving factories. The individual weaver suffers because he is still trying to carry on a complex series of operations without recognition of the advantages of sub-division of labour.

93. *Coir.*—The cocoanut palm is grown all over the Presidency, but it is chiefly on the West Coast in the districts of Malabar and South Canara that the manufacture of coir is carried on. The extraction of the fibre is mainly the work of women, and during the past ten years the number engaged in this trade has largely increased. Groups 24 and 25 in the occupation tables include all the workers in this industry together with those engaged in the extraction of other fibres, of which, however, only palmyra fibre is of any importance. In 1901 the number of workers were 50,202 and in 1911, 63,046—an increase of 25 per cent. The internal trade in coir products is not very large and each district probably supplies its own requirements. The export trade is from the ports of Calicut and Cochin, where numerous presses have been set up for baling the yarn. Weaving, mat-making, and rope-making, are also carried on to some extent both by European and Indian firms. The following statements furnish statistical information regarding the progress and volume of the trade during the past ten years :—

Exports of coir and cordage for ten years.

Year.	Coir.		Cordage.	
	Quantity.	Value.	Quantity.	Value.
	TONS.	RS.	TONS.	RS.
1901–02	19,151	35,81,685	652	1,19,430
1902–03	21,703	43,70,163	895	1,53,054
1903–04	23,664	46,78,050	741	1,34,591
1904–05	25,073	50,63,824	519	90,062
1905–06	26,755	53,01,459	771	1,37,696
1906–07	27,635	55,24,154	866	1,43,352
1907–08	25,072	53,09,131	381	71,381
1908–09	28,437	61,90,471	472	87,947
1909–10	33,621	72,27,705	779	1,44,319
1910–11	31,730	68,69,887	653	1,17,156

Statement showing the countries to which coir and cordage were exported in 1910–11.

Countries to which sent.	Coir.		Cordage and rope.	
	Quantity.	Value.	Quantity.	Value.
	TONS.	RS.	TONS.	RS.
TOTAL ...	*31,730*	*68,69,887*	*653*	*1,17,156*
United Kingdom	8,234	16,92,223	117	24,540
Germany	10,516	22,76,516	2	608
Belgium	2,808	5,78,431	...	...
France	2,626	5,56,130	...	...
Holland	2,985	6,45,422	..	...
United States	1,594	4,21,468	...	...
Turkey	175	26,099	179	29,339
Arabia	...	...	6	983
Persia	32	4,658	46	7,704
Other foreign countries	2,228	5,09,842	68	12,314
Other Provinces of British India.	532	1,59,098	235	41,668

94. *Dyeing.*—From the census returns this industry would appear to be in a decaying condition, as in 1901 it supported 10,061 people, and in 1911 only 7,208—a decrease of 28·3 per cent. The statistics of the trade, however, tell quite a different tale. In the following statement the value of the imports of alizarine and aniline dyes is given for the last ten years :—

Year.	Value. RS.
1901–02	11,47,479
1902–03	11,79,393
1903–04	13,56,255
1904–05	13,21,271
1905–06	13,60,300
1906–07	12,39,827
1907–08	16,64,534
1908–09	14,30,100
1909–10	15,75,533
1910–11	15,42,065

95. The average values during the last three years show an increase of 38 per cent. on the values of the first three years. This is very largely due to the, expansion of the dye-houses attached to the Buckingham and Carnatic Mills in Madras, and to development of the turkey red industry in Madura. In the Madras mills the industry is run on modern lines and under the control of expert chemists. In Madura it may be regarded as an indigenous industry, modified for working with chemical dyes. The modern phase of the industry is due to Mr. L. K. Tulsiram, a Souráshtra of Madura, who was taught the methods of dyeing cotton yarn with alizarine dyes in the laboratories of the Badische Aniline Fabriker in Bombay. Tuticorin is the port through which the bulk of the dye-stuffs intended for Madura passes, and in 1901–02 the imports were valued at Rs. 1,51,519 and in 1910–11 at Rs. 5,26,795. A rough estimate places the outturn of the Madura dyed yarn at about 2,000 bales per month, equivalent to an annual output of nearly 10 million pounds. Dyeing is carried on in a small way in almost every place where there are weavers, but the industry is not in a flourishing condition, chiefly owing to the lack of technical knowledge on the part of the dyers.

96. *Indigo.*—In 1900–01 the area under indigo was over 250,000 acres, and the production of the dye was estimated to be 46,100 cwt., whilst by 1910–11 the area had dwindled down to 72,000 acres, with a yield of 12,600 cwt. It is hardly necessary to point out that this is due to the competition of artificially-produced indigo, and it seems not unlikely that the cultivation of the plant for the purpose of producing dye-stuffs will in time cease altogether. This has been the fate of madder. In recent years great efforts have been made to improve the methods of cultivation of the plant, and of extraction of the dye-stuff, and with a considerable measure of success; but militating against these improvements are corresponding developments in the manufucture of synthetic indigo, whilst finally the increased value of other agricultural products has in no small measure facilitated the transfer of indigo plantations to other forms of cultivation.

97. *Jute.*—The real jute (*Corchorus capsularis*) is not grown in this Presidency, but what is locally known as "jute" is the "Deccan hemp" (*Hibiscus cannabinus*), which is largely grown on red soils in the Northern Circars. There are two jute mills in the Presidency, one of which at Chitavalsa, near Bimlipatam, was established in 1867, and contains 3,328 spindles and 154 looms, and gives employment to 1,180 work people. The second mill was established at Ellore in 1907, and is equipped with 1,704 spindles and 80 looms and now employs 630 workers. The local market for gunnies is said to absorb the whole production of these two mills. There is a considerable export of raw jute, chiefly from the coast ports of the Northern Circars. From 1901 to 1906 it averaged Rs. 10·48 lakhs per annum and from 1906 to 1911 Rs. 14·06 lakhs per annum.

98. *Leather.*—The census returns are included in groups 32 and 33 of order 7. The number of persons engaged in the manufacture of leather has increased from 9,268 to 13,754, or by 48·3 per cent., but the number of persons engaged in the

manufacture of leather articles has decreased from 50,795 to 37,028, or by 27·1 per cent. As already explained this result is partly due to the rise in value of leather, which has led to its being replaced by iron as the material from which *kavalai* buckets are made. There is also some tendency to the concentration of thie industry in factories, which is leading to the gradual extinction of the village *chuckler*, and a corresponding increase in the efficiency of production. Group 69 gives the number of boot, shoe and sandal makers, and these have increased from 111,585 to 123,253, or by 10·4 per cent. The leather trade in the Madras Presidency is of great importance as the following tabular statement in respect to the export trade will show :—

Year.	Raw hides and skins.		Tanned hides and skins.	
	CWT.	RS.	CWT.	RS.
1901–02	87,049	67,71,779	224,864	2,09,96,426
1902–03	76,135	52,08,957	218,846	2,33,89,128
1903–04	67,578	41,93,402	223,572	2,37,19,700
1904–05	97,924	71,80,409	215,702	2,30,27,813
1905–06	142,116	1,10,67,166	284,198	2,89,71,331
1906–07	125,173	1,08,19,204	309,955	3,62,94,296
1907–08	85,081	73,94,568	224,908	3,07,79,225
1908–09	85,618	62,13,990	261,961	3,42,86,921
1909–10	76,970	74,93,746	257,970	3,24,67,993
1910–11	106,562	72,09,838	242,060	3,35,23,358

99. The exports of raw hides are insignificant, but since 1898 there has been a large demand, chiefly on the part of American tanners, for raw skins. This is partly due to fiscal regulations, whereby raw skins are admitted free of duty, whilst tanned and dressed skins are excluded by prohibitive import duties. The introduction of the chrome process is also partly responsible for the demand for raw skins. It should be clearly understood that the whole of export trade in the Madras Presidency is in tanned hides and skins, and not in finished goods. The hides are tanned, but not curried ; and the skins are tanned, but not dressed. The returns from the Inspector of Factories show that, out of 18 tanneries in India employing over fifty hands, 14 aresituated in the Madras Presidency, but all the Madras tanneries are small compared with those situated at Cawnpore and at Sion near Bombay. No information is available as to the number of tanneries in the Presidency, and the state of the trade may be best gauged by the increased value of the exports. Hide tanneries are generally much smaller than those devoted to skins. The capital outlay involved in setting up a tannery, even of the largest kind, is not much and there are numerous small tanneries in which a few hundred rupees will probably cover the whole cost. As a natural consequence work is carried on in the tanneries very irregularly, all the more so as the tanners themselves have generally very little capital, and are almost entirely dependent upon advances from the export merchants wherewith to buy skins or hides to carry on their business. Tanning is carried on in the Madras Presidency in a very primitive way, and the first step towards improving matters was taken by the Madras Government when they sanctioned in 1903 the experiments in chrome tanning, which eventually led to the establishment of the Government Chrome Tannery at Sembiem. A considerable measure of success attended these pioneer operations, and eventually in 1910, two large private chrome tanneries having been established in the south of India, the Government factory was sold. The locally made chrome leather is mainly used for boots, shoes and sandals, and for water buckets, and *kavalai* trunks ; but the demand in the latter direction has not expanded so rapidly as it might have done owing to the introduction of iron water buckets.

100. *Manures.*—The demand for artificial manures in this Presidency has hitherto been mainly confined to planters, but the ryot is now, in a small way, beginning to appreciate the advantage of using suitable fertilizers, and the industry, though still a small one, shows signs of expansion. At the same time the following table shows that the foreign export trade is growing, and that the Presidency is parting

with large quantities of valuable manure, which could, with very much greater profit, be employed in increasing the productivity of the soil :—

Years.	Animal bones.		Fish manure.		Oil cake.		Other kinds.		Total.	
	Quantity.	Value.	Quantity.	Value.	Quantity.	Value.	Quantity.	Value.	Quantity.	Value.
	TONS.	RS.	TONS.	RS.	TONS.	RS.	TONS.	RS.	TONS.	RS.
1901–02	2,973	1,10,983	...	...	...	...	766	29,076	3,739	1,40,059
1902–03	3,270	1,29,250	...	...	...	...	2,861	1,15,435	6,131	2,44,685
1903–04	3,752	1,47,742	...	...	...	...	2,996	92,584	6,748	2,40,326
1904–05	3,792	1,65,422	...	...	...	...	7,322	4,74,634	11,114	6,40,056
1905–06	7,228	3,43,218	1,771	72,134	27,717	10,59,223	1,558	97,348	38,274	15,71,923
1906–07	11,154	5,55,595	7,694	2,30,571	38,767	26,48,395	949	52,313	58,564	35,86,874
1907–08	8,044	4,31,829	16,050	7,50,452	24,631	15,06,700	627	43,511	49,352	27,32,492
1908–09	10,723	5,58,428	8,171	3,10,677	30,046	18,39,537	1,666	1,84,861	50,606	28,93,503
1909–10	10,959	6,10,935	8,532	3,26,608	22,565	13,76,433	2,286	2,61,636	44,333	25,75,612
1910–11	8,181	4,26,994	14,061	6,30,745	23,690	15,06,866	2,286	2,62,327	48,218	28,26,932

101. The marginal figures furnished by Messrs. Parry & Co. in relation to the output of their works at Ranipet are interesting as showing the slow but steady growth in the local use of manures.

Year.	Fertiliser	Bone meal grists.
	TONS.	TONS.
1905	...	2,808
1906	194	2,035
1907	480	2,810
1908	578	4,498
1909	576	6,424
1910	1,314	3,855
1911	1,547	4,508

Ten firms are altogether reported to be engaged in the manufacture of artificial manures, and on the West Coast the preparation of fish manures is an industry of considerable importance.

102. *Metal workers.*—Under this head may be included all the artizans working in the non-ferrous metals, excluding gold and silver. Their numbers have increased from 19,578 to 20,857. The raw material with which these men work is mainly imported from abroad, and it is impossible to reconcile the small increase in the number of men employed in the trade with the very large increase in the imports shown in the following tabular statement: an examination of which discloses the fact that, whilst the imports of copper and yellow metal for the three years from 1900 to 1903 amounted to 74,444 cwt., in the three years ending March 1911 they amounted to 205,280 cwt. Similary the imports of tin have increased from 4,691 cwt. to 10,226 cwt. The expansion of the aluminium industry has already been noted. The increased consumption of these metals is a very certain indication of a widely diffused increase in the wealth of the people, as among the poorer classes the substitution of metal vessels for earthernware is an infallible sign of prosperity :—

Year.	Copper including yellow metal.		German silver.		Lead.		Tin.		Total.	
	Quantity.	Value.	Quantity.	Value.	Quantity.	Value.	Quantity.	Value.	Quantity.	Value.
	CWT.	RS.	CWT.	RS.	CWT.	RS.	CWT.	RS.	CWT.	RS.
1900–01 ...	14,889	8,14,706	1,094	1,09,627	8,486	1,36,913	1,060	1,04,886	25,529	11,66,132
1901–02 ...	26,528	13,87,961	2,953	2,90,402	10,498	1,45,837	1,763	1,66,892	41,742	19,90,592
1902–03 ...	33,027	15,70,440	4,082	3,53,262	8,050	1,03,266	1,868	1,64,334	47,027	21,91,302
1903–04 ...	34,501	16,03,829	3,254	2,93,257	9,554	1,18,409	2,286	2,19,406	49,595	52,34,901
1904–05 ..	44,628	20,54,219	2,538	1,89,940	9,351	1,22,479	2,104	2,02,985	58,621	25,69,623
1905–06 ...	21,443	11 07,131	1,678	1,31,554	10,599	1,30,889	1,355	1,49,451	35,075	15,18,525
1906–07 ...	21,205	12,54,411	1,295	1,05,276	6,197	94,897	998	1,42,065	29,695	15,96,649
1907–08 ...	30,691	20,61,635	2,337	2,22,255	8,153	1,33,009	2,049	2,62,587	43,230	26,79,486
1908–09 .	58,523	31,43,707	1,641	1,26,959	13,867	1,95,191	3,783	3,97,473	77,814	38,63,330
1909–10 ...	68,861	33,63,531	2,324	1,65,112	11,740	1,60,732	3,091	3,36,727	86,016	40,26,102
1910–11 ...	77,896	37,93,109	1,943	1,42,774	14,090	1,97,161	3,352	4,12,122	97,281	45,45,166

103. *Iron trade.*—The number of large engineering works in the Presidency is small. The locomotive and carriage building works of the Madras and Southern Mahratta Railway at Perambore and those of the South Indian Railway at Negapatam, besides smaller repair shops and running sheds at the more important junctions, represent the only big developments in this direction. The Public Works Department has engineering shops in Madras, Bezwáda, and Dowlaishwaram ; and there are five or six private firms, mostly under European management, which supply all the local engineering requirements. Repair work, and the manufacture of structural iron work, cover the bulk of the business done in this Presidency, but recently certain classes of machinery largely used in this country have been manufactured locally. No useful statistics regarding the state of the industry can be furnished, as the sea-borne trade returns on private account are altogether swamped by the inclusion with them of the railway imports. All that can be said is that during the last decade there has developed throughout the country a distinct tendency to substitute machinery for hand labour, wherever the work can be sufficiently concentrated to render it possible to find adequate employment to keep the machinery continuously at work.

104. *Sugar.*—In this Presidency sugar is obtained both from sugarcane and from palmyras. The area under sugarcane in 1910–11 is reported to have been 94,879 acres and the area under palmyras 88,740. The changes in the classification of the census returns prevent any comparison with the figures of the 1901 census. Group 62 shows that there are 18,212 people engaged in the manufacture of sugar, molasses and gur. Of modern sugar factories there are only five in the Presidency, three of which are under the management of Messrs. Parry & Co., the most important being at Nellikuppam in the South Arcot district, with an average outturn of 12,000 tons of sugar per annum. In addition to the local supplies of sugarcane from the surrounding villages, large quantities of jaggery are imported from Java, and converted into refined sugar, whilst, as by-products, spirits and carbonic acid gas are largely manufactured, the average outturn of spirits being 705,217 gallons of London Proof spirits per annum. Recently great efforts have been made to encourage the local cultivation of the cane, and from an average of about 600 acres per annum it has increased this year to considerably over 2,000 acres. In very few parts of the country is the cultivation of sugarcane sufficiently concentrated to justify the establishment of large factories for crushing the cane and converting it into finished products. There are but few individuals who cultivate a large extent of cane, and, in the absence of any co-operative movement among the cane growers, all operations connected with the industry are of a very primitive type, and there is not only a large waste of raw material, but the expenses connected with its manufacture into jaggery are unnecessarily high. As it is probable that the attention now being paid to the sugar industry will lead to considerable developments in the not distant future, the following tabular statement has been prepared showing the area under both sugarcane and palmyras in each district for the year 1910–11:—

Acreage in 1910–11.

District.	Sugar.	Palmyra.	District.	Sugar.	Palmyra.
PRESIDENCY TOTAL ...	*94,879*	*88,740*			
Ganjám	5,598	241	Chittoor	9,047	2,614
Vizagapatam	25,118	216	North Arcot	2,709	2,411
Gódávari	6,973	214	Salem	2,290	870
Kistna	575	5,663	Coimbatore	10,489	2,437
Guntúr	2	3.079	Trichinopoly	8,037	72
Kurnool	599	...	Tanjore	525	1,225
Bellary	10,493	103	Madura	2,304	663
Anantapur	2,825	2,355	Rámnád	306	9,605
Cuddapah	164	937	Tinnevelly	199	43,452
Nellore	121	2,258	Malabar	61	7,736
Chingleput	42	941	South Canara	1,826	280
South Arcot...	5,075	1,368	The Nilgiris...	1	...

105. *Silk.*—Sericulture is only carried on in the Kollegál taluk of the Coimbatore district, where the area under mulberries fluctuates from year to year for reasons which I have not been able to ascertain. This is clearly shown by the following figures for the last ten years :—

	Acs.
1901–02	8,902
1902–03	8,485
1903–04	9,345
1904–05	12,315
1905–06	13,994
1906–07	11,817
1907–08	14,793
1908–09	12,242
1909–10	10,937
1910–11	9,112

106. No information is available regarding the value of the outturn of silk, but it is insufficient for the needs of the Presidency, and there are large rail-borne imports from Mysore, of which only about 10 per cent. are exported *viâ* Madras, the remainder being used by the silk weavers of the Presidency. The following tabular statement gives the values of imports of raw silk and piece-goods during the last ten years :—

Year.	Raw silk.			Piece-goods.		
	Foreign.	Indian.	Total.	Foreign.	Indian.	Total.
	Rs.	Rs.	Rs.	Rs.	Rs.	Rs.
1901–02	1,365	34,72,339	34,73,704	2,637	1,98,537	2,01,174
1902–03	1,716	32,44,705	32,46,421	22,613	2,41,746	2,64,359
1903–04	3,569	35,15,180	35,18,749	679	1,69,403	1,70,082
1904–05	3,567	28,88,908	28,92,475	...	47,939	47,939
1905–06	8,673	39,37,343	39,46,016	...	75,572	75,572
1906–07	5,704	37,03,295	37,08,999	1,088	12,145	13,233
1907–08	6,384	48,18,815	48,25,199	4,737	15,583	20,320
1908–09	29,526	36,93,677	37,23,203	9,900	27,732	37,632
1909–10	68,235	32,98,533	33,66,768	11,711	2,74,482	2,86,193
1910–11	62,233	22,31,440	92,93,673	7,919	2,417	10,336

107. Apart from the transit trade through Madras, the exports are of insignificant value. From the occupation tables it appears that under group 27 the number of silk spinners and weavers has increased from 30,423 to 36,854, or by 21·1 per cent. It must not however be imagined that any very large percentage of these weavers are engaged in the manufacture of pure silk fabrics, as the majority of them only use silk for the borders of the cloths which they manufacture, or, in the case of women's cloths, unions are made consisting of cotton warps with silk wefts. There is, however, a certain amount of silk brocade manufactured, heavily decorated with gold lace. These cloths probably represent the highest development of the weavers' art in Southern India, and are chiefly made in the Tanjore district.

108. *Wood.*—Workers in wood, such as sawyers, carpenters, turners, cabinet-makers, etc., form an important section of the artizan population, and are enumerated in groups 36 and 74. Sawyers, carpenters, and joiners have increased from 131,244 to 146,583, or by 11·6 per cent., whilst cabinet-makers and carriage builders have increased from 805 to 1,885. This is a trade in which female labour is never employed, and the inclusion of 7,515 women must be regarded as a mistake due either to a number of dependents having been enumerated as actual workers, or to the inclusion of coolies working in conection with house-building and so forth.

The principal sources of supply of timber are the forests of the Presidency, and imports from Burma, which consist almost entirely of teak. Compared with most countries of the world, in India timber is very expensive, owing not so much to the shortage of supply, as to the inferior quality of the wood yielded by the timber trees in the forests. Teak is unquestionably for general construction work the best wood grown, but the local supply is very small, and most of it is imported from Burma. The chief defects of Indian timbers are their great weight, extreme hardness and rough fibrous structure. The largest saw mills in the Presidency were situated at Calicut, but they have recently gone into liquidation, and in various parts of the country, where large supplies of timber are dealt with, either of local growth or imported, small saw mills, worked by steam or oil-engines or, in the case of Madras, by electro-motors, have been established. There is probably room for development in this direction, as cutting up timber by hand is not only expensive, but involves a considerable waste, owing to the unnecessary amount of saw-dust produced through irregular sawing. Under European supervision, and in some few instances without it, the wood workers are capable of turning out excellent work, examples of which may be found chiefly among carriage builders and cabinet-makers. The wood carvers of the Presidency enjoy a high reputation, but, owing to their inability to adapt their art to modern requirements, the demand for their work is very much smaller than it otherwise might be.

109. *Vegetable oils.*—The cultivation of crops yielding oil as the principal product is carried on very extensively in most districts of the Presidency. Appendix VI furnishes information as to the area under each crop in each district of the Presidency. Of the produce a large amount is consumed locally, but the export trade to other parts of India and to other countries is very large and has been growing rapidly in recent years. Group 53 of the census returns relates to people engaged in the manufacture of vegetable and mineral oils. The numbers have decreased from 27,170 in 1901 to 25,095 in 1911. This, in face of a large increase in the export trade in oil, indicates either a decrease in the local demand, or the introduction of improved methods of extracting oil. It is probable that both causes have been at work to some extent, as the rapidly extending use of mineral oils for lighting purposes has of necessity caused a decrease in the demand for vegetable oils. The following table shows the average weight and value of the exports of oil-seeds during the last ten years, also the number of gallons and value of the vegetable oils similarly exported :—

—	Oils.		Oil-seed.	
	Quantity.	Value.	Quantity.	Value.
	GALLS.	RS.	CWT.	RS.
Gingelly	360,525	5,42,189	340,257	25,73,457
Groundnut	2,159,444	30,36,554	1,755,123	1,27,58,776
Castor	648,231	6,98,633	354,777	22,58,205
Cocoanut	6,460,179	91,77,651	369,561	52,07,622
Other sorts	78,158	96,379	......	......
Cotton	......	......	144,372	4,26,460

110. The following are the reasons which may be assigned for the fact that oil-seeds are exported and not the oils :—

(1) Oil-seeds can be packed in bags or carried in bulk, whereas oil must of necessity be carried in expensive casks.

(2) There is a much better market for oil-cake in Europe than in India, and the freight on oil-seeds is less than the freight on oil-cake.

(3) Protective tariffs encourage the importation of seed to the exclusion of oil, thereby securing to the importing country the business of extracting the oil.

A return furnished by the Board of Revenue shows that in 1899–1900 the District officers reported the existence of 16,018 oil mills, a much larger number than one would expect from the census returns, which, however, in all probability do not accurately reflect the existing condition of things. Oil-milling in rural parts is not often a separate business, and many of the ryots have oil mills which they run occasionally when cattle labour is available to work them. The old wooden mill is to be found in every part of the country, but, for the extraction of castor-oil, large iron screw presses worked by a number of coolies are employed, and there is a growing tendency to put down small groups of iron *ghani* mills worked by an oil-engine. On the West Coast, in connection with the extraction of cocoanut oil from copra, there has been a very large development of this trade, though most of the mills are situated in the Cochin State. Steam power is employed to drive them, and a typical plant consists of from 30 to 50 *ghanis*, or rotary mills, each extracting the oil from about 45 lb. of copra per hour.

111. *Mineral oils.*—Although no mineral oils are raised in the Presidency, and they are not themselves the raw material for other industries, the trade in them has become of very great importance, and its development to some extent is an index of the progress that is being made in the country. In appendix VIII, the import trade both by rail and by sea is summarized for the past ten years. Under each head it will be seen that there have been great developments. The expansion in the use of lubricating oils indicates developments of the use of machinery, and the introduction of fuel oils is coincident with the development of irrigation by pumping. Whilst the bulk oil trade has not appreciably increased in value, there have been large developments in the use of case oil. The trade is entirely in the hands of three large companies, and the arrangements for the delivery and storage of oil in every large centre of population in the country are very complete.

112. The census returns, supplemented by the vast amount of statistical information which is collected by the various departments of Government which deal with agriculture, industries, and commerce, throw a good deal of light upon the economic conditions of the people, and, whilst revealing in unmistakable terms the poverty of the country measured by a European standard, equally clearly show that there is a steady advance in almost every direction. When one takes into account the extraordinarily favourable conditions under which a mere animal existence can be carried on, due to the mildness of the climate, and the comparatively little labour required to procure all the necessities of life, it becomes obvious that no comparison based on statistical data places the position of the people of the Madras Presidency in a proper light. Excluding seasons of scarcity and famine, the bulk of the people are on the whole as well off as the peasantry in most countries of Europe, and nowhere does the misery and destitution exist which is to be found in almost every large town in Europe. It is true that the people here are even poorer, but their poverty entails but little hardship.

113. The census returns emphasize the fact that the Presidency is essentially an agricultural country, with only 5 per cent. of its population actually engaged in industrial work. Comparison with the figures of the previous censuses is not possible as the methods of classification have changed so often, but it may be surmised that the percentage of people engaged in industries is decreasing, or at the best stationary. It is well known that there has been no large industrial development of any kind, which would give occupation to a large number of people, whilst there has been a by no means insignificant development in the use of machinery, which has thrown out of employment much industrial labour of a low type. For instance hand-spinning is practically extinct, rice pounding is beginning to disappear, and in a number of other occupations small factories employing machinery are displacing hand labour. The change, however, is going on gradually, and the people have time to adjust themselves to the changed conditions, so that, if the cry regarding the scarcity of labour can be accepted as genuine, there is at any rate no lack of employment. It is doubtful, however, if there is any real scarcity of labour, as the cry comes mainly from those who refuse to recognize that a permanent rise in

the price of food-grains by not less than 50 per cent. necessitates at least a corresponding rise in the wages of the labouring classes. The emigration statistics show that during the last ten years more than three and a half millions of people have left the country, and that three millions have returned from foreign plantations, resulting in a net loss, on this account, of over half a million people. The loss, however, in the labour market is greater than this, as a large percentage of those who return have materially improved their position, and have not come back again to work as coolies in the fields. Even assuming however that emigration provides an outlet for 100,000 able bodied people per annum, this is slightly less than one-third of the natural increase in the population. So far the labour thrown on the market by the increased use of machinery probably does not amount to 10 per cent. of this, and it will certainly be a very long time before the outlets for emigration are insufficient to prevent over-crowding in the south of India.

114. During the ten years under review it may be fairly said that the people of India have become alive to the necessity for the creation of some measure of industrial life. Experiments, rash and ill-considered in most cases, have been made in all parts of the country, but the many failures have produced a smaller measure of discouragement than might have been anticipated. In the Madras Presidency progress has chiefly been in the direction of the establishment of small factories; and the majority of these have proved successful, mainly because the economies possible by the introduction of mechanical methods of working have more than counterbalanced the losses due to want of skill and experience. So far, however, the attempts to organize the hand-loom trade in small factories have met with but little success. Many factories have closed down, and the few that remain are struggling with the difficulties chiefly created by the hand weaver. There are approximately half a million people engaged in this industry, but their outturn averages not more than 112 lb. of cloth per head per annum. If the weavers were amenable to discipline, and willing to work eight hours a day in a factory, and if proper organization and sufficient capital were supplied, either one-third of the people now engaged in this trade would suffice for the present production, or a vast increase in the outturn of finished goods would be possible. It is not suggested that the most elaborate organization in the world will enable the hand-loom weaver to compete with the power loom in the manufacture of what may be termed typical power loom goods, but the hand weaver can turn out something which is altogether different from the output of the power loom, and it possesses certain advantages which enable it to command a higher price. If the difference in price between the two classes of goods be not too great, the hand-loom products will be in much larger demand, and there can be no doubt that the future of the hand-loom industry depends almost entirely upon the improvement of the hand-loom weaver himself.

115. The conditions in Madras are probably less favourable than in any other part of India for the creation of an industrial system on modern lines. Not only are its natural resources limited to agricultural products, but there is no concentration either of industry or population in local centres which would create favourable conditions for the disposal of local manufactures. For nearly every class of goods the market is widely diffused, and extremely vulnerable to imports owing to the extensive sea coast with numerous ports of entry. The Government may not unfairly claim that much of the progress between 1901 and 1911 is due to their efforts to give suitable assistance to private enterprise; they have accepted the policy that industries must exist before technical education can be of any use, and that the Education Department can only provide for existing wants and cannot create new openings. Whilst the work actually done under Government supervision was by no means inconsiderable since it resulted in the successful establishment of the Aluminium industry, of the chrome leather industry, of irrigation by pumping, of the rural industrial factory, and in the substitution of the fly-shuttle loom for the indigenous hand-loom over large areas, it may claim even indirect results of greater importance, as the operations of the Department of Industries have undoubtedly stimulated private enterprise in every part of the Presidency. This conclusion is

substantiated by the facts enumerated in this review of industrial progress during the past ten years, and may be best summarized by the progress made in the use of small prime-movers, whether they be worked by gas, oil or steam.

116. The swadeshi movement led to the establishment of not a few experimental enterprises which have unfortunately met with comparatively little success. Attempts have been made to establish factories for the manufacture of pencils, soap, candles, pens, matches and glass; but, for one reason or other, none of them have proved profitable, and the only developments due entirely to private initiative are the rice factories in the Gódávari and Kistna deltas, and the revival and expansion of the Madura dyeing industry.

117. The preparation of this chapter has necessitated examining the statistical information published by Government, and whilst it shows that there is a large amount of material available for the review from time to time of industrial progress, it also reveals the fact that in certain important directions the information available is inaccurate because it is incomplete. The unrest and discontent with the existing régime, which has marked the opening years of the twentieth century in India, is largely due to economic causes, and to ignorance of real facts. On the one side, too much attention is probably concentrated on the rapid expansion of the foreign trade of the country, whilst on the other, too narrow a view is taken of the land revenue administration and the effects of periodic revision of the land settlements. A wider and more detailed knowledge of the economic condition of the country on the part of the educated public is called for, and it seems possible that it would be advantageous to introduce legislation to enable this result to be obtained with greater accuracy than is at present possible.

118. Attention may be drawn to an English Act to provide for taking a census of production which was passed by Parliament in 1906. This Act empowers the Board of Trade to take a census of production in the year 1908, and subsequently in such years as may be determined by an order of the Board of Trade. It empowers the Board of Trade to call for returns from every factory or workshop under the Factory and Workshop Act of 1901; from every mine or quarry; from every builder; from every person who by way of trade or busniess executes works of construction, alteration, or repair; from every person who by way of trade or business gives out work to be done elsewhere than on his own premises; and from every person carrying on any other trade or business which may be prescribed. It provides that the returns so received shall be treated as confidential, and that the data derived from them shall be published in such a way as shall not disclose information which shall be detrimental to the individuals or companies furnishing the same. Finally, it authorizes the imposition of penalties for infraction of the clauses enumerated.

119. The enforcement of such an Act in India would be impracticable whilst the scale of production remains so extremely small. Moreover, the statistics of the sea borne trade, and the returns furnished by the cotton industry, supply a large amount of information from which very definite deductions may be drawn regarding a very large part of the industrial work going on in the country. From the register of licensed steam-boilers it should be possible to trace the gradual extension in the use of steam power, but at the present time there is no means of ascertaining the number, or power of the steam-engines actually employed; or, what is of even greater importance, the number or horse-power of the various forms of internal combustion engine, the use of which is so rapidly extending. It would, I think, be desirable that every prime-mover in the country should be registered. Information appears to be collected from time to time in the Revenue Department regarding such items as the number of hand-looms, the number of oil-mills, the number of wells used for irrigation and so forth; but there appears to be some doubt as to whether the returns furnished are sufficiently accurate, and it might possibly be useful to take power to carry out at convenient intervals a census of such items of production, chiefly in the way of tools and plant, which would furnish reliable data on which to base generalizations regarding economic questions. The tendency

is towards the introduction of power on a small scale in rural tracts, and we may look forward to a time when in almost every village these small prime-movers will be found doing work which is now performed by cattle power. Owing to the fact that nearly all the machinery used in this country is imported from abroad, much useful information could be obtained by a more detailed classification of the goods passing through the custom-house, especially under the heading "Machinery and Mill work." It would not be difficult to record separately details regarding such machinery as engines, whether steam, gas or oil, dynamos and electro-motors, pumps, rice-hullers, sugar-mills, and so forth. The monthly statement of imports and exports simply gives the number of cases arriving from foreign countries, and their value; whilst the sea borne trade returns attempts some classification, but of such a vague nature as to be of little practical use. The terms "unenumerated," "other sorts," "other descriptions" generally cover by far the largest items so far as value is concerned, and it is more detailed information on these points which is so urgently needed to enable the industrial changes going on in the country to be placed in their proper perspective. An examination of the trade returns of the last ten years reveals the fact that the imports of the five years ending 1910–11 compared with those of the five years ending 1905–06 show increases as follows :—

	LAKHS.
Machinery	71
Scientific apparatus	28
Chemicals	18

This is no doubt useful information as indicating a general tendency towards a higher state of industrialism, but its value would be greatly enhanced if the direction in which increasing use was being made of such imports was also indicated.

APPENDICES.

APPENDIX I.

Occupation.

Description of occupation.	Workers, 1901.			Workers, 1911.			Percentage of increase or decrease.
	Males.	Females.	Total.	Males.	Females.	Total.	
1	2	3	4	5	6	7	8
Order V.—Salt, etc.	...	...	...	*768*	*282*	*1,050*	...
19. Rock, Sea and marsh salt	...	...	...	483	78	**561**	...
20. Extraction of saltpetre, alum and other substances soluble in water.	1,296	1,125	**2,421**	285	204	**489**	− 79·6
Order VI.—Textiles	...	...	...	*455,181*	*290,872*	*746,053*	...
21. Cotton ginning, cleaning, etc.	12,648	11,446	**24,089**	20,067	12,486	**32,553**	+ 35·1
22 & 31. Cotton spinnsing, sizing, and weaving.	398,426	225,357	**623,783**	{ 385,124 1,203	193,584 410 }	**580,321**	− 6·9
23. Jute spinning, pressing, etc.	455	78	**533**	1,925	503	**2,428**	+ 355·5
24. Rope, twine and string	5,867	37,009	**42,876**	7,082	46,712	**53,794**	+ 25·5
25. Other fibres (cocoanut, aloes, flax, hemp, etc.).	3,672	4,214	**7,886**	1,476	7,776	**9,252**	+ 17·3
26. Wool carders and spinners, etc.	...	...	...	11,561	11,445	**23,006**	...
27. Silk spinners and weavers	14,219	16,204	**30,423**	21,402	15,452	**36,854**	+ 21·1
28. Hair, camel and horse hair, etc. ...	...	...	...	684	3	**687**	...
30. Dyeing, bleaching, printing preparation and sponging of textiles.	6,564	3,497	10,061	4,707	2,501	**7,208**	− 28·3
Order VII.—Hides and skins, etc. ...	...	...	...	*46,532*	*4,414*	*50,946*	...
32. Tanners, curriers, leather dressers, etc.	8,138	1,130	**9,268**	12,872	882	**13,754**	+ 48·3
33. Makers of leather articles	45,262	5,533	**50,795**	33,551	3,477	**37,028**	− 27·1
34. Furriers	...	...	...	9	29	**38**	...
35. Bow, ivory horn, shell, etc., workers ...	112	2	114	100	26	**126**	+ 10·5
Order VIII.—Wood	...	...	...	*198,036*	*82,480*	*280,516*	...
36. Sawyers, carpenters, turners, etc. ...	127,136	4,108	**131,244**	139,068	7,515	**146,583**	+ 11·6
37. Basket makers and other industries of woody material.	61,354	81,480	**142,834**	58,968	74,965	**133,933**	− 6·2
Order IX.—Metals	...	...	...	*73,967*	*7,102*	*81,069*	...
38. Forging and rolling of iron and other metals.	266	...	**266**	845	3	**848**	+ 218·8
39. Plough and agricultural implement makers.	951	39	**990**	551	137	**688**	+ 30·5
40. Makers of arms, gun, etc.	1,080	22	**1,102**	212	5	**217**	− 80·3
41. Other workers in iron and makers of implements and tools.	51,840	3,972	**55,812**	52,882	5,555	**58,437**	+ 4·5
42. Workers in brass, copper and bell-metal.	14,248	826	**15,074**	14,672	1 095	**15,767**	+ 4·6
43. Workers in other metals (tin, zinc, lead, etc.).	4,237	264	**4,404**	4,783	307	**5,090**	+ 15·6
44. Workers in mints, die-sinkers, etc. ...	190	...	**190**	42	...	**42**	− 77·9
Order X.—Ceramics	...	...	...	*85,147*	*47,799*	*132,946*	...
45. Makers of glass and crystal ware ... 46. Makers of porcelain and crockery ...	} 931	486	**1,417**	{ 482 88	124 7	**606** **95**	} − 50·5
47. Potters and earthen pipe and bowl makers.	57,927	31,613	**89,540**	75,301	44,239	**119,540**	+ 33·5
48. Brick and tile makers	6,897	2,940	**9,837**	8,432	2,797	**11,229**	+ 20·2
49. Others (mosaic, talc mica, alabaster, etc.).	17	5	**22**	844	632	**1,476**	+ 6,609·1
Order XI.—Chemical products, etc. ...	...	...	...	*20,614*	*8,189*	*28,803*	...
50. Manufacture of matches and explosive materials.	1,304	148	**1,452**	287	183	**470**	− 67·6
51. Manufacture of aerated and mineral waters.	123	3	**126**	527	15	**542**	+ 330·1

APPENDIX I—*cont.*

Occupation—concld.

Description of occupation.	Workers, 1901.			Workers, 1911.			Percentage of increase or decrease.
	Males.	Females.	Total	Males.	Females.	Total.	
1	2	3	4	5	6	7	8
Order XI.—Chemical products, etc.—*cont.*							
52. Manufacture of dyes, paint, ink, etc. ...	...	...	...	1,127	462	**1,589**	...
53. Manufacture and refining of vegetable and mineral oils.	20,202	6,968	**27,170**	17,884	7,211	**25,095**	— 7·6
54. Manufacture of paper, card-board, etc.	...	...	...	118	6	**124**	...
55. Others (soap, candles, etc.)	...	...	...	671	312	**983**	...
Order XII.—Food industries	...	...	...	***37,186***	***134,221***	***171,407***	...
56. Rice pounders, huskers, and flour grinders.	15,866	152,090	**167,956**	17,959	107,715	**125,674**	— 25·1
57. Bakers and biscuit makers	1,986	318	**2,304**	2,947	3,068	**6,015**	+ 161·0
60. Fish curers	...	...	...	1,196	1,340	**2,536**	...
61. Butter, cheese and ghee makers ...	...	...	...	136	87	**223**	...
62. Makers of sugar, molasses and gur ..	...	...	...	3,873	14,339	**18,212**	...
63. Sweetmeat makers, preparers of jam, etc.	..	...	...	5,437	4,855	**10,292**	..
64. Brewers and distillers	249	40	**289**	791	2,155	**2,946**	+ 919·3
66. Manufacturers of tobacco, opium and ganja.	6,183	469	**6,652**	4,847	662	**5,509**	— 17·1
Order XIII.—Industries of dress and toilet.	...	...	...	***134,185***	***30,457***	***164,642***	...
67. Hat, cap and turban makers	329	1,084	**1,413**	250	1,517	**1,767**	+ 25·0
68. Tailors, milliners and dress makers ...	20,888	10,727	**31,615**	25,549	12,001	**37,550**	+ 18·7
69. Shoe, boot and sandal makers	99,967	11,618	**111,585**	107,382	15,871	**123,253**	+ 10·4
70. Other industries pertaining to dress, gloves, socks, etc.	75	36	**111**	1,004	1,068	**2,072**	+1,766·6
Order XIV.—Furniture industries ...	...	...	...	***1,654***	***241***	***1,895***	...
74. Cabinet makers, carriage painters, upholsterers, etc.	762	43	**805**	1,644	241	**1,885**	+ 134·1
75. Upholsterers, tent makers, etc. ...	...	...	...	10	...	**111**	...
Order XV.—Building Industries	...	...	...	***199,883***	***83,988***	***283,871***	...
76. Lime burners, cement workers	2,674	3,240	**5,914**	3,567	3,076	**6,643**	+ 12·3
77. Excavators and well sinkers	99,816	81,311	**181,127**	75,496	54,585	**130,081**	— 28·1
78. Stone and marble workers	95,396	22,284	**117,680**	107,950	19,841	**127,791**	+ 8·6
79. Others (thatchers, tilers, plumbers, locksmiths, etc.	3,049	154	**3,203**	12,870	6,486	**19,356**	+ 504·3
Order XVI.—Construction of means of transport.	...	...	..	***1,561***	***13***	***1,574***	..
80. Cart, carriages, palki, etc., makers and wheel wrights.	...	...	...	512	11	**523**	...
81. Saddlers, harness makers, whip and lash makers.	107	38	**145**	159	1	**160**	+ 10·3
82. Ship and boat builders	356	8	**364**	890	1	**891**	+ 144·8
Order XVII.—Production and transformation of physical forces.							
83. Gas workers, electric light and ice factories.	47	8	55	419	13	**432**	+ 685·4
Order XVIII.—Industries of luxury and those pertaining to literature and the arts and the sciences.	...	...	...	***121,916***	***8,568***	***130,484***	...
84. Printers, lithographers and engravers ...	4,752	12	**4,764**	6,912	70	**6,982**	+ 46·5
86. Book-binders and stitchers	1,200	...	**1,200**	1,818	35	**1,853**	+ 54·4
87. Makers of musical instruments	117	6	**123**	233	10	**243**	+ 97·5
88. Makers of watches and clocks, etc. ...	472	...	**472**	610	9	**619**	+ 31·1
89. Workers in precious stones and metals, etc.	96,261	3,780	**99,991**	108,680	6,886	**115,566**	+ 15·6
90. Makers of bangles, rosaries, bead and other necklaces, etc.	...	...	...	3,360	1,494	**4,854**	...
91. Toy kite, cage, fishing cattle, etc. ...	497	141	**638**	303	64	**367**	— 42·4

APPENDIX I—*concld.*

Abstract of occupation tables.

	Males.	Females.	Total.
Total ...	*1,377,070*	*698,639*	*2,075,709*
Order V.—Salt, etc.	769	282	1,051
„ VI.—Textiles	452,081	288,372	740,453
„ VII.—Hides and skins	49,632	6,914	56,546
„ VIII.—Wood	198,036	82,480	280,516
„ IX.—Metals	73,987	7,102	81,089
„ X.—Ceramics	85,147	47,799	132,946
„ XI.—Chemical products, etc.	20,614	8,189	28,803
„ XII.—Food industries	37,186	134,221	171,407
„ XIII.—Industries of dress and toilet	134,185	30,457	164,642
„ XIV.—Furniture industries	1,654	241	1,895
„ XV.—Building industries	199,883	83,988	283,871
„ XVI.—Construction of means of transport ...	1,561	13	1,574
„ XVII.—Production and transformation	419	13	432
„ XVIII.—Industries of luxury, printing, book-binding, etc.	121,916	8,568	130,484

APPENDIX II.

Summary.

District.	Number of factories.	Horse-power installed. Steam. Engines.	Steam. Boilers.	Oil or gas.	Water power.	Electricity.	Total.
1	2	3	4	5	6	7	8
Total ...	*903*	*26,101*	*44,613*	*8,989*	*1,763*	*286*	*36,853*
Ganjám	7	165	1,199	...	...	...	165
Vizagapatam	23	785	2,166	144	...	...	929
Gódávari	49	877	3,400	249	...	...	1,126
Kistna	89	1,493	3,485	2,138	...	...	3,631
Guntúr	62	607	2,540	81	...	...	688
Nellore	18	148	302	59	...	...	207
Kurnool	12	42	787	15	...	...	57
Bellary	24	377	1,782	35	...	...	412
Anantapur	12	161	1,117	48	...	...	209
Cuddapah	15	26	402	62	...	...	88
North Arcot and Chittoor ...	41	118	394	356	...	...	474
Chingleput	67	141	322	1,051	...	...	1,192
South Arcot	93	20	1,731	961	...	...	981
Salem	10	8	90	44	...	...	52
Coimbatore	54	1,282	2,304	928	27	...	2,237
Trichinopoly	24	369	364	161	...	...	530
Tanjore	30	370	615	235	...	...	605
Madura	16	1,125	1,047	65	...	...	1,190
Rámnád	10	610	872	363	...	95	972
Tinnevelly	33	2,531	3,155	270	1,150	...	3,951
Nilgiris	30	40	1,000	200	586	.	826
Malabar	51	1,185	2,840	183	...	...	1,368
South Canara	26	339	859	46	...	...	385
Madras	107	13,282	11,890	1,295	...	191	14,577

APPENDIX II—*cont.*

Details.

District and industry.	Number of factories.	Horse-power installed. Steam. Engines.	Steam. Boilers.	Oil or gas.	Water power.	Electricity.	Total of columns 3, 5 and 6.
1	2	3		5	6	7	8
Ganjám	*7*	*165*	*1,199*	...	...	..	*165*
Rice mills	4	72	252	...	...	...	72
Sugar mills	1	93	815	...	...	...	93
Electric generating stations	1	...	110	...	...	...	...
General engineering works including portable plant.	1	...	22	...	...	...	...
Vizagapatam	*23*	*785*	*2,166*	*144*	...	...	*929*
Manganese mines	2	149	487	189	...	...	338
Jute mills	5	550	1,020	...	...	...	550
General engineering workshop including portable plant.	6	10	215	...	...	...	10
Rice mills	5	31	317	...	...	...	31
Salt refining	1	...	25	...	...	...	...
Distilleries	1	...	80	...	...	...	...
Pencil factory	1	...	22	...	...	...	...
Irrigation	1	...	...	5	...	...	5
Railway workshops	1	45	...	...	...	...	45
Gódávari	*49*	*877*	*3,400*	*249*	...	...	*1,126*
Cotton ginning factories	4	58	...	...	...	...	58
Jute baling presses	1	45	115	...	...	...	45
Rope works	1	100	55	...	...	...	100
General engineering workshops including portable plants.	3	75	519	15	...	...	90
Petroleum storage and refinery	2	19	55	10	...	...	29
Rice mills	20	450	1,685	16	...	...	466
Municipal water works	1	130	147	...	...	...	130
Sugar mills	1	...	810	...	...	...	...
Salt refining	1	...	27	...	...	...	...
Irrigation	13	...	37	169	...	...	169
Fibre extracting	1	...	...	3	...	...	3
Saw mill	1	...	...	36	...	...	36
Kistna	*89*	*1,493*	*3,485*	*2,138*	...	...	*3,631*
Jute mills	1	750	290	...	...	...	750
General engineering workshops including portable plants.	7	20	576	...	...	...	20
Rice mills	48	487	2,370	331	...	...	818
Dye works	1	...	17	...	...	...	...
Aerated water factory	1	...	25	...	...	...	...
Weaving factory	1	...	12	...	...	...	...
Cotton ginning factories	2	...	60	...	...	...	...
Cotton presses	2	...	105	...	...	...	...
Municipal water works	1	200	30	...	...	...	200
Irrigation	25	36	...	1,807	...	...	1,843
Guntúr	*62*	*607*	*2,540*	*81*	...	...	*688*
Cotton ginning factories	18	76	532	...	...	...	76
Cotton presses	9	116	634	...	...	...	116
Cotton pressing and ginning factories	1	29	115	...	...	...	29
Rice mills	32	386	1,227	...	...	...	386
Oil mills	1	...	32	...	...	...	...
Irrigation	6	...	...	81	...	...	81
Nellore	*18*	*148*	*302*	*59*	...	...	*207*
Mica mines	9	51	182	24	...	..	75
Rice mills	3	40	120	...	...	...	40
Municipal water works	1	57	...	...	...	...	57
Irrigation	5	...	...	35	...	..	35
Kurnool	*12*	*42*	*737*	*15*	...	...	*57*
Cotton ginning factories	8	...	385	...	...	...	...
Cotton presses	3	...	330	...	...	...	...
Municipal water works	1	42	22	15	...	...	57

APPENDIX II—*cont.*

Details—cont.

District and industry.	Number of factories.	Horse power installed. Steam. Engines.	Steam. Boilers.	Oil or gas.	Water power.	Electricity.	Total of columns 3, 5 and 6.
1	2	3	4	5	6	7	
Bellary	***24***	***377***	***1,782***	***35***	...	...	***412***
Cotton ginning factories	9	192	650	...	...	...	192
Cotton presses	6	128	937	12		...	140
Cotton pressing and ginning factories ...	2	57	135	...	...	...	57
Oil mills	1	...	...	5	..		5
Grass farm	1	...	35	..	...	...	...
Sugar mills	1	...	15	...	...	...	...
General engineering works includin portable plant.	1	...	10	...	...	...	...
Irrigation	3	...	...	18	...	..	18
Anantapur	***12***	***161***	***1,117***	***48***	...	...	***209***
Cotton ginning factories	3	93	232	...	...	...	93
Cotton presses	1	68	65	...	...	..	68
Gold mines	3	...	820	...	...	...	...
Irrigation	5	...	...	48	...	.	48
Cuddapah	***15***	***26***	***402***	***62***	...	...	***88***
Weaving factories	1	6	17	..	...	...	6
Municipal water works	1	20	30	...	...	...	20
Cotton presses	6	...	335	...	...	...	...
Saffron works	1	..	20	...	...	...	...
Irrigation	6	...	...	62	...	...	62
North Arcot and Chittoor	***41***	***118***	***394***	***356***	..	...	***474***
Joinery works	1	...	...	7	...	...	7
General engineering workshops including portable plants.	1	.	...	80	...	...	80
Chemical works	1	24	80	37	...	...	61
Rice mills	4	80	237	..	...	...	80
Irrigation	31	.	77	208	...	...	208
Oil mills	1	...	...	20	...	...	20
Ice manufacture	1	...	...	4	...	...	4
Municipal water works	1	14	...	...	...	...	14
Chingleput	***67***	***141***	***322***	***1,051***	...	...	***1,192***
Tanneries	2	11	27	...	...	...	11
Tobacco factories	1	12	35	...	...	...	12
Quarries	2	12	65	...	...	...	12
Dye works	1	...	35	...	...	...	...
Rice mill	1	8	20	...	...	...	8
Bone crusher	1	...	40	...	...	...	...
Gold thread factory	1	...	35	...	...	..	...
Municipal water works	1	98	65	...	...	...	98
Irrigation	56	...	...	451	...	...	451
Railway workshop	1	...	...	600	...	...	600
Madras	***107***	***13,282***	***11,890***	***1,295***	...	***191***	***14,577***
Cotton spinning mills	2	1,500	1,025	...	...	...	1,500
Cotton spinning and weaving mills	2	4,750	4,175	...	...	...	4,750
Jute baling press	1	10	27	...	...	...	10
Leather baling press	1	12	...	...	...	...	12
Forage baling dress	1	...	.	6	...	...	6
Tanneries	1	15	30	10	...	...	25
Saw mill	1	...	...	...	...	50	...
Joinery works	4	22	15	38	...	8	60
General engineering workshops including portable plants.	14	292	3,472	174	...	...	466
Aluminium factory	1	...	...	105	...	...	105
Tin plate factory	1	...	...	32	...	...	32
Glass factory	1	7	17	...		...	7
Aerated water factory	7	29	135	8	...	7	37
Oil mills	2	...	...	7	..	15	7
Petroleum storage	4	20	80	40	...	..	60
Chemical works	1	20	80	...	...	...	20
Rice mills	3	65	182	...	...	...	65
Tobacco factories	1	...	...	5	...	...	5
Tailoring	1	...	...	4	...	...	4
Cement works	2	900	570	10	...	5	910

APPENDIX II—*cont.*

Details—cont.

District and Industry.	Number of factories.	Horse-power Installed. Steam. Engine.	Steam. Boiler.	Oil or gas.	Water power.	Electricity.	Total of columns 3, 5 and 6.
1	2	3	4	5	6	7	8
Madras—*cont.*							
Boot and shoe factory	1	...	...	8	...	...	8
Ice factories	2	15	160	...	...	...	15
Printing presses	23	83	200	186	...	76	269
Coach building works	3	...	35	7	...	18	7
Garrages	3	...	...	8	...	7	8
Jewellery shops	1	...	...	...	...	10	...
Tile works	1	...	30	...	...	...	...
Distillery	1	...	40	...	...	...	...
Electric generating stations	9	4,800	1,667	252	..	...	5,052
Municipal water works	1	32	...	...	...	...	32
Do. sewage pumping plant	...	700	...	340	...	...	1,040
Irrigation	10	...	...	55	...	...	55
Railway workshops	1	10	...	...	...	...	10
South Arcot	***93***	***20***	***1,731***	***961***	...	...	***961***
Rice mills	2	10	82	...	...	...	10
Sugar mills	1	...	1,597	300	...	..	300
Oil mills	1	...	52	...	...	...	...
Salt refinery	1	...	...	10	...	...	10
Irigation	87	...	...	651	...	...	651
Railway workshop	1	10	...	...	...	...	10
Salem	***10***	***8***	***90***	***44***	...	...	***52***
Coffee plantations	2	...	...	10	...	...	10
Magnesite works	1	..	60	...	...	...	...
Municipal water works	1	8	...	...	...	..	8
Irrigation	6	...	30	34	...	...	34
Coimbatore	***54***	***1,282***	***2,304***	***928***	***27***	...	***2,237***
Coffee factories	4	...		56	27	...	83
Coffee curing works	4	50	286	18	...	...	68
Cotton ginning factories	1	20	47	...	...	...	20
Cotton presses	2	...	105	...	...	...	...
Cotton pressing and ginning factories ...	2	152	550	22	...	...	174
Cotton spinning mills	1	...	42	525	...	...	525
Cotton weaving mills	2	290	355	...	...	...	290
Cotton spinning and weaving mills	1	700	810	...	...	...	700
Brick and tile works	1	...		36	...	...	36
Saltpetre refinery	1	40	...	...	...	...	40
Breweries	1	...	...	3	...	...	3
Rice mills	2	...	75	...	...	...	...
Dye works	1	...	17	...	...	...	...
General engineering workshops including portable plant.	1	...	12	...	...	...	...
Irrigation	29	...	5	268	...	...	268
Railway workshop	1	30	..	...	...	...	30
Trichinopoly	***24***	***369***	***364***	***161***		...	***530***
Cotton ginning factories	1	26	65	...	...	...	26
Tanneries	1	3	7	...	...	...	3
Joinery works	2	...	...	35	..	...	35
Rice mills	1	110	57	...	...	...	110
Electric generating stations	1	10	...	...	...	...	10
Printing press	1	...	...	4	...	...	4
Municipal water works	1	190	190	...	...	...	190
General engineering workshops including portable plant.	1	...	45	...	...	...	...
Irrigation	14	...	...	122	...	...	122
Railway workshop	1	30	...	...	...	...	30
Tanjore	***30***	***370***	***615***	***235***	.	...	***605***
Rice mills	21	175	420	193	...	...	368
Oill mills	1	...	50	...	...	...	...
Municipal water works	1	120	145	...	...	...	120
Irrigation	6	...	...	42	...	...	42
Railway workshop	1	75	...	...	...	...	75

APPENDIX II—*cont.*

Details—cont.

District and Industry.	Number of factories.	Horse-power Installed. Steam. Engine.	Steam. Boilers.	Oil or gas.	Water power.	Electricity.	Total of columns 3, 5 and 6
1	2	3	4	5	6	7	8
Madura	*16*	*1,125*	*1,047*	*65*	...	*95*	*1,190*
Cotton spinning mills	2	900	695	...	...	...	900
Joinery works	1	...	...	8	...	...	8
Tobacco factories	1	...	...	6	...	...	6
Cotton ginning factories	1	80	82	...	...	..	80
General engineering workshops including portable plant.	1	...	40	...	...	...	...
Municipal water works	2	135	230	...	...	...	135
Irrigation plants	5	..	...	56	...	...	56
Aerial ropeway	1	..	...	...	...	80	...
Railway workshop	1	10	...	...	...	...	10
Telegraph workshop	1	...	...	...	...	15	...
Rámnád	*10*	*610*	*872*	*363*	...	...	*973*
Cotton ginning factories	5	380	540	...	...	...	380
Cotton presses	2	...	67	...	...	...	...
Cotton ginning and pressing factories ...	3	230	265	363	...	...	593
Tinnevelly	*33*	*2,531*	*3,155*	*270*	*1,150*	.	*3,951*
Cotton ginning factories	4	115	157	180	...	...	295
Cotton presses	7	375	922	...	...	...	375
Cotton ginning and pressing factories	2	350	322	...	...	...	350
Cotton spinning mills	3	1,600	1,075	...	1,150	...	2,750
Petroleum storage	2	7	77	10	...	...	17
Rice mills	1	12	80	...	...	...	12
Sugar mills	2	60	515	...	...	...	60
Distillery	1	...	...	6	...	...	6
Tile works	1	...	30	..	...	...	...
Bone crushing	1	12	27	...	...	...	12
Irrigation	9	...	...	74	...	...	74
Nilgiris	*30*	*40*	*1,000*	*200*	*596*	...	*836*
Tea factories and estates	15	18	95	151	64	...	233
Coffee do.	6	...	...	45	22	...	67
Breweries	2	19	117	4	...	...	23
Cordite factory	1	...	472	...	500	...	500
Lenndry	2	3	22	...	...		3
Quinine factory	1	...	187	...	...	...	...
Electric generating station	2	...	100	...	...	...	...
Mineral water factory	1	...	7	...	...	...	...
Malabar	*51*	*1,185*	*2,840*	*183*	...	...	*1,368*
Tea factories and estates	7	20	77	156	...	...	176
Coffee do.	5	25	...	9	...	...	34
Coffee curing works	6	106	382	...	...	...	106
Cotton weaving mills	2	32	117	...	...	...	32
Cotton spinning and weaving mills	1	500	352	...	...	...	500
Coir yarn presses and works	6	79	495	...	...	...	79
Coir mat factory	1	10	110	...	...	...	10
General engineering workshops including portable plant.	3	10	37	...	...	...	10
Brick and tile works	9	278	720	...	...	...	278
Oil mills	4	77	212	18	...	...	95
Rice mills	2	23	137		...	...	23
Ice factory	1	...	22	..	...	...	...
Fish curing	1	...	20	..	..	...	...
Cocoanut desiccating factory	1	...	22	...	...	...	...
Saw mills	1	...	187	...	...	...	...
Railway workshop	1	25	...	...	...	...	25
South Canara	*26*	*339*	*859*	*46*	..	...	*385*
Coffee curing works	7	96	270	1	...	...	97
Cotton weaving mills	1	11	87	...	..	...	11
Joinery works	1	...	...	5	...	...	5
Brick and tile works	14	220	502	32	...	...	252
Printing presses	2	..	..	8	...	...	8
Railway workshop	1	12	...	...	...	...	12

APPENDIX III.

District.	Number of factories.	Horse-power installed.			
		Steam engine.	Boilers.	Oil or gas engine.	Total of columns 3 and 5.
1	2	3	4	5	6
TOTAL ...	*317*	*36*	*149*	*4,186*	*4,222*
Vizagapatam ...	1	...	...	5	5
Gódávari ...	13	...	37	169	169
Kistna ...	25	36	...	1,807	1,843
Guntúr ...	6	...	..	81	81
Nellore ...	5	..	...	35	35
Bellary ...	8	...	.	18	18
Anantapur ...	5	...	...	48	48
Cuddapah ...	6	...	...	62	62
North Arcot ...	31	...	77	208	208
Chingleput ...	56	...	...	451	451
Madras ...	10	...	...	55	55
South Arcot ...	87	...	...	651	651
Salem ...	6	...	30	34	34
Coimbatore ...	29	...	5	268	268
Trichinopoly ...	14	...	...	122	123
Tanjore ...	6	...	...	42	42
Madura ...	5	...	...	56	56
Tinnevelly ...	9	...	...	74	74

APPENDIX IV.

List of Boilers.

District.	Number.	Horse-power.	District.	Number.	Horse-power.
1	2	3	1	2	3
TOTAL ...	*805*	*44,613*			
Ganjám ...	22	1,199	Madras ...	207	11,890
Vizagapatam ...	38	2,166	South Arcot ...	28	1,731
Gódávari ...	61	3,400	Salem ...	2	90
Kistna ...	78	3,485	Coimbatore ...	82	2,304
Guntúr ...	51	2,540	Trichinopoly ...	11	364
Nellore ...	9	302	Tanjore ...	14	615
Kurnool ...	14	737	Madura ...	14	1,047
Bellary ...	24	1,782	Rámnád ...	10	872
Anantapur ...	20	1,117	Tinnevelly ...	38	3,155
Cuddapah ...	10	402	Nilgiris ...	24	1,000
North Arcot ...	10	394	Malabar ...	53	2,840
Chingleput ...	11	322	South Canara ...	24	859

APPENDIX V.

Statement showing quantity of yarn taken up by hand-loom weaving industry for the period 1901–10.

—		1901–02.	1902–03.	1903–04.	1904–05.	1905–06.	1906–07.	1907–08.	1908–09.	1909–10.
1		2	3	4	5	6	7	8	9	10
A.—Twist and yarn imported and produced in the Presidency.										
TOTAL A.	lb.	***662,31,590***	***63,542,596***	***59,151,960***	***65,940,001***	***70,944,793***	***71,781,615***	***75,298,278***	***79,973,136***	***73,455,497***
Sea-borne traffic	„	9,865,164	10,685,731	7,879,398	9,696,345	10,819,278	11,148,108	10,309,525	11,186,116	8,594,822
Coastal traffic { Indian	„	5,838,654	7,690,207	7,333,110	4,142,492	3,102,754	3,810,469	3,783,674	5,069,543	4,621,712
Coastal traffic { Foreign	„	123,582	183,887	145,012	187,080	116,914	318,810	176,358	158,267	198,940
Rail-borne ... { Indian	„	11,645,614	11,698,451	11,058,864	12,069,130	13,318,614	12,468,787	13,141,581	12,096,371	12,735,184
Rail-borne ... { European	„	6,642,762	2,028,218	4,121,419	9,770,409	8,405,049	7,611,916	10,951,249	11,827,415	6,708,849
Yarn produced in mills in Madras	„	32,120,814	31,256,104	28,714,162	30,124,685	35,282,189	36,723,575	36,935,891	39,635,423	40,595,990
B.—Twist and yarn exported and consumed in cotton mills in the Presidency.										
TOTAL B.	lb.	***14,080,567***	***13,003,550***	***9,906,779***	***13,368,582***	***16,635,927***	***14,699,441***	***13,618,963***	***16,596,858***	***18,938,636***
DIFFERENCE SHOWING QUALITY OF YARN TAKEN UP BY HAND-LOOMS.		***52,151,023***	***50,539,046***	***49,245,181***	***52,571,419***	***54,308,866***	***57,082,174***	***61,679,315***	***63,376,277***	***54,516,861***
Sea-borne trade { Indian	lb.	3,800,066	4,187,524	1,228,859	3,237,010	4,156,057	3,364,725	2,262,314	3,654,633	6,061,274
Sea-borne trade { Foreign	„	213,500	116,889	112,386	35,515	3,075	930	1,700	32,658	33,400
Coastal trade { Indian	„	1,454,682	959,130	751,575	583,021	595,565	116,428	295,041	1,769,666	1,460,175
Coastal trade { Foreign	„	38,219	48,819	49,412	10,322	9,044	49,205	8,817	8,922	6,290
Rail-borne ... { Indian	„	1,173,483	1,496,460	1,373,504	1,787,809	2,477,747	2,058,467	2,393,037	2,525,575	2,766,761
Rail-borne ... { European	„	1,023,729	949,906	780,286	807,116	851,228	764,507	685,065	628,772	495,363
* Weight of goods woven in cotton mills in the Presidency.	„	6,376,988	5,244,822	5,610,755	6,907,789	8,543,211	8,350,184	7,972,989	7,976,682	8,125,273

* Margin of 5 per cent. wastage is allowed in the figures.

APPENDIX VI.

Statement showing the area under cultivation of each kind of oil-seeds for 1910–11.

District.	Gingelly.	Groundnut.	Castor-oil.	Cocoanut.	Cotton.
1	2	3	4	5	6
TOTAL ...	*815,100*	*934,654*	*497,702*	*543,112*	*2,317,045*
Ganjám	65,192	7,000	6,776	8,155	1,563
Visagapatam	137,914	624	8,050	2,540	17,958
Gódávari	77,545	25	12,047	40,975	9,424
Kistna	101,971	535	26,950	6,067	68,603
Guntúr	1,891	641	45,474	245	180,970
Kurnool	4,757	8,832	47,655	65	398,165
Bellary	17,454	4,385	50,629	2,456	488,354
Anantapur	42,116	26,170	92,040	872	155,220
Cuddapah	5,341	30,241	28,966	247	96,473
Nellore	4,897	354	61,116	316	43,306
Chingleput	28,964	33,002	152	6,806	......
South Arcot	18,570	375,769	1,383	5,759	2,213
Chittoor	4,754	20,436	16,084	2,449	635
North Arcot	53,748	181,597	11,004	7,878	13
Salem	68,432	42,774	26,248	8,588	12,694
Coimbatore	24,039	35,567	28,510	6,809	245,932
Trichinopoly	40,107	83,766	15,898	5,842	61,304
Tanjore	9,015	72,608	685	19,709	2,155
Madura	43,449	50,315	15,013	5,177	160,193
Rámnád	18,404	7,943	3,580	6,746	216,254
Tinnevelly	19,133	322	3,428	4,015	299,422
Malabar	25,728	1,111	410	357,086	11
South Canara	2,126	37	649	44,315	154
Nilgiris	63	...	5	...	29

APPENDIX VII.

Import of mineral oils.

Year.	Fuel oils.		Lubricating oils.		Kerosine oil in bulk.		Kerosine oil in cases.		Other kinds.		Total.	
	Gallons.	Value.	Gallons.	Value.	Gallons.	Value.	Gallons.	Value.	Gallons.	Value.	Gallons.	Value.
1	2	3	4	5	6	7	8	9	10	11	12	13
		Rs.		Rs.		Rs.		Rs.		Rs.		Rs.
Total ...	*3,038,968*	*2,66,135*	*1,644,874*	*11,88,678*	*66,047,865*	*2,26,86,624*	*136,906,922*	*6,26,66,555*	*3,438,174* Cwt. *8,906*	*24,36,707*	*211,078,793* Cwt. *8,906*	*8,92,46,699*
1901-02	...	...	...	...	9,037,804	30,47,981	6,302,785	31,82,784	424,822 Cwt. 22	99,977	15,764,911 Cwt. 22	63,30,742
1902-03	...	...	...	...	8,052,945	26,04,027	7,682,104	35,83,113	308,077	3,20,599	16,043,126	64,07,739
1903-04	...	...	..	.	6,909,022	23,49,177	9,284,454	51,43,678	424,443	2,23,072	16,617,919	77,15,922
1904-05	...	...	...	...	8,576,790	27,30,651	11,181,790	54,04,696	437,998	1,92,213	20,196,578	83,27,560
1905-06	260,205	36,509	144,090	96,023	4,375,915	13,24,924	8,647,990	44,44,787	141,524 Cwt. 2	1,65,579	13,569,724 Cwt. 2	60,77,822
1906-07	276,744	30,385	149,413	1,18,456	2,922,074	9,39,408	18,308,082	90,27,548	140,764 Cwt. 11	1,36,878	21,797,077 Cwt. 11	1,02,52,655
1907-08	350,218	27,175	343,300	2,51,827	4,223,629	15,24,989	18,919,261	75,98,900	292,750 Cwt. 131	2,40,975	24,129,158 Cwt. 131	95,53,866
1908-09	745,228	61,069	394,874	2,59,009	9,115,756	33,70,191	17,334,231	82,04,189	342,525	2,93,188	27,932,614	1,21,87,641
1909-10	563,897	44,385	244,664	1,93,948	5,088,487	18,87,350	19,657,248	79,66,626	396,430 Cwt. 8,359	3,60,362	25,900,676 Cwt. 8,359	1,04,52,671
1910-11	842,666	66,632	368,533	2,69,415	7,795,998	28,99,926	19,590,977	82,00,239	528,841 Cwt. 171	5,03,869	29,127,010 Cwt. 171	1,19,40,081

SUBSIDIARY TABLES.

I.—General distribution by occupation.

Class, sub-class and order.	Number per 10,000 of total population.		Percentage in each class, sub-class and order of		Percentage of actual workers employed.		Percentage of dependents to actual workers.	
	Persons supported.	Actual workers.	Actual workers.	Dependents.	In cities.	In rural areas.	In cities.	In rural areas.
1	2	3	4	5	6	7	8	9
Class A.—Production of raw materials.	*7070·7*	*3712·5*	*52·5*	*47·5*	*0·5*	*99·5*	*164·4*	*90·1*
Sub-class I.—Exploitation of the surface of the earth.	7066·3	3710·4	52·5	47·5	0·5	99·5	164·4	90·1
Order 1. Pasture and agriculture—								
(a) Ordinary cultivation.	6835·8	3577·1	52·3	47·7	0·4	99·6	171·4	90·8
(b) Growers of special products and market gardening.	37·3	17·3	46·3	53·7	4·5	95·5	176·9	113·1
(c) Forestry	16·9	7·7	45·7	54·3	5·7	94·3	111·4	119·4
(d) Raising of farm stock.	119·2	84·0	70·5	29·5	0·8	99·2	90·0	41·5
(e) Raising of small animals.	0·1	0·0	48·0	52·0	2·5	97·5	75·0	109·2
„ 2. Fishing and hunting ...	57·0	24·3	42·6	57·4	6·3	98·7	144·5	133·9
Sub-class II.—Extraction of minerals ...	4·4	2·1	47·8	52·2	1·9	98·1	179·4	107·9
Order 3. Mines	2·4	1·1	44·2	55·8	1·7	98·3	206·5	124·9
„ 4. Quarries of hard rocks ...	1·3	0·8	59·1	40·9	0·4	99·6	176·9	68·9
„ 5 Salt, etc.	0·7	0·2	38·2	61·8	7·1	92·9	152·0	162·6
Class B.—Preparation and supply of material substances.	*2132·0*	*987·8*	*46·3*	*53·7*	*7·2*	*92·8*	*153·9*	*112·9*
Sub-class III.—Industry	1335·3	645·4	48·3	51·7	6·2	93·8	136·9	104·9
Order 6. Textiles	333·9	177·6	53·2	46·8	8·7	91·3	111·7	84·3
„ 7. Hides, skins and hard materials from the animal kingdom.	33·5	13·5	40·4	59·6	2·8	97·2	213·2	145·9
„ 8. Wood	152·4	67·5	44·3	55·7	4·1	95·9	162·3	124·2
„ 9. Metals	52·2	19·6	37·5	62·5	8·6	91·4	189·0	164·8
„ 10. Ceramics	59·6	32·0	53·8	46·2	2·5	97·5	99·4	85·5
„ 11. Chemical products, properly so called and analogous.	14·6	6·9	47·3	52·7	5·6	94·4	122·9	110·7
„ 12. Food industries	147·9	71·2	48·1	51·9	6·3	93·7	124·3	106·7
„ 13. Industries of dress and toilet.	295·0	149·7	50·8	49·2	3·3	96·7	146·8	95·2
„ 14. Furniture industries ...	1·2	0·5	39·2	60·8	25·4	74·6	148·6	157·2
„ 15. Building industries ...	144·9	68·9	47·5	52·5	4·5	95·5	157·6	108·3
„ 16. Construction of means of transport.	0·9	0·4	43·6	56·4	29·9	70·1	174·6	110·1
„ 17. Production and transmission of physical forces (heat, light, electricity motive power, etc.).	0·3	0·1	37·1	62·9	95·4	4·6	167·8	200·0
„ 18. Industries of luxury and those pertaining to literature and the arts and sciences.	88·2	31·7	35·9	64·1	14·1	85·9	188·0	177·0
„ 19. Industries concerned with refuse matter.	10·7	5·5	54·8	45·2	19·3	80·7	77·2	83·9
Sub-class IV.—Transport	135·7	54·1	39·9	60·1	19·7	80·3	177·9	144·6
Order 20. Transport by water... ...	18·0	7·5	42·2	57·8	21·7	78·3	145·9	126·6
„ 21. Transport by road	81·8	34·7	42·4	57·6	15·5	84·5	158·0	131·5
„ 22. Transport by rail	27·7	9·2	32·9	67·1	32·3	67·7	220·2	195·8
„ 23. Post office, Telegraph and Telephone services.	8·2	2·7	32·7	67·3	25·8	74·2	227·8	196·2
Sub-class V. —Trade	661·0	288·3	43·6	56·4	7·2	92·8	174·2	125·7
Order 24. Banks, establishments of credit, exchange and insurance.	27·4	9·6	34·9	65·1	10·1	89·9	171·8	187·9
„ 25. Brokerage, commission and export.	4·7	1·5	31·3	68·7	31·7	68·3	240·4	210·4
„ 26. Trade in textiles	23·5	10·3	43·7	56·3	13·6	86·4	182·6	120·1
„ 27. Trade in skins, leather and furs.	12·0	3·9	32·4	67·6	7·0	93·0	266·3	204·6

I.—General distribution by occupation—cont.

Class, sub-class and order.	Number per 10,000 of total population.		Percentage in each class, sub-class and order of		Percentage of actual workers employed.		Percentage of dependents to actual workers.	
	Persons supported.	Actual workers.	Actual workers.	Dependents.	In cities.	In rural areas.	In cities.	In rural areas.
1	2	3	4	5	6	7	8	9
Class B.—Preparation and supply of material substances—*cont.*								
SUB-CLASS V.—Trade—*cont.*								
Order 28. Trade in wood	8·0	3·4	42·0	58·0	7·5	92·5	263·6	127·8
" 29. Trade in metals	0·9	0·3	30·5	69·5	22·6	77·4	271·8	215·0
" 30. Trade in pottery	5·6	2·9	51·3	48·7	1·7	98·3	148·8	94·1
" 31. Trade in chemical products.	4·3	1·7	39·9	60·1	11·8	88·2	213·8	143·4
" 32. Hotels, cafés, restaurants, etc.	32·9	13·5	40·8	59·2	8·5	91·5	176·1	140·8
" 33. Other trade in foodstuffs ...	437·2	195·7	44·8	55·2	6·1	93·9	156·4	121·8
" 34. Trade in clothing and toilet articles.	21·5	7·6	35·2	64·8	7·9	92·1	312·9	172·9
" 35. Trade in furniture	6·9	2·5	36·6	63·4	13·7	86·3	209·6	167·8
" 36. Trade in building materials.	6·2	3·0	49·3	50·7	5·5	94·5	232·7	95·4
" 37. Trade in means of transport.	6·7	2·7	40·7	59·3	3·3	96·7	184·1	144·5
" 38. Trade in fuel	20·6	12·2	59·4	40·6	4·3	95·7	128·4	65·7
" 39. Trade in articles of luxury and those pertaining to letters and the arts and sciences.	21·1	8·5	40·3	59·7	12·6	87·4	201·6	140·3
" 40. Trade in refuse matter ..	0·1	0·0	43·9	56·1	43·0	57·0	57·8	180·9
" 41. Trade of other sorts ...	21·4	9·0	42·8	57·7	13·9	86·1	173·2	130·4
Class C.—Public administration and liberal arts.	***317·8***	***111·7***	***35·1***	***64·9***	***13·7***	***86·3***	***209·5***	***180·7***
SUB-CLASS VI.—Public force	50·0	17·1	34·2	65·8	12·4	87·6	167·1	195·7
Order 42. Army	3·9	1·9	48·3	51·7	49·8	50·2	91·6	122·5
" 43. Navy	0·1	0·0	11·1	88·9	4·1	95·9	11,300·0	35·5
" 44. Police	46·0	15·2	33·1	66·9	7·9	92·1	220·9	200·5
SUB-CLASS VII.—Public administration } *Order* 45. Public administration ...	84·3	27·4	32·5	67·5	14·3	85·7	231·7	203·5
SUB-CLASS VIII.—Professions and liberal arts.	162·6	59·9	36·8	63·2	11·1	88·9	217·6	165·8
Order 46. Religion	61·3	22·8	37·3	62·7	6·9	93·1	214·9	164·8
" 47. Law	11·6	3·2	27·5	72·5	25·6	74·4	280·5	25·8
" 48. Medicine	21·4	7·6	35·2	64·8	14·3	85·7	213·7	179·0
" 49. Instruction	35·1	13·0	37·0	63·0	11·1	88·9	210·9	165·0
" 50. Letters and arts and sciences.	33·2	13·3	40·1	59·9	13·0	87·0	198·4	142·3
SUB-CLASS IX.—Persons living on their income. } *Order* 51. Persons living principally on their income.	20·9	7·3	34·8	65·2	36·0	64·0	188·4	186·6
Class D.—Miscellaneous	***479·5***	***278·1***	***58·0***	***42·0***	***8·0***	***92·0***	***118·2***	***70·3***
SUB-CLASS X.—Domestic service ... } *Order* 52. Domestic service	49·2	26·4	53·6	46·4	24·3	75·7	106·8	80·2
SUB-CLASS XI.—Insufficiently described occupations. } *Order* 53. General terms which do not indicate a definite occupation.	364·9	209·2	57·3	42·7	6·4	93·6	136·2	70·2
SUB-CLASS XII.—Unproductive	65·4	42·5	65·1	34·9	5·6	94·4	48·7	54·0
Order 54. Inmates of jails, asylums and hospitals.	3·2	2·9	92·6	7·4	24·3	75·7	12·0	6·8
" 55. Beggars, vagrants and prostitutes.	62·2	39·6	63·6	36·4	4·2	95·8	64·5	56·8

II.—Distribution by occupation in natural divisions.

Occupation.	Number per 10,000 of total population supported in					
	Agency.	East Coast (North).	Deccan.	East Coast (Central).	East Coast (South).	West Coast.
1	2	3	4	5	6	7
Class A.—Production of raw materials	***8,350·0***	***7,225·3***	***7,389·9***	***7,137·3***	***6,726·8***	***6,588·7***
SUB-CLASS I.—Exploitation of the surface of the earth ...	8,349·8	7,218·3	7,381·8	7,134·9	6,724·9	6,581·3
Agriculture	8144·6	6,961·8	7,185·0	6,984·4	6,578·3	6,826·5
Pasture	187·2	172·6	158·9	100·2	95·8	35·2
Fishing and hunting	3·5	75·1	9·5	33·8	41·2	178 5
Others	14·5	8·8	28·4	16·5	9·6	46·1
,, II.—Extraction of minerals	0·2	7·0	8·1	2·4	1·9	7·4
Class B.—Preparation and supply of material substances.	***929·6***	***2,154·6***	***1,963·2***	***2,070·3***	***2,202·7***	***2,640·4***
SUB-CLASS III.—Industry	529·0	1,374 3	1,349·6	1,312·7	1,347·0	1,558·6
Wood industries	48·2	165·3	104 1	117·4	149·1	301·7
Metal industries	88·3	35·2	25·3	52·0	68·6	65·8
Food industries	21·6	96·1	48·4	128·6	182·7	379·7
Industries of dress and toilet	78·1	439·7	370·2	259·2	231·8	200·4
Other industries	292·8	688 0	806·6	755·5	714·8	606·0
,, IV.—Transport	20·8	97·8	68·3	147·8	142·2	281·9
,, V.—Trade	379·8	682·5	565·3	609·8	713·5	804·9
Trade in food stuffs	271·7	523·7	390·5	406·2	476·9	633·2
Trade in textiles	9·0	18·7	21·9	22·4	28·5	33·5
Other trades	99·1	140·1	152·9	181·2	208·1	138·2
Class C.—Public administration and liberal arts ...	***118·2***	***272·2***	***241·6***	***336·9***	***370·4***	***393·3***
SUB-CLASS VI.—Public force	51·6	54·0	70·9	50·5	47·5	25·7
,, VII.—Public administration	28·3	73·8	73·8	94·2	100·3	76·1
,, VIII.—Professions and liberal arts	36·5	125·6	86 3	156·2	207·4	276·0
,, IX.—Persons living on their income	1·8	18·8	10·6	36·0	15·2	15 5
Class D.—Miscellaneous	***602·2***	***347·9***	***385·3***	***455·5***	***700·1***	***377·6***
SUB-CLASS X.—Domestic service	40·2	37·3	36·0	52·5	37·4	112·2
,, XI.—Insufficiently described occupations ...	520·0	206·7	207·2	358 8	629·2	221·2
,, XII.—Unproductive	42·0	103·9	142·1	44·2	33·5	44·2

District and natural division.	Agriculture.				Industry (including mines).				Commerce.				Professions.			
	Population supported by agriculture.	Proportion of agricultural population per 1,000 of district population.	Percentage on agricultural population of		Population supported by industry.	Proportion of industrial population per 1,000 of district population.	Percentage on industrial population of		Population supported by commerce.	Proportion of commercial population per 1,000 of district population.	Percentage on commercial population of		Population supported by profession.	Proportion of professional population per 1,000 of district population.	Percentage on professional population of	
			Actual workers.	Dependents.			Actual workers.	Dependents.			Actual workers.	Dependents.			Actual workers.	Dependents.
1	2	3	4	5	6	7	8	9	10	11	12	13	14	15	16	17
Agency	**1,284,830**	**814·5**	**57·7**	**42·3**	**83,489**	**52·9**	**53·9**	**46·1**	**63,188**	**40·1**	**54·4**	**45·6**	**5,756**	**3·6**	**41·2**	**58·8**
Agency, Ganjám ...	285,281	818·9	61·9	38·1	23,095	65·9	53·6	46·4	20,295	57·9	55·5	44·5	769	2·2	51·4	48·6
Do. Visagapatam ...	830,757	814·3	57·2	42·8	45,446	44·5	54·7	45·3	34,678	34·0	54·8	45·2	3,702	3·6	39·8	60·2
Do. Gódávari ...	168,792	815·8	53·1	46·9	14,948	72·2	52·2	47·8	8,215	39·7	50·3	49·7	1,285	6·2	39·5	60·5
East Coast (North) ...	**7,316,691**	**696·2**	**52·7**	**47·3**	**1,451,662**	**138·1**	**51·5**	**48·5**	**820,064**	**78·0**	**48·5**	**51·5**	**132,027**	**12·6**	**38·6**	**61·4**
Ganjám	1,285,745	687·3	52·3	47·7	197,856	105·8	51·6	48·4	165,714	88·6	52·9	47·1	41,980	22·4	36·6	63·4
Visagapatam	1,571,654	724·4	60·0	40·0	273,597	126·1	53·2	46·8	172,325	79·4	54·7	45·3	14,458	66·6	37·2	62·8
Gódávari	961,350	664·9	50·1	49·9	220,637	152·5	51·2	48·8	131,987	91·3	46·1	53·9	16,647	11·5	36·0	64·0
Kistna	1,440,285	721·0	48·5	51·5	270,469	135·4	50·2	49·8	121,498	60·8	42·4	57·6	25,313	12·7	40·6	59·4
Guntúr	1,181,500	696·0	49·8	50·2	274,694	161·8	51·8	48·2	116,847	68·8	43·5	56·5	19,814	11·7	41·4	58·6
Nellore	876,157	659·7	54·3	45·7	214,409	161·4	50·8	49·2	111,698	84·1	47·3	52·7	13,870	10·4	41·7	58·3
Deccan	**2,740,881**	**718·5**	**57·4**	**42·6**	**517,927**	**135·8**	**53·8**	**46·2**	**241,699**	**63·4**	**47·9**	**52·1**	**32,939**	**8·6**	**43·8**	**56·2**
Cuddapah	639,616	715·5	52·2	47·8	134,840	150·8	51·7	48·3	51,950	58·1	46·6	53·4	6,754	7·6	38·5	61·5
Kurnool	683,914	731·3	58·6	41·4	105,542	112·9	54·7	45·3	56,218	60·1	45·9	54·1	7,090	7·6	37·3	62·7
Banganapalle	24,719	628·3	65·8	34·2	6,475	164·6	53·8	46·2	3,285	83·5	47·7	52·3	489	11·2	48·3	51·7
Bellary	720,239	742·9	56·6	43·4	120,465	124·3	54·6	45·4	57,432	59·2	47·2	52·8	8,965	9·2	41·6	58·4
Sandúr	8,604	636·1	48·7	51·3	2,720	201·1	57·4	42·6	1,036	76·6	51·8	48·2	246	18·2	38·6	61·4
Anantapur	663,789	689·1	61·9	38·1	148,385	154·1	54·4	45·6	71,783	74·5	51·0	49·0	9,445	9·8	54·4	45·6
East Coast (Central) ...	**7,941,420**	**698·4**	**51·1**	**48·9**	**1,495,231**	**131·5**	**46·0**	**54·0**	**861,396**	**75·8**	**41·4**	**58·6**	**177,646**	**15·6**	**35·9**	**64·1**
Madras	23,879	46·0	37·3	62·7	140,334	270·6	40·3	59·7	152,301	293·6	36·8	63·2	35,460	68·4	32·5	67·5
Chingleput	969,136	689·3	42·1	57·9	179,278	127·5	42·3	57·7	106,581	75·8	41·3	58·7	23,088	16·4	34·7	65·3
Chittoor	937,074	756·5	54·8	45·2	145,887	117·8	49·1	50·9	72,185	58·3	40·6	59·4	13,716	11·1	37·5	62·5
North Arcot	1,446,941	787·9	53·3	46·7	226,097	115·3	48·1	51·9	148,008	75·5	37·8	62·2	23,012	11·7	36·1	63·9
Salem	1,295,372	733·2	57·5	42·5	237,923	134·7	49·1	50·9	89,961	50·9	44·7	55·3	18,062	10·2	37·7	62·3
Coimbatore	1,351,564	638·6	53·4	46·6	371,747	175·6	46·5	53·5	174,438	82·4	45·6	54·4	35,971	17·0	37·3	62·7
South Arcot	1,917,454	811·6	46·7	53·3	193,965	82·1	44·2	55·8	117,932	49·9	43·5	56·5	28,337	12·0	37·2	62·8
East Coast (South) ...	**6,751,667**	**657·6**	**51·7**	**48·3**	**1,384,460**	**134·9**	**44·4**	**55·6**	**878,180**	**85·6**	**40·2**	**59·8**	**212,896**	**20·7**	**35·2**	**64·8**
Tanjore	1,495,753	633·1	44·3	55·7	282,253	119·5	43·5	56·5	250,352	106·0	38·4	61·6	76,120	32·2	33·4	66·6
Trichinopoly	1,379,069	654·5	55·5	44·5	252,329	119·8	45·3	54·7	130,039	61·7	41·8	58·2	40,124	19·0	36·9	63·1
Pudukkóttai	300,012	728·4	64·0	36·0	30,260	73·5	50·6	49·4	35,382	85·9	42·5	57·5	7,637	18·5	39·9	60·1
Madura	1,451,816	751·1	57·6	42·4	234,408	121·3	45·9	54·1	130,194	67·4	43·3	56·7	24,593	12·7	36·1	63·9
Rámnád	1,092,673	658·9	49·0	51·0	197,064	118·8	47·6	52·4	173,321	104·5	38·9	61·1	27,782	16·8	36·6	63·4
Tinnevelly	1,032,344	576·5	48·0	52·0	388,146	216·8	41·5	58·5	158,892	88·7	39·6	60·4	36,639	20·5	34·8	65·2
West Coast	**2,742,251**	**632·7**	**48·4**	**51·6**	**676,625**	**156·1**	**49·8**	**50·2**	**471,088**	**108·7**	**37·5**	**62·5**	**119,633**	**27·6**	**36·9**	**63·1**
Nilgiris	65,342	550·9	55·7	44·3	10,468	88·2	42·4	57·6	9,658	81·4	53·5	46·5	2,602	21·9	35·4	64·6
Malabar	1,829,786	606·9	42·5	57·5	541,217	179·5	49·3	50·7	367,386	121·8	34·6	65·4	91,582	30·4	35·7	64·3
Anjengo	651	116·8	27·2	72·8	1,277	229·2	50·4	49·6	1,317	236·4	44·1	55·9	330	59·2	23·6	76·4
South Canara	846,472	706·2	60·7	39·3	123,668	103·5	52·7	47·3	92,727	77·6	47·2	52·8	25,119	21·0	41·3	58·7
Cities*	**161,258**	**119·6**	**36·8**	**63·2**	**396,012**	**294·3**	**42·2**	**57·8**	**362,872**	**269·7**	**36·3**	**63·7**	**88,458**	**65·7**	**31·5**	**68·5**

* Including Madras.

IV.—Occupations combined with agriculture (where agriculture is the subsidiary occupation).

Occupation.	Number per mille of actual workers who are partially agriculturists.						
	Province.	Agency.	East Coast (North).	Deccan.	East Coast (Central).	East Coast (South).	West Coast.
1	2	3	4	5	6	7	8
TOTAL ACTUAL WORKERS ...	*27·9*	*13·3*	*41·5*	*35·9*	*23·3*	*22·0*	*17·2*
Class A.—Production of raw materials ...	*26·8*	*1·9*	*43·8*	*2·7*	*2·1*	*1·7*	*2·5*
SUB-CLASS I.—Exploitation of the surface of the earth.	2·6	1·9	42·7	2·7	2·1	1·7	2·4
Agriculture	0·6	0·5	0·6	0·1	0·4	0·7	1·6
Pasture	63·1	52·1	76·2	82·6	64·8	88·1	17·2
Fishing and hunting ...	72·7	100·3	131·1	188 4	46·5	84·0	21·8
Others	83·3	129·8	94·5	114·2	73·8	108·5	51 3
,, II.—Extraction of minerals	80·2	45·4	128·0	10·6	122·4	52·5	46·0
Class B.—Preparation and supply of material substances.	*104·0*	*107·4*	*150·0*	*139·0*	*90·3*	*78·2*	*50·3*
SUB-CLASS III.—Industry	112·4	98·1	166·4	138·2	99·4	82·4	55·4
Wood industries	106·4	95·2	142·0	118·8	114·8	102·0	52·8
Metal industries	118·9	74·8	144·4	139·2	138·1	128·3	40·8
Food industries	82·7	62·3	121·5	81·6	62·9	61·9	96·0
Industries of dress and toilet.	162·8	148·8	216·9	187·0	185·1	108·5	46·6
Other industries	97·2	96·2	148·5	121·6	91·8	71·7	87·3
,, IV.—Transport	58·9	106·9	87·9	99·1	49·7	64·0	30·2
,, V.—Trade	93·4	120·2	128·4	145·2	78·2	72·1	44·9
Trade in food stuffs	90·5	142·4	119·7	141·3	76·1	64·9	45·8
Trade in textiles	92·7	92·5	151·8	111·0	88·3	65 8	48·2
Other trades	102·6	60·9	132·6	158·4	82·2	98·3	89·6
Class C.—Public administration and liberal arts.	*156·9*	*132·3*	*230·1*	*173·9*	*139·3*	*153·5*	*74·6*
SUB-CLASS VI.—Public force	149·0	82·2	215·8	12·9	120·3	173·6	12·2
,, VII.—Public administration ...	219·4	235·9	317·9	234·5	187·2	207·0	125·0
,, VIII.—Professions and liberal arts ...	187·3	124·7	206·6	168·7	122·8	130·7	69·4
,, IX.—Persons living on their income.	101·0	144·2	149·8	92·5	85·3	85·6	71·2
Class D.—Miscellaneous	*42·8*	*19·2*	*72·4*	*126·2*	*35·0*	*25·0*	*14·3*
SUB-CLASS X.—Domestic service	37·3	37·8	103·4	54·8	17·3	38·5	5·8
,, XI.—Insufficiently described occupations.	36·8	11·2	45·8	147·2	38·8	24·7	19·8
,, XII.—Unproductive	75·7	108·4	112·8	111·6	26·2	19·5	13·0

V.—Occupations combined with agriculture (where agriculture is the principal occupation).

Non-cultivating landowners.		Non-cultivating tenants.		Cultivating landowners and cultivating tenants.			Farm servants and field labourers.	
Subsidiary occupation.	Number per 10,000 who follow it.	Subsidiary occupation.	Number per 10,000 who follow it.	Subsidiary occupation.	Number per 10,000 who follow it among cultivating landowners.	Number per 10,000 who follow it among cultivating tenants.	Subsidiary occupation.	Number per 10,000 who follow it.
1	2	3	4	5	6	7	8	9
TOTAL ...	*2,788·4*	TOTAL ...	*1,993·4*	TOTAL ...	*1,228·7*	*1,211·9*	TOTAL ...	*318·1*
Agriculture	711·7	Agriculture	555·7	Agriculture	465·6	406·1	Agriculture	84·2
Artisans	482·5	Artisans	349·6	General labourers ...	90·5	98·7	General labourers ...	18·3
Traders (other than of money-lenders, grain and pulse dealers).	436·4	Traders (other than of money-lenders, grain and pulse dealers).	340·5	Government servants (other than village watchmen).	35·6	17·5	Village watchmen ...	1·2
Priests	223·9	Priests	112·7	Money-lenders, grain and pulse dealers.	28·7	27·0	Cattle breeders ...	2·5
Money-lenders, grain and pulse dealers.	174·4	Money-lenders, grain and pulse dealers.	110·7	Traders (other than money-lenders, grain and pulse dealers).	141·1	146·8	Milkmen	2·7
Government servants ...	177·3	Government servants ...	84·3	Fishermen	7·5	14·8	Mill hands and weavers.	13·2
Miscellaneous labourers.	103·0	Schoolmasters ..	37·2	Boatmen	1·4	1·9	Fishermen	6·9
Schoolmasters	82·4	Clerks (not Government)	19·3	Cattle breeders ...	4·4	7·5	Boatmen	0·3
Clerks (not Government)	52·4	Medical practitioners ...	18·2	Milkmen	5·9	7·0	Rice pounders ...	7·2
Cart owners, drivers, etc.	37·3	Agents, managers of landed estates, etc.	66·9	Village watchmen ...	9·1	8·6	Traders of all kinds ...	48·7
Medical practitioners ...	34·5	Lawyers	4·6	Weavers and mill hands	31·9	18·8	Oil-pressers	0·7
Growers of fruits, flowers, etc.	33·9	Others	293·7	Barbers	21·7	15·3	Potters	2·2
Agents, managers of landed estates, etc.	33·7			Oil-pressers	1·7	9·7	Leather workers ...	2·4
Lawyers	6·1			Washermen	32·5	28·9	Washermen	6·0
Others	198·9			Potters	19·1	15·7	Blacksmiths	0·5
				Blacksmiths	5·7	4·6	Carpenters	2·7
				Carpenters	19·4	14·8	Others	118·4
				Others	306·9	368·2		

VI.—*Occupations of females by sub-classes and selected orders and groups* (1911).

Group number.	Occupation.	Number of actual workers. Males.	Number of actual workers. Females.	Number of females per 1,000 males.
1	2	3	4	5
	GRAND TOTAL ...	*12,932,854*	*8,379,378*	*648*
	Sub-class I.—Exploitation of the surface of the earth.	*9,179,226*	*6,356,393*	*692*
	Order 1.—Pasture and agriculture.	9,093,813	6,339,935	697
	(*a*) Ordinary cultivation ...	8,715,575	6,261,731	718
1-a	Non-cultivating landowners.	223,941	112,973	504
1-b	Non-cultivating tenants ...	41,563	17,617	424
2-a	Cultivating landowners	4,107,154	2,264,228	551
2-b	Cultivating tenants	1,994,758	1,104,904	554
3	Agents, managers of landed estates (not planters), clerks, rent collectors, etc.	23 554	1,629	69
4	Farm servants and field labourers.	2,324,605	2,760,380	1,187
	(*b*) Growers of special products and market gardening.	53,770	18,597	346
5	Tea, coffee, cinchona and indigo plantations.	16,772	9,723	580
6	Fruit, flower, vegetable, betel, vine, areca nut, etc., growers.	36,998	8,874	240
	(*c*) Forestry	22,515	9,754	433
8	Wood-cutters; firewood, lac, catechu, rubber, etc., collectors, and charcoal burners.	15,786	9,743	617
	(*d*) Raising of farm stock ...	301,842	49,807	165
9	Cattle and buffalo breeders and keepers.	45,215	8,259	183
10	Sheep, goat and pig breeders.	52,904	11,682	221
12	Herdsmen, shepherds, goat-herds, etc.	202,758	29,653	146
14	*Order* 2.—Fishing and hunting.	85,413	16,458	193
	Fishing	83,597	16,039	192
	Sub-class II.—Extraction of minerals.	*6,396*	*2,366*	*370*
	Sub-class III.—Industry ...	*1,801,286*	*900,950*	*500*
	Order 6.—Textiles	457,052	292,076	639
21	Cotton ginning, cleaning and pressing.	20,098	12,548	624
22	Cotton spinning, sizing and weaving.	386,598	194,350	503
24	Rope, twine and string ...	7,151	46,741	6,536
25	Other fibres (cocoanut, aloes, flax, hemp, straw, etc.).	1,479	7,777	5,258
26	Wool carders and spinners, weavers of woollen blankets, carpets, etc.	11,619	11,579	997
27	Silk spinners and weavers ...	21,407	15,452	722
	Order 7.—Hides, skins and hard materials from the animal kingdom.	46,619	4,415	95
33	Makers of leather articles, such as trunks, water bags, etc.	33,596	3,478	104
	Order 8.—Wood	199,825	82,836	415
36	Sawyers, carpenters, turners, joiners, etc.	140,649	7,603	54
37	Basket makers and other industries of woody materials, including leaves.	59,176	75,233	1,271

Group number.	Occupation.	Number of actual workers. Males.	Number of actual workers. Females.	Number of females per 1,000 males.
1	2	3	4	5
	Sub-class III.—Industry—*cont.*			
	Order 9.—Metals	74,771	7,137	95
41	Other workers in iron and makers of implements and tools, principally or exclusively of iron.	53,511	5,584	104
42	Workers in brass, copper and bell metal.	14,793	1,100	74
	Order 10.—Ceramics	85,674	48,521	566
47	Potters and earthen pipe and bowl makers.	75,707	44,878	593
	Order 11.—Chemical products properly so-called, and analogous.	20,696	8,241	398
53	Manufacture and refining of vegetable and mineral oils.	17,922	7,236	404
	Order 12.—Food industries ...	157,370	140,636	894
56	Rice pounders and huskers and flour grinders.	17,993	108,379	6,023
62	Makers of sugar, molasses and gur.	3,874	14,339	3,701
64	Brewers and distillers ...	791	2,155	2,724
65	Toddy drawers	111,242	3,187	29
	Order 13.—Industries of dress and toilet.	415,594	211,414	509
67	Hat, cap and turban makers.	250	1,517	6,068
68	Tailors, milliners, dress makers and darners, embroiderers on linen.	25,682	12,018	468
69	Shoe, boot and sandal makers.	107,562	15,888	148
70	Other industries pertaining to dress, gloves, socks, gaiters, belts, buttons, umbrellas, canes, etc.	1,004	1,068	1,064
71	Washing, cleaning and dyeing.	186,653	175,996	943
72	Barbers, hair dressers and wig makers.	94,074	4,074	43
73	Other industries connected with the toilet (tattooers, shampooers, bath houses, etc.).	369	853	2,312
	Order 15.—Building industries.	202,730	85,579	422
77	Excavators, plinth builders and well sinkers.	76,151	55,752	732
78	Stone and marble workers, masons and bricklayers.	110,027	20,230	184
79	Others (thatchers, building contractors, house painters, tilers, plumbers, lock-smiths, etc.)	12,946	6,486	501
	Order 18.—Industries of luxury and those pertaining to literature and the arts and sciences.	123,883	8,718	70
89	Workers in precious stones and metals, enamellers, imitation jewellery makers, gilders, etc.	109,727	6,943	63
90	Makers of bangles, rosaries, beads, and other necklaces, spangles, lingams and sacred threads	3,370	1,495	444
	Order 19.—Industries concerned with refuse matter.	13,432	11,100	826
	Sub-class IV.—Transport ...	*207,779*	*18,789*	*90*
	Order 20.—Transport by water.	30,658	826	27
97	Boatowners, boatmen and towmen.	20,456	518	25

VI.—Occupations of females by sub-classes and selected orders and groups (1911)—cont.

Group number.	Occupation.	Number of actual workers.		Number of females per 1,000 males.
		Males.	Females.	
1	2	3	4	5
	Sub-class IV.—Transport—*cont.*			
	Order 21.—Transport by road.	129,049	16,375	127
98	Persons employed on the construction and maintenance of roads and bridges.	10,238	5,185	506
99	Cartowners and drivers, coachmen, stable boys, tramway, mail carriage, etc., managers and employés (excluding private servants).	84,139	3,777	45
102	Porters and messengers ...	33,093	7,320	221
	Order 22.—Transport by rail...	36,844	1,519	41
103	Railway employés of all kinds other than construction coolies.	31,513	403	13
	Sub-class V.—Trade	***758,557***	***446,596***	***591***
	Order 24.—Banks, establishments of credit, exchange and insurance.	26,644	13,377	502
106	Bank managers, money lenders, exchange and insurance agents, money changers and brokers and their employés.	26,644	13,377	502
	Order 26.—Trade in textiles ..	36,384	6,727	185
108	Trade in piece-goods, wool, cotton, silk, hair and other textiles.	36,384	6,727	185
	Order 27.—Trade in skins, leather and furs.	14,431	1,771	123
109	Trade in skins, leather, furs, feathers, horn, etc.	14,431	1,771	123
	Order 28.—Trade in wood ...	8,522	5,552	648
110	Trade in wood (not firewood), cork, bark, etc.	8,522	5,522	648
	Order 30.—Trade in pottery ...	6,702	5,408	807
112	Trade in pottery	6,702	5,408	807
	Order 31.—Trade in chemical products.	4,860	2,380	490
113	Trade in chemical products (drugs, dyes, paints, petroleum, explosives, etc.)	4,860	2,380	490
	Order 32.—Hotels, cafés, restaurants, etc.	37,990	18,442	485
114	Vendors of wine, liquors, ærated waters, etc.	29,958	15,045	502
	Order 33.—Other trade in foodstuffs.	486,256	333,128	685
116	Fish dealers	49,436	63,160	1,278
117	Grocers and sellers of vegetable oil, and salt and other condiments.	245,577	106,973	436
118	Sellers of milk, butter, ghee, poultry, eggs, etc.	15,373	28,318	1,842
119	Sellers of sweetmeats, sugar, gur and molasses.	24,822	42,025	1,693
120	Cardamom, betel-leaf, vegetables, fruit and arecanut sellers.	60,311	45,865	760
121	Grain and pulse dealers ...	54,823	28,607	522
122	Tobacco, opium, ganja, etc, sellers.	21,452	4,661	217
123	Dealers in sheep, goats and pigs.	10,054	2,629	261
124	Dealers in hay, grass and fodder.	4,408	10,890	2,471

Group number.	Occupation.	Number of actual workers.		Number of females per 1,000 males.
		Males.	Females.	
1	2	3	4	5
	Sub-class V.—Trade—*cont.*			
	Order 34.—Trade in clothing and toilet articles.	25,980	5,737	221
125	Trade in ready-made clothing and other articles of dress and the toilet (hats, umbrellas, socks, ready made shoes, perfumes, etc.)	25,980	5,737	221
	Order 38.—Trade in fuel ...	21,777	29,411	1,351
130	Dealers in firewood, charcoal, coal, cowdung, etc.	21,777	29,411	1,351
	Order 39.—Trade in articles of luxury and those pertaining to letters and the arts and sciences.	26,136	9,411	360
132	Dealers in common bangles, bead necklaces, fans, small articles, toys, hunting and fishing tackle, flowers, etc.	17,683	8,417	476
	Order 41.—Trade of other sorts.	29,824	8,052	270
135	Shop-keepers otherwise unspecified.	23,452	6,610	282
	Sub-class VI.—Public force.	***71,552***	***3***	...
	Order 44.—Police	63,787	3	...
142	Police	32,656	3	0·1
143	Village watchmen	31,131	...	...
	Sub-class VII.—Public administration.	***114,313***	***534***	***5***
	Order 45.—Public Administration.	114,313	534	5
144	Service of the State ...	47,514	21	0·4
146	Municipal and other local (not village) service.	11,174	514	46
147	Village officials and servants other than watchmen.	51,496	2	...
	Sub-class VIII.—Professions and liberal arts.	***212795***	***37,912***	***178***
	Order 46.—Religion	84,180	11,484	136
148	Priests, ministers, etc. ...	26,674	1,968	74
149	Religious mendicants, inmates of monasteries, etc.	1,772	1,543	871
151	Temple, burial or burning ground service, pilgrim conductors, circumcisers.	52,329	7,538	144
	Order 47.—Law	13,339	3	0·2
	Order 48.—Medicine	24,432	7,172	294
154	Medical practitioners of all kinds, including dentists, oculists and veterinary surgeons.	22,018	3,090	140
155	Midwives, vaccinators, compounders, nurses, masseurs, etc.	2,414	4,082	1,691
	Order 49.—Instruction ...	47,566	6,764	142
156	Professors and teachers of all kinds, and clerks and servants connected with education.	47,566	6,764	142
	Order 50.—Letters and arts and sciences.	43,278	12,489	289
160	Music composers and masters, players on all kinds of musical instruments (not military) singers, actors and dancers.	25,788	11,684	453

VI.—Occupations of females by sub-classes and selected orders and groups (1911)—*cont.*

Group number.	Occupation.	Number of actual workers.		Number of females per 1,000 males.
		Males.	Females.	
1	2	3	4	5
	Sub-class IX.—Persons living on their income.	*20,973*	*9,420*	*449*
	Order 51.—Persons living principally on their income.	20,973	9,420	449
161	Proprietors (other than of agricultural land), fund and scholarship holders and pensioners.	20,973	9,420	449
	Sub-class X.—Domestic service.	*63,073*	*47,329*	*750*
	Order 52.—Domestic service ...	63,073	47,329	750
162	Cooks, water carriers, door-keepers, watchmen and other indoor servants.	55,865	47,074	843
	Sub-class XI.—Insufficiently described occupations.	*392,569*	*483,251*	*1,231*
	Order 53.—General terms which do not indicate a definite occupation.	392,569	483,251	1,231
165	Cashiers, accountants, book-keepers, clerks and other employés in unspecified offices, warehouses and shops.	56,417	3,446	61
167	Labourers and workmen otherwise unspecified.	329,834	479,347	1,453
	Sub-class XII.—Unproductive.	*104,335*	*73,816*	*707*
	Order 55.—Beggars, vagrants and prostitutes.	92,462	73,265	792
169	Beggars, vagrants, procurers, prostitutes, receivers of stolen goods, cattle poisoners.	92,462	73,265	792

VII.—Selected occupations (1911 *and* 1901).

Group number	Occupation.	Population supported in 1911.	Population supported in 1901.	Percentage of variation.
1	2	3	4	5
	Grand Total ...	*41,870,160*	*38,633,340*	+ *8·4*
	Sub-class I.—Exploitation of the surface of the earth.	*29,825,702*	*27,675,819*	— *7·8*
	Order 1.—Pasture and agriculture.	29,586,787	27,482,122	+ 7·7
	(*a*) Ordinary cultivation ...	28,621,449	26,488,155	+ 8·1
1(*a*)	Non-cultivating landowners.	960,194	796,842	+ 20·5
1(*b*)	Non-cultivating tenants ...	163,396	42,621	+ 283·4
2(*a*)	Cultivating landowners ...	13,168,009	13,509,901	— 2·5
2(*b*)	Cultivating tenants ..	6,423,909	4,394,658	+ 46·2
3	Agents, managers of landed estates (not planters), clerks, rent collectors, etc.	74,508	103,359	— 27·9
4	Farm servants and field labourers.	7,831,433	7,640,774	+ 2·5
	(*b*) Growers of special products and market gardening.	156,261	171,134	— 8·7
5	Tea, coffee, cinchona and indigo plantations.	37,379	51,376	— 27·2
6	Fruit, flower, vegetable, betel, vine, arecanut, etc., growers.	118,882	119,758	— 0·7
	(*c*) Forestry	70,638	92,046	— 23·3
8	Wood-cutters; firewood, lac, catechu, rubber, etc., collectors, and charcoal burners.	51,177	77,428	— 33·9
	(*d*) Raising of farm stock ...	499,097	536,978	— 7·1
9	Cattle and buffalo breeders and keepers.	74,647	80,313	— 7·1
10	Sheep, goat and pig breeders.	102,622	110,411	— 7·1
11	Breeders of other animals (horses, mules, camels, asses, etc.).	2,684	2,888	— 7·1
12	Herdsmen, shepherds, goatherds, etc.	319,144	343,366	— 7·1
	(*e*) Raising of small animals..	327	112	+ 192·0
	Order 2.—Fishing and hunting.	238,965	193,697	+ 23·4
14	Fishing.	234,080	188,153	+ 24·4
15	Hunting ...	4,885	5,544	— 100·8
	Sub-class II.—Extraction of minerals.	*18,336*	*16,814*	+ *9·0*
	Order 3.—Mines	10,051	8,002	+ 25·6
	Order 4.—Quarries of hard rocks.	5,536	4,588	+ 20·7
	Order 5.—Salt, etc.	2,749	4,224	— 34·9
	Sub-class III.—Industry ...	*5,591,058*	*5,312,321*	+ *5·2*
	Order 6.—Textiles	1,406,286	1,394,060	+ 0·9
21	Cotton ginning, cleaning and pressing.	59,253	43,478	+ 36·2
22	Cotton spinning, sizing and weaving.	1,118,628	1,169,876	— 4·3
23	Jute spinning, pressing and weaving.	5,564	855	+ 550·8
24	Rope, twine and string ...	74,294	60,851	+ 22·1
26	Wool carders and spinners, weavers of woollen blankets, carpets, etc.	37,415	21,554	+ 73·6
27	Silk spinners and weavers ...	74,773	55,126	+ 35·6
28	Hair, camel and horse hair, bristles work, brush makers, etc.	1,359	1,057	+ 28·6
29	Persons occupied with feathers.	991	723	+ 37·1
30	Dyeing, bleaching, printing preparation and sponging of textiles.	17,096	23,061	— 25·9
	Sub-class III.—Industry—*cont.*			
	Order 7.—Hides, skins and hard materials from the animal kingdom.	132,232	163,896	— 19·3
32	Tanners, curriers, leather dressers and dyers, etc.	32,331	25,323 }	+ 26·6
		...	207 }	
33	Makers of leather articles, such as trunks, water bags, etc.	99,309	132,000	— 24·8
34	Furriers	59	6,000	— 99·0
35	Bone, ivory, horn, shell, etc., workers.	533	366	+ 45·6
	Order 8.—Wood	638,284	529,003	+ 20·7
36	Sawyers, carpenters, turners and joiners, etc.	415,983	312,832	+ 33·0
37	Basket makers and other industries of woody material, including leaves.	222,301	216,171	+ 2·8
	Order 9.—Metals	218,594	210,727	+ 3·7
39	Plough and agricultural implement makers.	2,703	2,635	+ 2·6
41	Other workers in iron and makers of implements and tools, principally or exclusively of iron.	158,072	152,359	+ 37·5
42	Workers in brass, copper and bell metal.	41,871	41,118	+ 1·8
	Order 10.—Ceramics	249,413	190,235	+ 31·1
47	Potters and earthen pipe and bowl makers.	224,053	167,709	+ 33·6
	Order 11.—Chemical products properly so-called and analogous.	61,162	92,335	— 33·8
53	Manufacture and refining of vegetable and mineral oils.	53,302	58,386	— 8·7
	Order 12.—Food industries ...	619,298	625,535	— 1·0
56	Rice pounders and huskers and flour grinders.	204,922	256,830	— 20·2
57	Bakers and biscuit makers...	12,995	6,601	+ 96·9
58	Grain parchers, etc. ...	5,906	20,153	— 70·7
59	Butchers	25,865	28,573	— 9·5
60	Fish curers	4,114	3,317	+ 30·1
62	Makers of sugar, molasses and gur.	25,093	23,651	+ 6·1
63	Sweetmeat makers, preparers of jam and condiments, etc.	19,889	7,867	+ 152·8
64	Brewers and distillers ...	4,335	710	+ 510·6
65	Toddy drawers	303,420	263,052	+ 15·3
	Order 13.—Industries of dress and toilet.	1,235,134	1,136,065	+ 8·7
68	Tailors, milliners, dress makers and darners, embroiderers on linen.	83,777	71,660	+ 16·9
69	Shoe, boot and sandal makers.	277,702	270,319	+ 2·7
71	Washing, cleaning and dyeing.	603,630	556,359	+ 8·5
72	Barbers, hair dressers and wig makers.	260,537	233,527	+ 11·6
	Order 14.—Furniture industries.	4,866	1,825	+ 166·6
	Order 15.—Building industries.	606,841	607,116	— 0·0
77	Excavators, plinth builders and well sinkers.	229,892	303,428	— 24·2
78	Stone and marble workers, masons and bricklayers.	322,824	283,444	+ 13·9
	Order 16.—Construction of means of transport.	3,616	2,635	+ 37·2

VII.—*Selected occupations* (1911 *and* 1901)—cont.

Group number.	Occupation.	Population supported in 1911.	Population supported in 1901.	Percentage of variation.
1	2	3	4	5
	Sub-class III.—Industry—*cont.*			
	Order 17.—Production and transmission of physical forces (heat, light, electricity, motive powers, etc.).	1,166	167	+ 598·2
	Order 18.—Industries of luxury and those pertaining to literature and the arts and sciences.	369,364	319,976	+ 15·4
89	Workers in precious stones and metals, enamellers, imitation jewellery makers, gilders, etc.	330,566	288,161	+ 14·7
90	Makers of bangles, rosaries, bead and other necklaces, spangles, lingams and sacred threads.	9,839	9,048	+ 8·7
	Order 19.—Industries concerned with refuse matter.	44,802	38,746	+ 15·6
93	Sweepers, scavengers, dust and sweeping contractors.	44,802	38,746	+ 15·6
	Sub-class IV.—Transport ...	***568,701***	***597,357***	**— 4·8**
	Order 20.—Transport by water.	74,966	84,132	— 10·9
95	Ship owners and their employés, ship brokers, ships' officers, engineers, mariners and firemen.	15,912	10,043	+ 58·4
96	Persons employed on the maintenance of streams, rivers and canals (including construction).	1,778	2,060	— 13·7
97	Boat owners, boatmen and towmen.	51,983	71,208	— 27·0
	Order 21.—Transport by road.	342,676	382,742	— 10·5
98	Persons employed on the construction and maintenance of roads and bridges.	31,638	36,666	— 13·7
99	Cart owners and drivers, coachmen, stable boys, tramway, mail carriage, etc., managers and employés (excluding private servants).	215,475	166,528	+ 29·4
100	Palki, etc., bearers and owners.	2,857	4,883	— 41·5
101	Pack elephant, camel, mule, ass and bullock owners and drivers.	1,060	5,555	— 80·9
102	Porters and messengers.	91,646	169,110	— 45·7
	Order 22.—Transport by rail.	116,511	100,822	+ 15·6
103	Railway employés of all kinds other than construction coolies.	101,504	83,431	+ 21·7
104	Labourers employed on railway construction.	15,007	17,391	— 13·7
	Order 23.—Post-office, telegraph and telephone services.	34,548	29,661	+ 16·5
105	Post-office, Telegraph and Telephone services.	34,548	29,661	+ 16·5

Group number.	Occupation.	Population supported in 1911.	Population supported in 1901.	Percentage of variation.
1	2	3	4	5
	Sub-class V.—Trade	***2,767,356***	***2,588,075***	**+ 6·9**
	Order 24.—Banks, establishments of credit, exchange and insurance lenders.	114,562	102,852	+ 11·4
106	Bank managers, money lenders, exchange and insurance agents, money changers and brokers, and their employés.	114,562	102,852	+ 11·4
	Order 25.—Brokerage and commission expert.	19,872	29,482	— 32·6
107	Brokers, commission agents, commercial travellers, warehouse owners and employés.	19,872	29,482	— 32·6
	Order 26—Trade in textiles ...	98,575	130,047	— 24·2
108	Trade in piece goods, wool, cotton, silk, hair and other textiles.	98,575	130,047	— 24·2
	Order 27.—Trade in skins, leather and furs.	50,055	39,189	27·7
109	Trade in skins, leather, furs, feathers, horn, etc.	50,055	39,189	27·7
	Order 28.—Trade in wood ...	33,423	32,498	+ 2·8
110	Trade in wood (not firewood), cork, bark, etc.	33,423	32,498	+ 2·8
	Order 29.—Trade in metals ...	3,852	1,175	+ 227·8
	„ 30.—Trade in pottery ..	23,621	41,471	— 43·0
112	Trade in pottery	23,621	41,471	— 43·0
	Order 31.—Trade in chemical products.	18,136	7,418	+ 144·5
113	Trade in chemical products (drugs, dyes, paints, petroleum, explosives, etc.).	18,136	7,418	+ 144·5
	Order 32.—Hotels, cafés, restaurants, etc.	137,597	113,550	+ 21·3
114	Vendors of wine, liquors, aerated waters, etc.	109,072	95,434	+ 14·3
115	Owners and managers of hotels, cookshops, sarais, etc., and their employés.	28,525	18,116	+ 57·5
	Order 33.—Other trade in food-stuffs.	1,830,411	1,718,221	+ 6·5
116	Fish dealers	220,740	203,190	+ 8·6
117	Grocers and sellers of vegetable oil, salt and other condiments.	853,756	693,607	+ 23·1
118	Sellers of milk, butter, ghee, poultry, eggs, etc.	81,407	87,586	— 7·1
119	Sellers of sweetmeats, sugar, gur and molasses.	128,694	121,279	+ 6·1
120	Cardamom, betel-leaf, vegetables, fruit and arecanut sellers.	226,513	252,678	— 10·4
121	Grain and pulse dealers ...	200,859	219,572	— 8·5
122	Tobacco, opium, ganja, etc., sellers.	66,291	61,634	+ 7·6
123	Dealers in sheep, goats and pigs.	28,717	30,896	— 7·1
124	Dealers in hay, grass and fodder.	23,434	47,779	— 51·0
	Order 34.—Trade in clothing and toilet articles.	90,079	16,907	+ 432·8
125	Trade in ready-made clothing and other articles of dress and the toilet (hats, umbrellas, socks, ready-made shoes, perfumes, etc).	90,079	16,907	+ 432·8

VII.—Selected occupations (1911 *and* 1901)—concld.

Occupation.	Population supported in 1911.	Population supported in 1901.	Percentage of variation.
2	3	4	5
Sub-class V.—Trade—*cont.*			
Order 35.—Trade in furniture.	28,983	32,059	− 9·6
Hardware, cooking utensils, porcelain, crockery, glassware, bottles, articles for gardening, the cellar, etc.	21,263	29,351	− 27·6
Order 36.—Trade in building materials.	25,808	25,644	+ 0·6
Trade in building materials (stones, bricks, plaster, cement, sand, tiles, thatch, etc.).	25,808	25,644	+ 0·6
Order 37.—Trade in means of transport.	27,999	30,124	− 7·1
Dealers and hirers of elephants, camels, horses, cattle, asses, mules, etc., sellers (not makers) of carriages, saddlery, etc.	27,999	30,124	− 7·1
Order 38.—Trade in fuel .	86,234	135,203	− 36·2
Dealers in firewood, charcoal, coal, cowdung, etc.	86,234	135,203	− 36·2
Order 39.—Trade in articles of luxury and those pertaining to letters and the arts and sciences.	88,179	88,490	− 0·4
Dealers in precious stones, jewellery (real and imitation), clocks, optical instruments, etc.	22,602	29,134	− 22·4
Dealers in common bangles, bead necklaces, fans, small articles, toys, hunting and fishing tackle, flowers, etc.	59,839	55,039	+ 8·7
Order 40.—Trade in refuse matter.	440	—	—
Order 41.—Trade of other sorts.	89,530	48,745	+ 104·7
Shop-keepers otherwise unspecified.	71,688	23,258	+ 208·2
Other trades (including farmers of pounds, tolls and markets).	5,489	6,182	− 11·2
Sub-class VI.—Public force ...	***206,805***	***247,136***	− ***15·5***
Order 42.—Army	16,083	25,773	− 37·6
Army (Imperial)	15,154	25,186	− 39·8
Army (Native states) ...	929	587	+ 58·3
Order 43.—Navy	..	23	...
Order 44.—Police	192,722	221,340	− 12·9
Police	100,995	101,392	− 0·4
Village watchmen	91,727	119,948	− 23·5
Sub-class VII.—Public administration.	***353,164***	***396,610***	− ***11·0***
Order 45.—Public administration.	353,164	396,610	− 11·0
Service of the State ...	160,087	160,723	− 0·4
Service of Native and Foreign States.	13,380	11,163	+ 1·9
Municipal and other local (not village) service.	33,768	33,859	− 0·3
Village officials and servants other than watchmen.	145,929	190,865	− 23·5

Group number.	Occupation.	Population supported in 1911.	Population supported in 1901.	Percentage of variation.
1	2	3	4	5
	Sub-class VIII.—Profession and liberal arts.	***680,896***	***595,694***	+ ***14·3***
	Order 46.—Religion	256,639	221,646	+ 15·8
148	Priests, ministers, etc. ...	83,783	65,738	+ 27·4
149	Religious mendicants, inmates of monasteries, etc.	6,424	4,975	+ 29·1
150	Catechists, readers, church and mission service.	13,329	13,960	− 4·5
151	Temple, burial or burning ground service, pilgrim conductors, circumcisers.	153,103	136,973	+ 11·8
	Order 47.—Law	48,580	36,368	+ 33·6
152	Lawyers of all kinds, including kazis, law agents and mukhtiars.	20,723	20,569	+ 0·7
153	Lawyers' clerks, petition writers, etc.	27,857	15,799	+ 76·3
	Order 48.—Medicine	89,738	84,937	+ 5·7
154	Medical practitioners of all kinds, including dentists, oculists and veterinary surgeons.	75,295	68,571	+ 9·8
155	Midwives, vaccinators, compounders, nurses, masseurs, etc.	14,443	16,366	− 11·7
	Order 49.—Instruction ...	146,746	123,745	+ 18·6
156	Professors and teachers of all kinds, and clerks and servants connected with education.	146,746	123,745	+ 18·6
	Order 50.—Letters and arts and sciences.	139,193	128,898	+ 8·0
159	Others (authors, photographers, artists, sculptors, astronomers, meteorologists, botanists, astrologers, etc.)	28,400	24,971	+ 13·7
160	Music composers and masters, players on all kinds of musical instruments (not military), singers, actors and dancers.	81,809	84,779	− 3·5
	Sub-class IX.—Persons living on their income.	***87,306***	***123,409***	− ***29·3***
	Order 51.—Persons living principally on their income.	87,306	123,409	− 29·3
161	Proprietors (other than of agricultural land), fund and scholarship holders and pensioners.	87,308	123,409	− 29·3
	Sub-class X.—Domestic service.	***206,095***	***250,004***	− ***17·6***
	Order 52.—Domestic service ...	206,095	250,004	− 17·6
162	Cooks, water carriers, doorkeepers, watchmen and other indoor servants.	186,959	222,457	− 16·0
163	Private grooms, coachmen, dog boys, etc.	19,136	27,547	− 30·5

VII.– Selected occupations (1911 *and* 1901)—concld.

Group number.	Occupation.	Population supported in 1911.	Population supported in 1901.	Percentage of variation.
1	2	3	4	5
	Sub-class XI.—Insufficiently described occupations.	***1,527,876***	***679,417***	***+ 124·6***
	Order 53.—General terms which do not indicate a definite occupation.	1,527,876	679,417	+ 124·6
164	Manufacturers, business men and contractors otherwise unspecified.	14,764	15,447	– 4·4
165	Cashiers, accountants, book-keepers, clerks and other employés in unspecified offices, warehouses and shops.	162,653	151,935	+ 7·1
167	Labourers and workmen otherwise unspecified.	1,343,639	509,169	+ 163·9

Group number.	Occupation.	Population supported in 1911.	Population supported in 1901.	Percentage of variation.
1	2	3	4	5
	Sub-class XII.—Unproductive.	***273,828***	***344,481***	***– 20·5***
	Order 54.—Inmates of jails, asylums and hospitals.	13,424	11,438	+ 17·4
168	Inmates of jails, asylums and hospitals.	13,424	11,438	+ 17·4
	Order 55.—Beggars, vagrants, prostitutes.	260,404	333,043	– 21·8
169	Beggars, vagrants, procurers, prostitutes, receivers of stolen goods and cattle poisoners.	260,404	333,043	– 21·8

VIII.—Occupations of selected castes.

Caste and occupation.	Number per 1,000 workers engaged on each occupation.	Number of female workers per 100 males.
1	2	3
Balija	...	*551*
Traders	117·7	563
Non-cultivating landowners and tenants.	30·8	481
Cultivating landowners and tenants.	503·9	456
Field labourers, wood-cutters, etc.	169·0	1,269
Artisans and other workmen...	73·6	544
Others	105·0	302
Billava	...	*996*
Toddy drawers	53·3	...
Cultivating landowners and tenants.	646·8	988
Field labourers, wood-cutters, etc.	175·4	2,156
Artisans and other workmen...	38·0	955
Others	86·5	829
Bráhman, Tamil	...	*135*
Priesthood	122·2	14
Non-cultivating landowners and tenants.	332·2	199
Cultivating landowners and tenants.	195·6	92
Traders	99·1	496
Lawyers, doctors and teachers.	63·1	1
Public administration (other than gazetted officers).	62·5	...
Others	126·8	110
Bráhman, Telugu	...	*257*
Priesthood	107·6	38
Non-cultivating landowners and tenants.	386·3	406
Cultivating landowners and tenants.	328·6	276
Lawyers, doctors and teachers.	49·5	43
Public Administration (other than gazetted officers).	46·0	...
Others	82·0	238
Bráhman, Malayálam ...	..	*78*
Priesthood	268·8	2
Non-cultivating landowners and tenants.	483·0	136
Cultivating landowners and tenants.	71·2	78
Lawyers, doctors and teachers.	28·7	...
Others	148·2	61
Bráhman, Canarese	...	*281*
Priesthood	59·8	71
Non-cultivating landowners and tenants.	141·3	297
Cultivating landowners and tenants.	713·1	271
Others	85·8	570
Bráhman, Oriyá	...	*209*
Priesthood	85·7	185
Non-cultivating landowners and tenants.	188·7	248
Cultivating landowners and tenants.	419·7	82
Field labourers, wood-cutters, etc.	43·2	254
Artisans and other workmen...	64·0	6,076
Traders	89.1	160
Others	114·6	193
Chakkiliyan	...	*704*
Leather workers	222·6	63
Cultivating landowners and tenants.	17·6	404
Field labourers, wood-cutters, etc.	468·1	928
Labourers, unspecified ...	258·5	1,588
Others	33·2	636
Cheruman	...	*1,102*
Farm servants and field labourers.	956·3	1,148
Artisans and other workmen...	16·2	1,914
Others	27·5	101
Dévánga	..	*760*
Weaving	735·6	785
Field labourers, wood-cutters, etc.	55·3	1,754
Artisans and other workmen...	60·6	1,112
Traders	88·3	313
Others	60·2	504
Holeya	..	*1,377*
Field labourers, wood-cutters, etc.	797·1	1,516
Cultivating landowners and tenants.	28·0	1,029
Raisers of live-stock, milkmen and herdsmen.	24·6	169
Labourers, unspecified ..	85·8	1,273
Others	64·5	1,069
Kaikólan	...	*660*
Weaving	538·4	459
Cultivating landowners and tenants.	121·2	526
Field labourers, wood-cutters, etc.	34·5	714
Traders	100·2	1,076
Labourers, unspecified... ...	106·2	2,712
Others	99·6	749
Kallan	...	*641*
Cultivators	901·8	622
Artisans and other workmen ...	21·9	1,651
Traders	18·2	1,557
Labourers, unspecified ...	23·6	1,542
Others	34·4	203
Kammálan	...	*318*
Metal and wood workers ...	602·9	23
Cultivating landowners and tenants.	241·8	908
Field labourers, wood-cutters, etc.	75·4	3,379
Others	80·4	2,155
Kamsala	...	*186*
Metal and wood workers ...	699·6	84
Cultivating landowners and tenants.	94·9	589
Field labourers, wood-cutters, etc.	38·9	6,066
Artisans and other workmen...	88·2	68
Others	78·4	585
Mádiga	.	*707*
Leather workers	173·5	248
Cultivating landowners and tenants.	74·7	191
Field labourers, wood-cutters, etc.	661·4	1,063
Others	90·4	435
Mála	...	*855*
Agricultural labourers ...	790·6	1,042
Cultivating landowners and tenants.	118·8	491
Raisers of live-stock, milkmen and herdsmen.	24·1	55
Artisans and other workmen...	22·3	348
Others	42·2	250
Maravan	...	*670*
Cultivators	786·5	654
Artisans and other workmen...	53·4	1,070
Traders	18·7	1,378
General labourers	72·0	1,853
Others	69·4	74

62

VIII.—Occupations of selected castes—concld.

Caste and occupation.	Number per 1,000 workers engaged on each occupation.	Number of female workers per 100 males.
1	2	3
Sále	...	***686***
Weaving	638·1	690
Cultivating landowners and tenants.	73·6	427
Field labourers, wood-cutters, etc.	136·8	1,283
Artisans and other workmen	39·6	448
Traders	61·5	462
Others	52·4	459
Shánán	..	***469***
Toddy drawers ...	139·5	...
Cultivating landowners and tenants.	520·4	391
Artisans and other workmen ...	98·4	2,648
Traders	72·6	565
General labourers	110·3	1,193
Others	58·8	352
Tíyan	...	***709***
Toddy drawers	72·0	...
Cultivating landowners and tenants.	204·3	242
Field labourers, wood-cutters, etc.	438·0	1,179
Artisans and other workmen.	176·1	2,441
Labourers, boatmen, carters palki bearers, etc.	27·6	47
Traders	32·3	10
Others	51·7	235
Anglo-Indian	...	***309***
Artisans and other workmen...	130·0	467
Owners, managers, ships' officers.	112·0	83
Boatmen, carters, palki bearers, etc.	180·6	9
Lawyers, doctors and teachers.	94·9	2,304
Persons living on their income	115·7	706
Anglo-Indian—*cont.*		
Contractors, clerks, cashiers, etc., otherwise unspecified.	140·8	125
Government servants	60·9	38
Others	215·1	328
Indian Christian	...	***633***
Cultivating landowners and tenants.	237·5	475
Field labourers, wood-cutters, etc.	174·4	2,066
Fishing and hunting	31·9	42
Artisans and other workmen...	236·4	499
Traders	59.5	921
Lawyers, doctors and teachers.	29·5	527
Domestic service	27·7	723
Contractors, otherwise unspecified.	21·4	149
General labourers	88·9	828
Others	92·8	214
European	..	***161***
Agents and managers of landed estates, planters, forest officers and their clerks.	33·7	63
Owners, managers, ships' officers, etc.	88·5	18
Boatmen, car, palki bearers, etc.	42·2	18
Traders	49·1	218
Public force	360·7	...
Public administration ..	42·0	12
Religious professions	125·9	547
Lawyers, doctors and teachers.	75·3	1,379
Other arts and professions ...	39·2	50
Persons living on their income.	52·5	625
Contractors, clerks, cashiers, etc., otherwise unspecified.	43·9	116
Others	47·0	288

IX.—Number of persons employed on the 10th March on Railways and in the Irrigation, Post Office and Telegraph Departments.

Class of persons employed.	Europeans and Anglo-Indians.	Indians.	Remarks.
RAILWAYS.			
TOTAL PERSONS EMPLOYED ...	***2,825***	***59,035***	These figures exclude the lines in the French territory and in Cochin and Travancore. There are no railways in the other three Native States.
Persons directly employed	***2,817***	***49,440***	
Officers	142	6	
Subordinates drawing more than Rs. 75 per mensem ...	961	303	
" " from Rs. 20 to Rs. 75 " ...	1,483	7,292	
" " under Rs. 20 " ...	231	41,839	
Persons indirectly employed	***8***	***9,595***	
Contractors	7	976	
Contractor's regular employés	1	1,016	
Coolies	......	7,608	
IRRIGATION DEPARTMENT.			
TOTAL PERSONS EMPLOYED ...	***66***	***45,857***	These figures exclude those relating to the three Native States.
Persons directly employed	***66***	***9,810***	
Officers	33	22	
Upper subordinates	18	249	
Lower "	3	261	
Clerks	......	506	
Peons and other servants	9	5,591	
Coolies	3	3,181	
Persons indirectly employed	......	***36,047***	
Contractors	......	1,494	
Contractors' regular employés	......	1,260	
Coolies	......	33,293	
POSTAL DEPARTMENT.			
TOTAL ...	***84***	***13,496***	These figures include the three Native States also.
Supervising officers	11	70	
Post masters	22	711	
Miscellaneous agents	1	2,259	
Clerks	42	1,406	
Postmen, etc.	1	4,878	
Road establishment	1	2,986	
Railway Mail Service.			
Supervising officers	4	10	
Clerks and sorters	......	423	
Mail guards, etc.	......	195	
Combined offices.			
Signallers	2	142	
Messengers, etc.	......	416	
TELEGRAPH DEPARTMENT.			
TOTAL ...	***227***	***1,405***	There are no 'departmental' telegraph offices in any of the three Native States.
Administrative establishment	11	2	
Signalling	208	238	
Clerks	5	103	
Skilled labour	1	266	
Unskilled labour	2	423	
Messengers, etc.	......	373	

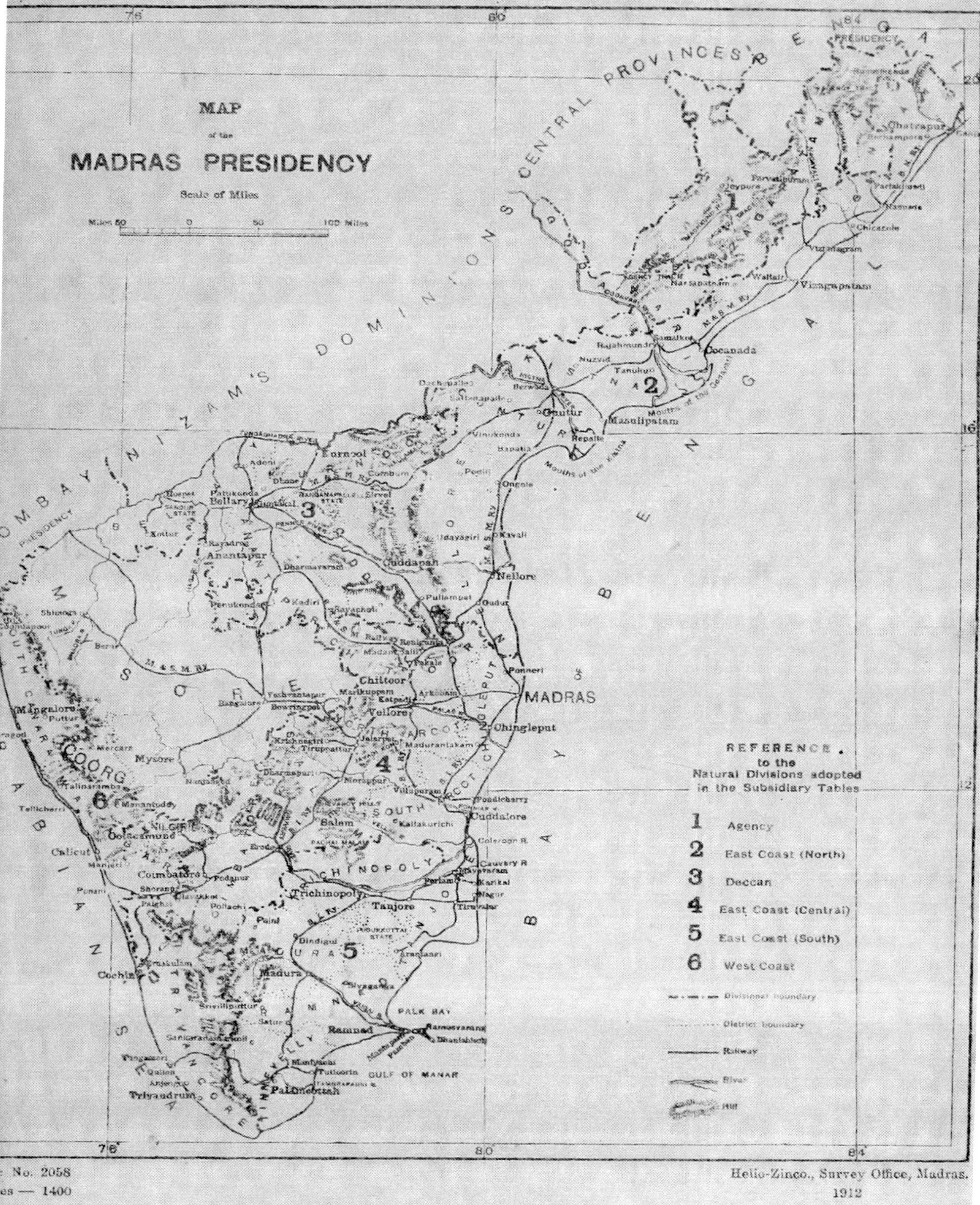

g: No. 2058
pies — 1400

Helio-Zinco., Survey Office, Madras.
1912

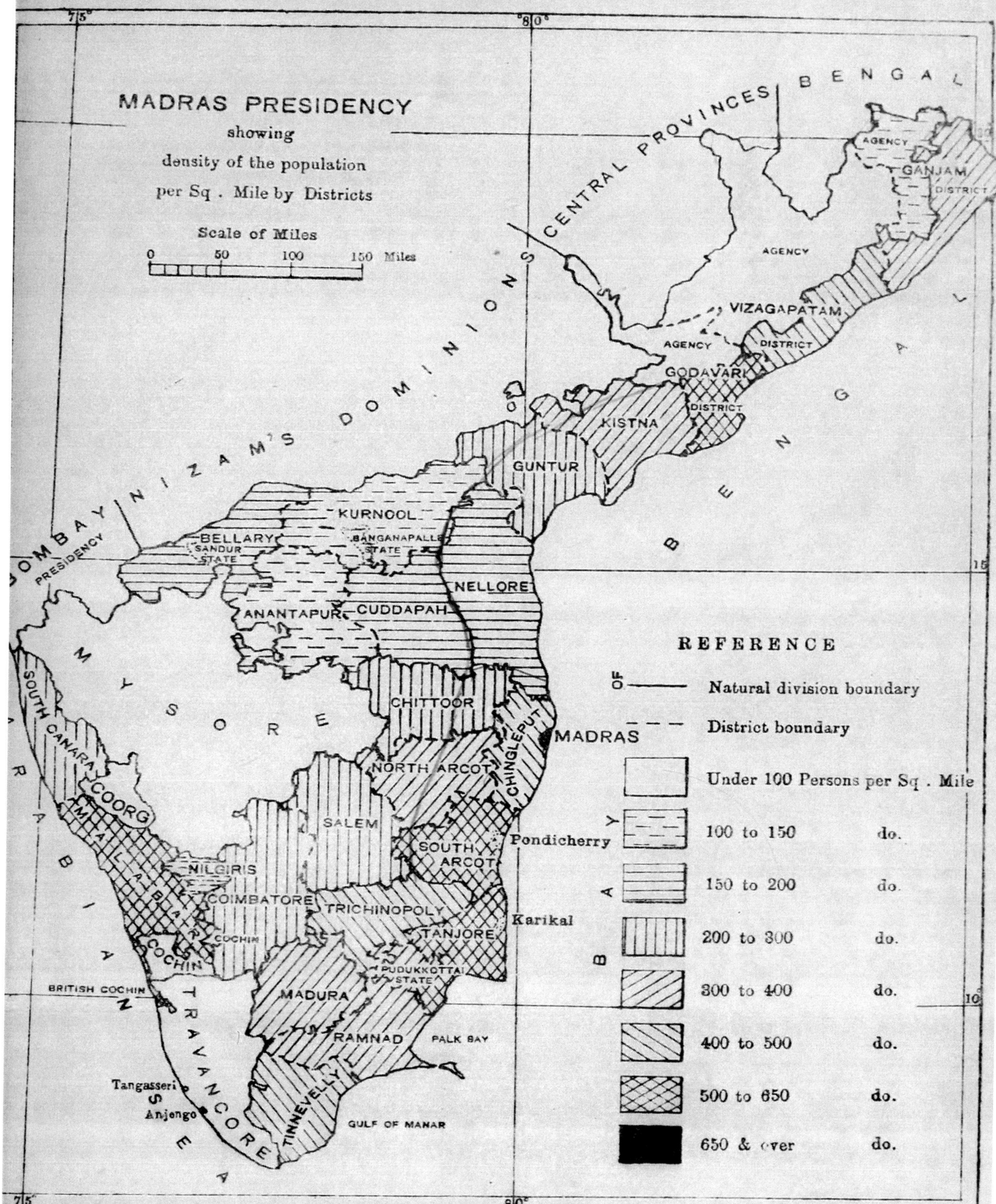

Reg. No. 2123
Copies —1400

Zinco, Survey Office, Madras.
1912

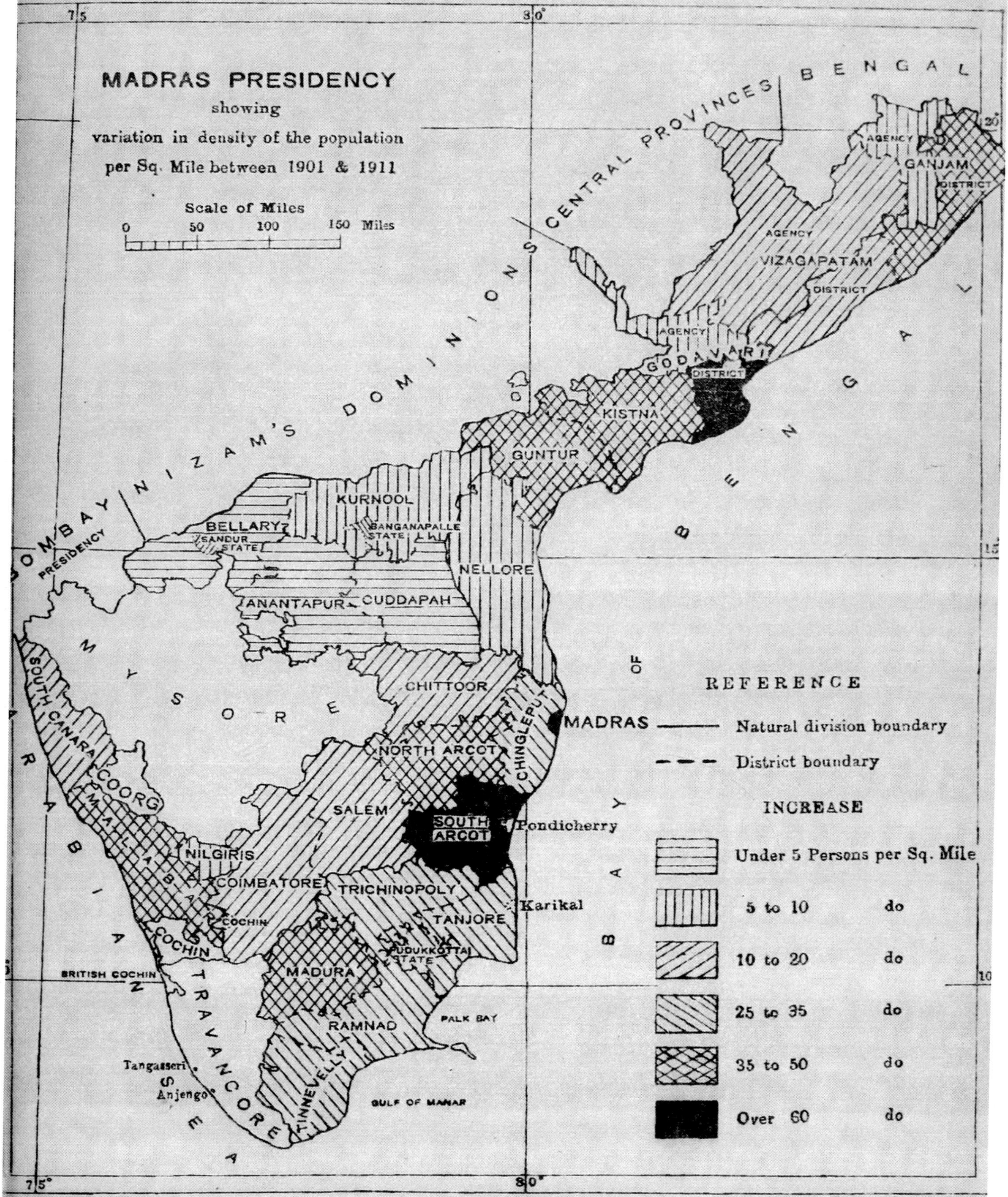

Reg. No. 2125
Copies — 1400

Zinco., Survey Office, Madras.
1912

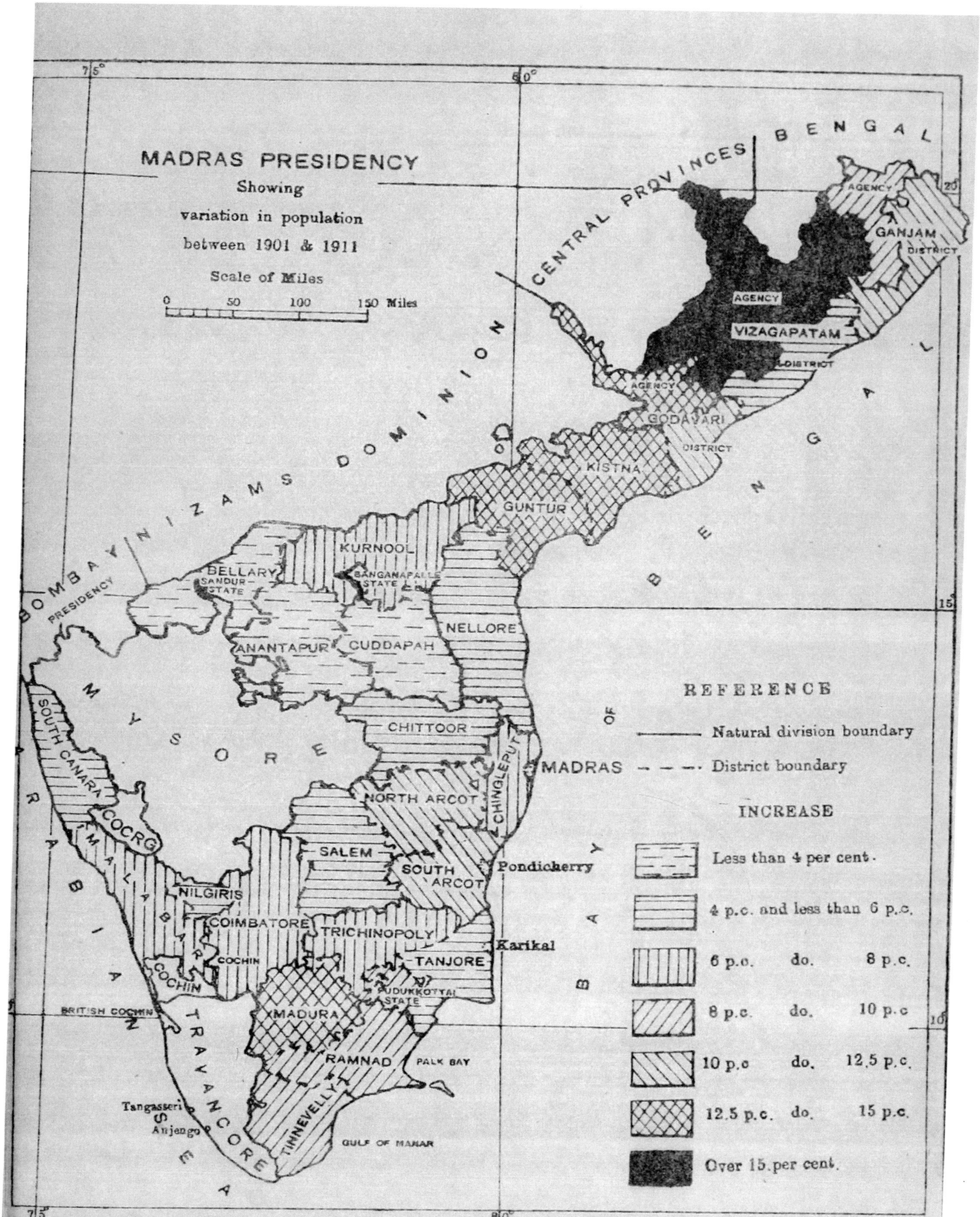

Reg. No. 2124
Copies -- 1400

Zinco, Survey Office, Madras.
1912

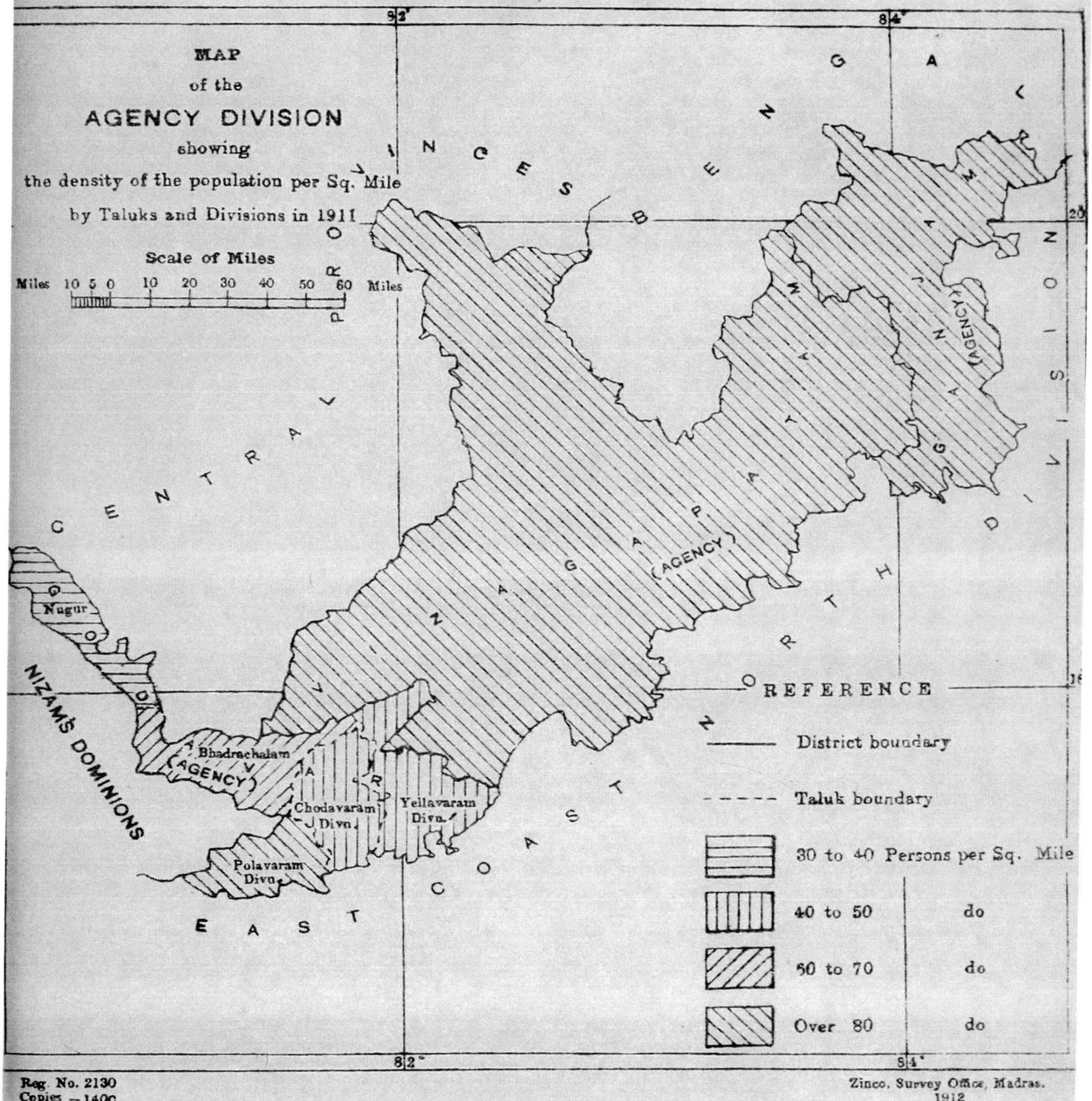

Note:—In Ganjam the taluk areas, and in Vizagapatam their boundaries, are not accurately known, and the density shown is that of the agency as a whole.

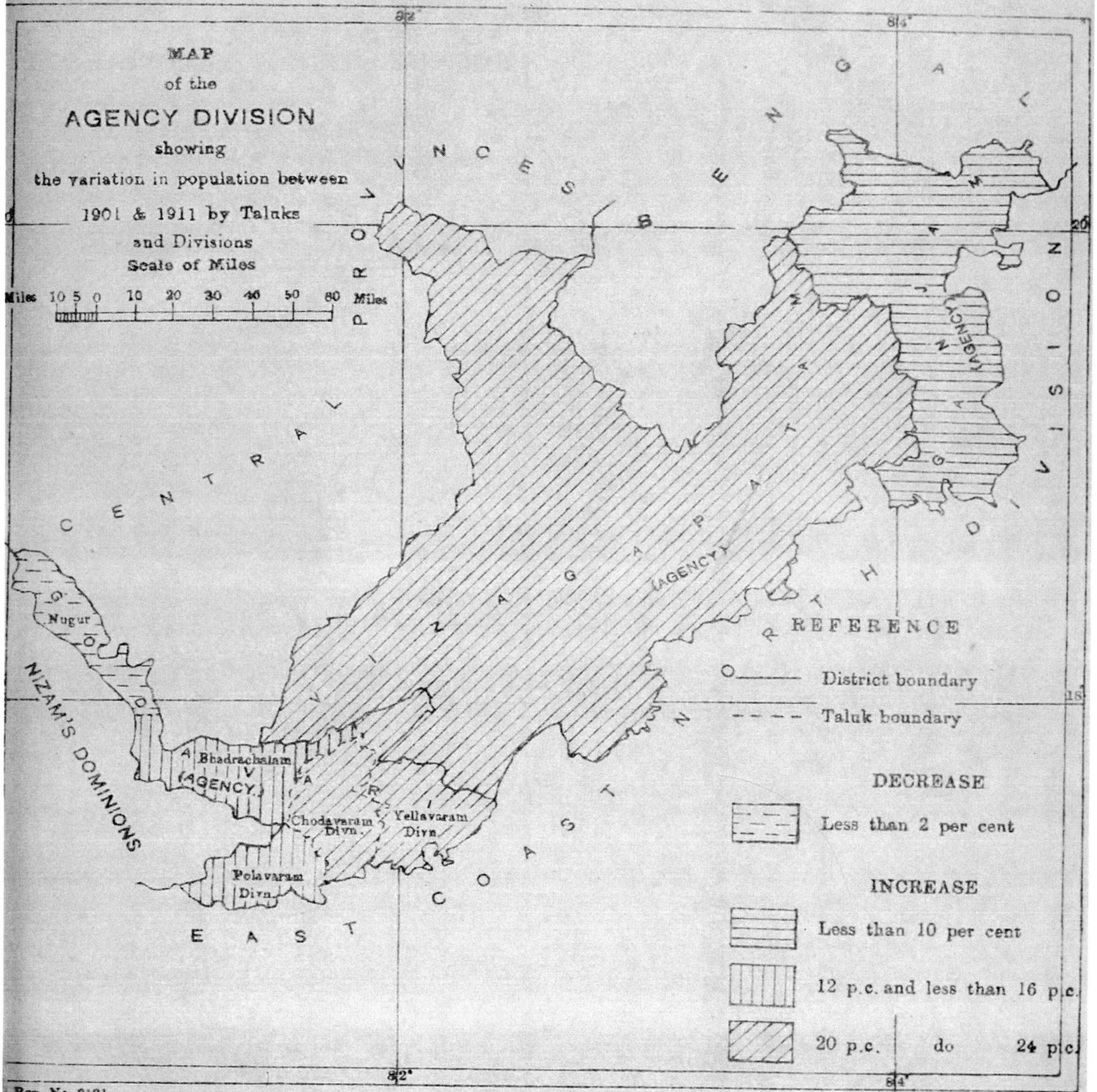

Reg. No. 2131
Copies – 1400

Zinco. Survey Office, Madras.
1912

Note:—In Ganjam the taluk areas, and in Vizagapatam their boundaries, are not accurataly known, and the variation shown is that of the agency as a whole.

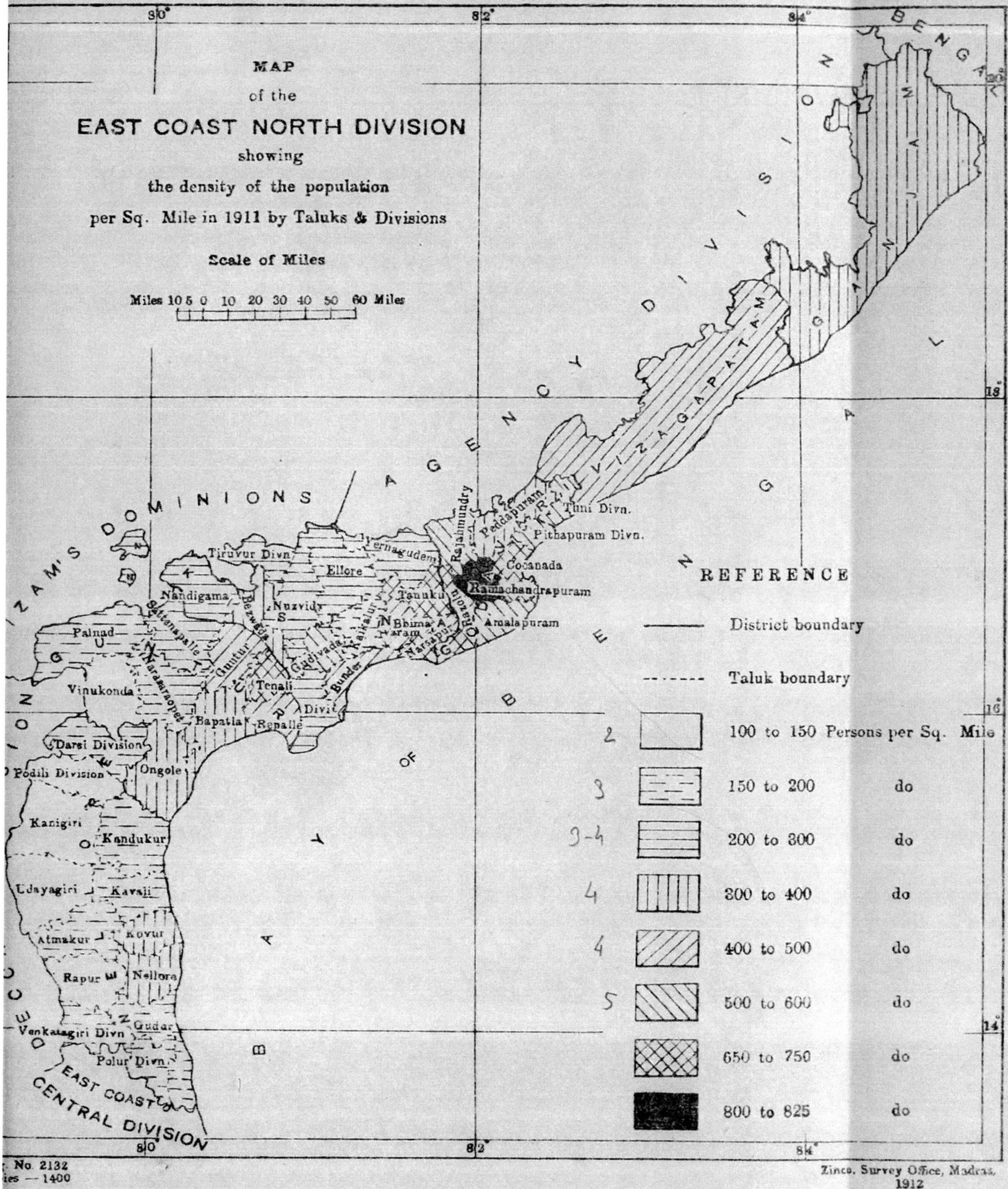

In Ganjam the taluk areas, and in Vizagapatam their boundaries, are not accurately known, and the density shown is that of the district as a whole.

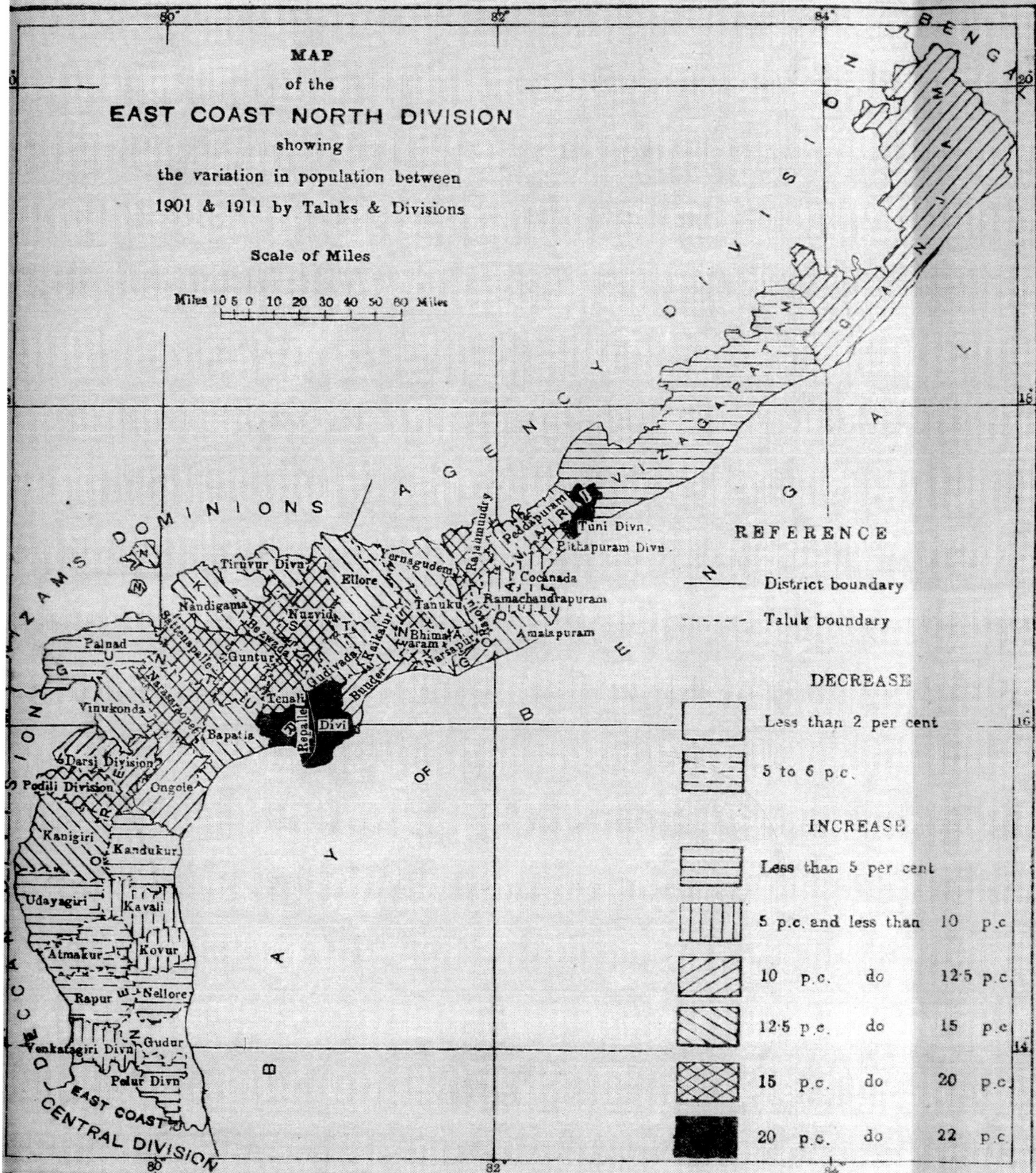

Reg No. 2133
Copies — 1400

Zinco. Survey Office Madras
1912

Note:—In Ganjam the taluk areas, and in Vizagapatam their boundaries, are not accurately known and the variation is that of the district as a whole.

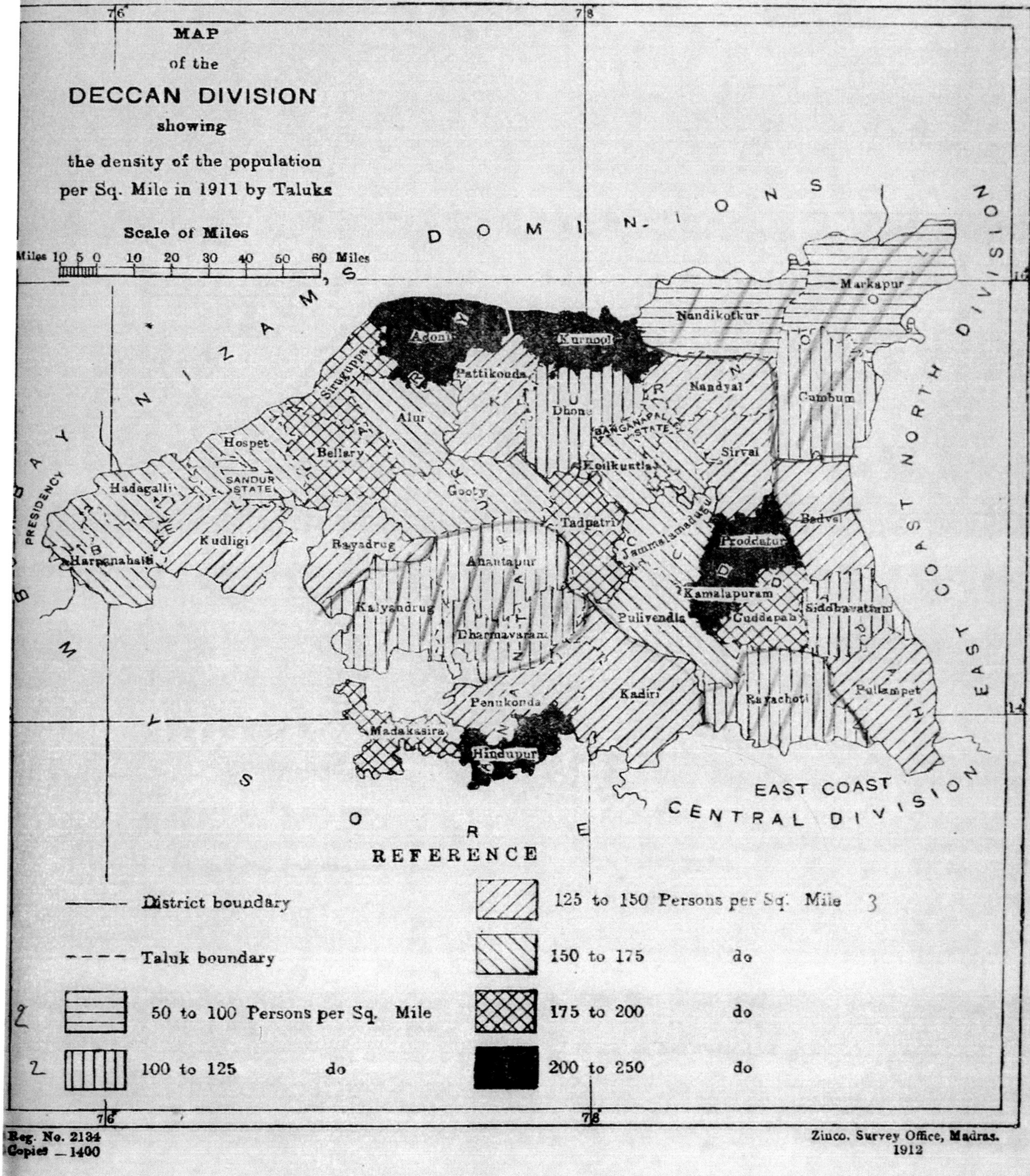

Reg. No. 2134
Copies — 1400

Zinco. Survey Office, Madras.
1912

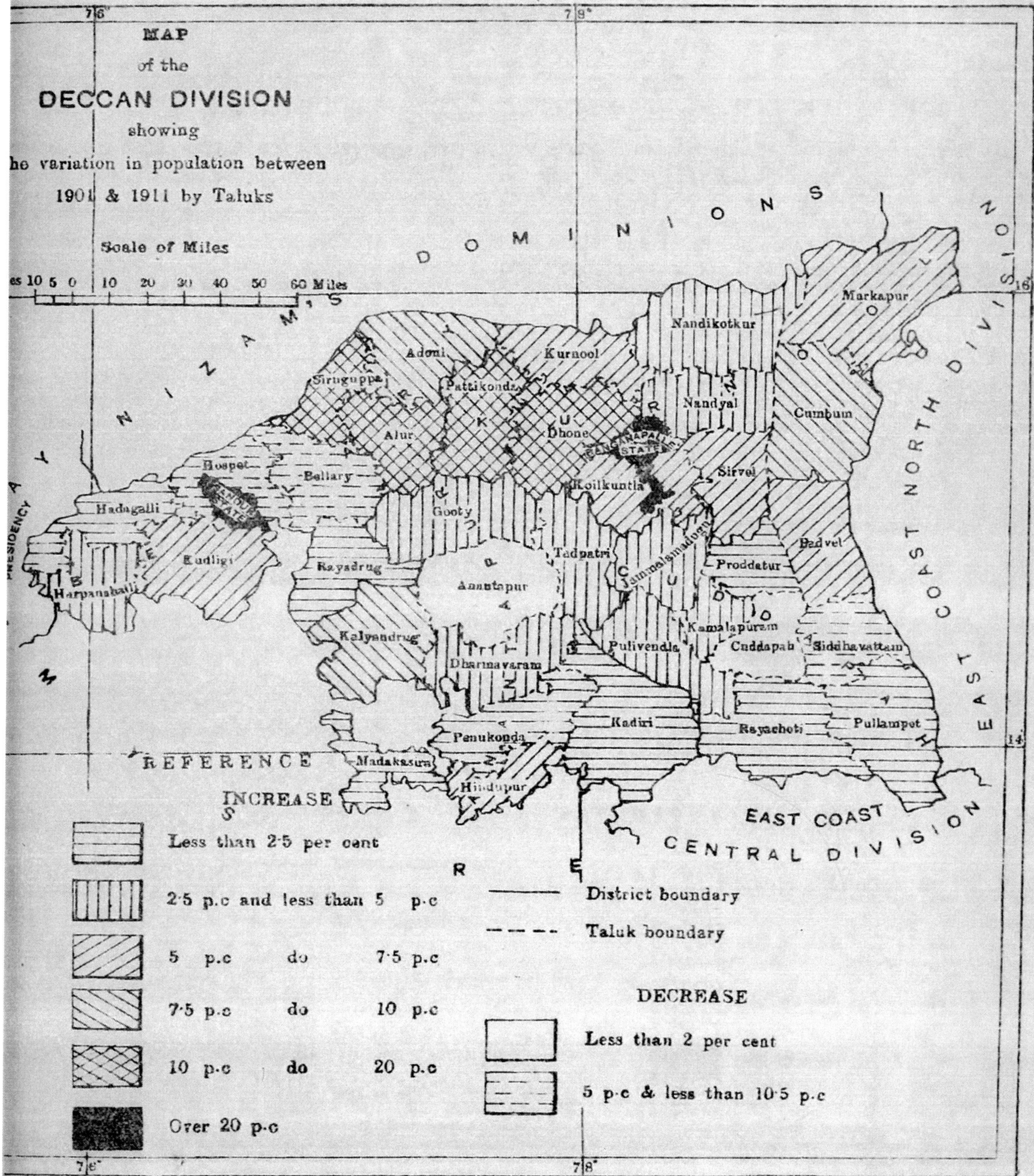

g No. 2135
pies _ 1400

Zinco. Survey Office, Madras.
1912

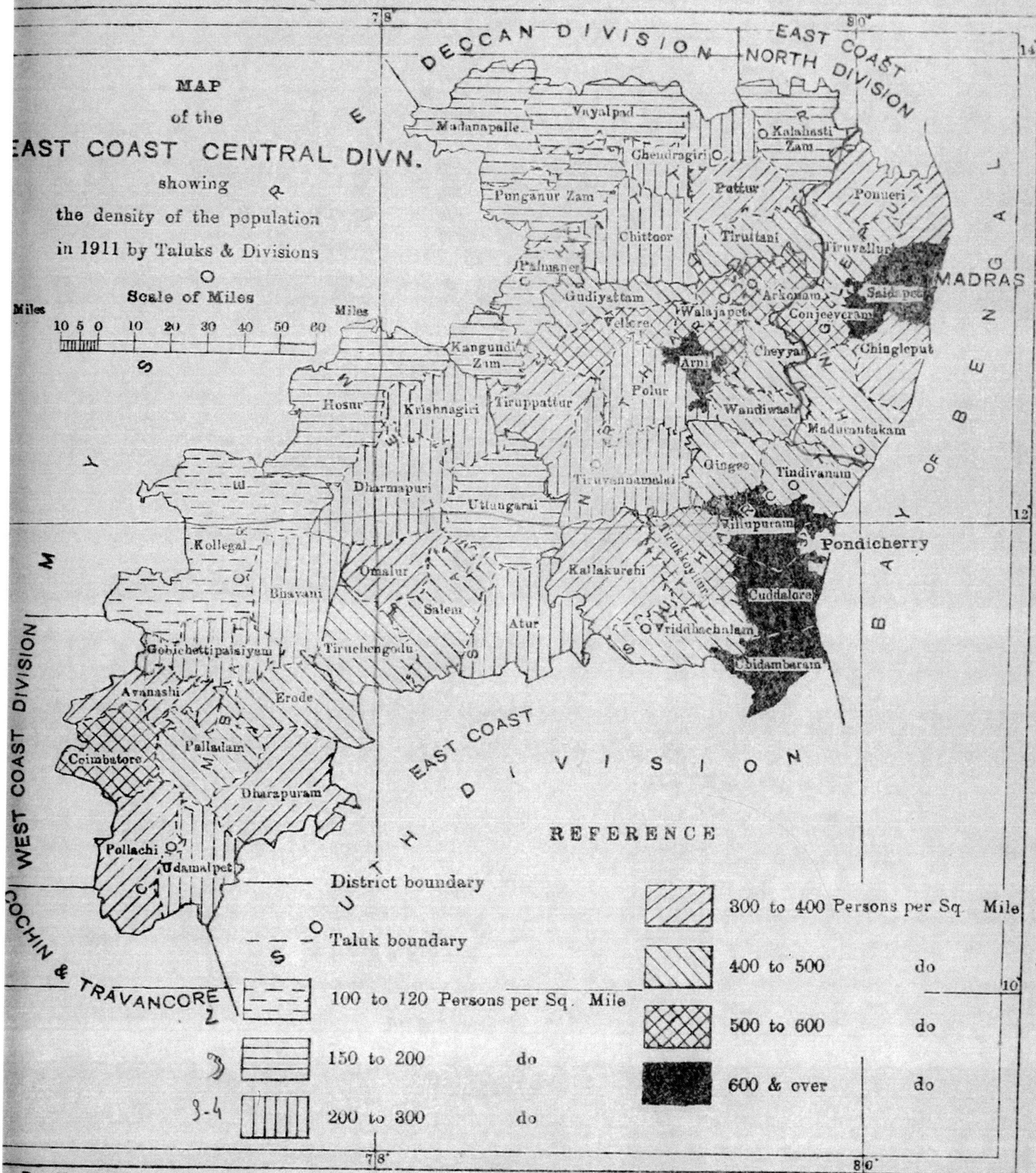

Reg. No. 2136
Copies — 1400

Zinco. Survey Office. Madras.
1912

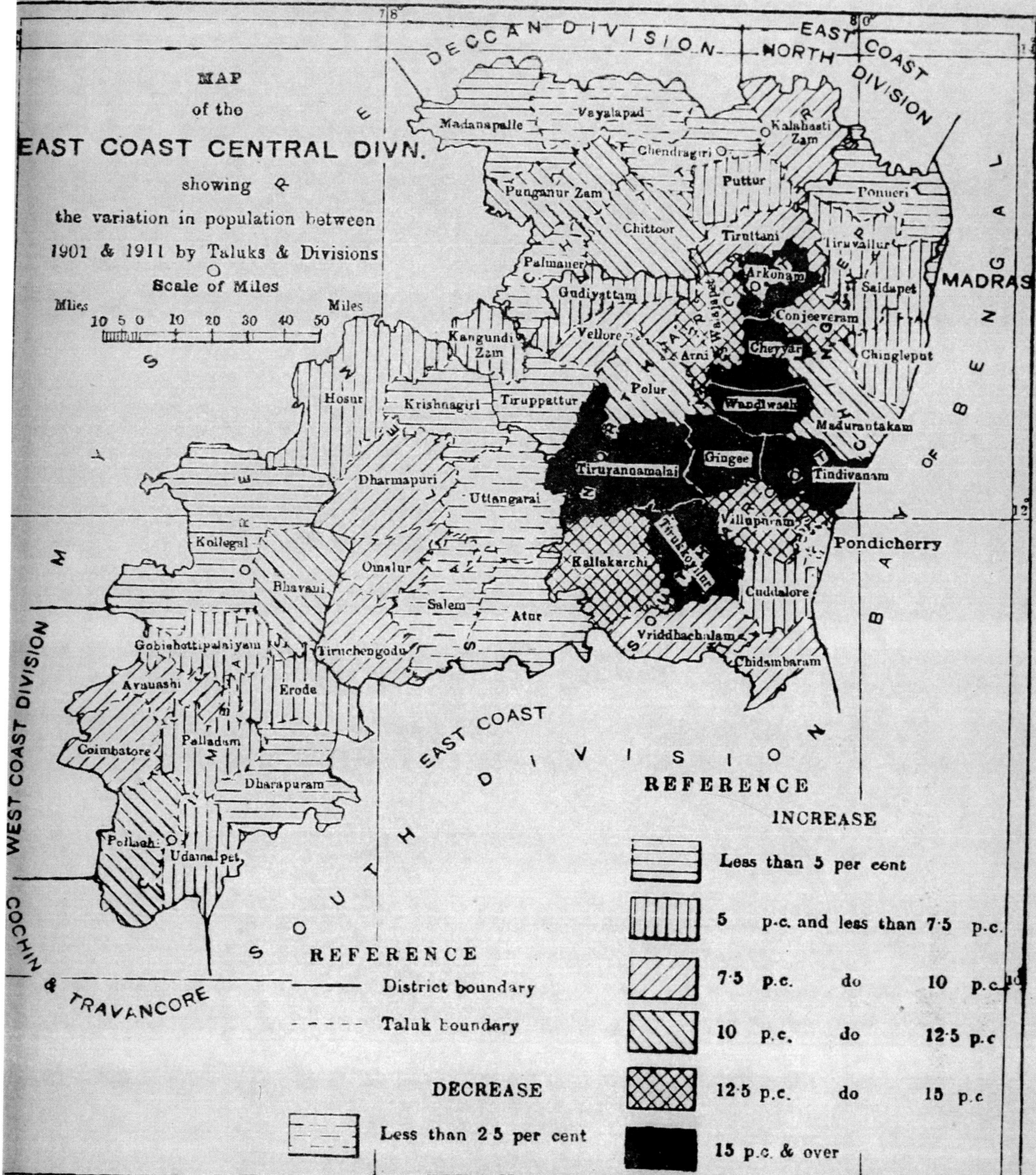

g. No. 2137
gies — 1400

Zinco. Survey Office Madras.
1912

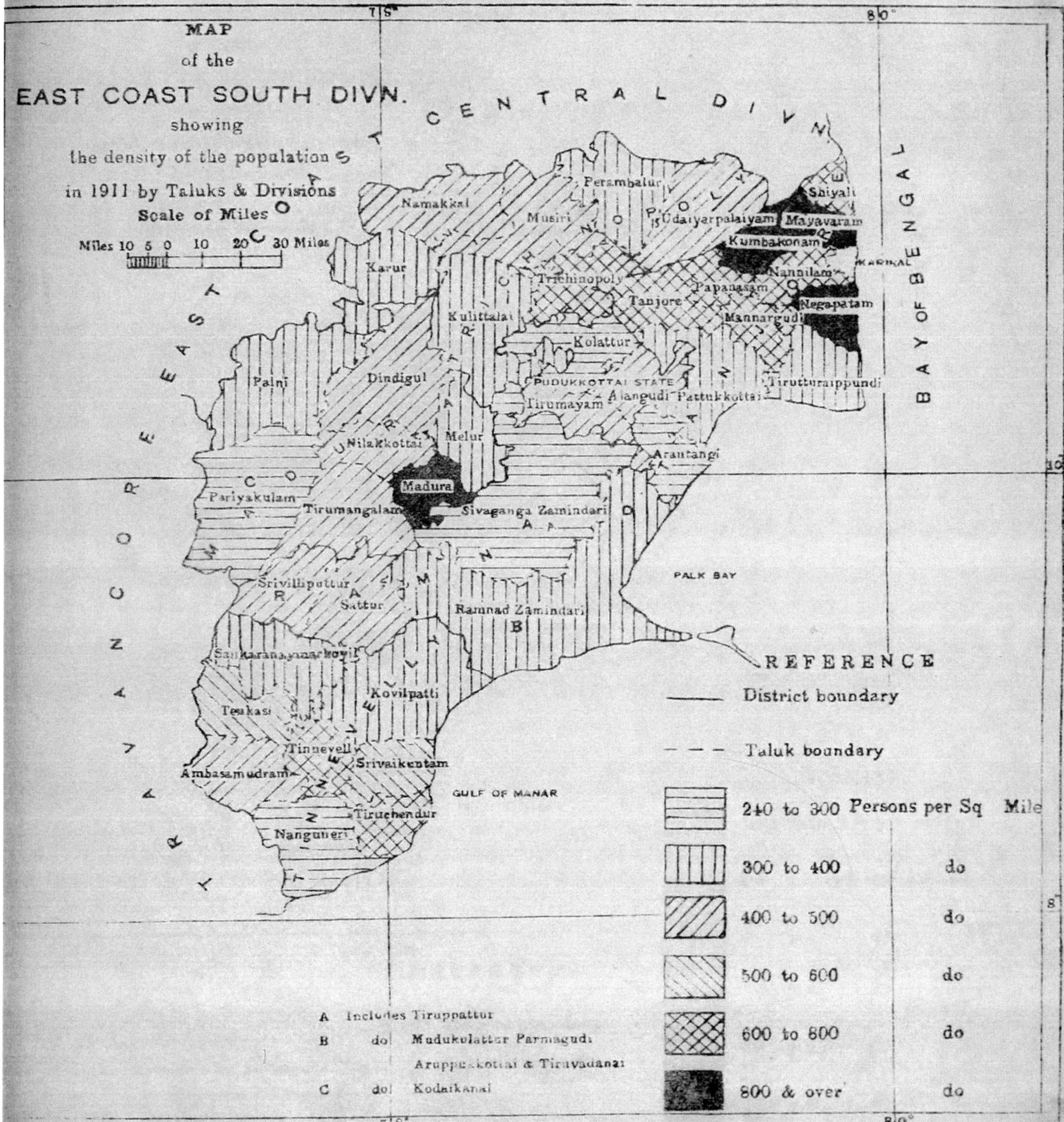

Reg No 2138
Copies – 1400

Zinco, Survey Office, Madras.
1912

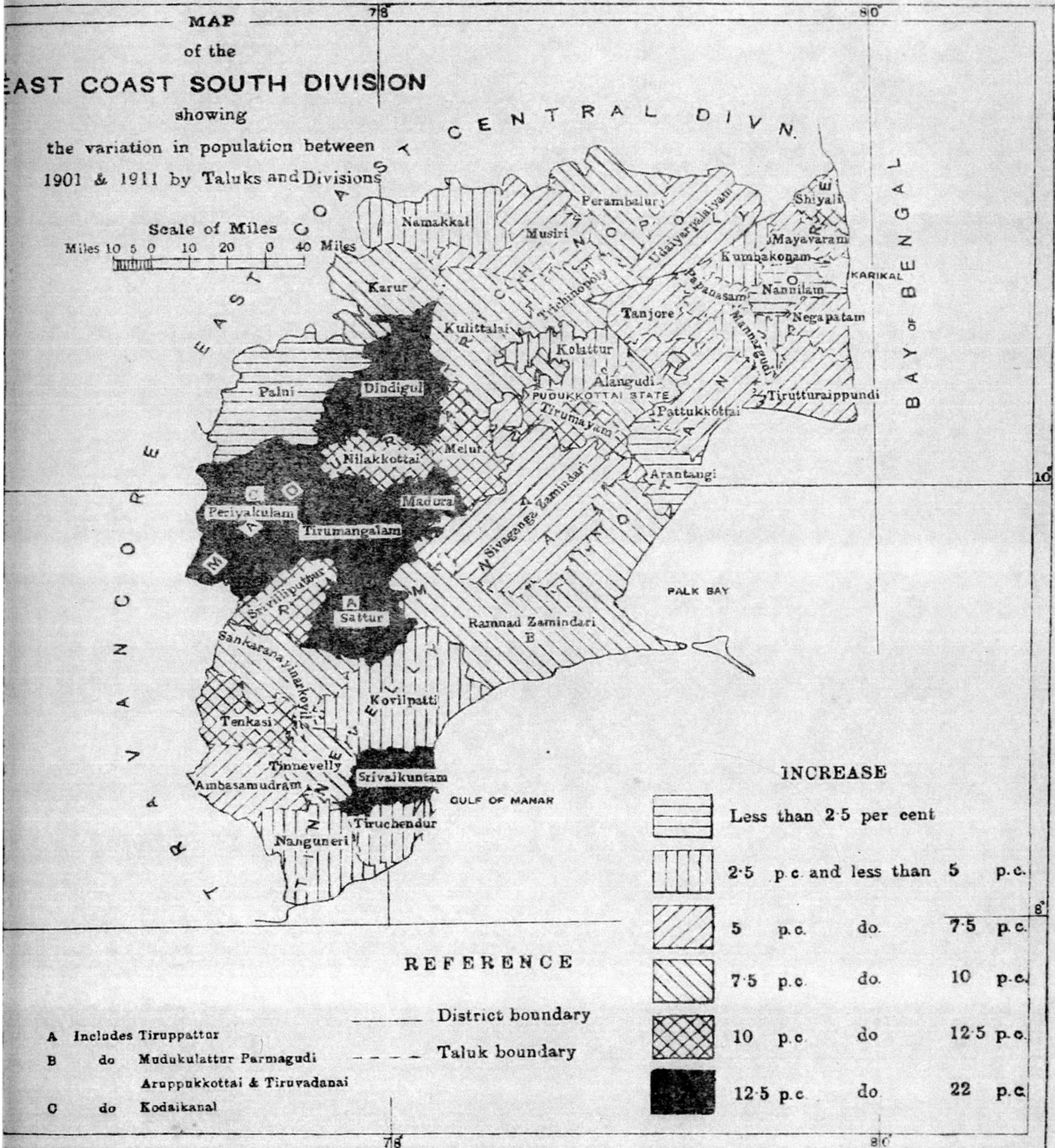

Reg No. 2139
Copies — 1400

Zinco Survey Office, Madras.
1912

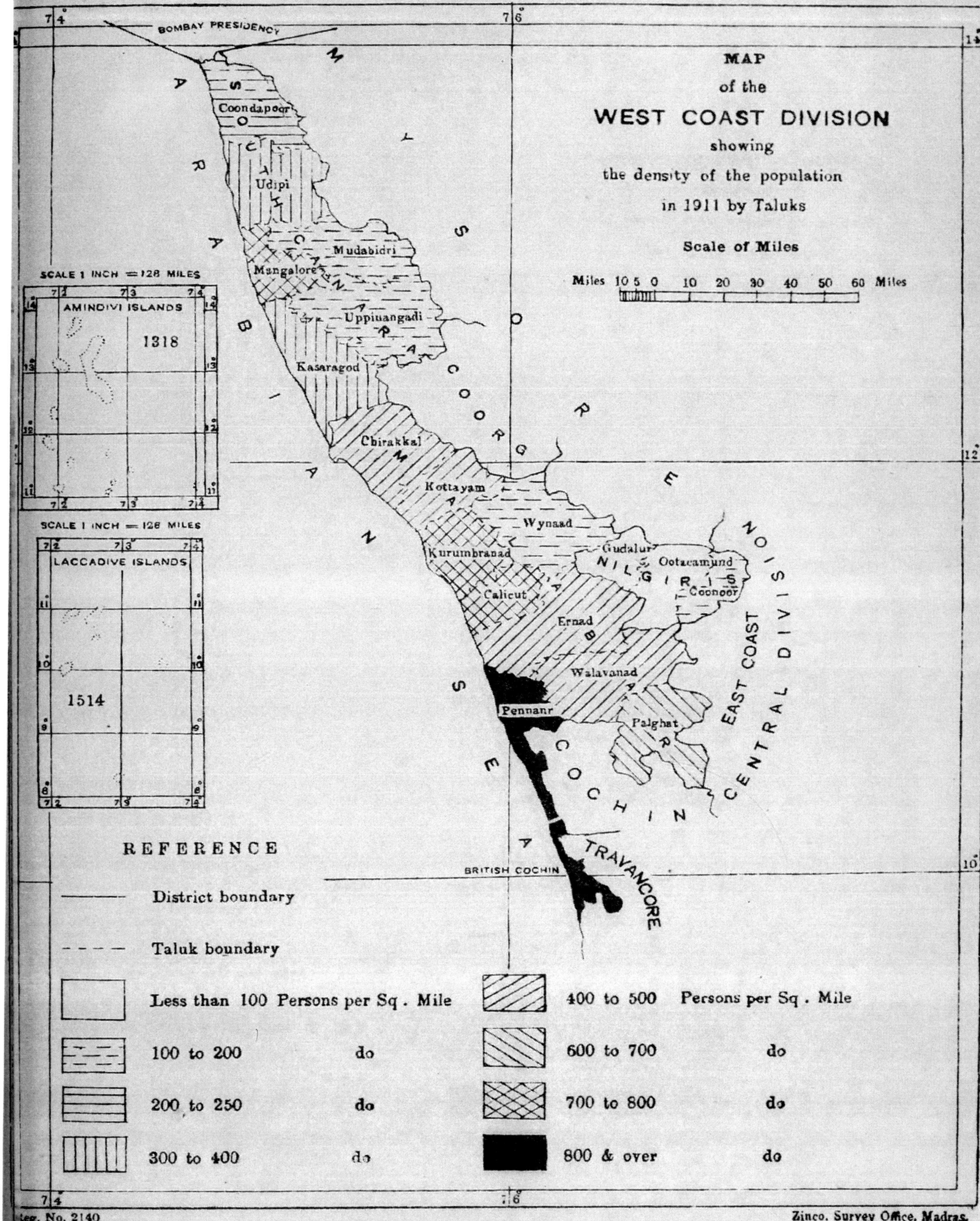

Reg. No. 2140
Copies — 1400

Zinco. Survey Office, Madras.
1912

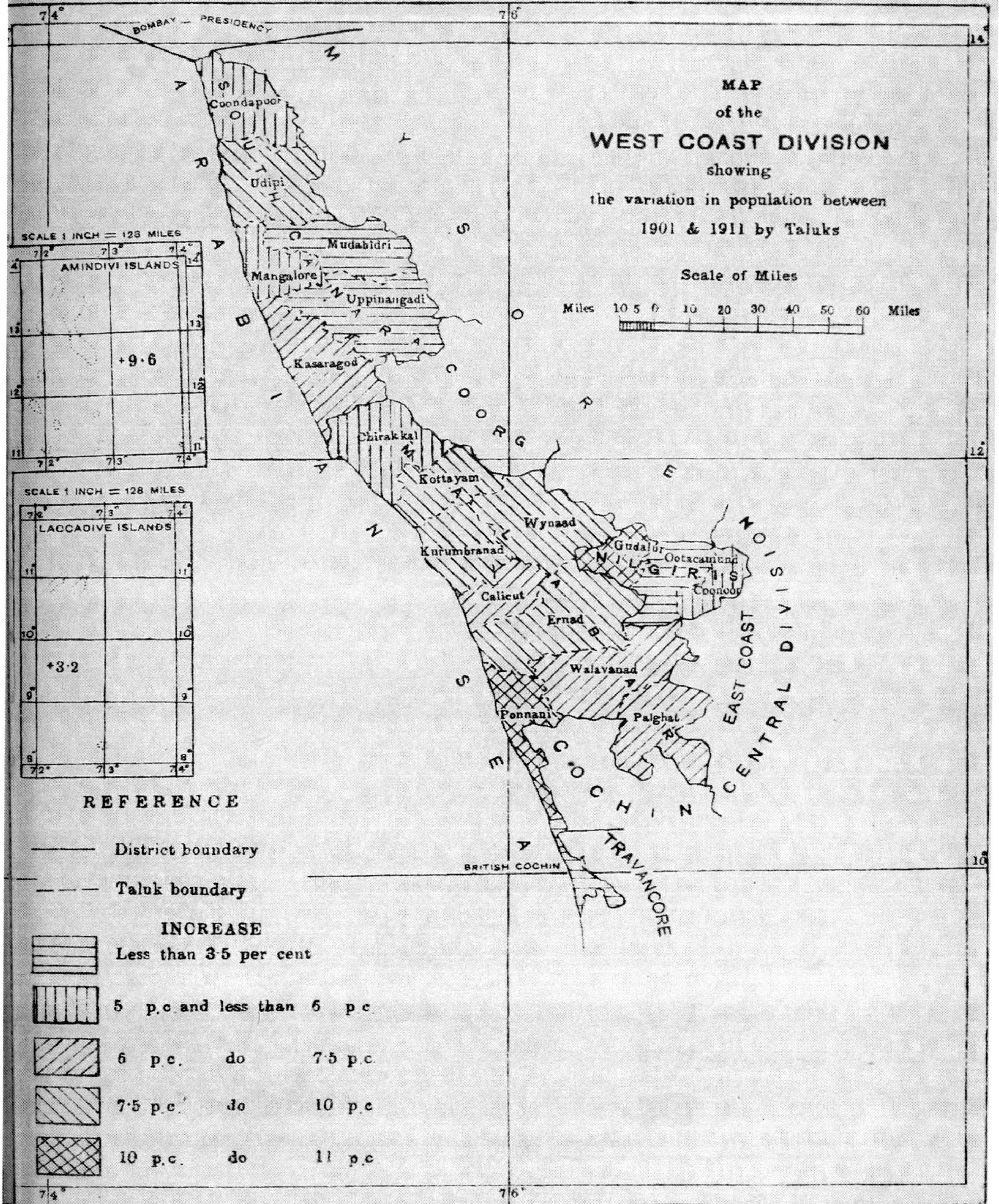

Reg. No. 2141
Copies — 1400

Zinco, Survey Office, Madras.
1912

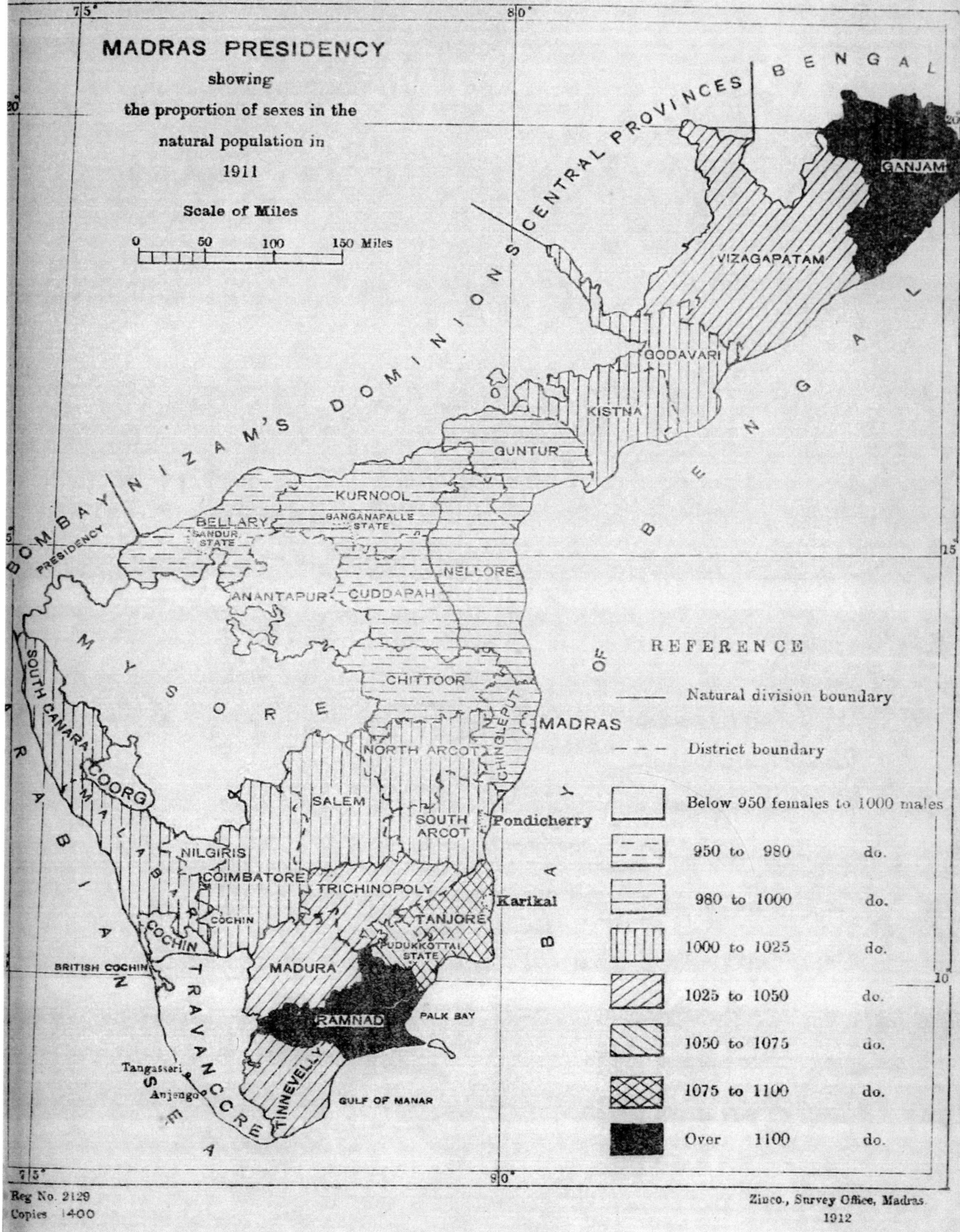
MADRAS PRESIDENCY
showing
the proportion of sexes in the
natural population in
1911
Scale of Miles
0 50 100 150 Miles
BENGAL
CENTRAL PROVINCES
GANJAM
VIZAGAPATAM
GODAVARI
KISTNA
GUNTUR
NIZAM'S DOMINIONS
BOMBAY PRESIDENCY
KURNOOL
BELLARY
SANDUR STATE
BANGANAPALLE STATE
NELLORE
ANANTAPUR
CUDDAPAH
MYSORE
SOUTH CANARA
COORG
MALABAR
CHITTOOR
CHINGLEPUT
MADRAS
NORTH ARCOT
SALEM
SOUTH ARCOT
Pondicherry
NILGIRIS
COIMBATORE
TRICHINOPOLY
Karikal
TANJORE
COCHIN
PUDUKKOTTAI STATE
BRITISH COCHIN
MADURA
TRAVANCORE
RAMNAD
PALK BAY
Tangasseri
Anjengo
TINNEVELLY
GULF OF MANAR
ARABIAN SEA
BAY OF BENGAL
REFERENCE
Natural division boundary
District boundary
Below 950 females to 1000 males
950 to 980 do.
980 to 1000 do.
1000 to 1025 do.
1025 to 1050 do.
1050 to 1075 do.
1075 to 1100 do.
Over 1100 do.
Reg No. 2129
Copies 1400
Zinco., Survey Office, Madras.
1912

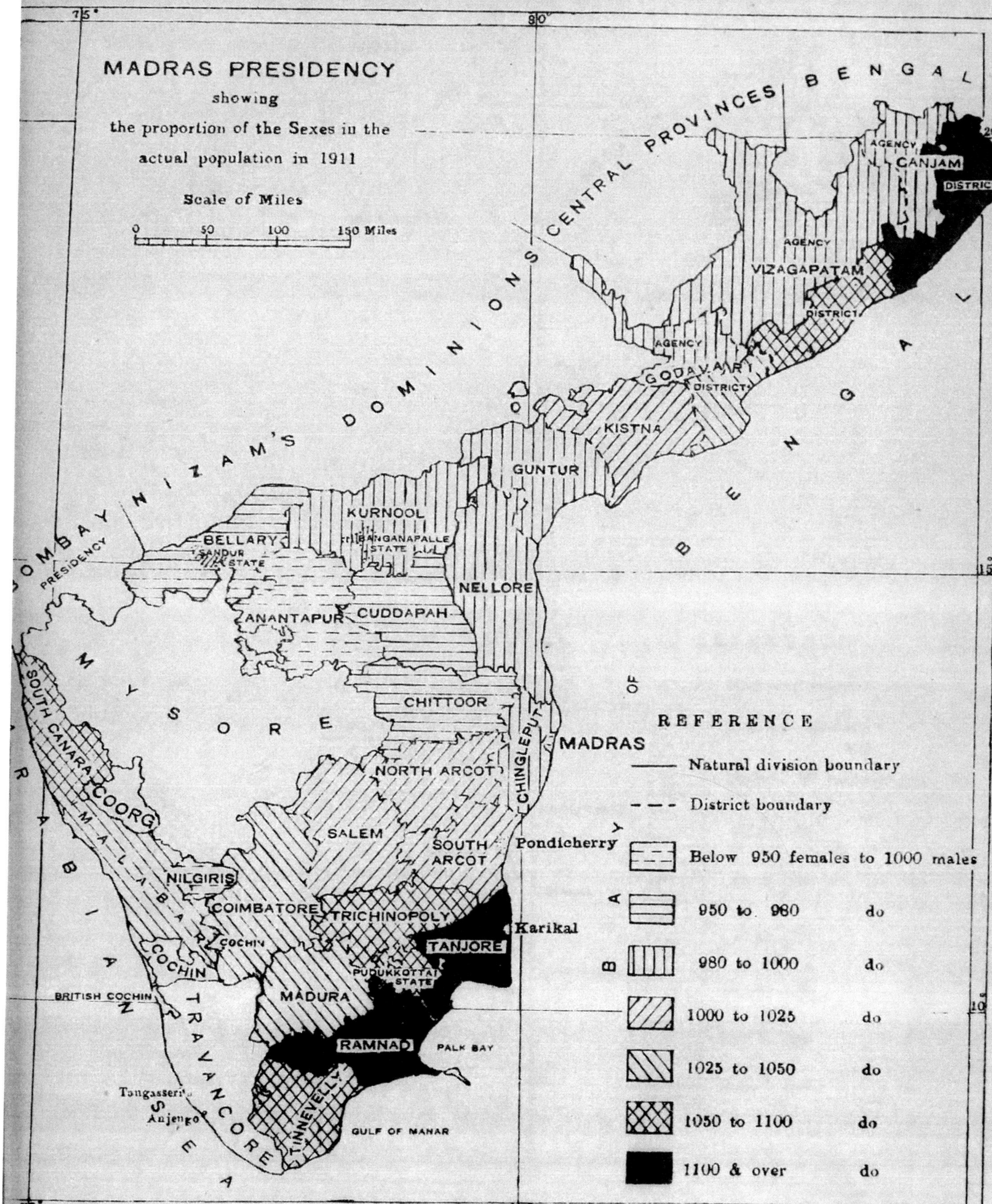

...g No. 2127
...opies 1400

Zinco Survey Office, Madras
1912

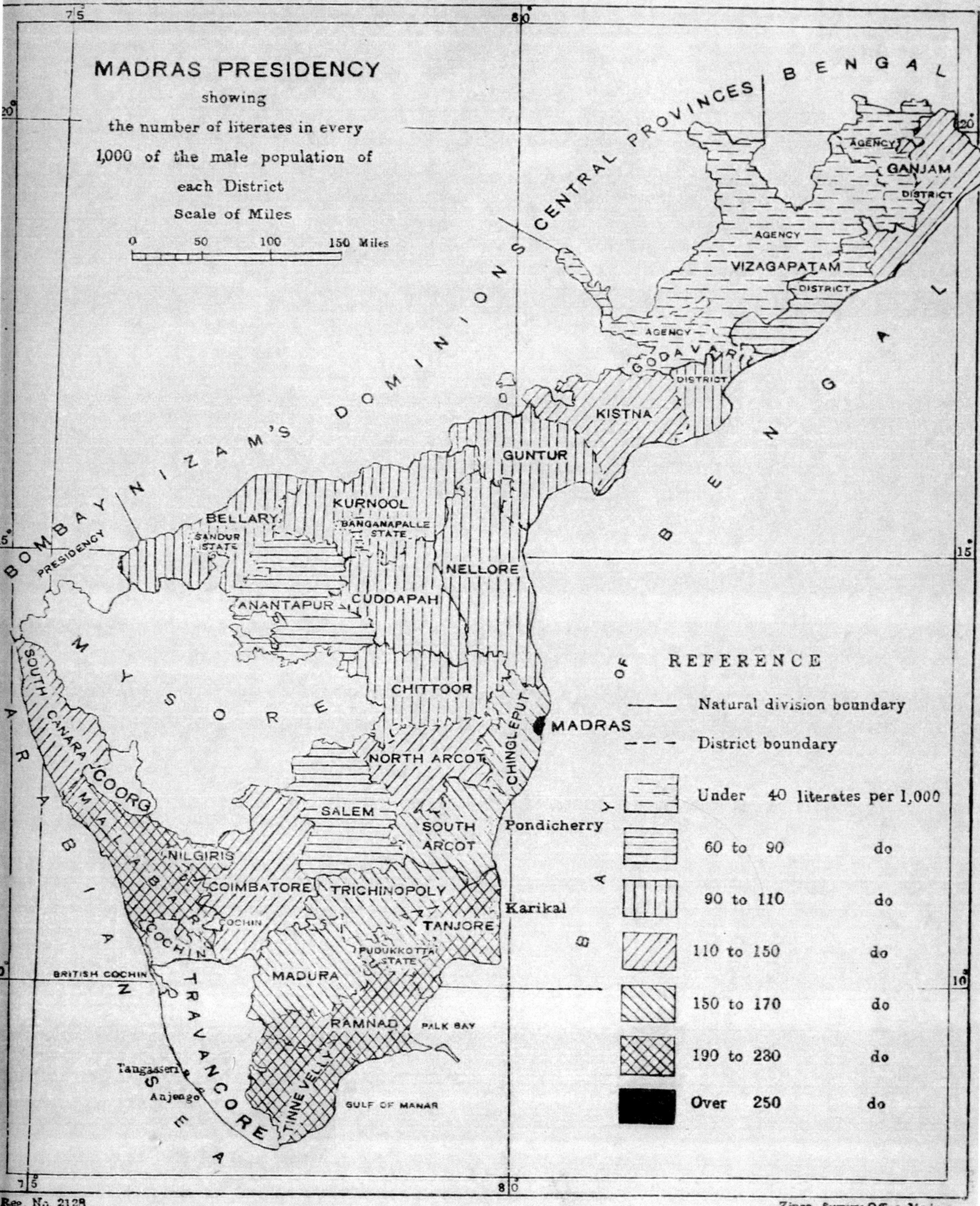

Reg No. 2128
Copies —1400

Zinco, Survey Office, Madras.
1912

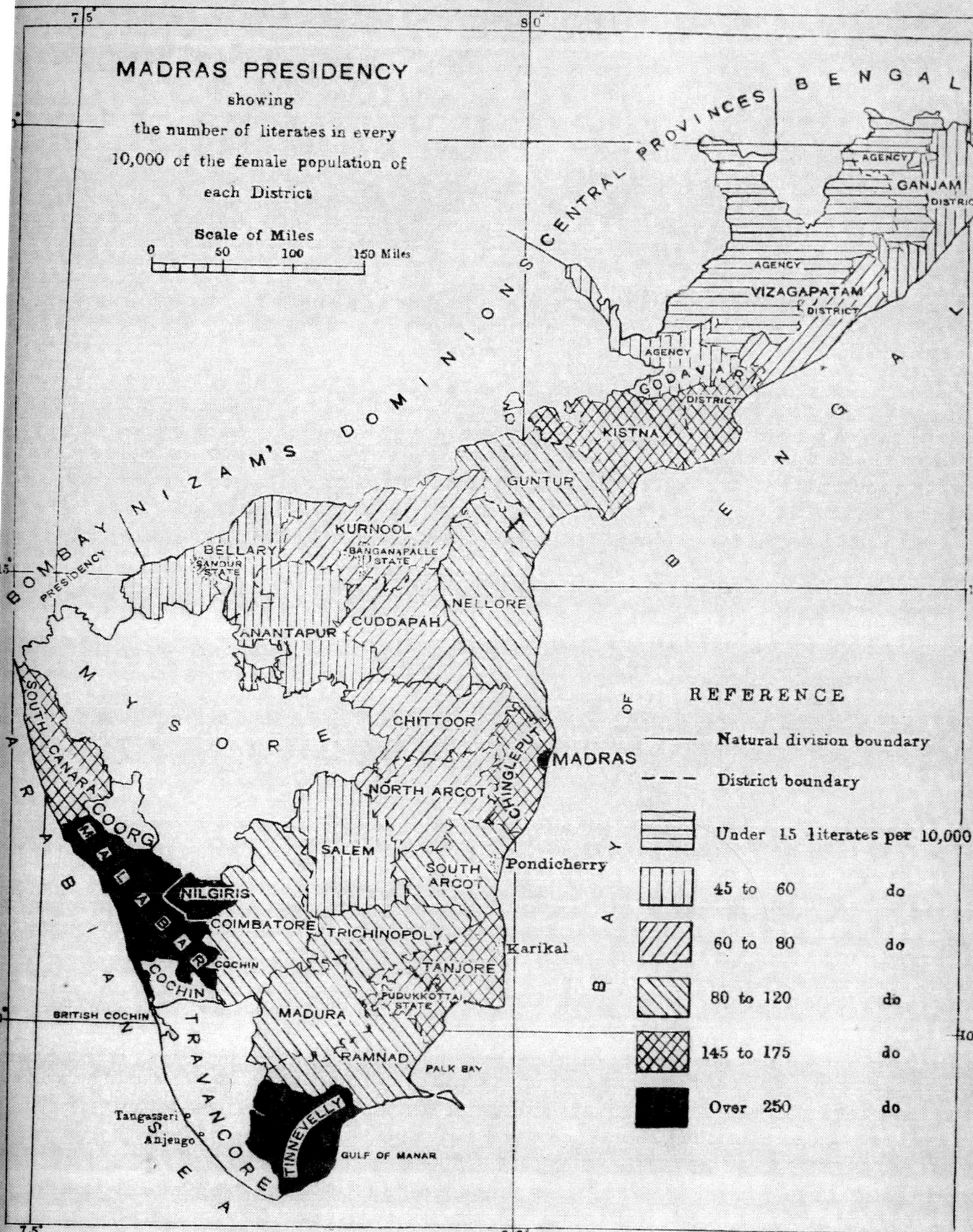

Reg: No. 2126
Copies — 1400

Zinco., Survey Office, Madras
1912